D1383161

VISIONS OF THE PEOPLE

VISIONS OF THE PEOPLE

Industrial England and the question of class 1848–1914

PATRICK JOYCE

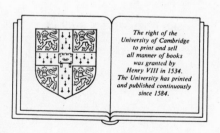

The right of the
University of Cambridge
to print and sell
all manner of books
was granted by
Henry VIII in 1534.
The University has printed
and published continuously
since 1584.

CAMBRIDGE UNIVERSITY PRESS

Cambridge
New York   Port Chester
Melbourne   Sydney

WITHDRAWN

HN
388
.E53
J69
1991

Published by the Press Syndicate of the University of Cambridge
The Pitt Building, Trumpington Street, Cambridge CB2 1RP
40 West 20th Street, New York, NY 10011, USA
10 Stamford Road, Oakleigh, Melbourne 3166, Australia

© Patrick Joyce 1991

First published 1991

Printed in Great Britain at the University Press, Cambridge

British Library cataloguing in publication data

Joyce, Patrick 1946–
Visions of the people: industrial England and the
question of class, 1848–1914.
1. England. Social conditions, 1837–
I. Title
942.081

Library of Congress cataloguing in publication data

Joyce, Patrick.
Visions of the people: industrial England and the question of
class, 1848–1914 / Patrick Joyce.
p.   cm.
Includes bibliographical references.
ISBN 0-521-37152-X
1. Social classes–England–History–19th century.   I. Title.
HN388.E53J69   1990
305.5′0942′09034–dc20 89-77387 CIP

ISBN 0 521 37152 X hardback

MAR 1 1991

This book is dedicated to the memory of
Catherine Joyce (1910–1982),
John Joyce (1907–1962),
Hugh Malone (1920–1988),
and to Elizabeth Malone,
my parents and my wife's parents

Contents

Appendices

Plates

Acknowledgements

A number of people read and commented upon drafts of parts of this book and I should like to take this opportunity of thanking them warmly. Among my own and colleagues' postgraduate research students at Manchester University, Tony Taylor and James Vernon gave me the benefit of their knowledge of popular politics. From Simon Gunn I learned much about class and the middle classes, and benefited from his friendship in perhaps more ways than he imagines. Of my Manchester colleagues, Iorwerth Prothero and John Breuilly have contributed much to this book over the years. Others who commented upon earlier versions of particular chapters were Peter Bailey, David Mayer, Dorothy Thompson, Rohan McWilliam, Dick Leith, Tom Paulin, John Belchem, Lesley and James Milroy, and Peter Burke. Edward Thompson did the same, and gave generously of his time during his 1988–89 tenure of a Simon Fellowship at Manchester. What value this book has owes much to the comment of those named. Its shortcomings are due solely to my own persistence in error.

I owe a special debt to Keith McClelland and David Vincent, who gave generously of their time and support at critical times. I also owe much to Robert Gray. My biggest debt is to my friend John Seed, whose critical intelligence, and enthusiasm for a serious and creative social history, have meant much to me. Others I should like to thank are David Harker, Paul Salvesen, Louis James, K. C. Phillips and Douglas Reid. Parts of this book were presented as research papers at seminars at All Souls College, Oxford; the Institute of Historical Research, University of London; Manchester University and the Max-Planck-Institut für Geschichte, Göttingen, which I visited in 1988. To all who listened and spoke at these meetings, my thanks. I owe special thanks to Alf Lüdtke, not least for his Göttingen hospitality; from his colleagues Hans Medick and Jürgen Schlumbohm I learned about the sense of the past and about the history of language.

John Coles of the Local Studies Library, Rochdale; Joe Gingh, Museums Officer of Tyne and Wear County Council; and above all Alice Lock of Tameside Local Studies Library, Stalybridge, were more than generous with their time and expertise. I should like to thank the staff of the British Library and of the many north of

England libraries I visited, especially the Manchester Central Reference Library, Newcastle-upon-Tyne Central Library, and the central libraries of Leeds, Bradford, Bolton and Oldham. The helpfulness and efficiency of the staff of the John Rylands University Library of Manchester at all times smoothed the way. Tina Reid and Liz Dyckhoff of the Manchester History Department Office and Margaret Riley of Broadbottom word-processed my laborious hand with remarkable speed, accuracy and good humour. My warmest gratitude is due to them. It is due to others not mentioned here. All academic labour is unoriginal, the product of a thousand borrowings. Authors are often the least well placed to know what has mattered in the gestation of their work. In the nature of things much of what really mattered is lost. To all those not mentioned here who contributed to this book I extend my thanks and apologies.

This book is based on research funded by the Economic and Social Research Council (ESRC) reference number GOO 23 21643, and by the award of a Nuffield Foundation Social Science Research Fellowship. Research was also facilitated by the award of study leave by Manchester University.

Acknowledgements and thanks for the photographs are due to the following: Chris E. Makepeace, Edith Olive, Manchester and Leeds Central Libraries, Tameside Local Studies Library, Audrey Linkman and the Documentary Photography Archive, Manchester. Cover photography kindly supplied by Chris E. Makepeace of Disley, Cheshire. Thanks also to Trudi Tate of Cambridge University Press.

My undying thanks to Rosaleen, who kept the pot boiling.

Patrick Joyce
Department of History
University of Manchester

1

Introduction : beyond class?

Until relatively recently, 'class' in British history was a settled matter. The periodisation given to the 'class consciousness' of workers had assumed fairly distinct lines. Despite the large amount of subsequent scholarship, the work of E. P. Thompson and E. J. Hobsbawm remained, and remains, central, fixing the historical sequence of class development. Thompson's enormously influential *The Making of the English Working Class* presents a picture of class consciousness as substantially 'made' by around 1830, the outcome of the effect of early industrialisation and political change upon the plebeity or common people of late eighteenth-century England.[1] Hobsbawm looks to the consolidation of industrial capitalism in the late nineteenth century, rather than to its inception.[2] Whatever the differences, class is seen as probably the major cultural and political expression of the prolonged sequence of nineteenth-century industrial change, if not determined by such change then developing roughly in step with it.

This has now taken the form of received wisdom. However, while there is no denying that class was a child of the nineteenth century, when it comes to how the social order was represented and understood, there were other children too who were every bit as lusty as class – indeed, in many respects stronger and more fully part of their time. Received wisdom has in fact become a dead weight, the fixation with class denying us sight of these other visions of the social order. This fixation has recently come under direct fire, significantly from the left rather than from the right: both empirically and analytically, the concept of class has been attacked as inappropriate and inadequate.[3] This scepticism is to be applauded. It informs the present work, though the fire here is less direct. Class will not go away. It has its place, and an important one, though it does from time to time need to be put in it. A good part of this disciplining of the class concept involves attention to the actual terms in which contemporaries talked about the social order, and to the means through which they communicated their perceptions. In short, it involves attention to language, to the means and content of human communication. This, therefore, is as much a book about language as about class. At least in part it is a product of its post-structuralist

1

times. It is necessary, however, to begin with the concept of class. And here, of course, it all depends upon how one defines class.

It also depends on how one conceives of industrialisation, and before coming to the question of definitions something needs to be said about this. Anglo-American scholarship on class has emphasised cultural and political factors so strongly that the last thing one may call it is economically determinist. Indeed, it can be accused of neglecting the dimension of economic change. Nonetheless, industrial change implicitly informs many such accounts: for instance, there is a telling analogy between metaphors of class development and economic change, ideas of biological growth informing both, with classes and industrial capitalism alike growing to 'maturity'. Now, this is not a book about industrial change and its effect on class formation. Nonetheless, because prevailing ideas about the industrial revolution have been influential, they need to be questioned. This can be done only briefly here.[4]

Britain was the seat of the 'industrial revolution', and continues to be widely seen as the epitome of new systems of production, and hence of a new consciousness of class to which these systems gave rise. Recent notions of economic development serve to question accepted ideas of a convergence of economic organisation around large-scale factory production and an attendant homogenisation of condition and outlook among the workforce. The picture of capitalist industrialism that has emerged in recent years is fairly familiar, though the ramifications of this view and its implications for the social outlook of workers have not been explored. Very briefly, what has been termed 'combined and uneven development' can be seen as involving the incorporation rather than the supercession of earlier forms of industrial organisation. For instance, outwork and small workshop production continued to be of great importance at least as late as the 1914–18 war. In supposedly 'modern' forms of organisation (for example in engineering, shipbuilding and even textiles), it is the 'archaism' of organisation that is evident, especially the reliance of employers on the strength, skill and authority of the workforce. The labour process is seen to involve not a linear process of 'de-skilling', and an homogeneous working class, but a multiplicity of outcomes, including continuity in the worker's experience and outlook. Explorations of capital reveal the paternalist values and strategies of employers, the force of inter-capitalist competition, and the relatively small-scale and fragmented pattern of industrial ownership. The Victorian and indeed the Edwardian economy in many respects was irregular and diverse. So too was the nature of the individual occupation and the pattern of the individual's work life.

The consequences of all this are evident in the revelation of a very diverse and fragmented labour force, one to which the term 'proletarian' applies with only a good deal of qualification. By that term one denotes, among other attributes, work for wages, usually life long, and usually manual. Workers are subject to contract rather than to extra-economic compulsions and traditions. Above all, ownership and control over the means of production are lost. However, the great variety of forms of industrial organisation, and in particular the complex permeation of authority within industry, involved a multiplicity of situations in which the worker had more to lose than his or her chains. As well as a stake in the ownership and control of production (sometimes vestigial to us but not for the workers involved), he (rarely she) also often had a stake in how production should be governed. The term 'proletarian' does not do justice to the range of experience involved, or to the great array of skills and statuses so clearly evident in what, in the singular, is clearly a distinctly tenuous 'working class'. This questioning of the idea of the proletarian is furthered by new considerations of the relationship between labour and capital.[5] Instead of an overmastering, trans-historical tendency towards conflict – along classical Marxist lines – what is evident is the inter-dependence of capital and labour, alongside the dependence and independence of labour which also mark the employment relationship at other times. Relations depend upon historical circumstances. Capitalists need to secure consent. The vested interest workers and employers have in co-operation is at least as great as any tendency towards conflict.

The upshot of all this for many received ideas about class is evident enough. Just as linear notions of economic development seem untenable, so too do linear notions of class development. Indeed, socio-economic class position or situation emerges as so fractured and ambiguous that the very notion of class may itself be questioned. This questioning becomes even more urgent when proletarianisation is set in its broader contexts.[6] The experience of residential community is often taken to complement the shared experience of work in cementing class solidarity. Yet when the British case is looked at it is the lateness and the ambiguous form of developments that are evident. For instance, the great coalfields, supposed bastions of 'traditional' working-class consciousness, did not emerge as fully coherent social and cultural entities until the late nineteenth and early twentieth century, particularly in the case of south Wales. In earlier forms of urban industry, above all in textiles,[7] the intimate relationship of work and community produced attitudes of mind often far removed from those of class. One could go on to detail other areas beyond labour mobility and urban morphology, looking for instance in the socio-economic sphere at patterns of immigration (particularly of the Irish), or at the very late development of the uniform working day, week and year, a late emergence of a uniform work experience paralleling the late emergence of uniform occupational communities.[8]

However, aspects of this kind of revisionism may suggest that all things being equal, and the conditions enabling the development of class consciousness emerging earlier, then a class outcome would have been evident earlier. There is a sense in which the answer to questions about the periodisation of class may be that everything (proletarianisation, consciousness) merely happened later and more gradually than was thought. However, one is still left with the evident anachronism of imagining that given the 'correct' combination of conditions class would be the outcome. Alternatives to class are left out of the account and historical situations are correspondingly misread.

In fact, once the question of proletarianisation is put in a radical manner then the concept of class comes under heavy fire. If we postpone class to the twentieth century this still leaves a rather large question mark over the nineteenth century. For, in order for the concept of class as usually understood to have a purchase, it surely must in some sense be anchored in the socio-economic condition of workers. The 'in some sense' is of course the rub. The emphasis on the study of class in Britain has strongly emphasised struggle, and the cultural agency of the individuals involved. Certainly, class needs to be seen in cultural and political terms of the playing out of values and traditions in changing circumstances. This, indeed, is one of the main arguments of this book. But before entering into the great array of questions and difficulties evident in this area, it is as well to maintain, without of course being in any sense determinist or production centred, that for the notion of class to hold then something other than cultural or political factors needs to be in play. That is to say, if class 'position' is not considered in the light of the very problematic nature of proletarianisation, then one is led to ask in what respect is the phenomenon to hand a matter of 'working-class consciousness' (presumably an outlook based on the perception of workers' shared experience as manual proletarians), rather than cultural and political traditions *per se*, or extra-proletarian identifications such as 'the people', or the primary producers. Of course, we can define class as we like, in terms as cultural as we wish, but we should be aware that we are doing this, and that this will change one of the major meanings of class, both within Marxism and beyond it.

Of course, the 'in some sense' comes into play here, too, and it is in practice impossible to dissociate the representations and beliefs of people from their experience of nineteenth-century industrial capitalism. The condition of the proletarian at the time was indeed complex and ambiguous, though there were important respects in which it *was* a shared condition of powerlessness. So, the matter is perhaps one of degree, and in other work I pull back from the verge of denying class, arguing the need to balance tendencies towards fragmentation in work experience with those towards unity.[9] One simple instance would be the strike in pursuit of the sectionalist interests of workers, an activity self-interested in character but at the same time directed against employers and so capable of various meanings and results. The main significance of trade unions would in this argument be not that they were sectionalist in character but that they existed at all.

Tendencies towards a unity of labour experience and a resulting unity of class sentiment can be geographically and industrially localised, or emergent and declining at different times and under different conditions. To admit this, and to recognise the formative role of periods of economic and political crisis, is not to disallow the notion of class consciousness, unless we wish to apply hopelessly idealised criteria. At the same time, there were elements of continuing force and moment in workers' conceptions of themselves which imply the persistence of a consciousness of being workers. Such a notion, considered in chapters 4 and 5, was that of the trade, allied to the concept of the 'artisan' or 'craftsman', which conveyed important distinctions of honour and worth often far beyond the ranks of craft workers alone. Therefore, tendencies towards unity and fragmentation in socio-economic position and in values cannot be resolved arbitrarily in one direction or the other. So, in pulling back from the brink one is not doing so in order to retain the fig-leaf of Marxist decencies. There is life after class. The reasons are mundane. Simply, class mattered.

However, in pushing home the implications of revisionist notions of the development of industrial capitalism, one recognises not only that there is life after class, but that this life is vastly more important and colourful than has been thought. Before considering the nature of popular conceptions of the social order other than those of class, I shall complete this genuflection to the economy by posing the question: if the greatly ambiguous nature of work experience often has negative implications for both the concept and the consciousness of class, does it perhaps have more positive implications for alternative popular understandings? I have spoken briefly of cultural and political traditions cutting across identifications based on the experience of proletarian labour, of extra-proletarian identifications such as 'the people'. When we come to the matter of definitions, it will be seen that if class has a rival it is perhaps that of 'populism', of 'the people'. Now, as I argue below for the need to take seriously the formative role of language and ideas in the formation of attitudes to the social order, I can hardly regress by treading again the path of 'economism' by explaining a populist vision in terms of the heterogeneous, ambiguous nature of so much labour experience. In fact, except in chapter 5, I have little to say about the character of the economy in relation to non-class models of the social. Perhaps too little. Certainly, the temptation is too great to resist here: the very ambiguity of many people's experience as labour – of being a worker by hand and for wages yet having a great deal in common with others who were not – surely made for the successful appeal of notions like 'the people' which often depended upon just such sorts of ambiguity. At the same time, the logic of ambiguous 'class position' certainly lent itself well to the many models of harmonic class relationships evident at the time.

So, this discussion clears some of the ground for a consideration of alternatives to class before 1914. More can be cleared by looking at the revised but still orthodox argument that class did come but came late and gradually, after 1880, say, or 1900 or 1918. With this one has some sympathy, particularly with the somewhat less orthodox notion that it was the years after 1910, and especially after 1914 and the war that mattered most here. If the 'same but later' argument holds, this inevitably colours our idea of the Victorian and Edwardian years: events and values may be seen as precursors of class, and their real character and effect may be lost. So, even though this means trespassing on what may be regarded as the matter of a conclusion rather than an introduction, I shall briefly look at aspects of change after the 1880s, so that these may be registered without driving an alternative narrative from our minds. The period between 1880 and 1920 certainly did see considerable changes, but more perhaps at its end than at its beginning.

Increasingly, if slowly, the Victorian and the Edwardian economies lost much of their heterogeneity over this period. If the experience of labour did not become more intensive in the sense of the erosion of the place of the skilled worker, then it seems to have become in a sense more 'extensive', a term employed by Mann in one of the best accounts of 'class formation' in Britain.[10] Semi-skilled work increased, and with it a uniformity of experience at that level. This was in turn related to changes in the organisational sphere which helped produce a clearer perception of being a manual proletarian; it also changed perceptions of the relationship of capital and labour as one more marked by conflict than was hitherto felt to be the case. In the form of mass organisations working on a national level the role of institutions was greatly important in bringing about changes in outlook. Political parties, particularly the Labour Party, employer organisations and above all trade unions, which increased in membership to a quite staggering extent between 1910 and 1920, were greatly important here.[11] Again, the decade from 1910 seems to have been most significant, obviously in terms of war, but also in terms of the growth of the Labour Party and the unions.

Nonetheless, the growing national integration and concentration of the economy had made itself evident earlier in organisational changes which made it possible and indeed necessary for workers to have a view larger than that of their immediate *milieu*.[12] It was from the 1890s that strikes and lock-outs on a *national* scale developed, and only between 1890 and 1920 that negotiated, nationwide collective industrial agreements were arrived at (though the Labour Department of the Board of Trade had been set up early in this period, in 1893). The emphasis on the role of organisations is of historiographical interest in its own right, and will be returned to: contrary to the drift of the social history of only a short time ago, changes in outlook now tend to be seen as the outcome of changes in organisation rather than the other way round.

This is not to suggest that broader social and cultural changes were not important, nor effective over the long term. Historians have pointed to changed patterns of consumption, which were perhaps as important as changes in production. Changes in the buying power of workers and in the organisation of retailing meant a more uniform pattern of behaviour, something also seen in the use of leisure time, such as the increasing popularity of organised sport and the seaside holiday. All this in turn involved a culture that was more uniform than hitherto, and was highly specific to workers.[13] More uniform kinds of housing and more segregated forms of residential settlement were evident within towns, a process going a long way towards breaking down the employer controls evident in earlier manifestations of the symbiosis of work and community. One could go on to list other changes which point to the plausibility of the argument that a more firmly delineated class consciousness emerged before 1914; for example mass, compulsory elementary education, and the mass literacy that resulted. Less frequently noted aspects would include the re-formation of the late Victorian middle-classes, a process we know very little about, but one surely closely linked to the structural re-formation of the labouring population.[14]

Plausible as the argument might seem, what few half-way systematic accounts we have of the 'class' outlook and values of workers do in fact suggest that it was the First World War and its immediate aftermath that was most crucial in re-forming attitudes. Waites' work is by far the best available.[15] This makes obeisance to pre-war developments, yet it is pretty clear that the war saw striking developments: it greatly hastened structural changes, such as a narrowing of wage differentials within manual labour, but most of all it saw the growth of dichotomous images of society turning upon the opposition of labour and capital. These replaced the old three-tier, and very fluid, pre-war system of an 'upper', a 'middle' and a 'lower' or 'working' class or classes.[16]

This evidence is striking not only because of its systematic attention to languages of social classification, but also because its very rigour throws into contrast the tenuous nature of much of the evidence for a changed 'consciousness' of class before 1914. The question is nothing if not an open one, but it must be said that the evidence presented for a change of this character is often thin. Many of the changes so far considered were of a structural or cultural sort, and while they may have been predisposing factors they are not evidence of the realisation of class consciousness. The evidence is stronger in some places than in others, for instance as regards the effect of organisational changes (though it must be said that these are often easier to track than other changes). In fact, our understanding of change over this period still rests heavily on Hobsbawm's work: suggestive as this is, it deals mostly with the emergence of what can be described as a 'working class culture', but this is not the same as the emergence of a working-class consciousness of class. Because manual workers chose to wear cloth caps and support football teams it does not follow that they saw the social order in terms of class. As chapter 6 below suggest, it is perfectly possible to have a culture which can be defined as 'working class' but yet for the consciousness associated with this culture to have little or nothing to do with class. As so often, the category of class has tended to drive other possibilities out of the account. Again, the teleological assumptions behind many accounts are not hard to find.

Waites' work is useful in countering these too. An emphasis on the onward march of class, or class as the only or the main outcome of historical change, obscures the fact that ideological versions of 'classlessness' constantly reproduce themselves. If class waxed so too did responses that denied it. Even if the latter were stronger in an earlier period than in early twentieth-century Britain, as Waites shows, governments, unions and employers, also intellectuals, both in war-time and in its immediate aftermath were influential in promoting notions either of the harmony of labour and capital or the essential classlessness of the nation.[17] New as these were, they had a strong relationship with pre-war politics and culture. This emphasis on continuity is in fact an important one, and applies more widely to the entire nature of British society. As this book will suggest, the mental universe of workers and others in the 1920s, 30s and later was shaped by the legacy of the Victorian and Edwardian years. Even if class was the outcome of the inter-war years, it was itself still powerfully shaped by that experience. In order to understand how that experience gave rise to popular conceptions of the social order it is necessary first to consider what our terms mean, particularly the term 'class consciousness'.

The term has indeed an antiquated ring to it, one redolent of a time, not so long ago, when class was seen in terms of patterns of belief and action of a uniform, indeed, cut-and-dried kind. Actual values and behaviour were understood in terms of what were in fact hopelessly idealised categories such as 'revolutionary' or 'labour' consciousness, notions emanating from an earlier Marxism but not at all its exclusive preserve.[18] The reason why such notions of consciousness have become superannuated is above all the effect of the new historical interest in theories of language and ideology. Instead of monolithic types of 'consciousness', the latter is resolved into a series of different, overlapping and often competing 'discourses'. This new interest in language is considered more fully in parts I and II, where it is related to the political and economic conditions of Victorian England. But it is worth emphasising here something of what is at issue.

Above all, what has become evident is the dissolution of the old assurance of a formative link between social structure and culture. Class is therefore increasingly, and rightly, seen less as objective reality than as a social construct, created differently by different historical actors. The seemingly simple recognition that the category of 'experience' (out of which historians such as E. P. Thompson argue comes class consciousness) is in fact not prior to and constitutive of language but is actively constituted by language, has increasingly been recognised as having far-reaching implications. In the disaggregation of 'class', deconstruction has taken this route of language, ideology and identity. This is the route of this book. Another route is that of organisation, it being argued for instance that 'class consciousness' should be seen as the attribute of organisations and not individuals.[19] According to this argument what matters is the capacity of a class to behave as a 'class actor'. 'Class organisations' enable this, transforming a 'latent' class 'identity' into class consciousness. Consciousness, then, is the capacity, through organisations like parties and unions, to convert sectional, conflicting struggles and interests into solidaristic and political forms. This emphasis on institutions can, however, be both excessive and crude. No one disputes the significance of organ- isations: the first two parts of this book emphasise their role, but they do so, one hopes, not by pre-judging the issue, or by defining in advance what are to be 'class actors', 'class organisations' and class consciousness.

Those historians who have done most to direct attention to 'languages of class' have done most to explode this evident anachronism. American historians of France such as William Sewell and William Reddy have been influential.[20] Reddy's researches in particular have unearthed workers' notions of work, family and community that were often far removed from the values ascribed to them by contemporaries and by posterity – as much by the workingmen leaders of the labour and socialist movements of the time as by less ostensibly sympathetic commentators, then and since. What his work points to most forcefully is the whole area of those facets of belief and value often *not* articulated by organisations, those aspects of life buried in the subsequent historical record because they were not perceived, or were mis-perceived, at the time. Now, such instances might be the ones where history simply failed to turn. They have been neglected because they failed to lead anywhere. But more often they have been neglected because of unwarranted assumptions about where history led. In both respects they were important. This sense of suppressed alternatives and neglected possibilities informs the present work.

It also informs the work of the British social historian who has done most to open up the question of class 'language', Stedman Jones. The considerable body of criticism his work on Chartism has given rise to will be considered in subsequent chapters.[21] This work has been rightly criticised for its formalistic account of political language and for its lack of attention to the contexts in which 'class' languages are used. In many respects, despite its bracing effect, it does not go very far either with language or with class.[22] However, it does begin to suggest alternatives to the notion of class, even though its account of these is not far developed. In short, along with other recent work,[23] his writing suggests the presence of a powerful 'populism' behind the rhetoric of early-century popular radicalism. With the employment of the term 'populism' it is at last time to come to the matter of definition, and in turn to some discussion of possibilities other than that of class.

The sense in which 'class' is used in this work is already to some extent evident. A common socio-economic condition as proletarians, or dependent, manual, waged workers, would in fact seem central to any definition of what 'working class' might mean, as would a shared perception of this common condition. Now, the actual nature of proletarianisation in practice varied considerably, but nonetheless a certain level of common condition and outlook would have to prevail. Therefore, broadly speaking, 'economic' criteria would seem to be uppermost. 'Class' also usually connotes relations of exclusion, of fairly clearly demarcated boundaries. In this respect Hobsbawm supplies us with a robustly empirical account of what the class outlook of British workers amounted to: it was based on a 'profound sense' of the separateness of manual labour.[24] Now, the sense of a shared condition need not automatically issue in an understanding of social relations as tending inherently towards conflict: this book gives many accounts of class identities and the use of class vocabularies which were heavily consensual in character. Nonetheless, the sense of being part of a class almost by definition involves being part of a society made up of more than one class: the sense of class is defined in relation to, and usually over and against, other classes. Again as Hobsbawm has put it for the British case, there is a readiness to fight for rights and for what is considered just treatment. Therefore, if a sense of conflict and struggle are not necessarily omnipresent, then in most definitions of class this sense would be fairly marked. Of course, in Marxist terms 'struggle' is seen as the defining mark of class. It would also be the case, given a shared perception of manual labour as central, that conflict would be chiefly viewed as the conflict of capital and labour. If not the only cleavage in society, the class cleavage turning upon this 'economic' opposition would be the main one.

What is apparent here is a rough definition of class as economic, socially exclusive, and connoting conflict. By contrast, 'populism' points to a set of discourses and identities which are extra-economic in character, and inclusive and universalising in their social remit in contrast to the exclusive categories of class. As intimated earlier, extra-proletarian identifications such as those of 'people' and 'nation' are involved. As well as, or instead of, conflict, chiefly evident are notions combining social justice and social reconciliation. The accent on social concord and human fellowship is very strong, as will be evident later in a variety of historical settings. Now, this sort of definitional exercise raises a number of difficulties and objections, some of which I in fact support. But on balance the exercise is valuable.

The first difficulty would be that after objecting to one over-arching social category, that of class, one is in turn in danger of erecting another, that of 'populism'. In the light of post-structuralism would this not be illusory? Should not terms like these be 'deconstructed' into the constituent discourses or identities that make up social consciousness? Sometimes allied to this is the argument that identities and discourses are in fact never coherent but always cross-cutting and contradictory. In turn this argument is at times accompanied by the notion that 'culture' is itself never coherent, but is an ensemble of discordant meanings, each specific to its own social context.[25] People are husbands, mothers, voters, members of classes or of football teams, or whatever, and these do not necessarily form between them coherent wholes. Whether 'deconstruction' takes these 'soft' or 'hard' forms it raises valid questions about supposedly coherent social identities.

In practice, however, it is quite apparent that social identities do overlap, and this goes for the major categories of 'class' and 'people' considered at some length in this book. It is clear that it is a plurality of language and identities we have to deal with, and a plurality of contexts and uses applying to these. Indeed, as the argument develops, the increasing complexity of the relationship of these major elements alongside nation, region, gender and community will become amply evident. But it still seems to make sense to speak of these large generic categories simply because they seem quite clearly to have been there, part of historical experience, as well as elements in a definition. In themselves, individual aspects such as class, people and nation were fusions of different loyalties, but they do nonetheless seem each to have had recognisably distinct forms, and culture was not the incoherent, discordant thing it is sometimes taken to be. Similar sorts of response could be made to the objection that the category of populism is simply too open-ended, encompassing too much, and in a sense referring to everything that is not class. To this two further things may be said: first, a coherent populism can be seen in this period, though in fact it is much more useful to talk about a variety of populisms (as is done in chapter 3); and secondly, the definition given *is* in some respects too baggy but that it is a necessary and useful heuristic device.

Before considering this let me briefly deal with another possible objection, namely that the term 'populism' contains too many connotations, is already too coloured, to be of use. There is a good deal in this argument, and it is with some hesitation that I use the term, for in the following account what so often presents itself when popular conceptions of the social order are considered is not quite 'populism' and not quite 'class'. But alternative terms are not readily available, and the present ones need to be used, purged as far as possible of associations automatically attaching to them. For instance, the automatic association of populism with demagogic politics needs to be guarded against. The term has been closely associated with particular kinds of politics and social movement, in the American farming midwest, for example, or in nineteenth-century Russia, and this is as it should be. The use of the term in this book is generally much looser, however, and is a means of contrasting certain sorts of outlook with that of class. The matter is discussed further in chapter 3 where the different senses of 'populism' are discussed: in fact the narrower (or 'classical') sense of populism was by no means completely out of place in nineteenth-century England, complete with conspiratorial notions of rule and with ideas of a vanished golden age and a virtuous people in battle with a manipulative elite.

To return to the heuristic aspects of the definition of class and populism, it will no doubt be objected, especially in relation to the definition of class, that this is all hopelessly idealised and unhistorical. Again, I have some sympathy with this view. In practice 'class' and 'populism' were so closely related that defining them as separate things may be unwise. As Stedman Jones has shown, workers in the 1830s and 40s looked upon the true 'people' as the workers, and a populist vocabulary certainly had a 'class' meaning at this time, at least in part. Similarly, a class vocabulary could have many of the attributes associated here with populism. For instance, workers in mid-nineteenth-century England and France had a clear idea of their identity as manual labourers, and they often employed a vocabulary of social description which used the explicit terms of class. But it has been frequently noted that they gave this vocabulary a decidedly moralistic and universalistic set of meanings,[26] one in which the accent was often upon fraternity and social reconciliation. Their conception of class can be regarded as specific to their time, and there is a sense in which this definitional concern can be avoided by seeing class languages and identities as developing over historical time, from the Enlightenment-influenced universalism of the mid-century, for example, to the more exclusive, 'economic' criteria of later times. At all events, as is suggested in chapter 5, it seems obtuse to refuse the term class to these movements and views of the mid-century. From one point of view this is valid, and it does not much matter what label is attached so long as the term class does not obscure the real character of what was there.

However, the problem is that the employment of the term usually does this. It is also the case that once we start defining class with more and more latitude, as it increasingly takes upon itself the terms of 'populism' as defined here, it becomes less and less useful. In particular, once a strong connection with the economic, with notions of social exclusion and with conflict rather than fellowship is lost, then one is led once again to ask in what useful sense the term 'class' applies at all. The matter of definition would not perhaps be seen as pressing by those who see class as the historical eventuation of social struggles, albeit of struggles in some degree rooted in the economic sphere. Here the influence of E. P. Thompson has been seminal, and one bears in mind his tireless strictures against the idea of idealised, platonic notions of class, or, in another key, notions of 'true' as opposed to 'false' consciousness. But that is not what is being urged here. Quite the contrary in fact.

It is among scholars influenced by the Thompsonian view of the priority of class struggle that the problem of the infinite elasticity of class most strongly asserts itself. It is also there that the most interesting interpretations of class are evident. A good example of this is the recent work of Epstein on early nineteenth-century popular radicalism.[27] In brief, it is argued that the constitutionalist rhetoric of popular radicalism was an expression of class. Citing the Marxist aesthetician Fredric Jameson, Epstein notes that 'the dialogue of class struggle is (normally) one in which two opposed discourses fight it out within the general unity of a shared code'. This matter will be discussed in chapter 4.[28] This is in fact potentially a productive way of looking at class. Dorothy Thompson suggests a rather similar approach in noting how it was 'working-class' people who spoke the language of political equality and of universal suffrage in Chartism, and the 'middle class' who held to a more restricted notion of political rights.[29]

But the great problem with this, summed up in the ambiguity evident in Jameson's 'general unity of a shared code', is to know in what sense it is class when the discourse in question is, on the face of it, not a class one, but one in which below, or beside, the level of a 'working-class' appropriation of a political discourse there may be large areas of thought and sentiment obtaining between different social groups (based for instance on ideas of citizenship and political rights). It is not that such a popular appropriation cannot be evidence of class. It is simply that a class connection needs to be shown, and to my mind it cannot be shown unless the discourse or values under discussion show a considerable affinity with the attributes of class as defined here. In neither of the two cases mentioned, Epstein and Thompson, is class demonstrated in this way. Of course, what all this raises directly is the relationship between class struggle and class consciousness, the emphasis on the formative role of struggle being central to the work of E. P. Thompson.[30] As Thompson argues, classes do not have pre-given identities, a 'true' consciousness. This is so. They acquire a consciousness of class identity in historical eventuation, very often in struggle. But the problem is to know what class identity looks like, and where it starts and stops. One cannot simply ascribe a class consciousness to the social struggles of subordinate groups simply because they are in struggle. Thompson's description of the gentry–crowd relationship in the eighteenth century as in some sense a 'class' struggle is a case in point: there seems little point employing the term when the attributes of class seem to have been so little present to the historical actors involved (not to mention the difficulties of applying a socio-economic class analysis to terms like the crowd, or the plebeity). Of course there may be polemical, argumentative force in choosing the term 'class struggle' instead of the seemingly more neutral 'social struggle', but that is another matter, and one removed from the substance of the argument.

Now, there is in these nineteenth-century examples a sense in which class can be allowed here, the sense that popular constitutionalism say can be pretty clearly the expression of a defined social group we call the working class. As has been seen, in practice identifying this group in the nineteenth century is often far more difficult than is sometimes thought. Nonetheless, we can talk of a peasants' or a workers' movement or set of values as 'class' ones in the sense of their being the expression of such groups. This is a reasonable usage, and one to which I return in the conclusion, when what might be meant by the making of the English working class in this period is discussed. Nonetheless, in the body of this book, however rashly, my money goes on an alternative method, that of applying an analytical definition of class, the better to understand the plurality of interpretations evident at the time. For, quite simply, the consciousness of *a class* need not be the consciousness of *class*.

Although social constituencies we might choose to call classes express certain values, this does not make the values *themselves* ones of class. Meanings are an altogether different matter. To assume that they can be gratuitously given a class label merely by dint of their social constituency is to open the door to almost any cultural manifestation as the expression of class. Hence the need for some kind of definition to prevent this sort of academic language game. What is evident here, and indeed in almost the whole response to Stedman Jones, is a steadfast recourse to the rock of class, a return to earlier positions, however re-defined, instead of an attempt to look for new directions. In importing class once again as holy writ, discussion of the real nature of the popular values involved is too often foreclosed. In the particular case of popular constitutionalism it may be that populism rather than class is the best descriptive term to apply.

Now, to Marxists of a less 'cultural' disposition than those discussed here all this would perhaps be regarded as a storm in a teacup. The forces of production create 'class position' or 'situation', a location within capitalist or pre-capitalist modes of economic exploitation which produces no necessary or given outcome in culture and consciousness. Theoretically, almost any outcome can be given a class label, or indeed refused one. Arguable as this position is, it runs up against the same difficulty as the previous position in that there is little or no control over what a class outlook should look like, except for the definition of the observer. In practice, such positions argue a 'strongly conditioning' role for class position, a relation of 'logic if not of law' as Cohen puts it.[31] In fact, advocates of a structural definition of classes impute very strong historical consequences to the 'class position' of people: people exist within exploitative relationships, and come to have interests in common in prosecuting or repelling exploitation. In such arguments, indeed, class is seen as *fundamentally* a relationship of conflict: as a Marxist historian of the ancient world observes, 'class conflict (class struggle) is essentially the fundamental relationship between classes, involving *exploitation* and resistance to it'.[32] Now, this is not the place to prolong theoretical discussion, though it should be said that this sort of position has the merit of delivering something that is recognisable as class, even though, accepting the exploitative nature of economic relationships for the moment, it seems to me entirely gratuitous to argue that such relationships are simply given to people in the form of conflict and antagonism.[33] Here the language of 'interests' breaks down: economic relationships, however exploitative (in the technical or moral sense), present themselves to people in countless ways, conditioned by culture and circumstance.[34]

In the remainder of this introduction, I will forswear 'theory' and outline the approach to be taken in what follows. In fact, the large number of topics considered below, and the considerable problems each of these topics reveals, mean that while attention to the matters so far discussed is always maintained, the historical material throws up a host of issues every bit as important as those already considered. Having made a claim to extended scope I should immediately follow this by saying that the remit of what follows is limited. This is a book chiefly about social identities and about discourses concerning the social order. It tries, especially in the first two parts, to say something about how these were related to movements and organisations, but it makes no pretence to putting social structure, organisations and identities back together again. Nonetheless, existing accounts of how this might be done, based on the idea of class 'interest', seem to me feeble in the extreme. Interests are not somehow given in the economic condition of workers, but are constructed through the agency of identities. Indeed, such identities are as real as any 'interests' ever were. The formation of social identities is not therefore something peripheral to a broader social and cultural history but is quite central to it. And this formation was something accomplished in and by language.

The various meanings of the term 'language' form a major

principle around which this work is organised: indeed, the strong interest in popular conceptions of the social order is equalled by the interest in the means by which these conceptions were constituted. This concern with language is pursued closely, so considerable, and fascinating, are the questions involved. The book is arranged in four parts: on politics, on work, on culture and on art and the imagination. In the first two parts language is considered in the sense of the 'discourses' which pertained at the time to popular politics and to labour, especially to trade unions. Discourse in this sense is seen as bodies of utterance of a relatively formal, public sort, often associated with institutions. Language in this sense of 'discourse' is to be differentiated from the symbolic, less formal and public, often assumed and unspoken, ways in which the social world is given form by people. In chapter 6, on custom and the symbolic structure of 'everyday', community life (a structure seen in dress, gesture, the built environment for example, in non-verbal as well as verbal forms), the meaning of this sense of language (as opposed to the earlier sense of discourse) will, I hope, become plain. However, there is no hard and fast distinction between these two senses, and the distinction at best is a rough one.

What I am trying to do is to expand the senses in which language might be considered by historians. Chapter 6's expanded sense of language as a sign system – of what might be called the semiology of the social order – is not allowed to detract from the conventional sense of language as spoken or written verbal communication. This sense of language, in this case of the national language, English, in its standard and dialect forms, is the subject of chapter 8, under the title of 'The People's English'. In the long, final part the 'language' of popular art is considered, the forms of art chosen being primarily discursive literature, as well as the performed arts of melodrama and music hall, particularly music hall. This part enables me to pursue the most subtle and the most complex of all the forms of sign system.

This is a big agenda. The drift of the parts on politics, work and art will be fairly self-evident. The kinds of literature considered in the last section on art are the broadside ballads and the many forms of dialect literature, especially in the industrial north, and in particular in Lancashire. Chapter 9 considers some of the problems of historical interpretation concerned with using imaginative material, and dwells on the justification for choosing these kinds of literature: they followed each other in historical sequence in this period, and had much in common. In turn, music hall more or less followed as the next step in the sequence, and had much in common with its two predecessors. The drift of the part on 'culture' will, however, be less immediately apparent.

When we consider language in the broad sense of a sign system, embracing verbal and non-verbal forms, and both literal and symbolic meaning, then we are in fact close to certain definitions of culture itself. The sense of culture as a symbolising activity, a giving of meaning to the world in order to control it, is one that seems to me especially productive. Therefore, because language in this broad sense is arguably so close to what culture actually is, my interest in language translates directly into an interest in culture. But 'culture' has, notoriously, many meanings, and in chapter 8, on national language, as in chapter 7 on how the sense of the past was constituted at the time, it becomes evident how ideas about language and history were also ideas about 'culture'. This is so at any time, but in the nineteenth century language and history were very closely related, history being seen in terms of language development and 'national' literatures, and language becoming perceived in historical rather than idealist terms, an historicism which was in fact to characterise many of the forms of knowledge at the time. Given the nature of nineteenth-century intellectual life, a discussion of history and language gives a tolerably accurate account of what contemporaries felt culture to be.

So, ideas about language and about history have been suffused in judgements and prescriptions concerning 'culture' in this second sense of the term, namely culture as *ideas* about the (chiefly) non-material formation of peoples and nations. This therefore warrants systematic attention to language and history, thus enabling a consideration of ideas about culture which were themselves in turn riddled with assumptions about how the social order was and should be made up. So, one approaches culture with this perhaps oversimplified distinction between the local, anthropological sense, and the ideological sense. Anyway, I do not wish to labour distinctions which will become fairly self-evident in due course. The former sense is more evident in chapter 6 on custom, the latter in the following two, though chapter 8 on the national language embraces both senses, with language use here often seen to be symbolically encoding valuations of the social in all sorts of implicit and assumed ways.

This is not merely a big agenda, but may be too prolific and ambitious as well. I am aware of the dangers: each of the topics chosen has its own intrinsic difficulties, and its own experts, historians and others. However, the opportunities presented by working across such a broad canvas are at least as great as the difficulties encountered. The result of the new historical interest in language is to direct attention back to what used to be called the 'close analysis' of particular 'texts', verbal and non-verbal. This is all to the good, and can yield rich results. At the same time, there is the parallel danger of paying too much attention to the individual text or instance, and shying away from the long-term and the synthetic account. One result of the 'deconstruction' of class is that we understand better the parts but not how they fit together. Of course, it may be fairly argued that the time for more synthetic accounts has not yet come. The work has simply not been done. This may be so. Nonetheless, however crude may be the present attempt at a synthesis, it is probably worth making. There is a need for some account of the larger English picture throughout this period, and for some foray into art, for example, as well as politics.

The breadth of interests evident in what follows is in fact given a reasonable measure of direction and coherence. A concern with identities and with language cannot for long abstract itself from particular times and particular places. The particular instance in this case is the industrial Lancashire of the years between the decline of Chartism in the 1840s and the First World War. However, the industrial north more widely is also the object of concern, the manufacturing districts of the West Riding of Yorkshire and the industrial north-east also figuring in the account. So, the 'industrial north', and in particular the textile districts and textile workers of Lancashire, are the means by which the diverse strands of this book are drawn together. In one sense my grand design is quite limited: the account is in many ways concerned with millworkers and with how they saw the world. This restriction is both necessary and inevitable if the real questions are to be answered. Anything else would be lifeless and, literally, meaningless. At the same time, while recognising the uniqueness of industrial Lancashire, I have at all times tried to locate it within broader, national patterns.

Asking Lancashire to stand proxy for England while continuing to acknowledge its uniqueness of course presents many problems. The time period chosen perhaps presents fewer difficulties: the years from the decline of Chartism to the First World War do have a certain unity. They were bracketed by periods of crisis and conflict. They were, broadly, years of consolidation, the consolidation of industrial capitalism, of political democracy, of a new urban culture. They were the years which shaped the character of the century that followed. However, one does not wish to impose a false unity upon them: it is simply that they have a kind of rough logic of their own.

The same may be said for choosing my industrial examples. However, Lancashire has a clear relevance to my subtitle. Lancashire was as good an example of 'industrial England' as anywhere. Indeed, to contemporaries for much of this period Lancashire *was* industrial England, its factories and mines the *locus classicus* of a new urban, industrial civilization. However, there were many sorts of industry, and attention was to shift away from Lancashire (and Manchester) towards the end of this period. It shifted towards London in the 1880s and 90s, and to what were in fact equally 'industrial' occupations, though the term 'industry' was to retain its provincial, and usually northern, connotations. There was industry in London – that of outwork and of the debased artisan – the industry so often of the sweated trades. There was the industry, too, of the Midlands, growing in size and importance throughout this time. It gave rise to its own particular political and social structures, and its own distinctive culture. The example of Lancashire cannot hope to do justice to this distinctiveness, nor to that of the other possible examples. These examples extend only to England. This is because the experience of Wales, Ireland and Scotland was even more distinctively different when compared to that of the English regions. To handle these differences would have involved writing another book at least as long as this one.

Nonetheless, for England as well as for Britain, the experience of Lancashire was not at all unrepresentative. If Lancashire was not the England of the capital, of the ports, of the small, 'traditional' manufacturing towns, least of all the England of the land and the county town, then it was the new England of town and industry, and these forces transformed the nation. It was also an example of the new provincial England, and the nineteenth century was the century of the English provinces to an extent that is not always recognised. Although attending closely, and necessarily, to the uniqueness of a particular setting, this is in the end an account of developments at a national level. In this respect, any of the English regions throws light on processes working fairly uniformly across the nation – developments such as the spread of the party system and the extension of political democracy; the growth of unions and new forms of factory labour; the spread of literacy, education and new kinds of popular taste; as well as the consolidation of a new kind of urban community life and the distinctive culture, marked by forms of popular entertainment such as the music hall, to which it gave rise. One could go on at length to describe such changes. They form, in fact, the subject matter of this book, and Lancashire is a particularly good way of getting at them. At the same time, while looking north, several of the chapters take in development at a broader level. This is especially so of the two chapters on politics, and to some extent too in the chapters on custom and history. The study of popular literature and the music hall also ranges broadly across the country, though Lancashire is central to my argument.

There is also a certain logic in choosing Lancashire in a book about class. It was there that industry and the town had reached their most developed form. It was there too that Marx and Engels found what they took to be the industrial proletariat and the class war in their most advanced and starkest forms. There is a very real sense, 'idealizations' of class notwithstanding, that it is in the England of the textile factory and the mill town that one would expect to find class in its most developed form. If it was not present there, or present to a lesser extent than has been thought, then this suggests that its significance elsewhere also may have been limited. In choosing fairly specific subjects of study – Lancashire operatives or more generally manual workers in the northern, industrial districts – one also runs into linguistic problems it is necessary to acknowledge if difficult to avoid. The problem of describing groups is a tricky one. The use of 'working class' or 'class' as adjectives is almost second nature to historians. But it pre-judges and colours the issue. I have avoided it here, and have tried to steer clear of substituting other, equally tendentious terms. This is difficult, try as I might not to lead the witness. Here, as everywhere else, our language constructs our understanding of the world.

The first of the two chapters on politics deals with 'political language' in two senses: it considers the workings of what might be called political communication, matters such as political rhetoric, style of leadership, the press; but it is also concerned with how two discernibly different political discourses or 'languages', those of popular radicalism and Liberalism, were in fact intimately related one to the other. One is concerned with the problem of political change, particularly in the British key perhaps; how new political discourses emerged but were yet still organically related to older ones. There are, I fear, even more senses of 'language' here. Chapter 3 pursues the transmutation of popular radicalism through Liberalism (and Toryism) into socialism. It begins by acknowledging the significance of a distinctively 'class' language in politics and beyond: class was a very important part of the vocabulary of social analysis at the time,[35] at all social levels, and the ways in which terms, and realities, were handled are discussed here. So too is the nature of the various 'populisms' that can be contrasted with class perceptions, but which were in practice often closely related to them.

The chapters on work concern what are called the 'moral discourses' of labour: in chapter 5 these are pursued in terms of the application of the rhetoric and values of the trade to the later trade unions. In chapter 4 popular valuations of labour are set within the wider moral universe of which union discourse was a part. I go beyond the institutional realm here, while recognising the fundamental role of unions in structuring discourse about labour and society in the fifth chapter. As in the political chapters, there is an interest in how popular institutions both shaped, and were shaped by, the broader culture of which they were a part. The character of discourses about and perceptions of the social order is tracked by a close attention to the experience of textile workers. The old legacy of the trade, and its many new applications and alternatives, are seen to result in singular, complex and perhaps unexpected versions of 'class'.

So, 'populism' and 'class' receive much consideration in these sections. Enough has already been said about the make-up of the chapters in part III: these begin to point to other dimensions of social identity, and other sources of collective mobilisation, political and otherwise. In particular they point to the new dimension of the 'nation', but almost at once suggest how this differed from yet was intimately related to other socio-geographical dimensions of identity such as the local, neighbourhood community, the town, and the region. By the end of part III the reader will be aware of the very varied elements involved in creating popular understandings of the social order, including the dimension of gender, which cuts across but also complements these other aspects. He or she will also know something of how these different elements of class, people, nation, town and so on were differently combined at different times and in different circumstances. The last section offers the chance to extend this discussion, by deepening our understanding of the elements involved and how they were combined, but also by moving towards the question of whether there was a dominant framework of mind, something like a dominant English tradition. The brief chapter introducing part IV, called 'Investigating popular art', is a good strategic point to draw breath: readers are directed to it for a re-capitulation of the argument by then developed, and for some indication of how this argument may be taken further in the light of popular art.

The last section is much concerned with what was a very powerful current of utopian feeling at the time, already evident in the previous discussion. The force of the term 'vision' in my title becomes evident here. 'Visions of the People' denotes versions of 'the people' created by those who were outside the ranks of the kind of people mostly considered in this book. It also denotes 'the people' envisioned by the people themselves, and this business of the labouring poor, seeing, and so making, themselves is the great concern of the last part. This seeing itself involved something akin to a vision strictly defined, a thing seen in a dream, something prophetic, a product of the imagination and the outcome of hope and desire. Utopian aspirations involved the idea of justice yet also the possibility of human reconciliation and fellowship. The feelings involved were often 'religious' in character, if little to do with organised religion. Though fellowship was most often realised in the masculine form of fraternity, this was by no means always so, the beliefs of the poor embracing all who were the children of God and of man.

These currents of belief, along with the multitude of insights about the geography of belonging thrown up by popular art, enable us to make some sort of judgement about the different sorts of social identity evident at the time. They strongly suggest the necessity of looking beyond class. But in looking beyond class for the other ways in which contemporaries conceived of the social order, we also need to incorporate class in our view. It was part of the landscape. However, it should not be taken for granted: it is necessary to look at it as well as beyond it. When we do that, what seemed familiar often appears strange. The picture that emerges at the end can, however, only be provisional. Like everything else in this book its conclusions represent work-in-progress, pointing back to the need to extend our knowledge of the nineteenth century and forward to the inter-war years and later. Then, perhaps even more than for the previous century, the extent of our ignorance is revealed once we begin to look beyond class.

Part I

Power and the people : politics and the social order

2

The languages of popular politics:
from radicalism to Liberalism

The study of popular radical politics in early nineteenth-century England has recently resulted in productive discussion of how the social order may have been seen by the labouring populations of the time. Writing on Chartism, Stedman Jones has argued that radical discourse was not an expression of underlying 'experience' but itself actively served to constitute this experience.[1] Rather than being the outcome of the economic and social situation of early industrialism, the terms of reference of Chartism were political. Rather than a 'class' language of an economic, proto-socialist kind what was evident was the category of the 'people', and with it – though Stedman Jones is not clear on this – a 'populist' politics. But as I have argued in the introduction, this is in many respects an inadequate guide to class, to language and to politics.

Nonetheless, it does pose some very important questions. The question of populism will be directly addressed in the following chapter. In chapter 4, the relationship between politics and economics in the formation of discourse and values will be explored in a more systematic fashion. This chapter is concerned with the nature of political programmes and appeals, with what are here called political languages. The success of political movements and parties may be said in large part to turn upon the elaboration of effective political languages, and something of this is traced here in terms of the transition from radicalism to Liberalism in the third quarter of the nineteenth century. For the sake of discussion, such languages can be taken as having two aspects. On the one hand, they can be understood as actively creating both political appeals and the objects of such appeals, the political constituency itself. It is this creation of political constituencies, or collective political subjects, which is of particular concern here. Unities of sentiment and action had to be created which overlaid the differences obtaining within political groups, and these depended on the elaboration of unifying identities, such as 'peoples', 'classes', or 'nations'. Political languages and the subjects they created thus had their own effect and were not the simple outcome of social 'experience'.

On the other hand, such languages needed in some way to make sense of people's conditions and outlook. To work effectively they had to comprehend social and economic situations. And, of course, they might relate to people's lives in unforeseen ways, perhaps failing, perhaps succeeding, in an unexpected fashion. At all events, the active role of political subjects was always important and, *pace* Stedman Jones, political languages took their meaning, or were eloquent, to the extent that they resonated with the preoccupations of those who received them. The interplay of these two aspects of political languages is thus very important. So much may seem self-evident, but the ramifications of this perspective for politics have not in fact been widely considered by historians.

This is clearly related to the question of class. For instance, 'non-class' appeals based on the virtue of independence and the subject of 'the people', for example, might accentuate tendencies telling against class in the broader culture to which politics appealed. Political languages had considerable force in their own right. On the other hand, in bringing their own viewpoints to bear, different segments of a political audience might inflect the constituent parts of political appeals with different meanings, including those of class. This interaction of an appeal and its reception is part of what was meant earlier by speaking of categories like 'class' and 'people', for instance, as not discrete but always in a relationship one with another.[2] This understanding of the sometimes very diverse sets of meanings contained within political languages alerts us to the difficulties of interpretation. For instance, very few political appeals have been based on an unalloyed appeal to class. But this does not mean that class was not a constituent of such languages, nor that parts of a political constituency did not bring their own class interpretation to what might seem to be a political discourse having little to do with class. So, one cannot assume from the character of political appeals that class was insignificant. Nonetheless, such extra-class appeals were and are mounted because of the need to transcend differences within political constituencies through the creation of higher unities. This need has often arisen from the irrelevance, dangers or inadequacies of class. Therefore, just as it would be unwise to minimise the significance of class, so would it be absurd to underestimate the strength of other identities which political languages in part created, and in part responded to as a vital part of the culture outside politics.

There is already some consideration of these aspects in the secondary literature. In particular, the capacity of the seemingly 'political' language of Chartism to be in practice about a range of matters beyond politics has been noted: this raises questions which are best considered under the heading of work and politics in what follows.[3] The burden of the argument is that new wine was to be found in old bottles. The identity of 'the people' could in fact take on a class character, turning upon the idea of labour as a 'working class' in conflict with capital. This was indeed so, and something similar is evident in the French case, where Sewell has shown how the ideological inheritance of the Revolution and of the corporate idiom of the trade – both ostensibly not of a class character – elaborated a class identity for workers in France up to 1848.[4] It is in fact arguable that despite obvious differences there are surprising similarities between the actual character of class outlook in the two countries, at least among certain groups of workers.

This takes us into the matter of the actual character of what was a clear, unambiguous class vocabulary. The argument above is that new wine was to be found in old bottles. It is also the case that alongside old vocabularies of social description and prescription were to be found new ones, or at least relatively new ones. One such vocabulary was that of class, which in the early and mid-nineteenth century became very marked in public discussion. This distinctively class terminology will be more systematically approached in the next chapter, where its character will be evaluated. What will be evident there is how class in England took diverse forms, which could be 'economic' and conflictual in the strict sense defined in the introduction, but which perhaps more often were political, moralistic, and quite capable of understanding society in ways to which conflict was foreign. The latter was especially the case when this pointedly 'class' language was linked, as it so often was, with conceptions of the social order not of a class kind. As will be apparent in the next chapter, class could be fitted into other, sometimes older, versions of consensual social relations. It could be shaped thus by those who feared its disruptive consequences, and this was not always difficult because popular preconceptions themselves often permitted it. This being so, one is tempted to say new bottles could contain old wine. However, it would be wrong not to recognise how certain aspects of the 'new' class discourse could be divisive and disruptive, expressing a sense of bitterness, loss and conflict, as well as a sense of independence. The consequences of class often presented themselves to those in authority in this light: as will be apparent, class was acknowledged in various degrees as a real and enduring feature of the new industrial, urban England, and had in many respects to be managed and controlled.

I do not therefore wish to deny class, but it is necessary to get it in perspective as one, and probably not the greatest, among a range of possible social and political identities available to and used by the labouring populations. Debate in the secondary literature, has, however, got little further than the rush to defend the idea of class by asserting that the seemingly 'traditional' in fact cloaked the new. This has obscured the extent both of the marked degree to which old languages were retained, and the reasons for this retention. The notion of 'the people' – which together with class would seem to be the chief candidates for consideration – continued to be very powerful beyond the mid-nineteenth century. As political and economic circumstances altered from the mid-century onwards the idea of 'the people' seems to have been emptied of a good deal of the class content it had accrued earlier. This sequence of events is considered in chapter 4. It suggests that 'the people' was earlier given a class character in rather an unfixed and provisional way. It is evident that the language and associations of 'the people' were the major terms in the relationship and had the greatest staying power. What needs emphasis in all this is that the category of the people stuck not only or mainly because politicians wanted it to stick but because, quite simply, it continued to make sense to people, in their daily and political lives. So, when the king has no clothes, it is necessary to say so: class did not lurk behind the image of the people. What was there was nothing other than the body of the people itself. So, it is once again tempting to continue the vinous analogy and observe that old bottles most often contained old wine.

This would be inaccurate, however, because the equation of 'class' with 'new' and 'people' with 'old' is misleading. Instead, if populist aspects were dominant this did not mean that they were conservative, embedded in the past, or incapable of change. Quite the contrary, for what is striking in the transition from radicalism to popular Liberalism is how within the terms of a radical discourse that did indeed owe much to the past, new meanings and uses were constantly created. Old versions of 'the people' gave way to new ones, as did old to new sorts of populism. Liberalism in large measure succeeded by feeding off this radical past. But Liberalism was a creed that was essentially to do with values other than class ones; indeed, it in many respects turned upon the denial of class (which did not mean it was above using class for its own ends). If Liberalism was integrally related to popular radicalism in this way, and was essentially a non-class creed, this strongly suggests that both the older traditions and the living present of radicalism were also not of an essentially class kind. The very success of Liberalism in building upon the radical inheritance to become the major party force in popular politics suggest that the social vision of popular radicalism was not primarily a class one, but was of such a kind as to facilitate the accord with Liberalism.

Therefore, the sense of 'political language' as used in this chapter refers to class in that political discourses served variously to strengthen, evoke or deny particular conceptions of society, depending in large part for their success on how they appealed to these: they thus tell us a good deal about the sources of social identity and collective action in a society. But they also concern how power was transacted and experienced. Therefore, a second sense of 'political language' lies in the relationship of one such language to another, that of Liberalism to radicalism, and how Liberalism built upon and annexed, but was also defined and limited by the latter. This concern with language also involves the various forms of political communication, the symbolic as well as the literal. One is in fact first concerned with the desires and needs met by politics and addressed by political languages, though in the process the aspirations and satisfactions focused upon particular popular conceptions of the social order will be amply evident. It is necessary now to turn from these generalities, and it is to the character of popular radicalism before the mid-century that attention will first be directed.

Here I shall draw on work-in-progress on the cultural aspects of popular radical politics in a range of English constituencies:[5] popular radicalism was not of course all of one piece, but it is striking in this research how in towns as diverse as Oldham and Boston, for instance, radical discourse was similar. It is with these uniformities of emphasis that I am chiefly concerned, indicating as they do the broad lines of a coherent, seemingly nationwide radical discourse. What is first of all striking is how little class terms or a class analysis seem to have been evident. If there was a place in contemporary England where these might have been expected, then it was surely ultra-radical, factory-manufacturing Oldham. If these aspects were absent, what was present?

Here the advantages of a cultural approach to politics are evident: diverse aspects of politics, such as organisation and discourse, were in fact intimately related. Organisation had a symbolic character. For instance, radical politics in 1830s and 1840s Oldham seems to have functioned by using organisation to symbolise the ideals of the radical cause in action. The practice of participation, representation and accountability was built into the modes of radical organisation, demonstrating to friend and foe alike the ideal, democratic constituency at work. What was above all conveyed to radicalism's followers was a sense of their collective strength and of the rightness of their cause. In particular, in appealing to the non-elector as a truly political person, the sense of a people excluded from their natural birthright was especially strong. In both organisational and discursive ways this sense of exclusion (and of power, pent force and rightness) were elaborated and dramatised through a series of oppositions which seem to have characterised radicalism nationally – tyranny and freedom, liberty and slavery, knowledge and ignorance, each of which was often painted in the religious and moral hues of good and evil, light and darkness.[6]

Now, while these terms could be, and sometimes were, employed in expressing class antagonisms, the extent to which political languages actively helped constitute the political subjects they addressed suggests the advisability of looking at the object of radical address as existing outside class. Democracy, freedom, the excluded heirs to constitutional liberties – these were the key terms, concerning the just and free man (a man, seldom a woman) who was part of a virtuous 'people' (the term most often used at the time). These and the allied terms of independence, honour and manliness – together with their opposites – seem removed from what we usually understand as the economic, socially exclusive terms of class.

Turning to the reactive character of political languages, popular radicalism obviously brought out elements of a social design already present in work and religion. Given the nature of the evidence, it is difficult to get at this design, if anything so finished as a design was in fact present. The term 'moral economy' has been taken by historians as a shorthand, though unsatisfactory, proxy for these popular conceptions of society and social relations. In chapter 4 on work and class something of this is explored more fully than here: the often utopian aspects involved seem to have seen an early 'moral economy' infused with democratic sentiment and radicalised by the early nineteenth-century experience of economic and political injustice. What resulted was not, however, class, at least in any conventional sense of the term: democracy seems to have sat side by side with ideas of society as a system of interdependent functions, often of a hierarchic or at least not a levelling character. Something of these notions can be briefly considered here, excited into more overt expression, as they so often were, by political events.

They show how powerful was the idea of independence. Ideas of 'the cottage economy' among early nineteenth-century factory workers indicate how for new as for old elements in the workforce, above all when fused with idealisations of the handloom weaving community, these ideas of independence, of what was 'natural', and of what were proper social relations between master and worker, served as a powerful critique of the factory system.[7] This critique was directly and forcefully articulated in politics, especially in Chartism. Among national leaders, such as O'Connor and McDouall, as among operative Chartist spokesmen, ideas of 'the cottage economy' and of

the 'natural' labour and life symbolised by the handloom and
especially by land, clearly produced an extraordinarily powerful
response in the popular constituency of the movement.[8] The
significance of these aspects needs to be established here, especially
for land, precisely because they were not to vanish but to remain as
important elements in Liberalism's utilisation of the radical
tradition, and indeed far beyond this.

In turn, they were linked to popular religion and morality, which
also served as bridges between one political tradition and another.
Nowhere is this more clear than in the case of Joseph Rayner
Stephens, the Tory Radical Methodist preacher, who from his base
in the cotton town of Ashton established a national reputation in the
1830s and 40s. Like Oastler, Stephens was not in the radical
mainstream (his rejection of Chartism and political solutions was
clear enough), but his impassioned 'physical force' rhetoric, his
missionary zeal for the Factory Acts cause, and above all his religious
rhetoric can be seen as articulating elements powerfully present in
popular mentalities. His 'political sermons' of 1839 drew large and
enthusiastic crowds in London and the factory towns.[9] It is not that
Stephens was a typical radical leader. His outlook was in many ways
highly individualistic. Rather, it is the obvious purchase of his
rhetoric on popular sentiment that is revealing. It is impossible to do
justice to the richness of his language here, but the dominant
patterns may be briefly indicated (see the example given in appendix
1). The 'cottage economy' of domestic industrial/agrarian production was as emphatically associated with family, home and
community as was the case with the Chartist spokesmen, but the
'natural' and the 'unnatural' were given religious form in the shape,
quite literally, of the devil, associated in turn with the 'unnatural'
cruelty of the worst of the millowners and the depravity of the
aristocracy. Stephens' self-dramatisation as martyr and messiah
enacted this religious message, but it was the language and
associations of the Bible – permeating his 'political pulpit' – that
perhaps chiefly served to express the aspirations and identity of his
audiences. They were the Chosen People, the despised and excluded
Israelites, whom God the Emancipator would save from the
diabolism and gross impiety of their persecutors.[10]

Again, this could serve as a class language: the titanic religious
struggle described with such violence by Stephens was frequently
applied to the actions of millowners and operatives in his home town.
But there is surely a necessary limit to the ingenuity with which every
manifestation of popular discontent can be seen as evidence of
'class': the forms of public, political expression are vastly more rich
and complex than this. If they are considered only in so far as they

expressed some 'underlying' reality of class – the husk, as it were, thrown away once the kernel is found – then everything that is important about them is lost. Although Stephens and the others often expressed grievances that sprang from the workplace, they did not usually present these in a class way – one in which the sources of evil and oppression were seen to spring from a new industrial system. On the contrary, their expression of grievances found such a powerful response because it resonated with popular understandings other and more powerful than those of class alone. For spokesmen and audience alike, the religious, moral, utopian and customary elements mattered in their own right. It was as a rejected people, a despised flock, or as independent beings dispossessed of their birthright that people saw themselves, and those terms cannot just simply be equated with class. For Stepehens himself, certainly, the terms that mattered were those of 'people', and 'rich' and 'poor', linked in turn with a defence of the patriarchal family that itself clearly found a powerful echo in operative opinion. This point need not be laboured here, as there is too much of value and interest in the languages of popular politics to be diverted any longer from a closer consideration of them.

There is, for instance, what may be termed the sensibility of feeling evident in written and other expression, which needs to be considered alongside the sources of popular imagery and of social designs already considered. Historians are now beginning to notice the pervasive presence of what may loosely be termed 'romanticism' in the political discourse of the time.[11] Notions of nature were themselves drawn from a romantic critique of industrialism and utilitarianism amply present in Chartism: in O'Connor for instance, the distinction between 'natural society' and the 'artificial society' of industrial capitalism was of crucial significance.[12] It was not, however, simply a case of 'high culture' penetrating 'low'. There was, long before the 1840s, a 'popular' romanticism, evident in melodrama and gothic-influenced romances.[13] Oastler and Stephens, among others, played upon this, in their invocations of 'vampires', 'fiend-begotten monsters' and such like. And, of course, the specific emotive object of this romanticism, and thus the one having a claim to be as real as class, was humankind itself, the suffering and wronged humanity evident in the grand and eloquent terms earlier seen – liberty against tyranny, light against darkness, or freedom against slavery – terms inherited from the fusion of romanticism and enlightenment coming out of the period of European revolution and revolutionary war. Romanticism supplied an ideology, certainly, but more than this it supplied a kind of language of feeling.

However, before moving to the transcendental realm of feeling, to the pervasive tone of moral exaltation and aspiration, let me descend to the low and vulgar, for there were many other facets to the languages of politics beyond those already mentioned. Whether or not Oldham was vulgar, it was certainly rough, and it is to Grime's contemporary account of the turbulence of popular politics from the 1830s to the 1850s that I shall turn in order to make some brief observations about the wider character of popular politics.[14] This detailed and almost verbatim amount of stump speeches, wall propaganda and political satire gives a good idea of these other dimensions of politics, for example the significance of drink, gain and violence.[15] In the transition to party politics described in this account these aspects may with only a little exaggeration be regarded as elements in political discourse, associated as they were with particular political occasions and appeals. Grime's account also indicates the need to attend in detail to the means of political communication as well as to the form, to the placard, to the speech and the crucial oral dimension,[16] but also to the newspaper which was to become such an important element in the consolidation of party politics. Some account of this political literature of the streets will be found in appendix 2. However, as well as considering the workings of political language, it is necessary to give some idea of tactics, alliances and developments, and Oldham is a good place to do this. Therefore, before turning to the forms of politics in terms of romanticism and the means in terms of the press, Oldham will be used to suggest something of the route to party politics.

Foster has traced something of how the radical cause split between the Tories and the Liberals from the mid-century.[17] Liberalism was the majority faith in the nation at large, but popular Toryism was always important, particularly in industrial Lancashire. The concentration of this chapter is on Liberalism, but Toryism demands consideration. Paradoxically, perhaps, as I have shown elsewhere, it was the anti-*laissez-faire*, pro-Factory Acts elements in Toryism which made it more the repository of class feeling than was Liberalism.[18] However, popular Toryism in many respects is misunderstood as chiefly a form of class politics: these 'class' elements were combined with patriotic and ethnic currents, as well as with the politics of factory paternalist influence and with an often forthright belief in the verities of Church and State, to make up an often volatile mix that might better be described as 'Tory populist' rather than as class politics.[19]

The cultural reputations of the nascent parties were quickly established, as Grime makes plain.[20] The Liberals were the party of education and respectability, the Tories were associated with drink, violence and what may be termed the politics of bonhomie, of the good time. There was much special pleading in this, especially by the Liberals, who were sometimes as wedded to drink and violence as the Tories. Nonetheless, the emergent personalities of the parties were true enough to this casting. What is evident, therefore, especially on the Tory side, are aspects of political style – very important constituent parts of political language – that drew directly on aspects of popular culture which the dominant emphasis here, on Liberalism, should not obscure. The Oldham example shows, for instance, how personalised politics was – in Oldham one was a Foxite, a Fieldenite, a Cobbettite. On the Tory side, especially, great capital was made by identification with the sporting, masculine culture of drink and the pub (against respectable, often Non-conformist, 'namby-pamby' Liberalism).[21]

Two things stand out forcibly from Grime's account. First, it shows how early it was that mass party politics were pioneered; the association with public opinion being made, and that with 'faction' and 'dictation' being qualified, in the 1850s. The connection of political activity with the life of the newly incorporated boroughs was another example of this shift. Secondly, however, and against Whiggish notions of political change, the new party politics fed directly off the old.[22] The personalisation of politics continued, not only around the names of old tribunes of the people (evident well into the 1860s), but also in terms of the parties' cultivation of local men as the representatives, indeed the symbols, of local interests and identities. The politics of the borough were themselves as much about the politics of reputation, influence and largesse as they were about radical, democratic nostrums. The symbolic Tory language of beef, beer and Old England also drew on aspects of some antiquity in popular culture.

Nonetheless, though these features were important, mid-Victorian politics revealed a very different side in its characteristic romanticism, especially in popular radicalism and Liberalism. The romanticism of the early nineteenth century was a powerful influence on early workingmen radicals, especially Chartists. It was, however, but one among a range of influences, and it is the sheer eclecticism of the learning of workingmen Chartist leaders that is chiefly evident (and, often, their sheer erudition): literature, religion, philosophy, politics and science, from the ancient classics onwards, were plundered in the relentless desire to re-write the history of humankind as the history of the pursuit of liberty. Nonetheless, the romantic influence was great, even if the term itself is invariably used in an eclectic manner. The romantic sensibility is clearly evident in those aspects touched on earlier; the ideas of nature, of the mighty struggle of moral opposites, of a virtuous, pure 'people', and of the dominant note of exaltation and aspiration. The latter was a part too of the profoundly religious caste of mind of the age, and it is clear that religion and romanticism met in a particularly volatile mix which produced a sensibility but also a framework of social interpretation.

One can see this at work among the radicals. William Aitken of Ashton was a representative figure: the outstanding popular Chartist leader of his district, his life between 1814 and 1869 shows how the romantic temper, and the broader role and style of local, plebeian leadership, spanned both radicalism and Liberalism, cementing their shared vision of the world.[23] Romantic perceptions were grafted on the old stock of the worship of reason: Aitken's writings and 'spiritual addresses' are full not of the struggle against capitalism but against priestcraft, superstition and the slavery of body and soul.[24] As in the general Chartist culture of this town[25] (and Ashton had claims to being the most Chartist town in England), in the celebrations, songs, toasts and the memorabilia of the movement it is a suffering people in struggle with the age-old forms of darkness that is evident. It is clear that the old notion of 'the people' had by the 1840s long lost its former associations with the property-owning classes – contrasted with the dependent 'poor' – but if 'people' and 'working classes' became increasingly coterminous at this time, the aim of the struggle was still the liberty of humankind.[26] The influence of the English Romantic poets was slightly later to have its fullest effect and it was Burns (Aitken's favourite poet) who then, and later, most fully elaborated for self-educated workingmen the classless humanism of this view of liberty,[27] while at the same time asserting the special rights of workingmen to be a part of humanity.

Aitken went on to lead the potent Chartism of the town into Liberalism, and it is clear from his autobiography that he saw no fissure between the two: Liberalism was completing the business of Chartism, and both were yet one more step in the history of liberty. In this Aitken was no different from the workingmen leaders who reproduced this effect throughout the industrial districts and throughout the country. The history of Rochdale and of 'Alderman' Livesey is essentially the same: Thomas Livesey, the self-styled follower of 'Billy Cobbett', was if anything even more pervasive a presence in Rochdale politics than Aitken in Ashton. Livesey lived to be the confidant of Bright and Cobden and to cement the historical accord with Liberalism.[28] Forty thousand turned out for his funeral in 1864.

This is some indication of the hold of these leaders. At first sight it is surprising that their intensely elevated romantic language touched an audience often not even literate. (Aspects of this language will be explored in chapter 4.) Aitken's obituarist in fact observed that: 'He had acquired an excellent style – clear and animated – and the elevated sentiments with which his mind was filled were expressed with energy. As one who had sprung from the people, he knew intimately their feelings and their wishes, and could express what the many felt with fullness and point.'[29] He 'had read much', in poetry, history, and popular science. Adorning his speeches, this learning articulated 'with fullness and point' the feelings of his audience in such a way as to leave on them the characteristic marks of the intellectual temper of the age. One need look no further than the Chartist *Northern Star* for corroboration of the popular hold of the language of romanticism, and of high literature and learning more generally. The *Star* was fond of telling its poor contributors that their letters or reports were 'illiterate', 'overstrained' or not of poetic interest. Yet the *Northern Star* was voraciously consumed by its enormous popular audience. This closeness of fit between aspects of high and low culture need not surprise us (the romantic infusion in popular literature and entertainment has been noted): self-educated workingmen, until the age of popularisation, had literally nowhere to go but to the canon of 'high' culture, especially literature. As Thompson has shown, illiteracy and high levels of self-culture often sat happily side by side in early radicalism.[30] Aitken's was indeed a good example of this compatibility: after leaving politics he set up as a very popular teacher in the town, directly shaping a new generation of operatives.

It is, however, in the style and intellectual formation of the great national leaders – so important for these local men – that the romantic aspects of politics are most clearly discernible. O'Connor has been noted, and the figures of Ernest Jones and George Reynolds are of equal importance. Especially in the north of England, Jones was crucial in creating the accord of radicalism with Liberalism. Reynolds was of some note himself as a popular leader in the days of late Chartism, and his *Reynolds News* was of seminal influence in popular radicalism after 1850.[31] All three were outside the social world of urban industrial society, either of military (Reynolds) or landed origin. As with O'Connor's view of 'natural' society the land was of great importance in their politics. (O'Connor's view of the redemptive power of small-scale ownership was indeed directly influenced by his understanding of his native, Irish peasantry.)

This concern with the land question was of course eminently practical in many respects: until the twentieth century the issue figured in Liberal and socialist politics simply because Britain was still in many respects an agrarian and aristocracy-ridden country.

But the concern with land went deeper. This is Jones in 1867: 'Back to the land! It is the shield of freedom. You talk of unchaining yourselves – unchain the land and all the rest will follow. Back to the land! It is a moral, a physical, a political, a national regenerator.'[32] This was in a lecture ostensibly on 'Labour and Capital'. The constant emphasis on land as the source of 'redemption' and 'regeneration' argues a more potent attachment to land than that of anti-aristocratic politics alone, and land was indeed a fixation for these leaders. Their own background, their own estrangement from urban industrial society, suggests this, and this predisposition of social position made them highly susceptible to the romantic critique of urban industrialism. But no more susceptible than workingmen, to whom popular access to land ownership continued to have a profound emotional and symbolic appeal down into the twentieth century.[33] With workingmen, as with national leaders, one should not write this off as the politics of nostalgia: the issue had plenty of political currency, but more than this the vision of the land was a means of evaluating and understanding the present, and planning for the future, rather more than it was a reactionary reverie. The customary notions of independence and of community relations which were so closely linked to the land issue in early nineteenth-century radicalism, like the religious aspirations also articulated by radicalism, need to be seen in this light.

Jones was a poet, Reynolds reputedly the biggest-selling author of popular fiction in the nineteenth century (for an example of Jones' romantic rhetoric see appendix 3). Chartism thrived on its poets: poetry and song were integral to its associational life. The literature that the likes of Jones and Reynolds imbibed in their youth was the romantic literature of liberal-nationalist Europe in its golden age. Jones was steeped in German romanticism,[34] Reynolds in French. In turn, in *Reynolds News*, but more in his fictional work, Reynolds returned to radical workingmen in the later nineteenth century an inherently romantic conception of the world, coloured especially by Hugo and Eugene Sue. O'Connor himself was steeped in the legendary poetry and mystical spirit of a romantic Ireland.[35] These leaders, just like the Tory Radicals – whose notions of the 'organic' community of 'Altar, Throne and Cottage' were every bit as strong as the vision of the land in men like O'Connor and Jones – also lived out their own political careers as romantic heroes, and this is of considerable significance in understanding how the new politics of Liberalism so effectively built upon the old.

These leaders presented themselves as exiled and spurned by their own sort, doing battle in the cause of their similarly exiled but poor fellow man. Representation in the guise of the 'lion of freedom'

(O'Connor), 'the Champion' (Stephens), the 'prophet of the North' (Jones) presented the hero-politician as doing battle in a cause to which he was a martyr, having forsaken his own kind in order, paradoxically, to affirm the underlying unity of all people. The religious and romantic overtones are amply evident here, as is the transcendence of class in the universal name of humanity. These aspects would take us further on in time to the central place of the land and of the romantic critique of Victorian industralism evident in Carlyle, Ruskin, Morris and others. Of course, the romantic current was also quite central to socialism from the late nineteenth century.[36] However, in this context, it is less these intellectual currents that matter than the styles and presentation of leadership and of political parties in the era of nascent Liberalism.

Before turning to this, however, the technology and cultural consequences of language need to be considered in terms of the press. Agitation against government interference in press freedom continued in the 1850s and 60s. This was a continuation of a theme central to popular radicalism: the association between knowledge and power, even in the earlier period of mutual suspicion, had drawn the middle classes and workingmen together around the central Englightenment tenets of progress and reason.[37] In the altered climate after mid-century the union of the classes against ignorance and reaction was symbolised by Liberal campaigning for press freedom, especially on the part of Richard Cobden.[38] This bore fruit in the new local and provincial press of the 1850s. Both Vincent and Lee have shown how important for the new Liberalism was the co-ordinating political effect and the ideology of this press.[39]

The effect of both aspects was secured by the content of the press but still more by its structure, the way in which its character actively promoted some ways of seeing the world and relegated others. Again, one is aware how political languages, this time in their means as much as their form, served to shape the political subjects they addressed. This needs to be looked at fairly closely, and the example of the Ashton press is as good a guide as any to the new provincial press of the 1850s. This didactic, 'tutorial', eminently serious press, was not the sole preserve of Liberalism. The Tories shared in the expansion of the 1850s as well, and their press was similar in character to the Liberals'. One cannot therefore attach party labels with complete accuracy, but the 'free press' was undoubtedly closest to the heart of popular Liberalism.

The Liberal *Ashton Reporter* was typical of the new press of the 1850s. Perhaps rather more than other newspapers of its type, it came under the control of owners who were openly sympathetic to labour, the Hobson family in the 1860s and in the 1880s the

Andrews, who founded and owned the textile operatives' union journals. Other papers were less sympathetic, and for all of them, Tory as well as Liberal, the centre of social gravity tended to be the active, respectable, small property-holders of their towns. Nonetheless, the papers were commercial concerns. As they grew they increasingly depended on a working-class readership, and so came to represent more evenly the varied social mix of these towns, themselves often new ones like their newspapers. Their effect lay in a peculiar mix of this cultural and social inclusiveness with marked characteristics of exclusiveness as well.

After their early bias to property had been partly eroded, they came to represent the town to the town. They were indeed part of a new sense of civic identity and civic pride growing up in England, especially in the new industrial towns. They were at once local and defiantly provincial, proclaiming to the world not just the virtue of the town but the integrity of the culture of provincial England, a culture significantly different from and superior to that of the established centres of power and privilege. Popular Liberalism was importantly an assertion of provincial identity, and the press (the big city press as well) was the voice of this identity.[40]

The sense of social inclusiveness that Liberalism stood for was enacted directly in the content and structure of the press. People of course read the national press, the great provincial press (the *Manchester Guardian* for example, or the *Leeds Mercury*), as well as the local press (though working people would probably have been more inclined to read the provincial and local rather than the national press, with the exception of the popular Sunday papers). But it was the local press that most effectively created the sense of social community Liberalism rested on. It should not, however, be thought that the local equated with the parochial: both the local and regional press combined local, British and world news in a way wholly unlike today. Again it is the ecumenism of Liberalism that is evident in this combination of internationalism and the local.

The sense of both the readership and the town as a community of interests was built up by the reporting, in minute detail, of town council affairs, of the law courts, of local market information, of local events of all sorts; a reporting that opened out to the institutional world of labour, to the unions, co-ops, friendly societies, burial societies, and the other institutions of working-class life. It should not be thought that labour's view, or the perspective of the poor, was directly presented. The ideology of the press was that no special viewpoint should be presented (though in practice the respectable world of petty property, sometimes of big property, often dominated). Nonetheless, often for the first time in these communities there existed a single, ever-changing mirror of events, reflecting the composite life of the town and its people.

As well as this reporting, simple matters like the announcement of meetings, dances, discussions and such like served to develop the sense of joint if not always common activity. The political role of the press served to reconcile the different factions of employers, unions, and Nonconformists that made up the alliance that was Liberalism.[41] The emphasis was continually on the reconciliation of differences, under the banner of progress and reason. From the sublime to the ridiculous, reconciliation and amelioration were the keynote. The actual language of the press put this into practice: the emollient, cliched language of reporting – familiar to readers of Joyce's *Ulysses* as the 'Deasyism' – seems to have been pioneered around this time, before 'journalese' reached one of its many apotheoses in turn-of-the-century Dublin. This, however, is perhaps a little hard on the Victorian and Edwardian press. In comparison with the con-temporary press, newspapers were models of rectitude, innocent of 'features', 'human interest' and sensation: they did in fact report at great length and often almost verbatim, and there was no sense of news being 'presented'.[42] Reporting was reporting. The 'tutorial' press is a fair description, despite the stock phrase and the flattering comment.

However, these papers were unashamedly biased in other respects, though in ways which were mostly transparent. Along with the sense of inclusiveness, went that exclusiveness mentioned earlier as characteristic of the way in which the newspaper served to shape the world of its reader. The press was openly and unashamedly party political, and this was echoed in equal strength in religion. However, people at this time were, or grew to be, emphatically partisan in politics. They were always partisan in religion. To some extent, therefore, the press simply reflected existing loyalties. Nonetheless it also hardened these, and had a very important role in attaching them to support for the political parties. Being a Liberal involved the universalistic and ecumenical, but it also involved an often fierce attachment to religion, indeed sometimes a sectarianism, equally evident on the Tory Anglican side. Outside politics and religion, the press for the most part presented events reasonably impartially, but within these areas – in the choice of events and the character of their reporting – the picture of town community that emerged was one highly coloured by deep-seated sectional loyalties. These did not contradict the notion of the urban community, but they did present it in particular ways.

Therefore, a press that was read by all classes served to facilitate the concord of popular radicalism and popular Liberalism. A full account of this process would need to involve other aspects of the fusion of democratic and urban sentiment, and to attend to the spoken as well as the written nature of political communication. This was the age of oratory and of the speech, even more perhaps than it was the age of the press. These oral dimensions of political culture have been considered by Matthew.[43] Noting how central to the whole Liberal ethos free and rational public discussion and oratory were, he remarks,

> ...for Liberal party workers the rhetorical appeal was not merely the centrepiece but the distinctive characteristic of liberal politics. Liberals persistently gave speeches on the nature of Liberalism: the Tories avoided rationalistic articulation of the underpinnings of their appeal.

And again,

> Men such as Gladstone, Morley and Asquith had no base for power within their party save their rhetoric and their legislative achievements...Their standing in the party depended on their success as rhetoricians and legislators...The absence of a formal party structure allowed them and the policies developed in their rhetoric to become the national focal point, the unifying and determining element in what made up the Liberal party in the late nineteenth century.

Noting how in Gladstone's speeches the ethical substance of his policies became fused with the ethical character of his personality, Matthew observes that this points to

> the means by which a university-educated, non-industrial, intellectual elite succeeded in co-ordinating the working of a great political movement in a predominantly industrial and commercial state. They did so by expressing the rationalistic values which the Liberal 'hundreds' regarded as the stuff of national politics.

But the stuff of national politics was prefigured in the localities; in the party organisation, which Matthew underestimates, in the press, but also in the 'town meetings' that regularly punctuated the political life of English towns, especially those recently incorporated and keen to advertise the mediating role of lord mayors and the importance of the town hall as a new venue for public debate. Not that this venue was always freely given: in Chartist days the sheer strength of popular radical feeling often scared the local authorities into granting access, or calling town meetings. In the following decades it was a concession that sometimes had to be fought for, but nonetheless the town meeting came, and with it another instance of how town institutions were presented as responsive to the democracy and emblematic of the shared urban community. And, as one surveys the sheer number, the high degree of popular participation, and the wide range of issues involved in these meetings, it is clear that their place in the ideology of neo-Athenian urban democracy was not without real foundations.[44] For working people so long excluded from the life of the nation all this was of some importance. In London vestry meetings had similar functions, though radical Liberals had nothing like a monopoly on these.

These oral and printed dimensions of political communication were closely related: the press made the political speech available across the nation, yet its verbatim reporting, a kind of frozen rhetoric, served to perpetuate the forms of oratory in political life. This is very apparent in the case of national Liberal politicians, who were very quick to see the potential of the press. Bright's 1859 Birmingham speech has been acutely described as the first example in British political history of the speech as a press conference.[45] Bright spoke to a carefully prepared text with a national audience in mind. Some fifty reporters were in attendance. Gladstone was to follow the same path to even greater effect: the press created for the nation the possibility of sharing in Gladstone's rhetoric, the Midlothian campaign being perhaps the best-known example of this.[46] The politician became in the process a new kind of national hero, and politics, with religion, the great passion of the people, akin in a later day to the excitement surrounding the stars of mass sport and entertainment.[47]

Gladstone's gift was to get his audience, present and distant, to feel that they participated in his oratorial effort. He invariably addressed his audiences as 'gentlemen', and as moral and intellectual beings capable of judging cases on their (exhaustively detailed) merits. In being drawn into a sense of participation in his efforts people were also drawn by his vein of high seriousness into the life of the nation. As Matthew has remarked, ethical substance and ethical character were fused in his speeches. This was especially potent for working people. Gladstone flattered and in turn exalted his auditors, bringing the erstwhile excluded back within the political pale. A brief example of the Gladstonian speaking style is given in appendix 5. One discerns here in Gladstone's oratory and its effect the great importance of political leadership at the time, and it is to this I shall now turn. In the process of exalting the political individual as a moral and intellectual being Gladstone also served to exalt the political institutions of the country, both old and new, Parliament as well as the new kind of mass political party. The matter of leadership is therefore intimately related to what with only a little exaggeration may be termed the invention of party and of modern, parliamentary democracy. In so doing, the great, popular Liberal leaders, pre-eminently Bright and Gladstone, can be said to have invented their own political subject, 'the people'.

The importance of political leadership in the form of the 'gentleman' is evident in the leading figures of early radicalism, 'Orator Hunt' and Feargus O'Connor.[48] However, far from dying out, the 'gentleman leader' continued to be of real importance well into the era of Liberalism: John Bright can be seen in this light, and in some respects Gladstone too. Continuities in styles of leadership, and in popular expectations of leadership, are indeed one major strand linking radicalism and Liberalism. However, it is important to acknowledge the importance of the local leadership of working-men politicians,[49] and not to be led astray by the 'gentleman' tag into underestimating the recriprocal nature of leadership.[50] Nor should one fail to notice the growing degree of organisation in politics, evident in the later development of Chartism and thereafter in nascent party politics of a popular sort. Politics as a continuously organised activity served in part to obviate the need for leadership of the older sort. Nonetheless, until the later 1860s party organisation was still fairly rudimentary, and even then the 'gentleman leader' retained sufficient symbolic power to remain important.

This leader figure in fact served quite pragmatic purposes, and it would be wrong to imagine that one is dealing with a 'primitive' politics, the charismatic leader dominating the spellbound led. In the absence of formal organisation and given the strong attendant tendency to disunity in popular movements, it was essential that issues and activities be personalized and dramatized through the leader (in a sense Chartism in its northern heartlands *was* O'Connor in his passage through the people). In the frequent absence of an educated and experienced following, it was the gentleman leader who knew the forms and language of high politics. The forms of the old radical 'politics of the platform' invited the activity of such leaders, in particular the great political demonstration. If the petitioning arm of this politics fell into decay after the 1840s, this was not the same for the other elements.

Something of the peculiar attraction of the gentleman leader will be evident from the account of the leader as romantic hero and as martyr given earlier (in which the religious undertones were also marked). His power turned on his internal exile, his revocation of high society in the cause of those in low society who were similarly exiles in their own land. The rapprochement of the state, the middle classes and the working poor was indeed real in the 1850s and 60s, but at least until the Second Reform Act the sense of exclusion continued to be great, and, as the next chapter will show, currents of a fierce populist distrust of the state and of respectable society continued to flow strongly much later than this. Nor, perhaps at any time in British history, was the sense of the working classes as strangers in their own land ever completely lost.

The self-consciousness of the gentleman leader is early on evident in O'Connor's reworking of the legacy of 'Orator Hunt'. And of course so many of the radical leaders, of all social levels, actually suffered in the popular cause, either by trial or imprisonment (Jones, O'Connor, Oastler, Stephens come to mind, as well as the much longer list of workingmen). Notions of leadership, and radical politics more generally, were shot through with the theme of suffering, with the letter from prison, the triumphant release from captivity, and so on. Above all, the evocative associations of the martyr are evident, combining forcefully with those of the gentleman. And, while one must assert the truly representative nature of this leadership, and the very marked political awareness of the led, one cannot fail to detect a note of real deference among some followers, a belief in the superior capacities of 'the quality'. This is indeed apparent in the writing of those historians rightly wishing to defend the truly democratic nature of radicalism: a popular distrust of the workingman political activist is noticeable sometimes,[51] and Thompson has noted in early nineteenth-century radicalism a tendency to hyperbole and denunciation among the politically excluded,[52] a sense of powerlessness that could perhaps elevate supposedly superior and inherited qualities of leadership. Whatever the precise source of the magic of this figure, the gentleman leader ultimately represented the transcendence of class: by the high becoming low he showed that all people were as one. However, this utopian world-turned-upside-down – so powerful a theme in the broader popular culture[53] – was neither conservative nor consensual in its implications for political conduct. But it does suggest that this conduct had rather more to do with 'populism' than with class.

If the most resonant, the gentleman leader doing symbolic battle with the people's enemies on their behalf was only one among a range of styles of leadership. As with the gentleman, these owed much to the continuing force of the romantic current, above all as this was expressed in the liberal nationalism evident in European liberation struggles. Figures like Kossuth and Garibaldi held a powerful fascination, and were rapidly appropriated to the Liberal cause. Other figures in the pantheon could take a more homespun form, in which rather different associations of the gentleman were evident. This was especially so in popular Tory politics, throughout the century in fact, though the Liberals (and the radicals before them) could also draw on figures such as 'the fine old English gentleman', the bluff, inarticulate but honest military man, the honest squire and the just employer.[54] With the onset of mass party politics in the 1860s, Members of Parliament and aspirant candidates were often invested with the qualities of the hero, unlikely as this casting sometimes was. The political forms and emotional needs of an earlier politics were grafted upon the new, something evident in the ritual fêting of politicians, when carriages might be drawn through the street in triumphal passage, and also evident in the fêting of their constituents by politicians, when often quite massive celebratory and consolatory gatherings were held, in which the largesse of leaders was employed in order to cultivate their personal reputations.[55]

These rather unheroic heroes represent a more hidden and mundane current in popular politics that was to figure alongside the aspects given most attention here. The latter are apparent in the re-emergence of styles of leadership in 1860s and later radicalism and Liberalism which owed everything to the continuing cult of the gentleman leader, though now a cult increasingly serving the ends of party politics. Edmond Beales was president of the Reform League, set up in 1865 to agitate among workingmen for the vote. The League had a rudimentary sort of organisation but Beales' martyrological style mattered just as much. Beales' workingmen followers explicitly referred to him as a 'martyr', one of a long line of martyrs in the cause of liberty going back to the time of the 'Norman Yoke'.[56] Beales, a barrister, had lost a good deal of his livelihood because of his political involvement. At another meeting in the same year,[57] Beales cited with approval the words of a Polish patriot to the effect that activity in the cause of the people did not bring reward in this life. But it certainly brought popularity: at this time Beales was appearing throughout the country in a series of receptions in his honour and for his financial support. In the political Reform agitation the suffering gentleman leader was a surrogate for a dispossessed people: at the same time as Beales, Ernest Jones was stumping the country presenting the working people as the insulted and the injured of England.[58]

It was above all Bright who worked with this sense of injustice, now including the insulted multitude in the body of the nation. This he in large part did by making the political party the vehicle of this sense, enormously extending and deepening the range of meanings support for a party could have,[59] and bringing workingmen within the fold of parliamentary, liberal democracy. If Gladstone was the Christ of popular liberal democracy, Bright was his John the Baptist.

Bright presented himself very much in the guise of the old gentleman leaders. In 1859, his return to politics after illness was presented by his supporters as evidence of the hand of Providence.[60] The figure Providence revealed in Bright's speeches was that of the unwilling hero of the multitude, called back to his political mission not by base motives but by support for the moral right represented in the people's cause. Bright began his systematic flattery of his audiences early; in 1859 the reluctant returnee exalted elector and non-elector alike. It was his privilege to represent them.[61] In 1866 he was the man without ambition,[62] who had not sought the lionisation of the great cities and the workingmen.[63] His was the moral energy that came from his audiences: at Birmingham he was despondent until he looked at the great throng before him and drew energy and will from it.[64] The sense of suffering in the cause of justice, of unwillingly taking up a burden that must nonetheless be borne, was very strong in Bright, as was the sense of political leadership as a trust or a stewardship in a higher cause.[65] For an example of Bright's rhetoric see appendix 4. All these linked new to old styles of leadership, as – above all – did the idea of the leader doing battle against privilege on behalf of the excluded many.

The continuing liveliness of old aspects of politics, and their appropriation to party politics, is evident too in the political demonstration (the term 'demonstration' in fact seems to have been coined in the 1860s). There is for instance a good deal more than a hint of the old politics of the platform in the great series of reform meetings of the mid-60s, and in Bright's mastery of this great public stage. The tactic of subtly threatened force, of the might and right demonstrated by numbers, was much in evidence, and Bright was not afraid to ride the tiger. In his Manchester speech of 1866, speaking of the 'transcendentally great' open-air meeting held earlier in the day, he went so far as to declare, 'It is not more immoral for the people to use force in the last resort, for the obtaining and securing of freedom than it is for the Government to use force to suppress and deny that freedom.'[66]

The careful management of these great reform meetings needs closer consideration than can be given it here,[67] as do the great occasions of party political solidarity that followed,[68] but it is the emergence of new alongside old themes that is perhaps most striking in the politics of Reform. At Manchester in 1866 it was the association of numbers and 'public opinion' that was the dominant note, and this association was characteristic of the age. The days of Bright's audience were a new age: two hundred thousand people could gather peacefully at Knott Mill in Manchester and this was a sign of the advance, hand in hand, of morality, intellect and the people. Gladstone, for all his patrician aloofness that denied his role in the making of liberal democracy,[69] was no less adept than Bright in employing his audience as a living demonstration of the Liberal cause. His south Lancashire electioneering of 1868, carefully orchestrated for the press as well, shows this clearly.[70] It also shows, as with Bright, that the Liberal cause was the cause of moral right. What was new about this accent on numbers, public opinion and morality was its setting in the terms of mid-Victorian individual and social improvement.

Indeed, moral right was the fundamental Gladstonian formula of reform. By 1864 Gladstone had hit on the notion of moral entitlement, a formula, as the historian of the second Reform Bill remarks, charged with the aspirations of the age.[71] The trap for the opponents of reform was a clever one: to oppose the vote for workingmen was to deny their morality. To support the vote was to exalt the voter as a moral being. The age of natural right was followed by the age of moral right: the banners of the workingmen that greeted Gladstone in the Lancashire of 1868 gave every sign that the moral exaltation of the worker by Gladstone and Bright was reciprocated in popular sentiment – 'Principle Not Place', 'An Honest Man's the Noblest Work of God', 'Be Just and Fear Not', 'Measure for Measure', 'Justice for Ireland'.

The new politics was the politics of principle and not of interests. In terms of issues popular Liberalism spoke for itself: Ireland, a just foreign policy, the removal of religious disabilities, these were what mattered. Working-class 'interests' were gestured at (the Tories could benefit from this neglect),[72] but Liberal politics were about other matters. The Liberals in many respects paid only lip service to what might be understood as workers' needs or interests, yet theirs was the ardent political faith of the great majority of working people, despite the aridity of their programme of 'retrenchment' and economy. Popular adhesion to Gladstonian Liberalism should not, however, be seen as the evangelisation of a pliant mass: the great Liberal leaders and their workingmen followers needed each other, and in a sense invented each other, for workingmen also created the leaders that fitted most closely their desires and aspirations. In a similar manner, Gladstone and others invented the working class they most wished to see. There was much in Liberalism that did not match up to popular aspirations, and after Gladstone the political faith that had so closely attached to him went in search of new gods, including socialism. But it remained substantially the same faith, one forged from the mutual needs and aspirations met in the marriage of the Liberal tribunes and the people.

The cult of Gladstone was the chief expression of this marriage. This took form from the 60s to at least the end of the century in popular autobiographies, political ephemera (like mugs and mottos), as well as the deliberate utilisation of Gladstone's family seat, Hawarden Castle, in north Wales. The romantic and melodramatic overtones of the castle were in evidence, and indeed Gladstone was himself represented in the vein of the Byronic romantic hero. However, this was romanticism transposed to the era of Christian respectability: the 'people's William' was known above all through the image of his spare-time pursuit, the eminently respectable, muscular activity of tree-felling. The 'woodman' at home was a harbinger of more modern cults of the politician as one of us. This cult was actively facilitated by railway excursions to Hawarden to behold the woodman at play – Hawarden was within easy reach of industrial Lancashire by rail. It was also facilitated by what seems to have been Gladstone's own ready response, a response that tells us more about Gladstone's oratorical style and his popular appeal. As Bagehot, and later R. H. Hutton, observed, he did not impose himself on his age. Rather, he responded to it, all the better in the end to lead the 'colours and hopes' of his time. Becoming aware early in his career of being a cult figure, knowing he was able to lead and move the multitude, his oratory took on the tone of 'democratic optimism' felt by these contemporaries to be so characteristic. Gladstone saw himself as the voice of a democratic people, and this people as the voice of God.[73]

Bright was, however, one of the first to understand how the party might be re-created. It was he who most effectively made Liberalism a creed. The emotional and imaginative dimensions of party loyalty are not always appreciated by political historians. Such dimensions are of course evident far beyond the example of popular Liberalism, though they were very evident in that case. John Vincent is one who has seen this aspect: Liberal politics gave its constituency a sense of agency in national politics, at once a sense of their own audacity and shrewdness and the chance of service to a higher cause.[74] From the other end of the political spectrum, Raphael Samuel has also grasped these aspects of politics, noting how party loyalty is about symbolic reassurance as much as about real or imaginary gain.[75] A party, like a church, must 'in some sort be a projection of our own ideal selves', serving a real human need for self-transcendence. The Marxist Samuel has indeed always had a keen awareness of Tory historians' almost intuitive understanding of these pre-cognitive aspects of politics.

It should not be thought that this transcendentalism was not politically self-serving. Bright in his tour of 1866 deliberately set out to constitute the Liberal Party around the Reform issue, equating the Tories in the process with party in the old sense of faction, 'dictation' and self-interest.[76] Gladstone's critical formula, equating the vote with moral right and moral worth, of course immeasurably helped him in this task. In this mid- and later Victorian period moral right was most often religious right, and the religious dimensions of Liberalism have often been noted. They obviously owed much to the Nonconformist wing of Liberalism, which brought to the party the organisational strength and emotional power of the embattled sect, complete with its own sense of history and of mission. But religion also worked in a more pervasive way, as the often unstated and assumed 'common sense' of how the world was thought about and felt. In this regard religion might have little to do with organised religion. It is necessary to recall the force of religion in the appeal of popular radicalism earlier in the century, particularly the language and associations of the Bible. Liberalism drew both on this generalised religious sentiment and on formal, organised religion.

However, a 'religious' sensibility at this time often had little to do with religion at all. Moral aspiration and exalted feeling have been seen to dominate much of popular politics of the radical Liberal sort: this is evident beyond religion in the romanticism previously considered, and in the utopian vistas evident in the 'moral economies' of workers articulated within and beyond radicalism. The resources that Liberalism drew upon were therefore deeply rooted in the life of the poor, both secular and religious. However, Liberalism represented a particular distillation of these resources, and one that, in its earnestness, was sometimes far removed from the utopian longings explored in a later chapter. Bright for instance frequently employed religious terminology in his speeches. This went far beyond the Nonconformist constituency alone, involving the superiority of 'the moral law',[77] and presenting the struggle for political reform in terms familiar from radical days, those of darkness and light, good and evil (the unreformed institutions of England were evil and corrupt).[78] Reform became almost an end in itself, the source from which would flow 'just law' and 'enlightened administration'. More than this, ignorance and suffering would lessen, and in Bright's impassioned words, Eden would be raised up in the wilderness.[79]

Far from the self-evident truth that reform had not secured Eden deterring the faithful, the aftermath of reform served only to strengthen a faith based on hope (and on the manifest truth that justice had not been secured for working people). Gladstone of course took up Bright's mantle, and became the greatest of all exemplars of moral populism. Not quite the 'gentleman leader' – though a good deal of this remained – Gladstone was a new version of leadership, the embodiment of the moral claims of the people's

cause, claims newly strengthened but still insistent. The formerly
excluded had now enlisted in the armies of the just. To his popular,
especially labouring audiences, Gladstone was variously 'conquering
hero', 'idol', 'champion', 'grand old man', 'grand old warrior',
also the 'woodman' (chopping down Disraeli's 'tree of state'). It is
impossible to do justice here to his peculiar appeal. The autobiography of John Wilson conveys some ideas of this.[80] Wilson was
a leading exponent of Liberal–Labour politics and a major leader of
the miners of the north-eastern coalfields of England. In giving the
working classes a stake in the nation, Gladstone had allied them with
'the great social forces which move onwards in their might and
majesty', and which were in turn inseparable from the moral
elevation and transcendence of the individual. Quoting Mazzini he
went on to declare that education was everything, 'the bread of our
souls', and the key to understanding both one's political role and
one's 'mission' in life. Quoting Mazzini quoting Gladstone, life was
seen as a great and noble calling to an elevated destiny in which all
the human faculties would at last be unlocked.

This drew on so many strands in the culture both of the self-
educated workingman and the broader labouring population that it
is impossible to follow all the trails laid down. Many will already be
evident, less so perhaps the ways in which popular conceptions of
justice were invoked. The deeply pervasive sense of 'fair play' in
popular culture will be considered later.[81] This animated elements in
politics beyond Liberalism alone, but it is evident enough in the
mottoes of the banners greeting Gladstone in 1868, the content of
which was mentioned earlier (to these could be added 'Let the Best
Man Win' and 'We Respect Law Not Privilege').[82] In their various
nuances they reflect the secular and religious roots of the popular
sense of justice. Gladstone's declaration for reform in 1864 seems to
have had an electrifying effect,[83] the expectation of political reform
existing independently of Gladstone, and finding reflection in the
hunger for justice expressed in the addresses of workingmen which
immediately fell upon Gladstone in some number.[84] The radical co-
operator G. J. Holyoake said of Gladstone that the multitudes of
working people who turned out on Tyneside to greet him on his 1865
visit had come to witness 'the only English minister who ever gave
the people right because it was just they should have it'.[85]

The radical Sunday, *Reynolds News*, observed in 1866 that
workingmen were so used to the rude and insolent treatment of their
'betters' that they tended to exaggerate the courteous reception of
those few gentlemen and aristocrats who showed them respect.[86]
There is indeed something out of all proportion in workingmen's
veneration of Bright, Gladstone, and – for a time – J. S. Mill. This

background of disrespect goes some way to explaining this – in the next section the themes of 'respect' and 'disrespect' will be seen to be of great significance in industrial life.[87] One of the greatest gifts to the reform cause in the 1860s was in fact Lowe's disparaging remarks that the workingmen of England were 'the great unwashed'.[88]

Liberal tactics depended on playing up this sense of insult and exclusion by emphasising the innate virtues of the labouring poor. Workingmen were true citizens of their country, indeed, the flattery continued, perhaps the truest citizens of all. This process of exalting the people took a religious and moral form: Gladstone's criticism of class took the form of claiming that the poor were better and wiser than the rich.[89] This exaltation of poverty and its virtues in fact found a powerful response in the popular art of the time.[90] One form in which the poor would inherit the earth was that of England and its institutions (rather than Britain, in fact), and the political form of popular virtue was at least as strong as the moral and religious. What Liberalism did, therefore, was to make working people feel that they were indeed true citizens, an integral part of the perfectible institutional life of England. At least this is what Liberals set out to do, though there is every sign that in the form of English citizenship they found a ready response in their popular audience.

Bright relentlessly hammered home to his audiences that 'you', the 'very cream' of workingmen, fought and paid taxes and yet had no vote (70,000 of 'your brethren' now served under the burning sun of India). It was 'you' who had built up the towns and industries that made Britain great.[91] This sense of pride in achievement was echoed by workingmen. It can be seen at work in the great Reform demonstrations of 1866–7 (over 200,000 were at Woodhouse Moor in Leeds): this capacity to take over public space in a peaceful way was seen by the organisers as a sign of their political and moral equality with anyone in the land. Public space was indeed a visual analogue of the vote. The Hyde Park 'riots' of 1866 showed how the insistence on reclaiming public territory as the right of workingmen could electrify the whole reform cause.[92] Popular emphasis on the peace and order of their public assemblies were of course grist to the mill of Liberal politicians' arguments for the vote on the ground of moral entitlement (a moral *right* and not merely a moral trust).

The Reform League made great play of its respectability, sobriety and peacefulness, and these instances of moral virtue were translated into political terms through the idea of citizenship. This was realised in part through the issues raised by conflicts over public space, but in the main through the idea of the constitution as as much the property and legacy of the workingman as were public places. Workingmen in 1866 made it plain (as did Bright) that they had no wish to destroy the institutions of their country because they were in fact their property as much as anyone else's.

The resonances of this with the character of an older radicalism are striking: there is the same veneration of a supposedly ancient constitution, which though subverted enshrines the liberties of Englishmen. If industry made Britain great it should be noted that it was the constitution that made England great, and as in the discourse of Liberalism it was politics that mattered more than economics, it followed that England signified more than Britain (at least, that is, in England). Between old radicalism and new Liberalism there is, then, the same emphasis on the political explanation of oppression. Beales of the Reform League emphasised how the people's rights were enshrined in the constitution if only its purity could be realised: statute after statute showed that no laws could be passed without the consent of the whole commonwealth.[93] For Beales, Bright was the man who could maintain all that was best in the constitution, and for Bright the House of Commons was to be the house of the 'common people', the house it was designed to be, so giving the people back their ancient heritage. All this was a matter of 'national honour' and the 'public interest'.[94] The monarchical part of the constitution was not left out: Bright played up the theme of the people's Queen, and radical banners bore the legend 'The Queen and the People'. If we look for an anthem for the 1860s Reform movement then we need look no further than 'Rule Britannia'.[95]

Notions of the lineage of English liberties convey something of the strong historical sense involved. Bright was rooted in the long, intertwined history of religious and political dissent.[96] So too were many in his working-class audiences. Above all, and forming perhaps the most striking of all continuities with radicalism, was the idea of the long history of liberty and slavery, which has been seen to be of such importance in earlier popular radicalism. At the great Woodhouse Moor meeting of 1866,[97] as at the other reform meetings,[98] the notion of the 'battle' or 'struggle' for liberty as something handed down 'from sire to son' was crucial to workingmen's conceptions of reform. What, on this account, seems not to have been crucial was a sense of class conflict, or indeed much of a sense of class at all. Bright's idea of class was clear enough, and it was shared by very many workingmen. What 'we', 'the people', wanted was justice. However, justice could not be got from a class. It is, however, easy and certain when it comes from a whole people. Class rule had been tried and had failed. This was the class rule of the aristocracy and the governing classes. Bringing 'the rich' into communion with the people would assure the end of class rule.[99]

What popular Liberalism, and in large measure popular radicalism, turned upon was this appeal to collectivities other than class, this desire to transcend and negate what were seen as its divisive and destructive effects. But class was seen in other ways too, and the sense of class simply cannot be dismissed as irrelevant to popular politics. Class also had positive and benign associations, ones that enabled it to co-exist with, and often promote, other versions of the social order; versions which emphasised social co-operation and accord, even as they frequently offered powerful denunciations of the prevailing injustice of the social order. Class also had implications of conflict and social exclusiveness that are equally not to be denied, even though these seem not to have been uppermost. The language of class was itself a political intervention, actively shaping political and social realities. Class was an aspect of the social and political discourse of the time upon which contemporaries fixed with fascinated attention. This concentration, and the uses and indeed 'management' of class, form the subject which begins the next chapter.

3

Class, populism and socialism: Liberalism and after

Managing class

By the 1870s Gladstone had made the crusade of the'masses' against the 'classes' a central part of national politics.[1] However, Bright's flattery of the 'working classes' (the plural was usually used) involved a concentration upon the collective attributes attached to a class, and contemporaries and politicians of all sorts were fond of dwelling upon the 'energy' of the middle classes, the idleness of the aristocracy, or the morality and 'industry' of the workers. The familiar tripartite division was much used, and this indicates the extent to which class distinctions were recognised as real in British society. But it is how these were used, and how much they counted that matters. Here, popular Liberalism, the creed of so many of the 'working classes' of the time, provides us with our best guide. It seems that the positive attributes of class were accepted, in so far as they contributed to the realisation of broader and more inclusive social and political identities. The 'negative' and divisive aspects of class were anathematised, by all classes. Popular Liberalism, and in fact popular Toryism as well, were about the union of the classes against class.

Gladstone shows this in action. Addressing his parliamentary constituency in 1865 he returned to his auditors their own building analogy:

> society is as you describe it...like a well-built, well-ordered fabric, – many stones, many timbers, many doors, many windows, many parts and portions of that fabric, all having their separate offices, some of them above and some of them below, some of them larger, and some smaller, but all built and framed by the mind of the builder to serve a common purpose.'

As he concluded, 'The interest of every class is to have justice done to all.'[2] Gladstone's image of classless inter-dependence, or the inter-dependence of the better selves of the classes, varied between this building analogy, that of the factory system when visiting the factory districts (the factory was also the image of self-order),[3] and that of an

56

idealised farming community when visiting the country districts.[4] At an engagement with the volunteers the military metaphor was dominant, as was the idea of the 'middle class' as the cement between the 'upper class' and the 'lower class'.[5] As this shows, class was itself used in different ways, often with reference to the attributes of work, but also in this more fluid, spatial sense, which has only a tenuous relation to the economy. Whatever the analogy, the message was the same. It is worth remarking further that in Gladstone, as in Bright, the doctrine of class was given a great deal of its coherence through the idea of citizenship. Gladstone's public pronouncements dwelt much on the workingman as citizen and rightful heir to the long history of England. Again, it was England rather than Britain that was more powerfully resonant.

Languages of class were clearly as much prescriptive as descriptive. The few accounts we have of such language indicate a retreat from the vocabulary of class after the 1840s until the period leading up to the Second Reform Act,[6] when public discussion and public concern again pushed it to the forefront of attention. However, in all sections of society[7] this renewal of interest took the form of a concern with divisions *within* as much as *between* classes, especially those of a moral–occupational sort, most of all the 'respectable artisan' and 'labour aristocrat'. This figure and the agitation of meanings surrounding the Reform issue clearly show the active role of language in constituting the social order.

It has another role, perhaps, in fooling historians, for it is clear that the labour aristocrat so beloved of recent social history was rather more a rhetorical than an economic construct. Recent work on the period shows how the artisan figure was in many respects socially constructed,[8] particularly in his 'respectability', which, as Bailey has shown, differed greatly in meaning according to social context.[9] The social construction of the artisan can in fact be followed in the political debates of the time. These reveal a ruling class marked by anxiety, as well as by the confidence of the Liberal tribunes (also by downright ignorance about the size of the working classes and the shape of the new electorate). Ignorance and fear were fixed upon the notion of 'the residuum', the obverse of the 'respectable artisan'. The 'dangerous' or the 'criminal' classes, supposedly severed from all links with the civilising influence of their betters, was also a notion employed by Bright. He too – along with other radical Liberals of the time – made much play with the figure of 'Rochdale Man', an apparition which looms powerfully over the whole debate on Reform, and indeed over the 1860s and 70s as a whole. 'Rochdale Man' (a subsequent coinage) was used by the radicals to cajole opinion, the 'residuum' to bully it.

The mythology of 'Rochdale Man' was culled from the example of Rochdale's co-operating, self-educating, respectable workingmen (Rochdale was of course Bright's home town). It was also culled from Liberal images of the stoical, principled operative enduring the deprivations of the Cotton Famine.[10] 'Rochdale Man' symbolised all the Liberal 'advances' made since 1832, serving of course the language of social reassurance as well as Liberal politicking. As the positivist friend of labour E. S. Beesley remarked of the 1860s, it was then that the terms 'working man' and 'artisan' came to mean not the whole of the working classes but the 'skilled, respectable working man'.[11] Of course, these versions of respectability often differed greatly from those of working people themselves[12]: nonetheless, there was sufficient ground in common among the different meanings of the term to invite the widespread class co-operation noted by historians of this period.[13] However, contrary to the exponents of the 'labour aristocracy' notion, this co-operation sprang not from 'the co-option' of a 'reformist', skilled working class but out of the values and social imagery of the workers' own culture.

It should not be thought, however, that this emphasis upon the 'positive' or harmonic aspects of class identity was the only popular understanding of class to spring from this culture. The divisive and 'negative' aspects of class could in fact be embraced rather than anathematised. The sense of class identity established in the earlier decades of the century had very powerful overtones of independence and conflict which were not altogether lost at this time, though they were eclipsed. Among intellectuals and leading politicians at the time of the 1860s debate on political reform one discerns this recognition of class as a feature of urban, industrial society which – unlike in Bright and Gladstone for instance – had to be worked with and in a sense accepted rather than transcended. This awareness of class as a fixed social condition is evident in Grey's reform proposal that workingmen should be represented *as a class* in the House of Commons, or in J. S. Mill's view that they should have half the votes in a reformed House. Cobden's acute sensitivity to class represents another current, the dread of its divisive implications and the desire to employ an alternative vocabulary of social description.[14] If politicians worked with the grain of popular preconceptions in employing other social vocabularies or accenting harmonic notions of class, this did not mean that from whatever position they viewed class – as benign and malleable or as threatening – they were not much concerned with the question of managing it.

The need to manage class testifies to the continuing threat of conflict and division posed by class. Harrison has documented the scepticism with which some groups of skilled, politically active workingmen greeted the overtures of class conciliation made in the

1860s.[15] An older rhetoric of class conflict was still significant, the control of capital taking precedence over the control of privilege. Deliberate attempts at class conciliation on the radical side, such as Jones' 1868 Manchester candidacy, revealed a good deal of mutual class suspicion between workingmen radicals and middle-class Liberals.[16]

Nonetheless, even in the few and halting attempts at labour representation seen at the time (strongest probably in the coalfields of the north-east), the idea of labour was primarily that of an 'interest', the 'labour interest' being one interest among many, and the link between labour and class either not being made or taking socially co-operative forms. As Harrison has noted, as the 1860s wore on alternatives to the politics of Liberalism and of class union were weakly supported and not strongly articulated, even among the politically aware, skilled unionist workers and political leaders with which he chiefly deals.[17] In Manchester Jones had achieved the politics of class union by 1868, in the process marginalising the old rhetoric of class conflict and full manhood suffrage.[18]

The latter example suggests the importance of the local and provincial dimensions of politics, for it was indeed in these contexts that the politics of class union was pioneered. This politics, especially in its popular Liberal form, was much less characteristic of London, and something of the rather special case of the capital will be considered in the next section of this chapter. The efforts of the great Liberal tribunes were successful only because they were rooted in these local advances. Nowhere was advance more striking than in the factory towns and the northern, provincial cities, and it is to the example of the spinning town of Ashton-under-Lyne I shall turn in exploring the management of class.

Ashton combined 'advanced' industry with as advanced a radical bourgeoisie as could be found in the country. As has been seen, in the early nineteenth century its popular radicalism and class consciousness were as developed as in any town in Britain. Ashton was at once the most difficult and the most propitious ground for class union, its legacy of class hostility being matched by the radical drive to transcend class. Though somewhat precocious, the town nonetheless exemplified changes going on across the nation.

What is first of all striking is the sheer weight of the cultural offensive directed at working people from the early 1850s: by the mid-50s, in the winter months especially, a seemingly endless stream of lectures and talks, covering every conceivable subject, was provided by local clerics, employers, professional people and party leaders. This was accompanied by the opening of institutions of moral and educational self-improvements (Mechanics Institutes, mutual improvement societies, reading rooms and libraries). The

Liberals led the way in this, and there were marked differences between Liberalism and 'anti-improvement' aspects in popular Toryism,[19] but there was also a substantial degree of concord between the parties on the essentials of this liberal world view, namely the joint belief in reason and faith, progress and revealed religion.[20]

Even in secular manifestations of this cultural liberalism the 'religious' infusion was not far to find, for instance in that note of moral exaltation that resounds throughout Victorian England, as loudly among workingmen as among the upper-class purveyors of Improvement. For instance, when self-educated Ashton workingmen made their views on poetry public, it was its 'holy mission' that mattered above all.[21] The moral exaltation, the 'holiness' of this mission, might not be formally religious at all, but the effect of heightened emotion and aspiration was the same, and nowhere is this clearer than in the religion of knowledge. Knowledge made men free (sometimes, though not usually, free of religion, especially organised religion), and if bourgeois and workingmen's visions of Improvement differed – the one individualist, if social, the other more collective – then there was sufficient in common in this legacy of Enlightenment rationalism and romantic aspiration to cement considerable common feeling in the town.[22] For instance, by 1857, William Aitken, the chief popular radical leader, was eulogising Charles Hindley, an employer and the town's MP, as a foremost champion of the liberating power of self-improvement now abroad in the land.[23]

Hindley was a strong supporter of the Factory Acts, and it has been seen in the previous chapter how in the industrial north the issue became very much part of the nascent party conflict of the time: the Liberals appropriated these 'improving' aspects, the Tories others. In turn the Liberals fused the religion of Progress with the advance of democracy. In 1856, the Oldham Lyceum was opened, the institutions of municipal self-government (along with the support of the new, 'democratic' press) lending their weight to the education offensive.[24] The opening was indeed a set piece of the new democratic populism of Liberalism. The local radical MP, W. J. Fox, took a leading part. It was Fox, the self-styled 'Norwich Weaver boy', who had earlier developed the idea of the 'masses' against the 'classes' (long before Gladstone), and who now dwelt on the idea that 'all great men sprang from the people'. At Ashton meetings of a similar sort the same extension was made from knowledge and freedom to the progress and happiness evident when all the town's inhabitants blended their voices into that of 'a single family', 'the people'.[25]

The Liberals were also adept at annexing foreign affairs to democratic radicalism, an especially potent extension of nascent popular Liberalism in the era of European liberal nationalism. In 1857, for instance, the Liberal leaders engineered Kossuth's Ashton visit.[26] Unlike their European cousins, the English people were at last exerting themselves, and with the help of their supporters Parliament was showing itself responsive and 'liberal ideas' were making progress.[27] The break with the pure doctrine of Cobdenite foreign policy was much in evidence in the town[28]: Tories and Liberals joined together to extol Palmerston's forward foreign policy. In turn anti-aristocratic politics were fused with patriotism: Britain was the home of liberty and civilization, and both commodities were available for export. In linking the people's crusade against Privilege with national identity, class boundaries were still further dissolved.

Political Liberalism as much as cultural liberalism depended in part upon the appropriation of the past to the cause of Progress, an appropriation already evident in the area of the nation. Political Liberalism set out with much success to annex the radical past: there is no more telling a symbolic expression of this than the construction of the Free Trade Hall on the site of the Peterloo massacre.[29] In a different sphere, the work of Gray has recently shown something of how public discourse about labour and the factory displaced or marginalised the operatives' understanding of the factory system of the time,[30] and this liberal accent on the factory as 'rational' and 'progressive' is equally in evidence in the political area.

As the previous account of popular politics has shown, working-men would in fact have needed little prompting to envisage the struggle for liberty in the 1860s and 70s as part of a centuries-old history, one marked by the progress of reason evident in reformed political institutions as well as in the march of Improvement.[31] The autobiographies of Liberal, ex-Chartist, workingmen activists bear witness to this sense of the seamlessness of the old cause.[32] The 1840s, for instance, was cast as the 'hungry forties', caused by protectionism and cured by free trade. Free trade was in fact perhaps the most powerful single exemplification of the Liberal doctrine of economic and political progress. Toryism was cast in the guise of ignorance and darkness, Liberalism as the symbol of the fatherhood of God realised in the brotherhood of man. Liberalism was seen as the logical extension of Chartism, itself an episode in a far older story.

Of course, the Tories had their own versions of history and progress, and, again, these received expression at provincial[33] and local[34] levels in such a way as to serve as a crucially important base for the national advance of organised party politics in the 60s and 70s. These emphasised church and state as the embodiments of a nationally unified people, and the Tory party as the guardians of the pristine British constitution, a constitution suborned by Whig oligarchy in the past and Liberal factionalism in the present. The accent on nation and on the past was clearly greater than in the Liberal case, but just as with the Liberals ideologies of class union were much in evidence, as were attacks on the divisiveness of the unacceptable aspects of class. Notions of progress were by no means absent, for instance those of progress as embodied in the alliance of the Tory aristocracy, the commercial middle classes and the workers, an alliance responsible for and embodied in the industrial advance of the nation.

In Ashton the Liberal offensive of the 1850s bore fruit in the politics of the 1860s: by 1867 Brightean rhetoric permeated the language of public political address in the town,[35] reproducing all the characteristic marks of emerging popular Liberalism. This was as much the case with Liberal workingmen as with their better-off co-Liberals.[36] For workingmen spokesmen 'class legislation' and 'class representation' were attacked, political reform heralding the end of class rule and the reign of 'the universal brotherhood of man', also the realisation of 'rich and poor' as 'one happy family'.[37] Working men at Reform meetings were prone to emphasise how material and mental labour went hand in hand,[38] and when class terms were used they were invariably not of an exclusive or conflictual sort.[39] Much of the time the universalistic vocabulary of 'people', 'brotherhood' and 'humanity' was employed. In 1867 the new Liberal tribune Ernest Jones reinforced this stigmatisation of 'class rule' in the town,[40] and it is evident how in the sphere of trade unions as of political affairs,[41] large demonstrations in the same year gave forcible expression to this populism. The idea of England as the 'land' or 'home' of the free was much in evidence, and it is worth remarking that this embodiment of the people as the nation (not as a class) was, later on, apparent in public debates on the secret ballot. In industrial Lancashire, at least, these were carried on in terms of whether the measure was un-English (not un-British) or not, an idea in turn linked to whether it was 'un-manly'. The endemically male-centred nature of political language is again amply in evidence.

Ashton was representative of the nation at large: as the following accounts of other, non-party continuities in radicalism will indicate, the same attack on the aristocracy as the chief enemy of the people, the same emphasis on political rather than economic explanations of wrong, and the same desire to transcend class in the name of broader social unities were as evident on the national as on the local stage. This was especially evident in the pages of the chief organ of this radicalism, the popular Sunday newspaper, *Reynolds News*.[42] It was evident, too, in the leaders of the Reform League agitation: for Edmond Beales the great struggle was that of the rights of man against property rights; for the 'Edmond Beales of the North', Jones, that of the people against oligarchy.[43]

On the few occasions when workingmen, or at least radical Liberal leaders of labouring origins, elaborated on the ways in which they understood society, one sees very similar emphases to those present in this political dimension. The 'moral force' Chartist Henry Vincent lectured in Stalybridge in 1856 on his conception of the social system of the time.[44] In one sense this was a class system, of 'higher', 'middle' and 'working' forms. But the composition and relations of these classes were only in a secondary sense economic, and in no sense conflictual. Rather, the categories in which Vincent thought are primarily moral (also politico-moral): the different classes are related by ties of obligation and duty which have been morally degraded by the gross materialism of the age. The classes are also morally as well as socially composed. The 'middle classes' include those one would expect but also the workingmen who respect themselves, who do not squander their money, and who bring up their children in the word of God. The really wealthy among the business groups are in fact consigned to the 'higher classes', the 'middling orders' (a term also used by Vincent) holding the moral high ground of the nation, as much against the degraded workers below the ranks of the respectable (the 'criminal' or 'outcast' classes) as against a degraded aristocracy.

Clearly, in this system economic categories take much of their force from, and are usually overlain by, moral notions. Now, this sort of view is not surprising from those of Vincent's stamp, a man whose Chartism led him into educational and temperance activity and thus into the politics of class union (also into the lecture mania of the 1850s). Nonetheless, it was the perspective of men like Vincent that became dominant in this period, and it is evident (for instance in the case of Thomas Wright cited above)[45] that this ascription of moral (and political) causes and attributes to the social system was wholly characteristic of the time.

This characterisation of class in popular politics need not surprise us when we look back to the popular radicalism of the early nineteenth century. Putting the 1860s and 70s in this context serves to indicate the importance of broad continuities in the outlook of the time, particularly among the more politically aware and active workers, but probably also among the labouring poor at large. Considerations of a wider temporal span also invite a broader geographical comparison, and it is useful to examine the social outlook of French beside British workers, as evident in their political

movements.[46] (A fuller examination of the English example follows
in the later account of work and class.)[47]

In both cases, the language of class was well developed, but
attention to its actual form reveals how necessary it is to avoid
anachronistic understandings of class as primarily 'economic' and
conflictual in character. In both cases 'the people' tended
increasingly to be defined in terms of manual workers, manual
labour serving more than hitherto as a crucial symbol of collective
identity. This perhaps developed more rapidly in France, where it
was linked to rather more collectivist – and decidedly more socialist
and revolutionary – aims and activities. Nonetheless, in England as
in France, the language of class was applied by workers seeking to
forge alliances among quite varied groups of workers. This was
especially so in England in the aftermath of the 1832 Reform Act,
when the sense of 'betrayal' by the 'middle class' appears to have
hastened the use of these class terms.

More particularly, radical political economy in the 1830s and 40s
increasingly defined exploitation as capitalist in character, and came
to employ a labour theory of value. The focus was shifted from 'Old
Corruption' and taxation to capitalism and profit. However, as the
secondary literature on the British case is increasingly making
clear,[48] it is the limits to all this that are most evident ('limits', I
hasten to add, does not imply that the radical analysis was somehow
historically false or inadequate). Limits are evident in a social sense:
the degree to which this alternative political economy percolated to
a wider audience was probably limited, for very many the old
terminology of priests, landlords, tax-eaters, and the like, continuing
to be uppermost. Indeed, the radical analysis of capitalism did not
itself look towards production as central, but concentrated chiefly on
the areas of economic exchange and distribution. It was not an
awareness of opposed interests rooted in production and thrown up
by a new capitalist economic system that mattered. Rather, for the
rank and file as for the radical leadership, the source of and solution
to social injustice lay in the political sphere. The conception of
production held by even the advanced radicals was in fact essentially
reciprocal in character, viewing labour and capital as having quite
basic interests and identities in common. Nor was the end of private
property seriously envisaged. In these various aspects the leadership
also had much in common with the broader popular view.

In these respects, also, Britain was different from France, yet in
comparing the idiom of class in the two it is the similarities that are
striking, the obvious and marked differences notwithstanding. The
terms of reference of the 'class consciousness' of French workers, as
of their British counterparts, were universalist rather than exclusive

in character. 'Class' was more often than not seen in a negative way, as a reprehensible and selfish denial of the common interests of all people.[49] It was only later – in England much later and always incompletely – that 'class' came to have the positive attributes of exclusiveness: solidarity, struggle, also a clear sense of sub- and superordination. 'Class' simply did not carry the charge other terms had. These other terms may have carried a class charge, but their meaning – as in the term 'the people' – was not exhausted thereby. On the contrary, they carried their own associations, not least the universalist ones of the Enlightenment legacy.

Thus it was that the social outlook evident in the early nineteenth century both permitted the co-existence of diverse forms of social description and social identity, and emphasised in its 'class' manifestations elements other than conflict. This did not mean, however, that this outlook was 'reformist' or not markedly critical of the status quo. Indeed, it carried powerful visions of the social order against which the present was judged, visions to which the terms of 'class' do poor and partial justice. The terms of 'populism' perhaps do better justice and it is to these I shall now turn.

Varieties of Populism

So far the term 'populism' has been used rather loosely, and somewhat sparingly, to describe a set of values and ideas inadequately described under the heading of class. Popular radicalism, and especially popular Liberalism, are better explained as populist in this loose sense of the term. And this applies to the popular radicalism of the later nineteenth century as well. For, far from falling into decline, popular radical traditions continued to live on, largely subsumed in party politics, but also partly distanced from party allegiance. The conception of politics involved was far from outmoded, though this is the way it is often treated by historians. Anti-aristocratic politics, and politically centred notions of oppression and injustice made much sense (even in the industrial districts) in a Britain still dominated by aristocracy and traditional forms of mercantile and manufacturing capitalism. As has been suggested, the very uneven experience of 'proletarianisation' itself contributed to non-economic and populist readings of society.

Aspects of these continuing radical traditions, however, merit the designation of 'populist' in a somewhat more precise and narrow sense than that so far adopted. In what follows, therefore, the continuing popular radicalism of the second half of the century will be traced in these two senses of populism, the broad and the more precise. Behind the populist radicalism effectively if not at all completely integrated in Liberalism (and Toryism), lay a more 'classical' populism, too protean and tumultuous to be easily absorbed in party politics. But first I shall look at later radicalism, the history of which has been rather neglected in the literature. Only some of its characteristics can be discussed here. Perhaps its clearest expression was the massively popular Sunday newspaper *Reynolds News*.[50] Something has already been said of G. W. M. Reynolds, who served as a crucially important bridge between the old radicalism and the new.[51] *Reynolds* was but one example of the mass-circulation Sunday: *Lloyds Weekly Newspaper* reached sales of one million in the mid-1890s, and this and the *Weekly Times* dealt in a politics more moderate than *Reynolds*, though every bit and more removed from a class understanding of society. As much as the sheer size of circulations (over 300,000 for *Reynolds* by the mid-1860s), it is the readership that is striking: *Reynolds* was the special favourite of the 'old', often London-based artisan trades, but had a wide readership among workingmen of all sorts throughout the country. 'Lower middle class' elements were also much in evidence, though more in *Lloyds* than in *Reynolds*.[52] The very social heterogeneity of the readership itself suggests the utility of the populist label, and the dangers of ascribing clear-cut geographic and socio-economic designations to the different strands of popular politics.

Nonetheless, in the latter respect, it is evident that the provincial–London distinction is useful: the heart of popular Liberalism and Toryism was in the provinces, London being more strongly linked to the old radicalism, apparent in what seems to have been a strong, lingering Chartist influence, but also in the newer *Reynolds*-style popular radicalism. The reasons for this are not far to find. The sort of radical bourgeoisie seen in the case of Ashton was much more widely developed outside the capital, particularly in the industrial areas of England. The 'provincial' England I describe in this contrast is obviously an industrial one, based on Lancashire, but extending to Yorkshire, the industrial Midlands and the north-east, which were in fact even more emphatically centres of popular Liberalism than Lancashire. Nonetheless, the 'non-industrial' provinces were probably closer in this regard to industrial England than to London. The political effect of a radical, reforming bourgeoisie, bent on the politics of class union, were obviously complemented by the social and political effects of the employers among these groupings: new forms of employer influence and control attended new forms of industrial organisation, particularly the factory. Modes of economic, cultural and social influence were reflected both in the politics of 'opinion' considered here, and in the politics of influence and even deference. One would also need to consider the importance of Nonconformity in all social levels in English provincial society (not to mention Welsh or Scottish society). The comparatively weak hold of Nonconformity in the capital is very striking.

Along with these factors, the different character and social constituency of early nineteenth-century radicalism in London and elsewhere would need to be considered (the artisan–factory worker distinction is very crude, but will suffice for now). Later developments such as the delayed emergence of a London popular Toryism were important. Popular Toryism served as a powerful spur to popular Liberalism in a number of English areas, most notably but not at all exclusively, Lancashire. A closer look at London and provincial economy and society would uncover many other reasons for these differences. These also bear on the broader question of the social character of the audiences popular politics at large addressed. It seems fairly evident that the better off, the most skilled, and the best organised and educated among workers were those most attracted to the politics of 'opinion' discussed here; whether radical, Liberal or Tory. Such labelling should, however, only be done in a very qualified way. Large numbers of the poorer, less politically articulate kinds of worker were attached to the party (and non-party) currents so far considered and this was sometimes for the same reasons as their better-off fellows, such elements perhaps drifting in and out of political activity. For the most part, however, these workers may have been influenced more by other considerations; party politics being made up of the politics of influence and deference, of ethnicity and religion, and of patriotism, beer, bonhomie and corruption, as well as of the politics of opinion. However, crude as it is, the distinction, like the London–provinces one, probably conveys something of the reality. Of course, the mainly 'higher' working-class social constituency of this politics was numerically very large as is evident given the 'archaic' and skill-dependent character of Victorian industrial organisation.

Returning to *Reynolds News*; though a genuine newspaper it was intensely political in character. It was recognised at the time as the organ of 'ultra radicalism', a creed widely disseminated among workingmen,[53] if perhaps chiefly those of the artisan and highly-politicised sort. Clearly, if *Reynolds* worked sytematically to promulgate a particular vision of society this corroborated the deep-seated predilections of its readership. The character of this understanding of society may be briefly outlined[54] (it is already very familiar from early nineteenth-century radicalism). There was no analysis of production as the source of oppression, nor of classes, and no conception of an industrial bourgeoisie. In so far as class was

mentioned, and a 'middle class' was identified or attacked, this was
chiefly in the moral and political terms applied to the enemy *sans
pareil*, the aristocracy. Political conceptions of wrong were uppermost, as indeed was much of the 'old analysis' of a predatory
ruling class: the terms 'placeman' and 'patronage' were almost as
much at home in the 1880s as in the 1820s.

Elements of that more 'classical' populism mentioned earlier can
also be discerned. (It should be emphasised that these and the other
characteristics mentioned are evident in *Reynolds* reporting of
workingmen's social and political meetings and activities as well as
in its leader and letter columns.) Ideas of a lost golden age emerged
frequently ('Norman Yoke' ideas were commonplace), and were
themselves linked with the long historical view always characteristic
of radicalism. Utopian evocations of the virtues of the land were
much in evidence, though these also had practical relevance, given
the politics of contemporary agrarian radicalism and the salience of
land reform on the political agenda. The second major aspect of
'classical' populism was the pronounced anti-statism of *Reynolds*, its
distrust of the state and its vaunting of voluntary activity. Distrust of
the state often took the form of distrust of the law, the armed forces
and the police. Far more potent than divisions arising from
production were divisions of another, older, 'economic' sort, those of
rich and poor, around which also turned ideas of rulers and ruled,
expressed in such forms as there being one law for the rich and one
for the poor. However we interpret these attitudes their longevity is
very striking.

Berridge's account of the content of *Reynolds* suggests a more class-
based conception of society developing in the 1880s, but a reading of
the newspaper in this and subsequent decades up to 1914 suggests
little change. The 'capitalist' might figure more than hitherto in
radical demonology, but this did not generate the terms of economic
class or of a capitalist *system*. (Capitalists not capitalism remained the
adversary, though the employer as capitalist could often be viewed
in harmonic economic terms.) Class terms were in fact chiefly
remarkable by their absence,[55] and hostility to the state was
unabated,[56] government frequently being associated with scandal
and corruption.[57] By 1905 the central struggle was still that between
the democracy and the classes, and the paper's banner – '
Government of the People, for the People, by the People' –
continued to testify to this and to the primacy of politics.[58] The same
valuation of the land was evident as earlier, divorce from the land,
'the soil', being the source of all social woes.[59] The same historical
vista and conception of lost rights was also evident.[60] The aristocracy
was the abiding enemy, enmity being characteristically mixed with

fascination for the doings of the well born.[61] This heady mix of political distrust, sensation and voyeurism did not of course die out: on the contrary, as anyone familiar with the Sunday popular press in Britain in quite recent times will be aware, it has marked a wider populism, though the ingredients have been mixed in different proportions; the accent on scandal and voyeurism being evident most famously in the *News of the World* – itself a nineteenth-century Sunday – and the emphasis on political radicalism being apparent in *Reynolds* itself, the paper surviving to be a major advocate of the Labour Party.

Before taking up our narrower definition of populism it is necessary to say something about the relationship between the radical current so far traced, and the political parties themselves, especially the Liberals. There were undoubted differences between this neo-radicalism and Liberalism, but also considerable affinities, as well as differences which on closer inspection turn out more apparent than real. Popular radicalism and popular Liberalism differed in terms of how the state and political institutions were seen, Liberalism evincing a more positive attitude. The rapprochment of the two politics was accompanied by a general lessening of that popular sense of exclusion from the institutions and civil society of the nation so marked in the early nineteenth century. Successive administrations to 1914 passed much ameliorative legislation, and this served to present the state and political parties in a more benign guise. The feeling that British institutions and British law were responsive to working people's needs certainly became more marked.[62] The growth of political reform and of the party system contributed to the same end.

Yet one ought here to differentiate between the 'state' and the political system. It was the latter that reflected the greater shift in popular attitudes: the anti-statist *Reynolds News*, for instance, was fairly amenable to political parties, especially the Liberals. When one looks more closely at attitudes to the state it is the suspicion and hostility shared between radicalism and Liberalism that is evident. It is true on the one hand that the local and central state presented a more acceptable face after the 1840s: regulation and legislation in trade union affairs and factory conditions, as well as municipal self-government, are examples of this. Nonetheless, even in the more positive and mellowed reception of the state evident among workingmen Liberals, it was the limits of the state that were constantly emphasised: the state was in fact seen as rather more neutral than positive, its intervention securing the conditions in which workingmen and their institutions could operate freely, whether these be unions, or friendly and burial societies. While the self-help of workers was rather more collectivist than individual (or at least not individualist in the bourgeois liberal sense), the state was valued only in so far as it allowed expression to the cardinal virtue of 'independence'. Beyond this, the interventionist state was looked upon with much distrust. This was as true of popular Toryism as of the radical and Liberal currents. The institutions of church and state might be venerated in Toryism, but there was much hostility to the 'centralist' state.[63] Popular attachment to free trade, spanning all the parties, represented an economic analogue to non-intervention in the political sphere.

Radicalism and popular Liberalism shared sympathies in common. The very success of Bright and Gladstone in creating a sense of social inclusion among a virtuous and embattled 'people' para-doxically depended on playing to and keeping alive the very sense of exclusion itself. The political drama in both politics was substantially the same, that of the struggle against a privileged, corrupt and manipulative ruling class. If 'the people' in Liberalism was much more a matter of the union of classes than previously, then the undercurrent of more radical and explosive versions of an excluded people, of the excluded 'masses' against the 'classes', was not far below the surface.

It erupted in the full-blown populism so amply evident in the second half of the century, and yet so remarkably neglected by historians until very recently. It is necessary to demarcate differences between popular Liberalism, the continuing popular radical tradition, and this more emphatic populism. But what is rather more interesting than the obvious differences are the similarities that cut across these, forming something like a continuum, with Liberalism at one extreme and 'classical' populism at the other. In describing ultra- or neo-radicalism I have already touched upon two chief characteristics allying it with this more strictly defined populism, namely anti-statism and the idea of a golden age. It will be amply apparent from the account of popular politics so far presented that these aspects were by no means foreign to Liberalism. Above all, the continuing potency of beliefs in the elemental struggle of the dispossessed against the powerful few served as a bridge to the populism of populism.

What was this and where was it to be found? An answer to the second question will already be partly apparent – in all political parties and in none. It was a current pervading all of English popular politics, suggesting by its existence the centrality of the populist tradition, however conceived, rather than the tradition of class. It was chiefly evident, however, in certain mostly non-party agitations, the most revealing of which was the 'Tichborne Case'.[64]

An account of this in turn serves to answer the question as to what this essential populism was. The case has been considered in some detail in the secondary literature (manifestations of its appearance in the broadside ballads of the time are considered below).[65] Very briefly, the case concerned 'the claimant', one Charles Orton, and his struggle to regain his supposed standing and fortune as Sir Roger Tichborne. Orton emerged from the Australian bush in 1867 to be abetted in his claim to be the true Tichborne heir by Thomas Kenealy, QC. Most of the Tichborne family fought tooth and nail to repulse the claims of Orton. It speaks volumes for the sensitivities of the time that the case convulsed the nation, and went on to convulse it from the late 1860s to the early 80s. The serried ranks of the powerful, the propertied and the respectable drew up battle lines against the claimant, aware that the forces he had unleashed were a threat to the maintenance of property and order. On the other side, the case drew the even more diverse ranks of the unpropertied together in their fight against the privileged few. The force of *vox populi* was as strong as the fear and loathing expressed for it by the privileged.

The case reveals the distinguishing marks of populism in its narrower sense: ideas of a corrupt ruling class and legal system, of rule by conspiracy, of an excluded people against a corrupt state apparatus, of messianic leadership and a lost golden age were all very much in evidence. So too was a pronounced martyrology. The strong echoes of much of this in popular radicalism and Liberalism (also Toryism) will already be evident. The notion of a vanished Eden was reflected in an idealised England, a radical patriotism that took the form of a powerful attachment to suborned liberties (Kenealy in fact set up Magna Carta Associations throughout the country). These often spoke in terms of a return to a golden age of craftsmen and yeomen. The form of Eden may have differed from other manifestations – that of Bright, for example – the fact did not. Similarly, the anti-Catholicism and messianism evident in the agitation may not have been precisely duplicated in 'respectable', 'legitimate' party politics, but they are amply evident below the surface, for instance in the extreme (and violent) Protestant Evangelicalism of the 1860s and 70s, so closely linked to popular Toryism,[66] and in the styles of leadership already noted in radicalism and Liberalism.

The case brought to the surface many other popular suscepti-bilities. The theme of one law for the rich and one for the poor was especially strong in Tichborne. There were strong echoes of the attitudes seen in *Reynolds News*, such as distrust of those institutional expressions of law, the police and the legal profession. The distrust of political parties evident in the Tichborne agitation was not so apparent elsewhere, though accompanying popular allegiance to party was also a certain distrust of the self-serving partisanship of party politicking (this will be looked at later).[67] Broader echoes may also be found in the distrust of war and armies evident in the case, in the exaltation of the values of the land, and in the extreme prurience matched in a wider sphere by the love of scandal and sensation evident in popular radicalism (the case was in fact taken up with great gusto, and passion, by *Reynolds News*).

The state was looked upon with deep distrust. It was seen as the preserve of corrupt manipulative elements, lawyers, politicians, 'ministers', aristocrats or 'capitalists'. The theme of the machinations of the 'moneyed interests' was marked, a variant of conspiratorial notions of rule of some moment in most populist movements, and one taking anti-semitic form here if not more widely.[68] The machinations of the state could at one moment be seen to be directed at the drinking and sporting classes, who could in the next moment see themselves as the paragons of industry. Dislike of government regulation of drinking and gambling was equalled by contempt for the idleness and indulgence of the 'ruling classes', above all the aristocracy. The case also became linked to such anti-interventionist causes as the agitations surrounding the Contagious Diseases Act, the Income Tax Act, compulsory vaccination and the institution of the population census.

The political struggle of the ruled and the rulers, the many and the few, was accompanied by a social struggle that took the various but essentially similar forms of 'the people' against 'Society', the public against the 'upper ten' (thousand), 'the masses' against 'the classes', also, on another tack, 'Mammon' versus 'the rights our fathers fought for'. It also took the form of the opposition of 'the rich' and 'the poor', the rich being viewed in terms of 'influence', respectability, 'fashion' and 'show' (the 'half-bred swell' was a special term of abuse). As will be seen later,[69] this opposition of the vices of the rich and the virtues of the poor was much more central to the popular culture of the time than has commonly been recognised. In the Tichborne case the hypocrisy seen to be synonymous with wealth and respectability was the special object of popular contempt, and this had profound echoes in the broader political culture of the time, though often below the level of organised party politics. I have dwelt elsewhere upon the grass roots, extreme political Protestantism of the time, which in its assault on respectability seems to have appealed to many among the poorest and most outcast in society.[70] Akin to popular Toryism as it was, it nonetheless (like Toryism) appealed to a wide range of social levels, including those beyond the rank of workers. So too did the Tichborne agitation, which if it may have carried a proto-political message to the very poorest, represented the sentiments of the great mass of workers, skilled or unskilled, better off or poor, Tory or Liberal.

Such values seem removed from class. Far from being the residual or anachronistic sentiments of an 'advanced' industrial workforce, it is quite apparent that this extreme populism was one of a range or family of populisms united by the common themes discussed above. Yet it is as an anachronism that populism has mostly been discussed by historians. The problem with these accounts is that they are themselves anachronistic, fixated as they are with class as the sign of modernity. Calhoun's work represents the most systematic attempt to apply the notion of populism.[71] *Pace* E. P. Thompson, early nineteenth-century radicalism is seen as an example of populism rather than class: the defence of 'traditional' trades and communities is contrasted with the supposed 'class' movements of Chartism and trade unionism. These are held to be the political expressions of a new industrial proletariat, the 'reformist' expression of a new acceptance of the capitalist economic system. The problem with this is that it turns on a series of highly schematic, anachronistic and ultimately spurious oppositions; those of 'artisan' and 'factory worker', 'revolutionary' and 'reformist', 'traditional' and ' modern', and 'class' and 'populism'. Rubinstein's recent examination of the populist current in early popular radicalism raises similar difficulties,[72] the notion of the inevitable retreat of populism before the modernising force of class being even more marked.

To a considerable extent this anachronistic view is shared by the only serious, synoptic account of the ideology and practice of populism that we have,[73] though there is also present in this account the eminently sensible view that populism is a cluster of attributes the proportions of which differed considerably as to time and place. Present too is the equally sensible view that populism is not somehow foreign to British political traditions.[74] The latter misconception is of a piece with the view that populism is an expression of the strains of 'modernisation', the reflex action of groups excluded or marginalised in this process, particularly in industrialisation, and especially peasants, small farmers and artisans. Not without considerable condescension, populist movements are usually labelled nostalgic, conservative, 'irrational' and 'primitive'. But this view in turn rests on a mistaken view of industrialisation, utopianism and British political development.

Industrialisation and proletarianisation were, as has been seen, vastly more complex than the linear view employed here. Even from the account of utopian currents so far given it will be apparent that the conservative label just will not do. And British political development was about a good deal more than the growth of a class-conscious proletariat. The contrast between third-world nationalism, small-farmer midwest American populism, or nineteenth-century Russian populism, and the 'advanced', industrial west, is almost certainly overdrawn, resting as it does on these bogus and Euro-centric assumptions about industry and class. As for the assumption that unlike mainstream British political development populism was demagogic, all one can reply is that demagogy is in the eye of the beholder. It is remarkable how judgemental ostensibly neutral accounts of populism are. If conservatives often embrace populism for what it is not (conservative) then liberals and socialists reject it on equally false grounds, as at once 'irrational' and contrary to the manifest destiny of the proletariat.

The extreme or classical populism found in the Tichborne case, and so similar to the broader stream of world populism, can be detected as a powerful and persistent if subterranean current in this period, even if its chief interest lies in pointing to the family of populisms across the whole political and social spectrum. This current is subterranean in part because populist feeling did not readily accept incorporation in formal movements and ideologies, and in part because of historians' neglect of it. Within the present compass only a few of its manifestations can be briefly referred to. This includes aspects such as the mixture of Russophobia and radicalism evident in Urquart's workingmen's Foreign Affairs Committees of the 1850s, the Sunday Trading riots of 1855, the Anti-Vaccination and Contagious Diseases Act agitations of the 70s, and the popular opposition to the 1872 Licensing Act. In the same decade, the Royal Parks and Gardens Act saw a continuation of this same sense of popular grievance about interference with the livelihood, pleasures and privacy of the poor and the workingman.[75] One might also point to the politics of land reform and rural radicalism in the last quarter of the century, emphasising as these did the themes of dispossession and the values of the land. Below this level of public agitation lay the substratum of continuing popular distrust of the state, in many respects the chief raw material of populism. Consideration of this takes us towards the end of the century when the development of socialism and welfarist Liberalism might suggest a changed outlook among both the active workingmen politicians and the wider labouring population. However, the old spirit of populism was abroad in both, even if its chief impact was evident in Liberalism and radicalism.

The old and the new in socialism

The impact of Liberalism upon socialism has been much considered by historians, though not that of popular radicalism or populism. At the risk of some repetition, then, it is necessary to amplify the influence of the Liberal inheritance if the place and character of class in politics is to be understood. But first something can be said about the links of extreme populism and certain kinds of socialism, links that were closer than is often thought. As Roe's account of the Tichborne case makes clear,[76] individuals and associations linked the old Chartist days with the formation of the Social Democratic Federation in the 1880s (the Tichborne agitation forming the element of continuity). One of Kenealy's foremost lieutenants was John de Morgan, red Republican, associate of Bradlaugh, anti-Vaccinationist, and tyro of the Magna Carta Associations. De Morgan was connected with late Chartism and with 'red' radical elements in the artisan, club life of London radicalism. The marriage of intellectual Marxism and artisan proto-socialism was presided over by H. M. Hyndman, its offspring being the SDF. What is so striking, however, is the extent to which the SDF was rooted in the Tichbornite kind of populism: Hyndman, de Morgan and others were members of the Kenealy circle, active in the Magna Carta Associations, and founders of the SDF. The relatively limited appeal of the SDF notwithstanding, the exoticism of this political mixture ought to put us on our guard against too ready an association of socialism and class. It was, however, in other forms of socialist politics, chiefly the more popular Independent Labour Party, that the more important influence of the previous politics was to be found, especially that of popular Liberalism and radicalism.

Before this, however, popular attitudes to the state need further attention if the effect of the older anti-statist political legacy is to be fully appreciated. What limited systematic evidence there is suggests that far into the twentieth century the desire for voluntary effort and independence was very pronounced, in the institutions as in the culture of workers. Cheap food and stable employment seem to have mattered more than welfare schemes. A more benign view of the state emerged, but this may have been as late as the 1930s and 40s, and even then the preference was for welfare schemes with strong elements of self-regulation and local democracy.[77] Looking at the culture of workers, Hoggart's account of the 1950s, and previous generations, tends to confirm this, indicating as it does the force of 'Us' and 'Them' distinctions, a socially rather undifferentiated 'Them' being defined as those in authority, local and national. For 'Them' was reserved not so much fear as mistrust, and the desire of people to keep to their own sort, helping themselves as best they could.[78] People and not views or ideas mattered, and there was a distrust of public and general life.[79] In this as in all other aspects of his account, it is the Victorian and Edwardian roots of these values that are striking. The broadly populist character of this twentieth-century outlook does not need labouring here.

This distrust of the state characterised workingmen socialists too, if to a lesser degree, but before pursuing this something of the broader traditions of the Labour Party may be considered. Foote's recent account of the political thought of the party seeks to defend the idea of 'labourism' as the central tenet of that thought against those who would see Labour as a set of diverse ideological influences and historical circumstances.[80] In this I think he is right but the term 'labourism' is an unfortunate one, employed as it usually is by those on the left who wish to condemn the supposed 'reformism' of the party and the unions. I shall not dwell on the large measure of philosophical idealism in this view, except to remark that this account makes amply plain how working within the terms of existing institutions and values was compatible with often profound aspirations to change. This aside, Foote indicates what seems to be the case of Labour thought and values capable of rejecting Liberalism on the right and Marxism on the left. These core values were based on the trade union, and on the wider associations of labour value, and while the redistribution of wealth to its creators was sought, the capitalist social and economic systems were for the most part unquestioned. For instance, though 'capitalists' might be criticised, given the lack of an economic analysis of capitalism, capitalists and employers might be distinguished, employers having a useful role and being distinguished in turn as good or bad.

The early nineteenth-century roots of 'labourism' will already be evident, and will be more closely looked at in due course.[81] It is amply plain that 'labourism' was quite compatible with a range of political ideologies and parties, including those that had little to do with class. However, this labourism does need in certain respects to be distinguished from what went before, and those characteristics marked the more 'economic' and 'class conscious' politics and popular attitudes that seem to have emerged after 1918. Briefly, what was new in turn-of-the-century 'labourism' was the emphasis on the independent role of labour, and the association of labour and class, an association now seen in terms of a growing sense of the historical role of the working class. These aspects will be considered presently: clearly they differentiated Labour from Liberalism, but while these differences were important there was a deeper similarity between political Liberalism and Labour, especially in the radical legacy.

This legacy was obviously richer and more complex than this thumbnail sketch of 'labourism' suggests. A major bridge between Liberalism and Labour was the Independent Labour Party, and it is to Howell's account of the political values and social analysis of the ILP that I shall turn. Howell's is an account not just of the lineage of ideas but of the assumptions, values and social situations of the workingmen and women who gave life to the party.[82] The work at once makes it plain how labels like 'labourism' and 'ethical socialism' are plainly inadequate, for there was also much interchange between union and labour values and demotic socialism.

As Howell observes,[83] at a local level the socialism with which he deals was strongly marked by the features of local Liberalism, especially where Liberal politics had 'domesticated' traditional radical sentiments. This radical-Liberal legacy was strongly evident in the intellectual sphere, especially in the formation of the ILP cadres. The romantic, moral and aesthetic critique of 'industrialism' was taken over intact by socialists. The pantheon of Liberalism and radicalism was the pantheon of socialism – Dickens, Bunyan, Carlyle, Ruskin, and, later, Emerson, Thoreau and Tolstoy. Marx and Morris were not much bothered with.[84] Strands of socialist thinking influential beyond as well as within the ILP preached a similar message: MacDonald's anti-urbanism was as evident as Blatchford's evocation of a 'merrie England' in which 'pre-industrial values' were exalted. Edward Carpenter attacked 'modern civilisation' rather than capitalism as a system.[85]

Workingmen, leaders and committed followers both, grafted their own visions of the past onto this romantic stock. The talismanic figure of Robert Burns has already been noted, and the vision of the ease, dignity and delight of labour evident in his 'Cotter's Saturday Night' was overwhelming for many workingmen, evoking notions of the cottage economy and the independence of labour as well as the virtues of the land, elements already seen to have been such a powerful presence in early nineteenth-century radicalism. Hardie's vision of the 'independent collier' was a version of this, and was paralleled in the industrial north by mythologies of work, ranging from that of the handloom weaver in Lancashire and Yorkshire to the pitman and keelman of the north-east. The significance of this plebeian invention of tradition cannot be too much emphasised,[86] not least in attaching the sentiments of working people to the socialist cause by fusing their own traditions and socialist thought. However, the social outlook evident in these mythologies, and in the literary means that gave these and so many other popular aspirations expression, was rooted in the radical and popular tradition rather than in class.

Looking for the moment at the more formal elements of political thought evident in the ILP, it is apparent that its conception of society was one in which the idea of 'community' was uppermost. Evolutionary and biological metaphors abounded, and with them the belief that present society could evolve towards a reformed end (for instance the idea that industrial struggle could change the minds of employers as well as of workers). Marxism was rejected in favour of liberty, equality and fraternity. In line with aspects of populism discussed here, the critique of capitalism was moral and not economic, despite a more marked emphasis on production and capitalism as sources of wrong. Kier Hardie, for example, understood work under capitalism to be morally alienating. The root of the worker's situation was arbitrary, impersonal authority and a deadening system of production generated by the immorality of competition: there was little or no sense that the drive for profits systematically robbed the worker.[87]

In many respects, therefore, the economic analysis and pre-scriptions of the ILP differed hardly at all from those evident in 'labourism'. As Howell suggests,[88] the economic thought of the ILP indeed represented little advance on Liberalism (when, that is, there was any interest in economic thinking at all). In line with Hardie's perspective, more widely there was little or no notion of capitalist crisis or breakdown, no idea of capitalism's dissolution under its own contradictions. In line with evolutionary conceptions, the belief was that the transition to socialism would come about through collective ownership and social responsibility overcoming present capitalism, and – by uncharted means – leading on to higher social forms. These forms were not those of class, for complementing socialist economic thought was a social analysis that ultimately denied class in the present or in the future. The working class were warriors but the war was not about class: rather like Gladstonian notions of class, the morally acceptable side of class might assert itself, but only in the end to deny the rightness of class distinctions and the privileging of any one class. For the ILP 'class interest' and 'class struggle' did not produce the unity of workers, but represented the limited, self-interested concerns of the trade unions. Despite the new sense of the independence and agency of labour and of class, class struggle was not the motive force of history. What mattered instead was the moral energy of the whole people or the 'commonwealth'.[89] For Hardie socialism was a crusade against materialism, and the class war reduced it to a faction fight.[90]

Early ILP socialist values were representative of popular socialism more widely, and this goes as well for its strong religious and moral aspects. As Yeo has shown,[91] among a wide range of socialists, personal and structural change were seen as ultimately the same.

The full realisation of community might be the end goal, but its means lay with the individual as much as with the collectivity. For Hardie, again, talk of class made people look outside themselves for the cause of their oppression and misery. Socialism was less about state intervention than self-help, albeit self-help made possible by the state's adjustment of the profound inequalities of present, capitalist society. As Howell has argued,[92] the line between collectivist and non-collectivist measures ran more through Liberalism than between it and socialism. It is indeed arguable that it was more the socialists' desire for independence at an institutional than an ideological level that separated Liberalism and socialism. This gradually imposed its own logic, cutting down room for manoeuvre with the Liberals, and in the end accentuating the quite limited ideological and policy differences between the two.[93] It is quite clear that socialist versions of 'self-help', expressed above all in the virtue of independence, differed in their collectivist nature from the marked individualism of superficially similar notions present among the middle classes and insistently relayed to the poor, not least by certain sections of Liberalism. Nonetheless, in other versions of popular radicalism and popular Liberalism, 'independence' served to express that fusion of the personal and the communal evident in later socialism.

Thus it is clear that socialist conceptions of the economy, of class and of society and the individual had a great deal in common with radical Liberalism. This similarity of outlook and the relative absence of class perspectives, could be traced rather more systematically in other spheres too, particularly in attitudes to the state, where despite the emphasis on collective ownership a marked anti-statism continued in socialism. In the ILP a distrust for the state went together with a benign view of British history, institutions and traditions that was very reminiscent of radical Liberalism.[94] Of course this account of the outlook of the ILP gives only a partial description of British socialism at the time, though it does probably describe the strand that was most characteristic of socialist workingmen, especially in the industrial north of England. Other valuations of the state were evident in socialism, most evidently in the Marxian and Fabian strands, but in other currents too.[95] However, Fabianism itself set liberal and individualist limits to the role of the state,[96] and in the most powerful element of all, that of the 'labourism' of the trade unions, distrust for the state was very marked. However, in revealing the Victorian roots of Edwardian socialism it is less this abstract account of intellectual developments that is compelling than descriptions of party politics at a local level.

Smith's recent account of Victorian and Edwardian Liberalism in Glasgow shows its profound influence on socialism.[97] This was perhaps more emphatic in Scotland and Wales, but the example is undoubtedly of general relevance. Home Rule and nationalism had a particular resonance as issues linking the two politics, but if the hatred of landlordism (more marked than of capitalism here) drew some of its inspiration from the local setting, it was widely typical of the anti-privilege, democratic tradition bequeathed to socialism. Free men, free trade, free land were the issues of a deeply entrenched Liberalism, rooted in the traditions of local working-class self-help institutions, and expressing precisely that fusion of personal and collective 'independence' noted above. These traditions were in turn attached to a sharp feeling for the democratic, radical past; one embodied by Liberal workingmen in impressive public ceremonial.[98] As will be seen subsequently, there was in the industrial north of England especially a similar sense of a radical, dissenting past, which despite its Englishness could make common cause in something like a north British democratic patriotism. Similar too was the belief in progress (perfectly compatible with attachment to the 'good old cause'), a belief very marked in the Glasgow example, and one obviously of central significance in socialism, not least in that new sense of the 'forward movement' of labour increasingly evident by 1900.

Above all, it becomes evident that once Liberalism and socialism are seen in these ways, the argument that it was the new 'progressive' Liberalism of the late nineteenth century that served as the bridge between the two begins to appear distinctly unsound. In fact, it was the old and not the new Liberalism that served this purpose. However, it is plain that there were elements of the new in socialism and that the break with Liberalism was often a sharp one. But this was essentially an expression of dissatisfaction with what was taken to be the ossification of Liberalism, its denial of its true radical credentials, especially among its middle-class proponents and the local and regional party chiefs. The old Liberalism was denied in the name of the old Liberalism. Of course, prior to the First World War this denial was muted, and this emphasis on socialism is somewhat misplaced in neglecting late nineteenth-century Liberalism, still easily the majority creed, whether in 'old' or 'new' forms. Particularly culpable is the neglect of Lloyd George, the next after Gladstone in the line of great radical-Liberal tribunes of the people, and perhaps the clearest example of all of the continuing potency of the underlying populism of the radical tradition. In this respect, let me refer in passing to Stephen Reynolds' 1911 account of working-class political loyalties and aspirations, one of the most impressive 'insider' accounts of the time. For Reynolds the political opinions of workers were perfectly expressed in Lloyd George's recent City

Temple speech. There the figures of Dives and Lazarus were called upon to summon up the fundamental contrast of rich and poor. The speech expressed the simple fellow-feeling of the poor for those 'down under', and an impatience with the endless 'tinkering-up' of social wrong. The call for justice was, however, between man and man, not rich and poor: men were all born the same way, and had but one life to live.[99]

The persistence of Liberalism and populism notwithstanding, the new in socialism was registered in the emphasis on the independence of labour, and with it the attachment of the values of labour to class, a sense of class which in turn specified a stronger awareness of the historical agency of the working class than hitherto (as well as the heightened sense of optimism and moving ahead noted above). Work on the example of south Wales shows this in action, and indicates again that tussle about meanings seen in the last chapter to be so important in politics.[100] In south Wales, as in so many parts of industrial England,[101] socialism broke in upon the entrenched power of local, paternalist industry, breaching the decades of control it had built up. This control was in part expressed in a politics, variously, of economic dependence, deference and fatalism, a politics below the surface of the chiefly formal politics so far considered, and one already noted in earlier times. It was also expressed in decades of political understanding built up between the local magnates and workingman Liberals. This influence had to be broken: the external, critical stance of socialism, while necessary in undermining the local status quo, carried in turn the danger of too freely spurning local traditions and values. To succeed best, its message had to adapt the garb of the known and the familiar. One can see something of this, especially in south Wales but more generally, too, in socialism's articulation of the thought and institutions of religion, and its very experience as a form of religious conversion and of the 'new', truly 'religious' life.[102]

As in the transition from early century radicalism to Liberalism and the transformations of populism, old terms took on new meanings. The Welsh case shows how important conflicts about language were, in this case not religion so much as the meanings and values of 'labour'. Of course, this invigoration and re-definition of old discourses functioned best when older traditions had ossified, as was the case with much of elite-dominated south Wales Liberalism. Socialism in south Wales drew on the old cutting edge of popular radicalism in transforming the previous associations of the 'labour interest' (as one interest among many) into the new associations of independent labour. It was socialists like Kier Hardie, themselves steeped in radical traditions, who pointed to the Liberal leaders' betrayal of their own claims to be the friends of labour, and who most effectively tapped those older associations of labour which best lent themselves to the idea of independence. In the latter respect it was as much the figure Hardie cut as the policies he followed that preached the gospel of independence; his emphasis on the plainness and dignity of the workingman, and not least his 'cultivated air of insubordination'.[103] Hardie was active in Wales, but the wider activism of Hardie and the others like him testifies to the representative character of this case.

In Wales as more widely industrialists and Liberal leaders fought back by playing perhaps their strongest card, their reputations as custodians of the community's interests and identity, especially in their industrial form. Later chapters will reveal how important were these representations of local community, and how they had markedly different political and social forms and uses. Workingmen socialists made way by hitching not only religion and labour values to their star, but also these versions of local, regional and indeed national identity, potent as these already were in the radical legacy. But if these people translated a past they were still its children. They gave old terms a new meaning, but they did this chiefly by exploring the full dimensions of the radical inheritance, rather than by pioneering a new way of seeing society. Philip Snowden, later to be the first Labour Chancellor of the Exchequer, is a good example of this. For all his originality he was a product of Victorian industry, Victorian religion and Victorian radicalism.[104]

Born in 1864 in the former handloom-weaving, mill village of Cowling in the West Riding, the memory of domestic industry – its legacy of values but also its deliberate re-creation – was central to Snowden and to countless other political workingmen, radical and socialist. In many ways it was the vision of Cowling, then and now, that shaped Snowden's socialism in its emphasis on co-operation replacing competition, on thrift, and on plain living and in-dependence. Snowden's quite astonishing effect on working-class audiences owed much to this,[105] and to the extraordinarily powerful message of emancipation he carried. This was in turn derived from the Nonconformity of Cowling imbibed in his youth, in the spirit if not the letter. In terms of the understanding of labour and of religion involved, particularly in the marked utopian elements of both, it is apparent how much there was in common between the outlook of the early nineteenth-century workers considered earlier, and that of their children and grandchildren in Snowden's time. Moreover, it is the profoundly northern character of English socialism that is evident in men like Snowden, who was known as 'the prophet of the north' long before his reputation was more widely made. Ernest

Jones before him, of course, bore the same title. The industrial north was the bastion of the ILP, and outside London Lancashire was the greatest centre of the SDF. Robert Blatchford and the 'Clarion' movement, perhaps the single greatest source of mass inspiration in early socialism, were also distinctively northern in character. This socialism was inextricably interwoven in the whole, existing culture of northern workers, reaching back to the moral and social vision that had informed the radical tradition throughout the entire century.

There were, however, elements in that culture of a darker, more intractable character than has perhaps so far been indicated. Snowden sought to transform the central value of 'independence', rooted as this was in work, religion and community. But he also saw the more sombre side, how independence and respectability could turn in upon themselves as the obsessions of the poor, leading in the end not to emancipation but to enslavement and fatalism. The present account has only hinted at elements of dependence and resignation in popular political culture. Something of how poverty twisted aspiration into the shape of a deep fatalism will be looked at later.[106] Snowden understood this, and how the legacy of independence could be disabling as well as enabling. In 1895 he wrote movingly of Cowling, attacking the claim that thrift was the source of the village's advance:

> It [thrift] represents injustice doubly-damned, because inflicted on those whose virtues are made instruments to scourge them. It is that sturdy spirit of independence, that desire to be self-respecting and respected, the inherent trait of emulation, which we as Socialists expect to be such powerful forces of social regeneration. It is these virtues which, struggling for material embodiment and yet being too weak and ignorant to make a fitting environment, sacrifice everything to the hope of being able, by incessant toil, to preserve that same independence and self-respect when physically unable to provide for it from day to day... They are heroes, these despised factory men and women. They are resigned to their lot; scarce ever a murmur is heard. They are full of hope and faith – hope that they may be able to struggle to the end; faith, that God's eternal justice and love has provided rest when their earthly toils are over. I have heard them sometimes in their prayer meetings, when seemingly their suppressed anguish could no longer be restrained, utter in a frantic shout, whose pathos has made the flesh creep on my bones, 'Thank God there are no Monday mornings in Heaven'. But they rose the next morning[107]

One could dwell on other examples of how the early socialists sought to forge a language that would make working people no longer feel resigned and in so doing re-working older traditions and legacies. Blatchford's re-working of the idea of the nation,[108] the widespread influence of his writing as almost religious in its power to convert, and his at times unashamed jingoistic populism, are all important. But to dwell on these influences and on the rank-and-file socialists would give a distorted picture. Snowden's account of Cowling suggests the rather different politics of the majority of workers, and in any account of early socialism and the Labour party it is the unions and their rank-and-file that need pride of place. The unions were not uninfluenced by socialism before 1914–18, nor were they totally lacking in a class perspective on politics and on labour affairs. The advances they made in these respects prior to the Great War should not be underestimated. Nonetheless, as the following chapters will suggest, when all qualifications have been made, it is the limited penetration of socialism and of class independence and conflict,[109] indeed of the very terms of class themselves, that is most of all evident.

Part II

*Moralising the market : work
and the social order*

4

Civilising capital: class and the moral discourses of labour

If class was a somewhat elusive presence in the political sphere then commonsense would tell us that in the world of work it found its true home. Surely, the accelerating pace of proletarianisation in the nineteenth century led to the widespread development of class identities which were rooted in the economic categories of labour and capital and gave rise to conflictual conceptions of society which, unlike in previous times, were anchored firmly in the area of industrial production, rather than economic exchange or distribution? This was so, but only partly so. It represented one among many tendencies of development, and was not as single or overarching as it is so often taken to be. In themselves, the forms of class manifest at the time turn out on closer examination to be somewhat different from what we might expect.

In this section I have chosen to concentrate chiefly on cotton factory workers, the manifestation of the new in the contemporary economy. With these workers we would expect to find most clearly expressed a sense that the social order had resolved itself into the antinomies of labour and capital, and that the customary values of the past had given way to the economic and class values of the capitalist marketplace. We find something of this, and the rise of 'economic', 'market' categories is a subject broached in this chapter, and pursued in the next. But we find much else too – namely, the intertwining of custom and the market, and the continuing dominance of the former, albeit often in much re-worked forms, right down to the end of our period in the early twentieth century. The nature of custom in the present sphere of work is pursued in this chapter and the next. Both are concerned with what I term the moral discourses of labour: the attempt by workers to address work and economic life in a humane and just way. This attempt is traced in the next chapter chiefly in terms of the trade union, and the role of institutions in shaping the discourses of labour (and hence the discourses of the social) will be evident. The ways in which the union redeployed the old, customary language of the trade is one instance of the fate of custom discussed more generally later. But the discourses of the trade and the role of the union was only part of the larger moral universe of labour, and it is with this broader current that I am concerned in the bulk of this chapter. Workers' valuations of labour extended beyond work, the economy and institutions, and in tracing these we learn much about how the social order was seen at the time.

The time in question here is the second quarter of the century, a period of acute crisis in both the political and economic arenas. The next chapter moves on from the third quarter of the century to say something about the period down to 1914. Before considering the very early years, therefore, it is perhaps sensible to say something here about the mid-century, in particular the 1850s to the 70s, setting the scene for what went before and what was to come: in doing so I also have the opportunity to expand a little on what terms such as custom and the market might mean.

Amid the very considerable diversity of industrial organisation and work experience evident across the mid-Victorian economy, there emerged chiefly in the northern, industrial districts a new uniformity marked by increased capitalist control of the workplace. This took organisational and technical forms, for instance in the factory and the steam-powered machine, and seems to have been accompanied by the sense among workers both of the intensification and the insecurity of labour, as well as by the feeling that industrial capitalism was here to stay and that for good or ill the fate of the worker was tied up with its fate. These developments have been discerned in the advanced industrial forms of factory textiles and the iron shipbuilding and engineering of the north-east.[1] Given the unevenness of British industrialisation,[2] in no sense can these industries be regarded as typical of the nation at large. Nonetheless they are illustrative, both of tendencies evident elsewhere in somewhat different forms and at different times, and in terms of their own internal structure. On closer examination, however, this structure turns out to be removed from conceptions of a monolithic 'modern industry'. Textiles is a good example, cotton for instance containing a myriad of wage levels, occupational statuses, distinctions of gender and age, and capacities for power in the workplace. In fact, cotton reproduced aspects of work experience to be found quite widely in Victorian England, beyond as well as within the manufacturing sectors. Therefore, in drawing from the example of modern craft production on Tyneside and applying this to the example of the factory the wider relevance of this discussion should be evident.

In this examination of Tyneside industry McClelland has provided an important account of how workers saw their work and the social relations work gave rise to.[3] Workers' recognition of the seeming permanence of capitalist industry brought with it a changed outlook on the capitalist market. Labour was still regarded as the source of wealth and value but was increasingly seen as only one element in the production process: if labour was the arch, capital was the keystone of industry. As McClelland suggests, this acceptance of the legitimate role of capital was linked to political considerations, particularly the eclipse of the more anti-capitalist aspects in popular radicalism. Whatever the full sequence of events, ideas of the legitimacy of capital seem to have brought with them notions of rightful profits, and the belief that wages were derived from increases in capital. Among trade unionists what were increasingly seen as determining the share of capital and labour in the product of industry were the governing 'laws' of political economy, especially of supply and demand.[4]

Now, it seems to me that there is nothing much new about ideas of the legitimacy of capital and profit (also of the 'fair' employer), though the influence of political economy consequent in part upon increased employer control in the workplace was a new departure. To my mind rightly, McClelland is at pains to emphasise that the unions' acceptance of central tenets of political economy went beyond mere pragmatism. Similar points have recently been made by Biagini,[5] whose examination of trade union and radical opinion in the 1860s and 70s (including *Reynolds News*) shows how widespread beyond the north-east were beliefs in a 'natural' order of interests obtaining between employers and workers, beliefs buttressed by a selective recourse to political economy.[6] As McClelland suggests, there was a sense in which workers took the 'economic' as a discrete sphere of activity, the market serving as the premise and limit of trade union action. The union came to be seen as modifying but not abolishing the 'natural' movements of the economy.

The importance of these developments is apparent in historians' accounts of industrial relations at the time, accounts which emphasise the increasing importance of market categories and the wage form in unions' and workers' justifications of their roles.[7] Attention has also been drawn to the increasing tendency of unions to accept the legitimacy and efficiency of the private ownership and managerial organisation of industry.[8] Turning to the wider political sphere, the argument that Chartism represented a political analysis of economic ills has brought with it the recognition that the demise of the movement may have led to a sundering of political and economic modes of explanation.[9] The failure of Chartism to explain the character of the mid-Victorian state and economy meant that political explanations of economic phenomena were less credible. Instead, 'economic' explanations of such phenomena became marked, and with this the tendency to conceive of the economic as a discrete sphere of effect. For instance, trade unions tended to restrict themselves to economic interests, and economic ideologies – particularly free trade – came to have a powerful influence. The non-interventionist character of the Victorian state and of Liberal politics tended to reinforce this divorce of politics and economics.

On the face of it, then, custom waned and the 'market' waxed. There is indeed a good deal in this picture that cannot be denied. However, it conveys only a very inadequate idea of how workers saw their labour and thus how this vision shaped their wider social outlook. In particular, it gives no account of how new valuations of labour co-existed with, and were indeed embedded in, old valuations. Custom and the market formed a relationship – sometimes complementary, sometimes contradictory. In most respects, however, it is the strength of the moral categories of custom rather than of the economic categories of the market that is most evident. To understand this relationship more closely the very suggestive work of McClelland may again be utilised. It was the union that above all gave voice to both the new and the old sentiments of labour, reformulating the old in terms of new demands and opportunities. The new trade union was created out of the old organisational and discursive resources of the trade. A central aspect of the trade mentality, going back far into the eighteenth century and beyond,[10] was the notion of skill as the property of the worker. Proprietorial notions of skill carried with them the idea of the worker having a 'vested interest' in the trade. Such values, argues McClelland, were somewhat weakened in the second half of the century, but nonetheless still carried an extremely powerful charge for the new trades of engineering and shipbuilding emerging in the north-east. Indeed, as well as constituting the widespread belief that labour was the fundamental source of value in society, they also underpinned much of what it meant to be a man for these workers, initiation into the trade being a good part of initiation into manhood.

However, the legacy of the trade had another major aspect, less stressed by McClelland but of equal importance with proprietorial notions of skill. Such notions operated in terms of the idea that the trade comprised a community of interests of masters and men. The trade was an arena of reciprocal rights and obligations, which defined a kind of partnership in which each side had its proper role to play.[11] Both aspects of the trade outlook were powerfully present into the late nineteenth century, and indeed beyond, the notion of the community of interests long perpetuating older and very powerful ideas of rightful profit, just employers and proper trade practice. Now, these ideas could be expressed in opposition to ideas of the market, but the relationship of the two was usually more complex. McClelland sees market categories as being the 'ultimate determination' of trade union action in this period. Yet he also notes that such ideas were accompanied by a profound belief that the system could and should be subject to human intervention. What the unions were concerned with was the construction of 'a world of "reciprocity" pivoted on a morally regulated exchange of labour against capital'.[12] As ideas of state intervention and co-operative production shrank from view after mid-century, union activity certainly came to be about hours, wages and conditions. The unions could be narrowly instrumental and exclusive, but as McClelland puts it they also saw themselves as 'a kind of morally purifying agency which would dissolve the bad and the corrupt' at work, as much among the men as among the masters, whose duties to capital they stressed as much as those that flowed in the opposite direction.

These aspirations to order in the disordered world of the market seem to have been of quite crucial importance, as the following account will attempt to show. Aspirations to a harmonious world of production encompassing master and man, in which both sides would live up to their responsibilities, existed, however, in a world in which the actions of employers often belied the attempt at concord. As capitalist industry increased in scale and sophistication of organisation, and as free market ideologies made headway among employers, the opportunity and motive for abrogating trade responsibilities and interests were amply evident in the camp of the capitalist. Yet aspiration mattered nonetheless (and of course very many employers behaved in ways often departing widely from the precepts of the free market). Aspiration mattered, and it is necessary to emphasise this against accounts, widely prevalent,[13] that would see the meanings of work as exhausted by explanations of economic 'interest'. Union practice was dictated by real, observable behaviour, but it is also true that practice and behaviour were interpreted by cultural values, especially of the trade, that always framed labour in a wider moral and social setting. Aspiration mattered, again, simply because in this age it mattered in the wider culture of workers: it will already be apparent how important moral and religious values were in the political setting, and this was no less so in the economic. As McClelland argues so persuasively, the unions had a 'moral cosmology' which was central to their purpose. The market had to be moralised, capital had to be civilised.

The moral discourse of the union did not somehow float free of the tumult and demands of action and organisation. Far from it, for, as in the political realm,[14] discourse was a means of organisation. The moral claims of the union were a means of justifying the actions and standing of the leadership and of building the union. Such claims looked outward to public opinion and the public realm in this, but also inward in the attempt to control and influence the action of an often divided and refractory membership. The union claimed to lead by emphasising the importance of collective, not of individual interests, and sustained itself also by a rhetoric of unselfishness which stressed the responsibilities of capital to labour and labour to capital. Therefore, union values were not simply an expression of some underlying unity of sentiment or interests, for instance an underlying 'class consciousness', but were through their discursive and organisational forms a means of bringing about such unities. As in the political area, discourse was an active intervention in how the social order was understood.

Therefore in what follows it will be apparent that the values of the trade often ran up against rank-and-file opposition: short-term was put above long-term interest, and informal, customary modes of regulation were put before the need for formal, continuous and disciplined organisation. The latter is a nice illustration of how a model drawn from custom, that of the trade, could in fact conflict with the realities of custom. Union leaders had to work with often recalcitrant material, but they knew their job: evidence of disharmony between the spokesmen of union values and the rank and file cannot be denied, but what is usually more striking is the success of the unions in working with the grain of their members' values and expectations. Again, as in politics, a public discourse shaped values but only by reflecting them in a creative way. To a surprising extent, given the diversity of work experience at the time, the model of the trade was effective in building the union. But it had its limits. Particularly in the case of cotton, it is evident how the model had to be adapted, and in some respects rejected in favour of other possibilities. It had its defects as well as its merits. Other models also mattered.

It is also the case that the discourse of the trade set up distinctions within labour, as well as creating solidarities: it demarcated the union man from the non-union man, one tradesman from another, the tradesman and the skilled from the unskilled and the 'dependent', and also, often, men from women. These distinctions were apparent in the crafts proper, and were also evident in the application of the trade idea to the situation of the factory. But what is striking is how the notion of the trade, suitably modified, served as a principle of unity and social inclusion, these divisions notwithstanding. Nonetheless, the perceptions of class emerging were always stamped with the mark of a part, not the whole, of labour. As McClelland has suggested, the figure of class derived most fully from the craft-based trade model – that of the skilled, male, head-of-household – was one predicated upon powerful elements of animosity and division within the ranks of workers.[15] What might be called the paradigm of class emerging from the textile factory and its utilisation of variants of the trade model, while in some respects less divisive was highly particular in another sense, rooted as it was in a strong sense of the industry, factory life, and the region.

This talk of class, however, tends to pre-empt later discussion. In many respects the terms of class do scant justice to the moralised notions of economic relations beginning to emerge so far. Before pursuing these notions of the trade the wider social setting of labour needs to be considered, for it was not merely in the terms of the trade that labour defined itself. To be a worker was to be a member of a community, of a family, of a nation, as well as of a trade. In tracing what may be termed the extra-economic meanings of work the recent writing of Reddy has been pioneering.[16] Unfortunately, Reddy is so keen to deny the validity of conflicts about market criteria such as the wage that he fails to appreciate what is amply evident here, namely that market and non-market criteria exist in a relationship and not as antitheses.[17] Nonetheless, Reddy's emphasis on the significance of aspects such as 'honour' and 'shame' in the behaviour of unions and workers points up the significance of the broader cultural context, and it is to this I shall now turn in search of workers' perceptions of the social order in early nineteenth-century industry. These perceptions have been almost universally seen by historians in terms of class. When we go back to the second quarter of the century in search of the roots of the attitudes that have been briefly explored here it is apparent that something more ambiguous and elusive than class was in fact present.

The search for what was present must, however, be acknowledged as exceedingly difficult: given the amount of research on the labour history of the period it is surprising how impressionistic are accounts of these perceptions. This impressionism of course inheres in part in the nature of the evidence, but it has been compounded until recently by a rather simplistic resolution of the evidence by historians into signs either of class or of its absence. What is there has tended to be lost in the middle. I rely here on piecing various accounts together, rather than on direct analysis of the actual terms in which workers may have viewed their society; obviously, not a very satisfactory procedure. A good place to start is Stedman Jones' account of the economic components evident in popular radicalism.[18] Despite the shift to an understanding of exploitation as based on capitalism and profit (itself perhaps only partly registered among the rank and file), the radical analysis was directed more to exchange and distribution than to production. The conception of production was in itself reciprocal in character, viewing labour and capital as inhabiting a would-be harmonious world of production in which many interests were held in common.[19] The 'economic' critique of capitalism put forward was far from a class-based, economic reading of exploitation. These views have been explored by Stedman Jones, and their implications may usefully be brought out in this context. The politically engendered rigging of the economic system posited capitalists as 'middlemen', coming between producers and consumers; a reading of capitalism in fact quite accurate for the vast numbers of workers involved in mercantile, non-factory forms of production. The populist implications of the radicals' view of the economy for such workers should not be forgotten in this concentration on factory workers. The political and other alliances that the logic of their economic position suggested to so many workers in the 'archaic' industrial England of the time were those with their employers against the ruling class, not those against them. The capitalist as employer might in fact have a useful role in production (as opposed to the cardinal, chiefly aristocratic, vices of idleness and parasitism). He might be entitled to 'fair' profit on his provision of capital. Employers were not identified as a class, and thus it followed that they were differentiated individually, by their actual behaviour. The industrious, efficient and honest employer could be as much singled out for praise as his opposite for blame. And, if competition was attacked, it was unfair competition and not competition *per se*.[20]

There was, therefore, nothing in the radical critique representing an inherent block to understanding the relationship of workers and employers as one of mutual interests, however often in practice this was tested by events. If in the 1830s and 40s, employers, and especially textile masters, put themselves outside the pale of the 'industrious' and 'the people', then there was nothing irrevocable about this. If they adjusted their political and economic behaviour they might be brought back within the pale again. And, of course, from the mid-century onwards capital presented a decidedly changed face to labour, especially in the textile districts.[21] Now, this reading of events presents two things to view. First, it suggests that the changed tenor of social relations in the mid-century is in need of re-thinking. Once it is recognised that the popular movements of the first half of the century were not of a production-based class sort then the transition to mid-century social reconciliation is in a sense less remarkable than has usually been thought: the two sides, labour and capital, were seen as having much in common, and given the right circumstances what was held in common could be capitalised on. The second aspect that is suggested in this account of the radicals' understanding of production is the presence of a less sharply defined but nonetheless powerful vision of society widely dispersed in the labouring population of the time: for the radicals there existed what is clearly evident on this account as a populist interpretation of the economy just as of the polity, and this may have influenced, just as it also drew sustenance from, rather similar popular understandings of the economy.

However, Stedman Jones' account has with justice been exposed to considerable critical comment for its formalistic account of language and of political ideas, and for its attention to a rather narrow range of public political utterance.[22] What matters is the appropriation and use of radical ideology and rhetoric, the particular social and political contexts involved. Workers and their spokesmen may have charged shared terms with rather different meanings from others in society. In particular, a 'political' discourse about oppression could be applied with inventiveness and gusto to economic life and economic exploitation. It is also the case that given the interventionist character of the early Victorian state workers' ascription of economic wrong to political sources was not far off the mark.[23] Many criticisms of Stedman Jones have been drawn from the example of the factory districts, where industrial capitalism was most advanced, and labour and political conflict most marked.[24] The burden of these criticisms is that inter- and intra-trade differences were resolved in the common recognition of a class identity. The combined force of early century industrial capitalism and an oppressive state are held to have created an awareness of political exclusion emanating from 'class rule'. Class terms were used, becoming both emblems of solidarity and negative, pejorative epithets. Class identity and class language were based on workers' recognition that what they felt to be their oppression was related to the new industrial system of the factory as well as to political causes. There is, I think, a good deal in this, though the picture still leaves the shape of workers' views of labour and of economy very indistinct. Class in this 'economic' sense needs to be related to the wider discursive realms in which the social visions of workers were enfolded. Kirk's 'defence' of the idea of economic class offers a good way into these questions.[25]

Usefully enough for present purposes, Kirk bases his discussion on the example of south-east Lancashire, perhaps the most radical of all the factory districts. (It should be noted that this precociously advanced area may be a kind of limit-case – class, if it was present, probably being less developed in less 'advanced' areas.) Kirk argues,

unexceptionably, that workers recognised that political and economic power was conferred on employers by their ownership of the
means of production as well as by political means. Among workers'
leaders there was an awareness of factory production as a 'system',
a clear anti-capitalist recognition of power flowing from economic
means. But in fact Kirk is forced to cede the major part of the
argument in recognising that among radical spokesmen and their
audience the key to, and major cause of, exploitation was still felt to
be an oppressive political system. Nor do workers seem to have
disputed the right to capitalist ownership of industry. There were no
moves towards the appropriation of industry, and production-based
explanations of exploitation, if present, seem to have been
surprisingly little developed. Above all, perhaps, even if there were
primitive forms of such explanations, class was still in large measure
seen as an unnatural disordering of human relationships[26] (again,
the negative aspects of class usage assert themselves very strongly).

How the social order may have been seen by workers is in fact
interestingly revealed by Kirk's evidence. Before pursuing this,
however, it is appropriate to consider here further work criticising
Stedman Jones' viewpoint. In Epstein's recent article the emphasis
is on political discourse, but a familiar point about the plasticity of
public discourse is being made.[27] It is argued that ostensibly political
or 'populist' terms such as 'people', 'patriot' or 'industrious' were
indeterminate signs, the meanings of which were often constructed in
opposition to the accents given them by other, dominant, social and
political groups.[28] Epstein goes on to quote the Marxist literary
theorist Fredric Jameson to the effect that 'the dialogue of class
struggle is (normally) one in which two opposing discourses fight it
out within the general unity of a shared code'.[29] In the historical
situation with which Epstein deals – that of the radicalism of the first
quarter of the century, particularly in industrial Lancashire –
popular, oppositional appropriations of a pervasive constitutionalist
rhetoric and ideology are held to be evidence of class.

This claim, however, seems to me to be entirely gratuitous. The
subtlety of Epstein's account of political language is to be applauded,
as is the theorisation of class, but it must be emphasised that all
Epstein finally shows is no more than different versions of an
ideology at work. For all the sensitivity of the analysis class is simply
'read off' from the character of discourse. The claim has all the
boldness and baldness of another example in this same vein of class
'defence' quoted in a previous chapter,[30] namely, the contention
that Feargus O'Connor's use of the symbolism of fustian cloth, his
appeal to 'unshorn chins' and 'blistered hands', may stand as
evidence for class consciousness. On the contrary, what is demon-

strated is the employment of a particular appeal, the character of which can be open to all manner of interpretations. We can talk of a peasants' or a workers' movement or set of values in the sense that these are held by recognisable social groups (problems of defining such groups aside). But although social constituencies we might choose to call classes express certain values, this does not make the values themselves ones of class. We need to distinguish again between the consciousness of *a class* and the consciousness of *class*. A good deal of the argument under review here not only gratuitously abstracts class from discourse, but – despite all the protestations of new departures – then returns to familiar paths in abstracting meanings from socio-economic phenomena.

In Epstein's case what is presented is a popular constitutionalism, not class consciousness. Indeed, for all his emphasis on the 'multivocality' of the sign, Epstein's argument does not seem far removed from Stedman Jones' position, namely the argument that a populist discourse took on class meanings at particular times, just as constitutionalism may have taken on such meanings. but the point is that populism and constitutionalism, both, had a wide variety of meanings. It is not that Epstein's claims for class are necessarily wrong, only that he does not demonstrate his case, and in not demonstrating it, in turning again to the tarnished idol of class, he, like others, forecloses discussion on what the real nature of popular values might have been. In this case, a kind of populism rather than class might seem a rather more appropriate way of seeing popular constitutionalism, especially when the capacity of a later popular, and populist, Liberalism to capitalise on the still lively inheritance of radicalism is borne in mind. This successful appropriation in turn prompts the recognition that 'multivocal' signs also carry histories, layers of meaning and association that are persistent and cannot be easily sloughed off. The new emphasis on the plasticity of language is in danger of forgetting this power of language to create enduring worlds.

However, let me return to the particular in search of how conceptions of labour may have informed views of the social order. Kirk's 'defence' of class turns much on the views of operative and middle-class radical spokesmen in south-east Lancashire, and especially in Ashton-under-Lyne. When these views are more closely considered it is evident that central to radical 'economic' under-standings was a moral opposition between the factory and the 'natural' order of work, an order closely related to popular ideas about the 'cottage economy'.[31] For the surgeon, McDouall, one of the most advanced of the radicals active in Ashton and the manufacturing districts, the factory system produced the 'White

Slaves of Great Britain'. It was contrasted with what the factory system had destroyed, which was above all symbolised by domestic industry. The handloom weaver, parlous as his plight had become, stood for a freedom or 'independence' in work which was integrally related to views about the integrity of the family and the standing of the family head. This vision of labour was also tied up with the idea of the worker as the inheritor of nature's bounty and glory. This was of course an idealisation, though it is very striking that McDouall is at pains to argue that it is the whole truth and not fancy, something to which 'the experience of living men' testifies.[32] Idealisation or not, or rather all the more because an idealisation, such views begin to reveal the character of the operatives' social outlook (an extract from McDouall's 'White Slaves' is given in appendix 6).

The very close association of popular movements of social and political protest with the defence of particular trades and communities has been noted by many historians of early nineteenth-century England.[33] The discourse of such movements worked because it articulated the values involved in people's immediate situations, particularly those customary values which in fact linked work and community very closely together. Long ago Edward Thompson pointed to the extraordinary force of such values in textile handloom-weaving areas and how they imparted to the radical movement their own particular character.[34] Part of this character involved the realisation in radical discourse of often unstated but nonetheless powerfully held customary notions of what social relations should be. Historians have been very quick to label such notions as evidence of class,[35] or, latterly, of populism,[36] but this has in the process distracted attention from their actual character. They may have lent themselves to both sorts of discourse, as a 'language of class', say, but in themselves they were in fact neither quite one thing nor the other. It is, however, in their very uniqueness that they were most important.

What may have been the social design evident in these customary notions is suggested by Stedman Jones' account of the radicals' understanding of production relations, and by ideas concerning the integrity of work, families and communities emerging among men like McDouall and the operative radicals of Lancashire. Again, one must emphasise how this popular social design has not been systematically explored by historians. Nonetheless, the remarks of the feminist historian Alexander on class and sexual differences in the 1830s and 40s are suggestive.[37] Arguing that early century radicalism drew on the idioms of the leaders of such communities, she nonetheless indicates how important for popular politics was their construction of community. It was a male construction certainly, one of artisans, domestic workers and small masters (in varying stages of economic dependence), but this does not mean that it was not without great effect in the community at large.

The language employed was one of disinheritance from control over work and family life. The outlook involved emphasised independence and a social organisation of labour centred upon kin and household which permitted the natural affections to flow simultaneously from work and domestic life. This conception of labour allowed for a continuing dialogue of master and man, and was part of a broader picture in which egalitarian currents were accompanied by ideas of social balance, of reciprocal rights and duties obtaining between those with different social functions and responsibilities. The ideas that the weak should be protected and that each person should have his or her proper place seem to have been strong, as was the idea that the whole was sanctioned by a benevolent constitution through which power would be exercised with responsibility.[38] Accompanying Stedman Jones' account of radical conceptions of production are rather similar, and it must be said similarly sketchy, indications of a customary outlook in which ideas such as those of a balance between town and country, and of the freedom of the truly industrious from government interference, accompanied the aspiration to a harmonious, interdependent world of production.[39]

Smail's account of the language of labour in the woollen textile districts of Yorkshire in the first decade of the century offers a sharper picture and suggests the longevity of these attitudes.[40] According to Smail, workers at the time dropped older, 'moral economy' forms of protest, asserting instead the validity of a 'corporate discourse' which they evolved in opposition to the language of employers, where language was increasingly taken up with the market, and indeed proto-class, categories of 'labour' and 'capital'. In the workers' outlook the link between conceptions of labour and wider social concerns was as usual an intimate one: the interests of the 'commonwealth' (the term used) were put before those of the individual, worker or employer. The aim seems to have been the preservation of the legitimate place of different individuals and their functions within a morally and socially satisfying conception of social relations.[41]

In more discriminating terms than many previous accounts Gray's exploration of the language of factory reform in the 1830s serves to further unravel workers' perceptions of labour and society.[42] Examining the ways in which the public address of the reform movement picked up on popular concerns Gray indicates again deeply rooted ideas of labour as property, of fair employment and patriarchal authority, also of society as a just balance between different interests and functions. He has also noted that supposed 'artisan' ideas of fair exchange and the fair employer were in fact firmly ensconced in the textile industry, within the factory as well as without. This indication of the extension of supposedly 'traditional' values into the experience of factory labour is most important. These ideas of labour were part of the attempt (also evident in notions of the trade mentioned earlier) to moralise employment relations through the conception that there were mutualities of right and obligation obtaining between master and man. As Gray notes, these ideas survived powerfully into and beyond the mid-century, serving to underpin on the operatives' side the understandings involved in the operation of the new, employer paternalism so evident in the textile districts from the 1840s and 50s.[43]

These glimpses are tantalising, and one needs to turn to the considerable range of spokesmen who amplified these customary sentiments at the time. Tory Radicals like J. R. Stephens and Oastler seem to have had a good sense of them, as Gray indicates in the latter case.[44] Stephens' re-iteration of the values of the 'cottage economy' will be called to mind: if Stephens' Tory Radicalism may have counted for relatively little among the operatives, his powerful religious message and his invocation of the natural order of work were of great effect (just as his leadership and standing continued to be important in Lancashire until his death in 1877). The terms in which mainstream radical leaders like McDouall and O'Connor saw things differed little. Epstein has noted the sympathy of O'Connor for Oastler's and Stephens' defence of the family, and his belief that family life was being broken up under the impact of the factory.[45] At his trial O'Connor dwelt on the factory as a 'living tomb', a sentiment also echoed by operative spokesmen who spoke of the contentment of the 'cottager', and the bastille-like qualities of the factory.[46] To O'Connor, of course, and to so many of his workingmen followers, the land symbolised a superior way of life to the present experience of the servitude of the factory. However, this usually went hand in hand with an eminently pragmatic response to the demands of factory labour on the part of the operatives. Idealised social relations might be used to condemn the factory system *tout court* but more often it was unacceptable aspects of that system which were objected to. As time went by, this structure of myth and memory was employed to judge and manage a factory system the operatives well knew was there to stay.

In all of this, two aspects should be borne in mind, the first being the decided absence of production-centred explanations of oppression. One may look again to the trial of O'Connor for a brief illustration of this: the evidence of the south-east Lancashire Chartist delegates dwelt upon how in this 'class-ridden country of ours', the 'middle classes' riot in voluptuousness, 'as the swine wallows in the mire'.[47] The moral degradation flowing from parasitic idleness is here and elsewhere a constant theme, though the chief exemplars of such degradation were of course the aristocracy. Recent work on how the radicals utilised the broadside ballad indicates these aspects at work: the theme of the aristocrat as seducer of the worker's kin was extraordinarily widespread, giving voice to an enduring moralism in such a way as to tap fears about patriarchy and family life.[48] In turn, ideas of purity were closely linked to ideas of what was 'natural', whether in the realm of sexual behaviour or of work. Oastler and Stephens for instance were fond of contrasting the natural in these senses with what they took to be the cruelty, impiety and rapacity of the people's oppressors, who, as has been seen, they frequently dubbed 'fiends' and 'monsters'.

What was so in Lancashire and Yorkshire was so in England. In considering the example of the north-east coalfields Colls has shown the significance of this moral understanding of labour into the third quarter of the century. Use of the biblical language of oppression and salvation, of notions of natural right, and of the moralistic discourse of custom were blended together in a theory of exploitation as based on moral actions and imperatives. As Colls pithily puts it, the great coalowner Lord Londonderry was opposed as a despot not as a capitalist, and 'the proof of labour value was the pudding of ostentatious wealth'.[49] By his deeds was the tyrant known, and no deeds were darker than the irresponsibility of authority, and the ostentation and condescension of heedless wealth.

The matter of moral perceptions of social relations bears on the central question of whether these amount to class or not. Ideas of social balance, of interdependencies of social function, do not equate with class in the sense employed in this book. Quite what they equate with is not, however, clear: the terms 'moral economy' and 'corporate discourse' have been used to describe the sentiments and social conceptions described here. Both have their uses and their limitations: the former term is taken from the specific context of eighteenth-century English society,[50] and has been widely used in a rather indiscriminate way to describe almost any instance of folk morality or sanction, or any custom-derived understanding of society. Its blanket use obscures the need for more contextualised descriptions of popular conceptions of society. The kind of view explored here is perhaps best seen as specific to the first half of the century, arising out of the moral economy of the eighteenth century and capable of articulation with class models, but not a class view in itself. If the term 'moral economy' has difficulties, the idea of custom is still useful and has been retained here. There seem to me to have been communally based ideas of society contained in custom, but custom should be seen as a constantly changing *activity* in popular culture, rather than a characteristic of a particular period. Employed in this way, as it is here in terms of the evolution of customary understandings of the trade, it suggests that if custom-derived understandings of society achieved a particular form and salience in the circumstances of the early part of the century, then they were not entirely lost later on. Whatever concepts we apply, it seems clear that the corporate, reciprocal, 'commonwealth' visions of society discerned here simply cannot be equated with class without emptying them of their true character.

However, customary perceptions of work and the social order were always part of the broader discursive world of the labouring populations of the time. In order to consider this it is necessary to return to the experience of cotton factory workers in the mid-century. The customary understanding of society evident in the early part of the century, like all views of society, was most emphatically, vocally and coherently put when it was most under threat, and when the worker was viewed, and viewed himself or herself, as the outcast of society. In the industrial and political conditions of the 1850s and 60s, this was no longer felt to be the case. Therefore, something of the force and coherence of older views was lost: quite simply, factory production had irrevocably strengthened its hold on older forms of production and many of the views and practices associated with the older forms no longer made sense to workers. New justifications of labour, above all those of the market, were evident. Yet when one turns to the discourse of organised factory labour in the 1850s and 60s, what is most evident is the vitality of older conceptions in negotiating these new justifications, and the new circumstances of these years.

A valuable collection of handbills and proclamations issued by the Ashton and district Short Time Committees in 1853 enables us to trace the continuities and discontinuities involved. These committees extended across the textile districts of Lancashire and Yorkshire, those of that year representing the last round in a decades-long popular agitation to limit the hours of factory labour and regulate the conditions of work. This agitation continued to involve great numbers of factory operatives, so the deliberations of the committees are an especially good guide to how workers conceived of the world in which they were operating. This material is supplemented by a similar collection of material issued by the spinners' unions, in the Ashton district but also more widely in Lancashire and Cheshire.

This extends from the 1850s into the 60s.[51] Of course, in no sense is this the 'spontaneous' voice of labour. The language employed is that of the leadership, though this leadership was uniformly of the ranks of labour, and almost always made up of factory operatives. The auto-didact element was strong, and one is reminded of the intellectual formation of the popular radical leaders.[52] Indeed, William Aitken, so active in Chartist politics, was a major figure in the local Short Time Committee. In this activity as in his political work there is ample testimony to the hold of his rhetoric over the operatives at large, not least of the battery of romantic imagery and high learning that he brought to bear. A testimonial of the local Committee in 1854 spoke of the force of his 'intellectual oratory', how he was the instrument of 'the poor', applying in their cause 'the vast powers of the mind' granted to him by 'the Almighty Maker'.[53]

In other respects, too, it is clear that the language of the leadership had a strong popular hold (leaving aside the fact that the discourses of 'high culture' were in fact much more widely dispersed in low culture than is often thought). Factory reform organisations and unions at this time had few resources other than their members' goodwill. Their spoken and written addresses were indispensible weapons in their armoury which they could not afford to use unwisely. If collective actions are anything to go by then these addresses were highly successful: thousands of people were frequently mobilised in large and enthusiastic meetings, processions and demonstrations, especially in the Factory Acts cause.

This was also done through the means of music in the form of brass bands, of the marching column, and of the banner. Banners were in fact a kind of frozen rhetoric, the words of which were often abstracted from the printed addresses. The discursive material of the addresses was thus deployed in a way designed to achieve maximum effect, particularly in a society where literacy was not always highly developed. The proclamations were frozen rhetoric in another sense too, being clearly designed for public speaking as well as public reading. Their highly declamatory form was reinforced by the frequent and judicious capitalisation of key phrases, tags as it were to lodge in the mind of a partly illiterate audience: 'Lift Up Your Hearts and Down with Your Jackets', 'From Six to Six with One Hour and a Half Out', 'The People are the Grand Moving Power'. (Examples of the placards are given in appendix 7.)

In considering the Short Time Committee material the first discontinuity to note is that there is less emphasis on the threat to the integrity of family life. The factory reform legislation made unsteady progress, hence the existence of the Ashton Committee, but by the early 1850s enough ground had been made to lessen the earlier anxieties. Instead, what was newly apparent is summed up in the title of one placard, 'The Accomplishment of Freedom and Social Advancement Exists Within the People'.[54] The real 'moving power' (this play on the associations of powered machinery was constant) is held to be an 'industrious people', who are 'the source of every great advance in arts, in sciences, and all that testifies to the elevation of a free and independent country'. In 'The Queen, The People and the Ten Hours Bill', with the passing of the Factory Acts, factory life will be 'endurable' and the 'serfs of mammon' will be no more. In another example,[55] the long hours system 'circumscribes the intellect and impedes the social advancement of mankind'. The 'life-destroying, mind-stunting system of long hours' is challenged in the name of Christianity, 'science' and 'reason'.[56]

The change here is evident: factory legislation is foreshadowing the stress on moral and social 'Improvement' so characteristic of all social levels in mid-Victorian Britain. There is a move beyond the body and the family life of the worker to a new concentration on the mind, and the cultivation of the full human potential of the factory worker. The gospel of Improvement was of course a major ground upon which social and class tensions were resolved at this time, though the meanings of Improvement varied greatly according to who promoted it. In industrial Lancashire it often signified freedom, indeed the gaining of a full humanity: as another Ashton placard put it, factory legislation was the source of a new beginning 'in which the name of slave (in this slave-ridden district!) will be unknown'.[57] The wider character of the rhetoric is evident in the address to the workers and employers of Mossley on the results of the Factory Acts:

> The whole people will be more happy and contented than at any former period, and our own loved island of the West shall continue to shine out proudly from the sea, the freest of the free, and its merchants, manufacturers and populace be models of all that makes a nation great, glorious and industrious in the eyes of an admiring world.

Patriotism is linked here specifically to social and moral improvement, but is pervasive throughout the Short Time literature. It is for instance persistently linked to the idea of the industrial progress of the nation, a progress of which employers are as much a part as workers. At first sight this may seem surprising in an industrial Lancashire so recently racked by labour conflict and the destruction of domestic industry. It marked a new departure, certainly, but was nonetheless firmly rooted in older values. The right of workers to have their role in industrial advance recognised is pressed with unvarying persistence: for too long they have been treated as slaves and outcasts, their part in events unrecognised.

This claim to inclusion in the body of the nation – so closely paralleling the new populist shape of politics at the time – was, however, couched in the old garb of popular constitutionalism.

Pace Epstein, this could encode the aspirations of labour, but this did not make it necessarily a class 'language'. An address of the Stalybridge Short Time Committee spoke of 'our free and commercial country' in which the will of a free people must be heard.[58] In addressing the manufacturers of Ashton and neighbourhood these operative spokesmen showed themselves keenly aware of and sympathetic to the anxieties of those with a great deal of capital sunk in the area.[59] There is praise for the 'application, sagacity and ambition' of the capitalists of Ashton, and an exhortation to join the operatives in reducing hours and thus equalising competition so as to prevent the overweening problem of overproduction. The Ashton employers have nothing to fear from foreign competition, where the lack of liberty is the chief cause of industrial inefficiency, whether in Russia, France or Germany. The emphasis on national progress in alliance with employers is here complemented by a new emphasis on efficiency – 'with the industry of the people and your own indomitable industry, the British Manufacturers can bid defiance to the world'.

Judged by the criterion of this patriotic constitutionalism (in which the patriotic note is more insistent than in the 1840s and 30s), employers would be found wanting, like the Mossley masters who were castigated for not being 'English gentlemen'. To be such a 'gentleman' (a motif of some interest in itself, the genuine article here being distinguished from the shoddy), was in this case to defend the constitutional right to public procession. This right went back to 1688, and was indissolubly linked to 'The Protestant Religion and the Liberties of England'. The venerable term 'Free Born Englishmen' is also frequently used.[60] The great constitutional authorities are invoked – Coke, Erskine and Blackstone. Shades of feeling later apparent in popular Toryism are present in the Protestant emphasis, evident in the stress upon the love of freedom of the 'Anglo-Saxon race', for which the nation is 'famed throughout the world'.[61] This was accompanied by the appeal to 'the spirit of your fathers', 'that has carried you to victory in many a...field'. John Milton figures elsewhere as 'The Blind Minstrel of England', who evinced the knowledge that 'truth was never put to the test in a fair and open encounter with Reason'.

As in the political sphere so in the industrial; there is an increasing sense among workers that appeals to lost constitutional rights are bearing fruit in the present. In 'The Queen, Her People and the Ten Hours Bill', the Queen is called the best monarch this land has known. In defying her (as a supposed advocate of reform) the

Glossop masters defy 'all law human and divine'. If human and divine law is spurned, an outraged people will rise in majesty, swearing upon 'the constitution and altar of the country'. The suggestion of force here is very unusual. More often rights are held to be attainable within a reformed polity, and the present polity is seen as capable of reform. The old popular constitutionalism in turn received a new expression in the emphasis on 'public opinion' and 'the spirit of the age'. The operatives made adept use of this newer appeal to the present. The Glossop employers could not 'set at defiance the principles of the age in which they live'. It is the employers who defy the times, a nice outflanking of the employers' deployment of political economy as the sign of modernity. Another placard tells of the Mossley employers who, like Julius Ceasar and Charles I, failed through a contempt for public opinion. This vigorous anachronism of thought indicates the great flexibility of the old constitutionalist rhetoric.

Ideas of law were central to this rhetoric. Interesting differences here emerge among operative opinion in the 1850s, the Ashton Committee going more for local action and communal regulation of the Acts, the Oldham men pressing for more parliamentary intervention. Here Gray's exploration of the language of factory reform in the 1830s is of great interest,[62] the operatives' leaders making much in their appeal of what seem to have been popular ideas of law. These ideas saw law as an expression of the consensus of local communities rather than as the simple enactment of external bodies. The opponents of the Factory Commissions emphasised the voice of the community as opposed to 'expert' knowledge. Legislation was seen as endorsing communal norms. Clearly, custom and popular conceptions of law were closely linked. This sense of the moral and communal legitimacy of law surfaces powerfully in the 1850s material. In the Ashton Committee's appeal to Victoria it is the people's law which if flouted will be enforced by the people themselves. To go to Parliament is to place 'factory labour' at the mercy of 'quibbling lawyers'.[63] The 'moving power' is not in Parliament's hands but is located in human hearts and hands, in 'the transcendental mechanism of the human frame', which is in turn the expression of God, 'The Great Moving Power of the Universe'. Ours is a 'moral movement', and the people of communities such as Ashton, Stalybridge and Oldham, not Parliament, are the real force behind everything that creates wealth and England's glory. It is they who should have responsibility for regulating the Act.

Despite this, there is a discernible shift towards a new confidence in Parliament and established legal structures. As will be seen, this was part of a larger sequence of events that served to undermine (or at least partly marginalise) custom. The attitude of the Oldham Committee indicates this, and the Ashton men could also address the Oldham operatives with the sentiment that if 'our institutions are faulty then they are still praiseworthy. England is still the freest country on Earth'.[64] As in the political sphere, factory legislation did not betoken an enlarged view of the state. Government, for all its more benign face, was still seen in minimalist terms as ensuring rights to liberty and 'independence'. The literature is full of the emphasis upon the Factory Acts as releasing the reserves of 'manly independence' so characteristic of the 'British People'. The perseverance and energy taken as virtues in the Ashton employers are applied to the operatives as well: these were contrasted with the dependent situation both of those on parochial relief and the enslaved foreign worker. The central radical oppositions of tyranny and liberty, freedom and slavery, were much in evidence.

The links to the early part of the century were strong: the independence at issue was still very much a 'manly' one, the emphasis on traditional family roles receiving no criticism in this literature. The independence to be secured was at once individual and communal: as subsequent consideration of imaginative representations of work reveals,[65] the invocation of a lost golden age of the individual weaver and the handloom weaving community was central to the outlook of generations of factory and other workers down into the twentieth century. The notions of independence involved were in part rooted in living memory and in part in invented tradition. Therefore, the vision of independence could take new forms, sometimes more individualist than previously, or undermining custom as part of a new view of liberal progress and reason. The notions of communal integrity rooted in earlier, customary versions of independence could also take new forms, not least in new views of the legitimacy of employers' activities as partners in and to some degree leaders of the new factory neighbourhoods and towns. Leaving communities to get on with their own lives, and so enacting their own sense of reciprocal rights and responsibilities, was a powerful element in operative opinion, and one that perpetuated older, customary notions of community identity in often unexpected ways, such as the new industrial paternalism of the mid-century.

Turning more directly to the conceptions of society evident in this material, class terms are in fact noticeable by their absence, as indeed is discussion of matters in 'economic' terms. Very revealingly, this applies to the spinners' union material of the 1850s and 60s every bit as to the factory reform placards. The religious dimension, not so far much stressed, was greatly in evidence. The

lack of unity between different cotton trades is regarded as
'ungodly'. An address from late 1850s Preston prays that when the
struggle with the masters commences, 'May God Protect the
Right'. Similar terms are used to address employers and the
employment relationship as are used to address workers themselves.
In eulogising the ideal employer, John Fielden of Todmorden,[66] it is
maintained that the great inventions of the cotton industry must be
regulated by laws based on the principles laid down by the
'Almighty Maker, from whom all human ability proceeds'.[67]
Another address from these supposedly hard-headed, 'economistic'
spinners dwells on how 'humanity blushes' at one employer's
reduction in wages, before going on in the most ornate language of
melodrama to tell of the fate of the de-sexed working mother with
her infant at her knee. This ends with an appeal to the 'Divine
Giver' for 'Our Daily Bread'. It also dwells on the workings of
earthly authority: 'property' (at no time attacked in the literature)
has its duties as well as its rights, 'and it is one of the wise laws of our
ancestors that the property of this country must maintain the poor
of this country'.[68]

Similar notions of mutual interests and reciprocal obligations
suffuse the union literature as the factory reform material,[69] in which
the strong emphasis on joint interests realised in industrial progress
and efficiency will already be evident.[70] There is again a clear
recognition that factory industry is an irreversible development, also
an association of this development with the well-being and future of
towns and communities. There are no signs of capitalist ownership
or control of industry being challenged. At the same time the
legitimate rights of labour are pressed strongly, and capital is given
its place on condition it accords to these. William Aitken's activities
inspired both the factory reform and union movements. He gave
expression to the role of capital thus:

> He would be a poor legislator and wretched well wisher to his
> country and his fellow man who could wish to permanently injure
> either capital or labour. Capital is the fruit of labour and all
> hoarded capital that is made reproductive proves advantageous to
> all classes of society...those who use their money in finding
> reproductive employment, in improving agriculture, in building
> mills, sinking mines, and all the various industries of the most
> industrial age the world has ever seen, are benefactors to all that
> come within their sphere of influence. The capitalist may benefit
> himself individually more than any one else, but useful em-
> ployment is found for others, blessings are multiplied more or less
> on every hand, and by their union and harmony they 'make the
> desert blossom as the rose'.[71]

The emphases on industrial progress and 'reproductive employment' represent the new departures of the mid-century period. The notion of the partnership of labour and capital in 'reproductive' industry was to become very important. The use of the terms 'labour' and 'capital' indicates the element of the 'economic' in these new departures. Yet the matrix of the new and the 'economic' was the old and the moral, above all the values of the trade. It seems that these were translated directly into the situation of the factory: many factory trades, particularly the spinners, were in many respects craft workers within the factory. Yet the notion of the trade was also extended to mean the industry at large, in its various manifestations at the level of town, region, nation, and even the immediate locality. The idea of the trade, as in 'the interests of trade', could hold both meanings at once, for 'skilled' workers but also for the unskilled majority, including women workers, who whatever the objective definition of their standing often thought of themselves as having a trade to hand. Therefore, far beyond the ranks of the non-factory trades, the older notion of the trade had penetrated the world of the factory, picking up on new ideas of industrial partnership and progress, in part employing the discourse of the economic market, yet still serving as the matrix of the new in attempting the moral regulation of capital, the moralising of the market. The old idea of the trade became the foundation for the new idea of the trade union.

Notions of property in skill suggested that the worker as well as the employer had a direct stake in the industry or the trade; indeed, that it was in a sense as much the worker's possession as the capitalist's. In the extracts already quoted it will also be evident that there was an element of stewardship in this: the trade or industry served the interest of communities and the nation as well as those immediately party to it. The Ashton spinners described themselves and their role thus: 'our mission is not to live for ourselves alone, but to make mankind happy and comfortable'. The society must be of benefit to mankind, aiming at promoting the interests of 'the trade', 'leaving it better than when we found it'.[72] These notions of proprietorship and stewardship were to continue at least until 1914: the populist overtones of the operative standing proxy for the whole people of the community or of the nation do not need labouring here. The society is keen to realise 'the unity of interest' between themselves and employers that obtains 'in the abstract'.[73] Of course the imperatives of the market and the actions of employers very often prevented this. Defending their conception of the trade often meant involvement in bitter conflict with employers. Capitalists would not easily be civilised. The values of the trade are not to be seen as consensual or conflict free. Quite the opposite: as so often in this study it is evident that deep-rooted beliefs in social fraternity could be the springboard of conflict. But however ignored or fought over, the dimensions of morality and aspiration were crucial, serving as the means by which the unions found their way in the changed circumstances of the time.

The way that they found was an 'economic' one in the sense that the cotton unions bargained long and hard about pay and conditions. Their reputation for hard-headedness is deserved, but this reputation has obscured not just the moral discourse of the trade, but the extent to which this was embedded in a much broader range of cultural values. Reddy's work on the industrial relations of the time is one of the few that has shown itself aware of these aspects, above all the extent to which industrial conflicts were about mastership and authority, respect and honour, as much as they were about material considerations.[74] If the spinners' appeal to the Glossop masters of the 1850s recognised the need for discipline in the highly capitalised mills then it was the exploitation of this need that was the source of the deepest hurt finding expression in the appeal: the fining system spoken of was objected to for the loss of wages involved, but still more for the want of 'respect' shown.[75]

An 1850s address to the Bolton spinners speaks of the 'insolence of office' as giving the most offence. On the other hand, the master most respected was not only the one who brought capital and work into the area, but the one who was 'plain', 'just' and 'honest'. John Fielden was such a man,[76] in the early part of the century standing as one of a few. This was to change after mid-century.[77] But this change occurred in the teeth of an hostility to organised labour that continued among many employers. Unions had to build their organisations in the face of this and hence conflicts about authority, honour and respect continued to be very marked in the third quarter of the century. Indeed, the idea of the union as the embattled champion of justice was a major means by which economic terms were translated into ethical ones, and the older labour values were adapted to new circumstances.

Something of this is evident in the Preston strike of 1853–54, the watchword of which was 'Ten Per Cent and No Surrender'.[78] Percentages were fast translated into a bitter conflict about union 'dictation' and employer 'tyranny' and 'haughtiness'. The principle of mastership was at issue for the employers here and more generally at this time.[79] On the operatives' side the whole rhetoric of industrial relations was shot through with the heightened emotion of a vocabulary of moral right and moral indignation. Workers were 'freemen' or 'slaves', employers 'tyrants'. This continued through the third quarter of the century and indeed beyond. Employer coercion of workers at municipal and parliamentary elections in the

1860s gave rise to 'Victim Funds' and 'Indignation Meetings' at which the rights of freemen to speak and vote freely were publicly defended. The proof of the pudding of labour value lay in ostentatious authority as well as in ostentatious wealth. The principle of mastership was settled on a more equitable footing in the 1860s and 70s in which workers' and unions' rights to a say in the affairs of the trade were gradually recognised. But this was often an uneasy compromise, a negotiated peace.

The incendiary properties of respect denied were also much in evidence in the daily experience of fining and pettifogging authority in the mill (in which, however, figures other than employers were often most prominent). The burdens of the factory were evident in the wider social relations of the factory towns. The considerable violence seen at times during the Cotton Famine seems to have owed much to insults directed at the pride and independence of the operatives. The insolence of office here took the form of relief given in the shape of clothing stamped 'lent', of reading classes in which grown men were locked in classrooms for the day, and of the injunction to those in receipt of relief to doff their caps to the relief authorities. This was accompanied by the use of what was felt to be harsh and disgusting language to wives and daughters. Accusations of capricious favouritism were also in evidence. The result was an explosion of anger which resulted in serious rioting and the 'popular taxation' of the premises and goods of those Poor Law and relief authorities who had dispensed insult instead of respectful relief.[80]

The level of violence in industrial disputes in cotton was greater than is sometimes supposed,[81] though it was the blackleg, the transgressor of communal codes of honour, rather than the employer, who was the object of this violence. The exception, and the most striking example of large-scale violence in the second half of the century, was the north Lancashire weaving strike and lockout of 1878.[82] In the epicentre of Blackburn the special object of the crowd's feeling seems to have been R. R. Jackson, the employers' leader, variously known as 'Stonewall Jackson', 'The Blackburn Warrior', and 'The Great I Am'. Jackson was widely regarded as the 'evil genius' and 'vindictive spirit' among the employers. The epithets applied indicate popular detestation of arbitrary authority and the lack of respect. Like Lowe before him in the political sphere, Jackson earned the special ire of workers by referring to them as 'The Great Unwashed'. Jackson's house was attacked and burned to the ground. However, those other symbols of arbitrary authority, the police, were considerably more the object of the crowd's displeasure than were the employers.

1878 was in many respects the last great example of large-scale, 'informal' industrial action rooted in community norms and practices, and expressed in communal forms of action such as riot, effigy burning and the anonymous letter.[83] It is very revealing that these forms of action were evident not among the highly organised and skilled spinners, but among weavers and others less subject to the discipline of the union. Nonetheless, the weavers' union had by then developed a successful union organisation that drew on these communal, customary codes of behaviour, yet also distanced itself from them as sources of indiscipline and disunion. The Blackburn unions were quick to condemn the violence and the rioters of 1878 as evidence of irrational conduct in the new era of a rational public opinion. It is this complex relationship between the union leadership, its discourse, and the proclivities of the rank and file that will be taken up in the next chapter. It reveals the failings and difficulties but also the creativity of unions. It also reveals much about the nature of class, but before considering the discourse of the trade unions, some clearer discrimination of the conceptions of the social order emerging so far is necessary, particularly in the very revealing wall literature of the factory reform movement and the spinners in the 1850s and 60s.

Class terms were in fact very infrequently used, and when they were employed, 'class' and the older term 'order' were sometimes used interchangeably. Much more in evidence was the rhetoric of 'the people', and the deployment of maxims drawn from literature which emphasised human fraternity. Rather than radical political economy it is the sentiments of Robert Burns that are employed by the Ashton factory reformers: 'Then let us pray, that come what may, and come it will for a' that; when man to man, the world all o'er, shall brothers be and a' that.'[84] In the literature, as in operative discourse more widely, such terms emanate from Enlightenment and romantic thought and literature. They also come out of religion, from the notion that all are the children of God.

Against the God of humanity had been set up the fake God of Mammon, and it is to the failings of human nature rather than to a new system of production that men and women of the time looked. As more widely, human greed, the vice of competitiveness, was the overweening sin, the source of tyranny and slavery. Factory workers were 'slaves' or 'serfs' not to an economic system so much as to the God of Mammon. Mammon worship was pernicious because it betrayed the fundamental rights and obligations upon which society rested. In the words of the spinners' union, 'it is one of the wise laws of our ancestors that the property of this country must maintain the poor of this country'.[85] To the factory reformers somewhat earlier the recalcitrance of the Glossop masters threatened to break the bond that tied society together and drive the people into rebellion.[86] These various sentiments, and their various sources, composed a picture of society primarily moral and socially inclusive in character. This was certainly an expression of labour, perhaps too an expression *of a class*, but whether it was itself a *class expression* is another matter. Perhaps it would involve distorting words less to call it something else and perhaps 'populist' is a better general description than class. Whatever term we choose, it is evident that the languages of labour in this period addressed economic life in a way which encompassed the whole culture of the worker. In the second half of the century the trade union was to be the chief heir to the moral discourses of labour, employing them in building the modern trade union.

In the process the union did much to create a sense of class analogous to the way in which class is understood in this book. Far from the supposedly timid and 'reformist' unionists of the second half of the century departing from the way of the 'true' class consciousness of the 1830s and 40s – the drift in fact of a good deal of the historical literature on the subject[87] – that consciousness very often had little to do with 'class' at all. The general argument of this book is to emphasise alternatives to class in popular perceptions. But where it was evident it should not be denied. It was evident in the sphere of work and union activity in the later part of the century, though it seems to me to have achieved this developed form mainly and perhaps only in this area. Even then it was deeply marked by an older legacy. Far from being unequivocally about class, the legacy of the labour discourse of the early and mid Victorian years, particularly in its customary manifestations, lent itself just as easily to populist as to class interpretations of society. In itself it simply did not add up to 'class consciousness'. Building on this past the sense of class issuing in important measure from the unions therefore lent itself easily to ways of seeing the social order other than that of class alone. Though class was in the ascendant, a similar plurality of work-derived interpretations of the social order still continued. The forms of class themselves often departed radically from those which posterity has mistakenly ascribed to the world's first industrial proletariat.

5

Building the union: 'the gospel of absolute and perfect organisation'

In the second half of the nineteenth century there is no denying the narrowing in the range of social concerns expressed in the ideas and values accruing around work. Many of the developments behind this have been noted, such as the tendency for politics and economic life to become to some degree separate areas of discourse, a tendency above all evident in the labour legislation of the 1860s and 70s. In securing the relations of labour and capital on a more equal footing, the state in effect withdrew from industrial relations. As has recently been observed,[1] this meant that the market was excluded from politics. Analogous to the effect of free collective bargaining was the ideological power of free trade, which as McKibbin pertinently remarks, before 1914 meant more than socialism did to the working classes. Both developments served to emphasise the same conception of politics and economics: they led towards the justification of market capitalism to workingmen, and to the idea of the autonomy and propriety of a working-class politics, in the limited sense, that is, of the politics of the labour interest as one interest among many.

If we turn to the example of factory industry, it is not difficult to find evidence for this narrowing of concerns, reflecting these changes at a national level, as well as local developments such as the changed attitudes of employers to unions and the success of the Factory Acts. The public addresses of the 'Fifty-Four Hours', half-day Saturday movement in 1870s Lancashire contrast with the power and diversity of the rhetoric of factory reform earlier on. There is a restriction of the appeal to the need for the worker to recover from the physical and mental 'prostration' factory work engenders, a clear sign this of the new contemporary concern with 'leisure' and its uses, a concern in turn reflecting the way in which work was ceasing to play quite such a central role in defining social relations and social identity.[2] The Oldham material of the 1870s also dwells on how legislation 'in this country is now dictated by public opinion', 'the people' increasingly having parliamentary power. In petitioning Parliament, government is asked to regulate hours without interfering with 'the legitimate enterprise and freedom of industry', the fruits of which it is hoped 'our manufacturing and mercantile classes' will long enjoy.[3]

114

The conduct of strikes presents evidence of a similar sort. The great spinners' strikes and lock-outs of the late 1880s and early 90s saw an explicit rejection of the old inter-mill marches and the factory gates collections characteristic of earlier forms of organisation. These were regarded as 'out of date', not consonant with 'modern civilisation'. 'Modern' industrial relations were a matter, precisely, of 'absolute and perfect organisation'.[4] The spinners' organisation came close to such perfection, the disputes of these times resolving themselves into patient waiting games, seemingly without the public forms of collective solidarity earlier evident. Solidarity was displaced to the institution of the union, and conflicts tended to be about percentages and profit margins. The Stalybridge Lock-Out of 1892–93 was indeed known as 'the battle of the margin'. The increasing significance of the economic language of the market is apparent: in the 1880s the Bolton spinners' unions, for example, seem to have been imbued with the idea that 'a reasonable and normal but constantly rising rate of profit' was the proper basis for wage increases.[5] Without such profits it was felt capital would go elsewhere. Unskilled cotton factory operatives were also wont to complain that their labour was not sold at 'market value',[6] and there was a widespread tendency to describe industrial relations as 'the wages question'. The awareness of being wage earners with labour power to sell was certainly present, and with it a clear conception of class as arising from the entities of labour and capital. In one sense this obviously represented an adoption of the language of the market. However, this was usually far removed from subscription to the 'laws' of the market, particularly those of supply and demand. The unions were clear that if there was a relationship between profit, demand and wages,[7] then the market did not operate as the political economists said it did. The unions were well aware that in practice it was trade unions that kept up wage levels. In the Stalybridge Lock-Out the unions' journal was emphatic that labour's interests were defended only by the unions, and that workers had the right to sell their labour on the best terms. The operatives, who were the 'producers' of wealth, had a 'right' to this as against the 'might' of the employers. A 'fair wage' was what the employer could be made to pay.[8]

We seem here to be far removed indeed from any 'moral discourse' of labour. Yet behind the partial adoption of market categories there was clearly a disbelief in the justice of unregulated capitalism, evident in the emphasis upon the need for the equitable operation of the market. Again, the emphasis was upon human intervention. And human intervention involved a set of moral imperatives which denied the notion that the free market carried its own justifications. Thus the unions' adoption of the language of the

market involved the idea of a moralised market. This becomes
evident when we explore the discourse of the cotton unions further.
In some respects those unions have claims to be the most
market centred of all. Yet when we plumb even this seeming depth
of hard-headed unionism, the vibrancy of moral conceptions of
labour and the trade becomes amply evident.

Before this, let me step back a little to look at two instances of how
such ideas were widely disseminated in industry beyond the cotton
factory example. W. H. Wood, the secretary of the Manchester and
Salford Trades Council, spoke to and on behalf of the whole range
of unions, but especially the craft ones, in his address of 1882,
'Twenty-One Reasons Why I Am A Trade Unionist'.[9] This was
both a public defence of the unions and an attempt to supply
unionists themselves with counter-arguments to the public criticisms
levelled against them. As such it reminds us of the strategic
dimensions to union discourse, its location within conflicts about
what 'public opinion' was and how it should be used. In the
material so far considered, especially the Short Time Committee and
union addresses, there was of course a calculative element at work in
the attempt to enlist the support of public opinion on labour's side.
Among the cotton unions, the weavers – who were less powerful and
less easily organised than the spinners – needed to cut the cloth of
their rhetoric with an eye to the weakness of their industrial position.
A rhetoric of industrial peace – emphasising the rationality, order
and lawfulness of the union – served to enlist public opinion on the
weavers' side, avoid wasteful local action of an unplanned and
divisive sort, and preserve the union recognition upon which their
existence so much depended. However, the merely calculative
aspects of such appeals should not be exaggerated.[10] An ethical
rhetoric always sought to bring about a goal, but this made it more
rather than less reliant on working with real moral values. After all,
as we have seen, the spinners – seemingly less in need of them – were
every bit as wedded to these moral conceptions as the weavers.

W. H. Wood certainly invokes the values of the trade in such a
way as to suggest its deep roots in the cultural self-definition of
workers. Like the engineering and shipbuilding workers of the north-
east, workers of the north-west are addressed as 'the natural
guardians' of the trades for which they have qualified by 'a period
of servitude'. This makes them the custodians of 'trade rules', the
masters of the 'secrets and intricacies' of their calling. The time
given to acquire trade knowledge represents so much 'capital' sunk
by the worker, capital in need of protection from the 'unprincipled'
who do not 'invest' such time. This telling example of the terms of
the market decking out a much older trade rhetoric goes on to dwell

on how the union (obviously building on the trade idea) 'teaches us the grand and noble principle of self-reliance and self-respect', and 'exalts the citizen and prevents his degradation'.[11]

W. H. Wood was a printer, and it was in such highly skilled trades that these notions were most developed. The example of the printers is in fact a good place to explore further both proprietorial notions of skill and the concept to which such notions were inseparably connected, namely, the view of the trade as a community of interests of masters and men. The printers' union journal served in the 1850s to police this relationship between employers and workers in the interests of the trade. Notions of fairness were much in evidence, whether the 'unfair shop', the 'fair master', or the 'unfair price'.[12] Fairness was equated with honour, as in the 'honourable' and 'dishonourable' trades, and both were deployed in opposition to the actions of those denying the observances of the trade, men and masters alike. To them, especially to 'scab' labour, was applied the term of 'rat': the journal hunted down the rat, referring to 'the rat's nest', the 'scent of the rat', indeed to individual workers as not leaving their last 'rat holes' clean. Non- and anti-Society men were 'rats', dishonourable workplaces 'rat offices'.[13]

The 'art and mystery' of the 'trade' or 'profession' of printing was defended against those who would destroy the confidence of employers and injure the interests of the trade. Such behaviour included drunkenness, the avoidance of work through laziness, theft, leaving bills unpaid, as well as transgressions in the workplace itself.[14] Some half a century later, the scope of the moral remit of the printers' union had not lessened. The journal still ran a 'Fair List', policing as best it could through public exposure the actions of masters and men. Union spokesmen dwelt on how the interests of workers and employers were identical. The complete defeat of one was the ruination of the other. That man who sees the great benefit of cementing the interests of labour and capital together is held to be vastly more use to society than he who annoys people with the 'remote possibilities' of a civil war between the classes.[15] Individual branches of the printers' union spoke of how so long as they got trade union wages and conditions they had no right to interfere with the employer's conduct of business.[16] Workers should consider it their duty to look after their employer's interests as well as their own.[17] It was likewise the 'duty' of trade unionists to look upon employers with 'equity and consideration'.[18] The unionist writers in the journal also spoke of the need to differentiate between good and bad employers. Employers were not the 'natural enemy of the work-man'.[19] Above all, in supporting the good employer the fundamental goal of 'the common good' of the trade would be consulted.

That these various writers felt moved to disclaim class war and the disharmony of the interests of masters and men is testimony to the appearance of precisely these claims, especially it seems among younger workers. At the opening of the new century these ideas were making progress here and elsewhere,[20] but the overwhelming force of opinion was still of another kind.[21] This was equally evident in the cotton industry. The unions at the time of the Stalybridge Lock-Out might speak of the right of the worker to sell his or her labour to the highest bidder but this was a right that was subordinate to what they also called 'the interests of the trade', interests that were the concern of employers and workers together. To be a waged worker was more than to be a mere 'hand' or a 'wage slave'. Here one begins to uncover that transposition of the identity of the trade to the industry at large spoken of earlier, though there long remained a fruitful confusion between the two terms in their factory usage.

The unions dwelt much upon these matters in the 1890s, but such attitudes were greatly in evidence long before, industrial conflict simply bringing them more clearly to the surface. The employers' federation was the 'capitalists' trade union', and talk of the 'tyranny' of capital over labour was written off by the cotton unions as 'bombastic', just as the idea of 'extinguishing' capitalists was 'rubbish'. Employer organisations properly conducted were 'in the interests of the trade'. The unions firmly set their face against outside interference in 'the trade', as it was only the masters and their workers who knew its inner workings.[22] This latter conviction went along with the sturdy belief that labour's interests were defended by the trade unions alone, the idea of 'identical interests' being employer propaganda. Here and elsewhere, as with the printers, it is evident that talk of the 'identity of interests' did not imply the ideas of a 'natural' unity evinced in the workings of the market. Nonetheless, that there were strong common interests and reciprocities involved was an idea everywhere apparent.

It was evident in the inaugural number of the *Cotton Factory Times* where the 'unity of interests' is held to be based on co-operation 'for the good of the industry'.[23] The unions were very aware of themselves as the policemen of this good. The notion that the industry, or trade, was theirs as much as the employers' was strong. Earlier notions of the proprietorial nature of skill were here translated into the situation of the factory, directly in the case of the skilled trades like the mule spinners but also more generally in the *Times* insistence that the workers were the real producers and labour the source of all wealth. These notions, inseparable from the idea of the employers as partners in industry, clearly had implications not at all necessarily conservative in character.

Policing the trade's good meant getting the best market for the sale of labour power, but it also involved creating fair shares for all, including the employer who had sunk his capital.[24] Checking unfair competition was aimed at securing the workers' fair share but also at enabling employers to compete fairly, so looking upon matters of common interest in a reasonable light.[25] In the same breath the language of fairness was transformed into that of friendship. A 'fair stand-up fight' between labour and capital was needed, with 'no blows below the belt'. The best man was to be the winner, both sides continuing in friendship just as before the conflict, with the conflict characteristically seen as a family one. In 1887, the *Times* emphasised how quarrels with employers in the past had been many, but that these were 'family quarrels', which in the presence of a 'common foe' were forgotten.[26]

The idea of an external enemy was in fact very strong in the industry, as in Victorian industry more widely. This was particularly so in industries dependent on foreign trade, subject to foreign competition, or reliant upon a range of middlemen. More than this, the very nature of industrial organisation as late as the early twentieth century served to reinforce these possibilities. The relatively 'archaic' nature of organisation meant that authority within the workplace was developed in a variety of ways, ranging from subcontracting to the multiplicity of tradesmen-helper or minder-helper systems characteristic of the workshop and factory trades alike. In other work, I have explored something of the effect of this,[27] in particular the displacement of authority, and hence often of blame, to a range of intermediaries between worker and employer. These might be foremen, managers, or in cotton the skilled, adult male trades, especially those 'Olympians' of the factory, the spinners. It is not always easy to tell who was regarded as the 'boss' in nineteenth-century industry. The effect of these structural character- istics was to accentuate the force of ideologies of work which emphasised the concord of workers and employers. It also accelerated the marked tendencies to compromise and co-operation apparent in the capitalist labour process. These tendencies were in fact particularly marked in Victorian and Edwardian industry, the skill- and labour-dependent nature of which involved employers and skilled workers in particular in a whole range of understandings and accommodations. These in turn facilitated ideas of the worker and the union being the proprietors or stewards of industry, or the partners with capital in the good of the trade: as has been noted, the populist possibilities in all this were marked; in the notion of the union of the 'industrious classes', say, or in liberal ideas of industrial progress as the progress of the whole nation, and the product of the efforts of all in the 'productive classes'.

Exploration of these structural factors would have to consider the degrees of internal competition within industries as well. For instance, the weaving sector in cotton, especially the small man, was partly dependent on the more highly mechanised and capitalised spinning sector, as well as upon brokers and agents at both ends of the production process.[28] The fierce competition so often evident in weaving could create fierce conflicts with workers. But competition and subjection to the vagaries of middlemen could also create solidarities between workers and employers, and not only in weaving. More generally in the industry the good of the trade was looked for in world markets: this often involved the joint activity of unions and employers in defending and developing overseas markets. It also frequently meant the direction of discontent at foreign competitors, or at home against merchants rather than employers. In turn this involved very deep-seated distinctions made by workers between productive (or 'reproductive') capital and parasitic, speculative, unproductive capital and wealth. The employer, whatever his shortcomings, in the end had a good deal in common with the worker.

In the Stalybridge dispute of 1892–93 for instance, it was speculating brokers, merchants and salesmen who bore much of the blame. It was believed that the employers, because of their fear of the speculators' vested interests, had mistakenly squeezed the operatives instead of their real enemies. Mawdsley the spinners' leader attacked the 'middlemen bloodsuckers' who took the profit out of the industry.[29] The periodic bursts of speculative mania on the Liverpool raw cotton market (in which some employers were in fact engaged) were sometimes the subject of joint employer–union action, as in 1887 when short-time working was agreed upon in order to counter the familiar machinations of what became widely known as the 'cotton corner crew'.[30] At other times the unions mounted a sharp attack on the 'money interest', defending useful industry against speculative capital.[31] The chief historian of the cotton unions has described in detail the joint activities and interests bringing the two sides together in defence of the industry in the late nineteenth and twentieth centuries.[32]

The general belief in the 1892–93 dispute was that masters and workers should be left alone to settle their own affairs. However, if the employers would not look after the industry then someone else had to.[33] This could involve state regulation, though the unions' involvement with the state was always more opportunistic than ideological,[34] the industry's need always taking precedence over the expansion of the state, socialist or otherwise.[35] The unions did not call for nationalisation until 1935, the employers for protectionism not until 1958. The destiny of the union in fact lay in what may be termed a collective individualism exemplified in the union, as well as in the Co-op of which so many union activists and rank and file were members. Co-operation fostered self-help, for the foundation of all genuine improvement lay personally with each individual. Thus the union was held to be against all manner of 'encroachateers', its leaders citing the radical and leading Co-operator, G. J. Holyoake, with enthusiasm: 'In these days of state socialism ... the co-operative movement however does not preach industrial despair, nor cling to the skirts of the state, nor envies other classes, nor preach war on property ... as do many in educated and well-to-do circles'.[36] Thus the experience of their own industry had taught these men that there was a possibility of moralising the market. This view created a sense of class – for surely one must call what ensued class – which was clearly rather different from the conceptions of class posterity has ascribed to these workers. Whether in textiles or in the trades proper, conceptions of class could be far removed from ideas viewing conflict as the essential mark of the social relations of capitalist industry. At the same time, such class conceptions allowed other notions of the social order to prosper.

These conceptions of society will be traced a little further in terms of how the discourse of the union actually worked in practice. But before this it is necessary to say something about workers' conceptions of employers. These have been widely misunderstood because interpretations of the labour process have viewed matters solely in terms of resistance and conflict. Yet tendencies towards compromise and co-operation between capital and labour have in fact been just as visible. Here it is necessary to depart for the moment from direct accounts of union and worker relations to consider the picture of work emerging in the literature that operatives and other workers sang, read and wrote, a literature considered systematically later on in this book. Notions of the value and dignity of labour, and the vice of idleness, were marked in the broadside ballads. These themes were reproduced in the dialect literature increasingly popular from around 1850. In this, as in the ballad, the employer was seen as a figure who when he fulfilled his true function was useful and productive. For instance, the Barnsley miners and their union were celebrated in the town's dialect almanac in 1873, *The Barnsla' Foaks Annual*,[37] but it was also understood that they had an obligation to labour honestly and hard for their employers, who were decidedly not numbered among the idle. In 1892 the almanac gave voice to 'Hah T'Soashalists Laid Sheffield E Ruins', echoing in the process many of the preconceptions of workers across the Pennines in the cotton industry:

> Theease a class a men theer at hev gotten sum queer noashuns abaht property, that is other foakes'es property, not their oan for they stick ta that. They're noan real Sheffielders for t'Sheffield grinders are hard wurking fellahs whoaz motto is live an let live, they honour ther mesturs, an t'mesturs honour them, and that is just as it owt to be.

The socialists only knew work in books, and sought to abolish 't' Dignaty o'Labour'.

Clearly, the 'dignity of labour' had many more uses and inflections than are usually recognised. The attitudes to work and employers evident in cotton Lancashire clearly had a hold with many other sorts of worker as well. The Barnsley instance was only one of many dialect almanacs and journals circulating in industrial Lancashire and Yorkshire at this time. One does not have to search far in this literature to find very similar attitudes expressed, though usually without the anti-socialist tone. The usefulness and virtue of the honest, hardworking master was frequently emphasised. On the other hand, the duty of the worker to work hard and do good work is widely apparent.[38] The term 'master' in its dialect variant is used in this literature, and this reflects everyday use as well, despite the frequent use of 'capitalist' and 'employer' in public discourse. The continuing use of the term 'master' far into the twentieth century indicates a relationship altogether more complex than does the use of the term 'employer'.

That complexity was in part reflected in the frequent idealisation in this literature of the caring, paternalistic, frequently elderly employer. And precisely the same kind of idealisations are evident in the unions' journals and in the writing of authors, especially dialect authors, who were either very close to union opinion or ardent socialists. Ben Brierley was in the former category, Allen Clarke in the latter. Both were hugely popular at the time. As will be evident later, their use of the paternalist fiction and the idea of a golden age was not nostalgic but represented a way of both interpreting and judging the present, and a powerful aspiration to realise in the sphere of work that sense of fraternity so widely evident in popular values at the time. It certainly points to the many-layered, often ambiguous relationship between worker and employer in a region where in fact paternalistic factory regimes were very much in evidence at the time.

For instance, Brierley figures in his writing the person of Aaron Hartley, the paternalist putter-out of the old days and the very embodiment of 'The Fine Old English Gentleman' (an anthem much sung at employer-sponsored factory outings and celebrations at the time). Through Hartley, Brierley imagines what should be the proper relations of masters and workers: Hartley has done right between the two, growing up alongside the workpeople, helping them at times of need, providing for them at a loss and vowing never to leave them.[39] Brierley's other employer figures, for example 'Sam Smithies', represent the genial, frank sides of the ideal employer. In the work of the socialist Clarke, far from being stigmatised as the class enemy *sans pareil*, the employer is celebrated as a useful figure, and his character and foibles are presented in a surprisingly favourable light. Clarke's mythical employers, though clearly drawn from life, included the grafting, no-nonsense 'Fred Factories of the Oldham Limiteds' (who was contrasted with the non-productive cotton broker), and the terse 'Lancashire spinner' who is both honest and mindful of his workpeople.[40] Such representations are all the more telling in coming from a man who was well aware of the politically disabling force of the employers' own self-representations when acting upon an often pliant workforce.[41]

It was, however, in the pages of the *Cotton Factory Times* and the *Yorkshire Factory Times* that perhaps the most revealing mythologies of employers worked. At the same time as they attacked the excesses of employers in their news columns the union journals ran romantic serials (in standard English) centred upon the experience of factory workers. Written either by ex-operative writers or professional pedlars of fiction these offer considerable insight, produced as they expressly were for an operative audience, and particularly an audience of women and young girls. Questions concerning the interpretation of popular literature will be raised later, particularly the genre of romance,[42] but what must be noted here is that this material cannot be written off as 'escapist', or as 'wish fulfilment'. Rather, these romances need to be treated seriously as a means of handling the present reality of their readers. Their marked 'realism' affirmed the integrity of ordinary experience, but at the same time they were fantastic, in rather the same way as melodrama was fantastic. It will be suggested later that the fantastic and the conventional (such as unlikely coincidences or the happy ending) should be seen as allegorical and not misjudged as aborted realism. Above all, these romances can be read as allegories about the way the world should be – as imaginative projections into demotic utopias, but also as judgements about how the world was.

They therefore offer insight into the views of the world handled by such means. Typical titles were 'Madge: The Factory Girl, Or Through the Fire', 'Sir Joseph Beckett, Weavers' Boss and Baronet', 'From Doffer to Millowner', 'A Factory Girl's Sacrifice', 'The Old Factory' or 'Fairies of the Factory'. Something of the themes will be evident from the titles – the trials of the ordinary mill girl, the success story, the idealisation of the factory and the 'factory community'. Pursuing the richness of these themes is impossible here, and only one fairly typical story, that of 'Madge', can be dealt with.[43] Madge yearns for more than the factory and falls for the caddish son of the local millowner, one Cecil. Inevitably Cecil jilts her, and Madge is cared for by the operative hero, Jim Cranston. Cecil is discovered and cuts his throat. The contrast between Cecil and his upright father, Honest John Warpley of Weft and Warpley, is a central one. Honest John is honourable, the patriarch of the mill community in which the fiction is set. He does his duty by Madge, recognising her as a daughter and looking after her and her new husband Jim in his will. As evident as the portrayal of the 'good old' employer is the careful patrolling of social boundaries. Madge aspires to leave her own kind and the perils of this are plain to see. Madge makes a real and symbolic return to the ranks of the workers. 'Class' distinctions are affirmed. Yet she is recognised as a daughter by Honest John. She becomes part of the symbolic family of which labour and capital are a part. At the same time she is both faithful to her own class and desirous of attaining both social reconciliation and a larger human identity. Far from being escapism, such stories served to handle the very real contradictions and ambiguities of class, resolving them, failing to resolve them, or simply presenting them to view. Whatever the result, the tension and mingling of the utopian and the realistic in the stories, the ought and the is, reflects perceptions of employers and the factory that divulge some rather unfamiliar faces of class.

These stories were one discursive means of organising values, ideas and actions. The discourse of the union was another, and it is to the application of this discourse that I shall now return, having earlier considered some of the central tenets of union belief. One needs to consider the obstacles in the way of building unions, as well as the solidarities they both created and drew upon. The cotton industry was as divided as any industry in the country,[44] despite the seeming uniformity of factory labour and of geographical concentration. The main branches of the industry were in fact geographically localised. Divisions existed on the basis of occupation, status, skill and pay, but also age and gender; and not least nationality, religion and political affiliation, in a very partisan part of nineteenth-century England. Perhaps the most fundamental distinction of all, at least in comparison with other industries, was that between men and women.

Through this account and that of the previous chapter there runs a persisting theme, that of the desire to defend the authority and standing of the male worker, especially the male as husband, father and head of household. The previous account of the meaning of the trade outlook in the industry of the north-east indicated how closely involved this was with ideas of masculinity. From the early nineteenth century, when the threat to the position of domestic and factory textile workers was in large part perceived as a threat to their standing as family heads, the peculiar conditions of the cotton industry – seen in the close propinquity of men and women in the workforce and in the protracted debate about the place of working women and children in the factory and the community – served to turn the predominating gender stereotype of masculinity into the channel of family life and values. However, as will be seen, the employment of the metaphor of the family, and of kindred ideas to this, did not express either a simple supremacy of men over women or a conflict between the two, even if it worked within the dominant values of the age.

Early on in the century, women were excluded from many textile trades. Towards the end of the century male union leaders made assiduous if rather laggard attempts to unionise them. The difficulties in the way of this were considerable, above all the dual call of work and home on women's time and energy.[45] These difficulties were hardly helped by the attitudes of male union leaders, these attempts notwithstanding. Articles in the *Cotton Factory Times* reflected this opinion: women were seen as so physically and psychologically different from men as to be almost a race apart.[46] And if women became trade union members in some number in the period after the 1870s, they were invariably led and organised by men. At union meetings women might attend and even make resolutions, but they seem very rarely to have spoken as organisers and leaders.[47] In cotton the public voice of labour was almost totally male. If the present account of union discourse emphasises the male voice, this is only because the voice of the union was a male one. Nonetheless, if the cotton unions were to make way, given the nature of the industry, they needed to organise women.

Before turning to some of the ways in which they accomplished this, other sectional divisions, as well as more general obstacles in the way of building the union, require some consideration. In the Lancashire of the time, and indeed in other northern industrial districts, political loyalties were closely linked to the loyalties of denomination and nation; those of church and chapel, the English and the Irish, the Protestant and the Catholic. The unions' studious avoidance of party political involvement is ample testimony to the force of these loyalties and to the profound danger to solidarity they represented. Their divisiveness is everywhere apparent: in the 1880s, for instance, a separate Tory-inclined weavers' organisation was set up in Blackburn in order to counteract the perceived radical complexion of the main body.[48] The strength of these loyalties was equally not far to find: in the same town in 1869 all union organising activity had to be set to one side so all absorbing was the popular interest in the parliamentary election of that year.[49] Indeed, political partisanship was an important barrier standing in the way of independent labour representation in the early twentieth century. Attempts at this constantly ran aground on the operatives' suspicions of political bias, suspicions often all the stronger when socialists were involved.[50]

Long before this time, the necessity for the union to present its affairs as either outside or above politics had laid the basis for the long-continuing and strong rank-and-file resistance to even the limited politicisation evident in these turn-of-the-century attempts. This necessity is indeed striking testimony to how political attachments might often be stronger than those emanating directly from work or from a labour identity, not least a labour identity of a class sort. The strength and character of political loyalties needs also to be attributed to the power of employers over workplaces and communities: this power issued in a partisan politics, but also reflected the economic weakness and dependence of labour which was the reverse side of the coin of employer influence and power. Perhaps more than any of the sectional divisions that plagued labour, including that of gender, it was the bedrock of economic dependence and poverty and the attitudes this gave rise to that limited union activity.[51]

This is how Allen Clarke described the operatives of Bolton in 1899:

> They have no true idea of life. They believe they are bound to work; they do not see that work is but a means to life... They think that the masters build factories and workshops not to make a living for themselves by trading but in order to find the people employment. They honestly believe that if there were no mills and workshops the poor people would all perish.[52]

Clarke was not alone in this view. J. R. Clynes, the Oldham operative union leader and later Home Secretary in the first Labour administration, also pointed to the operatives' shadowy picture of the world outside their own immediate range of experience: the men of his youth, even the skilled workers, believed that labour was dependent on the employers, and upon the almost magical workings of national and global capital.[53] The propaganda of the leading socialist writers similarly bears witness to how deep rooted these ideas were. The choice of Robert Blatchford's fictional plebeian antagonist is a telling one: the figure he invented to portray all that was most stubborn about the old order was one 'John Smith', the hard-headed, fact-loving Oldham spinner (again, it was the skilled who exemplified these attitudes as well as the unskilled). John Smith stood for all that was most intractable in making socialists, namely the beliefs that labour depended on capital for work, that capital would simply remove itself if labour protested too much, and that the employers' success in competitive world markets would ensure the well-being of the operative.[54] Blatchford blamed the unions for inculcating the latter belief – which, as we have seen, they very largely did. Yet the attitudes that are evident here were most often a bar to union activity. In some respects these attitudes can also be seen as bolstering market valuations of work and labour identity, yet they seem to me to have operated at another and deeper level than economic ideology alone. Dependence also served to breed a fatalism and a deference to employers that told greatly against the advancement of the union cause.

This was reflected in the operatives' mistrust of union activists: attempts to unionise weaving in Ashton in 1887 met with the frequently expressed belief that the leaders were profligate or dishonest with union funds. In turn, employers sometimes played ruthlessly upon such beliefs, in this instance not only exploiting the sectional differences among workers but employing their own spinners and overlookers to pressurise striking weavers back to work, weavers who were often women. These efforts were complemented by the usual recourse to the threats of eviction from employer-owned housing, discharge, or the refusal of promotion.[55] Across the Pennines in the textile industries of the West Riding the same difficulties were evident: Ben Turner's attempt to unionise the notoriously badly organised town of Batley in the 1890s met not only with suspicion of his motives, but with the belief that he showed 'impudence' beyond his station as 'only a weaver' in standing for Parliament.[56] The actual conduct of strikes and other industrial actions shows these difficulties in action. For every instance of inter-trade and inter-town solidarity there was at least one instance of poor support for striking workers, of levies and contributions not paid, of sectional discontent and suspicion of other workers and unions. The actions of key groups like spinners often put other, less skilled workers out of employment, and these were precisely the workers hardest hit by such action. In turn the fear, suspicion and resignation bred by poverty and dependence were underscored by the enormous social and cultural influence, as well as the economic power, exerted by employers. This in turn translated these attitudes into a deference that could be willing as often as unwilling.

Nonetheless, though many employers resisted for a long time, from the 1850s and 60s union recognition by employers became increasingly marked. This was often a matter of conviction, but also often a matter of necessity, a grudging admission of the *fait accompli* created by the power of some trades at the point of production itself. Trades other than that of spinning, such as the major branch of weaving, did not have this power to hand but for all trades in the industry the creation of a viable union organisation which would accentuate the strengths and obviate the weaknesses of the shop floor was an urgent necessity. Given the enormous difficulties the unions faced it is not their disunity but their unity that is most striking.

Obviously, a full account of the development of unions would need to consider practice and organisation. But of at least equal standing with these was the rhetorical appeal of unionism. However, this appeal was not disembodied but was created by individuals whose character and values imparted meanings to workers at large. Consideration of these individuals, all men, helps us understand the purchase of union discourse on its popular constituency. The job of building the union was most difficult in weaving districts, and evidence drawn from the example of weavers' leaders active in the 1880s in the Blackburn and north Lancashire area is therefore of relevance here.[57] Many of these men went on to be important figures in the regional and inter-trade organisations developing later.

First of all, these were men who sprang from the communities they represented. They were either handloom workers in their youth or came from handloom weaving families. They tended to share in the consequences of the coming of the powerloom, in particular the dispersal of families to new locations in search of work, and the eventual return to the place of origin. They were thus part of communities with a strong sense of local tradition and history. They were also men who had worked as operatives for much of their lives before becoming union officials. Most had very strong religious affiliations, reflected in close association with particular places of worship for most of their lives, especially with Sunday Schools. Many had strong political beliefs, mostly but not exclusively radical Liberal ones. In these respects, as in their origins, they were often close to the people they represented. But in these respects also they were to some degree men apart; the active, the organising, the articulate among their fellows. In a later chapter, the complex and ambiguous relationships between the autodidact and his fellow workers will be considered at greater length.[58] What can be noted in passing here is how such men, if part of the culture of their fellows, might also be out of sympathy with what they took to be its unregenerate traditionalism, its violence, its supposed ignorance and 'superstition', and its attachment to old and often customary ways.

But if one can detect a certain intolerance and impatience with their fellow operatives which stood in the way of union organisation, then in other respects the careers of these men served as living dramatisations of the rightness and justice of the union cause. It was in their capacity as symbols in themselves that they gave life to the discourse of the union. They embodied that association of the union with the battle for honour and respect which was such a powerful energising force in establishing unions in the third quarter of the century. These men came to the fore in that period as martyrs to the union cause: many of them had been systematically victimised by employers before finally gaining triumphant recognition for themselves and their unions. This was especially so in the less well-organised districts, especially Burnley. Joshua Barrows, Secretary of the Amalgamated Weavers' Association from 1883, spent his young life as a union activist in the 1860s in a peripatetic attempt to find work and avoid victimisation. This took him from Burnley to Rochdale, on to Oldham and then back to Padiham in the north-east of the county.

For all of these men 'the gospel of absolute and perfect organisation' (as one of them put it) was the guide to all their actions. When they looked to the past of the industry they very often compared it unfavourably with the present. The past was the time of tyranny, unlike the many benefits the gospel of organisation brought in the present.[59] At the same time this view was held alongside an idealisation of this relatively recent past: the seemingly contradictory view could be expressed that if hard, masters in the earlier days of the industry were honest and hardworking, in contrast to the failings of the present. On balance, if always in a somewhat ambiguous relationship to their rank and file, the cultural and social formation of these men enabled them to speak with powerful effect to the majority. It was men such as these who translated the values of the 'trade' into the context of factory industry, whether in the generalised sense of the industry at large or in the more specific sense of the individual factory occupation as a craft – as was the case with skilled workers such as the spinners, who in their union rules, dress and union regalia, and in their use of the language of the crafts, continued to act and think like craft workers. As we have seen, these different senses of 'the trade' were deployed by factory workers of all sorts, but it was among the less skilled that the adaptation rather than the adoption of earlier models was most pressing.

Nonetheless, the language of unskilled labour was very similar to that of the skilled, for instance the appeal to the poorly organised cardroom workers of the 1880s in terms of fairness and the defence of the operatives' liberties against the authority of unreasonable employers.[60] These appeals were often made to women, but to unskilled male workers the defence of their 'manhood' against 'tyranny' was also used as a rallying cry by officials.[61] These notes were struck alongside a firmly practical espousal of the financial benefits of union membership, of course, but the language of honour was never subservient to 'economism' (indeed the two aspects were inseparable in the unions' activities). This was so with the spinners of the 1880s as well, whose vulnerability in the labour market and the factory if less might still be considerable. In 1887 the conduct of overlookers to spinners was held by the latter to represent the 'oppression of the independence of the Lancashire operative' by 'the unreasonable conduct of men in authority'.[62] For all workers, for men as for women, there seems to have continued in the late nineteenth century the same sensitivity to the disrespect shown by bad language that was so evident earlier on.[63] Nonetheless, the domination of male power and of male perspectives in the unions is evident in their very uneven and reluctant attempts to combat the sexual harassment of women by their co-workers or those in authority.[64]

In the same way, the language of fairness was so often couched in a form that both appealed to and reflected the concerns of male officials and workers among the unskilled and unorganised. Ideas of the interests of 'the industry' already examined have been seen to involve ideas of fair shares and fair behaviour between family members. In 1887 the *Cotton Factory Times* maintained that while no friends to 'socialistic robbery' they were nonetheless 'hip-and-thigh' opponents of employers having the 'whiphand' over workers. In combat with the employers the operatives felt 'that stern joy which warriors feel / In foemen worthy of their steel' (foemen, that is, who did not strike 'below the belt').[65] While one should not write off the appeal to fairness among the female part of the unskilled, language such as this indicates how male preconceptions might create a union discourse that failed to elicit the concerns and aspirations of women, and so failed to build the union to its full potential.

However, through the means of the idea of the trade in particular, it is the notable successes of skilled and unskilled unions alike that are evident in the last quarter of the century. Transplanted notions of the trade were evident, for instance, in the concern to do right by master and man. This involved denouncing the operative if necessary,[66] particularly for conduct which lowered moral standards and damaged interests, such as laziness, theft and above all bad work.[67] In fact the *Cotton Factory Times*, just as the *Yorkshire Factory Times*, dwelt lovingly and at length on the hard-working nature of the operatives and of Lancashire and Yorkshire folk in general, as well as on their pride in the quality of their work.[68] This moralisation of the function of the union around the ideas of hard work and quality goods was a major means by which the traditional preoccupations of the trade were translated into the conditions of factory labour.[69] This translation was also effected by the unions' strong emphasis on encouraging technical advance, which was seen as a responsibility of capital and labour alike. This attention to the broader interests of the trade was in turn linked to the notion of industrial and social progress,[70] and reflected in the support given to technical education.[71]

Yet it was at a more fundamental level that notions akin to those of the trade took effect. And, in the end, in being adapted to the situation of factory workers these notions became so altered as to have little in common with their originals. To appreciate this one needs to know something of what has been called the 'interior' life of the workplace. In previous work I have described something of 'the culture of the factory', the existence of a vibrant social life within factories, as well as of important links between workplaces and the broader institutional and cultural life of communities.[72] Factories were much more than places of labour alone. They were the source of treats, teas, outings, demonstrations. They were linked to churches, chapels, schools. These aspects of 'factory culture' might express employer influence and power and be under the direction of the structure of authority in factories.

But there were other, more autonomous dimensions to factory culture as well, even if in practice it is often difficult to separate them out, the structures of employer influence often developing quite naturally from the spontaneous camaraderie of the workplace. Nonetheless, that camaraderie was the fundamental element from which sprang a range of uses and meanings. Paradoxically, perhaps, the unions as well as the employers were to erect their influence upon this foundation. Let us look briefly at the life of the factory. It comprised for instance benefit nights or factory collections for stricken workers (sometimes organised by unions, but very often not), excursions run by managers, overlookers, and workers – all expressing the *esprit de corps* of particular shops and occupations in the workplace – and presentations to long-servers or those leaving, whether workers or supervisors. Marriage, birth and death were also marked in similar ways that involved the initiative of workers themselves as well as those in authority. The weekly 'Voices from the Spindle and Loom' column of the *Cotton Factory Times* and *Yorkshire Factory Times* is full of these events, taking many other forms than those mentioned here (including football, cricket and the brass band).

Other accounts of mill life at the time suggest that a distinct way of life attached to the factory. One account of Bradford mill life in the 1870s noted the importance of clothing, the women for instance in functional 'harden' skirts, their finery adorning the upper part of their bodies.[73] The smocks and caps of overlookers set them off from production workers. (We have already noted the dress sense of the cotton spinners, a sense extending from the distinctive, functional garb of work to the wearing of bowler hats to and from work.) This report indicates that in mills with a less severe pace of work there might be time for the 'unfinished toilette', for gossiping and joking in work time, indeed for communal singing (in this case of hymns) as and when the task to hand permitted. Another account of factory life dwelt on the talk going on during breaks, but also on the capacity of highly skilled workers such as loom jobbers to make time and space for themselves during periods of work. This sort of freedom was relatively rare, though the feelings of one old Lancashire woman weaver were not: she looked back to her work life with pleasure, as offering opportunities for 'friendship' second only to those of the chapel and Sunday School. It was felt that in the mill women were 'free' compared to the servitude experienced in a shop or as a seamstress.[74]

Thus the culture of the factory reached down further still than the organised event, embracing the fundamental activities of human sociability. These aspects were of particular significance to women, the informal life of labour and the workplace involving them in the collective interests and actions of fellow workers whereas formal aspects of organisation very often excluded them. These accounts are unfortunately rather impressionistic, and to obtain something more systematic one needs to turn to more recent ethnographic work on the linen mills of Ulster in the early twentieth century.[75] The context was of course different, but there is every reason to believe the English situation would have been similar in essentials.

In the Ulster mills each of the different process rooms had its own particular lore and observances. Social relations within (and indeed outside) the workplace were worked out in terms of practical joking, of rituals surrounding weddings and so on, and of the varied social and subscription clubs or 'joins' (these were much in evidence). The 'joins' funded parties, many of which marked special occasions throughout the year such as 'Lighting Up' in the mills in autumn, or Halloween. Not least among these celebrations were the 'footings' we usually associate with the craft apprentice's passage to journeyman status. 'Footings' were a marked feature of English mill life, among women as well as men, and among weavers, warpers and creelers as well as the elite spinners. In Belfast the terms 'apprentice' and 'journeyman' were used explicitly to describe the full range of mill occupations, and this wholesale transfer of the language, rituals and practices of the trades to the situation of unskilled labour was widely characteristic of the English situation, marking indeed the twentieth-century development of the English motor car industry.[76] Women cotton weavers in Lancashire were conscious of having what they often termed a 'trade' to hand – expressed, for instance, in the pride of graduating from the working of two to three or four looms.[77]

It was upon this rich and complex culture of work that the unions drew, not upon some homogeneous *lumpenproletariat* of the factory. The leadership and discourse of the unions in large part depended upon working with the grain of this culture, in a sense in talking its language, in a rather similar sense indeed in which employers had done. This is a striking indication of how the same cultural raw material could be articulated in very different ways, serving very different purposes. The stuff of class was the stuff of deference.

For instance, union activity sought to control and canalise the solidarities based on 'informal' workplace activities such as the use of communal sanctions against workers and figures of authority, or 'spontaneous' actions like unplanned strikes and 'walkouts'. Such actions were often supported by collections made in the immediate neighbourhood of the strikers. Even though the unions came to organise strikes in a systematic fashion that involved a departure from earlier communal forms of solidarity, as in the Oldham strike of 1885 and the Stalybridge dispute of 1892–93, they continued to depend on communal sources of support such as co-ops, working men's clubs, music hall benefits and chapels, as well as the support of publicans and shopkeepers.[78] This was especially marked among those outside the ranks of the highly organised spinners.

But more than these forms of action and community resources it was the sense of communal identity involved in the culture of the factory that the unions drew upon. This involved the varied senses of 'the industry' and 'the trade', but to these should be added a further sense, that of 'the factory', or perhaps 'the factory community', allied to but distinct from the other elements in union discourse. To a considerable extent this sense was in fact realised through the operatives' union journals.

Founded in 1885, the *Cotton Factory Times* waxed as the fortunes of the unions waxed in the late century, union numbers increasing markedly among the ranks of the unskilled. The cotton journal and its sister, the *Yorkshire Factory Times*, helped cement the greater inter-local and inter-trade co-operation that marked union activity, if not always rank-and-file sentiment, at this time. It gave a public platform for the revelation of abuses and the exchange of information. It acted as the co-ordinator of union activity of all sorts,

1 Mirth in the mill: a homegrown postcard of the sort popular in Lancashire c. 1900.

from lobbying to strike action. It exploited the sense of the whole cotton community, imparting to this sense more of the meanings of unionism than had hitherto been the case. The older senses of 'the trade' and 'the industry' were in part turned in a new, more 'labourist' direction. The appellation of 'factory' or 'factory community' is, however, more appropriate than the term 'industry' or 'cotton community' because at its most fundamental level the identity the unions built upon was that of the ordinary life of the workers and the factory. This sense of 'factory foaks', like the other sources and models of union discourse, was itself protean, taking in the sense of the factory itself, but also the factory in its various communal settings of neighbourhood, town and region. The term 'factory foaks' in fact comes from the greatly popular dialect literature of the time, which reproduced a powerful sense of regional identity that was linked to the staple industry of cotton.

As will be seen,[79] many of the leading dialect writers were union activists, and both the union journals ran many dialect columns over the years, featuring for instance 'The Gradely Growlers' Club' or the musings of 'Pedar Tum' and 'Peter Pike'. Together with humorous columns in standard English these dwelt much on a specifically Lancashire (or Yorkshire) sense of identity, associated as we have seen with the virtues of hard work. 'Factory foak' were seen as the truest exponents of the Lancashire virtues of shrewdness and endurance and of a certain wry, disabused humour.[80] Dialect conventions and regional cartoon archetypes were directly employed by the union journals in mounting various agitations as well.[81]

It was, however, in the journals' reproduction of the range of people and interests that made up mill life that they most directly worked with the notion of the factory. They ran a 'Children's Corner', a woman's page ('To Wives and Maidens'), a household hints section, voluminous pages of fiction, gardening columns, accounts of sporting, friendly society and co-op news, as well as the humorous sections, and trade and union news. For over half a century after 1885 the *Cotton Factory Times* also ran a 'Mirth in the Mill' column in which ordinary operatives wrote in to give their account of the daily course of mill life. Now, the male-centredness of journals exclusively written by men is apparent enough in the title 'To Wives and Maidens', but notwithstanding this the unions sought to integrate women and all other members of the cotton workforce into a sense of attachment to the unions through these journals. In many respects the mechanism of this integration was the idea of the family, an idea reflecting the strong family character of much labour in textiles. In their children's column,[82] for example, both journals had a very strong sense of family life and family values.

2 Mirth outside the mill: holiday postcard sent from a mother in
Bolton to her daughter in Morecombe, c. 1920. Cards were sent *to*
the seaside then.

Through these means, even if only partly and from the point of view
of male unionists, women were brought within the remit of union
discourse. The idea of the family was a central element in the
broader idea of the factory community.

The unions in turn created an institutional parallel to this
emphasis on the community. If excluded from public discourse
women were not totally inactive in union affairs. Particularly in
cotton weaving, women – especially young women – were involved
as collectors of union dues. However, the central element probably
remained the 'interior' life of the workplace itself. From the 1860s
and 70s the less skilled trades began to organise tea parties, socials,
outings and galas,[83] which were a feature of spinner organisation as
well.[84] For the weaving and spinning trades this took a more
continuous form from the 1870s with the setting up of union
'Institutes'. These were not usually very elaborate but they
circumvented the old reliance on the public house by offering
reading and meeting rooms. With gathering pace up to the First
World War, the unions enlarged this association with the community
in other ways, expanding the sense of that term to cover the town as
well as the factory.

For instance, the unions became active subscribers to town
institutions and charities, such as hospitals and orphanages. Slowly

but surely, with the growing strength of the unions and the rise of independent labour representation, their officers became integrated in the whole fabric of local and national institutional life, as members of town councils, School Boards, the magistrates bench, and eventually of the House of Commons. Some indeed became Factory Inspectors and Correspondents to the Labour Department of the Board of Trade. By so doing they established for themselves and their unions a stake in a community wider than labour alone. This sense of involvement in the wider community was based upon a sense of labour identity to which the term 'class' seems wholly applicable. However, more important than this claim are the actual forms class took.

These were based very heavily on the threefold identities of trade, industry and community which the union both fostered and based itself upon. It is important to emphasise here the role of the union and of its 'moral cosmology', its organising discourse. This discourse was not simply the emanation of a pre-formed community sense. Forthcoming work on the miners of the north-east of England makes this point forcibly.[85] Indeed, it can be argued that the union, rather than the community itself, was the basis of collective identity both in the north-east and more generally. This overstates the case, though the claim calls attention to what is maintained with some emphasis here, namely that the ideology and practice of the unions played a central role in creating popular conceptions of the social order, particularly class perceptions. Union discourse was more than the reflection of the workers' world. It actively shaped it. And, as with the engineering and shipbuilding workers of Tyneside, or the Durham miners, in creating a sense of communal identity and solidarity it also paradoxically served to reproduce the divisions as well as the unities existing in the community beyond the workplace.

The previous account has indicated how much the sense of class in England turned upon the figure of the adult, skilled male head of household. Around the central element of the trade upon which this particular sense of class was built were in turn recreated the divisions upon which the trade subsisted, those for instance between the skilled and unskilled, the tradesman and the non-tradesman, the independent and the dependent.[86] In so far as craft-like versions of the trade made progress in the factory – and this was very considerable – these divisions were reproduced in textiles, where they were given an added emphasis owing to the importance of female labour in an industry whose union structure was dominated by men.

But as we have seen, the other elements of industry and community were also apparent in textiles. These served to reproduce both social solidarities and social distinctions in a rather different way. They led to a union structure and a labour force with a strong sense of a labour identity rooted in particular localities. The same could be said for the miners of Durham, the formative role of their unions notwithstanding: the strong sense of community that shaped the sense of class in this region echoed the marked particularism of the textile example. Indeed, whether one is dealing with the role of the union and the particular discursive themes it utilised or with factors outside the effect of unions, one is very forcibly struck by how locally (and regionally) conscious was the sense of class that began to emerge in England prior to the First World War.

No one example can do justice to the range of industrial and union organisation in Victorian and Edwardian England. But the textile industry is not at all unrepresentative, employing its threefold image of the union and representing in its make-up a wide range of work experience. Its example shows us something of the character of class emerging more broadly in the century. The social solidarities ensuing from a vision of labour so fixed upon a single industry and upon particular localities and regions are not far to find in English social and political history. The enormous power of the unions of the 'staple industries' and popular support for a Labour Party shaped in these unions' image were to be increasingly evident after 1900.

Again, there seems no reason not to call this class. It represented a strong sense of the local and the particular, but this sense of labour identity did not preclude the expression of common feeling with other regions and industries – such as miners with textile workers, for example. Many of the developments making for this inter-regional commonality of feeling were discussed in the introduction, among them the growing integration and concentration of the national economy, the growth of inter-regional organisations on both sides of industry (also the increasing role of the state in these), together with a host of changes in extra-economic spheres, such as changes in the socio-geographical configurations of towns and the growth of a national Labour Party. Hobsbawm provides a striking example of how these developments made a wider sense of solidarity both possible and necessary at the time.[87] W. P. Richardson (1873–1930) was born and lived all his life in the village of Unsworth, County Durham. Yet this man, 'as rooted in his village as any Hertfordshire milkmaid', helped to found the local ILP branch, joined the board of the *Daily Herald*, and became the national treasurer of the Miners' Federation. As Hobsbawm observes, there was nothing natural about this progression: the changes described here meant that for men of Richardson's generation it became easier, and in many ways essential, to see their local industry as part of a national pattern, and to perceive being a worker as being a member of a national working class. For earlier generations this was much less evident, men for instance like Henry Rust (1831–1902), the West Bromwich miners' leader, who never believed that his men had anything to gain from joining the rest of the Midland miners, much less the National Miners' Federation.

This expanded sense of class had, however, to begin somewhere: very often it began in the *milieux* of work, in the community of the factory, say, or in the local, in the neighbourhood, town or region. The *Cotton Factory Times*, for instance, provided a good deal of information about other markets and other unions. Like the wider union activity, it served to make the twentieth-century Labour Party the creation of these particularistic senses of industry and place, as it were the sum of the parts of industry, just as the class vision that emerged in England at the time was the sum of its several parts, rather than an integrated whole. But this implied division as well as unity: the *Cotton Factory Times* only went so far in publicising the affairs of others, just as its unions continued to agitate for its members' interests first and foremost, whether inside or outside the new Labour Party.[88] The rootedness of the sense of class in particular communities could therefore serve to work in different directions, enabling a larger inter-regional, inter-trade solidarity, but as often emphasising tendencies of an opposite sort. As in the sphere of other work-derived perceptions of society such as the trade, the symbolic bases of class reproduced distinctions and divisions as well as unity. To some extent, this was a matter of generations: before 1914 men like Henry Rust were perhaps more influential and numerous than men like W. P. Richardson, those born before Richardson's generation of the 70s being formed rather more in the image of old radical than new socialist times. This was also to some extent a matter of the difference between the labour and political leaders and their rank and file: the former were more alive to the implications of new circumstances than the latter.

It is also the case that though the emphasis would have differed in different industries, this ambiguous sense of class was also made up of strong ties between workers and employers. Versions of the relationship of labour and capital could as often take forms of compromise and consensus as of conflict. So could the class expressions that were built around visions of this relationship, though most accounts have failed to emphasise this. Some perspective can be gained on this by looking briefly at a situation in which the sense of class was rather different, that of French workers in this same period. Michelle Perrot has identified a set of attributes involving an awareness of being a victim, being cursed, being in misery.[89] French workers combined this sense of being outsiders with a very marked *ouvrierisme* that celebrated work and production as 'class sacraments'. This carried with it not only a celebration of being manual, waged proletarians, but also a strictly defined sense of class boundaries, a firm sense of social exclusion. This was inseparable from the notion of the employer as the principal 'enemy'. How different this was from the English sense! So different in fact that one is tempted to say that the English instance is not class at all. After according English attitudes the designation of class, I can hardly refuse it in the next breath, but it is clear that in many respects – in its tolerance, its sense of class harmony rather than of class war, its sense of social inclusion rather than of exclusion – the English instance of class was often perfectly compatible with all manner of social and political appeals, as well as popular identities of a non-class sort.

The banner cry of the *Cotton Factory Times* was 'The Peoples' Advocate', its motto, 'In all things Essential, Unity: In things Doubtful, Liberty: In all things, Charity!' To this were appended the words of Milton, 'Give me above all other liberties, the liberty to know, to utter, and to argue freely, according to Conscience.' By 1914 a more class-conscious, certainly a more socialist message is recognisable in the writing of the journal's opinion columns. The assertive tone of this is evident. The right of the employers to 'control' the life of the operatives is questioned. There is a keener sense that prerogatives for so long seen as those of the employers are now open to dispute and negotiation. There is also the more frequently expressed view that the industry has been built up more by trade union effort and state intervention than by the employers.[90] In many respects these were simply the playing out of the implications of the older notion of the trade and of skill considered as the proprietorial interest of the worker: the idea that the industry was as much the concern of the operative as of the employer could easily develop into the view that if the employers reneged on their responsibilities then right of ownership reverted to the other side. There were always radical implications in the morality of the trade.

However, these observations and assertions seem to have been the preserve more of labour's intellectuals than of its rank and file; and in the watchwords of the *Cotton Factory Times*, the continuing influence of the old radical, populist legacy is evident among these intellectuals as well. More radical conclusions concerning the trade were drawn in the early twentieth century, though these took the form of attachment to a union-backed rather than a socialist-inspired Labour Party. And, for the most part, it was not the newer and more radical lessons that were learned, at least before 1914. The

1906 election, for instance, was more notable for the joining of ranks on all sides in defence of free trade. Free trade defined the interests of what was referred to at the time as 'the great staple industry' of the region. More than anything else the defence of these interests, involving the alliance of all involved in the trade, defined the vision of the union and the resulting vision of class through the nineteenth century and far into the twentieth century as well.

Part III

*Custom, history, language:
popular culture and the social
order*

6

Custom and the symbolic structure of the social order

Consideration of how the social order was represented and understood requires attention to language. This is because language was at the centre of culture. To accord language this significance is today almost *passé*, though it must be said that in general historians have mostly paid only lip-service to its importance.[1] The expanded sense of language as a sign system is explored in this chapter, culture here being interpreted as the codes of symbols people use to confer meaning and order on the world. However, a dominating concern with the semiotics of the non-verbal has until recently drawn attention from words.[2] The fundamentally significant verbal character of language is therefore considered in chapter 8 in its broadest dimension of the national language itself.

This part begins, however, with a consideration of custom, using custom as one means of exploring the broader character of assumed, often unspoken knowledge of society. It soon becomes apparent how intimately custom was linked to the construction of the sense of the past. Custom was about the legitimation of social values and social practices, and this involved the deployment of the notion of precedent and hence of an historical sense. In the course of this period this sense interacted with more formal and conscious elaborations of history. Contemporary conceptions of language were in turn heavily historical in character (just as history turned much upon the idea of national histories being embedded in language and literature). Discourses about history and about language carried very powerful notions of both what culture was and what it should be: ideas about national history were for instance very often ideas about national culture.

Therefore, in moving from the symbolic realm of custom and the everyday to the intellectual world of linguistic and historical scholarship one moves, as it were, from the unconscious in culture to clearly enunciated ideas of what culture was. Approaching culture in these different ways is necessary to an understanding of how the social order was seen at the time, for perceptions of the immediate world and ideas about the larger realm of 'culture' both abounded with representations of the social. Any selection of characteristics defining 'culture' is bound to be arbitrary, but in the conditions of the nineteenth century there was a powerful logic connecting custom, history and language, enabling them together to give a tolerably full account of 'high' and 'low' culture, and the connections between the two.

Something of these connections will already be evident in the accounts of politics and work. Radical and populist political movements, union and other labour organisations all employed notions of cultural identity and of the past, appropriating and developing them to meet new circumstances. This activity, emanating from 'below' in large part, is evident in aspects such as popular constitutionalism, ideas of a prelapsarian golden age, and the applications of custom to be found in the legacy of the idea of the trade. In the transition from radicalism to Liberalism and hence to socialism, 'high' and 'low' cultural motifs were intertwined, 'high' versions of culture and history being brought to bear on the culture of the majority with unprecedented vigour and force. Again, the matter of culture is of the utmost relevance to the matter of class: with only a little exaggeration the history of representations of the social order can be written in terms of the decline or at least marginalisation of a customary popular culture and the rise of notions of progress and reason, notions which together with the values of revealed religion we may loosely term 'liberal culture'. Of course, the rise of liberal culture owed as much to influences emanating from within as from outside the culture of the labouring poor.

Nonetheless, in the cultural but especially in the political sphere liberal values made headway by working with the grain of what had gone before. A doctrine of progress and the future was remarkably successful at integrating and appropriating the past. For instance, the idea of a virtuous, dispossessed people and nation, struggling to realise its destiny in the attainment of liberty, was an extraordinarily fertile means of fusing old and new, within but also far beyond the area of politics. Liberal culture (which refers to more than Liberal politics, and to more than politics itself) was remarkably adaptable and capable of renewal. But as well as a flexible set of metaphors of feeling and of categories of thought liberal culture itself also had a past, being in its late century manifestations a realisation of its late eighteenth and early nineteenth-century roots in rational Enlightenment and romantic thought. It is both the capacity for renewal yet also the limits of liberal culture which become evident in what follows, though within the present compass only a very rudimentary discussion of the questions involved is possible. By 1900 it is a moot question as to which was most in evidence, limits or renewal. On balance, up to 1914, the old liberal world view was substantially in place: so much is evident for instance in socialism's debt to radical Liberalism. Nonetheless, flexibility had its limits and by 1914 what liberal culture had changed into often bore little resemblance to the values and outlook of the 1850s and 60s. In this transformation of liberal culture we can see both the persistence of old ways of seeing the social order and the emergence of new ones.

The development of new versions of culture and society also represented discontinuities with the past, and called out disagreement and resistance. Liberal culture did not have it all its own way, in high culture calling forth the critique of conservative thought and in low culture the resistance, or at least the persistence, of an unregenerate popular culture. Again, the limits to adaptability and renewal are evident. This is particularly apparent in the persistence of customary elements in popular culture, and it is to the unreformed plebeity that I shall now turn. The account so far given of popular political and trade union discourse was by no means exclusively concerned with the more educated, active and articulate among workers. Distinctions between an articulate, socially superior 'higher', and a 'lower' working class are sociologically dubious, and do scant justice to the actual operation of the discourses considered. Nonetheless, cultural, economic and social divisions were marked among workers, and if the distinction is a crude one it is probable that we have so far heard most from the educated and articulate, if not necessarily the most skilled and prosperous. Unearthing the symbolic dimensions of social life reveals something of the assumptions of people hitherto often hidden from view.

The category of custom has been a major means by which historians have sought to understand popular culture, particularly in the eighteenth and early nineteenth century. What is meant by the term is not always clearly defined, but what is involved are 'informal' practices and observances which regulated social and economic relationships existing within and between different social groups. One thinks for example of those customs that regulated the relations of landowners, farmers and agricultural workers, such as the rituals and ceremonies marking out the yearly calendar, or of customs of a quasi-juridical sort setting out parish boundaries or rights to land use.[3] An industrial and urban analogue would be the customs of the trades and the craft workshop. In rites of passage marking birth, death and marriage, say, custom obtained at an individual and familial as well as a communal level. Nonetheless, the association of custom with the regulation and reproduction of usually small-scale communal life has been most often made. Associated with these practices, rituals and observances have been the values and outlooks of the individuals and communities whose affairs custom regulated, reflected and shaped. In this way, custom offers insight into how people thought about their communities and societies.

Custom tends to be seen in particular ways by historians. It is often contrasted with the practices and values of the capitalist market, in leisure as well as in the workplace. Cultural practices once organised on a local, communal and participatory basis are seen as being displaced by market considerations, such as the provision of commercial entertainment and national media of communication. Above all, custom has been seen as everywhere in retreat in the nineteenth century, dissolved from within by the subscription of working-class leaders and autodidacts to the canons of rational reform, progress and revealed religion, and from without by the increasing structural limitations on time and space as industry and towns grew.[4] The growing significance of the regulative functions of an increasingly interventionist local and national state were important, as evident for instance in policing, the control of leisure and the provision of education. The confluence of utilitarianism and evangelicalism in upper-class attempts to reform popular manners also contributed much to the assault on custom. While there is much of value in this picture it does raise certain problems.

These can only be briefly considered here. The implied contrast between 'modern' (large-scale, complex) and 'traditional' (small-scale and local) society, gives grounds for unease. In particular, the idea that local and regional characteristics were subsumed in a nationally uniform mass culture is open to doubt, as is the notion that nineteenth-century industrialisation and state centralisation led to the eclipse of local and regional economic and political distinctiveness. Indeed, it has recently been argued persuasively that industrialisation, at least up to the last quarter of the century, actually increased the degree of economic and cultural distinctiveness.[5] The importance of regional factors will be evident from the treatment of unions. Like the cultural factors considered in the next section there is much evidence of the persistence of diversity until at least 1914. In fact, our thinking in this matter is bedevilled by rather whiggish notions of socio-geographical change. Some remarks may be in order here. First, the different social and spatial levels of the local, regional and national are *always* in a complex relationship with each other, rather than, as is so often emphasised, leading in a linear fashion to the 'modern' state and 'modern' society. In the formation of social attitudes these levels are constituted in people's experience in a much more composite and integrated way than is often imagined. The configurations of these levels are constantly changing, and 'stage model' versions of change which associate the develop-

ment of towns and industry with the eclipse of the regional and
local are unhelpful.

Turning more directly to custom, its presence in popular culture
was more tenacious than is sometimes thought. One may certainly
discern the two currents of outright suppression, and a more-or-less
deliberate higher-class remodelling of custom. The latter may be
seen in the nineteenth-century English countryside, farmers, landowners and the clergy remodelling older practices along neo-
paternalist lines as a means of handling agrarian social change.[6] It
was also the case that for a variety of reasons much of custom simply
became obsolete. Equally, a surprising amount of custom continued
in place: this was so in the area of workplace and trade custom,
particularly outside the factory,[7] but was evident too in the area of
leisure, for example, the persistence of wakes and fairs.[8] However,
something more complex than simple suppression, obsolescence or
continuity was involved – something akin to the remodelling evident
in upper-class agrarian circles, and in workers' deployment of the
legacy of the trade. This process of cultural adaptation is best
approached first by discriminating the nature of custom more
clearly.

Understanding custom in fact helps us understand the processes
by which culture is made. Custom should be seen as an activity or
a process rather than as a set of practices or attributes characteristic
of particular phases of social development. It has been approached
in this light by Hobsbawm,[9] where in contrast to the formalised,
repetitive practices that make up the 'invented tradition' of the state
and higher social classes, custom is flexible and may have a tendency
to social innovation. The requisite that custom be compatible with
precedent imposes limits on change. What Hobsbawm remarks, but
does not sufficiently emphasise, is that the activity of custom may be
as characteristic of 'modern' as of what he calls 'traditional'
societies. Appeal to custom may be restrictive, but has powerful
creative and innovative aspects too. The tendency to sanction as
custom what is in fact of very recent origin, hence re-assembling the
whole corpus of precedent in the process, has frequently been noted
in the literature. For instance, in the British labour movement
workers and unionists have continued up to recent times to sanction
action by appeal to the court of precedent. The persistence and
adaptation of the idea and organisation of the trade is one instance
of this. 'Custom' was, and is, in the eye of the beholder: one person's
customary rights are another person's 'restrictive practices'.

Now, there is no disputing the lessened force of custom in popular
culture, especially in the course of the second half of the nineteenth
century, and in the face of the changes described above. As a cultural
activity it became less public, more subterranean than before; in

ideological terms it became displaced, in a sense marginalised, by a new set of discourses turning upon extra-local, formal and institutional modes of organisation, such as those of law, of parliamentary politics, and indeed of the trade union itself. Nonetheless, when we think of custom as a cultural activity characterising recent as well as more distant periods in British history, then it is this relatively hidden face of custom which is revealing, exposing to view people's often unstated assumptions, especially the assumptions of the less articulate. These assumptions were often assumptions about the character of the social order.

How then can custom teach us about perceptions of society? First, in deploying precedent in the defence and elaboration of particular practices and values, custom very often invoked a popular sense of the past. Present change was managed by reference to imagined pasts,[10] and these notions of the past often contained versions of what proper conduct and proper treatment should be: in the foregoing account of the popular conceptions of society emerging around the defence of trades, families, and communities in the first half of the century, idealised versions of a past golden age were seen to be very important.[11] The chapters on popular literature that follow, especially on the ballads, make this activity plain, far beyond the mid-century in fact. This is one sense of 'history', though the broader question of the popular historical sense is approached more systematically in the next chapter. Custom in the context of early nineteenth-century industrialising communities was about what may be called popular law as well as popular history. In both senses it related practices to values in a very direct way.

Custom was both a way of doing things and knowing things. For instance, the insistence that traditional patterns of work and leisure be maintained was a means of handling encroachments on time in the present, but it was also shaped by the values and associations accruing around the regimes and strategies of these practices. Practice and values were interwoven in the pattern of a working day, week and year which provided a practical and emotionally satisfying structuring of time. Another example would be that of trade apprenticeship, the business of managing the labour market being intimately related to the business of being a man through the customary passage to journeyman status. As historians are increasingly aware, practices and values, interests and emotions[12] are inseparably involved one with the other. So, it is necessary to look at custom as practice as well as precedent. What all this points to is the realisation that the realm of everyday practice was, and is, inscribed with symbolic meaning.

Custom as symbolic meaning is, therefore, inseparable from an understanding of the everyday culture in which custom is embedded as itself symbolic in character. There are verbal languages of class, but also non-verbal, symbolic ones, a semiology of the social order. This approach to culture has not been much pursued by historians, and what follows must be regarded as almost entirely speculative in character. I shall return to custom subsequently, considering here the broader matter of culture as symbolic meaning. One has to start in the recent past, and work backwards as it were, not a very satisfactory procedure to be sure. This is because it is less to historians than to cultural sociologists that one may look for bearings in this matter.

Here the relatively little noticed work of Bernice Martin on cultural change in modern Britain is particularly useful. Drawing conceptually on the large armoury of contemporary cultural analysis, Martin also employs the 1950s and 60s sociology of community, and classic accounts of 'working-class' culture, such as Hoggart's *Uses of Literacy* and Robert's *Classic Slum*, to depict the symbolic character of this culture in the 1940s and 50s.[13] She also draws on her own experience, pertinent for us, of growing up in the industrial Lancashire of the time. Her definition of culture as itself primarily the symbolic ordering of the world has the virtue of emphasising that the ascription of meaning is not the frill on top of 'real' or 'material' interests but is at the very centre of culture. At the same time the inseparability of interests and emotions is evident: the culture she describes as one of order, boundary and control is seen to be rooted in the need to manage and bring meaning to the experience of poverty, endemic economic insecurity and ordered industrial production. This approach also stresses how the full range of cultural practices has symbolic meaning, from the uses of space within the home to the employment of leisure time (in pubs and on weekends for instance) and the practices governing sexual conduct, for example.

These are seen as having an internal symbolic coherence. Drawing heavily on the anthropological and linguistic work of Mary Douglas and Basil Bernstein on the meaning and effect of cultural boundaries and markers, that coherence is seen to turn upon an acute, almost consuming, sense of order, role and boundary demarcation. The disciplines of boundary and control made up a pervasive 'respectability', a concern with symmetry, matching and public face itself enforced by ritual and repetition. Moments of potential excess threatening to disrupt the prevailing sense of order (say in drinking, swearing or sexual behaviour) were themselves carefully ritualised and routinised. In the anthropological terms employed, this 'framed liminality', this policing of cultural boundaries, represents the most self-conscious and sensitive aspects of the need for order.

This need took the form of a series of strictly maintained

3 Faces of poverty: woman and child, Crumpsall Workhouse Infirmary, Manchester, 1897.

distinctions, pre-eminent of which were those between public face and private reality, work and play, the 'rough' and the 'respectable'. For instance, the home was presented to the world in such a way as to emphasise the maintenance of public face. Leisure was prepared for in advance and rigidly marked off from work time.

4 Faces of respectability: studio portrait of young Salford men in their best suits, c. 1905.

Ritual and repetition were the organising principles in every aspect of life: household chores, clothing or the consumption of food, for instance, were among the aspects managed and given meaning in an often highly moralistic way, a moralism itself given a ritualised and

5 Between respectability and roughness: man at ease outside Sale pub, c. 1905.

reptitive character in the shape of the prevailing love of sayings. Sex, age and social status were minutely mapped out by a series of cultural boundary markers, among them sayings, jokes and stories. The overwhelming concern was thus with the preservation of order. This was reflected in the maintenance of established gender distinctions even in the Lancashire of the waged woman millworker. It was also reflected in the consternation caused by the outsider, those who did not fit into prescribed categories, the homosexual, for instance, or the non-white immigrant.

Now, this kind of approach raises many problems, some of a theoretical order that can only be touched on here. The picture of culture presented is altogether too closed, introspective and conservative. The Durkheimian perspective of Martin precludes a closer attention to the broader dynamics of culture and power, such as would be evident in Marxist notions of culture, especially those of Gramsci on the struggle for ideological 'hegemony' in state and society. This sort of symbolic approach also tends to ascribe culture to a clear-cut social base, whereas what is 'popular' in popular culture is not necessarily a fixed set of cultural objects and categories but a *relation* to cultural elements which may be common to a wide range of social groups.[14] A 'relational' or transactional view of culture might well indicate a less coherent symbolic system and indeed the tolerance of a certain degree of disorder and incoherence in people's lives. However, these other kinds of approach tend to be either silent or superficial when it comes to these fundamental aspects. If flawed, the approach *via* symbolic meaning is richly suggestive.

In relation to this study, it is not so much a tolerance of incoherence as a positive attempt to transcend the constricting aspects of boundary and category that is so often evident. This attempt was more complex in its effect than the patrolling of liminal moments evident in Martin's account. The final part of this book deals with this utopian current, this desire to abjure distinctions and celebrate the fellowship of all people. The account of work and politics already presented indicates how important were the themes of tolerance and social inclusiveness in popular culture. Indeed, the popular culture of the period can in large measure be seen as the product of these two divergent tendencies, caste and social exclusion being in tension with these counter-currents. The rage for order needs to be set beside the aspiration to transcend it and the need to explore and even invert established categories. A culture of control might have fatalistic and conservative consequences, but the need for dignity and respect from which it sprang also led to claims for justice, equality and fraternity, claims that often led to the subversion of established social categories. As regards the question of class, as Martin observes, a 'proletarian culture of control' was a prerequisite of the organised labour movement throughout its long history, the dignity conferred on manual labour through the emphasis on respectability issuing in a class pride. Class identity could be rooted in a culture of order. However, this sense of boundary was a matter of category identity rather than simply of class solidarity.[15] Distinctions operated as forcibly within the ranks of the labouring poor as outside them. Their culture was internally fractured not only along the main line of 'rough' and 'respectable', but also along those of age, sex and other divisions.

Robert Robert's picture of the highly elaborate caste system of turn-of-the-century Salford is well known and helps to establish the relevance of twentieth-century perspectives for the nineteenth.[16] He explores the powerful sense in which social distinctions were taken as 'natural', part of the ordained order of things. As Roberts suggests, this sense of caste as preordained and ineluctable was probably most marked before the 1914–18 war.[17] Roberts vividly describes a consciousness of caste in which being respectful was as important as being respected. Defence of one's own position was accompanied by respect for those above one.[18] This sort of deference could be slavish, but also could be conditional upon respect being shown to one. This caste system stood 'natural, complete and inviolate' because it answered to people's needs. It expressed not the class struggle but the battle of life itself, the constant attempt to handle the daily realities of poverty by bringing order and meaning to life. Class could be one expression of this: Hoggart's account of 'working-class' culture at a later date is full of the major cleavage between 'Us' and 'Them' in authority,[19] though this cleavage could as easily lend itself to populist as to class expressions.[20] What is evident here is that a culture of control rooted in the exigencies of poverty and work was at the centre of a variety of expressions of which class was only one.

In Roberts' account social caste was played out in terms of the symbolic significance of the everyday: homes, streets, jobs, pubs all created the drama of the social. However, Roberts and Hoggart are perhaps too often drawn upon in this regard and it is necessary to turn to other late nineteenth-century accounts. Philip Snowden's account of the mill village of Cowling will be recalled, in particular the way in which the desire for independence and respect was made an 'instrument to scourge' the workpeople of his youth. Baulked in so many material respects, in this instance people sought by 'incessant toil' to bring dignity to their lives. The mixture of faith, hope and resignation that resulted is evocative of the condition of so many at this time. The situation in the factory town of the 1890s did not materially differ. Allen Clarke's description of how the operatives saw work – 'They have no true idea of life. They believe they are bound to work' – conveys an even stronger impression of resignation, of things as they are being almost preordained. Clarke moves beyond this account to show how social distinctions were symbolically enacted in the town,[21] and it is worth briefly following him in this respect.

One set of distinctions was enacted in the structuring of time: the mass of people rose and prepared for work around five o'clock, the shopkeepers and clerks at seven, and the higher classes showed their worth by getting to work two hours after the seven o'clock class. Space was structured in a similar fashion: the higher orders had Bolton's streets to themselves in the day. In going to and coming from work the streets reverted to the worker. It is clear that class could be one distinction expressed, and learned, through these means. (The distinction between those who got their hands dirty and those who did not was also very strong.) One could expand this to talk of styles of clothing, food, seating arrangements in churches and at public events, as well as classes of travel, particularly railway travel. A three-class model was much in evidence. But in describing what he called the caste system of the factory town, Clarke indicated how this tripartite division was very elaborate. The many symbols of social ordering set off a high class, a second class made up of the 'lower middle class' and the respectable workingman, and a third class of labourers and poor workingmen. Clarke then went on to add a fourth class, the very poor.[22]

In these ways, social differences were breathed in with the air of Bolton. This was especially so with the linguistic markers of social distinction, which had a powerfully symbolic as well as literal aspect. Speech was a great source of social anxiety, as Wells' *Kipps* and *Tono Bungay* make amply plain.[23] It was also one of the most sensitive boundaries patrolled by the British upper classes. Stephen Reynolds' account of the linguistic rituals of class interaction prior to the 1914–18 war is very revealing.[24] In meetings between the classes he reported how the rich would not give away the advantage whatever came. The upper classes took the upper hand without even knowing it, for this was inbred. Even the would-be liberated upper classes were condescending, expecting respectfulness, especially the use of the term 'Sir'. As his respondant reported, the best treated one like children, the worst like dogs. There was sensitivity to humbling oneself to the 'Likes o' they', but deference and its rituals were also often ground in, by schools, for example, or through the provision of philanthropy. More than a surface deference was evident: poor people were not able to help it, and 'our own sort' often upheld the philanthropist in his attitude to the poor. The poor had to 'lick up a living from somebody's boots': responses were a mix of the calculative and the ingrained, the habit of respectfulness being deeply lodged in the minds of the poor, who were respectful of the 'real gentleman' and suspicious of their own leaders. Again, the sense of social caste is more striking than that of social class.

Moving outwards from custom in these ways raises far more questions than can be tackled here, in particular the symbolic dimensions of what may be loosely termed middle-class 'languages of class'.[25] The chief task for the moment must be to establish a little more firmly the connections with nineteenth-century popular culture, particularly with the realm of custom. In fact Roberts' work on Salford is steeped in the sense of the formative influence of Victorian upon Edwardian popular mores, and Hoggart's account of the 1940s and 50s shows how much the popular culture of the time was rooted in the emotional and artistic earth of the later nineteenth century, in Nonconformity, in the music hall and the melodrama, in popular literature. The selectivity at work in the culture Hoggart considers seems to have operated by accepting the new only in so far as it was compatible with the needs and assumptions expressed in much older cultural practices and motifs.[26] One begins to discern a broad continuity in 'working-class' culture from the mid-nineteenth to the mid-twentieth century, the rise and decline, one might say, of a post-customary popular culture based on the new exigencies of larger-scale urban and industrial life. These are large generalisations, however, not the least sweeping of which is the notion of a post-customary culture. In some respects useful, the idea does scant justice to what we have seen to be the flexibility and continuity of custom.

Hoggart's work in fact offers us some insights which begin to unravel something of this continuity, and which point to the larger stream of symbolic significance of which custom was a part. Again, given the state of information on these matters, I am being extremely speculative. One of the most striking features of the culture of control considered here was the marked sense of stoicism and fortitude bringing order and dignity out of the implacable material of life. 'Putting up with things' was a cardinal virtue. This seems to have involved the removal of the uncertainties of life to the realm of what were almost 'natural' laws. It is important to be clear about this. The sense of fate did not necessarily imply fatalism: as Hoggart suggests, there was a basic and underlying optimism evident in the religious sense so closely tied to the sense of fate. So many depictions of popular culture, particularly Stedman Jones' influential picture of late nineteenth-century popular culture,[27] emphasise the importance of fatalism and consolation that it is necessary to stress what Hoggart grasps so movingly and sensitively. Religious conceptions of an after life were powerful. The sense of home, fatherhood, rest and peace was a crucial aspect of this. The hymn *Abide with Me* was, and to some extent still is, perhaps the single most revealing expression of this. Sung far beyond ostensibly religious circles, the hymn is something like an anthem. Its place in that most distinctive of English proletarian rituals, the FA Cup Final, has traditionally been a central one.

But it was equally the case that attitudes were marked by a sense of purposiveness, of life being lived in the present. 'Putting up with things' was also an aspect of the hedonism and toleration evident in the epithet, 'live and let live'. The sense of fate was neither inherently quietistic nor conservative. Nonetheless, the feeling that the condition of things had to be endured had powerful overtones of fate that were themselves of a religious character. As Hoggart expressed it:[28]

> Working people feel that they cannot do much about the main elements in their situation, feel it not with despair, or disapproval or resentment but simply as a fact of life, they adopt attitudes towards that situation which allow them to have a liveable life under its shadow ... The attitudes remove the main elements in the situation to the realm of natural law; the given and raw, the almost implacable, material from which a living has to be carved.

In Roberts' account of an earlier period this sense of the condition of things being part of the implacable order of fate is even more evident.

What this indicates most powerfully is that the business of imposing order on the world involved deep-seated beliefs, beliefs in part of a formally religious character, yet also of a 'religious' sort in a larger philosophical sense outside denominational terms, and indeed in some respects beyond Christianity itself. It is here that custom again suggests itself as a useful means of analysis bridging older and more recent phases of popular culture, though custom in the sense of customary beliefs, the mental framework in which customary practices were embedded.

And this touches on the other major aspect of this part as a whole – the development of new kinds of popular culture and of new ideas of what culture was, yet at the same time the counter-current of continuity and even rejection of the new, especially the new in the form of the liberal canons of progress and reason. This account indicates the surprising strength of older currents of belief, particularly among the less articulate in the historical record. It also

serves to elaborate the ways in which patterns of belief may have
been linked through the symbolic texture of everyday culture to
conceptions of the social order in such a way as to emphasise the
inevitability and even the necessity of prevailing social hierarchies.
The 'culture of control' we have considered was rooted in the new
circumstances of the mid- and late nineteenth century but it was also
shaped by older currents of customary belief about fate. From
whatever source, the conservative, indeed oppressive implications of
a fixation with the necessity of control and order will be evident. It
would be wrong to emphasise these in isolation, for example
separating them from other, more optimistic religious currents. It is
also unwise to stress only the conservative implications. A kind of
withdrawal from public life, a scepticism about power and social
hierarchy was one outcome. Nonetheless, though they may not be
necessary consequences of the belief in fate, aspects such as fatalism,
pessimism and deference should not be underplayed, the force of the
counter-current of egalitarian utopianism notwithstanding.

The persistence of older patterns of popular belief was much
stronger than is commonly allowed. Reporting from a late vantage,
Hoggart himself noted how his grandparents, moving into Leeds in
the 1870s, brought with them and long retained the remedies,
sayings and 'superstitions' of a rural life.[29] Later still Seabrook
records the memories and beliefs brought by his country kin into the
industrial settlements of the Midlands and long surviving there.[30]
But it was by no means a matter solely of 'rural' beliefs being
engrafted on urban, industrial life. Rather, such beliefs grew
spontaneously out of this soil as well. Of the mining north-east John
Wilson wrote in his autobiography of 1910 how witchcraft beliefs
had a powerful currency in his younger days, as did recourse to 'wise
women' and 'wise men' (one of the latter in Wilson's case was to be
found in the eminently modern city of Newcastle).[31] Wilson was a
leading unionist of his day, and a convinced Primitive Methodist.
Methodism was of course dedicated to the eradication of popular
'superstition'. Yet what is striking in Wilson's account is his decided
ambiguity in the face of such beliefs, part scornful yet also part
believing and fearful.

In fact the line between reforming Methodism and 'folk belief' is
not as sharp as contemporaries, or posterity, have claimed. As Rule
has shown for the example of early nineteenth-century Cornish
Methodism, newer patterns of belief obtained a currency not by
eclipsing but by building upon older ones.[32] Methodism made
headway among fishermen and miners by matching and mingling
the enthusiasm and anti-intellectualism of the faith with the flock's
pre-Christian ways of handling the vagaries of nature and of fate

(vagaries endemic in the hazardous life of fishing and mining). More than any other scholar, Obelkevich has helped us understand the persistence of older beliefs within the belly of the new in the England of this time.[33] His study of popular religion in rural Lincolnshire shows how pre-Christian and Christian motifs intermingled in a religion persisting longest and in its purest form among the very poor. It was a religion that was both efficacious and pessimistic, concerned with getting things done but full of a sense of the implacability of fate and the natural world. It directly echoes conceptions of fate clearly much in evidence in urban and industrial settings. Again, the rural is not as distinct as we imagine: as Obelkevich observes in respect of patterns of belief more widely, Lincolnshire was typical in its unoriginality. Even a cursory glance at the folklorists of industrial Lancashire in the second half of the nineteenth century would suggest that Obelkevich is right and that rural and industrial England shared more in common after the mid-century than is sometimes allowed.

It is evident that a belief in 'magic' subsisted long, often within the contexts of the ostensibly reforming and orthodox. 'Luck' and 'magic' had already been forced apart by the early nineteenth century, but by the end of our period a clear shift to the secularisation of magic as mere luck is evident. Nonetheless, a residual super-naturalism was much in evidence in Hoggart's Leeds of the 1950s, dream almanacs and fortune telling for instance enjoying much popularity.[34] Lancashire folklorists of the later nineteenth century indicate what seems to have been a more marked inclination to the magical. In a part of the world in which the liberal gospel of rational progress and improvement was perhaps more developed than anywhere else this is perhaps surprising.

In several accounts it is said that superstitution is alive but people are shy of talking of it, except among themselves.[35] Clearly, by the 1870s, the stigmatisation of such beliefs was for long evident, yet they were still a powerful hidden presence, one writer remarking that fortune telling and omens were believed in far more than 'educated people' would allow.[36] These reports should be treated carefully: it is necessary to read between the upper line of condescension towards 'popular delusions', and the bottom line of the romanticisation of supposedly ancient folkways. Doing so, there is fair evidence of persisting belief in ghosts, divination, astrology and the power of omens. These tended, by no means exclusively,[37] to be given a location in the outlying parts of the county, though by this time such areas were often quite heavily urban and industrial. Such beliefs were indeed increasingly seen as a matter of luck, but this does not seem to have stopped people acting upon them with great promptitude. For instance, people would travel miles out of their way to avoid places of ill-omen.[38] Manifestations of the supernatural could attract people as well as repel them. In 1856 thousands travelled to Melling, near Ormskirk, to see the tree in which sap was supposed to be rising in the shape of the head of Palmer, a notorious murderer of the time.[39] Palmer was buried without a coffin, mass perturbation arising from what was clearly a confusion of 'religious' and 'superstitious' beliefs. The fusion of these categories was in fact commonplace: it was evident for instance in the 'dream books' which continued to sell in vast numbers into the twentieth century.

Contemporary autobiographies and reminiscences tell a similar story, religious practice incorporating rather than superseding older beliefs and local traditions.[40] The eminently rational Chartist and Liberal William Lovett noted in the 1870s how the Bible was often used to give sanction to notions of evil spirits.[41] Autobiographies of a later generation like that of Thomas Burt of the Durham miners report that religion could itself become a source of 'superstition', men from the depth of their Bible belief inveighing against science as 'infidel'.[42] Lovett and Burt were not alone: what is striking in other accounts as well as theirs is the prevalence of what these rationalistic autodidact workingmen called 'superstition' down into the early years of the present century.[43]

The idea of powerful natural forces at work in the world which could yet be partly mastered is much in evidence in the attachment to seasonal lore apparent in the almanacs. Almanacs were perhaps the major reading item of the poor in the nineteenth century. As their historian has indicated, the divisions between religion, science and 'superstition' were not at all watertight. Prediction and rationality, science, religion and astrology were not viewed as opposites by the writers and readers of the almanacs,[44] however much rationalist radicals like Hone might guy them.[45] To do the matter of popular belief even scant justice would involve much further discussion, but what emerges from this brief account is distinctly reminiscent of what Obelkevich calls the 'folk protestantism' of the later nineteenth-century rural labourers. There is the same osmosis of Christian and 'pagan' beliefs, in which in the end it is by no means certain which had the upper hand. Above all, in industrial England there are clear signs of popular beliefs expressing a kind of animism, notions that the natural world was full of spiritual forces with which 'religion' had to deal. Again, as in rural England, these submerged aspects of popular belief involved getting things done, an efficacy contrasting with the comparative quietism of Christianity. At the same time, in contrast to the optimism of Christianity,[46] the prevailing pessimism of such beliefs suggests itself, or at least the notion that there were pre-ordained and implacable forces at work in the world.

The relation of such beliefs to conceptions of the social order in the way I have suggested cannot be shown without a great deal more research, if indeed it ever can be conclusively demonstrated. Nonetheless, the parallels are too insistent and suggestive to be ignored. A fatalism evident alike in patterns of belief and in some manifestations of a 'culture of control' surely can not but have contributed to ideas that prevailing social hierarchies were well-nigh immoveable and, indeed, pre-ordained and 'natural'. In respect of the discussion of popular culture itself it will already be amply evident how at least in terms of patterns of belief one may talk of a still-lively customary culture at least to the end of the nineteenth century. To some extent this is so with other aspects of custom as well. Lancashire and Yorkshire were typical of other industrial areas in seeing this persistence as most marked in the outlying industrial areas rather than in the cities. The Huddersfield area, especially the Colne Valley, and Clitheroe in north Lancashire are good examples of this.[47] In some cases as late as the 1914–18 war, country lore and 'moorcraft', special holidays and sports, marriage and funeral customs, all continued strongly. It should be emphasised that these involved industrial and not rural workers. In fact much industrial work was situated in rural or semi-rural situations, and the spatial distance between town and country was itself often short. So too was the cultural distance, the pursuits of the 'countryside villages', for instance on May Day, often spilling over into the towns, rather than the towns simply colonising the country.[48]

Nonetheless, while this persistence is striking, cultural change is best understood as a series of transformations involving the combination of old and new. One cannot deny the force of change. The old customary calendar was not only appropriated by new institutions (much as beliefs had been), but was in many cases altogether superseded. Church and chapel, the Sunday School, the factory, the range of self-help institutions such as co-operatives and friendly societies all were to displace older practices and routines. For instance, the discipline of factory work went far to change the uses and perceptions of time. 'Rational recreation' helped eradicate violent, communal sports and customs,[49] though what replaced those was less the culture of improvement wished by reformers than mass, organised sport, usually accompanied by gambling on an equally mass scale.[50] From within workers' own culture co-ops and self-help institutions helped disseminate the plebian versions of what was earlier termed 'liberal culture'.

The work of E. P. Thompson suggests a useful way forward in

approaching this blend of change and continuity a little more systematically.[51] In arguing against what he takes to be an ahistorical functionalist anthropology Thompson points to the changing function of old forms, so that continuities of cultural form should not be seen as carrying with them the meanings and uses of their previous contexts. The example he cites is that of *charivari* or 'rough music', a sanction against those transgressing communal norms, which was applied for different ends at different times. This sort of form–function distinction is helpful. Old forms may hide new functions, but old functions may also continue in new forms. The accent on boundary and order evident in interpretations of workers' culture as a culture of control indicates how older functions of communal self-regulation were continued in a new key in the new industrial towns. Nonetheless, new functions were also involved in the transition to large-scale urban industrial life, and with these new forms, too, just as in other respects, continuities of both form and function are quite striking.

Working out this distinction in terms of the broad range of cultural practices and values is beyond the scope of this study. A fuller account would certainly have to dwell on a very wide range of practices and their meanings in order to understand the ways in which the symbolic structure of everyday and material culture yields up an account of how people saw the social order of which they were a part. Alongside work practices, the symbolic content of consumption no less than production would need consideration. So too would the significance of familial and neighbourhood networks of support.[52] The role of women in all this was of course pivotal, whether the household is regarded as a unit of consumption or as a unit of production. In the latter respect, it is necessary to emphasise that even in the factory towns and certainly in the industrial villages the making of clothes and food (particularly bread), as well as to some degree the keeping of livestock (chickens, pigs), continued to be of importance in the second half of the century.[53] The management of the household involved the management of poverty, and hence the ways in which people saw themselves and their fellows:[54] the 'proletarian' condition and outlook was decidely more complex than is often allowed. Together with the producing household one would also have to consider the 'penny capitalist' provision of goods and services to industrial communities by workers themselves.[55]

However, in exploring attitudes to both culture and the social order I shall concentrate on public and communal occasions, especially those where functions of communal self-regulation and self-knowing can be seen to persist through a variety of new forms. Perhaps the best documented example of this is the popular holiday, particularly in its Lancashire form, the 'wakes'. Changing material and social circumstances certainly gave the wakes new functions, yet what is striking is the persistence of certain key communal purposes. Poole's account of 'Oldham Wakes' is the best account for our purposes,[56] tracing the phenomenon from its original church- and parish-based form into that of the commercial 'fair' and thence into the modern holiday, especially the extended stay at the seaside, above all at Blackpool, which was increasingly popular from the end of the century. In its original form of 'rushbearing', the custom involved the annual renewal of the rushes which carpeted the floor of the parish church.

In this transition there were considerable changes: the pubs took an increasingly important role in the fair, as did religious and secular institutions like the Sunday school and the co-op in the organisation of treats and excursions. The involvement of new or changed institutions reflects how the wakes took upon themselves new functions, the meaning of leisure now in part residing in the purposes of such institutions. There was also a new element of self-consciousness evident in the revival of earlier aspects of the custom, particularly the 'rushcart' that figured so prominently in the original wakes. As Poole observes, 'the rushcart became an object of commercial display, the product of specific initiatives rather than communal organisation, and embodying traditional sentiment rather than living custom'.[57] Nonetheless, though changes of both function and form were real, the wakes also appear to have retained crucially important functions.

Poole notes the striking degree of continuity in the town's growth, expressed in its expansion around the nuclei of established out-township settlements which long retained their own identities. Continuity was also evident in the composition of the town's social and economic elite. It is in fact becoming increasingly evident in the literature on these matters that earlier notions of the 'industrial revolution' as marking a sharp break with existing popular culture are misleading.[58] In Oldham these social continuities were expressed in cultural terms, as Poole notes in the tenacious attachment to local custom that seems to have marked the inhabitants throughout the century. This was most evident in the case of the wakes. Under the banners of 'progress', 'rational recreation' and industrial efficiency attempts at reform were made between 1879 and 1882. These involved unions and co-ops as well as the town council and the School Board. This sentiment ran into the ground of a popular opposition that took its force from the feeling that the wakes were the people's own possession. They were this in the sense that they gave the opportunity for families and communities to meet and socialise on a regular and ritualised basis. Rather than eroding this opportunity the railway in fact made it increasingly possible, just as it in many ways intensified rather than diluted the local character of the wakes. More than this, however, the wakes were the people's own celebration in the sense that they enacted the identity of Oldham and its various sub-communities. This in fact amounted to a communitarian or populist sentiment rather than to a class one. The 'Oldham working class' or the working class more widely were not the objects of the exercise, but 'the people', albeit often 'ordinary', 'poor' or 'working people'. As the latter term suggests, class elements were present, but only as one of a range of sentiments.

This elaboration of a communitarian, populist identity is evident throughout the transformation of the wakes. In the early phases the wake expressed village and out-township identity, reproducing the solidarities but also the lines of conflict within and between settlements that made up this sense of identity. What is striking is how this function appears to have been maintained through the lengthy transformation to fair and holiday. It is no accident that the old name of wakes continued to be used, and is used to this day. Blackpool during 'Wakes Week' became 'Oldham-by-the-Sea'. Whole streets appear to have transplanted themselves to the boarding houses of the town, reproducing the social configurations of Oldham in the new domain of pleasure. Street committees, pubs, chapels and factories organised this, though neighbourhood community was not the only principle of organisation, co-ops, unions and Sunday Schools reproducing communities of sentiment as well as of residence. Nonetheless, including special interests and elements of division as well as the prevailing solidarities, the seaside manifestations of the wakes continued to enact the sense of being the real people of Oldham. Back at home the upper classes of the town enacted their ambigious relationship to this sense throughout the century, but especially in the acrimony evident between 1879 and 1882,[59] some of them opposing the people's pleasures, others, Liberal and Tory, deferring to and identifying with this populist defence of the integrity of popular culture.

From the Gramscian perspective that has been influential in the study of British popular culture, Bennett has recently explored the symbolic meaning of Blackpool.[60] While it is good to see the social history of pleasure taken seriously in this way, there are serious problems with this interpretation. Drawing on my own work on nineteenth-century Lancashire,[61] Bennett equates a no-nonsense, down-to-earth northern 'populism' rather too much with the northern industrialist and not enough with the northern worker. The idea of a northern populism based on the identity and achievements of local industry is a productive one, but as my account of work and class above makes plain, workers were as much involved in this as employers.[62] It was not something based merely on the employers' social and economic dominance but involved the worker's own sense of identity and pride, including aspects of class feeling at times.[63] Bennett is also, I think, mistaken in claiming that a combination of 'northern populism' with what he calls the 'discourse of modernity', both alike evident in Blackpool's early twentieth-century cultural style, were responsible for dismantling or nullifying 'traditional forms of popular recreation'.[64] This is to deal in a false (and romanticised) dichotomy between the 'traditional' and the 'commercial', as well as to underestimate the degree of continuity between places like Blackpool and earlier forms of pleasure.

When one considers the symbolic structure of Blackpool it is the characteristic popular re-shaping of previous cultural styles, rather than the eclipse of the old and the rise of versions of 'modernity' based on Americanised ideas of technological wonder and of a technological future that is again evident.[65] It is not that such ideas were not evident in the text of Blackpool, above all in the design of the town's entertainment. Nor was it that they were not of influence, especially in the early twentieth century when they were fused with the idea of Lancashire industry as another embodiment of the modern. However, the text of pleasure was read according to the preconceptions of the pleasured, by whom it was indeed in large part written. For instance, the theme of carnival was much in evidence, particularly the inversion of everyday routines and manners. But what is most apparent is the way in which indulgence was limited and patrolled.[66] Again a culture of control is manifest, 'liminal' excess being carefully managed. Oldham was no less Oldham for being 'Oldham-by-the-Sea'. Under the eyes of family and neighbours from work and town, the operative visitors seem to have emphasised their 'respectable' and disciplined behaviour, unlike for example the reputedly rowdy Londoner.[67] Social boundaries were explored but also carefully controlled: the Tower ballroom permitted social mixing on the dance floor, but this was a highly ritualised environment in which convention was all important.[68]

Rather than the Americanisation of pleasure, it is perhaps the reproduction of the characteristics of the life of work and home that is more evident. Postcards are a good guide to this,[69] being as often sent *to* the seaside as *from* it before the First World War. A characteristic refrain was 'Don't Forget Work Next Week Owd Pal', a reminder of the inevitability of toil. Pictorial representation dwelt on the contrast between the mill girl in her holiday finery, and in her

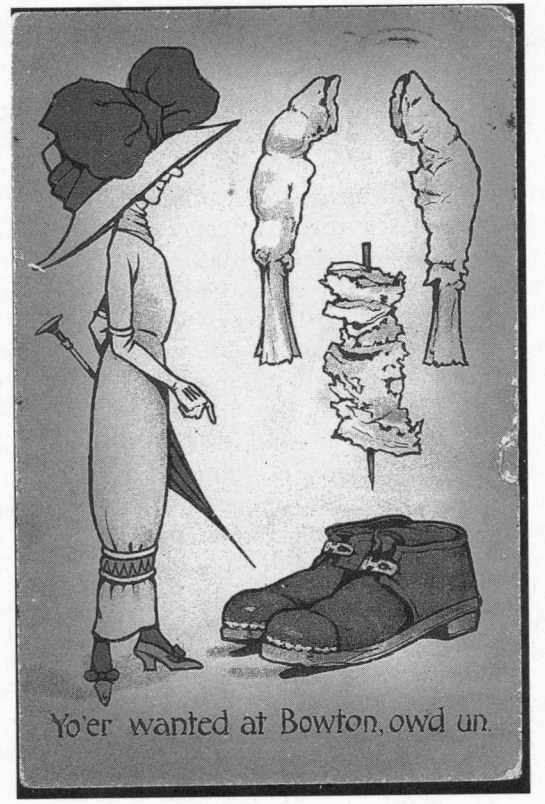

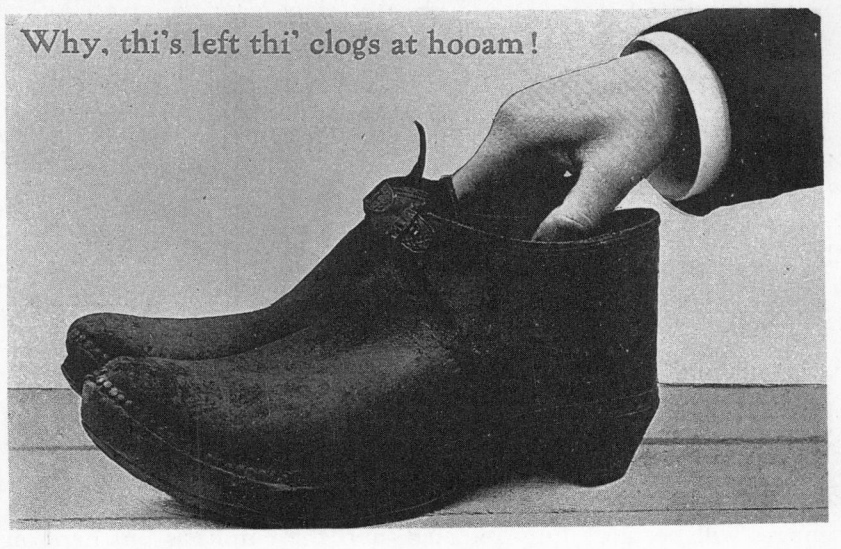

Why, thi's left thi' clogs at hooam!

6, 7 and 8 Lancashire holiday postcards of the Edwardian period.
The message on the card in plate 6 reads: 'Dear Bob, Hope you are
enjoying yourself. And don't forget that you have only gone for a week
and tha has to come whom and put thi' clogs on and start to look at
the other side. From J. Brady.'

shawl under the shadow of the mill chimney. Yet work was not an
intolerable presence: the pals at work beckoned one back to the
camaraderie of the mill as well as to the necessity of labour. A certain
pride in work and in the industrial town is also much in evidence in
these cards (which seem to have been produced locally with local
demand and expectations in mind). Bolton cards represent the town
through the device of the operatives' clogs and the popular town
emblem of the pig's trotter (the 'Trotters' is still the nickname of
Bolton football club). The refrains were often in town dialect – 'Yo'er
wanted at Bowton owd un'.

The Lancashire fairground emigrated to Blackpool, and with it
the unselfconscious enjoyment of the home town.[70] The Blackpool
landlady and her boarding house also reproduced much of this
ethos. What signified was the unpretentious, the homely, the
'gradely', a dialect term denoting a sense of the fittingness of things.
All this is very much in evidence in the dialect journals and annuals
proliferating at holiday time from around the end of the century.
There was no more popular author that Allen Clarke of Bolton,[71]
whose *Gradely Guide to Blackpool* was in its fifth edition by 1908.[72]
Again, the pleasures and freedoms of ordinary people served to

establish and reflect a sense of identity more of a 'populist' than a class sort. In the guide, the chief social distinction is between the 'aristocracy' and the ordinary visitor. The 'aristocracy' comprised the 'rich and ignorant' who frequented Blackpool in the autumn and who did not like the 'vulgar' low tides of the summer. The dominant note is that exalting ordinary 'Lancashire folk', indeed ordinary folk everywhere, for by then Blackpool was not solely the preserve of the Lancashire workers. The vision of bliss and the good life in all this is not the Americanised dream of technological advance but sleeping late in the morning, or having a breakfast of bacon and eggs.[73]

However, the distinction between class, communitarian and populist identities requires much more elaboration than can be provided here: images of society and the social conveyed through the symbolic ordering of pleasure are akin to those evident in the symbolic ordering apparent in popular literature and popular entertainment, and it is therefore in the final section that such images will be more fully pursued, and the emphasis put here on populism will be defended. But before this the conceptions of culture, and hence of society, evident in attitudes to language and history need to be considered. So too does actual language usage, for this embodied social identity in very powerful ways. Preparatory to this something of the connections between custom, language and history requires discussion.

First of all language. In drawing upon Roberts, Hoggart and other works on 'working-class culture' Bernice Martin dwells perceptively upon the central place of sayings and stories, the ritualised repetition of popular wisdom in oral form. These ritualised, metaphorical practices are 'the mechanisms by which the lore of the people is preserved and extended without benefit of literacy. They fix what is known and understood, they form the body of symbolic representations from which myth and meaning are taken.' They are the code 'which defines the contours of both dream and reality'.[74] These ritualised linguistic practices are inseparable from the whole stream of symbolic meaning of which custom is also a part. They are at once the mechanism of transmission and the content of the transmitted form. Verbal folk wisdom and folk knowledge, if I may employ the tendentious adjective here, were linked to custom in the sense that they often accompanied customary practices and expressed the customary beliefs attaching to these. But more than this, just as language is both mechanism and substance, they in a sense *were* custom. Sayings, proverbs and stories, just as much as the practices and values of the trade, say, were powerful symbolisations of history and identity. When custom seemed so often to be in retreat in the nineteenth century, what one may term 'linguistic custom' was often the most persistent and resistent element in popular culture. This was so in the sense of the ritualised verbal 'counters' Hoggart spoke so eloquently about much later,[75] but also in the sense of the vast residue of meaning and association attaching, often barely consciously, to ordinary language usage itself. In both senses language had a symbolic as well as a literal signification, and this lay very close to the creation of social and personal identity.

A good deal of this persistence lay in the fact that in so far as it was informal, localised and assumed, custom lay very close to the oral dimensions of culture. Despite the inroads made on the oral nature of popular culture these continued to be greatly important, and with them the values and associations that clustered around 'linguistic custom'. Before this is looked at more closely the links between custom and history need mention. The particular modalities of culture come to mind – orality, writing, print and post-print technologies of communication. There is a close and largely unremarked link between the character of oral culture and the character of custom. Much in the nature of custom becomes clear when it is related to the mode of linguistic communication in which it was so deeply embedded. The flexible use of precedent, the sloughing off of what is useless and irrelevant in the past, the ever-present modernity of custom considered as a cultural activity all appear to be integrally linked to how oral cultures semantically organise thought in the absence, or relative absence, of the semantic fixedness of writing, and especially of print.[76] The relevance of this for the popular historical sense is self-evident: oral-customary cultures appear to organise the past in a particular way, a way in which the past is as it were ever present and ever new (though the appeal to precedent may place limits on this). In oral culture, as in custom, knowledge and meaning are largely controlled by present use and present need. In contrast print makes possible linearity, sequence, finality. Knowledge and meaning are controlled by authority, power, learning. These generalisations are of course sweeping, but if we wish to understand how perceptions of the social order were encoded in representations of the past then the massive impact of literacy and print upon earlier modes of ordering the past needs to be appreciated.

7

The sense of the past

Given the very nature of oral means of transmitting and constructing the past, there is much in the popular historical sense which is for us unknowable. Nonetheless, there are various ways of approaching it. Even though they go in part through the unrepresentative route of self-educated working people, David Vincent's studies of popular autobiography and of literacy and popular culture are revealing.[1] He has shown how autobiographers drew on a rich and vital store of private oral histories, circulating within as well as concerning families and communities. Such histories were by no means solely oral, but sometimes drew upon a popular print culture apparent in chapbooks and ballads. Quite clearly, the idea of an 'oral culture' is a misnomer to the extent that it fails to register the centuries-old symbiosis of oral and printed forms of communication, an association particularly close in Britain and western Europe.

When applied to these 'histories' perhaps the term history is another misnomer. Vincent indicates that they served the needs of the present, very much in the key of custom.[2] They served to amuse, to intimidate and instruct new generations, and to console or edify older ones. These functions are evident enough in the history which writing and print made possible, but the differences between this and oral histories are clear enough. Contemporary consideration of 'popular memory' shows this selectivity and utility at work in present oral culture as well.[3] Oddly enough, particularly among oral historians, the questions of the content and the forces structuring the selectivity of memory have not been much considered.[4] When it comes to how people come to remember and recount their own lives certain characteristics have been noted, for instance the emphasis on narrative, on humour, on personalising events and on rendering them very much in terms of the immediate milieu.[5]

In turn these characteristics also seem to apply to the manner in which life histories are linked to broader historical events, and so to the ways in which these are interpreted. The dialect literature that will be considered later in fact offers insight into processes which are otherwise largely hidden. It drew on these resources of oral storytelling and reminiscence, reproducing an older manner of reconstructing personal and communal memory in new and more public, conventionalised, and widely disseminated ways. In its

172

closeness to popular sayings, proverbs and so on dialect also produced something of the content as well as the processes of memory, processes such as the constitution of collective memory through the emphasis on humour, the personal and the immediate world.

This was an example of print preserving oral characteristics of culture, albeit in an often highly changed form. For the most part, though, the explosion of print evident in this century threatened to undermine older ways of constructing histories. Even as workingmen autodidacts and politicians drew upon oral reminiscence they recognised its political limitations. In the cultural and political conditions of the early nineteenth century, it was not possible to sustain a satisfactory alternative history through the processes of oral transmission. Operating in a situation where the upper classes had a near-monopoly of print, and hence of the public forms of knowledge, especially historical knowledge, the radicals needed to create a history that could be sustained in the public sphere of print.

In the account given above of radical and Liberal politics, it was seen how important to popular radicalism was this elaboration of the unbroken, ages-old history of liberty and the radical cause.[6] In the massive effusion in print of popular radical sentiments in the early nineteenth century, particularly in the so-called 'pauper press', one can see something of this alternative historical sense worked out.[7] Before this time, as Olivia Smith's account of 'the politics of language' makes clear,[8] the emergence of a mass popular radicalism owed much to radical intellectuals' creation of an 'intellectual vernacular language' which would translate the protest and values of 'low culture' into the currency of dominant discourses, so enabling the people to fight on equal terms in the public domain of power. The elaboration of a radical sense of the past was itself part of a much larger process whereby both dominant and subordinate forms of knowledge were at once rejected and re-interpreted.

This process of re-interpretation offers us insight into the preconceptions evident in the popular culture upon which radicalism drew, preconceptions that often subsisted below the level of the more elaborate and intellectualised versions of history emerging in radicalism, and which were indeed sometimes held in the teeth of radicalism's rejection of them. In establishing the popular presence in public discourse the radical leaders drew on components of popular culture such as ballads, chapbooks and religious literature.[9] Paine drew on the Bible and Bunyan's *Pilgrims Progress*, Spence on the vast reservoir of folk tales and ballads and upon less distinctively verbal aspects such as the iconography of popular protest, especially that of the bread riot. Hone drew upon a similar legacy, which extended to Foxe's *Book of the Martyrs*. Now, Smith does not deal with the precise nature of the articulation of 'high' and 'low' elements in radical discourse, nor does she consider what light this radical fishing in demotic waters throws on the popular sense of the past. It seems to me that it does in fact allow us some revealing glimpses of this sense. (I speak of this sense in the singular, aware that there were many such senses, yet mindful of the great similarities that marked different strands.)

For instance, again and again it is the central texts of English Protestantism that emerge as important, the Bible, Bunyan and Foxe in particular. As Smith remarks, because vernacular texts were limited in number and accessibility after the Restoration, the literature of Protestant dissent occupied a quite disproportionate place in the mental outlook of the poor; 'the isolation of the audience with a few radical texts was an irony of the supremacy of the refined language'.[10] One is dealing here with printed texts of course, but these were often well known to illiterate or semi-literate audiences, through either public or private communal reading, or through other word-of-mouth versions. However, while one is certainly dealing with the idea of a common English, Protestant heritage, and in many respects with a literature of religious and often political dissent, it is by no means safe to assume as Smith does that this always had radical implications. A history turning around the sanctity and longevity of English religious and political liberties could have conservative as well as radical implications. Toryism in the eighteenth and nineteenth centuries, particularly in alliance with the more popular manifestations of Anglicanism, could be an expression of these sympathies.

Nonetheless, the idea of a free Protestant people was often volatile in its consequences, and radical in its conclusions. One may at this stage only conjecture, but it is easy to imagine the outlook of plebian Protestantism merging with the more limited time-frame of oral reminiscence, and giving an historical expression to wrongs remembered in more recent times. It was perhaps the very diffuseness of what I shall term Protestant libertarianism that gave this capacity to articulate all manner of grievance. The recent work of Snell points to aspects of the relationship between the structure and outlook of local communities, and the sense of the past they may have had.[11] It also shows the importance of factors other than religion. In particular, it indicates how regional differences were important. In considering the consequences of decreased labour mobility from around the mid-eighteenth century in the south of England he notes the increased inter-generational contact that resulted. This issued in what appears to have been a marked awareness of parish history and a greater awareness among the young of the political and religious proclivities of their parents. Snell suggests that the consequences of this were played out in the radical form of nineteenth-century agricultural workers' trade unionism.

By contrast the agricultural labourer in the north of England shared less in this growing sense of village history and communal identity. This, however, was not the case with the artisan and domestic-industrial sectors there, and with much justice Snell points to the example of the cotton handloom weaving community as the seat of a particularly powerful plebeian sense of inherited historical identity. This sense was linked to local custom, but also to the influence of local autodidact workingmen, men who were at once open to the claims of custom and of the vast corpus of established, printed knowledge; not least the knowledge that knowledge itself made men free, reason releasing them from the bonds of 'superstition' and ignorance. What begins to emerge here is a rather complex relationship between 'liberal culture' and custom, the rejection of custom as itself perhaps the seat of ignorance and superstition, but also a keen sense of and love for local history and traditions.

This was especially evident in the sphere of dialect writing and scholarship considered later,[12] where the evidence on balance points to the intellectuals of the labouring poor having a positive rather than a negative view of their own culture and its history. Old and new histories did not have to be in conflict but could produce a synthesis embracing history as rational progress.[13] Other autodidact working men might express a more jaundiced view of much of the culture from which they came. For such men, their appropriation of the Protestant past notwithstanding, history only fully began in the period of late eighteenth-century revolution. Literacy and their love of learning could separate them from much in popular culture: David Vincent has dwelt on these aspects of mutual suspicion and rejection, aspects which balanced the perhaps greater empathy with popular manners.[14] Versions of history in turn cut them off from their fellows, whose unregenerate behaviour associated them with a past of ignorance, deference and delusion, a past which the march of reason and progress battled to destroy. The thrust of so much of their endeavour lay in the belief that reason and its employment in the acquisition of 'useful knowledge' would make men free of the shackles of the *ancien regime*. Their frequently expressed belief was that in the course of the century they had lived through monumental and unparalleled change. Alongside an appropriation of the English past must therefore always be set the sense of a radical discontinuity with the past, and even a rejection of it in favour of the future.

The many-sidedness of the popular historical sense acknowledged, one so often returns to the religious current. A proper account of the place of religion would obviously have to dwell on the role of the different denominations and sects. Clearly, Nonconformity nurtured much that was dissenting in the Protestant heritage, feeding this with a sense of the seventeenth century that was a living presence in the nineteenth-century chapel. A full account would also need to dwell on the sense of continuity that emerged around particular churches and chapels, as around villages and parishes. The sense of history was often a matter of the traditions, leaders and families associated with these. In chapel culture this might involve a turning outwards to social and political involvement, or inwards to the sense of the congregation as brethren, a family, a 'connexion'. Everitt has suggestively pointed to these conceptions of the chapel as more than simply 'a temple made with hands',[15] and has discussed the introspection and exclusiveness that might result from the enduring socio-religious metaphors of the family, the home and the refuge.

A more diffused yet powerful sense of the Protestant heritage is evident in the staple literature of even the illiterate poor, namely the almanac.[16] Religion and 'superstition' often sat happily side by side in these. So too did the most jingoistic and radical expressions of the predominating historical current of Protestant libertarianism. The almanacs of the nineteenth century sold in vast numbers, for instance 560,000 copies of *Old Moore* in 1839. If the original *Old Moore* declined in the course of the century its place was taken by a new penny version with sales well in excess of the original as late as the end of the century. In both old and new forms what can only be called the populist emphasis is marked, the liberties and rights sanctioned in the constitution and the Protestant past being invoked in the name of the virtuous 'poor' and 'people' of England against the 'slavish tyranny' of popery and unconstitutional monarchy.[17] Yet as the century progressed almanacs developed in ways which indicate how new versions of history came to complement and also to challenge old ones.

This is evident in what may be termed the radical almanac. From the early nineteenth century radical spokesmen mounted an attack on the supposed 'delusions' evident in the old almanacs, William Hone's *Poor Humphrey* of 1829 being a case in point.[18] Mockery of the old was combined with an attack upon the traditional almanac diet of jingoism and Protestant sectarianism. Yet it was also combined with a certain regret for what was believed to be the passing of old ways, and indeed with a loving depiction of 'country lore' and traditional custom. This could take an extremely self-conscious form, in which respect, ridicule, literary artifice and an eye for the quick shilling came together: the craze for what would later be called 'folklore' was in full swing by the time the first edition of *Hone's Year Book* appeared in 1832, and Hone seems to have tapped successfully into this market with his mixture of literary artifice and somewhat bowdlerised rural folklore.[19]

Other examples of the genre, like the *Working Man's Almanac* for 1833,[20] fused secular with religious radicalism. Like almost all almanacs this gave a list of anniversaries, events, and notable dates. Given that the almanacs were a staple of popular reading, the potted histories this listing of dates and events conveyed were often the main source of a history for the poor, certainly a history broader than their own account of parish, village or place of worship. This was obviously less the case with those who would have consulted the 1833 almanac. There the radical cause was linked to a broader history, Tom Paine for instance joining the great figures of seventeenth-century religious liberty in the marriage of reason and religion.

The diversity of the almanac market can only be gestured at here, though its specialisation indicates that if in earlier times the almanac may have been directly formative of attitudes, later on it came more to reflect historical understandings gained elsewhere. Christian almanacs attacked both the impiety of prediction in the traditional almanacs and, sometimes, the impiety of radical politics.[21] The local press of the mid-century also began to issue almanacs. This effusion of almanacs is indeed a characteristic instance of the explosion of print at the time. This carried new versions of history, and nowhere was this more evident than in the case of the press.[22]

These almanacs complemented the ideological effect of the free, provincial press itself.[23] In more explicit historical terms they served to fuse the radical and dissenting Protestant tradition with a new emphasis on industry and the town (especially urban self-govern-ment), as the expressions of a liberal sense of progress. Even with the provincial Tory press this emphasis was present, though without the recourse to seventeenth-century history. Irrespective of party one begins to see emerging something like a popular version of the Whig interpretation of history, one in which town and self-help institutions, religious bodies and industry all join the march of representative political institutions as evidence of an unfolding design of national advance.[24]

It is evident that the gap between 'high' and 'low' histories was closing in the course of the nineteenth century. This owed most to the greater accessibility of formal, printed histories, itself the product of increased literacy and of increased provision in both the schoolroom and in private reading. It was, indeed, writing but especially print that gave rise to the possibility of history as we would know it, as a sequential, linear progression in time and as something relatively fixed, unlike the more malleable history evident in custom and in oral culture. And the embodiment of this sequential history was perhaps more than anything else the nation itself,[25] though the town was also greatly important. It was the nation, in the nineteenth century closely linked to ideas of the people and their culture, which provided history's master-narrative, and this obtained far beyond the Whig interpretation itself. So far the springs of a history emerging from below have been considered: when the history that emerged from above is explored, the forms the idea of nation took will be evident, and with them the versions of the social order they carried. But before this a little more must be said about self-taught workingmen, for it was they who stood at the junction of 'high' and 'low' versions of the past.

Such men mattered because they were leaders of institutions and communities, however much that leadership may have been questioned and often rejected or ignored. Irrespective of their hold on popular susceptibilities, and they did a great deal to mediate between 'high' and 'low' culture and history, they did much to shape the whole character of public debate about the nature of politics and society. Four fairly representative figures must serve to indicate the range of influences at work. Thomas Cooper and George Howell were nationally renowned figures in labour affairs and popular radical politics; Thomas Burt and John Wilson major influences in the north-east.[26] Burt and Howell were born in the 1830s, Cooper earlier in 1805, and Wilson in 1837. For all these men, different as their situations were, Bunyan, Foxe and the Bible were formative in their early years. Especially for Cooper and Burt, the influence of Primitive Methodism was central, as was the experience of conversion. This experience of Methodism could be either liberating or cramping: in Burt's case the Primitives met together with freethinkers and secularists; in Cooper's the sect was intolerant and anti-intellectual. For all four, the sense of a Protestant, dissenting past was important, religion in one case negatively and in one positively driving these men more deeply into the world of high culture.[27]

Grafted on to the Protestant stock was the English literary tradition. One cannot overestimate how much this mattered to workingmen. As more widely in English culture, history and a sense of English tradition was learned through literature. The figures that mattered most seem to have been the English romantics, and Burns, Shakespeare and Milton. It was Byron, as Mark Rutherford testified so eloquently, that taught the poor workingman to feel, liberating him from the mental and physical confines of poverty.[28] Burns spoke with special urgency of the nobility of labour, linking the liberated mind back to its origins. In Burns, morally and aesthetically pleasing visions of a golden age cottage economy established another dimension of the historical sense,[29] one as we have seen in tune with visions of prelapsarian utopias deeply held by workers at large. In terms of historical outlook, Milton seems to have mattered more than Shakespeare, for it was Milton who formed the main link with the religious and political struggles of the seventeenth century, so completing the circuit between Protestantism and literature.

Of more directly historical influences, the early and mid-Victorian literature of moral and educational self-improvement was a major influence. For Cooper, of an earlier generation, as for Burt later on, Channing's *Self-Culture* seems to have been important. Perhaps more significant, however, was the cheap, improving periodical literature that flooded from the presses of the 1840s and onwards. This was in part a response to the growth of radical literature in earlier decades, and in part an acknowledgement that the patronising tone of the no less voluminous didactic literature of earlier decades had alienated popular opinion. The Liberal-radical credentials of new journals like *The Working Man's Friend* or *The Working Man* were pronounced (both were published in the 1860s).[30] The message of these journals was overwhelmingly that of the Whig interpretation of history. Macaulay was central to this, figuring prominently in the journals and in the intellectual nurture of the four workingmen discussed here.

What becomes evident here, particularly for this mid-Victorian generation of workingmen leaders, is the familiar grafting of a new set of liberal presuppositions upon the old stock of radical ideas and values. In terms of both self-culture and the historical sense this fusion was involved in the rise of 'liberal culture'. Though the nature of radicalism was often greatly changed, its critical faculties were by no means completely eroded. Cooper is testimony to this, though it should be noted that he was from an earlier generation of Chartist critics of society. In the late 1840s and early 1850s he occupied himself as an itinerant lecturer, talking on a quite extraordinary range of subjects. This included fifty-one lectures on the history of England.[31] From Cooper, a new generation of young workingmen from London and the provinces would have learned a history that included accounts of Peterloo, Henry Hunt, and the early English freethinkers, subjects either ignored or sanitised in official versions of history, including many variants of the Whig interpretation.

It is to these versions, to history from 'above' as it were, that I shall now turn. There are two aspects that require attention, the history of the schoolroom and the pedagogue, and the range of historical representations more widely evident in society. Taking the latter first, it is evident that alongside the idea of the nation, and in fact often closely linked to it, the region played an increasingly important role from around the mid-century. This was reflected in the growth of folklore studies noted in the previous chapter. Likewise in the 1840s and 50s, the publication of town and to a lesser extent county histories became important. The same men were often involved in both kinds of venture, folklore and a pride in urban civilisation being perfectly compatible. The new histories were in fact especially evident in the new industrial towns of the north of England. There the rapidity of urban and industrial changes called into being both the awareness of a past believed slipping away, and a history in which town and industry figured as symbols of national and industrial progress. An interest in the past of custom and a belief in rationality and progress could be combined, though the antiquarian's and folklorist's versions of custom were often rather different from the actual experience of custom. These urban histories, published for almost every Lancashire and Yorkshire town of any size after about 1840, constructed a past very similar to that evident in the newspaper almanacs noted earlier (indeed several authors were newspaper editors, most others clerics and professional people). The industry and inventiveness of the town, its institutions of civic self-government, its social and cultural bodies all figured as expressions of what in retrospect now seems a quite astonishing optimism and confidence.

It seems likely that local histories of this sort had some effect on working people, especially on the autodidacts who to some extent moved in the social and cultural *milieux* of this local scholarship, publishing and adult education. Similar historical perspectives also owed much to similar political perspectives, the fusion of radicalism and Liberalism involving a shared outlook upon the past. The writing of William Robertson of Rochdale is typical.[32] Robertson produced many works on the history of Rochdale and district and a biography of Bright. Published in the 1880s and 90s, his work shows how new generations were for long shaped by the prevailing liberal view. The idea of progress was uppermost: the bad old days saw the domination of the drones, living parasitically on the people and leaving the working classes in poverty. The old days were ones of ignorance and violence: the local clergy were applauded for their efforts to reform popular manners. In such works there was an intense fear of 'superstition', which left unchecked would 'fester and corrupt' the lifeblood of the community.[33] As in autodidact culture, there was a similar sense of awe at the great changes taking place in the nineteenth century. More forcibly than before, this awe became linked to the industrial and engineering marvels of the age (marvels which towns like Rochdale evidenced in abundance).[34]

Yet the relation to the past is complex, here as among the self-educated. The fear of festering superstition accompanied a detailed and loving recreation of old characters in town life and of old customs and beliefs of the neighbourhood. This was often quaint and picturesque, evincing a nostalgia not so present among workingmen. But even here there is a sense of loss at what is daily disappearing.[35] What was being created here was a sense of the town as wedding past and present: economic and social advance were emphasised all the more by being given a pedigree. In Ashworth and more widely this pedigree often stretched back to Roman times and beyond, far further in time than the recent customary past. Yet it was that recent past that was chiefly drawn upon in creating the idea of the 'good old town', alongside notions of the 'good old days'.[36] Though nostalgia and regret were present in the town histories this did not usually lead to anxiety about the price of progress. Rather, the past served to sanction progress by measuring the distance it had come and the achievements it had made.

These achievements were methodically listed as chapels built, co-ops opened, representative institutions fostered, in the legion of town 'annals' and yearbooks published in the late part of the century.[37] Their listing of significant dates, like the older almanacs they replaced represented a potted history that was quickly digested and easily available. The yearbooks were a culmination of the earlier town histories, the town being even more firmly implanted at the centre of historical awareness as time went on. Like the new press of the mid-century years, the yearbooks and town historians created an urban identity that aimed to be above social differences, including class differences. It was recognised that different social groups had a stake in the town and had contributed to making it what it was. Thus, friendly societies, unions, co-ops and the like were chronicled alongside civic, educational and religious institutions. The 'good old' town became identified with the dynamic new one.[38]

The dominating optimism evident in these examples was not always registered elsewhere. A more questioning tone is evident beyond the urban histories. The Historic Society of Lancashire and Cheshire, meeting for the first time in 1848, was symptomatic of the new regional organisation and intellectual focus for history. Such institutions sprang up throughout the country around this time. The Lancashire body was made up equally of businessmen, clerics, professional people and some of the gentry. In the Society's 1848 deliberations an uncritical worship of progress is criticised, as is the overly scientific temper of the age.[39] By contrast, attention is drawn to the long pre-industrial history of the region, above all to the culture of 'the people'. It is from their example that lessons are to be drawn: the 'common people' are held in all ages to have been the same. In their retention of old habits and customs, not least the 'spirit of chivalry' lost to the rich, there is much to be learned.

This note of concern about progress is echoed in Manchester's representation of itself. It was evident, for example, in the organisation of the 1887 Jubilee Exhibition in the city. Those involved, some of whom were members of the English Dialect Society, were concerned with Manchester's reputation as the seat of Mammon, the home of 'ignoble purpose'. To counter this they established as part of the Exhibition a display of 'old handicrafts', costumes and buildings, establishing for the city a Roman pedigree, in much the same way as the town histories did.[40] If more qualified, the sense of optimism and achievement was strong in the city as well as in the towns. There is no more striking instances of this than the building and decoration of the new Manchester Town Hall of 1877. The architecture, external and internal, blended urban gothic with a pride in modern achievement, expressed for example in Ford Madox Brown's murals on Manchester history, or in the working into the internal decoration of the building of the symbols of the cotton flower and the industrious bee.[41] In the murals the industrial and scientific roots of the city are seen as one with the heritage of Protestant liberty:[42] the establishment of Flemish Weavers in the town in 1363, the trial in 1377 of Wyclif, the religious reformer, the defence of Manchester against the royalists in 1642; these are among the twelve murals, others of which included the figures of John Kay the inventor of the fly shuttle and John Dalton, in Madox Brown's words 'the inventor of Atomic theory'.

Clearly, the murals like the town hall testify to an industrial and commercial bourgeoisie that seems anything but an appendage of 'gentry' culture. Wiener's account of bourgeois culture as passive and reactive seems greatly wide of the mark.[43] What is evident here is a self-consciously urban elite creatively appropriating the past and its artistic legacy. In turn these sorts of visual representation were reproduced in print, in the many histories of the city written in the nineteenth century, and in the county histories – increasingly popular in the last quarter of the century.[44] In this form such conceptions would have impinged on working people's outlook, but this would perhaps have been evident more in the area of non-verbal, symbolic meaning, an area the symbolism of the town hall indicates. However, it was perhaps the living rhetoric of urban ritual rather than the visual rhetoric of art and architecture that mattered more here. Not that the historical sense inscribed in the new urban architecture of the time was not important. The new markets and parks, libraries, factories and places of worship, as well as town halls, would repay consideration.[45]

However, the ritualised public occasion is particularly revealing, and in recent years historians have directed attention to urban ritual itself,[46] and to urban celebrations of national events, including royal jubilees.[47] The 'invented traditions' of classes, political parties and states have also been considered,[48] such traditions often being enacted through urban ritual. Thus the identities of class and nation often flowed through the conduit of the town, just as the town sometimes acted not so much as the subject of public ritual as the venue for the expression of the institutional loyalties existing *within* towns, be these those of the Sunday school or the union and the friendly society. Nonetheless, a public rhetoric and a public ritual turning upon the town itself became increasingly important in this period, civic self-government and civic institutions breeding their own ritualised public life in the form of mayoral processions, the opening of town halls or parks and libraries, and the public side of municipal politics. It is also the case that seemingly national celebrations, such as the 1887 and 1897 jubilee celebrations in the towns and cities outside London,[49] were in fact often about creating and expressing town and city identity, and regulating the relationships of the social groups and the institutions that made up the town.

Given the rapid transformation going on in the industrial north of England, it is surprising that we have accounts of towns talking to themselves in this way in the south rather than in the north.[50] I shall concentrate on one particularly revealing instance, that of the Preston Guilds Merchant.[51] While the event is unusual the developments it enables one to chart were not. The Guilds was held every twenty years to celebrate the burgess freedoms of the ancient borough and the old guild system of the town. It outlived these purposes yet was retained to serve others and as such is a striking instance of an old cultural form expressing new meanings. At the same time, old and new celebrations in large part turned on the event representing the identity and continuity of the town and its trade.

In many respects the Guilds were concerned with the celebration of a bourgeois rather than a working-class identity. Whether in the town council or outside it, it was the middle-class notables of Preston who orchestrated the pageantry of the event between 1842 and 1922. On several occasions these men called on the services of antiquarian historians of the event in order to perfect their invented ritual. This seems to have been aimed less at incorporating labour than at presenting themselves and their like as the real expression, the real guardians, of town identity once the local gentry and aristocracy had in the early nineteenth century withdrawn from their previously important role in Preston life. By 1862, secure in having engineered the processions and celebrations in such a way as to express the industriousness and gentility of their kind, they felt free to welcome back the gentry, above all the greatest Lancashire landowners of all, the Derby family.

Nonetheless, institutions like friendly societies, co-ops, trade unions and Sunday schools always seem to have been keen to be involved, these bodies invariably marching in full trade, lodge and school regalia. There were in a sense two Preston Guilds, even if control remained in the hands of the better off. The institutions of workers expressed a sense that the Guilds belonged to all Prestonians, especially to the friendly societies and unions which were held to be the heirs of the old guilds. This complexity marked all of the public ritual of the period, different groups appropriating the event and the past it represented for their own ends, the great ceremonial opening of Manchester Town Hall in 1877 for instance expressing the pride of the bourgeois city fathers, and the claims of the 44,000 who marched (with bands, banners and full regalia) to be recognised as equally valid members of the civic community.[52]

Urban ritual, therefore, had the propensity to be viewed and used in different ways. In the Preston Guilds, the town marched as one in the processions but the celebrations that followed were divided between the decidedly genteel on the one hand and the decidedly 'popular' on the other. The Guilds and other similar events could express conflict as well as concord – conflict of a broad social kind but in fact more usually conflict of a politico-religious kind that cut across distinctions of social status. In Preston the celebrations of 1842, 1862 and 1882 were much marked by inter-denominational rivalry about the staging and content of the town processions. But even if such events represented an assertion of the right to be included in the urban community and even if they could express the divisions of town life, there is good evidence that when inclusion was duly accorded and popular institutions were integrated in these rituals, then working people seem to have shared with others the view that the town itself had interests and an identity that transcended the divisions of urban life.

In the Guilds it was 'proud Preston', 'the town and trade of Preston', that were repeatedly emphasised. Preston was above all symbolised by the cotton industry: the concept of 'the trade' as made up of the mutual interests of workers and employers which we have seen to be so influential in the sphere of industrial relations was here visually enacted in its urban dimension. Between 1882 and 1922 the organisers of the Guilds and the trade representatives worked together closely, the former becoming much more closely involved in the trades procession than hitherto. By 1922, when the Guilds had become larger than a solely Preston event, the *Cotton Factory Times* could remark that the celebrations symbolised the whole textile industry, and thus Lancashire itself. The re-enactment of trade practices and processes old and new, and the exhibition of trade machinery, had always been features of the procession, for all the trades as well as for cotton. So too had *tableau vivant* expressing what was taken to be the spirit and history of the trades. Thus labour deployed its own historical sense on these occasions. But after 1882 the emphasis was strongly upon the association of Preston with its staple trade, and the defence of that trade's interests. This was especially marked with the increasing exposure to foreign competition from this time, as was the association of the interests of Preston and its trade with the Empire. Nonetheless, the town itself remained a very strong element: in 1902, when the Coronation and Guilds coincided, the Guilds seem to have taken precedence, the town transcending the nation.[53]

So far what emerges may be broadly termed a liberal view of the present and a liberal construction of the past. Past and present were intrinsically linked in the advance of liberal culture, and nowhere was this more evident than in the social construction of the respectable artisan. We are already familiar with this figure, especially its deployment in the rhetoric of class and of political reform.[54] The views of autodidact workingmen suggest that the conception of history present in the pursuit of reason and knowledge was much more than the imposition of 'high' liberal culture. However, even if inflected differently in different social situations, the semantics of rational respectability permitted a view of history as progress which united social groups. As David Vincent has remarked of the mid-century years, 'the affinities in the commitment of the advance guard of both the middle and the working classes to the values of rational enquiry and moral improvement...in the calmer years that followed the demise of Chartism were to be vital elements in the creation of a more peaceful pattern of class relations'.[55] On a broader front, Tholfsen has argued that with the mellowing of an earlier, strident liberalism about this time, radical workingmen and middle-class exponents of rational improvement were enabled to realise the common perspective on progress they held.[56]

This process of *rapprochement* can be pursued in terms of the literature of self-improvement at the time – the literature, for instance, which served to nurture the likes of Burt, Howell and Wilson. This varied in character,[57] though its radical bite should not be underestimated.[58] Nonetheless, from whatever perspective, the belief in history as progress was overwhelming. However, it is necessary now to turn to a much more voluminous literature, that of the history book itself, especially the schoolbook, the influence of which was to be increasingly felt in the second half of the century. This influence serves to put the other currents making up the popular sense of the past into focus. In so far as we can find a common legacy in the notion of an English Protestant heritage, this was in part appropriated in radical discourse in such a way as to fuse Protestant libertarianism with a belief in reason and progress. Nineteenth-century Nonconformity represented an allied but not precisely similar development. In turn, both of these developments were re-worked in the second half of the century in the transition to 'liberal culture', the wider sphere of values which this term indicates being just as significant as the better-known political transition from radicalism to Liberalism. The predominating Whig caste of mind was worked through in themes such as the history of the town, but also, as will be seen, of the nation.

Now, it will be evident that the legacy of Protestantism was complex, by no means always taking radical, rationalist or progressive forms. As such it suggests areas of historical consciousness evident below the horizon of the articulate and educated workingman, and beyond the reach of the histories of progress. It is necessary to recall aspects of the mental world of the poor considered in the previous chapter; the continuing hold of customary practices, and what were called 'customary beliefs', notions which seem to have often been removed from the linearity of history and divorced in their fatalism from the belief in progress. Of course, the invocation of a 'Protestant heritage' leaves out of the account the many other currents in contemporary historical consciousness, for instance the structure and content of oral reminiscence and its complex links through print to parish, village and church or chapel history. Therefore, for the sake of argument, one may discriminate between what is perhaps the dominant, public sense of the past, that of the radical-liberal view of progress, and these many other currents, the origins and complexity of which can only be hinted at here. As we have already seen, the relationship of rationalist to customary notions, for instance, could be one both of accommodation and hostility. In many respects, as the account of dialect literature will reveal, it is striking how self-educated northern workingmen were able to fuse a belief in progress with a selective re-working of their customary past to produce a mythicised history which was of great effect in the industrial districts.

But here it is not this plebeian myth-making one is concerned with but historical pedagogy. Especially from the 1860s the schoolroom was to confront these various strands of history we have so far considered. Overwhelmingly it was to emphasise the liberal current, but it was also to turn this in new directions, away from a religious to a more secular viewpoint for instance, and most of all towards the dominant public myth of the nation. In this process one can see something of the longevity and adaptability of liberal notions of history, as these sought to incorporate order, radical notions, and as they developed in new ways. This responsiveness to the changed conditions of the end of the century is evident in new formulations of citizenship and new ideas of 'popular culture'. But schoolbooks reflected other currents of opinion, even if the whiggish caste of mind was predominant. They also contained more conservative and illiberal views of culture and the past, particularly when these aspects became linked with imperialist sentiment. Such views were not of course completely removed from the earlier cult of progress: indeed an imperial destiny was often seen as the ultimate expression of the spirit of progress. However seen, as the negation or the culmination of the cult of progress, as the corrosive anti-liberalism of conservative thought or as the expression of an underlying illiberalism in liberalism, by 1914 the limits of the old liberal culture were much in evidence.

But this is to speak only of the history text and the schoolroom, the significance of which it is easy to exaggerate. For most of the century, before and after the 1870 Education Act, elementary schooling was of a pretty rudimentary sort.[59] As regards books, pupils were often left to provide their own reading texts.[60] As with the commercial market for cheap versions of the classics of English literature and history, it was only after 1870 that schoolbooks began to be provided in large numbers. It was only after 1875 that the teaching of history was encouraged in schools, only in the 80s that historical readers were introduced in the upper standards of elementary schools. Even then, teachers were barely more able than their pupils to use the books, so woeful were the standards of teacher training.[61] As late as 1902 Manchester educationalists were typical in complaining about how poorly history was taught and how low was its esteem in schools.[62] Therefore, in considering schoolbooks of the period between 1870 or so and 1914, one has to recognise their limited effect, an effect felt often by generations who were to grow to maturity beyond the confines of the period considered here. Nonetheless, the books tell us much about the preconceptions of the educators if not always of the educated.

It is also the case, however, that prior to and after the Education Act of 1870, history was relayed to pupils in many more ways than in history books alone. The readers used to teach the basic skills of literacy are a case in point.[63] In these, it was as late as the 1840s that religious themes gave way to secular ones, and even then their moralistic, didactic tone was marked. The Bible itself continued to be used, and not until 1862 did the Codes of the Committee of Council on Education preclude this.[64] It is clear that the Bible was used in many ways, supporting the didacticism of established authority as well as the dissenting sympathies of Protestantism. The markedly propagandist character of the schoolreaders is striking, and this continued past mid-century, the 1861 parliamentary report on popular education emphasising that the purposes of education were religious and moral. The readers worked less by dealing directly with history, though texts were often taken from English history, than by emphasising a view of English society which formal history verified, one in which inequalities were pre-ordained, and obedience was enjoined upon the poor. In emphasising thrift and self-help, along with generous doses of political economy, crude versions of liberal progress were grafted upon earlier versions of the social order.

Chancellor's work on history textbooks throughout the century indicates the broad lines of how the past was 'officially' repre-sented.[65] The familiar onward march of British institutions is much in evidence. In some of the books the terminology of class could in fact be used, 1832 for instance being seen as a victory for the nascent 'middle classes'. The 'working classes' was used toward the end of the century, but 'the poor' or 'the people' seem to have been more evident. The period after 1870 marked a new emphasis in many ways: as well as the 1870 Act itself being seen as one among many measures that had secured the progress of 'the people', there was also a more favourable response to the popular politics of the early part of the century. Peterloo, for instance, was recruited in the cause of the Whig interpretation, just as in the political sphere it was appropriated by the Liberals. But the limits to this were marked, much more marked than in Liberal politics, say. Early century popular radicalism tended usually to be seen as either misguided, self-indulgent or seditious. Either this, or examples such as Chartism were ignored altogether. The exertion of the popular will was however acceptable when the passage of time was less uncomfortably brief. Chartism and the French Revolution were not permissible; the Peasants Revolt, or the religious and political struggles of the seventeenth century, were. Here, as in the radical-liberal past more widely, class was usually criticised, and certainly notions of class conflict, though the conflict of the energetic liberty-loving middle classes and a parasitic aristocracy was to some degree exempted from this criticism. The appropriation of Peterloo is a case in point: it was seen in the textbooks, where it was mentioned at all, as a result of 'bad government' or of hunger. These impeded the people's rights to representative institutions. The myth of Peterloo was in turn fused with that of the 1840s as the 'Hungry Forties'. The principle of progress in history was represented by Free Trade, that of reaction by Protectionism.[66]

The representation and actual memory of Chartism are subjects which are of particular interest. Rather like the fate of the operatives' own representations of the factory and of factory labour,[67] a kind of marginalisation seems to have been evident, a combination of silence and historical re-writing which secured the dominance or at least the currency of official accounts. A full picture of this would take us far beyond the school textbook and the schoolroom. What happened, as with factory reform and Peterloo, involved the weaving of the radical instance into the greater narrative of the triumphal progress of representative democracy in Britain. As Chancellor remarks,[68] in the school textbook history was seen in the revelation of religion: if not quite an Englishman, God was especially bountiful to the English. Triumphalist accounts of political progress became fused with the idea of the progress of Protestant liberties to produce a history that was in many respects akin to revealed religion. Late nineteenth-century liberal accounts of history therefore drew on a powerful religious legacy, reproducing in the schoolroom the kinds of intellectual appropriations of the past going on elsewhere.

It is immensely difficult to judge, but it is probable that a good deal of what was subversive and critical in the recent past was lost to the view of subsequent generations. In the late nineteenth century workingman radicals and others emphasised the necessity of written accounts of Chartism. It was noted that, given the relative absence of these, and the availability of unfriendly accounts compared to friendly ones, the memory of Chartism was either lost or re-shaped among working people.[69] Clarke's account of operative attitudes in the Bolton of these same years emphasises how deficient in the sense of their own immediate political history people were.[70] The *Cotton Factory Times* never tired of remarking how present generations were almost ignorant of the politics of their own communities in the first half of the century, a deficiency it sought to remedy by publishing many features on the early history of popular politics and textile trade unionism.[71]

In looking more closely at the period after 1870 I have drawn chiefly on history textbooks, but also on the very revealing literacy readers, histories of English literature, and books on English composition, as well as grammars and manuals of usage, all of which carried versions of the national historical past.[72] Very usefully, these are held in one collection, covering schoolbooks collected in and around the city of Manchester. They also cover the period before 1870, enabling a comparison over time for a particular place. While the early century crudities of historical 'cathecisms' gave way to a less offputting format,[73] the negative treatment of radicalism and Chartism is once more evident.[74] By the 1860s, 1688 was firmly in place in this popularisation of the Whig interpretation, prefiguring politically the unfolding of social and industrial progress in both Hanoverian and Victorian England.[75]

A more responsive and moderate line becomes evident from 1890 or so, for instance in Tout's *Short Analysis of English History* (1900), where the social and political legislation of the 1830s and 40s receives extensive treatment as a harbinger of the extended democracy of the present.[76] While the triumphal tone was still marked there was an emphasis upon the role of the ordinary person as a citizen, someone enjoying rights of ownership, as it were, in the political nation. Again, it is evident how quickly schoolbooks reflected broader changes of opinion, the interest in citizenship from the 1890s reflecting the prolonged public debate about democracy that flowed from the Third Reform Act and culminated before the 1914–18 war in Progressive Liberal attempts to transcend the individualism of classic Liberalism. Changed perceptions of the role of the state were also in evidence in this questioning of the mid-Victorian Liberal settlement. These developments were reflected in a more responsive, less censorious attitude to the history of 'the people' at large, and this was also seen in the other major development that marked the schoolbooks of the time, namely the new interest in the outlook and values of 'the people'.

These developments may be briefly traced. C. H. Wyatt's *The English Citizen and His Life and Duties* (1894) is a typical instance of the notion of citizenship. Wyatt was clerk to the Manchester School Board and the book was written for senior classes in elementary schools and for continuation scholars.[77] The author emphasises that government must be founded on the goodwill of the people. A nation is strong only in so far as its people aspire to freedom, mercy and justice. The aim is to prepare the pupil to be part of 'representative government' by teaching him about its workings, from the level of Empire down to that of local government. The latter emphasis is very strong, continuing the older emphasis upon civic virtue. The task of this pedagogy is fortunately made all the easier for the fact that the English (again the English, even at this late stage, not the British), are by nature and temperament fitted for self-government.[78] All sectional interests were to be sacrificed to the common good, neo-liberal versions of state and nation taking form here as elsewhere through the metaphor of the family.

The second emphasis, upon what would later be called 'popular culture', shows the dimensions of the central motif of the nation. The cultural identity and unity of the nation were perhaps the most telling of all aspects of culture in denying or moderating notions of social disunity and conflict. These cultural aspects of the idea of the nation will be more fully pursued in the following account of language, though they were everywhere apparent in the schoolroom. However, the idea of a national culture could take a radical form, one that sanctioned a place for the distinctive contribution of class. Something of this is evident in the school historians of the late nineteenth and early twentieth centuries who sought, in however qualified a form, to rescue the everyday culture and customs of 'the people' from the condescension of posterity.[79] Nevertheless, what is most evident in the schoolbooks of the time is their continuing condescension. The new emphases on citizenship and culture were on the whole exceptions to this rule.

And even some of the works in which the new emphasis on culture was apparent, extending to books designed for public examinations outside schools,[80] could elaborate an interest in 'national songs' and 'national manners'[81] which gave the idea of the English nation a mystical and conservative expression rather than a rational and liberal one. Uncritically patriotic notions of the cultural unity of the English marked liberalism even in its mid-Victorian heyday. An uncritical worship of progress also did little to combat a growing cultural chauvinism still more evident at the end of the century. The new sense of Englishness emerging was therefore in part the offspring of old liberalism. However, as has been recently suggested,[82] the hegemonic Englishness of 1880–1920 expressed the crisis of the old liberal culture, and in many respects was a direct denial of rational knowledge and the belief in social progress. Much of this found its way into the schoolroom, eclipsing the liberal-radical expressions of English culture, especially English popular culture, to be found in a few of the schoolbooks (but also to be found in great force outside education in the provincial ethos of turn-of-the-century radical cultural nationalism).[83]

Cultural chauvinism was much in evidence, particularly in those books aimed at the lowest levels of achievement. Heywood's *Manchester Readers* for standard III of the 1871 code,[84] deal in a geographical determinism in which the racial character of the English is exalted above all others. Notions of Englishness also turned on the racial figure of the Anglo-Saxon; no intellectual he, but withal brave, patient and cool-headed. The cult of Empire represented an apotheosis of the cult of progress and of the Whig interpretation, as well as a social and political conservatism that in fact denied that view. And if we are to judge by the experience of the children who might have read Heywood's *Manchester Readers* – the slum children of Salford around 1900, for example – then conservative manifestations of the cult of progress do not seem unimportant. A number of the schoolbooks considered here greatly moderated the earlier condescension and didacticism and attempted to appeal to the susceptibilities and capacities of children, but the overwhelming feeling one is left with is of an unregenerate pedagogy, the success of which for all its insensitivity could not have been completely minimal. In Salford children seem to have left school almost ignorant, save for the lesson of allegiance to the Empire and its institutions.[85] Elsewhere at the turn of the century, historians have testified to the great effort put into the propaganda of Empire, within but also beyond the schoolroom, particularly in the quasi-military youth movements of the time.[86] By this time, versions of the English past, carrying covert and overt versions of how the social order should be seen, had adopted ever more emphatic versions of a truly national culture. History was one guide to this culture. The other major guide to culture was language.

8

The people's English

Understanding language helps us understand culture and the representations of the social order evident in culture. Language will be approached here in two senses; actual spoken language – use and attitudes to this use – and more generalised notions of what language was and what it stood for. The two senses of course overlapped, attitudes to use evident for example in schoolbooks or manuals of language use being influenced by theories of language which were part of the general intellectual climate. Nonetheless, the distinction is a useful one, for it corresponds both to the sense of culture as a way of life and everyday social practice, and to culture in the sense of ideology. In the conditions of the period, ideas about language and culture were in fact almost interchangeable. Understandings of the social order also correspond to these two senses of language and culture: language use takes us to the heart of social identity, and ideas about language and culture were pregnant with ideas about society.

Let me begin with language use, and Shaw: 'It is impossible for an Englishman to open his mouth without making some other Englishman hate or despise him.'[1] The acute sensitivity of the English to the linguistic markers of class has long been noted. Playwrights and novelists are one guide to this: writing in the same Edwardian period as Shaw, Wells' novels offer much insight into sensitivities that had by then become almost morbid.[2] Contemporary sociolinguistics offers another guide, one not usually enlisted by historians.[3] What follows here is only a brief and amateur guide to a large and complex area of scholarship.

Sociolinguistic theory of one sort has concerned itself with the structuring of culture, in particular models of the social order, through language acquisition. Different social groups seem to have what Basil Bernstein termed different 'socio-linguistic coding operations'. Bernstein's seminal model of 'restricted' ('working-class') and 'elaborated ('middle-class') linguistic codes has been widely criticised,[4] yet in the broader domain of cultural symbolism it clearly is a suggestive means of approaching what was earlier termed a 'culture of control'. However, whatever the criticisms, Bernstein's strong emphasis on the active role of language in cultural formation is interesting, in the same way as in the discipline at large it is the recognition that linguistic phenomena are social realities that counts:[5] as one practitioner has polemically observed, the real difference between a language and a dialect is that one has the armed might of the state behind it, while the other does not.[6] Later elaborations of Bernstein's approach are revealing, particularly Halliday's work on language as 'social semiotics' – for instance, the idea of 'antilanguage', evident in extreme form in gang talk or thieves' cant.[7] Antilanguages serve functional ends for the groups and individuals involved, but they also constitute an alternative or counter reality to dominant discourses. This emphasis on language as metaphorical as well as referential is important, and calls attention to patterns of usage and of semantic habit and meaning specific to different social groups and contexts. (It also shows how, in the constitution of social reality, people both structure and are structured by language.)

These approaches have been developed and criticised in a range of empirical studies, most notably, perhaps, in the work of Labov. For instance, his impressive study of young, black English in New York has shown the crucial significance of language in the creation of group identity.[8] Ironically, the functions of language at opposite ends of the social spectrum become evident: like black English, Received Pronunciation (RP) is, or was, the code for a group similarly marked by a strong sense of territorial identity and an absence of social mobility, together with strong ties of kinship, school and economic interest. As well as supplying a corrective to Bernstein's account of a relatively impoverished proletarian speech, Labov's work goes far to correct the historical and evolutionary biases of nineteenth-century dialectology,[9] biases still very much part of the lay commonsense of language. Instead of linear notions of the development of dialect, its supposed decline in the face of inexorable pressures for cultural standardisation (evident for instance in 'mass' education, or the 'mass' media), what becomes evident is how dialects constantly undergo change. As will be apparent, regional dialects in England were in part eroded, but it is also the case that not only was there much persistence of old forms, but when older forms receded they were (and are) replaced by other non-standard varieties, which may be similarly localised and have similar sorts of value attached to them as the older vernaculars.[10] Dialectal change may also be a highly conscious affair, brought about in resistance to change.[11] Recent work on contemporary Belfast English has shown the special role of peer groups, particulary youth groups, in maintaining older dialects,[12] a conservatism of childhood and adolescence in fact long known to students of language (and observers of the playground). There was, and is, no such thing as a pure dialect form.

This being so, in the account that follows, as in the account of dialect literature, I have chosen to retain the term dialect, well aware that in the process of dialectal change in Britain over the last centuries dialects have become less numerous and more diluted: there has indeed been a process of standardisation, individual variants being recombined in new, particularly large-city, forms of speech. There has also been a marked decline in non-standard, dialect vocabularies. Standard English has advanced, and this is so for pronunciation as well: to some degree, from the mid- or late nineteenth century, one can talk of a regional accent, or a modified, regional standard. And yet in doing so one is in danger of missing a great deal that is of interest in dialect.

Dialects are usually oral variants of a language, denoted by a different vocabulary, pronunciation, grammar and syntax. It is too often assumed that with the decline of dialect vocabulary, dialects themselves decline into mere accent or regionalised versions of the standard. But dialect is contained in the vast resources of language structure and presentation as much as in vocabulary, in the cadences and order of speech for instance, or in the specific resources of humour, irony or intimacy dialect can call upon. 'Dialect' is perhaps itself an unfortunate term, carrying its own silent apology, so powerful is the domination of the standard in our thinking, or at least in the thinking of middle-class intellectuals. But the term is preferable to the inadequacy of 'accent' or 'regional'. Of course, in practice people had, and have, several spoken languages, degrees of 'dialect' itself, which at one end modulate into regional standard and thence perhaps to received pronunciation. Dialect literature was itself another thing, a deliberate and self-conscious conventional-isation of language which sometimes had relatively little to do with spoken use.

In charting the operation of these differences of spoken usage, sociologists have called attention to the social and personal strategies and contexts that determine the choice of use. They alert historians to important dimensions they have previously ignored, even if, given the nature of so many historical sources, there is often not much that can be done to rectify the omission. The richness of this material can only be hinted at here,[13] for instance how even when respondants attach no positive value to aspects of their use of language these aspects may nonetheless compose patterns of symbolic meaning which are very important for the identity of groups.[14] The significance of language use may be pre-cognitive as well as highly conscious. Just as often, it is both, as in the management of the many social settings in which language enacts and reinforces social differences; in the 'switching' of codes by social superiors for instance, speaking dialect to or joking with supposed social inferiors and using the standard form for social equals (but also often reserving dialect for private life).[15] Language, especially dialect, transacts relations between groups but also within them: Milroy's account of Belfast working-class speech shows how language functions to symbolise identity through means such as the use of gesture and precedence in speaking, or the management of silence itself.[16]

When set beside this sort of study historical accounts of usage are bound to be impressionistic. Even so, they permit the clear observation that then, as now, the obituary of dialect has been prematurely written. This observation also applies to the most systematic account of nineteenth-century language change, that of Waller.[17] There is no doubting the dialectal changes already mentioned; the greatly decreasing importance of dialect vocabularies, the erosion of local, rural dialects in favour of new, urban ones (especially the linguistic imperialism of cockney), and the rising importance of standard forms of pronunciation. The reasons for this undoubted decline of dialect are not far to find, among them increased migration and education, new and improved systems of transport and cultural communication, and the development of large-scale towns and industry. Changes in values and ideas were also significant, among them the decreasing hold of customary practices and beliefs. The period when dialects seem most quickly to have gone through this process of standardisation was that from the 1880s to about 1914.[18] On the face of it, then, a familiar class scenario is revealed in this account of dialect: the standardisation of demotic speech is evident at the same time as a supposed political, economic and cultural standardisation of experience along class lines. There is a sense in which this is true. But rather than arguing for the destruction of dialect, we should acknowledge its partial weakening but insist, along with the sociolinguists, on its continuing capacity for change and regeneration.

With this capacity in mind, may we hold on to the notion of 'class' in the sense of a more uniform linguistic experience? If we can, then it must be with the proviso that the linguistic experience of the majority in this period was never uniform in any conventional sense of the term. Rather, in the industrial districts of the time, dialect did not simply decline but took new forms based heavily on the experience of labour and common living in these new regions. It was standardised, but standardised around what were still powerfully regionalised and localised forms.[19] Some of this can be explored with reference to industrial England, especially the example of Lancashire.

As early as 1850 Samuel Bamford bemoaned the decrease in dialect use and popular custom.[20] However, if we move forward to

9 Strategies of speaking: the persistence of the oral; two women talking, Salford, c. 1900.

1917, the sentiments of Bamford are again echoed, this time for the 1850s and 1860s: people were then held to be more 'parochial', and dialect terms then in use were reported as no longer current.[21] A shrewd observer of Black Country dialect in the 1930s recognised this constant tendency to exaggerate the decay of dialect, a tendency closely related to the mythologising of the past as the 'good old days', of interest in itself but not especially revealing about actual usage.[22] Some sixty years after the institution of mass elementary education, daily use among the Black Country working classes strongly reflected nineteenth-century patterns.[23] Even as early twentieth-century observers mourned the passing of older forms of dialect it was recognised that in Lancashire alone there were at least twenty different dialects, especially individual town ones which were not only strong but markedly different one from another.[24] Actual change probably owed more to the processes of migration into the factory towns than to education or the media. Modern dialectologists indicate the rapid mixing of surrounding dialect in urban speech.[25] Given the nature of migration into many of the new industrial districts, often short-range and by a series of steps,[26] an element of continuity in styles of speech seems likely.

The 1861 parliamentary reports on the state of popular education offer considerable insight into spoken use and attitudes to it.[27] Among the Education Commissioners the culture of the populace is regarded as a species foreign and exotic to educated opinion. Popular manners are invariably depicted as rude and barbaric. Language is very often presented as the index of this cultural state: in Rochdale, for example, speech was represented as being blunt and abrupt. Primitive customs were said to abound in the district, particularly the inclination to dispense with surnames in favour of dialect patronymes and similar forms. For two miles around the centre of Milnrow, a district of Rochdale reputedly the centre of the south Lancashire dialect, it was said that a stranger would find it almost impossible to understand the 'broad, unadulterated pro-vinicialism' of the natives.[28] The attitude of 'educated opinion' is clear enough here, as it was some three decades later in the town when an unusually progressive school inspector maintained that dialect should be used in elementary education. This drew down the wrath of the educated classes of Rochdale for whom the rootedness of dialect was the greatest difficulty in the way of advancing 'a good English education'.[29] The more common attitude among school inspectors seems to have been one of contempt for dialect, a contempt that was framed in what for Lancashire people was the 'foreign tongue' of the inspector.[30]

The association of strong dialect attachments and thriving local cultures apparent in the case of Rochdale, and evident also in the sociolinguistic literature, is reflected in the other districts considered in the 1861 reports. In the case of the Cumberland lead miners, and the smallholders of that county known as 'statesmen', these attachments went hand in hand with long traditions of literacy and book ownership. Where literacy was less marked, and where the social distance between the classes was greatest, as in the colliery villages of Durham and Cumberland, it was said that 'the language of books is an unknown tongue to the children of the illiterate, especially in remote situations. It is utterly unlike their vernacular dialect, both in its vocabulary and construction, and, perhaps, not less intelligible than Latin was to the vulgar of the middle ages.'[31] It is indeed striking how little formal schooling eroded dialect.[32] The Commissioner for Durham and Cumberland noted that educational success was achieved only in the Sunday school, where teaching was done in 'one of the most uncouth dialects it was ever my lot to hear'.[33] The link between modes of thinking and modes of language was perceived by the Commissioner: Scots teachers in the far north of England had best success as through their language they had access to the minds and the culture of the children, and he noted of himself that without a familiarity with Lowland Scots he would have had no 'free or satisfactory discourse' with the labouring classes of the region.[34]

Clearly, language use, especially the employment of dialect, expressed strong social distinctions and stood for decidedly different ideas of what 'culture' was. The differences evident here, in both language use and attitude to use between the 'labouring classes' and 'educated opinion', are very strong. But in no straightforward sense are these class differences. The contempt of the educated for the people's English argues a clear class distinction, but only in the elementary sense of class seen in distinctions like rich and poor, or educated and uneducated. It is not that this sense of class was not real or very important, though it will be evident enough now that the 'populist' label applies better. Applying the class label in a more pointed way runs into difficulties, however: these instances of dialect expressed the cultures of labouring communities, but neither the activity of labour nor the identity of being working class provided a complete definition of what such communities were. They were made up of different social elements and of varied cultural traditions, not least linguistic ones. These traditions were not exclusively those of workers. As some of the instances so far given have shown, language might cross social boundaries as well as accentuate them. This cultural ambiguity of language use applied both before and after the partial standardisation of dialects which seems to have accelerated from the 1880s. If we call the modified dialects of this time urbanised, 'class' dialects, then this important proviso must be borne in mind. 'Class' or not, it is also true that the very rootedness of language in the local and the particular might at all times tell against the larger solidarities of class.

This ambiguity extended to attitudes to use. It also extended to notions of language and culture. Both in practice and in theory things were more complex than a single, prescriptive current of upper-class opinion and practice. Beside, and often opposed to, the veins of differentiation and condescension were more responsive and subtle attitudes at work. Before considering these, however, it is necessary not to lose sight of the better-known tendencies to social differentiation in language use. Historians of language have identified the stages and many of the processes by which particular regional variants obtain a national hegemony of use and prestige, both in written and spoken form. This is intimately tied up with the emergence of the centralised state and of dominant social groups, and closely related to the development of national identities (an association with nationalism until recently ignored in work on the English and British cases).[35] This process began early in England, standardisation of the written form of the language preceding the spoken. The end of the eighteenth century saw a significant acceleration of the standardisation of written English, evident in the contemporary concern with the codification of a prescriptive grammar, the obsession with logical 'rules' and the clear separation out of the 'vulgar' and the 'polite' tongues.[36]

It was not until the end of the nineteenth century that spoken use began to catch up with written convention. The association of Received Pronunciation – that variant by definition 'socially acceptable in the best circles' – successively with the 'Queen's English', the 'King's English', 'Oxford English' and 'BBC English' has seen a hardening of the association between language and class from the late nineteenth to the mid-twentieth century. The emergence of RP as the 'class' dialect of the south of England educated upper-middle class has in turn meant the close association of pronunciation with power, learning and authority, so much so that many have lived with the corrosive illusion that their own speech was somehow 'wrong' or 'ignorant'. As with the partial standardisation of lower-class dialects, the period after the 1880s seems to have been crucial, though the process had begun long before. In considering the question of class in relation to demotic speech it is necessary not to lose sight of the larger speech community in which this speech was embedded. The class potential of developments lower down the social order was certainly reinforced by those higher up. By the end of the century, G. K. Chesterton was indeed suggesting that by the 'enormous importance' they attached to speaking correctly the middle class had cut itself off from the classes above as well as below it.[37]

This varied, however, from one region of Britain to another. In the

English provinces, particularly the northern industrial districts and among employers continuing to be in frequent contact with workers,[38] this was a good deal slower to occur than in the south of England. In the late nineteenth-century industrial north, particularly in Lancashire, employers and other middle-class elements constructed a demotic style, drawing much on demotic speech, which was of great importance in the maintenance of factory paternalism and the management of party politics.[39] There was always a gap between the attitudes and the practices of 'educated opinion'. It is quite clear that dialect was spoken by a wide range of middle-class people, among whom regional characteristics of speech are indeed still marked, especially in the north. This was to some extent a matter of degree and of strategy. The most emphatic dialect was probably used by the poor and the lower classes. The switching of language codes has already been noted.[40] Employers were indeed adept at this, as Arnold Bennett shows so revealingly in the case of the Potteries.[41]

So too were those lower down the social scale, not least the labouring poor themselves. Lancashire workers inhabited at least two language worlds at the time – in this regard there is nothing so revealing as the appearance in dialect books and pamphlets of advertisements for guides to how to speak and write in the 'correct' standard way.[42] The manifold strategies of popular speech can only be adverted to here:[43] the foregoing account of language as a symbolic marker of class, especially of the rituals of social interaction, suggests the great contemporary significance of language use for the poor as well as for the wealthy.[44] Of course, far more than dialect alone would have to be considered when exploring the strategies and resources of popular speech. Slang, for instance, was of great importance.[45]

Slang might be critical and subversive, yet it is also a means of bridging social distinctions. But the use of language should not be seen solely or mainly as a matter of social strategem. The employers that Bennett's fiction reveals are, for instance, wedded to dialect at the same time as they deploy it for social effects, and this applies to much of middle-class, northern provincial speech as well. Social elevation might mean the trappings of gentility but the retention of dialect. Bennett writes of one Josiah Curteney, a big pottery manufacturer, whose wife is intent on eradicating all evidences of his humble origin. She refuses to listen to Josiah when he talks dialect. Clara manages to put a stop to other habits associated with belonging to 'the people', but she meets stubborn and victorious resistance here (as she does with Josiah's retention of the sacrosant plebeian custom of high tea).[46]

Lower down the social ladder, dialect was often used without self-consciousness. Barlow Brooks' account of his upbringing in late nineteenth-century Lancashire speaks of lesser millowners, mill managers and mill cashiers all speaking dialect as part of the linguistically undifferentiated communities of the chapel and the mill.[47] These men and women also made free use of dialect songs and stories as a way of holding the attention of the children who made up their Sunday school and temperance audiences. The Blackburn historian, newspaper editor and Liberal leader, W. A. Abram, stated that in early nineteenth-century Blackburn businessmen and professional people not only spoke but thought in dialect.[48] This in fact took a long time to change. The case of Lancashire employers is revealing.[49] The consolidation of RP was slow. The public school education in which dialect was lost and polite manners and speech acquired was the experience of only a minority of even the largest employers in the third and last quarters of the century. For the others local education would have left the mark of earlier generations of speech fairly intact. Even with a public school education, employers frequently returned to the family firm and to a still-lively speech community: it seems to have taken several generations for RP to root itself among employers to any depth, a process evident more in the 1920s and 30s than the 1880s or 90s.[50]

The ambiguous nature of language and of class is therefore evident. A similar ambiguity attended ideas about language and culture, ideas in part derived from attitudes to the use of the language commentators daily experienced. The less prescriptive among these ideas were, however, not so evident in the literature of the schoolroom. This strongly echoed the opinions of demotic language and culture evident in the parliamentary reports of 1861. Throughout the century the 'educated' had struggled to respond to the culture of the 'uneducated', for most of that time reacting in a hostile, moralistic and didactically unimaginative way. This was so in the teaching of literacy as in the teaching of history. As David Vincent has observed,[51] there was a rejection of the home environment of the child, in particular the linguistic community. Pronounciation was to be in the mode of the 'intellectual and educated classes', and the criteria of 'intelligence' were defined in terms of 'established knowledge', as opposed to the 'sensuality' of the local and home environments. The deliberate attempt to undermine the knowledge gained in those areas is evident in the attitudes of the educationalists of 1861, for instance in their equation of 'provincialism' of language with 'barbarism' of culture.

As Vincent's work has further shown, this attempt through both the means and the ideology of literacy and print foundered on the rock of the orality of popular culture.[52] In the nurture of children formal schooling was usually subsidiary to the acquisition of skills and knowledge which were orally communicated and orally transmitted between generations. This was so in the learning of moral values, in learning about one's community, and in the development of the imaginative faculties, though here the effect of reading was more marked. It was also the case with the skills acquired for work. However, change was evident by the 1860s and 70s as educationalists came to the belated recognition that the grand educational engine of moral regulation and social order was not working. Payment by results was one consequence, an acknowledgement of the market principle which in fact accorded more closely with parents' somewhat utilitarian view of education. There was also an increasing tendency to work with the child's linguistic and cultural environment. Nonetheless, the impact of a more liberal regime which sought to make the home the source of moral regulation and the school the centre of mental training had by 1914 made little headway in formal teaching. However, the very existence of these attitudes is testimony to the permeation of new views of popular culture and language outside the schoolroom. And, in fact, it is outside rather than inside the schoolroom that we need to look to find the other major, responsive current of upper-class thought about these matters.

But first, a brief consideration of late nineteenth-century schoolbooks makes it evident how slow the change was in education.[53] Elocution books and manuals of usage circulating far beyond the school show how the older, prescriptive current was strong outside education as well. Within school it was ever-present, appearing in the most seemingly neutral texts such as grammars. Perhaps the foremost nineteenth-century school grammar, Lindley Murray's (in its fifty-second edition by 1842), intersperses the rigours of grammar with examples that actively teach the canons of moral and social duty, and 'habituation to subordination and control'. However, as well as the fact of pedagogic method as cultural propaganda, it is the class assumptions in these works which are glaringly present. Especially in the first half of the century correct English was associated with 'polite' usage and society in the grammars,[54] and the differences of 'vulgar' and 'polite' discourse were strongly emphasised, as was the superiority of written over spoken language. Formal language skills and grammatical skills were themselves associated with moral virtue. This is evident in elocution and reciting books as well: language skill is associated with entry to 'respectable' walks of life.[55] To get good pronunciation one should associate with those of education and refinement.[56]

10 Some uses of literacy: the limits of the moralising schoolroom; wares of a Salford newsagent, c. 1920.

Manuals of usage, and the increasing crop of books concerned after 1860 to define and defend the purity of the 'mother tongue', are full of these preoccupations.[57] They are evident in J. R. Seeley and E. A. Abbot's aptly-named *English Lessons for English People*.[58] From at least Henry Alford, Dean of Canterbury's *The Queen's English* of 1874, one sees emerging a new association of the language with English national identity which was to be full of implications for the future. In works such as this, as in Froude's *The King's English* of 1906,[59] these implications were highly conservative. But this was not always so, and in order to understand this it is necessary to turn back to the late eighteenth century and the genesis of later attitudes to language and culture. In tracing the increasing split between ideas of 'vulgar' and 'polite' language at this time Olivia Smith has pointed to the importance of language theory.[60] Theory served as an anchor for wider preconceptions about the nature of the social order. In order for what Smith terms an 'intellectual vernacular language' to emerge it was necessary to dislodge the theoretical edifice of 'Universal Grammar'. In this corpus of theory, influential in the schoolroom far into the new century, words were regarded as the symbols of timeless ideals, and what was significant about language was its manifestation of mind or spirit. The 'universal' languages were exalted above 'mere, native English', and the general, the abstract and the timeless above the concrete, the particular, and the historically situated.

Horne Tooke and other radical intellectuals provided a critique of this idealism, in which the relationship between language, power and authority was established very much at the forefront of radical politics. As Cobbett so clearly saw, language mattered. To be free it was necessary to get grammar, and have access to standard English and established intellectual discourse. However, the new century was to see the development of new paradigms of language and culture. Smith does not dwell on these, and one is left with a picture of the growing divergence of 'high' and 'low' culture, the temporary alliance of radicals and literati not withstanding.[61] It is certainly the case that the emergence in Britain of the new European historical philology was blocked until the 1830s. The appropriation of Horne Tooke by the Utilitarians stressed his materialist philosophy of mind and not his historical approach. Nonetheless, the Germano-romantic critique of Utilitarianism, particularly in Coleridge, paved the way for notions of culture which stressed the community of interests of all those making up the nation. That community was sought in 'culture', and the root of culture was very often found in language. The eighteenth-century revolution in language study was central, the historical philology of the nineteenth being its foremost flower.

It is easy now to lose sight of just how significant for contemporaries was the model of culture and history to be found in language. Notions of language shaped the whole mental framework of nineteenth-century intellectual life. For the great language scholars of the German Enlightenment language was the key to culture.[62] For Michaelis, etymology was 'the voice of the people'. Language was essentially democratic, no one person's use being privileged above any other person's. From Michaelis, through Herder, Sir William Jones and Schlegel, one sees developing an attention to the 'organic' structure of language; its revelation, contrary to idealist and mechanist modes of thought, of the historical unfolding of cultures. It was not the origin of language, nor its relation to universal, philosophical truth that mattered but its historical evolution and the factors that determined this. If for Michaelis language was the people's archive, for Herder it was the revelation of the spirit of the folk. There was an interest in spoken as well as written language, in the illiterate, in dialect, and in early poetry, for, as in Herder's *Stimmes der Völker in Liedern* ('Voice of the People in Song') of 1778, song was near to the origin of speech, and hence near to an understanding of the people.

This approach to culture was a broad river, fed by many tributaries, among them the rise of German scholarship in historical and classical studies and, much more widely, the interest in popular custom and antiquities evident across Europe from at least the time of the publication of Percy's *Reliques of Ancient Poetry* in 1765.[63] The river flowed in many directions. Its democratic force will be evident already, and this could take both radical and liberal forms. This linguistic populism could also take conservative forms. All these manifestations were evident in England, in much the same ways as in the received wisdom of the history schoolbook in the late nineteenth century the emphasis on the cultural unity of the English nation took on a plurality of interpretations.[64]

The reception in England of the new language scholarship can only be briefly indicated here.[65] The broadly romantic conception of culture it stood for was reinforced greatly by the works of Sir Walter Scott, themselves owing much to the late eighteenth-century antiquarian craze. Scott's fictions dwelt on the language of 'the people', just as Burns took language to be the most expressive vehicle of culture. In England – and the rest of Britain – the link between literature and language was crucial, literature most fully expressing the language, which in turn expressed the culture. In Macaulay's massively influential *History of England* the historical identity and integrity of the English was expressed in their literature. In fact, not only was the study of language historical in the nineteenth century, so too was the study of literature. And, again, the narrative of this history was a national one, just as in Macaulay it is a *national* literature that gives expression to English history and culture. This suggests only some of the influences at work: in Coleridge and Wordsworth one also sees the term 'culture' itself emerging as an object of discourse, a process described by Raymond Williams.[66] For Wordsworth and Coleridge people were cut off from their 'traditional past' and needed to be put in touch with their cultural heritage. This idea of 'culture' as the yardstick by which a utilitarian, industrial present was measured and found wanting of course took many forms, becoming increasingly conservative when the utilitarian present was also seen as the democratic present. Matthew Arnold is one exponent of this talismanic view of culture, the present being judged by appeal to a past couched in terms of the development of English literary history.

The new language study itself had to make headway against the entrenched orthodoxy of the old universities. From the start it had a radical, heterodox edge because of this.[67] It found an early home in the congenial climate of King's College and University College, London. The influence of the Dissenting Academies was also important in shifting to an historical approach, away from the age-old rhetorical method, and from the idea of literature as polite learning. T. H. Kemble (1807–1857) and Benjamin Thorpe (1782–1870) were seminal figures, formed by the historical philology of the late eighteenth and early nineteenth century. They were instrumental in setting up the Philological Society in 1842, which was the driving force behind that great totem of English cultural identity, the *Oxford English Dictionary*, the first volume of which was published in 1886. The line from Michaelis to this monument to the historical method was an unbroken one.

This is to say something of the world of learning. What of the popularisation and reception of these ideas? Here a crucial figure seems to have been Richard Chevenix Trench.[68] Trench, later dean of Westminster, studied at Cambridge alongside Kemble and Thorpe, Tennyson and the later Christian Socialist, F. D. Maurice, a band of 'Apostles' liberal in politics and romantic in poetry. His *On the Study of Words* (1851) was in its nineteenth edition by 1886, his *English Past and Present* in its fourteenth by 1889. Trench's work was greatly influential in the training of teachers, as well as in popularising the new language study for a lay audience. Furthermore, he gave this study a distinct religious ring. For Trench the spiritual and moral life of the English was disclosed in their language. Love of language was synonymous with love of country. Quoting Frederick Schlegel, Trench intoned that 'the care of the national language I consider at all times a sacred trust and most important privilege of the higher order of society'.[69] The class assumptions of liberal culture are again in evidence.

But popularisation took many forms and had diverse consequences. Palmer has outlined some of these,[70] considering the spread of new notions of English studies to provincial centres like Owens College, Manchester, and from the 1870s and 1880s into the University Extension courses where they would have reached educated workingmen. F. D. Maurice, typically Professor of *both* English Literature and History at King's, promulgated these ideas through the London Working Men's College. The wider effect on education was quite rapidly felt, the study of the English literary inheritance taking precedence over language study, perhaps, though the two, together with history, were often barely indistinguishable. By the 1850s important public examinations added English literature to their list of subjects. Textbooks and cheap editions of the English 'classics' followed. By 1872 English literature was recognised as an approved class subject in the upper three grades of elementary school.

By this time the philosophical outlook of the eighteenth century had been translated into the commonplaces of the English school textbook. Grammars and grammar histories after 1850 expressed their debt to, and arranged the corpus of their knowledge along the lines of the new historical philology.[71] Language was recognised as growing naturally and 'organically', and there was a clear association between the mother tongue and the English literary tradition.[72] In the work of the principal of the National Society's Training College in Battersea, ideas, history and morality were held to be enshrined in words. Knowledge of 'the science of language' enabled the tabernacle to be unlocked.[73] In the school readers used in elementary schools in the 1850s and 60s, Macaulay is widely chosen as himself just such a key.[74] Extracts from his *History* were used to show the emergence of the English national race in the thirteenth century, wherein was to be found the origins of the glorious English constitution, of which all others were pale imitations. Institutions were in turn linked to other aspects of the English make-up, to the 'British Sailor', the 'Ancient Colleges', the Common Law, but above all to the language and the literature. The language was forceful and rich, the most durable of the glories of England, and the primary exemplar of the national character.[75]

As with some of the history schoolbooks there is at times evident a decidedly liberal, in some respects radical, hue; particularly in the construction of notions of culture as popular in character, ideas about culture also evident in some of the history books. In the 1850s in Henry Reed's *Introduction to English Literature from Chaucer to Tennyson* the idea of a national literature was developed strongly,[76] but was seen as spreading to the common human condition of all people.[77] The emphasis on literary culture as truly human was fused with a more radical perspective in which eighteenth-century *belles lettres* were attacked as polite in favour of an older and deeper democratic aspect to literature. This view is evident elsewhere, for instance in Stopford Brooke's *English Literature from A.D. 670 to 1832* (1896),[78] one of a series of literary primers edited by J. R. R. Green, author of *A Short History of the English People*, a notable landmark in the history of the 'common people', and rightly claimed by today's 'people's history' as a radical ancestor.[79] But for the most part, as far as this incomplete look at school and allied textbooks permits, the more radical variants, as in the history books, are eclipsed by the triumphal, uncritical tone, whether this is liberal or conservative in sympathy. The custodial attitude evident in Trench seems uppermost. It is there in the manuals of usage, in Froude for instance, and in Alford's *Queen's English*, where the 'mother tongue' is seen as 'the land's great highway of thought and speech'; what the nation 'in the secular unfolding of its will and habits has agreed to speak and write'.[80]

And the nation here is decidedly England, rather than Britain. Tom Paulin has recently adverted to the close association of language, English ethnicity and the glorification of national institutions. In citing H. W. Fowler's *Dictionary of Modern English Usage* he reminds us of the continuing propagandism of the language manual, and recalls us to a sense of the longevity and rootedness of English linguistic patriotism[81]:

> But it must be remembered that no Englisman, or perhaps no Scotsman even, calls himself a Briton within a sneaking sense of the ludicrous, or hears himself referred to as a BRITISHER without squirming. How should an Englishman utter the word *Great Britain* with the glow of emotion that for him goes with England? His sovereign may be Her *Britannic* Majesty to outsiders, but to him is Queen of England; he talks the *English* language; he has been taught *English* history as one continuous tale from Alfred to his own day; he has heard of the word of an *Englishman* and aspires to be an *English* gentleman; and he knows that *England* expects every man to do his duty. 'Speak for *England*' was the challenge flung across the floor of the House of Commons by Leo Amery to the leader of the Opposition on 2nd Sept. 1939. In the word *England*, not in *Britain*, all these things are implicit. It is unreasonable to ask forty millions of people to refrain from the use of the only names that are in tune with patriotic emotion or to make them stop and think whether they mean their country in a narrow sense or a wider sense each time they name it.

As Paulin observes, the platonic standard of Standard English is not free and transcendental, but has an actual location in the British House of Commons.

The conservative, the patriotic and indeed the mystical are evident enough here. But whether or not ideas about language and nation took a radical, liberal or conservative form, through this period they certainly offered something a lot more complex than the divergence of 'high' and 'low' culture that seemed to be evident in the aftermath of the Napoleonic Wars. In their various forms they also offered something rather more responsive and accommodating than the solely critical, patronising and didactic account seen already to be evident in the attitude of educationalists and so much 'educated opinion' towards the language and culture of the people. Nonetheless, ideas about language were probably most effective where they most unreservedly engaged themselves with the real as opposed to the imagined culture of 'the people'. This is not, however, to write off the effect of the more conservative pedagogy of the schoolroom: the assault on the values of the labouring poor was so various, long lasting and unremitting (indeed almost subliminal in its many sidedness and persistence) that it is unlikely that a good deal of it would not have stuck. Nonetheless, it was in their more radical manifestations, where they accorded some real autonomy to popular culture, that ideas about language were most influential. This was most evident among autodidact workingmen and in the cultural milieux of provincial England. So far most attention has been given to established institutions such as schools and the established world of high learning and literature. However, far from movement being, as it were, from the centre to the periphery, many of the developments noted here had quite early in the century percolated into provincial England[82] and the mental world of the articulate workingman. There they found a ready and energetic response, the provinces (especially in the industrial north), being not at all abashed by their provincialism, and indeed using it as a badge of their superiority over the centres of power and high culture.

James Murray was editor-in-chief of the *New English Dictionary*, later called the *Oxford English Dictionary*.[83] Joseph Wright was editor of the *English Dialect Dictionary*.[84] Yet these men straddled two worlds, the world of high learning, and the world of provincial, autodidact culture. Both were of radical, dissenting backgrounds; Wright from the handloom weaving culture of village West Yorkshire, Murray from a similar rural-industrial background in the Scottish Lowlands. They were men of two worlds in another sense, too, rooted in their own communities but partaking in the world of the book. They both drew a sense of purpose, and much of their scholarly material, from the still-lively oral cultures they were nurtured in. They both had a very lively sense of the history and traditions of their immediate communities, one gained from the stories and sayings of their kin and neighbours. Their biographies reveal a keen sense of 'the people' having their own valid traditions and culture. To this sense of local history they wedded a large sense of history, in both cases one derived from the Nonconformist vision of the Protestant heritage. The people's own English was in fact perhaps the chief sign that this tradition and history lived. Language was the source of special concern and endless fascination to these men. In this they were joined by many thousands more workingmen, the influence of whom upon their fellow, unlearned labourers was to be great. Their influence was felt particularly in the area of dialect literature, and it is through this literature that these matters are best explored further. Something of the complexity of the relationship between custom and autodidact ideas of progress and reason has already been seen.[85] This might extend directly to language, many self-taught workingmen making a point of abandoning their dialect, just as they had put custom and 'superstition' behind them.[86]

But with men like Wright and Murray this was not so, and a more fruitful relationship between past and present was worked out. The nature of that relationship is to be sought in provincial England. This England was increasingly that not of the villages and small towns of Wright and Murray's youth, but of the city and the large industrial town. Nonetheless, the vibrancy of the provincial culture of late nineteenth-century urban England was to owe much to its earlier counterpart.

Part IV
Kingdoms of the mind: the imaginary constitution of the social order

9

Investigating popular art

In late February 1933, Gracie Fields visited her home town of Rochdale. This is how the special correspondent of the *Sunday Chronicle* described those wintry days:[1]

> I write in humility of Rochdale, and of Gracie Fields, the great comedienne. Something has been happening in this mill-haunted town this week which could not happen in any other place in the world.
>
> Once – and not so very long ago – Gracie Fields wore real clogs and a real shawl, and worked in a mill in Rochdale.
>
> So she left Rochdale and became well known. Then famous. Then world famous. Her income grew larger and larger...
>
> And, six days ago, she came home to Rochdale to stay for a week in order to raise money for the local unemployed by singing for nothing at the Rochdale Theatre Royal.
>
> ### HER PEOPLE'S HOMAGE
>
> Now I, who have been watching these happenings here this week, tell you that no queen in her own country ever received greater homage or was more ecstatically cheered and adored by her people.
>
> But it was not in civic welcome, visits to institutions, receptions etc., that made her Queen of Rochdale. It was the breathless joy of everybody in her presence.
>
> Did she walk in the park – then a hundred and fifty mothers walked proudly after her. Did she call in a shop – then a crowd quickly collected outside. Did she wave a hand – then scores of hands and hats and handkerchiefs waved back. Yes, every day this week.
>
> ### BEING HERSELF
>
> Why? Because, instead of staying at the best hotel in the town, she has been sleeping every night this week in a tiny bedroom over a tiny beer-shop in Milkstone-road, kept by Mrs. Schofield, her mother's oldest friend.
>
> Because she has talked to everyone in Rochdale's own tongue, not with the faintest air of being patronising, but with sheer, obvious enjoyment.

Because when she has gone into the park she has swung on the public swings and nursed the children and taken them with her to tea.

Mrs. Schofield, of the off-licence shop, has been the second happiest woman in Rochdale this week. Gracie Fields has been the happiest.

For who else in the world could have a whole Lancashire town at her feet simply by being herself?

What possible relevance can the career of this mistress of the popular style have for an understanding of how conceptions of the social order were created? Surely the real business of class was being fought out elsewhere; in the struggling cotton mills, in the mines and foundries, in the electoral politics of the period? Is not popular entertainment the merest froth upon the surface of what really mattered? It is the purpose of this final section to suggest that this is not so, and that popular art was really quite central to the question of how the social order was seen, and hence to the changing social history of Britain down into the twentieth century. William Reddy may have the next word, reporting upon the dialect literature of French textile workers, a literature every bit as formative as that evident at the same time among English workers. This literature will be a central concern in what follows. As Reddy observes,[2]

Interpretations of class are still confidently put forward that are utterly mythical in form...Groups are characterised by describing the outlook of a typical member of a group...as if such a thing could exist. All signs of rhetorical effort to make, mould, or alter community identities are systematically ignored...An entirely different view of working-class identity is possible, however, as soon as one begins to treat records of working-class experience as evidences of a continuous effort to create identity, as interpretations, as tentative proposals about self and others, with no particular authority and finality and formulated in the difficult material and political context that surrounded labourers in the nineteenth century.

It is this rhetorical effort to create identity which is at issue here, an effort traced first in terms of the broadside ballad, and then though dialect literature and the music hall. This selection is obviously only one among a number that could be made. The chief justification for making it is that for northern industrial workers, particularly in the textile districts of Lancashire and Yorkshire, it is a specially telling choice. It gives a good account of the sorts of popular reading and entertainment that mattered to these people, and hence of their rhetorical effort to make identity. That effort has first to be seen in relation to what has so far become evident in the consideration of politics, work and culture. Only then will the capacity of popular art to deepen our understanding of these matters be revealed. With this fuller appreciation also comes the possibility of discriminating between different ways of seeing the social order, of seeing how they were related, but also how certain ways of seeing may have been more important than others. However, a defence of the credentials of popular art requires more than spirited assertion and this chapter closes with an extended discussion of some of the problems and possibilities inherent in the subject.

The discussion of politics indicated the vital place of a populist political rhetoric and social identity. This sense of the political nation and of citizenship drew upon the loyalties of class and, to some extent, nation and was inflected with the meanings of these identities, especially of the former. Nonetheless, the controlling discourse and social vision seem essentially to have been 'populist' in character. It was evident that the roots of social identity lay very importantly in the sphere of politics, in particular in the traditions of popular radicalism and the transformation these subsequently went through. They also lay in work, and in the fusion of work and communal identities evident in valuations of labour. These gave rise to ideas that were 'corporatist' in character, akin in some respects to an earlier 'moral economy' but very much the child of their times. The term 'populism' is not inappropriate when applied to these, though they could form the basis of class identifications as well. The latter certainly grew in importance in the second half of the century, in line with the language of the market. But this language was itself powerfully shaped by the language of custom, particularly the idea of 'the trade', and this led to a fine balance between rights and duties when labour viewed capital.

A class understanding was one outcome. The emphasis upon conflict in these formulations was, however, often muted, and this meant that appeals of a non-class sort could often be integrated with such class perceptions (in much the same way, in the political sphere, as class was 'managed' by its insertion in the broader political currents seeking to transcend class in the name of constitutional rights, of party and of reform). In the sphere of work and unions class was evident in sectional and parochial terms, yet also had the potential for broader, more catholic interpretations, even if these do not seem to have been fully realised until after 1914.

The picture that emerges is certainly in line with a general argument that class was a fairly late arrival, and was for long subordinate to other ways of seeing the social order. Nonetheless, if the argument so far points away from class it is also suggested how

in practice elements like 'class' and 'people' were often closely
related. The argument also indicates that populism cannot be
viewed as static, conservative or traditional (as opposed to the
'modernity' of class): on the contrary, it is the capacity of populism
to mutate that is striking. The third part of this book, on culture,
begins to extend our terms of reference, though indeed something of
the force of the region, the town and the immediate neighbourhood
milieu are evident earlier. The discussion of custom dwells upon the
meaning of leisure-time activities such as wakes and holidays: the
term 'populism' is applied here, but postpones the question of what
terms like town and community meant and how they were related.
The discussion of the sense of the past dwells on the decided
'populism' of what is there called 'Protestant libertarianism', also of
'liberal culture'; in this manifestation the idea of history as the
unfolding of reason and progress. Again, the varied sources of
popular conceptions of society are evident, and it is as much the roots
of such conceptions and their particular forms that are the subjects
of interest as any type-casting of this variety. Certainly, the existence
of sometimes different conceptions in different areas of life is evident,
be these political, economic, or cultural.

Under the last heading, the consideration of custom and the
symbolic dimensions of the social dwells upon more conservative,
pessimistic and, indeed, fatalistic habits of mind, ones associated
with a culture of boundary, order and control. This is to be
contrasted with the already marked emphasis on utopian visions of
justice and human reconciliation evident in the accounts of both
politics and work, an emphasis drawing sustenance from many
aspects integral to popular culture, such as religious notions,
idealisations of community, or ideas of honour and fair play. This
introduces a note frequently evident here, namely, the distinction
between hope and aspiration on the one hand and fatalism and
accommodation on the other. I shall come back to this briefly at the
end of the chapter, when the significance of the utopian current in
popular literature is considered. The section on culture ends with an
examination of language use and attitudes to language: like views of
history, views of language carried a powerful message that 'culture'
was a realm unifying differing social groups around the theme of
nation but also around themes of town and region. Nonetheless,
ideas about these various manifestations of territoriality could also
produce a discordant note when compared with dominant versions
of the nation and its culture. This was also evident in the account of
language use, where the example of dialect began to reveal some of
the contradictions and affinities between these different socio-
geographical levels, also between class and other ways of seeing the
social order.

A discussion of popular art therefore enables one to explore these cross-cutting aspects of social identity and to see how they were related. For there is no doubting how profoundly important were regional and local differences in the work, culture and politics of the time. Because of the early formation and centralisation of the English state, this diversity is often lost to view. In the talismanic significance of figures like Gracie Fields one begins to appreciate something of this localism of spirit. Not that 'the north' or 'the industrial north' was all of one piece: the industrial districts of Lancashire, Yorkshire and the north-east were often profoundly different in their industrial histories and experiences. Lancashire towns were just not like Yorkshire ones: they had different sports, different sorts of architecture, different churches and chapels, different ways of speaking. The sense in which these differences mattered, yet were compatible with other kinds of allegiance, is something explored in what follows.

The chapter on ballads does its task of exploring the 'populist' theme further, and it also shows how there was something like a fairly uniform 'national' ballad culture which was yet inflected in very important regional and local ways. The locality could be the source of innovation and creative energy in its own right. It could be parochial as well as catholic. Something of the same goes for an understanding of dialect, and the two long chapters given the subject bear on its importance (and its neglect), an importance directly indicated at the end of chapter 8 on language, where the vitality of urban, provincial cultures, especially of autodidact workingman culture, is pointed to. Chapter 9 is given up mainly to an account of the development and organisation of the literature and its trade, and chapter 10 to matters of interpretation. A consideration of dialect enables one to make some very important discriminations between the overlapping aspects of social identity so far considered, showing for example the co-habitation of parochial and catholic, conservative and radical tendencies in popular culture. As was evident, for instance, in the chapters on politics, the provincial and the local could be very radical forces. The discussion of unions and work showed the power of the parochial and the sectional, but also the potential for broader sympathies. On balance, perhaps, the study of dialect evinces the dominant radicalism of local loyalties in their different forms.

The longevity of the forms of identity developed through nineteenth-century dialect is indicated in the music hall and melodrama chapter, though these were now formulated in the new key of an emerging 'culture industry'. This brought with it its own populist message, often far removed from localist loyalties. What has been termed 'liberal populism' emphasised the equality of all people

as consumers of leisure, and involved every person's right to the
'good time', a right especially potent in the era of nascent, mass
democracy. Nonetheless, in the north, the old localist message seems
to have held into the inter-war years, despite changes of emphasis
and changes in the material conditions of life and art. Chapter 13
enables us to put the preceding chapters of this part into some sort of
perspective, pointing, rather tentatively, to the reality of a dominant,
enduring, radical English populism, albeit one not divorced from
class. However, this is to pre-empt discussion, which itself needs to be
introduced by the defence of popular art promised earlier. But before
this attempt to argue the utility of popular art for the historian, it is
necessary to say something briefly about the forms of art chosen
for this discussion, their development and something of the
relationships between them.

The different forms of popular art considered in this section
coincided temporally with each other, particularly in the third
quarter of the century. This was true of the popular stage, too, in its
melodramatic variety, and in the music hall vein which is my chief
concern here. Thus contemporaries would have experienced all
three forms, which between them give a good account of the cultural
life of the second half of the century and beyond. They provide a
kind of map of nineteenth-century preoccupations. The relationships
between these forms of art offer further justification for using them
to get at the broad sweep of popular values at the time. The fully
fledged music hall dialect of the north-east was not evident elsewhere,
but dialect was everywhere to some degree a performed art, and
there was in Lancashire for instance a debt to the music hall in
dialect's public presentation.[3] The broadside ballad was filtered
through the changing forms of popular entertainment, to be returned
to a mass audience in the form of music hall song.[4] Melodrama did
something to maintain the decaying ballad tradition, reproducing in
performance the motifs and conventions of the ballads. The great
debt of dialect to the ballads will be seen, as will the equally
important changes of content and form between the two. There were,
however, also considerable substantive changes between all these
different forms of art, and emphasis on the area of temporal and
thematic coincidence should not obscure this.

The transition from ballads to dialect clearly gathered great pace
in the third quarter of the century. Dialect and the popular stage
continued side by side from the 1840s to the early twentieth century.
Nonetheless, to some degree music hall succeeded dialect: certainly
after 1900 or so it waxed while dialect started to wane, before music
hall was in turn subjected to the competition of radio, film, records
and television. Thus there is a rough temporal sequence in the kinds

of art chosen (melodrama was perhaps the only example to fully span the whole century). Popular theatre represents considerable differences in other respects from the examples so far considered. It was decidedly more commercial, indeed capitalist in its more highly elaborated late-century forms. It was more distinctly a performed art. Compared with the other two, the production of culture was less in the hands of audiences. This can, however, be exaggerated; and the ballads and dialect were not innocent of commercialism either, though it was a rather crude 'artisan' form that it usually took. However, the details of these distinctions will become plain and it is now necessary to turn to our discussion of the interpretation of popular art, permitting one of its greatest exponents to have the first say.

Charles Dickens observed of the popular theatre of his day: 'Those who would live to please Mr Whelks must please Mr Whelks to live.'[5] In the England of Dickens' day there were many who so lived. Popular entertainment and popular literature had for long been organised on a commercial basis, and this was to accelerate through the nineteenth century. Thus in order to understand the significance these forms of imaginative life had for Mr Whelks and his like it is necessary to attend to what may be termed the conditions of their production. It is by now unnecessary to labour the point that the content of popular art cannot be properly interpreted as the unalloyed expression of popular 'mentalities': there were many intermediaries between a 'text' and how it was received.[6] To interpret the music hall, for instance, one needs to consider not only the performer and audience but also the mediations of managers and impressarios, as well as those of the local and national state, whether as licensing or censoring authorities. These all helped shape the finished text, and one ignores them at one's peril. This said, however, Dickens gets it right: the customer was the final arbiter, and texts only prospered in proportion to how eloquently they spoke to their audience. In short, it is necessary to give some account of the conditions of their reception, the ways in which texts were actively possessed by those who made use of them. For it is in fact a matter of an active audience, and the force of what is said here will be to deny the validity of interpretations which rest upon both the notion of the autonomy of the text, and that of the passive consumer of the products of a mass, 'culture industry'.

In considering popular, oral poetry – ostensibly the most tradition-laden, anonymous, and conservative of arts – Ruth Finnegan has rightly insisted on the innovatory aspects of even this form, and on the way it continually recreates the social world of which it is a part.[7] This business of what she calls 'making it again' seems to me just as characteristic of other, and later, forms of popular entertainment and literature. But this 'making it again' exists within a social and artistic context. One needs to insist on the creativity of the user, while recognising that this operates in contexts defined in part by the conditions of 'literary' production indicated above, and in part by the collective expectations and traditions of audiences. In considering the ballad Peter Burke gets at some of these difficulties of interpretation.[8] It is in a sense impossible to know who is the author of a ballad; the writer, the seller (and singer), the printer, the publisher or the buyer (who again reproduces authorship in singing). Yet the author, if not an anonymous, collective entity, is not quite the individual either. Performer and audience are aware of a certain weight of expectation or precedent into which the work must fit. As Burke remarks, audiences exercise a kind of 'preventive censorship': in an 'oral culture', 'the individual may invent but "the community" selects'. This, I think, is much more true of later culture, and of literate cultures, than is sometimes recognised. In what follows I shall try and capture something of this blend of innovation and precedent; a mix of adaptiveness and conservatism itself very evident in popular culture more widely considered.

There are considerable difficulties of interpretation, of course, but the existence of what may be termed collective reception, and of the blend of individuality and impersonality in literary creation, make the ballads a particularly revealing source for understanding popular conceptions of the social order. In considering other forms of popular imaginative life it will be apparent that the ballads are not alone in this. All the forms of art considered in this section, through their collective nature, tell us about popular understanding of collectivities. In order to explore these conceptions it is first necessary to consider the setting or situations of use. Here I shall be brief and descriptive, prior to addressing the question of interpretation and meaning. In considering cheap, popular literature in the USA Michael Denning has recently pointed to the importance of situating reading in this way.[9] In this example it is settings other than the individualistic one that are striking, whether these be familial or communal. The 'private' reader is less apparent, and this strongly suggests the persistence of oral traditions of story telling into the era of mass literacy and a mass fiction market.

These observations may be made with even more emphasis about the broadside ballads (and about the dialect literature that followed them). Ballads were commissioned, published and sold by commercial printers but the conditions of their sale, reading and performance were decidedly public rather than private.[10] In this respect there were clear differences with 'high' culture, and one can detect in the nineteenth century a progressively marked bifurcation of reading habits and settings, in which the 'private' reader in the 'high' tradition is synonymous with the development of 'psychological realism' and the naturalistic narrative. It is unwise to over-state the class-specific nature of modes of reading however. Ballad singing in familial and public settings, together with the immense popularity of the 'art' of recitation, characterised most social levels in British society.[11] So too did a sheer delight in verbal play.[12] Nonetheless, the differences between 'high' and 'popular' ways of reading were marked. As will be seen, ballads had specific social, public functions too, and these served further to emphasise differences.

The public and participatory aspects of the settings in which popular imaginative life was formed are just as evident in the case of the music hall. To some extent elements in the evolution of the halls threatened these aspects. One may note here the concentration of ownership and the more elaborate managerial organisation evident in the late nineteenth century, as well as a 'star system' of national dimensions among the performers. However, even in its most highly organised and 'capitalist' phases around 1900, the meanings of the music hall resided in the context of performance, and were a product of the interplay of audience and performer.[13] Indeed, it can be said that the more that outside elements intervened in this relationship the more were they circumvented by audiences. Performers and audiences rose to the occasion; a nod was as good as a wink. These partners in the cultural transactions that characterised the halls should not be regarded as unaware of the intervention of managers, local authorities and cultural entrepreneur-impressarios that together made up 'the business of the halls'. There is every evidence that people knew the rules of the game. Only by knowing the rules could they be bent.

In emphasising the significance of what has been called the 'transactional' nature of meaning in the halls, it is also necessary to discriminate between the big city-centre halls and the host of smaller, provincial establishments. Particularly in the latter, audience participation was at a premium. In historical writing on the music halls, the former have received undue emphasis. A contemporary account of what were called 'low-class' halls in the industrial Lancashire of 1900 is particularly revealing here.[14] Familiarity and intimacy obtained between performers and audience and within the audience. Audiences were a real part of many of the stage performances. More direct involvement was evident in the encouragement of amateur 'turns', especially in the form of the Lancashire speciality of clog dancing. In Lancashire performances were scheduled to fit with the working times of the mills and factories. This closeness between the music hall and its popular constituency was also reflected in the content of performances.

Commentators blanched at what was termed 'the naked revelation of sordid aspects of domestic life' in these 'poor people's' music halls. Alongside the male and female 'swell' of fashion (themselves often offering commentary on proletarian life), were sympathetic stage figures such as the aged miner or the 'street arab', and the unsympathetic figures of authority, above all the policeman. Performers were quick to respond to the expectations of audiences, inflecting their performance to meet local demand. Twentieth-century accounts testify to the longevity of these characteristics. In inter-war Britain the renowned northern comic Sandy Powell adopted the manner and costume of the Scots when in Scotland, and of the miner when playing in the pit districts.[15] Writing in 1925 on the patter comedians' 'poetry of the gutter' D. C. Calthorp noted this acute responsiveness to popular tastes, especially in the case of the perennially favoured dialect turn. These took the forms of Scots, Cockney, Irish, 'Mummerset' and 'Lancashire Lad'. The latter, invested with the cultural symbolism of football, clogs, and the whippet, was the very epitome of heartiness and honest forthrightness.[16] Beyond these small-scale and informal, often less 'respectable' halls, were the still more informal entertainment pubs, in which amateurs and professionals were often pitched in together.[17] These particular settings or situations of the reception of popular art therefore put a very great emphasis on the collective and participatory.

Peter Bailey has perhaps done more than anyone to enable us to understand contemporary modes of perception in popular art, in this case the music hall. The 'transactional' nature of meaning is evident in his analysis of the 'swell song' of the later nineteenth century: the songs were essentially defined in use, exploiting a range of cues that drew the audience into 'an active dramatic recognition of its various social selves'.[18] This radically contextualised understanding of the generation of meaning at once serves to question notions of 'collective' authorship or reception. Audiences are, as it were, disaggregated: different elements of an audience defined themselves differently in relation to the performance, but also in relation to each other, for, as Bailey has indicated,[19] 'the language of the halls' was spoken within the audience as well, the audience also being in a sense performers. Audiences are disaggregated in another sense too, for it is important to emphasise that it was the 'various social selves' of audiences that were re-combined in the performance. Rather than reflecting or creating fixed and uniform patterns of identity the halls are better regarded as a laboratory of social style and self-definition in which both old ways and new possibilities were constantly explored. The performed arts of music hall and melodrama naturally set the highest premium on these dynamic aspects of meaning, yet they were also present in the ballad and dialect forms.

This contextualised perspective on meaning in fact makes one keenly aware just how important for an understanding of class discourse these forms of imaginative life were: the social order was not simply 'out there' in social and economic structures, but 'in here', being actively constructed in the imaginative life of audiences, albeit in the realisation of 'social selves' brought from outside. One is also aware, particularly from the specific example of the highly complex 'swell song', just how difficult the historian's talk of reconstitution is, representing as it does a hermeneutic operation upon a hermeneutic operation that was the audience's. As with the language of the halls, more widely was it the case too that meanings were often highly specific to particular contexts. Nonetheless, if not 'collective' in a simplified or monolithic sense, this term is still of considerable use in considering the nature of popular responses.

This is all the more the case when one turns from the settings or situations of use more directly to the manner of interpretation. If the 'selves' of individuals and audiences were not 'collective', then they were inherently social. Denning's recent work on popular fiction is again useful here.[20] Contrary to the private, individualised reader of naturalistic and realistic literary convention, 'pre-naturalistic' modes of presentation and reception suggest a more collective or at least 'social' reader. Unlike the hermeneutic code of the narrative in the 'high' fiction form of the novel, Denning emphasises how in 'low' fiction narrative should not be read as a developmental sequence (with truth lying at the end of expectation in a framework of psychological realism), but as allegory or metaphor. For instance, sensational fiction dealing with the 'working girl' become 'lady' and heroine should not be interpreted as wish-fulfilling, escapist fantasy. To do so would be to apply the irrelevant tenets of psychological realism. Rather, the working girl in question is both working girl *and* lady, a unity represented in the form of allegory. Understanding how narrative itself, as well as the literary character, can be read as metaphor and allegory enables us to understand how readers used fiction to explore personal life and social identity. The 'working girl' fictions Denning describes involved the reader in affirming both the daily life of the working girl and exploring the relations between the poor and the rich.

One is reminded here of Darnton's comment on another example of allegorical, pre-naturalistic fiction, the folk tale of the French peasant. Such tales were 'good to think with',[21] and also in a sense *goods* to think with, just as more widely in French peasant life, ritual, custom and proverbs comprised a kind of symbolic capital to be expended in handling, and making sense of, the work, family and community life of the peasant.[22] In the case of the English ballad, for instance, this instrumentality might be very direct: as Vicinus has shown, ballads were a means by which migrants in nineteenth-century urban England got to know the workings of city life, of shopkeepers, for example, or of landlords.[23] But the means of handling poverty, economic insecurity and the relative absence of power lay as much in the imagination as in simply learning the city ropes. The example drawn upon by Darnton is revealing in this respect. The cunning of the low-life trickster of the folk-tale helped him secure on the part of the poor a kind of psychic revenge upon the rich, the well-born and the powerful, a revenge engineered through ridicule and humiliation.[24] Thus it can be seen that popular art and the imagination concern the possession of knowledge about and hence control over one's circumstances. They are, in short, a form of knowing and empowering, functions which if magnified for the powerless poor are in fact intrinsic to all art, 'high' or 'popular'.

This business of empowerment goes far beyond 'escapism' or 'wish-fulfilment', yet these remain the terms in which popular art is so often seen. Darnton is a typical case, arguing that the effect of the peasant folk tale was in the end a kind of wish-fulfilment of no danger to the status quo of established power. In terms of British popular culture, Stedman Jones' account of late nineteenth-century music hall is still arguably the dominant one, not only of the halls but of popular culture more widely considered.[25] Escapism, consolation, wish-fulfilment; these are the terms to which the functions of the imagination are reduced. A more subtle variant on this theme is given in Sharrat's interesting account of melodrama.[26] He inverts the usual notion that melodrama was an escape from everyday life. Rather, the escape into the horrific and tempestuous world of melodrama enhances the familiarity and normality of the everyday. The 'normal world' is sanctioned and this is at the root of what (quite gratuitously) is taken to be the conformism and acquiescence of the working class. Related to this is the idea that melodrama offers a kind of pretended knowledge which displaces real knowledge and compensates for it.

A valuable corrective to all this is gained from Radford's recent treatment of romance, a genre particularly prone to this sort of misapprehension.[27] Using Northrop Frye's work, Radford dwells on how the wish-fulfilment present in the romance genre dissolves the boundaries between the actual and the potential, offering a vision of the possible, the future, the ideal. This utopianism is what makes romance such an important and representative form. Whether romance was enabling or disabling for the reader was a matter of personal and historical circumstance. The same may be said for the effects of melodrama we have noted (and of course applies to popular art more widely). Knowledge might be real and active; affirmation of the quotidian might be anything but acquiescent and conformist. Imagined utopias seem in fact to have been quite central to the workings of imaginative life at a popular level, releasing the ideal in order that it might be thought about, explored and used in all manner of ways.

This demotic utopianism should be differentiated from its better-known relatives, those well-documented utopias of literature, politics and social experimentation. On the contrary, little is known of this current. Its importance has been obscured by anachronistic accounts of popular *mentalité*, above all the mentality of a 'true' class consciousness. Similarly, the longing and aspirations involved in the utopian current were often ignored or misunderstood by contemporaries, not least the would-be leaders of popular opinion.[28] Before moving to a closer exploration, some general points may be made. The force of demotic utopianism may have been direct and overt: one thinks here of the aspiration to human fraternity, the desire to transcend the exclusiveness of class, so evident in nineteenth-century popular Liberalism. But the effect may have been indirect and in a sense hidden, a silent but strong force against change: what comes to mind here is the general failure of English socialism to comprehend the mental universe of the music hall, from which for the most part it held back aloof, judgemental and disdainful.

Existing accounts of popular literature begin to point to the significance of this utopian thinking and feeling. Denning's account shows how the allegories of cheap fiction are allegories of social redistribution, of justice and the just society. Yet they are just as much allegories of social reconciliation, the aspiration to justice taking the form of the aspiration to the realisation of human fellowship. In existing work, informed by prevailing class theory, this tends to be noted and forgotten. On the contrary, as will be seen, the emphasis on reconciliation was ever present and points to the essential character of popular conceptions of the social order. Dime fiction is in these respects very similar to the example of the ballads, with their theme of 'mundus inversus', the world turned upside down, though these themes are very old and evident far beyond the ballads. It should be added that this emphasis on equity and reconciliation, in which present society is interrogated at the bar of fantasy, is as likely to be radical as conservative.[29]

This account of the projections and functions of popular art immediately raises questions concerning the relationship between fatalism and hope, quiescence and utopian aspirations. The matter was broached earlier,[30] where the conservative implications of the culture of the new urban, industrial world of the late nineteenth-century worker were emphasised. A culture marked by order, boundary and control certainly had these implications, particularly when driven inwards by poverty and the demands of industrial discipline, so that a concern with 'station' or caste became obsessive, and the social order came to seem fixed and immutable. This outlook and its frequently conservative social and political consequences have been illustrated in several places in this book.[31] In central ways, therefore, the material experience of poverty, economic insecurity and work discipline was formative in the making of the culture of workers. But this experience and culture were not, of course, uniform.

Fatalism may often have been the opposite of hope, pulling in a contradictory direction. It may have characterised some more than others: the possibility was raised earlier that it may have characterised most the poorest and the most dependent. But in the end it is the broad uniformity of condition and outlook in the culture of the labouring poor that is striking, and it is rather the case that power and powerlessness, hope and fatalism, aspiration and accommodation, were not opposites but different sides of the same coin of poverty. It is this dialectic of poverty that popular art enables us to trace so closely. In the end, it is the utopian current that seems uppermost, in art as well as in life. A culture of control was about controlling adverse circumstances by gaining and giving dignity and respect. A concern with creating a sense of control over life led outwards as well as inwards. It involved a claim to be like all people, and so it involved a claim to justice. But it also involved the desire for human fraternity and reconciliation which sprang from this recognition of a basic human equality.

The need for power in often overwhelmingly hostile circumstances sometimes led to fatalism. The deformations of poverty were real but so was the vision of hope. Out of the conditions of industrial labour come the acknowledgement of boundaries but also the attempt to transcend them, an attempt that went far beyond some 'liminal' patrolling of boundaries all the better to clamp people back into their fixation with order. This section of this book therefore gives ample testimony to the desire to transcend social differences, to turn the world upside down and re-make it in a better image. Art reflected this but also enabled it. It involved, as I have argued, an empowerment of the poor that was real, not imaginary; or, more properly, real *because* it was imaginary.

At the same time, as was argued earlier, an account of the culture of urban workers as defined exclusively by poverty and labour is far too narrow a conception. People were not sealed in some hermetic condition of order. Like everyone else in society, they were open to the whole range of influences that made up the society of the time. They were members of parties, unions and congregations, readers of books and newspapers. As is amply plain, utopian influences emanated powerfully from all these areas. If the experience of poverty and labour refracted these influences it gives nothing like a full account of them. That kind of account is most evident in popular art, the means so often of combining together the diverse currents of hope and aspiration evident outside art. In exploring the various social selves of audiences art made this sort of exploration and synthesis possible.

10

The broadside ballad

The popularity of the broadside ballad continued much later than is commonly allowed. Far from being a hostile environment the industrial town seems if anything to have been congenial to the ballad. The banning of street music in 1860s' London hastened the ballad's decline there, but in regions such as industrial Lancashire one many note a living practice in the street ballad singing of out-of-work operatives in the 1860s Cotton Famine. Men toured Lancashire and Yorkshire singing traditional songs as well as songs especially composed and printed for the occasion. In normal times, too, as late as the 1870s and 80s, the streets of Lancashire mill towns were reported to be full of street singers.[1] In 1879 the citizens of Oldham got up a petition against the 'profane and debauched' singing of ballads in the street, especially on Sunday and by women as well as men. Ballads were published and sung to aid the victims of industrial accidents in mid-1880s' Bradford. Party political agitation relied on the ballad form to the end of the century. The proponents of the Manchester Ship Canal, advocates of economic modernity in the 1880s and 90s, turned with alacrity to the old-established ballads in propagandising their case.[2] The longevity, and something of the uses, of the ballad will be apparent.

The collections of the big printers seem to have been broken up and sold off in the 1870s and 80s. The effect of legal regulation, cheap newspapers, and the growth of alternative, commercial entertainment all took their toll, but it was only with the approach of the twentieth century that this centuries-old tradition was finally extinguished. Up to then press and music hall had in fact temporarily retarded the decline they were eventually to accelerate: the ballads fed voraciously off the newspaper press, as did the music hall, which in turn picked up streets ballads as well as feeding its own creations back into the literature of the streets.[3]

Something of the difficulty of interpreting ballads will already be evident. These difficulties are compounded by the vagaries of nineteenth-century collectors, who often employed their own peculiar principles of selection. I have used several local collections, and the great Madden collection at Cambridge University Library for ballads dated or in circulation in the nineteenth century up to the 1850s.[4] Covering ballad printers and sellers throughout the British

Isles – and going back to the 1770s – the very size of the collection suggests a representativeness compensating for any editorial bias on the part of the collector. The Madden collection has been examined to explore the typicality of the regional and local collections which are chiefly drawn upon in the analysis that follows. This typicality seems to be evident, though the local collections have a specificity of time and place lacking in the larger collections, and this is most important, enabling one to locate the workings of the ballads more exactly.

Most attention in what follows is given to the very specific example of the Pearson collection in Manchester Central Library, and to other collections covering (roughly) the period 1820s to 1870s.[5] The special value of the Pearson collection is that it forms the entire holdings of one ballad shop at one time, the seven hundred or so songs on sale in Pearson's Chadderton Street shop in central Manchester in 1873. It is not so much the size as the variety of the collections that daunts the ballad student. Very old ballads were sold alongside ballads commenting on current events. Some ballads can be dated, others cannot. Old ballads themselves might go through many reincarnations. Do old ballads and their themes signify continuities of outlook and expection? Are they merely the vestiges of former time, the stuff of nostalgia perhaps, the memories age had of youth (aspects which have considerable interest in their own right)? Many questions suggest themselves. Much remains to be known about sales, for example, about age and sex differences in the audience addressed, indeed about almost every aspect of ballad production and reception.[6]

One is aided in knowing what significance the broadside ballad had for nineteenth-century contemporaries by the comments of collectors and interested observers. Their enthusiasm is, however, immediately suspect. In the preceding discussion of custom it was seen how 'folklorists' and antiquarians invariably re-fashioned elements in popular life in the image of their own preconceptions. Nonetheless, the list of those describing the ballads as the true literature of the poor includes observes like Henry Mayhew, someone who had a closer and more realistic understanding of the poor than almost any of his contemporaries.[7] Lower down the social scale, the self-educated chronicler of Manchester popular manners and low life, Fred Leary, was adamant at the end of the century that the ballads had been the essential literary voice of the working class, especially the operatives, though it is revealing that 'the educated part' of the community was not immune from influence either.[8] Recent research on cheap ballad literature indicates that the writers, printers and publishers of the trade were socially fairly close to their popular audience, and extraordinarily sensitive to its tastes and expectations.[9]

Though part of the commercialisation of culture, the trade seems to have been led by, rather than leading, popular taste. This is evident in a rare glimpse into the provincial ballad trade of the 1850s by one 'Felix Folio'.[10] In reporting on the ballad shops and 'flying stationers' of Manchester (the hawkers seem to have been more important than the shops, though they dealt in the same material), ballads were said to be the special preserve of the lower and often illiterate working class. This may be so, but the matter was probably one of degree only. The ballad was so ubiquitous in popular culture, and so diverse in theme, that it seems very likely it reached all levels of the labouring population. In Felix Folio's acount the truly popular character of the literature is in fact clear. Tastes were often highly specialised. Dialect ballads were popular throughout the region, but – in standard English or in dialect – in weaving districts weaving songs, and in Irish districts Irish songs were in demand.

The spatial configurations of this literature are of considerable interest. Chapman distribution routes from the main provincial centres, but especially from London, were long established by 1800. The big London printers also had agents throughout the country. A high degree of plagiarism obtained, London being liberally pillaged by the provinces. However, there were limits to these metropolitan tendencies: the big provincal centres (for example, Preston, Newcastle, Manchester, Leeds) represented autonomous influences at work over regions and sub-regions,[11] and the small-town ballad trade was highly developed, as the Madden collection testifies. This balance was reflected in the content of the ballads. In terms of subjects and themes treated and conventions used there appears to be a fair degree of uniformity throughout the country (beyond England, too), so much so that it may be just to speak of a national ballad culture. The analysis of the content of the ballads that follows draws on the Pearson collection, but it is apparent that this highly specific example nonetheless reflected broader patterns (evident, for example, in the treatment of themes such as labour and nation).

These recurrent trans-local elements were, however, most often given a sharper definition by local concerns. There were distinctive regional and local traditions. For instance, in the industrial villages of early nineteenth-century Lancashire, or the pit villages of the north-east, there were village songs, taking up the themes of local occupational life, and of local amusements, especially fairs and wakes. In Littleborough, for example, just outside Rochdale, these songs circulated as part of an oral culture before being printed as broadsides.[12] Perhaps the most powerful of all local traditions was the dialect one, and long before the mid-century development of a self-conscious dialect literature in the northern industrial districts the dialect ballad was greatly popular in these same regions. One of many examples is that of Oldham, large towns as well as villages having distinct dialect traditions.[13] Usually anonymous local authors, together with local printers, turned out songs on local politics, on work, and on events in town life. Those productions drew on a range of references known only to those initiated in the mysteries of Oldham.[14] Despite broader changes in the tone of popular literature and entertainment, these very local ballads continued to be popular. For instance, the 'respectability' characteristic of dialect literature was accompanied by the older ballad .vein of bawdy and violent writing. This is evident in the Manchester and Oldham collections, and in the latter there is good evidence of strong internal traditions in the employment of a figure like 'Gentle Jone' (Gentle John), in the 1870s and 80s picking up the persona of early-century Oldham heroes to provide comic and satiric commentary on the present.[15]

The local and the regional could indeed be introspective and parochial. Certainly, for their full effect such ballads depended on local knowledge, as is evident in the Oldham case. Nonetheless, what this local knowledge often did was to re-work 'national' events and figures, and broader processes, in local terms: elections, wars, trade depressions, technological change, all these were made vivid and sensible to local experience. At the same time local experience was perfectly *au fait* with national developments. The Littleborough example is a good case: there were decidely local songs of limited currency, but also local songs reworking broader currents, and as such typical of what was going on in settlements throughout the country. At the same time, at one extreme from local songs in the oral culture, patriotic and 'British ballads' and the songs of Burns circulated, works uniform in character across localities. Indeed, as the example of dialect literature will show, nineteenth-century urbanisation and industrialisation in some respects created a greater regionalism if not parochialism in popular culture. Contrary to received wisdom in this matter, the ballads provide suggestive evidence of a rather homogeneous, extra-local popular culture long before the supposed emergence of a uniform working class in the 1830s and 40s. Perhaps the eighteenth-century 'plebeity' was more cosmopolitan than we give it credit for, the nineteenth-century 'working class' more introspective.

Thus, local and extra-local elements co-existed,[16] the 'national' being realised through the 'local', and the 'local' itself being in part assembled by means of conventions drawn from a broad tradition.

Both dimensions mattered: a Geordie or Tynesider might have felt peculiarly at home in the north-eastern ballad idiom, but he or she would not have felt completely at a loss when venturing far from home. This interplay of different levels indicates something of the living, innovative character of the ballads, an adaptiveness intimately related to how these songs were used by contemporaries to talk and think about the society they lived in.

Underlying these uses were more pragmatic ones, some of which have already been indicated. Whether pragmatic or not, the alacrity with which contemparies utilised ballads itself argues the resonance and malleability of the form. It needs to be emphasised, in this respect, that men and women frequently made up their own songs. Emphasis on the ballad trade should not obscure this, such home-made songs often subsequently entering the printed ballad canon. The closeness of the ballad form to popular culture, as well as its innovative potential, is reflected in these ordinary uses, say in the philanthropy of the poor to the poor, or in their frequent use in labour disputes, for instance in the great Preston dispute of 1853–54.[17] Ballads might be part of highly localised, neighbourhood agitations, and as such a weapon in the armoury of customary sanction. An example of this from the 1860s was the pillorying of a Leeds magistrate for persecuting a servant. The theme song of placards and 'rough music' seems to have been the rough, satiric rhymes of a ballad called 'Oh don't I love my dripping' (the servant girl was sentenced for giving away the JP's dripping).[18] As noted previously, the ballads were a means of handling the workaday vicissitudes of city life, arming the unwary in their transactions with landlords, for example, or publicans.

Ballads were also employed in managing more intimate aspects of everyday life: the themes of courtship (romantic and traumatic), and marriage (usually traumatic) were the largest staple of the ballad trade, an aspect of the songs that cannot be considered here. The ballads were a literature of advice, warning and admonition, a moral commentary on the life of the people that emerged from the settings of that life. Something of this is evident in accounts of ballad performance, accounts which are extremely rare. Flora Thompson's description of later nineteenth-century rural Oxfordshire indicates how through the evening different groups would sing different songs, songs of youth being sung by youths, middle-aged men taking up graver themes, and at the end of the evening songs which represented, and celebrated, the community as a whole were sung by the old or by all the singers combined.[19]

The more instrumental use of ballads involved the public and formal, as well as the informal life of communities and the private lives of individuals. Political ballads are the best example of this. These might emanate from the local party leaders in co-operation with the local 'party printer', but just as often these political ballads avoided the more routine and regimented aspects of political propaganda. They were an integral part of the loyalties bred by partisanship, especially when they were couched in the dialect idiom. Something of the capacity of the ballad to echo popular predilections is evident in Benjamin Grime's account of Oldham politics in the 1850s, this prim and disapproving Gladstonian Liberal looking back from the relative calm of the 1880s. The cries and ballads of the extraordinarily violent and feeling political culture of the 50s 'were too expressive of the struggles and emotions that animated the body of the people during these periodical conflicts, and they enabled the great untaught to give vent to sarcasm and turbulent passions which ardour and zeal aroused within them. These rhymes were an easy way for the masses to express their sympathies and their antipathies. Reduced to verse in the native language of the locality, and adapted to some popular tune, the populace sang aloud or hummed their hopes and aspirations in a style of language suited to their intelligence.'[20]

This 'singing of aspiration' spoken of by Grime was important. It indicates the capacity of the ballads to serve as a vehicle that could be adapted in many different ways. Yet there is the other side, too, the element of precedent, defined by the expectations of audiences and the conventions of the ballad form itself. The latter in a sense set limits to what could be expressed in the guise of conventions of style, theme and so on. Despite their flexibility, the ballad privileged certain views of the world and denied others. The same could be said for other forms of art: the melodrama, for example, dealt in conventions that lent themselves to clearly delineated moral opposites, especially those of good and evil, also perhaps to notions of individual rather than 'social' causality and responsibility. Conventions of style were not divorced from the sense of precedent enforced by audiences. In what follows these two aspects, the capacity for innovation and the weight of precedent, will be traced. The flexibility of the ballads was operative within precedent. Indeed, it could be argued that simply *because* the ballads were so flexible in use, the attachment to conventions of form and of outlook is all the more striking. People *chose* to work within expected frameworks of artistic convention which in turn represented rather old and long-established ways of seeing the social order.

If the weight of the present argument falls rather more on the side of precedent, the aspect of innovation nonetheless needs to be forcibly urged, and, if one identifies the tenacity of older ways of

representing the world under the heading of 'populism', then this
populism was itself never static. Rather, it was capable of great
development in its various appropriations and uses. The innovativeness of the ballad tradition is apparent in its function as a form
of social commentary and, indeed, of social morality (as we have
seen, the ballads both distilled and proffered popular wisdom). This
is apparent in the actual form of ballads. They might have spoken as
well as sung parts, or other internal flexibilities of structure, which
allowed for extemporary commentary on passing events. This
function of commentary can best be illustrated by discussion of one
particular ballad from nineteenth-century industrial Lancashire, the
ballad of 'Jone o'Grinfilt' (John of Greenfield, Greenfield being a
weaving village near Oldham). The Lancashire ballad collector
John Harland published six versions of the song, and mentions a
total of thirteen.[21] The original version recounts the enlistment of the
starving 'Owdham' weaver to fight in the French wars. He fights
willingly if under the spur of poverty. The qualified, ironic patriotism
is balanced by the sharp realisation of poverty, and by Jone's
attachment to his town and trade. 'Jone o'Grinfilt's Return' was
more decidedly patriotic. The whole text of the original 'Jone' is
given here, after Hollingworth's 1977 edition:

Jone o'Grinfilt

Says Jone to his woife on a whot summer's day,
'Aw'm resolvt i' Grinfilt no lunger to stay;
For aw'll goo to Owdham os fast os aw can
So fare thee weel, Grinfilt, an' fare thee weel, Nan;
For a sodger aw'll be, an' brave Owdham aw'll see;
An' aw'll ha'e a battle wi' thi' French.'

'Dear Jone,' said eawr Nan, un' hoo bitterly cried,
'Wilt be one o' th' foote, or theaw meons for t' ride?'
'Od eawns! wench, aw'll ride oather ass or a mule,
Ere aw'll keawer i' Grinfilt os black os th' dule,		*hide away, devil*
Both clemmin', un' starvin', un' never a fardin',	*being hungry and cold*
It 'ud welly drive ony mon mad.'

'Ay, Jone, sin' we coom i' Grinfilt for t' dwell,
Wey'n had mony a bare meal, aw con vara weel tell.'
'Bare meal, ecod! ay, that aw vara weel know,
There's bin two days this wick 'ot wey'n had nowt at o';
Aw'm vara near sided, afore aw'll abide it,		*decided*
Aw'll feight oather Spanish or French.'

Then says my Noant Marget, 'Ah! Jone, theaw'rt so whot,
Aw'd ne'er go to Owdham, boh i'England aw'd stop.'

'It matters nowt, Madge, for to Owdham aw'll goo,
Aw'st ne'er clem to deeoth, boh sumbry shall know: *somebody*
Furst Frenchmon aw find, aw'll tell him meh mind,
Un' if he'll naw feight, he shall run.'

Then deawn th' broo aw coom, for weh livent at top,   *hill*
Aw thowt aw'd raich Owdham ere ever aw stop;
Ecod! heaw they staret when aw getten to th' Mumps,
Meh owd hat i' my hont, un' meh clogs full o' stumps
Boh aw soon towd 'um, aw're gooin' to Owdham,
Un' aw'd ha'e a battle wi' th' French.

Aw kept eendway thro' th' lone, un' to Owdham aw went, *straight on*
Aw ax'd a recruit if they'd made up their keawnt?
'Nowe, Nowe, honest lad' (for he tawked like a king),
'Go wi' meh thro' th' street, un' thee aw will bring
Wheere, if theaw'rt willin', theaw may ha'e a shillin'.'
Ecod! aw thowt this wur rare news.

He browt meh to th' pleck, where they meaurn their height, *place*
Un' if they bein height, there's nowt said abeawt weight;
Aw ratched meh un' stretch'd meh, un' never did flinch:
Says th' mon, 'Aw believe theaw'rt meh lad to an inch.'
Aw thowt, this'll do; aw'st ha'e guineas enoo.
Ecod! Owdham, brave Owdham for me.

So fare thee weel, Grinfilt a soger aw'm made:
Aw getten new shoon, un' a rare cockade;
Aw'll feight for Owd England os hard os aw con,
Oather French, Dutch, or Spanish, to me it's o' one;
Aw'll mak 'em to stare, like a new-started hare,
Un' aw'll tell 'em fro' Owdham aw coom.

On the other hand, 'Jone o'Greenfield Junior' is a searing indictment of the effect of the post-war depression on the handloom weavers, in which the parson and the putter-out are bitterly criticised. This version was very popular at the time, and Harland mentions that the last three lines had become household words in the Lancashire of his own day. Harland's first edition was 1865; this follows Hollingworth's 1977 edition:

Jone o'Greenfield Junior, or Th' Owdham weyver

I'm a poor cotton weaver, as many a one knows,
I've nowt to eat i' th' house and' I've worn out my cloas   *clothes*
You'd hardly give sixpence for all I have on,

My clugs they are brossen and stockings I've none,   *bursted*
You'd think it wur hard to be sent into th' world,
To clem and do th' best 'ot you con.   *starve*

Our church parson kept telling us long,
We should have better times if we'd hold our tongues,
I've houden my tongue till I can hardly draw breath,
I think i' my heart he means to clem me to death;
I know he lives weel by backbiting the de'il,
But he never picked o'oer in his life.   *threw a shuttle (i.e. wove)*

I tarried six week an' thought every day wur t' last,
I tarried and shifted till now I'm quite fast;
I lived on nettles while nettles were good,
An' Waterloo porridge were best of my food;
I'm telling you true I can find folks enew,
That are living no better than me.

Old Bill o'Dans sent bailiffs one day,
For a shop score I owed him that I could not pay,
But he wur too late, for old Bill o'Bent,
Had sent tit and cart and ta'en goods for rent,   *horse*
We had nou bur a stoo', that wur a seat for two,   *only*
An on it cowered Margit and me.

The bailiffs looked round as sly as a mouse,
When they saw aw things were ta'en out ot house,
Says one to the other, "All's gone, thou may see,"
Aw sed, "Lads, never fret, you're welcome to me;"
They made no more ado, but nipp'd up th' owd stoo',
And we both went wack up' th' flags.   *stone floor*

I geet howd of Margit, for hoo wur strucken sick,   *she*
Hoo sed hoo ne'er had such a bang sin hoo wur wick,   *alive*
The bailiffs scoured off with owd stoo' on their backs,   *scampered*
They would not have cared had they brook our necks,
They're mad at owd Bent cos he's ta'en goods for rent,
And wur ready to flee us alive.   *flay*

I sed to our Margit as we lay upo' th' floor,
We shall never be lower in this world, I'm sure,
But if we alter I'm sure we mun mend,
For I think in my heart we are both at far end,
For meat we have none nor looms to weave on,
Egad, they're as weel lost as found.

Then I geet up my piece and I took it 'em back,   *piece of woven cloth*
I scarcely dare speak, mester looked so black,   *employer*

He said, 'You wur o'er paid last time you coom,'
I said, 'If I wur 'twas for weaving bout loom;   *without*
In a mind as I'm in I'll ne'er pick o'er again,
For I've woven mysl' to th' fur end.'   *far*

Then aw coom out and left him to chew that,
When aw thought again aw wur vext till aw sweat,
To think that we mun work to keep them and awth' set,
All the days o' my life and still be in their debt;
So I'll give o'er trade, an' work with a spade,
Or go and break stones upo' th' road.

Our Margit declare if hoo'd cloas to put on,
Hoo'd go up to Lundun an' see the big mon,   *i.e. the king*
An' if things didn't alter when hoo had been,
Hoo swears hoo'll feight blood up to th' e'en,
Hoo's nought again th' King, but likes a fair thing,
An' hoo says hoo can tell when hoo's hurt.

The bitterness and the claim to fairness evident in this song, and especially clear in the last three lines, signify feelings that took a more ostensibly political and radical form in 'Jone o'Grinfilt's visit to Mr Fielden' and in 'Dialogue and Song, Between Captain Swing and Jone o'Greenfield'.[22] The latter is in fact a nice illustration of the relationship of local and regional to broader currents mentioned above. In the symbolic meeting of these two popular heroes, the agitation of the rural is joined to that of the industrial districts, the northern ballad writer showing a keen and nuanced awareness of the national pattern in the process. Swing is rendered in standard English, 'Jone' in dialect, the cutural identity of the region on the large stage thereby being asserted. One suspects a radical hand here, but the point could be made for non-political ballads with equal force.

A radical hand seems decidely present in 'Jone o'Grinfilt's Ramble...', a skit on the Queen Caroline Affair, and in a 'Jacobin' parody of the original, noted by Harland but not printed. In the 1850s the patriotic vein re-asserted itself again in 'Jone o'Greenfield Gooin To Th' Rooshan War' (the Crimean War). Regional associations are here appropriated to new versions of the national cause, ones less radical than hitherto. What is amply evident here is that the ballads were not the creation of an anonymous, collective 'people'. In the case of 'Jone o'Grinfilt' the original was written by Joseph Lees, a Glodwick (near Manchester) weaver, perhaps with the help of Joseph Coupe, barber, spinner, tooth drawer, carder and turner.[23] Looking more closely at the emergence of ballads what

becomes evident is the importance of particular individuals, families
and locations. John Grimshaw of Gorton is a case in point. For a
good deal of the first half of the century still a domestic-industrial
village, Gorton seems to have been fertile ground for popular song,
much of which eventually found its way into the printed ballad form.
As with centres of dialect literary production slightly later on,[24] these
older (especially handloom weaving) *milieux* seem to have been
particularly significant.

Individual singers were said to have come to Gorton to sing the
'Jone o'Grinfilt' ballads in local pubs. Known as 'Common'
Grimshaw, John Grimshaw composed some of the finest early
nineteenth-century ballads dealing with the effects of economic
changes, such as 'Hand Loom versus Power Loom' and 'The Hand
Loom Weavers' Lament'.[25] John Beswick of Gorton, known as
Parish Jack, was a singer, flautist and fiddler at the village 'stirs', for
which he was paid in kind, not in cash. He also sang in the local
church choir and composed many songs. A nephew of Beswick's is
reported to have carried on the tradition of singing (if not of
writing), one sighting being made in a Gorton pub in the 1860s, at
the unlikely event of the christening of a favourite dog. Long before
this, one 'Lucas' of Gorton, an illiterate textile worker, composed
the very popular 'Grimshaw's Factory Fire' in 1790.[26] In Ashton,
the slightly more literary hand of John Stafford published a book of
songs in 1840.[27] Some of these were decidely radical and political,
others provided humorous and satiric commentary on local religious
sects like the 'Joannas', or on the life of the local pitmen. In form and
content these were very similar to the ballad, but it is not known if
these circulated as ballads before 1840. These indications of local
traditions show the presence of individuals behind the abstraction
'tradition'. At the same time, the strong roots of these individuals in
particular communities suggest the more collective, selective and
precedent-enforcing activity already noted.

This active use of the ballad as a kind of social commentary seen
in the case of the 'Jone o'Grinfilt' songs overlapped with the
function of moral commentary. Both functions were in turn
intimately related to what is for present purposes regarded as the
most important function of the ballad, namely its role in the
cultivation of social identities. Ballads circulating in mid-nineteenth-
century Manchester illustrate the coming together of all three
aspects.[28] Songs like 'Bell Vue Goal', The Sewing Machine',
'Tinkers Gardens' or 'The Manchester Omnibus' dwell, amongst
other themes, on young love and its perils (chiefly pregnancy and
enforced marriage). The first three verses of 'The Manchester
Omnibus' are given here, also the fifth, out of a total of six verses:

In Manchester lived a servant girl,
And whose mistress sent her to Belle Vue,
And she thought as how she might do worse,
Than ride in a Manchester Omnibus.
    A green and yellow omnibus,
    A regular Manchester omnibus,
    So she thought as how she might do worse,
    Than have a ride in an omnibus.
                    With a rum, tum, etc.

She sat in a seat against the door,
Because there was no room before,
And as she was just sitting thus,
She looked at the conductor of the omnibus;
    She laughed at the conductor of the omnibus,
    She winked at the conductor of the omnibus,
    She thought there might be men much worse,
    Than conductors of a Manchester omnibus.

Now this conductor was not so green,
As not to know what she did mean,
And though for her he didn't care a fuss,
Yet he chatted with her in the omnibus.
    He popped his head in the omnibus,
    He kissed her in the omnibus,
    'And', says 'meet me tonight you must',
    As he handed her out of the omnibus.
        [Spoken – Never mind the bob]

...

At length the time arrived, egad,
When this servant girl was brought to bed,
'O lawks! O dear!' exclaims the nurse,
The child's marked on the back with an omnibus.
    A green and yellow omnibus,
    A regular Manchester omnibus,
    And the nurse she said to make things worse
    That the accident happened in an omnibus

...

Such songs formed a literature of exhortation, admonition and advice, all in a comic mode. At the same time the songs also comment freely on the new sights and sounds of Manchester life. Commentary and morality come together, and in so doing the forms and motifs of the traditional ballad are transposed to the streets of Manchester where they celebrate city life and the character of the city dweller. This celebration in turn deals in quite deliberately orchestrated popular identities, which were also reflections of the ballad audience's expectations. In the ballads already cited this affirmation of identity in new social surroundings is apparent. It is also evident in ballads dealing with work and new industrial conditions. Songs such as 'The Dashing Steam Loom Weaver', 'Flare Up Factory Girl', 'The Girls of Lancashire' or 'Sam Shuttle and Betty Reedhook' convey in their titles alone this capacity to adapt traditional motifs to enunciate and celebrate new identities, in this case that of the collective life of the worker in factory industry.[29] The first three verses of 'Sam Shuttle' give the flavour of these:

> I'm going for to give you
>> A very strange narration;
> But what I tell is really true,
>> Of my own observation.
> A lass there was and as nice a one
>> As any on you'd need look,
> She was a steam loom weaver,
>> And they called her Betty Reedhook.
>>> Tow, row, row, &c.

> There was a chap in love with her,
>> He said quite to distraction,
> And wanted ill to marry her
>> In spite of all objection;
> This was an overlooker,
>> That came aft her loom to fettle,, *adjust*
> He worked at th' top o' th' Lacky Moor
>> And they called him Sammy Shuttle.
>>> Tow, row, row, &c.

> Now Betty couldn't bear this chap,
>> Tho' some fine things he took her,
> A spark ith' warehouse won her, slap,
>> He was a sly Cut Looker;
> And when she took her cuts to him,
>> They'd so much fun and prate, sir,
> He always past o'er all her faults,
>> And never used to bate her. *fine*
>>> *Tow, row, row, &c.*

The same process can be seen at work in the various appropriations of the 'Jone o'Grinfilt' character. There the motifs of the handloom weaver and handloom weaving were not transposed but directly retained. This was reflected, for instance, in the continuing popularity, well into the second half of the century, of 'Jone

O'Greenfield Junior' in particular (late re-christened 'The Oldham Weaver'). But as will be apparent in the discussion of dialect, the extraordinary resonance of the hand-working heritage and the talismanic quality of the handloom weaver, particularly in his 'Jone' manifestation, did not betoken a residual conservatism or a sense of nostalgia. Rather, they point to the use of the past to create social identities which handled present questions and conditions. Something of the creativity and innovativeness of the ballad form will be apparent, and this in turn indicates the necessity of approaching with caution the idea that ballads enshrined unchanging patterns of thought or uniform outlooks on the world.

In turning now to a closer examination of the nature of the social identities, and hence of the understandings of the social order, revealed in the ballads, it will be apparent that if such caution needs to be applied it is nonetheless clear that fairly coherent patterns do emerge. These suggest the limits precedent set to innovation. The 'populism' that describes this coherent pattern was an outlook which if varying in meaning over time nonetheless reveals a considerable degree of consistency as well. Exploration of ballad themes and their applications suggests this persistence of older ways of seeing the world. In considering conceptions of social identity and the social order the Pearson collection offers the most revealing insight into the dominant themes. The representation of England as 'Old England' was pervasive, and many of the ballads convey a rather uncritical patriotism in their praise of military glory (Admiral Nelson's victories, for example), of the monarchy, and of the glories of British institutions, especially the Constitution. It can be noted in passing that many of the ballads are about Old Ireland as well: in these the sense of past become present is perhaps even stronger than in the English case. Old rebel and new Fenian songs jostled for prominence with representations of a romantic Ireland found especially in love songs and songs of emigration. The patriotism evident in the English songs is by no means solely uncritical. It often took the form of what can be termed a libertarian constitutionalism, which powerfully echoed the popular radicalism of the early nineteenth century. In the later nineteenth century this current flowed in the direction of popular Liberalism, as well as popular Toryism.

In 'Success to the Derby Statue', the frequently used convention of the notables' visit to the locality is evident. In this case a party political use of the ballad is evident, Lord Derby being exalted as the great aristocratic hero of Lancashire popular Toryism. Tory sentiments of the organic union of altar, throne and cottage were reflected in ballads such as 'My Ancestors were Englishmen'. Across the political divide, 'Garribaldi and Freedom' echoed an alternative vision of liberty, nation and progress. Both political parties, however, emphasised how British institutions were the guarantee of liberty.

In doing so they clearly drew upon widely prevalent beliefs, present far beyond the party sphere alone. Ballads such as the early nineteenth-century 'White Cliffs of Albion' continued to be very popular, the liberties of Albion being the historically sanctioned inheritance of the 'Free Born Englishman' (the antique term is used quite frequently in the ballads of the 1870s).[30] The first three verses of the 'White Cliffs of Albion' go as follows:

> On the white cliffs of Albion, as musing I stood,
> Surveying the waves of the rough swelling flood,
> I saw from the surface a female arise,
> And with wings like an eagle she mounted the skies.
>
> Her figure was noble, and comely her mien,
> I looked and knew it was Liberty's Queen;
> With sword in her hand she shouts as she flies,
> Ye rulers of Britain be prudent and wise.
>
> For this island I chose, long before you had birth,
> For the seat of my empire, the freest on earth;
> And tho' you have forged them, no chains will she wear,
> Nor e'er be enslav'd whilst a sword I can bear.

In turn, this idealisation of 'Old England' sits beside notions of the 'good old days' of youth, and the 'good old town', though the chief embodiment of the past seems to have been the nation in its constitutional guise. This libertarian constitutionalism was an important vehicle for the wider representations of society made in the ballads. It is a current that was decidely 'popular', or populist, for it was the liberties of the English (less so the British) people as a whole that were at issue. While, as we have seen, 'the people' could at certain times be equated with the working people of England, the populist element is the most striking. This is especially apparent in the way English liberties are held to be inseparable from characteristics of temperament seen to be the preserve of the nation as a whole (an obvious example being the figure of a frank and hearty John Bull).

Representations of the monarchy are also of interest. The crown is positively, even fulsomely, regarded, yet the ballads very characteristically tend to humanise the mighty by presenting them in the guise of ordinary people. In a sense the subject of such ballads is not the monarchy at all but 'ordinary people' themselves. Ballads presenting royal and aristocratic visitations not only re-cast the persona of the great, but also celebrate the day itself and people's enjoyment of it. This humanising of the mighty, conferring upon them honorary plebeian status, is characteristic far beyond the ballads. So too is the self-celebration. Together with a libertarian constitutionalism in which the sense of the people's birthright was immensely strong, these aspects betoken that sense of control or mastery over the world spoken of earlier as so characteristic of popular literature. The people were held to be a part of the great world, their exaltation stemming from inversions of the established order which involved their inclusion in the company of their equals, the mighty, or in the great traditions of the nation.

The 'freeborn Englishman' was but one manifestation of a mythologised England. Pervading these various recuperations of a mythical past was a powerful sense of loss. Yorkshire ballads of a period somewhat earlier than the Pearson collection, Manchester, convey this well. The 'Fine Old English Gentleman' summons up a world of paternalist obligations in 'the olden time', and this is contrasted with the abrogation of such obligations in the present time conveyed in 'The Fine Young English Gentleman', or 'The New Fashioned Farmer'. 'Then and Now' explicitly links the New Poor Law to new-fashioned farmers and to the police. In the Manchester ballads, as more widely, the New Poor Law was a potent symbol of change; the measure of a present criticised by reference to the evocative symbolism of past plenty, above all in the shape of the roast beef of Old England.[31] This striking contrast of plenty and want, of the open and the closed hand, persisted long after the immediate implementation of the New Poor Law of 1834. One variant of these themes was the notion of the 'good old town', and the full text of 'Our Merry Town' in the 1870s Pearson collection is given in appendix 8.

In imagining a past to negotiate the present such ballads also constituted imagined futures, and these took the form of the utopian current that was such a central aspect of the imaginary constitution of society. The past directly informed the future, infusing it with the sense of lost rights, of an ideal England of the old times in which respect for rights was accompanied by respect between farmer and labourer, gentleman and commoner, high and low. What seems to have been present was a hoped-for world in which what was lost might be found again: the ballads clearly convey a strong attachment to what might be termed 'paternalism', though the uses and different versions of the myth of a paternalist past were numerous, and were always accompanied by the sense of lost rights. However, perhaps the most significant framework for this kind of imaginative projection into utopia was the moral contrast of rich and poor. These categories were in fact quite central to the representation of society evident in the ballads. As such they seem rather different to the categories of class.

The category of 'the poor' was decidely given content by the values and attributes of labour. It might be made up of the 'labouring poor' or 'the workingman'. Nonetheless, if honest toil and the good of the workingman are seen as respectively the root and purpose of a properly functioning society, then there is little or no sense of labour and capital as the basic social dichotomy, let alone a distinction conflictual in character. Exploitation in turn is seen as extrinsic to production, being located in moral and not economic realms. The use of an explicitly class vocabulary is notable by its absence. Indeed, the emphasis on the value of labour has perhaps more in common with the centuries-old, European-wide depiction of labour as part of a society of orders or ranks: the lord fights for all, the priest prays for all, and the labourer (or peasant or workingman) pays for all. What appears to be the case is that the value of labour is recognised and asserted yet is subsumed in the larger and looser terms of rich and poor, the content of which extends far beyond the attributes of labour alone and shapes the conception of society directly and in its own ways. Before turning to this it is worth dwelling briefly on some of the aspects of labour seen in the ballads.

The use of motifs and conventions to represent the present life of the worker has been noted, yet this went hand in hand – in industrial Manchester – with the association of labour with rural England. The poacher was a principal character in the ballads of the city dweller. 'The Claughton Wood Poachers' dwells upon game as the gift of God, the property of all men and not the landowner. The very popular 'Bonny Moor Hen' – a miner's song and so a reminder of the agricultural links of many industrial workers – speaks of the miner as bred to hunt game. Locked in battle with the mineowner the pitman will die for the bonny moor hen. The rights of labour are linked to the idea of rights to the natural produce of the land, but above all, perhaps, to the notion of freedom and independence summoned up in the idea of the pursuit of game on the free, open moors. It will already be apparent how potent this set of themes was among the articulate and active working class:[32] here their powerful popular resonances are evident.[33] Rural and urban labour in the 1870s in fact forged bonds of sympathy: the songs of Arch's agricultural labourers' union circulated in Manchester and were sung at large union gatherings.[34]

It is also worth remembering that the stock-in-trade of the ballad seller remained the vast array of romantic, rural love ballads. This was so in Manchester as in all the urban centres. Such ballads were populated by conventional heroes and heroines such as squires, milkmaids, farmers, sailors and so on. The stereotyped squire-aristocrat was the central symbolic figure here, and in particular it was he – and not the capitalist employer – who was the chief enemy of the labouring man or 'the people'.[35] Of course, this roll-call of rural England was the stuff of an already ossified convention in many places. Even so, the dead weight of convention had its own inertia, and of course – as has been seen – rural England was by no means a dead letter in the urban England of the 1870s. This aside, it is apparent how important for the urban worker the mythology of the rural world was: the paternalist world of the rural past might be summoned up, but so too was the attendant symbol of the poacher, limiting and defining the mutual obligations of that world by the recourse to rights and freedoms.

Returning to the theme of rich and poor, Colls has aptly commented on the outlook of north-eastern workers in this period that 'the proof of labour value was the pudding of ostentatious wealth'.[36] What this betokens is that injustice and social failings were understood not in economic terms, but in what may be termed moral ones, above all in terms of the moral oppositions summoned up by the concrete forms wealth and poverty took. The attributes and values of labour were an important part, but only a part, of this moral constellation. As Colls sees in the north-eastern case, it was not so much the capitalist employer who figured as the opponent, but the despot and the hypocritical, unproductive and ostentatious rich. In the ballads, songs such as 'The Loom and the Lathe' shout hurrah for the sons of toil: the happy man lives by the sweat of his brow. The rich, who do not, are troubled and are rather to be pitied than despised.

The 'Loom and the Lathe' goes as follows, the middle two verses being omitted here:

> Like most other men who've been knocking about,
>   Strange places and persons I've seen,
> Sometimes I've had plenty, sometimes been without,
>   And frequently hard up I've been.
> But still tho' dame fortune has been a sad jade,
>   And baulked me of many a prize,
> What I see I remember, and some say I've made
>   A pretty good use of my eyes.

> CHORUS
> Then hurrah! for the loom and the lathe.
>   Hurrah! for the spade and the plough.
> The happiest man I have met with is he
>   Who lives by the sweat of his brow.

The laywers, with eagerness, pocket the fees,
    But look at them well and you'll find,
Tho' they live in great style, and appear at their ease,
    They're frequently troubled in mind;
The parsons have duties from morning to night
    If they do them but yet I'm afraid,
The living is that, in which most they delight,
    And they make their religion a trade

...

The higher the station the more we require,
    And the more we're expected to do,
The greater the income, the more we desire,
    I'm sure you'll acknowledge that's true,
The more we possess, the more anxious we get,
    For fear that our wealth should be lost,
The path of the rich is with troubles beset,
    As many have found to their cost.

So! Happy is he on himself who depends
    If he has but contentment and health,
For industry more to his happiness tends,
    Than either position or wealth.
I envy not those who great riches have got
    For wealth is often a ban,
For he has the best and the happiest lot
    Who works – gets – and speaks as a man.

The 'Factory Girl' contrasts the dignity of toil with the idleness and
gentility of the rich, but as in 'The Loom and the Lathe' where the
themes of content and trouble suggest wider vistas, so in this song the
idea of labour introduces opposites shaped by the larger categories of
rich and poor, in this case the contrast between the falsity and
frippery of the rich and the honesty and integrity of feeling evident
among the poor.[37]
    The ballads mounted a kind of investigation and celebration of
poverty and its lessons. Poverty was rendered from the inside. 'Days
When I Was Hard Up' enjoins the auditor to wear the ragged coat
of poverty with pride; and 'Poor Married Man' combines this with
a clear awareness of the extremities and humiliations of poverty:

In the days when I was hard up, I bowed my spirits down,
And often I've sought out a friend, to borrow half a crown.
How many are there in the world, whose evils I can scan,
The shabby suit of toggery, but cannot see the man.

In the days when I was hard up, I found a blissful hope,
It's all the poor man's heritage, to keep him from the rope;
But I've found a good old maxim, and this shall be my plan
Altho' I wear a ragged coat, I'll wear it like a man.

and, from 'Poor Married Man',

He has no shirt, especially on one day,
When he lays at home without it on Sunday,
While the old gal rubs it out for Monday,

He live [*sic*] on sodgers, rashers, faggots,
        Poor married man.
When in luck black ornament and chances the maggots,
        Poor married man.
Dreams of blows out, kitchen cleanings,
Fancies he's Lord Mayor when eating tongue parings,
And longs for the time of cheap fresh herrings,
        Poor married man.

Last scene that ends the man's history,
        Poor married man.
He died, how he liv'd has been a mystery,
        Poor married man.
Grim death comes loudly to releive [*sic*] him,
Friends so poor, no time to grieve him,
And a parish egg chest perhaps may receive him.
        Poor married man.

The besetting sins of the rich are deviousness and hypocrisy: in 'How to Get Rich' the acquisition of wealth is indeed seen as inseparable from these failings. Thus it is that the superiority of poverty to riches is innate: the poor are inherently the moral superiors of the rich, in 'Rich and Poor' (and how characteristic the titles are!), hypocrisy is joined with an unfeeling ostentation represented in the conspicuous consumption, the deliberate flaunting, of wealth.[38] It is the external signs of pride in riches that enrage the author. The full text of 'Rich and Poor' will be found in appendix 9. The tendency to symbolise wealth in its concrete expressions is marked throughout popular art, not unexpectedly, given that for poor people poverty might be an empty table, riches a full one (the great emotive force of food is considered in the next chapter). Political songs circulating earlier than these ballads in the Ashton area of the early 1840s indicate the importance to the radical critique of oppression of the themes of ostentatious idleness: those who eat while we starve are berated, their vices being symbolised in the pheasants, turtles and champagne they consume.[39] In the 1870s, in 'An Imaginary Dialogue Between Mr Gladstone and A Working Man', ostentation and idleness are inverted to figure again the moral poor, useful and temperate in contrast here to the parasitic and grinding rich.[40] The poor now demand their rights as in the sight of God rich and poor are all alike.

This note of a common humanity indicates something of the complexity and, indeed, the contradictions which accompanied these representations of poverty. (Such contradictions, if they are such, are not surprising; the ballads were not a treatise or programme.) The emphasis on the innate superiority of poverty would suggest the belief that distinctions of wealth should be obliterated. Yet there is also present in the idea of ostentatious wealth the implication of proper or just wealth. Indeed, one attitude emerging strongly is that if rich and poor recognise their common humanity, then distinctions of wealth are acceptable. This is so because in recognising fraternity the obligations of fraternity will naturally follow. Both attitudes to differences of wealth are, however, present in the ballads.

The centrality of the rich and poor distinction is amply apparent: in 'Rich and Poor' society is explicitly described as made up of these two great 'classes'. The familiar theme of one law for the rich and one for the poor is evident. The religious dimension is also apparent again: the question is asked, 'where shall the rich be on Judgement Day?' In the 'Dialogue Between Mr Gladstone and A Working Man' the belief that in God's sight all men are alike is the cue for a powerful denunciation of the cruelties of the rich, but what the song also points to most forcibly is the time when rich and poor will unite and act as brothers. The song wishes God-speed to the time when pride and distinction will be gone and all men shall act as the brothers they will be in heaven. This theme is present in 'Remember the Poor':[41] in the Second Coming the rich and poor must lie down together. The last two verses of 'Remember the Poor' are followed by the final two responses in the Gladstone dialogue,

> But a thaw will ensue when the waters increase,
> And the rivers again they will flow
> When the fish from confinement obtain a release,
> And in danger the dwellers do go;
> When your paths are annoy'd by the proud swelling flood
> And your bridges are useful no more,
> When in peace you enjoy everything that is good,
> Do not grudge to remember the poor.
>
> The time it will come when our Saviour on earth
> And the world will agree with one voice,
> All Nations unite to salute the blest morn,
> And the whole of the world will rejoice;

When grim death is depriv'd of its hardkilling sting,
And the grave reigns triumphant no more,
Saints, Angels and Men, Hallejuhahs will sing,
And the rich must lie down with the Poor.

The vision of the springtime of human fraternity is echoed in the Dialogue;

Working Man.

'We do not crave for gold,
But all we ask is right,
Of better times we have been told
By men like *you* and *Bright*;
You may be clever, honest men,
Of course we must not doubt it,
We tell you what we want, and then,
Like rebles [*sic*] we are routed,
You must not think that we are fools,
Devoid of understanding,
For years gone by we've been your tools,
But now, we are demanding;
The rights of men, who toil each day,
Though not of noble station,
And Justice, demands a fair days pay.
To the supportes [*sic*] of your nation.

I trust the time will not be long,
God speed the happy hour,
When pride and distinction will be gone
Between the rich and poor;
From pride and all such nonsence [*sic*] part,
From you forever more,
Would it not move the hardest heart,
To see the suffering poor.
Mortals starving day by day,
Midst cold and bitter jeer,
Deserted to their God they pray,
And find relief in tears;
Be kind and never wound a heart,
But heal thy brother's sore,
And when from worldly care we part,
We'll meet to part no more.'

In 'Things I Should like to See', as the title suggests, the implicitly utopian becomes the explicitly utopian. The utopia in question is once again one in which fraternity matters as much as equality, and social distinctions such as those of wealth are seen as a bar to social reconciliation and the realisation of a common humanity. However, the millenarian expectation is that distinctions of wealth will somehow be ended.

Perhaps of equal note in representations of poverty is the acceptance of distinctions of wealth when the rich recognise their humanity and its obligations. Disparities of wealth exist in the real world and are to some extent accepted. The vision is not a communistic, levelling one. Wealth is moral when the wealthy behave with respect and recognise their duties to the poor. Francis Crossley, the great carpet manufacturer and philanthropist, is a clear example of the workings of wealth and the wealthy in the contemporary world figuring in the ballads. In 'An Elegy on the Death of Crossley',[42] Crossley embodies a basic humanity speaking to the humanity present in all, rich and poor alike. (The full text is given in plate 11.) The notion that the rich have duties to their brethren the poor is widespread in the ballads. It goes with the idea of true 'friends' of the people (of course an old idiom of radical politics), whether these be philanthropists or politicians like Gladstone. If the people had true friends, they also had, as it were, true enemies, the rich who had betrayed their responsibilities to the poor. These ideas, especially the treason of the rich, came together in a particularly explosive manner in the Tichborne case. Perhaps the most remarkable of all Victorian *causes célèbres*, the case reflects very closely the mental universe of the ballads and the marked populism present in ballad portrayals of the social order.

The case drew forth shoals of ballads which were very similar in character throughout the country, irrespective of localist traditions in the ballad form. The work of Rohan McWilliam on Tichborne and the broadside tradition – upon which the following account draws heavily – indicates that the case was a ballad cause *par excellence*.[43] With astonishing force it elicited all the primary themes of the ballad's way of representing society already considered here. The very capacity of the case to orchestrate ballad idioms of representation in this way suggests that these idioms made up a consistent whole, and not an incoherent series of responses. This ballad framing of the Tichborne case also suggests the longevity and antiquity of the social outlook portrayed. As the foregoing account of the case has suggested,[44] the link between representations, values and beliefs would appear to have been a strong one.

The capacity of the ballad to reflect the currents of feeling so powerfully evident in the case shows that the broadside spoke eloquently to the feelings of the multitudes who rallied behind the people's hero. In the Tichborne ballads the broader ballad emphases were all present – the depiction of labour, the sense of loss and of a

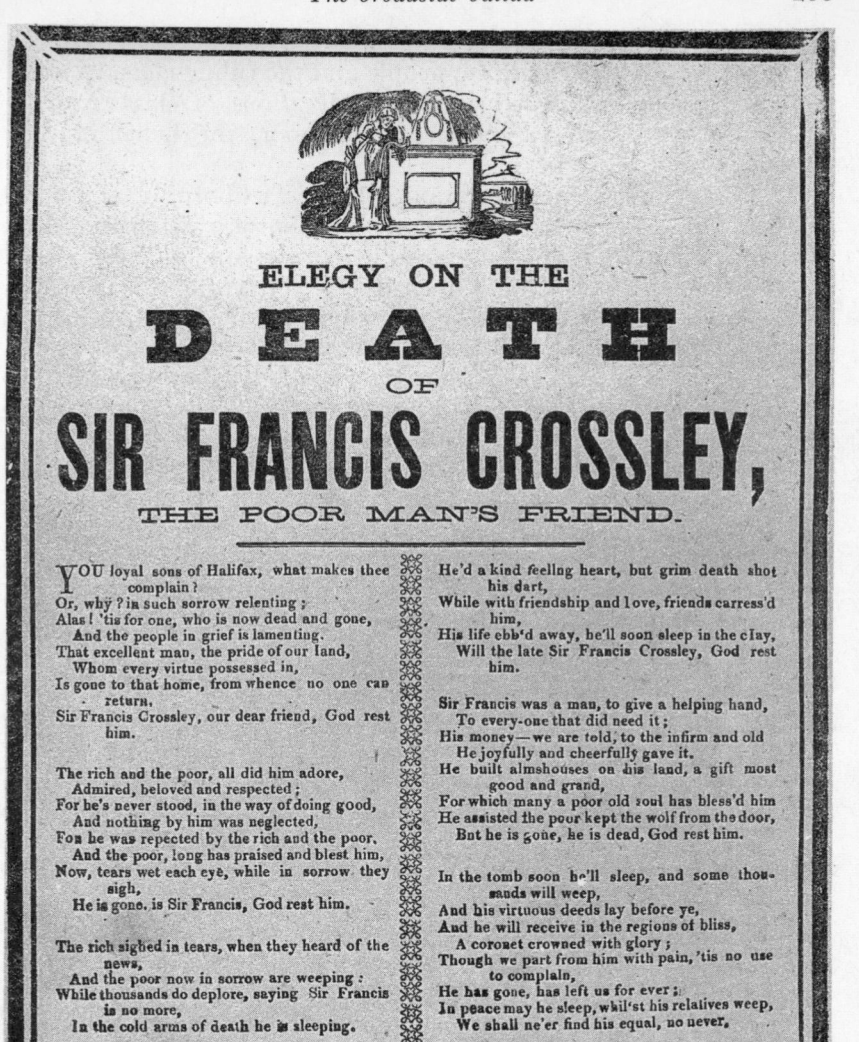

11 Elegy on the death of Sir Francis Crossley.

vanished golden age, the attachment to rights and to the figure of 'the freeborn Englishman'. Anti-statism was a strong aspect, and one of many elements decidely of an orthodoxly populist stamp. The nation was exalted over the state, and a radical patriotism took precedence over popular radicalism *per se*, though the link to this and other long-established currents was close. The cause of the people was defended against the conspiracy of the great and powerful, a conspiracy in part reflected in the idea of political parties as a device of the rich. Rich and poor, the people and the ruling class, were the dominant elements, rather than considerations of class. And we again see the moral exaltation of the poor, the belief in their superiority over the rich.

Thus the ballad representations of the Tichborne case echoed broader ballad themes. However, the Tichborne case elicited these broader currents of feeling in its own heightened and particular way. It worked with the theme of inversion, of the world turned upside down;[45] a theme of course amply evident in popular literature down the ages, and present too in the contemporary ballad (seen for example in the treatment of monarchy and of rich and poor). The Tichborne agitation was fuelled by the idea of *vox populi, vox dei*: it gave the people a sense of their own strength and agency. In short, it empowered them and gave them a sense that they had control over their destiny. The will of the people was symbolically enacted in the process of making the low high and the high low. The claimant was himself a marginal figure, one caught between two worlds; the aristocrat emerging from the bush of Australia, the man who had known the low – and been dependent on their succour – before his rightful reclamation of the high. There are obvious links to the bandit hero and to the exaltation of the criminal as hero in the ballads, similar figures often caught between two worlds. The claimant was given the garb of freedom perhaps most readily present to the minds of the poor, that of nobility. Hence the success of a figure so unlike the poor in many respects: the garb of nobility was the garb of freedom. In this role of the marginal figure and the emodiment of freedom and independence, there are many parallels with marginal, anarchic figures in popular art more widely – with the costermonger figure in the music hall, for example, with Mr Punch himself, or with that enormously popular hero of the comic art of the 1880s, Ally Sloper.[46]

As McWilliam observes, the causes espoused in the Tichborne agitation were themselves heavily marked by the theme of inversion. In reiterating the familiar theme of one law for the rich, one law for the poor, it was frequently emphasised in the Tichborne ballads how lawyers could prove right was wrong. In terms of sexual inversion, the claimant was represented as a kind of Victorian satyr (he was grotesquely fat), the people's phallic symbol, defying prevailing sexual customs by standing them on their heads. In the process the licence and the hypocrisy of the aristocratic and the 'respectable' were vehemently attacked. As noted earlier, this hatred of the sham world of upper-class respectability was all consuming in the Tichborne case.

Behind all this lay those utopian longings, those aspirations to a just and fraternal society emphasised earlier. In the anthropological literature the marginal or liminal figure is seen as ushering in the possibility of 'communitas', the realisation of a communion of equals who submit to the same reign of justice. The Tichborne case in particular, and the ballad literature and popular art more generally, figured these aspirations in terms of the notion of 'fair play', a greatly potent and greatly pervasive term in the popular parlance. In making the low high and the high low what was brought into being were these apprehensions of utopia. Through the portal of the eminently earthly and profane, a realm of feelings distinctly religious in many of their manifestations was entered. The longings expressed through the symbolic figure of the Tichborne claimant were similar to those wider utopian desires, both secular and religious, seen at work in the broader ballad tradition.

In the 1870s and early 80s the Tichborne agitation represented perhaps the last great flowering of the ballad tradition. By then decline had long set in, and in the industrial regions of the north the ballads from the 1840s were replaced by a new kind of dialect literature. This literature of course overlapped in time and readership with the ballads, and it owed a good deal to the older form, especially to its strong dialect component. Nonetheless changing social and economic circumstances brought about new possibilities and needs, and it was these that dialect explored. Social change itself also helped shift the balance between the national and the local evident in the ballads, combining these dimensions in new and rather unexpected ways.

11

The voice of the people?
The character and development
of dialect literature

From around the 1840s there developed in Lancashire, Yorkshire and the north-east of England a dialect literature of wide appeal to the working people of these industrial districts. A popular tradition was apparent in some other English regions, but these examples were overwhelmingly the most significant. In other regions, too, dialect was written by and for those outside the ranks of manual workers: this aspect will be considered later, the main emphasis here being upon the popular current. If decidedly popular, however, this dominant form was in no sense the direct expression of some authentic 'working-class' voice. Rather, its genesis and character were culturally and socially diverse: while there were two distinct strands in the literature these were in practice sometimes woven together. Unpicking this weave helps us explore people's self-images and the ideas they had of other social groups.

It is first of all necessary to convey briefly some of the main characteristics of what I take to be the dominant, popular current in dialect. It was a new literature, yet was also intimately related to the ballad tradition and oral culture that preceded it. What was new was the emergence of known, no-longer anonymous authors, writing in an often 'literary' way for a mass audience. With more justice than with the ballad, one may use the term 'literature' in the sense of awareness and pretentions extending from 'low' to 'high' literary culture. What was also new was an increasingly literate audience, and one that made up a more commercially developed market than hitherto. This market was exploited by sometimes quite large-scale publishing entrepreneurs. Changes of content and style were also evident: more elaborate and ambitious forms (extended prose, for example) spoke much more directly than hitherto about the everyday life of working people. The literature looked inward, as it were, to register and celebrate this life, specially in its domestic manifestations. The resulting picture was often more 'realistic' than the ballad, the tone more 'respectable'. Yet all this said, the links to prior developments were still considerable. One is in fact dealing with a rather primitive form of commercial culture. In terms of feeling and preconception, realism and respectability also hid close affinities with what went before. Similarly, and especially in terms of the elaboration of social identities, there were continuities of function between old and new genre.

These and other continuities were expressed in terms of form. The leading Lancashire writers of the first generation – for example Samuel Laycock and Edwin Waugh – originally published in penny ballad sheet form, and in their late writings continued to write to be sung or declaimed.[1] In the new prose tales there was a great debt to traditional, oral practices. Stories took fable form, characterisation was limited, and the prose was heavily based on conversation. Additive, formulaic methods of composition are apparent, which mirrored the formulaic quality of the traditional moral tale.[2] As will be seen, the printed dialect literature of the late nineteenth century was always rather more a spoken and public than a read and private literature. If during this time print and literacy became greatly more important in popular culture, dialect was still heavily indebted to oral dimensions of communication. And, as has been seen, the dialect element in the earlier ballads was already a very strong one.

Not that the ballads themselves were straightforwardly 'oral' or proletarian in character. The authorship and patronage of ballad writing, including dialect ballads, had by the mid-century long involved higher social elements, in particular what might be termed the literary intelligentsia of provincial England, people such as schoolmasters, professionals and the clergy. Research on the example of Newcastle and the north-east reveals the existence of important provincial publishing centres, which dealt in local song collections in part penned by such people.[3] This is an example of the more socially exalted strand of dialect, which clearly aimed at an audience other than that of workers alone. However, even when so aimed, this literature could be taken up by a popular audience and given a new set of values in its new settings. Colls' work shows this in action;[4] the workingman rake or spreer for example being commandeered, or tamed, according to the different secular or religious setting of popular life in which the figure was re-deployed. Nonetheless, the seemingly proletarian hero (in this case 'Bob Cranky') might have a surprisingly unproletarian literary lineage, and with it a similar set of original values and associations. Something similar was evident in Lancashire (though there this higher-class inheritance seems to have been much weaker). In Lancashire, John Collier the Rochdale schoolmaster (known as 'Tim Bobbin') was a major influence on subsequent generations of writers. His dialect glossary, the associations of his pseudonym, but above all his comic dialogue, *Tummus an'*

Meary (1750), established a tradition of conscious literary endeavour in the textile districts and the north more widely.

The broader cultural *milieu* of dialect also involved borrowings from 'high' culture. The point needs the fuller consideration it will be given later, but in this account of formative influences upon dialect it may be usefully made with reference to Edwin Waugh, perhaps the most influential of the first generation of the new, popular writers. The son of a shoemaker, he drew heavily on this experience of Rochdale town and moorland life. Yet he also drew on Collier, and his trade as a printer drew him into the society of 'gentleman' antiquarians who had long been friends of the dialect and devotees of what later came to be termed 'folklore'. As early as the 1830s Waugh met and was influenced by figures like Henry Roby, whose influential *Traditions of Lancashire* came straight out of the folklorist imagination.

Existing accounts of the development of the literature bear testimony to this access to friends and influence outside the immediate spheres of workers' lives.[5] Friends were to be found in the various literary associations and periodicals typical of the nascent lower-bourgeois provincial culture of mid-Victorian England. Influences were apparent in provincial, amateur philology; in the writing of local history and the general cultivation of regional cultures; in older higher-class dialect balladry, but also in the essential figure of Robbie Burns.[6] Burns was indeed very characteristic of this indeterminate social and cultural mix, signifying in the nineteenth century all things to all people, symbol both of a radical, plebeian tradition and of socially soothing visions of the rural. In its later days, too, for instance in the Lancashire Authors' Association, (LAA), founded in 1909, the social milieu of much dialect writing continued to involve a high degree of social mixing. In the LAA, cotton employers, teachers and socialist trade unionists met amicably together to foster the language and culture of the region.

Having considered the varied social and cultural elements in the gestation of the new dialect, attention can now be given to its dominant strain as this developed from the 1840s to the 1920s. The major writers were decidedly children of toil. Waugh, together with Ben Brierley, Samuel Laycock and Allen Clarke in Lancashire, and John Hartley and Ben Preston in Yorkshire, were the leading among scores of dialect writers. Hartley's father was a Halifax tea merchant, though Hartley spent his early working life as a pattern-maker in an engineering works. The others came directly from the ranks of manual workers and knew poverty at first hand in their early days. Aside from Waugh, the others worked as textile operatives, Laycock and Preston being unable to emancipate themselves from the factory for most of their working lives. Waugh, Brierley, Hartley and Clarke were exceptional among the run of dialect writers in managing to earn some sort of living from their writing.

This living could be precarious, especially in the other great centre of dialect, the north-east. There, dialect was more closely linked than it was further south to traditions of popular entertainment. Except perhaps for Joe Wilson in the 1860s and 70s – near in style and outlook to the Lancashire authors – dialect grew originally out of the club and 'free-and-easy' culture of Tyneside. In 1827 it was reported that in Newcastle and Gateshead (not counting about 50 Christmas savings clubs), there were 121 male and 45 female mutual insurance clubs.[7]

The music hall of the 1840s drew on the music and dialect songs of these and of the pub 'free-and-easies' to which they were related. Like the more literary Wilson, earlier figures such as Bobby Nunn and Ned Corvan were decidedly working class in origin. Their dependence on the stage and the club platform meant at best a precarious income (even Wilson, a popular author as well as a music hall performer, experienced this insecurity).

In this account of the character and development of the literature I shall, however, dwell mostly on Lancashire and Yorkshire, the major centres. Justification for this choice also lies in the seminal nature of writers from these districts, especially Lancashire: Waugh was a major inspiration for Joe Wilson and John Hartley, respectively probably the most renowned writers in the north-east and industrial Yorkshire. However, as noted in the north-eastern examples, there were very important local roots. Waugh for instance brought a new literariness, new accents on domestic life and on particular invented plebeian pasts, but this always ran alongside local currents of equal and perhaps greater strength.

Such a current in the West Riding of Yorkshire was the dialect almanac. In published accounts of the literature much attention is given to the likes of Waugh and Brierley, very little to the almanacs. *The Barnsla Foaks' Annual an Pogmoor Olmenac* of 1840 and the *Shevvild Chaps' Annual* of 1836 were probably the earliest. By 1877 the English Dialect Society estimated that there were forty dialect almanacs currently published, all but four of them in the West Riding.[8] The most famous of these was Hartley's *Halifax Illuminated Clock Almanac*, begun in 1865 and selling 80,000 annually by 1887. Hartley's almanac continued publishing, and selling well, until after the Second World War, though many were fairly short lived. A simple listing of almanac titles perhaps conveys best their indisputably demotic character, and their strong local flavour: *Dewsbre' Back at Mooin Olmenac*, *T'Bag o'Shoddy Olmenac* (Batley), *T'Nidderdill Olmenac*

(Nidderdale), *The Weyver's Awn Comic Olmenack or Pudsa Annewal* (Pudsey), *T' Leeds Loiners Comic Olmenac*; or in another vein, *Tommy Toddles' Comic Almanac, The Chimney Nook, The Tykes Own Almanac* (a late one this, 1923–25), *Bob Stubbs' Original Comic Yorkshire Almanac.* These were complemented by even more highly localised and ephemeral journals, such as the *Batley Comic Almanac* (1867), for the 'rag pickers and powerloom weavers' at a particular Batley mill.[9] The heyday of the dialect almanac was between the 1860s and 1914. They were written by workingmen with a little education (such as Hartley) or, often much the same thing, by small printers or stationers who also published them. They were hawked or sold in a range of retail outlets such as grocery shops, news vendors or the very rudimentary 'bookshops' of the time. They represent an extra-ordinary outpouring of 'penny capitalist' production, part of a 'market', yet one decidedly primitive and plebeian in character.

Authorship, however, is in a sense irrelevant. The almanacs tend to be derivative, feeding one off the other, specially off Hartley's Halifax almanac. Authors could be of decided loyalties: Hartley was a radical Liberal, Charles Rogers of the *Barnsla Foak's Annual* an ardent Tory. However, such loyalties did not intrude much, at least not in a partisan way. Instead, there is a marked uniformity of theme, method and appeal which is very striking. This goes beyond inter-textual influences; or rather, such influences were under-pinned by massive uniformities of expectation among audiences. The almanacs succeeded so well because they gave people what they desired, a set of representations figuring their own mythologies. Of course, authors colluded in and embellished these mythologies, but they did not invent them.

The almanacs are an especially clear example of the earlier emphasis placed upon popular art as endowing knowledge, empowering the powerless. 'Bob Stubbs', 'Tommy Toddles' or 'Uncle Owdhem' (the list is very long) were comic, avuncular, wise, of the people. Above all, perhaps, they expressed the knowingness of their audiences, their refusal to be fooled. The complement of the knowing uncle was the wise fool: he or she could be guyed, but often foolishness hid an innate knowingness about essentials which expressed the wisdom of ordinary working people. All this was complemented by the content of the almanacs: they chronicled the minutiae of daily life, but did so in a comic yet moralising vein. Clearly, they continued many of the functions of the ballad. Above all they aimed to amuse, to lighten the burden of work and poverty. The story form they took often owed much to stories and jokes current in the communities the almanacs served, embellishing these and inventing others, and so perpetuating in a cyclical pattern of

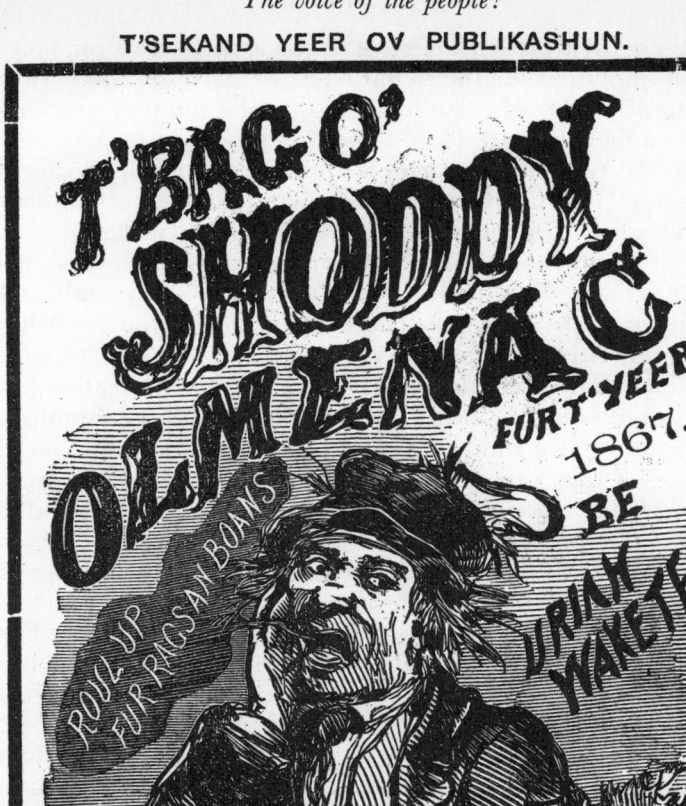

12 Cover of a Yorkshire dialect almanac.

mythical creation the self-image of the people. These almanacs need extensive quotation for their character to be appreciated. In order not to impede the discussion here several examples are cited at length in appendices 10–13.

The morality in the almanacs is implicit, not usually hectoring or proselytising. It is far removed from dominant modes of Victorian public morality. The moral lies in the tale and is brought out in the comic and sentimental telling: honesty, decency, hard work, helping one's fellows, avoiding the hypocrisy attendant upon wealth, above all dignity and fortitude in the face of adversity; all these are the stuff of the morality. It was a morality which if stoical was not quiescent, one in which individual dignity was inseparable from realising bonds of interest with one's fellows. The emphasis on local communities is of course strong: the almanacs retailed news and information about them, and in turn presupposed in their audience a high degree of local knowledge, about occupations, histories, individuals and so on.

Clearly, the medium was the message (here and elsewhere in the literature): it is difficult not to stray into meaning when discussing form and content. Meanings and the central aspect of created social identities will be systematically approached in due course. For the moment, it is the history of dialect's development and the character of its different forms that is under discussion. In Lancashire, the dialect journal and annuals were similar in form to the Yorkshire almanacs. The pseudonyms of writers echoed the informal naming practices noted earlier in the industrial districts: they corroborated practice in such a way as to play upon the sense of kin, friends and neighbourhood. Lancashire journals had titles like *Bill o'Jacks Monthly*, or *Bill o'Jacks Holiday Annual*[10] (Bill o'Jack was William Baron of Rochdale, not to be confused with Joseph Baron of Blackburn, 'Tom o'Dick o'Bobs'). Allen Clarke's pseudonym, 'Teddy Ashton', was similar to the various 'Bob Stubbs' figures of Yorkshire. Clarke in particular capitalised on the growing late nineteenth-century market for holiday annuals as the seaside holiday came within reach of workers.

As in Yorkshire, the journals and annuals tended to be local in character. (Brierley's Manchester *Ben Brierley's Journal* drew on a wider audience, but not a deeper one, its mix of comic dialect and autodidact Improving literature limiting its mass appeal.) Allen Clarke, Bolton operative, teacher and later writer and publisher of the dialect, turned out a succession of annuals and journals based in Bolton, and with strong Bolton affinities, yet also appealing to a wider, popular audience. Between 1889 and the 1930s his *Bolton Trotter* (the 'Trotters' was also a nickname for the town's football team), *Teddy Ashton's Northern Weekly*, *Teddy Ashton's War Journal* and his *Lancashire Annual* served to continue something of a Bolton tradition, William Staton's *Bowton Loominary* (1854–58, 1867–74) being one of the first dialect journals in the field.[11]

However, in Lancashire the variety of dialect literature was much greater than this, and these publications did not rival the Yorkshire almanacs in number and sales.[12] In all regions, but especially in Lancashire, expensive editions of leading writers such as Waugh and Brierley represented a select, higher-class market, served by introductions and annotations of the dialect. Disproportionate historical attention has been given to this form of dialect: both secondary and leading writers reached a much wider audience in the vast numbers of penny reciters and pamphlets, featuring poetry as well as prose. If those were increasingly published by the big provincial houses, such as Abel Heywood and John Heywood of Manchester, or Nicholsons of Wakefield, in other respects they represent a continuation of the penny broadside (they were also hawked or sold in local shops). The newspaper press served to enlarge this older market by reprinting popular items, as well as acting as an important source of dialect in its own right. As one commentator observed of Lancashire dialect after the Cotton Famine of the 1860s, 'Dow [dole] times ripened it, newspapers boomed it'.[13] Famine relief involved adult schooling, and street singing, increasing the audience for and the exponents of dialect. In the 1850s and 60s every town of any size gained its local newspaper, and often more than one, and these published large numbers of dialect sketches, poems and dialogues, often written by local authors, as well as the better-known writers. Again, the marked localism of dialect is evident, as it is in the strong traditions in dialect writing, such as the Bolton example already considered.

This localism of sentiment and creativity nonetheless went hand in hand with the larger influence and reputation of the leading writers. This is evident, for instance, in the appeal of Brierley. Like Dickens, Brierley went on speaking or performing tours which took him not only to different parts of Lancashire and Yorkshire, but to other parts of England where Lancashire emigres were to be found. (There seems to have been some appeal to non-northern audiences but it was fairly limited.)[14] This instance also serves as a reminder that dialect literature had very significant oral dimensions, and that rather than being eclipsed by the development of literacy and the new local press these factors served to perpetuate these aspects.

Oral performance was present in the way the literature was constructed. It was also evident in its reception. Dialect was recited in the home, and spoken or sung in all the venues comprising the institutional world of the labouring classes; at co-operative gatherings, at trade union, friendly society and Sunday school occasions, and in the ordinary run of social and political club life. The autobiography of Ben Turner dwells upon the place of the literature in the culture of West Riding millworkers in the 1860s and 70s (at a time when domestic production was a very recent memory): Turner's father sang and recited this literature and passed to his son a conscious love of the language and the 'homelyisms' it dealt in.[15] Groups of boys in his youth recited Waugh, Hartley and Laycock and the others at gatherings in houses and pubs. 'Yorkshire sentimental songs' were sung throughout the county, and by all ages, in pubs and music halls, as well as at 'homely' social gatherings of all sorts. A leading trade unionist and journalist of his day, Turner himself carried on the dialect tradition, becoming an author in his own right. The success of the more formal 'penny readings' at which dialect was performed was noted by Thomas Wright, 'the journeyman engineer', in 1867: in the manufacturing districts the popularity of these was matched by their freedom from oppressive patronage.[16]

On many of these occasions women were present, and it seems clear that if not usually written by women, dialect was read and listened to by them. This could hardly be otherwise if the literature was to reach a big audience in the textile districts, where women, as a major element in the workforce, had considerable purchasing power at their disposal. Home life and family relations were indeed a staple of a literature in which barriers of gender seem to have been as little marked as those of status within the working classes. It is of course difficult to judge the social standing of the readership. Nonetheless, the picture built up so far does point to this capacity to reach a massive and widely representative audience.

This is also borne out by what figures for sales we have. The oral reproduction of dialect makes us aware that such figures are not an especially good guide to the popularity of the literature. A single pamphlet or broadsheet might pass through many hands, many listened if they did not read or buy, and of course the newspapers gave a readership it is impossible to measure. Nonetheless, the figures for *Hartley's Halifax Almanac* are striking, and Clarke claimed to have a regular sale for his *Teddy Ashton's Northern Weekly* of 35,000 in the 1890s. Towards the end of his career Clarke claimed a sale of over one million of his penny *Tumfowt Sketches*.[17] The circulation of much dialect material was very localised – hence its impact was intense. Most writing did not scale these heights, but sales were still considerable: Laycock claimed 40,000 broadside and pamphlet sales for his cotton famine songs, and in the same period William Billington's 'Surat Weyver' alone sold 14,000.[18] Sales of some journals and of extended prose pieces regularly seem to have exceeded 10,000 copies.

The period between the 1840s and about 1920, or perhaps 1914, seems to have been the high point of dialect. Before this period there were limits of technology, distribution, literacy and need; later, the limitations posed by the counter-attractions of the popular press and the new forms of the mass media less shaped by local and regional interests and activity. This great outpouring of dialect literature was, as indicated, centred mostly on the industrial north. Other regions, for instance the West Country, had some significance, but there was nothing approaching the northern example. The best guide to the distribution of dialect publication is the English Dialect Society's listings of 1877:[19] of 156 pages covering the British Isles (131 pages on England, 22 on Scotland), Lancashire accounted for 35 pages of the bibliography, Yorkshire 23, Cumberland 15 and Northumberland and Durham 6. This underestimated the popularity of dialect in the north-east, where it was by then a music hall form.

The development of dialect literature may be traced into the late nineteenth and early twentieth century through a comparison of the different generations of writers. The early generation – men such as Waugh (born 1817), Brierley (1825), Laycock (1826) and even more Samuel Bamford (1788) – drew directly on rural and domestic-industrial culture, also on the traditions of popular radicalism. Hartley was a transitional kind of figure. Born in 1839, and only discovering Waugh in 1862, his fictions still deal in the pre-factory industrial pastoral, comic and pathetic, but are located more consistently in immediate circumstances and the present than with the preceding writers.[20] Writers of later generations still, such as William Baron of Rochdale (born 1865) wrote directly in his dialect monthly of current events (such as the machinations of the speculating 'Cotton Corner Crew') or dwelt in non-fictional terms on the present life of the factory operatives.[21] Yet he also dwelt lovingly on the old days before the factory and factory town: the influence of Waugh continued to be seminal.

The same could be said of his generation more widely: the same balance of engagement with the present yet loyalty to the old ways and masters is apparent. What this betokens will be considered in the next chapter. Here one wishes to register the change marked by later writers figuring more prominently than hitherto the present life of the worker and the factory. Clarke in his comic-satiric sketches of mill life is a good example of this: 'factory foak' (the dialect coinage of the time) became not just the object of the literature's appeal but also its subject. The Yorkshire almanacs of the 1860s see this happening rather earlier across the Pennines, while in Lancashire men such as Clarke, Samuel Laycock's son, Alan Laycock, Samuel Fitton (born 1868) and Joseph Burgess (born 1853) comprised a new generation of writers many of whom were also trade union leaders, founders of socialism in its ILP form and active in labour and union journalism. (Yorkshire's Ben Turner, or Durham's Tommy Armstrong, the 'pitman's poet', are examples in the same vein.)[22] These deliberately turned dialect towards their own ends,[23] showing in the process how malleable were the associations and identities it dealt in.

In the textile operatives' own journal, *The Cotton Factory Times* and *The Yorkshire Factory Times*, one sees these new appropriations at work from the 1880s, more in the union than in the political vein. When the journals sought to mount a union agitation, on 'time cribbing' in the mills, for example, it was to the dialect skit and the cartoon that they turned.[24] The journals also ran many columns of dialect comedy and commentary on current events. Brierley, Laycock junior, Fitton, Clarke, Turner and many others were dialect contributors to the *Cotton Factory Times*. Waugh also frequently appeared, long after his death. The role of dialect in the union's affairs and in its journal suggests its centrality in the wider popular culture: in the *Cotton Times*' 'Mirth in the Mill' column, ordinary readers wrote in about events in their own workplaces, couching their experiences in a dialect they used with little self-consciousness.[25] A convention had by this time become perfectly natural. Something of this is reflected in the odd and revealing instance of seaside postcards being written in a mix of dialect and standard in order to achieve the right balance of sentiment.[26]

This brief account of the development and character of dialect conveys something of its considerable longevity and range. It also provides a context in which to place existing accounts of the literature.[27] These tend to deal with selective and narrow aspects of a multifarious phenomenon, or else use a much fore-shortened temporal framework which leaves out many of the most important developments. They thus fail to appreciate the considerable significance dialect has for an understanding of popular attitudes to society. They do this because of a marked tendency to deal in anachronistic and idealised notions of class consciousness, measured against which dialect literature is seen to represent inadequate forms of social outlook. Older, and palpably inadequate, notions of popular art and popular attitudes as 'escapist', evasive or parochial once again raise their heads. Even the most subtle of these approaches[28] deals in a false polarity of protest and consolation, failing to appreciate that dialect was about the generation of meanings with which to manage daily life. The crudest of these accounts runs into the realms of the bizarre,[29] dealing in a fantasy world inhabited by 'class traitors', 'labour aristocrats' and other denizens of the nether world of 'false consciousness'. All accounts, to one degree or another, deal with a realm of 'real' or 'authentic' class or personal experience anterior to its verbal significations, rather than seeing that language is itself constitutive of this experience. In order to escape from anachronistic interpretations of class it is necessary to attend to what dialect had to say, to the actual historical form in which society got talked about and imagined. This form was not the icing on the class cake, but the cake itself, or at least a big part of it.

Something of the tradition of higher-class dialect writing will be evident, though the subject has been very little studied. Forthcoming work, however, points to a lineage reaching back at least to the seventeenth-century Interregnum.[30] Writing by the likes of clerics and better-off farmers' sons appears to have involved, through the utilisation of a kind of anti-pastoral, an idealisation of the independent farmer and agrarian smallholder. Much remains to be discovered, but the revelation here of dissenting currents articulated through dialect is particularly interesting. There is evidence of a rather long-established tradition of protest against social and economic change in the countryside, with links to political and religious dissent. To some degree one is in the small-town, semi-rural milieu in which 'radical artisans' such as Joseph Wright and James Murray were nurtured.[31]

The English Romantics, especially Wordsworth, represented one appropriation of this: Cumberland was an important centre of this small-town, small-propertied tradition in the late eighteenth century.[32] One may posit the existence, therefore, of a fertile and in some respects radical higher-class dialect current: the hugely influential Burns came out of a similar, lowland Scots background. It is no coincidence that Lancashire's Edwin Waugh was of a Cumberland family, and that Waugh made great play of this background in his writing, and of the tradition of the Cumberland independent smallholders known as 'statesmen'. (In the chapter on language the vibrancy of dialect use among the statesmen of the 1860s was noted.)[33] These instances show the liveliness of extra-proletarian dialect, and the danger of stereotyping it as the expression of a bourgeois class 'interest'. However, it had other aspects, and these are best revealed by turning briefly to its non-northern forms.[34]

Here, there was little comparable to the popular literature of the north, except perhaps that seen in the Potteries and the Black Country. And, it must be said, while there were clear connections between 'high' and 'low' forms in the north, it is the separateness of the two strands that is in the end most striking: popular, northern dialect developed primarily out of the cultural resources of the working poor. However, extra-northern English dialect of the upper, 'respectable' classes is of particular interest, especially as it tends to reflect the long-established dissenting pedigree already noted. This reflection went hand in hand with qualities that demarcated and accentuated social differences, showing how literary representations might be an important means of defining one's own group by defining those beyond its pale, in this case the agricultural labourer who, while part of the idealised rural world invented in the rural examples of non-northern dialect, was decidely put in his or her place as the object of the farmers' attentions, rather than the agent of his or her own destiny. Rural dialect, in examples drawn from Sussex and Wiltshire, makes this plain: the labourer's world is rendered from the outside.[35] The social *milieu* of this writing is revealed in the important West Country example: writers tended to be respectable (clerics, land stewards, school teachers, news-papermen, for instance), as did their means of public dissemination (lectures and readings, the latter – in one case – in the homes of leading Cornwall county families).[36] This was a literature written from the farmer's point of view, idealising the rural community as made up of labourer and farmer, but with the farmer very much in control. One is not far removed from the world of the then renowned dialect poet William Barnes of Dorset, closer still perhaps to Hardy's invention of Wessex.

But, if this were all, the literature would be of limited interest. It is the small farmer who is most often the focus of concern, a figure pivoted between the other elements in rural society, but in many respects closer to the labourer than the landlord. Paternalist myth and myths of rural community were very often directed against the big landowner. The labourer is presented as in need of advice and social advance, but he and his family are also seen with much sympathy and richness of detail. This often acute knowledge, both in the examples cited and in further instances drawn from East Anglia and the West Country,[37] reveals an empathy with the labourer and sometimes an angry radicalism alongside other currents emphasising separateness and distinction. These extra-northern examples deserve extended treatment: here, as well as illustrating a major current of political feeling, they must serve as an introduction to the industrial examples and to the ways in which social relations were conducted between and within the classes through the means of literature. A brief example of Sussex prose dialect is given in appendix 14.

The characterisation of north-eastern popular dialect as 'respectable' has led a number of commentators to doubt its proletarian credentials or see it as tainted by upper class influences, and if not this then to posit the triumph of a bowdlerising religion. Again, discussion of rather complex issues will have to be summary. There is certainly no doubting the change in tone between the ballads and popular, dialect writing. Early and mid-nineteenth century ballads are often bawdy. More than this, however, they are often startlingly violent, the details of violent sport and violent drinking being graphically and lovingly given.[38] Colls' depiction of the worker rake has been noted, particularly the way in which 'Bob Cranky' enjoyed a long lease of life into the late nineteenth century but was yet in the end suborned by local Methodist traditions. In fact, a fairly close reading of Tyneside material suggests that it is doubtful whether this took place. The representations of the keelman and other manifestations of the rake by leading music hall figures such as the dialect performer Ned Corvan show how in the earlier period (the 1840s and earlier) the rake was seen in a way which was both celebratory *and* critical. Corvan's 'Yer Gannin to be a Keelman' and 'The Happy Keelman' make the point, and are quoted in full as examples of the richness of Tyneside dialect.[39]

Yer Gannin to be a Keelman

Yer gannin to be a keelman, ye great big slaverin' cull,
Now luik how hard ye'll hae to work, and how hard ye'll
     hae to pull;
Ye'll hae to powey wiv a huik, till yor shoother's very
     sair,
But Jacky tyek a friends advice, and think of that nae
     mair:
When ye wear yor flannin' drawers, and yor stockins' made
     of blue;
As sure as aw is stannin' here, ye'll then begin to rue;
With your legs half down the huddock, and the pipe stuck
     in yor mouth,
Ye'll be gannin' doon the river, and ye'll not knaw north
     frae sooth.

The skipper he will byest ye sair, when he gets ye in his
     paws,
He'll myek ye work byeth day and neet, and often crack yor
     jaws;
Ye'll wish ye were at schuil agyen, or wanderin doon the
     burn,
I'steed of slavin' like a horse, sic nonsense man aw
     spurn:

Ye'll be comin' hyem at neets, with yor fyece all ower
　　　black,
And ye'll lie an snore aside the fire, and never gis yor
　　　crack,
But Jacky tyek yor friends advice, for aw's sure aw wish
　　　thou weel,
And never trim a shull of coals, or work aboard a keel.

When there is a gale of wind, ye'll begin to curse and
　　　sweer,
Ye'll hev girdle cyek and bacon, but not a drop of beer;
With trimmin' coals and smokin', ye'll be as stupid as a
　　　goose,
Smash, ye'll be sae tired wi workin, man, ye'll not can
　　　crack a louse:
If aw was Betty Todd, or yor canny uncle Ned,
Aw wad tyek a rope and skelp yor back, and set ye off to
　　　bed,
But Jacky tyek a friends advice, a porter pokeman be,
If ye gan to be keelman, ye'll rue till the day ye dee.

The Happy Keelman

Dayleet in the east was just peeping,
The stars seem'd to bid yen good neet,
As a poor honest keelman leet hearted,
Toddled off tiv his days wark aw reet;
Nae ambition or pride his mind troubled,
For he toss'd aw sick stuff to the deil,
He lov'd nought but his wife and his bairns,
His marrows, his beer, and his keel.

The pure morning air was sae caller,
A blessing he always enjoy'd,
For he like the lark gat up early,
Smash, he lik'd to be always employed;
For his bairns he toil'd hard day and neet, man,
There was nan like poor Geordie could feel,
He was happy, what mair could he want,
Wiv his marrows, his beer and his keel.

When his day's wark's aw dune he'd come hyem,
Wiv his feyce just as black as the deil,
While the bairns wad cry mother, here's daddy,
Coming hame wi Will Brown frae the keel;
His bit lassie with joy then would meet him,

And the younger bairn's creep to the door,
While his wife happy smil'd as he cuddl'd,
And kiss'd them aw ower and ower.

He hates aw teetotaler bodies,
That runs doon guid whisky and yell,
And he swears that good eating and drinking,
Brings ony man out of his shell;
He's fond of aw sorts of enjoyments,
Keelman-like, gox, they're aw rummy blades,
For he oft calls to hear the fine singing,
And hev a good gil at the Shades.

Now rich folks may slight a poor keelman,
And say, ignorance myeks him a brute,
But he mebbies knaws mair then they think on,
Though little of grammar ne doubt;
Great scholars and cockneys may scoff us,
But true friendship we never conceal,
We dee as we like to be dune te,
Tho' we work for wor bread in a keel.

The keelman, the pitman, and trimmer,
Through this world like the rest they mun pass,
And if poor, what the odds, smash my hoggers,
They can still treat a friend wiv a glass;
Nae ambition nor pride their mind troubles,
For they toss aw sic stuff to the deil,
They love their bit wives and their bairns,
Their marrows, their beer, and their keel.'

It was well known at what price (to the family) the spreer spreed. Similarly, in later decades, far from becoming extinct, this characteristic figure of Tyneside dialect remained an object of celebration.[40] There was a shift, but it was one of degree only, not of kind.

It is important to appraise closely what the difference of degree measured. Of course there was a more emphatic attack upon drink and popular manners from the mid-century onwards. But this 'respectability' was decidedly the province of worker's own efforts, and not a reflex of upper-class evangelisation. Rather, it was related to the new importance of a more settled (still precarious) domestic life for industrial workers, whether the engineers of Tyneside or the cotton workers of Lancashire. Joe Wilson in the former case and Edwin Waugh and Brierley in the latter responded to, just as they fostered, this new style of life. There is no doubting the shift of attention to family, home and neighbourhood in the dialect – indeed these are its essential marks. But what came out of this was far from a tamed, subservient respectability. The pitman poets and entertainers of the north-east show this best: the works of Tommy Armstrong or the lesser-known Alexander Barrass see something rather different from a Methodist taming of proletarian self-indulgence.[41] Instead, indulgence is criticised but the fellowship and sociability of the miner's social life is still uninhibitedly celebrated, the significance of family life notwithstanding.

Looking further at the Tyneside example, it is apparent that the notions of the triumph of Methodism and the injection of 'bourgeois' values are greatly exaggerated. Again, the line between the two strands in dialect needs to be emphasised. There was an upper-class dialect, and this catered to the images of workers and the self-images desired by those who were not workers. This invention of 'class' is of great interest: it can for instance be traced on Tyneside in terms of the dinners and entertainments held by those in the 'respectable classes' who patronised and practised dialect.[42] At these, 'Geordie' identities were reproduced in dialect performance, and colonised by those who wished to be included in them. This process goes on, of course, as do the very similar permanent inventions of Scots character, not least at respectable suppers and dinners, of the 'Burns Night' variety and otherwise.

This is one thing, popular dialect another. In fact, the line between the two while clear is not unbroken. If we look at the 'respectable' classes on Tyneside they turn out to be rather unrespectable. The friends of Tyneside dialect turn out unexpectedly. Theirs was the nether world of the travelling salesman, the publican, the 'caller' in the pub and music hall show, in short the bohemian rather than the Improving middle classes.[43] Nonetheless, in Victorian England it is difficult to elude entirely the cult of Improvement. The broken line between these two dialects works in both ways, as it were, respectability being diluted by the bohemian, but in turn edging over to shape the character of the popular.

Whether in terms of moral tone, or more widely in terms of the social character of the intellectual and aesthetic influences at work in popular dialect, dominant paradigms of knowledge and value were of effect and cannot be ignored. On Tyneside, for every bohemian friend there was another who had influence in the respectable literary world of publishing and newspapers, and these people drew their inspiration from a set of values lying outside popular life. Such values did enter dialect but in a limited and a particular way. The northern, and especially Lancashire, example is the best means of looking at the particularity of this way. Provincial society was not only the venue for this meeting of high and low cultures but also in a sense an active agent in the process: dialect in particular stood for the integrity of the provincial.

In respect of provincial life, it has been noted how local developments were in the van of national ones.[44] From around the middle of the century in the manufacturing districts, local histories began to appear in increasing number. These gave industry a history: the great revelation of progress, industry, was seen to be intimately linked to the character of the region. This character was definable in language, and in turn might be linked to an older history. The Lancashire and Cheshire Historic Society was formed in 1848: at its inaugural meeting dialect was seen as the means by which a popular culture in its present, industrial guise yet retained characteristics emanating from Elizabethan times.[45] Folklore, local history and language study were indistinguishable in these early initiatives. Nationally based and co-ordinated initiatives followed only later: the Folklore Society, for instance, was formed in 1878, the English Dialect Society (for long based in Manchester) in 1873. In all this the county was both a principle of taxonomy and of ideology. *The Victoria County History of England* which followed later continued this ideological arrangement of knowledge.

Samuel has recently considered the county as second only to the nation as the focal point through which national identity was constructed in the course of the nineteenth century.[46] (This was as present in Whig interpretations as in the Tory ones he describes). In terms of dialect literature Beetham has discerned a similar process, the region and nation functioning in a complementary way. The provincial 'folklorist' identification of the continuity and integrity of local cultural traditions fed powerfully into the ideal of a *national* culture supposedly rooted in the region.[47] This indeed is true and there is an important sense in which metropolitan culture was strongest precisely where regionally based enthusiasts were most determinedly local. However, this may underestimate the active and creative force of regional cultures, and important tensions obtaining between the regional and the metropolitan, taking the latter in its expanded sense to include other manifestations of southern privilege such as Oxbridge, as well as London itself.

Dialect figured importantly here. It was part of what may loosely be called a higher-class regional consciousness, which was not solely conservative in character. Here one may remark, necessarily *en passant*, the considerable degree of political devolution to the nineteenth-century provincial towns and their tenacious traditions of civic dignity and history. Of great relevance too were major manifestations of provincial, anti-metropolitan feeling such as the new, mid-century local press. This press was a central element in provincial Liberalism, which, particularly in alliance with sections of Nonconformity, was the greatest of all expressions of the provinces' dedication to the crusade against privilege. Historians of dialect have noted how it was interwoven with the rise of provincial cuture and consciousness,[48] on the part of the greater and especially the lesser bourgeoisie. This consciousness has been little traced: it can be seen for instance in the growth, after Elizabeth Gaskell, of the regional novel.[49] It is certainly evident in the social and political activities of contemporary capitalists,[50] and in the matter of language use itself.[51] Thus it is that the sympathies expressed and created by dialect could be rather complex in operation, representing in part the alliance of a coalition of anti-metropolitan, anti-privilege forces, rather than the permeation and domination of 'high' or 'bourgeois' culture.[52]

Not that aspects of this permeation were altogether absent. The importance of friends and influence in higher spheres has been noted. Waugh, for instance, was appointed to the Board of the English Dialect Society, and at various times lionised by the Manchester literary establishment, as was Brierley.[53] The list of those contributing to Hartley's (unsuccessful) application for a Civil List pension in 1904 reads like a list of the great and good of Yorkshire provincial society.[54] In Lancashire, as elsewhere, one sees much evidence for higher-class receptivity to aspects of a dialect found socially reassuring and ideologically beneficial: Mrs Burdett Coutts bought between ten and twenty thousand copies of Brierley's 'Come Whoam to Tha' Childer and Me' for distribution to the London poor, and Waugh's poem of praise to sobriety and the home was advertised for sale by the thousand to Manchester employers for circulation to their workpeople.[55] This is to say something of the reception and uses of dialect. At the level of the intellectual paradigms influencing its form one may also speak of a permeation of upper-class influences, or influences of a sort working against a sharp class emphasis in the literature (though the chief of these influences emanated from the popular culture itself).

Beetham has described the institutions and social relationships that helped mediate between the different social groupings making up the *milieu* of dialect writing in later nineteenth-century Manchester.[56] Local publishing and the local press were important here, helping to create the intellectual climate in which the literature developed. This climate may be considered in two aspects, the moral and the intellectual. Many of those who in their guise as journalists related 'high' and 'low' social worlds were self-made men with worker backgrounds, who frequently had a history of involvement in radical causes. The periodical literature associated with dialect in this region was full of the propaganda of moral and intellectual self-culture,[57] and self-help certainly impinged on journals such as Ben Brierley's. Nonetheless, this is mainly a reflection not on dialect writers, and especially not on readers, but on its friends in loftier places.

Perhaps rather more to the point than notions of hegemonic doctrines of 'respectability' through self-improvement is a certain moral earnestness, closely linked to religious feeling yet not necessarily formally religious. In the preface to Harland's influential *Ballads and Songs* of 1865 one is aware of a moral tone that would have found echoes in popular sentiment.[58] Literature is inherently moral, in senses combining both Carlyle and orthodox religion. It helps us to do the 'work' of life, which is to endure, love, and help the needy. Literature is a kind of work, therefore, and hence a kind of prayer, aimed at the aspiration to human brotherhood in this life preparatory to the life to come. The emphasis upon duty, responsibility, striving and endurance was widespread and emphatic in Victorian society at large: if much of the force of these virtues emanated from the daily life of the worker, then this was certainly corroborated by currents exalting brotherhood over class coming from outside that life.

Something similar is evident when one moves from the moral to the intellectual and aesthetic (though the distinction was obviously a fine one in Victorian England). Aesthetic justifications of dialect dwelt simultaneously upon its virtues of purity and simplicity, and its subservience to the great tradition of standard English literature.[59] This ambiguity was reflected in a number of workingmen authors,[60] deferential to 'literature' represented both as a timeless realm above and beyond considerations of class, and as a symbol of English cultural unity and continuity. The same was the case with considerations of the English language, the intellectual interest in which also involved notions of 'folk speech'.[61] Higher-class representations of dialect reiterated its role as a kind of Ur-language of England, which the humble classes carried in unbroken tradition down to the present. The various pre-Norman accretions of the language in the north of England symbolised a kind of north-British linguistic patriotism which, like aesthetic considerations, emphasised a past and a present free of social division.

While these ideas and values left their mark on dialect, it was from the culture of the working populations that it chiefly drew its meanings. It is necessary to attend to the points of concordance between 'high' and 'low' culture, but it should be clear that one is speaking of the intellectual, public discourse surrounding the literature, and even here applicable only to the outlook of some among the many who produced dialect. Even on this level, one needs to see the double-edged nature of these putatively dominant influences. The English literary tradition might often be seen by workingmen as in a sense theirs; 'Our Shakespeare', 'Our Milton' and above all Burns being requisitioned in the popular cause.[62] Literary traditions might be enabling not disabling. It has recently been argued that the romantic notion of the poet as the bardic representative of his community – much applied to dialect at the time – limited dialect poetry to the 'familiar' and the 'homely'.[63] In fact, when looking beyond poetry to the whole span of the literature, it was this very rootedness in the 'familiar' that gave it its peculiar strength, and enabled the poet to call upon the powerful associations of the bardic representative in the first place. Certain locations were great centres of dialect production – Bolton, Rochdale, the old domestic-industrial villages around Huddersfield, or the village of Failsworth, near Manchester – and in many industrial communities particular figures were regarded as local spokesmen and symbols of local identity.

Something of this strength is already evident in the account of the development of dialect. The next chapter will elaborate on this. However, a brief look at one representative figure, the Stalybridge operative poet Samuel Laycock, may be valuable in this respect. In Laycock's work one is aware how the emphases on self-help, social reconciliation, fortitude and striving are rooted in his own first-hand experience of poverty, as well as in his desire to raise his own brothers and sisters from material and spiritual want.[64] It is this recognition and cultivation of the dignity of the poor worker that explains his moralism and didactic quality, not the reception of dominant values. The moral urgency of his literature is drawn from literary sources, especially the moral idealism and egalitarianism of Burns. It is also drawn from politics, in particular a Gladstonian Liberalism concerned to place the general good above the particular interests of class. The politics comes out of the popular radical tradition, and its emphasis upon securing fraternity was not the result of any 'bourgeois' cult of respectability.

It is important to emphasise that all this went inseparably with a keen awareness of 'class', in the sense of pride in the working people from which he was drawn, and sensitivity to the divisiveness and inhumanity of class feeling directed from supposed superiors. When Waugh was feted by his wealthy admirers Laycock started a 'popular movement' for subscriptions to mark Waugh's seventieth birthday. Laycock wrote Waugh a poem attacking his 'twenty-five bob do' (a sum that would keep him and his like for a month or more). The poor could not be present at the 'do': like Laycock they had not the fancy clothes by which the rich measured the external man. If Waugh comes to Failsworth (home of dialect), 'An i' th' place o' thoose white-chokered flunkeys / Tha'll see lasses wi' bonny print frocks / An' maybe owd dames i' their bedgeans / An' labour-stained men i' their smocks'.[65] In this poem, as in Laycock and popular dialect as a whole, the constant theme is that the rich only see the outer man, the poor the inner. The links to the ballads are obviously very close. The quality of Laycock's writing is conveyed in 'Welcome, bonny brid', cited in appendix 15. His 'Bowton's Yard' is quoted in the next chapter.

The belief that dialect revealed to the poor their own 'inner voice' was one frequently expressed by workingmen authors.[66] In evaluating dialect, this belief ought to be attended to. In many respects it is true that dialect was restricted to particular 'domains', in the sense of particular social contexts or provinces of knowledge and expression.[67] Of course, standard English was the language of learning, of law, of religion, as of a wider range of literary expression and genre. Dialect literature was most often directed to a limited range of considerations, above all to daily, immediate life; and its chief forms were the comic, the pathetic and the ironic. From this, however, it would be a mistake – frequently repeated – to assume that this restriction of domain consigns it to the quaint and parochial.

On the contrary, for instead of having one language, it can be suggested that the dialect audience was enriched by having two, the standard and the dialect.[68] The range of the latter as expressed in popular dialect was in fact wide: the realm of the 'immediate' and 'daily' was in practice broad, dialect being the language of domestic life and neighbourhood, of leisure, and to a considerable extent of nature and of work. In fact, dialect writing, as in Laycock, often encompassed a range of issues beyond the immediate, especially religion and politics. Rather than being *the* language of daily life, it may be truer to say that dialect was *one* language, fertilising the standard, just as access to the standard meant the realisation of possibilities blocked to dialect alone. The advantages dialect brought should not be minimised, something too easily done by those who have lost, or never had, contact with its resources. It is not for nothing that dialect was the bearer of secular and perhaps also religious wisdom. Dialect was the bearer of popular philosophy because dialect speech itself enshrined so much of value and belief.

As Tom Paulin has observed of the operation of dialect in the Ulster of the present,[69] dialect may articulate rich fields of personal and communal experience which may simply have no point of reference in standard English. Dialect also carries discriminations of wit, humour and irony not present in standard literature, or dismissed as 'unliterary'.[70] Dialect was always to some extent marginalised by standard forms. Nonetheless, at certain times, above all between the 1840s and the 1920s, it entered the public domain in a singularly assertive way, releasing its hidden resources to be employed in the creation of the sense of themselves and of society working people came to have.

12

Dialect and the making of social identity

This chapter is about the effort to create identity; as Reddy puts it, the rhetorical attempt to 'make, mould and alter' community identities.[1] Language mattered in this. It mattered in quite central ways, ways embedded in the nature of culture itself, and broached already in the previous discussion of custom, its desuetude and its reproduction.[2] Language was the bearer of values and ideas, in stories and proverbs, for example. But it was more than merely a bearer or vehicle: it was in fact the embodiment or substance of values, itself a form of symbolic meaning standing for all manner of desires, associations, beliefs, conscious and unconscious. Dialect literature was thus embedded in the linguistic nature of culture itself and took its strength from this. That is one reason why it is such an important expression of popular culture. But it also represented a conscious articulation of desires and associations: working people deliberately identified their language as the central symbol of their culture and set out to elaborate this identification in the large number of ways making up the corpus of dialect literature.

Comparison with the French example of nineteenth-century textile workers studied by Reddy serves to delineate the English example. What Reddy has to say about language and the formation of social identities applies with equal force to the English case, though there were significant differences between the two, not least the much greater scope and complexity of English dialect. The simple fact that dialect developed among roughly similar sorts of workers at roughly the same time needs emphasis: the micro-local is in fact a phenomenon of international significance. Both examples were about the re-working of old traditions in new circumstances and for new purposes (the re-working of the spirit of farce in the French case is apparent). While not for the most part a literature of complaint or protest (though in the English case capable of these purposes), both cases were about the hope for justice and fairness. Both exemplified the finding of wisdom and self-respect, in large part by the portrayal of the ordinary worker or person as the exemplification of these attainments. Like so much in popular culture, dialect endowed the poor with knowledge and a kind of

279

control over the circumstances of their lives by presenting them as an active presence in imaginative life, particularly in that favoured form of the knowing, the simple and the stalwart.

The French example in turn also suggests the necessity of comparison between different English regions. The failure of dialect literature to emerge on anything like the scale of the north cannot be due to the destruction of dialects elsewhere: as far as one can tell dialect usage continued strongly in most parts of England. Developments in the standard language were important, however, for the emergence of dialect literature. The linguistic conventions and uniformities upon which dialect dependend, such as a widely comprehensible orthography, themselves depended on the con-solidation of the standard. With the explosion of both literacy and print from the early nineteenth century, standard English had a new prominence in popular life. The increase of the standard, in its spoken as well as written forms, may have contributed to a desire to maintain what was felt to be under threat. Yet something much more positive was at work than these defensive reactions. Print and standard language were themselves taken over to serve a still-lively oral culture and its non-standard forms. Even as dialect represented the increasing power of the standard form in print it offered new opportunities to undercut this power. A growing market for popular literature was also important. In the third quarter of the century in the industrial north a more literate and settled urban population, and one with greater spending power than previously, created a commercial market for dialect which was amply met by the new provincial publishing firms, and the new commercial music hall in the north-east. Demand and supply met in the new conditions of community life in these regions. These conditions are amply reflected in the themes of home and family life so marked in the literature.

The significance of particularly influential authors in dialect's northern popularity should not be minimised; nor should the influence of those outside the labouring populations be under-estimated, especially when it took the potent form of a populist antiquarianism. Dialect rose and prospered, especially in the factory districts, at a time when the middle classes were actively seeking to ameliorate the conditions of acute social tension of the 1830s and 40s. The reasons go deeper, however, and it seems necessary to turn to the particular blend of change and continuity in the economic and social structure of Lancashire, Yorkshire and the north-east. Dialect was made necessary by the degree of change undergone, yet it was made possible by the powerful continuities of structure and memory that obtained. The unevenness of the development of mechanised factory production has now become apparent to historians. Even within mechanised trades, such as cotton spinning, continuity was also more marked than is sometimes supposed – in work practices, for instance, and in 'craft' outlook.[3] Yet there was considerable upheaval as well, nowhere more than in the case of the cotton handloom weavers. This blend of industrial change and continuity was in process around the mid-nineteenth century, just at the time when dialect emerged. Continuity is above all evident in the simple fact that textiles and mining, albeit in often very altered forms, still continued as the dominant industries of these regions. In the north-east, the changing social geography of mining, attended by increases of scale and an altered pattern of location,[4] represented a rather similar blend of change and continuity. On the other hand, engineering workers represented a new breed of Tyneside worker, and departed somewhat from this pattern. Shipyard workers came somewhere between these two cases.

Changes in work organisation and outlook were reflected in the character of population movements. Contrary to older notions of industrialisation as syonymous with the breakdown of previous patterns of community and family life, recent research has emphasised the phased movement to large towns, the cellular growth of towns around earlier settlements, the similarity of environment between different urban-industrial situations, and above all the role of the family in mediating the transition to urban, factory life.[5] It is perhaps surprising to discover that mid-nineteenth-century Lancashire retained more of its native-born population than any other English county.[6] Yorkshire was slightly less retentive, but for both counties – as in the north-east[7] – immigration was mostly from contiguous counties. Nonetheless, the pace of population increase and the degree of demographical flux should not be minimised: there were differences between the cities and the factory towns, and everywhere the new scale and problems of urban life were apparent. Men such as Edwin Waugh and Ben Brierley were indeed children of their time: nurtured in a hand-working, part-rural culture they lived to see the proliferation of factories and the octopus growth of Manchester. Thus people handled change and created new identities, but they did so with a cultural legacy which was still living.

As with Joseph Wright and James Murray,[8] this may be seen in the close association of dialect with areas where such social and economic continuities were marked. The sense of the past involved was often a radical one, for it was in 'proto-industrial' northern Britain that plebeian Methodism made such inroads from the late eighteenth century.[9] The north-east is a case in point. Unlike the south of England, and like the upland manufacturing districts and the English south-west, small-scale farming was marked. Pastoral, upland farming and mining might be combined, the 'independent collier' being one expression of these cultural legacies, the Cumberland 'statesman' another. If Methodism and Nonconformity did not directly convert people, their anti-establishment ethos fitted well with these traditions of plebeian independence. This was especially so in the north-east, where the dominant landowners and coalowners were of the Anglican landed aristocracy and the legal writ of the Bishop of Durham and the Ecclesiastical Commissioners ran as late as 1832.[10]

The vitality of the popular culture of domestic-industrial communities has often been remarked,[11] but far less considered is the translation of this legacy into the new conditions of later nineteenth-century industrial Britain. Even as the handloom weaving village of Failsworth was engulfed by Manchester in the second half of the nineteenth century it gave rise to perhaps the single most notable group of dialect writers, of whom Ben Brierley was the most renowned. The woollen districts of Huddersfield, among the last to transfer fully to mechanised factory production, were an important location for dialect. From the late nineteenth century there also issued from the area a stream of local histories that testify to the keen sense of a customary, oral past evident in the likes of Wright and Murray.[12] In north-east Lancashire demographic stability, and continuity in the structural organisation of industry and in family structures themselves all indicate the existence of strong community cultures similar to those of the mining villages of Durham remarked upon by the 1861 Education Commissioners. In the mining villages, analogous to domestic-industrial communities, attachment to the spoken dialect was translated into the music hall form; in north-east factory Lancashire into the form of dialect literature. Recent work on industrial conflict in the north Lancashire of the 1870s indicates not only the link between tight community structures and such cultural continuities but also the exercise of communal codes of conduct in the prosecution of industrial disputes, an exercise akin to an earlier 'moral economy'.[13] Dialect was one element in a range of cultural practices extending beyond the rhetorical sphere alone.

This range of reasons for the development of dialect literature, in particular the blend of change and continuity in the social and economic spheres, does not seem to have come together in quite the same way in other English regions. Nonetheless, some of these conditions obtained, even if a mass dialect literature did not develop. In regions like the Potteries and the Black Country, a tight community structure existed and a strong spoken dialect. Even though the realisation of social discontinuity was much less apparent than in the north, a fairly lively dialect literature of popular appeal is evident. Birmingham seems to have given rise to little dialect literature, and that of the distinctly 'higher class' form noted earlier. This form was more generally typical, though this did not disbar its frequent radicalism being addressed to a wider audience. The subject is one that cannot be entered upon here,[14] but the case of London and the invention of the Cockney will be discussed in the next chapter.

In appropriating the past, however, dialect also ordered the present. It spoke to 'working folk' of all occupations and geographical locations, conferring upon them citizenship in the nationalities of 'Lanky', Yorkshire 'Tyke', or north-east 'Geordie'. The substantial numbers of Irish immigrants were included, but in their own way: their linguistic and cultural peculiarities were rendered in the very popular tales, skits and monologues figuring 'Pat, 'Mick' or 'Brigid' as comic heroes and heroines. Given the venom of anti-Catholic and anti-Irish feeling in Lancashire popular politics, the tone of these is strikingly affectionate.[15] Though dialect authors operated as the spokesmen of particular communities, and this was one of their strengths, the language they used was conventionalised in ways that made it accessible to wider audiences. Working people thus had a new form of communication in print that created somewhat different communal associations from those going before, ones broader and less localised in scope. People read, or listened, in different and more standard dialects than those in which they spoke. The locality, the area within the region (such as the clearly identifiable south-east and north-east Lancashire dialects), the region itself, and the exchange between regions (as with the popularity of Lancashire dialect in Yorkshire and vice-versa); all these represented different social and linguistic levels which were yet knit together in inclusive social mythologies. Differences were recognised, but around the central image of the region and its cultural and industrial identity these differences were subsumed in a unitary voice that was one of the most enduring of the nineteenth-century English labouring poor.

Dialect, like ballads, had functions of social commentary and social morality, as well as serving to form collective social identities. These functions were in practice linked. In the almanacs and journals, as in the prose tales of Brierley or Oliver Ormerod, the 'Rochda' Fellay',[16] there is a running commentary on events like elections, exhibitions and royal visits. Commentary was linked to morality, occasions such as the exhibition and the visit of the comic character outside the region offering the venue for moralising about the changing modes and manners of popular life; for instance about

holidays, excursions, drinking habits, also domestic and neighbourhood mores. However, it is the ways in which dialect constructed
and managed images of the people and of the social order that is the
chief concern here. Before examining in more detail the content of
these images, something needs to be said about two central aspects
of this creation of myth, namely, the manner in which the past was
handled, and the significance of created notions of 'community'.
Communal values, it should be noted, did not spring pre-formed
from neighbourhood life but were also rhetorically created.

This account of dialect has already dwelt on how the literature
very directly concerned the re-working of the past.[17] In this respect,
especially among the early generation of writers,[18] dialect picked up
on the energies of the ballad, where the idealised world of domestic,
industrial production continued to inhabit the late-century ballads
of the factory districts.[19] What is evident is the extraordinary force
and longevity of the vision of a lost Eden. This was above all
symbolised in terms of handloom weaving and the handloom
weaver. In the north-east the same kind of symbolic activity was very
characteristic, the key occupational identities being those of the
pitman and the keelman, the one a symbol of continuity, the other
the symbolic *locus* of a re-worked past.[20] Corvan's verses on the
keelman have already been quoted, and in George Ridley's very
popular songs the figure of the keelman was later on linked to the
present through their association with the great sporting heroes of
Tyneside (in sailing and footracing especially),[21] figures who long
before the advent of football symbolised the regional, industrially
specific identity of the Tyneside labouring populations. These
occupational motifs were closely related to the 'Geordie' and the
'hinny' or 'canny' lad, in the same way as in Lancashire and
Yorkshire they were related to 'Lanky' or the 'Tyke' and regionally
appropriate versions of the 'canny', such as the 'gradely' (a
Lancashire dialect word connotating, in the person, conviviality and
decency). There are countless symbolic utterances in the literature
about life and weaving, for instance in the way that the sorrows and
joys of life are woven together by God the great weaver.
Pseudonyms summoning up for generations of factory workers the
days of independent domestic production were legion, such as 'T'
Owd Weyver', 'Owd Shuttle', 'Owd Throstle', and – oldest of all –
'Tim Bobbin'. In the hands of Brierley and Waugh these creations
took their most elaborate and influential forms.

Brierley evolved his most popular comic character in the shape of
'Ab o' th' Yate' (Abe of the Gate). Within Ab's home village of
Hazelworth is lodged 'Walmsely Fowt', and it is within the home
'Fowt' (fold), a symbol central to the whole literature, that he

experiences the freedom of the loomhouse, the fellowship of the pub, and – with some upsets – the 'gradeliness' of home life.[22] 'Gradely is a fundamental dialect term, in this respect meaning contentment, enjoyment, the fittingness of things. A complete 'Ab o'th' Yate' tale is printed in appendix 16, though considerations of space restrict extensive quotation here. Brierley published scores of 'Ab' tales. The one cited is discussed later in this chapter. Waugh's principal character, Besom Ben, inhabits the same rural-industrial world, and there is the same stress on freedom of movement and self-sufficiency in the old order.[23] The literature as a whole was heavily influenced by Waugh and Brierley,[24] and was characterised by a similarly detailed and loving re-creation of custom and linguistic usage. The freedom of earlier days is used as an implied comment upon and measure of the greater confinement of present urban, industrial life, just as representations of nature interrogate present urban conditions.[25] Sim Schofield wrote at length of Failsworth, and the rich and varied popular culture in which Brierley and the local coterie of writers grew up.[26] Brierley's work drew heavily on this background; one in which, it is clear, the autodidact tradition complemented rather than contradicted its customary aspects. The tension between the two elements was noted earlier.[27] In the north it seems to have been less marked, though it is likely that the contrast is itself overdrawn: these writers did not reject the customary past of their communities, and the symbiosis of custom and self-education that has been noted for the early part of the century[28] seems to have survived later on, despite the mid-Victorian ethic of Progress and Improvement, and its attempt to drive a wedge between the two traditions.

Ultimately, this evocation of the freedom of a vanished Eden of the handloom weaver and rural artisan is anything but nostalgic. In the literature it sits cheek by jowl with a bitter realisation of the poverty and dependence that are also seen as characterising the old days. Brierley in fact explicitly inveighs against the tendency to sentimentalise 'the good old days'.[29] In his tale 'Owd Times An New' the past was a time when working people 'had to stare through a haupenny candle fro' neet to mornin, singing "Britons Never Shall be Slaves"', working constantly merely to stay alive.[30] In 'Hard Times' he described the recent past: it will be noted how in characteristic fashion the realisation of poverty and injustice is complemented, at the end, by the utopian and religious current.[31]

Hard-times
(Song)

'Yo may talk o'hard times,' said owd Abram o'Dan's,
'But yo'n nobbut touched th'fringe on 'em yet.
They'rn harder when bacon wi' th'scithors wur cut,
An' porritch no wayver could get;
When th'wynt would blow through yo' as if you'rn a sieve,
An' whistled the keener it froze;
When we'd nothing to fence eaur cowd bodies'gen th'cowd,
But creep-o'ers an' howd-teh-bi-th'-wohs.*

'They'n hard time when a crust o'Breawn George wur too hard
For rottans to drag i'their holes;
When childer wur moore scientific nur rats,
An' bored for 'it, like borin' for coals.
They made a big hole i'th'timbers o'er th'shelf,
Heaw they did it, wheay, nobody knows;
But th'crust o'Breawn George disappeared like a ghost,
Then 'twur creep-o'ers, an' howd-teh-bi-th'-wohs.

'It wur dangerous t'turn eaut wi' yo'r owler new graised,
For yo'rn sure to be tracked by dogs.
If they'd smelt mutton fat they'd ha' set yo' i'th'lone,
An' etten both tops off y'or clogs.
If a bakin'-day happened, though seldom one coome,
Mi feythr'd get ready for blows.
He'd ha' guarded th'oon dur like a sentry i'th'wars,
More creep-o'ers, an' howd-teh-bi-th'-wohs.

'No pawnbroker throve eaut o'th'custom he geet,
Becose folk had nothin' to pop.
They'd taken the'r rags till they'd noane they could spare,
Unless they'd ha' stript 'em i'th'shop.
Little help could be squeezed eaut o'th'rich i'thoose days,
Noather i'mayte, foire, nor 'thank yo' sir' clothes;
They walled reaund the'r heauses, an' shut up the'r hearts,
When we'd creep-o'ers, an' howd-teh-bi-th'-wohs.

'Aw've worn eaut mi owler i'lookin' for wark,
But of wark ther wur noane to be had;
When th'mice emigrated, an' deed upo'th'road;
An' wi' th'rottans – wheay, things wur as bad.
When th' brids come i' flocks to a cottager's dur,
An' showed 'em the'r frost-bitten toes,
An' heaw slackly the'r fithers hung on to the'r backs,
They couldno' ate howd-teh-bi-th'-wohs.

'Aw think it quite time these owd limbs wur at rest,
Or on the'r long journey to'ard whoam,
Wheere ther's no frost nor snow, an' no yammerin' hearts
Nor hauve naked bodies con come.
Aw yerd a voice sayin', 'Ye sufferers on earth,
Come hither, and try your new clothes!
For the poor shall be rich, and the rich all alike, –
No moore creep-o'ers, or howd-teh-bi-th'-wohs!'

* Creep-o'ers – 'Creep over stiles'.
Howd-te-bi-th'wohs – 'Hold-thee-by-the-walls', a kind of gruel sweetened with treacle.

The symbolism of food and of hunger (starving is 'clemming' in Lancashire dialect) is extraordinarily powerful in the literature: Brierley returns to it time and again, as a sign of progress (in food stalls in the street, for example), but above all as the essential sign of good or 'gradely' living.[32] Among contemporaries food was a potent symbol of the good life. It figured as the central element in ritual events; political, civic and philanthropic. Food was a material but also a symbolic currency: the typical, celebratory form of consumption was the roast beef, beer and plum pudding of Old England (the whole ox was ritually roasted in public). The political overtones of this were of course marked, not least in the Tory appropriation of John Bull as the epitome of this vision of content in patriotic garb.[33] The implications of this for 'class' outlook will be considered a little later.

Food was political in other senses too. The 'hungry forties' was an idea informing dialect, even among its socialist exponents. And of course it was a Liberal idea, part of the Liberal version of history, the bad old days of want and protectionism, the good new ones of plenty and free trade (the great historical force of the idea of free trade has already been noted).[34] There was a strong radical Liberal current among dialect authors, and where (as was usual) overt propaganda and active politics were not evident in writings and writers, the broader contemporary belief in progress and reason was strong. Laycock, for instance, invariably looked back to the early part of the century as a time of deference, when the parson was king, the poor paid the rich to think for them, and the gentry were almost worshipped.[35] Laycock's was a more evidently Liberal voice than most, though the idea that life had improved went hand in hand with a condemnation of the ignorance and 'superstition' of the past in the literature more broadly,[36] or in the culture of the autodidact worker more generally.[37]

Yet this Liberal (and liberal) version of the past was clearly far from the simple matter it is so often taken to be. Golden-age notions served constantly to undercut facile ideas of progress. One is of course discussing the writings and outlook of the autodidact worker here. Dialect is an extraordinarily good guide to the mental universe of the people's intelligentsia. But it is also far more than this. These writers created fictions that were of enduring popularity among masses of workers who did not share their background. They thus translated their own outlook and values into the popular currency, though only at the cost of acknowledging the presuppositions of a mass audience. Something of this is evident in the ways in which they developed their idealisation of the past to interrogate the present. The great power of the imagery of free, pre-factory production has been seen. More particularly, in Brierley, for example, or in John Hartley, one can see this acknowledgement of advance (measured by things such as excursions and technical change) yet also the recognition of the despoliation of the natural world and of older human feelings by the advance of town and industry, a recognition played out in terms of readers' own experience of change and of their everyday concerns.[38] The Liberal idea of progress could therefore give ample voice to the popular, more broadly liberal idea of progress, but only because its questionings and qualifications gave expression to misgivings among the mass dialect audience.[39]

Dialect therefore drew on the past in handling the present. It did so by re-working older motifs, and in the process it gave rise to new identities. The invention of the past was therefore one means of creating the present, above all in the sense of the values of communal association. Much of this will already be apparent in the account of the Yorkshire almanacs, which reflected communal life yet also returned to readers a fictional working-up of audiences' pre-dilections.[40] The almanacs are in fact a good illustration of how, among a mass audience, a liberal ideal of progress might go hand in hand with a powerful and critical idealisation of the past. The almanacs registered local events, such as the large number of feasts, fairs and 'clashes' which reflected the rich, ritualised associational life of the industrial West Riding.[41] They also registered events to do with the development of communities in what may be described as a Whig manner; representative institutions, reading rooms, co-ops and Sunday schools embodied a decided notion of political and social advance.[42] Yet the village also figured as a powerful symbol of lost childhood and of the costs of progress.[43]

This drawing upon the past is amply evident in Lancashire and provides important insight into the ways in which the social order was seen. Certain key poems, widely popular at the time, may be considered for the light they throw on the formation and content of

the outlook on community. Waugh's 'Eawr Folk' celebrates his own
family and by inference the families of his readers. Their varied
characters and (considerable) accomplishments are lovingly recorded. In Laycock's 'Bowton's Yard' the movement of sympathy is
outwards from kin and the immediate area of the home to the
broader community. In his 'Quality Row' and 'Second Visit to
Quality Row' Laycock returns to the same theme: the poorest and
the most stoical are the real heroes, though high and low are all part
of the same human brotherhood. Health and a contented mind are
to be prized above wealth. The theme of the street, yard or row
reproduces in the context of the factory town neighbourhood the
motif of the older 'fowt'. In Sam Fitton's 'Cotton Fowd' there is a
conscious re-working of this old constituent of mythological
neighbourhood, also a re-working of Laycock which reflects the
strong inter-generational debts in the literature. These poems of
Waugh, Laycock and Fitton are fairly long, and it would be unwise
to abbreviate them here: full versions are given in appendices 17–19.
The tone towards the better-off in Fitton is more critical but still
muted. 'Cotton Fowd' is a kingdom of its own, of 'fowks' good and
bad who in the end are 'nobbut human after all'. As with the
representations of the past these portrayals are not sentimental or
uncritical. They are accompanied by a sharp sense of the drawbacks
of such life in the conditions of prevailing poverty, for instance the
self-interest and intrusiveness of neighbours. Nonetheless, the
dominant role is one of celebration, and of triumph over near-
impossible odds.[44]

Dialect was very often about family life, about children, lodgers,
marriage and the joys and discords of the home. These are as present
in the *Halifax Illuminated Clock Almanac* of the 1940s as in the literature
of a century previously. It is clear that the dialect though written by
men was read and received by women. Much of it was indeed
written for a family audience, and this is echoed in its content and
form, the recitation being a private as well as a public event. The
representations of women do indeed draw on the dominant gender
stereotypes of the age, but the picture of women that is presented
lacks neither subtlety nor sympathy, as it would have to have
been in regions where many women worked and comprised part of
a paying audience. But, as with all other aspects, gender differences
are subsumed in the glorification of 'working folk' and their
community life. The home, as the centre of this life, is not a
sentimentalised retreat but is always part of the wider setting. One
is some distance from middle-class depictions of 'home-sweet-
home'. Waugh's famous 'Come Whoam To Thy Childer An Me'
enjoyed great popularity with all classes. Yet it is very characteristic

of the literature that it drew forth a string of parodies, the most renowned of which was Brierley's 'Go Tak Thi' Ragged Childer An Flit', a piece far removed from the conventional pieties.[45]

These accounts of the virtues of 'ordinary', 'poor' or 'working' folk broach the matter of the character of the social identities created in dialect. Considerations of what may be termed the *processes* of dialect creation (the employment of the past, the social construction of community), has in fact already revealed a set of representations which testify to a widespread outlook that is much less a class than a 'populist' one in the senses employed here: instead of a 'working class' one has 'people', 'working folk', or just plain 'folk'. Perhaps the best way of getting at the range of associations and intersecting loyalties expressed through dialect is to quote from Clarke's very telling 'In Praise o' Lancashire',[46] published in 1923. Certain qualifications should be made. This is late dialect written by an avowed socialist. It is thus a kind of limit case: if class was muted here, then this was even more the case with dialect in its earlier heyday. And, indeed, class is muted; Clarke, though a socialist, was a child of early dialect and of the intellectual and everyday world that gave it form. The poem helps us to isolate the terms of reference in so much of the literature.

In Praise o' Lancashire

Eur Lanky dialect's rough, but straight;
No lappin' up o' nowt;
Swift fro' th' heart to th' lips it runs,
Noàn hauve-a-mile reaund th' fowt.
We ha' not time to waste i' words,
We speik an' get it done;
An' Lancashire folk an' their dialect
Are as feyther an' as son.

There's gam an' prank in eaur dialect,
There's t' breeze an' t' breath o' th' moor;
There's allus a merry joke on th' jump,
There's pity for them 'at's poor.
There's bit o' skit, a bank o'wit,
An' sharp an' shut-up snaps,
For foes what thinks us gobbins, or
Tak's us for gawmless chaps.

...

For we were th' fust wi' railways, lads,
Machines, an' thrutchin' trade;
There's not a foreign market, lads,

But what its Lanky-made.
Eaur Lanky lads an' their gaffers
Has built aw th' bloomin' earth;
An' there isn't a job that's wo'th owt
But Lancashire gan it birth.

...

For Lancashire's clever fingers
Has sponned aw th' world wi' steel,
Y' con yer eaur dialect whirrin'
Wheerever there's a wheel.
An' England gaffers th' world, that's true,
But when aw's said an' spun,
It's Lancashire runs Owd England,
An' that's heaw th' trick's been done.

It weren't yore chirpin' Cockneys
That fit up th'world wi' gear,
Made Lancashire into th' engine-heause
An' Britannia th' engineer;
Made Britannia th' engineer, lads,
That sets th' fly-wheel agate –
Not cockneys-neow! but Lanky lads,
That's at it soon an' late.

An' though we're best at workin',
We're dabs at feightin' too,
For Lanky dialect an' lads
Fowt weel at Waterloo;
An' in th' Greit European War
Mony a victory were won,
By a bit o' Lanky dialect
At th' trigger-end o' th' gun.

For freedom, too, we've fowt'n,
An' been th' fust its flag to raise;
Eaur hondlooms wove its banner
I' th' brave owd Chartist days!
Strong unions shield eaur labour neaw,
An' its truth we're speakin' when
We say no workers nowheer
Lives like Lancashire workin' men.

...

So give us th' good owd dialect,
That warms eaur hearts an' whums,
That sawders us together,
An' that cheeans us to eaur chums.

It may be rough-and-ready stuff,
An' noan so fal-lal smart,
But it's full o' good an' gumption,
And it's gradely good at th' heart!

The region is obviously central. Its greatest expression is perhaps
its language, dialect, which 'sawders' (solders) us together, and
'cheeans us to eaur chums'. Language and people are 'feyther' and
'son'. The custodians of regional identity are very importantly
working folk, but this is not exlusively so (just as, earlier, it was seen
how spoken dialect accentuated as well as blurred group distinctions).[47] Working people are the backbone of the staple industry that
has made Lancashire and England great. Lancashire is the standard
bearer of labour and political freedom. Clearly, the region was a
vital, and subsequently largely unrecognised, element in the way the
world was understood: it was a kind of prism through which
England, Britain and the Empire were seen. It was also the means
by which history and tradition were focused. Political advance and
industrial progress, however, if owing much to working folk and
the moral value of labour, were the product of others in Lancashire
society too: it is Lancashire lads but also their gaffers (employers)
who have 'built aw' th' bloomin earth'. In this respect, as more
widely, 'Lancashire folk' was a key term, signifying a pride in labour
that was yet part of a broader range of affiliations, here the region,
elsewhere the 'people'. The class possibilities were obviously present,
and could be accepted at particular times, as with Clarke to some
degree. But even with Clarke, as will be seen, it is clear that class was
subsumed in broader moral and political values.

People, indeed, saw little contradiction between these different
elements, say of class, nation, people or region. They seem to have
made up a coherent popular outlook, with the regional as a very
strong element, often framing the other aspects. This did not mean,
however, that elements like the region could not be appropriated
and given new meanings and directions. For instance, employers in
the north-east were quick to emphasise the association between
regional and industrial advance represented by their own great
firms. They commissioned and otherwise encouraged dialect writing,
making these associations explicit.[48] But, as noted previously,[49] in the
very positive evaluations of employers made by operative spokesmen,
there was more to it than this, and Clarke's inclusion of the 'gaffer'
in the pantheon of Lancashire greatness was only typical of genuinely
popular, un-patronised Tyneside song which associated the greatness
of the 'coaly Tyne' with the great firms and the engineering
'miracles' of the age.[50] We have seen that progress could be

criticised, but it is also necessary to recall the extraordinary transformations plain to contemporary eyes in regions where, for once, the term 'industrial revolution' is not a misnomer.

If one looks beyond capital to the state, the use of regional loyalties is clearly evident in the 'county' organisation of the British Army. These loyalties were exploited in the formation of the 'Pals' Brigades' of the First World War, calling on town patriotism as well: if the success these had in getting young men to volunteer is any index, then the loyalties dialect expressed were very powerful. In earlier days the British Army was not slow to realise this: how widespread the example was is unclear, but in 1880s India the Loyal North Lancashire Regiment published *The Lancashire Lad* in various parts of the sub-continent as the regiment moved postings.[51] Thus dialect-formed regional associations could be built upon and altered in particular ways: this will also be apparent in the late-century socialist and union uses of dialect, as well as in employers' great success in utilising demotic associations for the ends of party politics and employer industrial paternalism.[52]

Although one can specify a fairly coherent popular point of view, this itself was not without its own nuances and complexities. This is especially evident in the place of the region in relation to other regions, especially in regard to their labouring populations. This is an aspect with obvious relevance to the theme of class. In the Clarke example dialect also stands as the marker of regional virtues, set against metropolitan stereotypes of the northerner as 'gawmless'. Lancashire stands for the true England and Lancashire people of all sorts may come together under this banner. What was not the true England, in all dialect literature, was London. In Clarke's piece the whirr of the dialect is contrasted with the chirping Cockney, and his 'snidey spiff and slang'. This contrasting of region and nation with London is a central motif in dialect: Tyneside writers and performers (Corvan in the 1840s, Ridley in the 60s) presented the cockney as superior and condescending. The anti-metropolitan tendencies of dialect have been noted already. What was often presented in the manner of a comic adversarial relationship could however hide rather deeper currents.

This was particularly the case with Brierley. In his dialect dictionary a Cockney is defined as 'A man ut thinks hissel th' first Englishman i' th' land, but conno talk English', calling everyone outside London a 'bladdy caintryman'.[53] The frequently used device of the 'caintryman's' visit to London is employed by Brierley to present deep-seated feelings of the superiority of the north over the south, especially London: in London it is the stark contrast of riches and squalid poverty that is most evident.[54] On the one hand there is an idle and profligate aristocracy. On the other, the demoralised slum dweller. There is nothing in between. The poor Cockneys are used to squalor, and for Brierley it is almost something in their nature. This picture of demoralised extremes is contrasted with Lancashire, where extremes of this sort are not the case, and where people are not sunk in vicious idleness but exalted by productive labour. As with Clarke, the true people of England are those from the industrial north.

Something of the complexity of the theme of region is evident here. The association of the north and its regions with work and productive enterprise represents that realisation of class *through* region and locale noted earlier.[55] The stress on the workers' contribution to regional and national advance is strong. But it is balanced by the inclusion of those outside the ranks of workers who also make industrial Britain great. They too may suffer the condescension of the south. If the region, its industry, its traditions, and the value of its workpeople may be the source of how class so often came into being in Britain, then in the London–Lancashire contrast there are also evident marked divisions within the ranks of labour. (Textile unionism often expressed its distrust and contempt for the workshy rabble of the London poor.)[56]

In the Yorkshire literature, for instance in the writing of W. H. Hampson, later editor of the *Halifax Illuminated Clock Almanac*, the contrast is equally apparent: if a chap could not be either from Lancashire or Yorkshire, he had better be a Scot.[57] Above all, he should not be a Londoner. Here one sees a reflection of broader inter-regional alliances against the centre, against its ruling class as well as its casual poor. The heritage of northern chauvinism was a double-edged sword. The idea of one true England was present from the early days of dialect: the *Barnsla Foaks Annual* gave it voice in 1840, and it marked the Yorkshire almanacs long into the twentieth century.[58] In the figure of Joseph Wright, compiler of the *English Dialect Dictionary*, one sees this northern consciousness at work: in his scholarly labours Wright encountered much snobbery directed at dialect, and in return he asserted the values of his own Yorkshire, not least in the form of that contrast between the northern 'grit' of Yorkshire and the effete south which is still very much a part of English culture.[59]

Moving on to the matter of direct depictions of the social order, as in the ballads the principal emphasis is not on class but on the distinctions between rich and poor. The ballads and dialect were both popular in the third quarter of the century, though dialect represented what was new and went on to supplant the ballads in popular affection. Thus dialect took over the terms of reference of the ballads, but developed them in the ways we have seen, adapting them to the experiences and needs of the new industrial workforce. A considerable degree of continuity is thus evident between the two forms and the social outlook they represented, but there is real change within this continuity as well. John Hartley, favourite of the industrial proletariat of the Yorkshire factory towns, will serve to begin exploration of the central theme of rich and poor and of this creative re-working of established ways of seeing the social order.

In the *Halifax Illuminated Clock Almanac* for 1888, under the title 'It's Wicked To Be Poor', he re-casts familiar themes with reference to horse-race betting, an activity by then deeply ingrained in northern popular culture. The theme of one law for the rich, one for the poor is as alive here as in the Tichborne case: in the literature more widely law, not capital, is the greater emblem of social injustice. Here, as with Tyneside writers such as Joe Wilson, the police are the butt of ridicule, to be blamed as executors of the law, yet pitied as its (mostly) workingman dupes: they are presented in dialect form in Hartley's story, like his workers, but the magistrate who jails the poor and ignores aristocratic betting speaks standard English. This association of privilege and the law is frequently found in the Yorkshire almanacs.[60] So are aphorisms expressing how readily the contrast of rich and poor was seen by contemporaries as basic: the *Weyver's Awn* for 1885 claimed that society was made up of two classes, those with more appetite than dinner, and those with more dinner than appetite (again the motifs of food and hunger are apparent).[61] Almanac wisdom also turned on a sardonic recognition of wealth ill-got: 'Many a chaps honest becos he's nivver had a chance to be owt else', or 'Ther's mony a fortune made, but few at's been earned.'[62]

Hartley is again characteristic in elaborating the moral virtues of poverty (rather more than of labour, though poor 'working folk' were important). In 'All We Had' readers are enjoined, of necessity, to make poverty their friends.[63] In the *Weyver's Awn* for 1881, though poverty has to be embraced, the ideal state is the avoidance of extremes.[64] 'T' middle state' should be aimed at. Success and failure equally spoil people. This is the ideal. The reality, that of poverty, provides its own wisdom and virtue: those born in clover do not know what it is to 'rep a bare pasture'. In the *Bob Stubbs* almanac (1911),[65] among the rich money replaces the free gift of love. The illusions of wealth are the obverse of the knowledge poverty and moderation bring: 'Rich for Twenty Four Hours' (*Tommy Toddles*, 1875) is a kind of precursor of twentieth-century folk wisdom about winning the football pool. The comic protagonist Billy Bunting inherits the cares and falseness money brings before his dream of riches dissolves in reality. In the same number 'A Pair O' Clogs' expresses something like a caste pride in poverty, Nancy the Dewsbury working lass choosing the man who wears clogs over the man who spurns them. The clog was of course a major symbol of popular identity in these regions.

Representations of poverty are linked to a selective attack upon the rich. The pretensions of the wealthy are singled out, representing a betrayal of what is a common human nature: muck in a carriage and muck in a cart are the same. In Hartley and Waugh it is the fop or dandy who is the special object of approbrium.[66] Brierley's *Ab o' th' Yate Dictionary* is, as often, the best guide: 'gentry', the quality, are above speaking to others, and are defined as 'arrogant, useless lumber'. The fop therefore symbolises the flaunting of wealth, its condescension, and is the obverse of 'gradely' humanity. Brierley heaps on the insults: an 'aristocrat' is a 'monkey', idle and vicious in his indulgence. 'Folk' is a word which connotes all that is genuine. There is no mistaking here the acute sensitivity to the vices of wealth, especially of the aristocracy, already seen in the ballad and the radical tradition itself.[67] In Hartley's stories these vices are linked to the arrogance of power. The man with power, especially a little power, is the worst sort.[68] What especially irks is the amount of bowing and scraping 'poor folk' have to do these days. They should speak out, difficult as it is, and in his 'Give it Em Hot' Hartley inveighs against vice, even if it is that of a lord.[69] The social order is seen in terms of moral attributes (pretensions, ostentation, arrogance, hypocrisy), and these are seen as distortions of a true humanity retained by the poor despite, yet largely because of, their poverty.

Hartley rehearses all these themes, and his work in turn reflects all the significant strands in the literature. In 'Nivver Heed' the central aspect of poor people's struggle to live is conveyed: 'bide' and 'biding' are key terms throughout dialect, and the emphasis here on stoicism is very characteristic.[70] 'Happiness cannot be bought with money.' 'If it is little you get its little you need.' The sayings are precisely those verbal counters of twentieth-century 'working-class culture' noted by Hoggart. The religious tone is marked: in 'The Honest Hard Worker' the worn hand is the passport to heaven. This is repeated in the almanacs where it could be very marked; typical mottoes were: 'Mak t' Best o' Life', 'Humility Inherits The Earth', 'God Will Reward Your Care and Toil'.[71] It would be a mistake, however, to regard this stoicism as quietism. Religion was usually accompanied by a deep-seated belief in human brotherhood: the almanacs look forward to its realisation in this life not the next.[72] Similarly, Waugh across the Pennines constructed a religion which was at once a religion of God and mankind, of the next world and this.[73] Whatever its ingredients, secular or divine, the exalted moral tone is ever present and deserving of the name religion, as well as of the term 'utopian'. It is a utopianism that irradiates the whole literature, informing the everyday experience and activities of 'poor folk'. The utopian aspirations to justice and reconciliation seen to characterise popular art are specially marked in dialect. This religious current is decidedly non- and anti-sectarian. This is so in Laycock,[74] and in Brierley's dictionary the parson figures as the hypocrite *sans pareil*. While the Nonconformist chapel formed many of these writers, there is a keen eye for the canting chapel hypocrite. The aspiration to human fraternity is accompanied by a fine eye for the hypocrisy of the well-to-do. Joseph Baron's 'Living on Sixpence A Day' is a minor masterpiece of satire against 'Kristian Fooaks' who think they understand the working people on the basis of a (canting) ten-minute weekly visit.[75] A consideration of some of the leading Lancashire authors serves to explore these aspects in a more detailed way, in particular the character of the social vision involved and the place of politics in this.

In Brierley's work the usual emphasis on the facade of riches is apparent.[76] In Brierley, as in the literature at large, notions of economic class carry little weight. It is interesting that in Brierley's dictionary 'cash' is accompanied by a drawing of Mammon, and 'pelf' by one of a laurelled and victorious £.s.d. figure. 'Economic' criteria continued to be seen in resolutely moral terms. However, in 'The Colliers' Spree' Brierley highlights aspects not yet directly treated.[77] The colliers' worth is seen to be as great as anyone's. However, when they depart from their accustomed sphere and imitate the manners of the rich they are seen as comically absurd. In 'Shoiny Jim's Kesmas Dinner' the prole as swell is mocked.[78] The mock-inversion of high cuisine as Lancashire cuisine serves to symbolise the cultural inversion accompanying the poor stepping outside their own boundaries. Interpretations of dialect, drawing on important conventions like the innocent abroad returning always to the comfort of his known environment, have rightly dwelt on a kind of self-denying ordinance, a limitation to the known and familiar.[79] There is indeed in dialect a strong vein of social conservatism. This echoed the inner character of popular culture: as was argued above, the significance of boundary, order and regulation made up both a strong conception of 'station' and a marked fatalism.[80]

Yet the culture we have looked at was marked by a profound tension between fatalism and aspiration. Dialect in particular shows how conservatism could be translated into something much more positive. Social distinctions were recognised but were met with in particular ways. In one respect distinctions of wealth and power are recognised so long as they can be given a moral foundation. In another respect, there is a desire to move beyond ideas of just and respectful wealth to the extinction of all distinctions in the way of communion between people. In both respects the similarities with the perspectives of the ballads are striking. The moralism and the 'religious' aspirations of the ballads have been adapted and developed for application in the growing industrial districts of England, yet the frame of mind is still recognisable as similar to what went before.

In Brierley those of the well to do who, as it were, invert their usual failings are accepted and applauded: in 'T' Oppenin of Manchester Teawn Hall' those 'high-ups' who do not put on airs, and who act as ordinary, decent folk, are fit to sit down with Ab at the Owd Bell in Walmsley Fowt.[81] The figure of the respectful, paternalist employer was, as has been seen, very powerful in dialect and the general culture.[82] In Brierley one also has the decent, dialect-speaking parson who, contrary to most representations of organised religion, is the opposite of the canting hypocrite.[83] In these representations moralised wealth is regarded as acceptable. Given certain kinds of behaviour the status quo was bearable.

But it was not just, and in this respect dialect did not aim at a revolution in politics or in social conditions. However, this did not mean that it was socially conservative. The search for justice began in the revolution of the heart. Dialect was a literature of aspiration suited to a culture where aspiration was integral: this broadly religious sense of humanity and society might take many forms, but though it involved ideas of how things *ought to be* we should not fail to see the capacity it had to underpin change in what *was*. Even if aspiration could not always be realised it informed thought and action. Utopias were of real effect in the world.

Brierley's account of a penny reading provides a kind of cameo of the social order:[84] at the reading the 'grands' and 'commons' are segregated by differently priced seats. The mirth of the 'commons' at the snobbery and moralising of the officiating parson and employer is not directed at the 'grands'. Rather, grands and commons laugh together. High and low are united in human sentiment, and the inference is that if the grands behave thus the social distinctions they represent can be accommodated. But Brierley – and the literature in general – go somewhat deeper than this. The religious form in particular pushes social distinctions aside to emphasise the falsity of the world and appearances: the conclusion of his 'Hard Times' will be recalled, 'Ye sufferers on earth / Come hither, and try your new clothes! / For the poor shall be rich, and the rich all alike / No moore creep—o'ers or howd-teh-bi-th'-wohs.'[85]

However, the social vision is usually rendered in a comic and secular way, not at odds with the religious sense – indeed part of it. Here the humanity of the wealthy is most evident when they are most like the poor, baptised again in the likeness of ordinary folk. What is apparent, therefore, is that ordinary folk are the truest measure of and guide to a proper humanity; notions of fraternity have their own decided 'class' hue. Nonetheless, if 'ordinary', 'poor' or 'working folk' know best what fraternity is, these versions of a just society abjure class as its denial. The picture of royalty in Brierley is revealing. The Queen is seen as at bottom one of the people – 'Th' owd mother o' princes', 'simplicity itself'. In his 'Th' Queen and Ab o' th' Yate' Brierley contrasts the home 'fowt' with Manchester,[86] where flunkeys are itching for knighthoods. The 'gradely' Queen finds refuge in the gradely 'fowt'. This fiction of the high rendered human is typical of the literature,[87] and is of course a variation on the theme of inversion we have taken to be so characteristic of popular art, particularly in its utopian moments. Here the moment takes the form appropriate to the condition and outlook of the new industrial proletariat of the north.

In 'A Royal Visit' this appropriation of the high goes together with a typically strong assertion of pride in 'working folk'.[88] (See the full text of this in appendix 16.) If the visiting prince, the royal 'lad', had to fight for his livelihood he would be stronger than he is. The ostentation of carriage folk is guyed as are the stereotypes the rich have of the poor. Times have changed, Manchester is not to be compared with London, where poverty is evident on the streets. The Manchester streets the prince visits form the quarter of the workers, not the swells: it is proud of its gradely lasses and its 'food of the people', as Brierley puts it (chiefly pig's trotters and tripe). In the end the 'royal lad' is accepted into the august company of the ordinary, working Lancastrian, ending his day, as his father before him, at the Bull in Walmsley Fowt. What is imaged in these religious and secular ways, in Brierley and elsewhere, is a popular definition of fraternity and humanity which dissolves social distinctions as artificial and onerous.

If dialect called for a revolution of the heart and not of the social order this immediately raises the question of the role of politics. The themes of self-help and self-improvement so strong in Victorian society were reflected in readers and writers alike, indicating as they did the revolution of the inner man. In Laycock's work this stress on the respectable receives expression in poems like 'Help Yo'rsels Lads' or 'A Respectable Man'.[89] The sense that the poor have their own failings and must set their own house in order before they criticise others is strong,[90] as is the idea that no man owes working folk a living. All must work. It would be wrong if the poor could pick up their bread from the streets.[91] Yet one is far removed here from the bourgeois pieties: rather than individual self-help it is 'our' house that must be set in order. It is the collective house of the poor or working folk that is to be reformed by the joint endeavours of people themselves.

These endeavours took collective form in political action. Many of the leading dialect writers were strong Liberals of the radical sort. Political action was far from precluded in the pursuit of the kind of society imaged in dialect. Yet the essential change was perhaps one of the heart, of moral reform (itself nonetheless collectively seen). In fact, the kind of moral regeneration desired was strikingly political. Liberalism and the socialism that followed it were first about moral and spiritual transformation, and only secondly about social change. They may not, however, be condescended to as simply 'reformist'. This would be akin to confusing the predominating stoicism of dialect with quietism. Rather than representing a mere acceptance of the reformed status quo, utopian aspirations often involved a more far-reaching spiritual change of heart than is compatible with the idea of reformism. This will be pursued below, where socialist appro-priations of dialect are considered.

Here one may dwell briefly on what was a rather ambiguous characterisation of politics in dialect. There was an underlying scepticism about the efficacy of politics that was widespread, and paradoxically enough this could also be present where political loyalties and activism were intense, as they so often were in the industrial areas of Britain at this time.[92] Even in a professed Liberal like Brierley, the sense of radicals and Tories for ever locked in argument, mindless of the welfare of the people, is a strong one.[93] In his *Ab o' th' Yate Dictionary* terms like 'vote', 'electors' and 'government' are defined in such a way as to depict politics as a mindless clash of partisan armies among the voters, and a corrupt game of 'ins' and 'outs' among the politicians. Much of this was accurate enough commentary on the state of party politics, and did not preclude a belief in political action of what was taken to be a purposeful or 'rational' form (especially among workingmen Liberals).[94] Yet the distrust of mere political change went deeper and is represented in the wide range of dialect texts that see 'party' as divisive. It is perhaps party feeling rather than political action *per se* that is scorned, yet the condemnation of parties and present electoral politics is so emphatic as to indicate the distrust of politics suggested. Clearly, this distrust sprang from both the conception of the priority of moral regeneration and the 'populist' distrust of politics and politicians noted already.[95] Partisan politics was seen as the product of ignorance and cheap drink,[96] ignoring the real interests of the working man;[97] a sectarian and manipulative exercise in which the 'high ups' and their parties were in it for what they could get.[98]

If sometimes retarded by this scepticism, socialists in Lancashire and Yorkshire were able to tap into the social identities elaborated in dialect, and give a new direction to them. The hugely popular Allen Clarke is evidence of this. An example of his work will be found in appendix 20. Around Clarke's various journals grew up something like a socialist subculture, with its own clubs and activities, akin on a smaller scale to that of Blatchford's *Clarion* movement. Dialect was a rallying point for a new, young generation of socialist activists, who saw in it evidence of a unique popular tradition.[99] However, it is Clarke's engagement through his literature with a much larger audience that is chiefly of interest. His overtly propagandistic writing had far less success than his popular applications of dialect seen in his comic writing. Here Clarke helped elicit a sense emerging in factory life itself,[100] namely the idea of the joint interests of 'factory foak'. As we have seen,[101] socialism and unionism draw on these dialect-created associations, the latter perhaps with more success than the former. Nonetheless, in Clarke's popular work, the socialist message was preached in a way particularly relevant to his audience: his stories dwelt upon what he termed 'industrial injustice', aiming through the use of comedy and ridicule to turn this sense of injustice into a larger awareness of their condition as factory workers. (His frustration at the conservatism and deference of factory workers, indeed his depiction of them as 'slaves' of a 'system', was the other side of the coin, militating against his great capacity to engage their sympathies.)[102]

Yet whether to the activist or the mass, and despite the newness of his socialism, Clarke represented very considerable continuities with the past. The novelty of his socialism, amply preached in his journals, cannot be denied: it is present in a strong sense of the agency of workers themselves, also of change being imminent, and in the employment of a class vocabulary with ideas of capital and labour as distinct interests. Yet the continuities were enormous. Clarke, like Turner for instance, was a child of the moral and emotional world of nineteenth-century dialect. Like Ben Turner, he learned from his father to love dialect literature and saw himself as the heir to Bobbin and to Waugh. (Waugh and Tolstoy were the strangely assorted icons in Clarke's spiritual life). Clarke was aware that the factory system and dialect literature grew up together: he

saw the intimate connnections between the two, connections of
which he was an expression.[103] The social and political outlook
present in dialect, and in nineteenth-century Liberalism, powerfully
informed his socialism, as it did that of so many of his generation.

His fictions echoed the same emphasis on the humanity of all
folks.[104] Even his accounts of a human, 'gradely' monarchy are
similar to Brierley.[105] His politics utilised a vocabulary of moral
regeneration which underneath the class rhetoric dealt with
universalistic conceptions of the social order. This was indeed the
reason for its successful appropriation of dialect. Clarke's emphasis
on the role of 'capital' and 'labour' took the forms which, as we
have seen, were far removed from class war.[106] He spoke of revolt but
it was 'democratic revolt' that he meant. Clarke's enthusiasm was
for Ernest Jones on democracy rather than for Marx.[107] Democracy
was not class rule, not the rule of the working class, but the rule of
the nation, embracing all and tempering different social elements
one with another. Democracy for Clarke was but Christianity
applied, and these democratic vistas were central to his socialism.
God is the God of all in society.[108] For Clarke, socialism was about
the reconciliation of all God's children in a commonwealth of the
people. The co-op movement represented one embodiment of this
commonwealth. It did not much concern a socialist appropriation of
production. Similarly, municipal government carried the same
message of reconciliation. The issue of municipal reform was above
the common concerns of party politics because of this. Despite the
newness of his outlook it is its debt to the radical tradition that is
uppermost. Similarly, despite the range of influences acting upon
Clarke, the values and associations present in the dialect tradition
were central. In this Clarke differed little from the masses of his
contemporaries, for whom he was a major spokesman.

The example of Clarke and of socialism reveals a set of values solid
and enduring, but also capable of changes in meanings and use. In
the next chapter this capacity for change becomes further evident,
particularly in the case of twentieth-century popular art. Of course,
the assumptions present in and created by dialect literature were
only one aspect of the varied life of the popular stage.

Before turning to this however, this account can be suitably
concluded with a selection of definitions from Brierley's *Ab o' th' Yate*
dialect dictionary of 1881. Brierley himself was not necessarily
typical of the audiences he spoke to, though the dominant radicalism
evident in what follows was characteristic of writers, if not of readers.
However, like all dialect fictions, this articulated the preconceptions
of the readers, and so serves as an invaluable guide to their views. It
is a piece of the dialect map which enables us to reconstruct the

whole. Its ironic tone and humour are not the least representative thing about it:

Archbishop ... It's thowt by some that he looks more after th' fleece than he does his flock.

Aristocrat. A useless hanger-on o' society. A gilded pauper, livin o' what his great-granfeythurs has stown off somebody elze. One ut looks deawn on folk ut are a great deal *nobler* than hissel. Sometimes a moneyed foo.

Atheist. A mon ut doesn' believe as another believes.

...

Folk. People. A very whoamly word, an means a great deeal. We liken saying – "eaur folk", "gradely folk", "owd folk" an' "young folk". We seldom say "bad folk". We liken to mean *good*, when th' words used.

...

Freedom. Th' opposite o' slavery. A state o' being more talk'd about than understood. A mon'll say 'Rule Britannia' ... when at th' same time he takken a hoss's place in th' shafts of a carriage, an' happen his dowter's working sixteen heurs a day wi' her needle, for just a bare livin'. An' this is a *free country*.

...

Labour. Work. Strictly spakin' it means hard work. It's considered by some to be a slovenly road o' gettin' a livin' ... Heawever a mon mit swager abeaut th' work he does, he wouldno like *labourer* to be at th' end o' his name. *Gentleman* an' thats supposed to be a mon ut gets his livin' by doin' nowt ... I wonder heaw it is work is so undignified ... there awt to be some dignity abeaut *labour* when th' Great Architect o' th' universe wur his own hod-carrier. After that, what is a gentleman but a sponge?

...

Land. Summat ut belongs to nob'dy unless they'n stown it, or their feythurs have stown it for 'em ...

...

Loom. A weyvers treadmill. My feythur passed sentence on me when I're fourteen, an' condemn'd me, for th' crime o' coming into th' world, to six days a week hard labour. I'm sarvin yet.

...

Magistrate. A mon ut's put in peawer fu t' fine drunken folk, if they're poor, an' go fuddlin hissel till he conno' see his road whoam... they kneaw no more abeaut law than a weyver kneaws about geaut (gout)...

...

Nonconformist. Some folk thinkin' he's a mon ut would like to have a whul chapel to hissel, or have every man to think as he does...

...

Pelf. Riches, in an odious sense. What's getten wi' thavin', or gamblin', or takin' it as their awn under the name o'reight. That uts gettin by squeezin' th' poor till they're flat... whichever way brass is getten it's glorified an' creawn't wi' th' bays o' a hero. I could do wi' an honourably-getten trifle or two on't.

...

Quality. Persons of high rank. Not aulus... They dunno' seem to remember what Burns has said,

'The rank is but the guinea's stamp;
The man the gowd for a' that'

13

Stages of class: popular theatre and the geography of belonging

The music hall indicates a more indirect relationship between the creation and reception of popular art than was the case with ballads and dialect. Popular theatre, and particularly the music halls, came to have a fairly uniform character throughout the country. In terms of organisation and performance one can speak of a 'national' form of art. Paradoxically enough, the early century ballads have a kinship here, but even they when compared with the music hall indicate how progressively in the century regional differences might figure somewhat less than national similarities. The case of the music hall therefore brings out the whole question of the relationship between the different social and geographical stages – local, regional and national – upon which the senses of belonging and solidarity were played out at the time. What is evident is something much more complex than the eclipse of the local and the regional by the national. If in some respects regional and introspective, dialect also pointed outwards to broader national horizons as well. The example of dialect in fact illustrates how these different levels or stages might be complementary: rather than disparate aspects of 'class' development it is a *relationship* which is chiefly evident. The changing character of this relationship will be considered in due course: it will be evident that the regional stage was to continue to matter greatly.

Nonetheless, the nature of the music hall in particular enables one to explore the character of social identities across the regions, where important new patterns were emerging in the late nineteenth century. To begin with audiences: these were in social character 'popular' rather than ostensibly 'working class', in melodrama as well as in music hall. Thus the social ambience of the theatre tended to emphasise one sort of image of the social order rather than another. Audiences were 'popular' in the sense that petit-bourgeois elements were drawn in (some higher social elements too), as well as all sections of the working classes.[1] This social mix makes music hall in particular a productive means by which to explore social attitudes. This is all the more the case in that within this arena of the popular classes social distinctions were marked and social differences were played out: there were differences between but especially *within*

305

the halls, different seating and pricing arrangements reflecting differences of socio-economic status in the community. The necessity of conceiving of the music hall as in fact a kind of laboratory of social style has earlier been emphasised[2]. Associations, beliefs and allegiances were brought *to* the halls, but the social order was not simply created outside and reflected in the theatre. Rather, the various 'social selves' of audiences were examined, undermined and re-created in the halls themselves. Imaginative strategies had an important role in managing 'real' life. The social order was created in, as much as outside, the venues of art.

Peter Bailey has done more than anyone else to make us aware of the role of music hall in actively transacting social relations. His exemplary account of the 'swell song' indicates how social distinctions could be both demarcated and subsumed.[3] The 'gentleman swell' might provide a model for the clerk, for example, in which sympathy and satire were combined. The 'coster swell' could function as the butt of lower-middle class elements in the audience. On the other hand, versions of the 'real gentleman' might play out notions of the 'natural' alliance of the aristocrat and the pleb, the real gent and nature's gent joining hands to worship at the shrine of pleasure to the exclusion of the middle-class do-gooder. But while the genuine swell might be admired and the pseudo-swell guyed by a popular audience, so too could the figure of the swell be the butt of anti-aristocrat feeling. Different styles of song and performance reflected different possibilities, but it was also the case that the performance and reception of almost all the swell songs embraced a high measure of ambiguity.

Songs on the theme of 'Jones and the working girl' reflected similar possibilities, distinctions between the lower middle class of Jones the clerk and the working girl being in this case the social border that was patrolled.[4] In this example gender distinctions were perhaps as significant as social ones. Inter-class sympathies based on the solidarity of male audiences were clearly evident. On the other hand, in the work of the renowned Marie Lloyd, the 'good bad' girl might symbolise a real aspiration to independence on the part of women.[5]

These instances are based on recent research on the music hall. This kind of cultural analysis is, however, only in its early days, and there is as yet insufficient of it to give more than a fairly rough-and-ready account of the dominant forms of social representation evident in popular entertainment. Music hall dealt in values which subsumed class differences. Orwell is of considerable interest on the halls, noting how they functioned as a 'second language' for all classes.[6] This 'Englishness' took the form of the language of parody, conceit, and above all innuendo. Its master was the twentieth-century comic Max Miller. As will be seen, the elevation of northern figures such as Gracie Fields and George Formby into the status of national icons shows how important the music hall was as a source of cultural symbolism. This elevation could be a rather deliberate affair, Fields and Formby, for instance, figuring as emblems of the kind of working people their superiors wished to see. The same process as in dialect is apparent. Something similar is also evident in superior, drawing-room appropriations of the broadside ballad.[7]

There were, however, rather more elusive forces at work, which produced notions of national and social character that were perhaps closer to the appeal of Max Miller and more deeply buried in the national psyche than the manufactured versions of the northern, industrial English evident in the cases of Fields and Formby. Similarities of sensibility between different social groups were evident: Victorians of many sorts shared a common love of the sentimental and the pathetic, for instance,[8] and for much of the century there was a common love of melodrama.[9] This is an area of great interest which needs much closer attention given it than has previously been the case. The nearest thing to an analogy with Orwell's comments on a national *lingua franca* is Darnton's treatment of the French peasant folk tale, and how by uncharted, subterranean means these have crept into versions of Frenchness. (If the English exemplify cheek and innuendo, the French are negative, detached, foxy.)[10]

Bratton's work on the Victorian popular ballad in its drawing room, music hall, and published forms helps take this a little further.[11] In considering the 'heroic ballad' she dwells upon the similarities of style and sentiment obtaining between high and low representations of Jack Tar, one of the first versions of the common man as hero to span class differences. The common British sailor symbolised patriotism, but it is in his guise as the obscure individual that he is most revealing. Though not anti-war, the heroic ballad did not usually glorify nation and empire. Rather, it exalted the ordinary man fighting against the odds, conquering himself and – often – the incompetence of his superiors. The potency of these notions of the common man is especially evident in the case of Kipling's ballads. The cult of the common man thus took forms emphasising populism rather than class. There were, however, 'class' differences apparent in the 'ballads of the common man' examined by Bratton, but these were of a character congruent with the dominant 'populist' reading of the social order traced in the other forms of popular art. Figures like the outlaw, the criminal and the costermonger often emblematised for the poor a sense of social

differences and opposition to the higher classes or the rich. As we
have see, they also symbolised aspirations to independence on the
part of working people.[12]

It is Bailey's work which throws most light on the social outlook
evident in music hall.[13] The themes of feast, plenitude and profusion
were central to the ethos of the halls in their late century
manifestation. These reflected changed patterns of spending and of
the use of time among audiences. With a number of qualifications,
one may speak of an increasing 'consumerism' in the later nineteenth
century, in which the demand side of increased wages and less work
time was met by the supply side, not only in the realm of
entertainment, but also in the marketing and distribution of
consumer goods.[14] The ethos of the halls also reflected the increasing
material and ideological separation of work and non-work time
evident later on in this period.[15] 'Leisure' came to be a subject of
intense public debate and concern. Music hall was one of the most
important expressions of the problems and possibilities thrown up by
these changes. The halls emphasised the celebration of consumption
in terms of their exaltation of style: the figure of 'Champagne
Charlie' was in these respects an evocative one. At the same time the
halls emphasised 'family' entertainment and respectability, or at
least paid lip-service to these goals.

The halls attempted to reconcile indulgence and restraint. In his
work on the comic art of the 1880s, especially on the cartoon figure
of Ally Sloper, Bailey shows how widespread were these concerns
beyond the music hall alone.[16] The figure of Sloper represented an
attempt at balancing release and constraint, all within the larger
creation of social mythologies which turned upon the idea of 'the
good time'. In the music hall the principal guardian of the good time
was the entrepreneur or impresario. Bailey dwells on the example of
Billy Holland. Holland as entrepreneur symbolised the merits of the
market and of competitive self-advancement. He and his like dwelt
on the ·ideas of success and social mobility as well as upon
respectability. Yet they were capitalists of a strange sort, of the ranks
of the gambler and *parvenu* rather than of respectable wealth. In
establishing the idea of the good time, and in elaborating the themes
of feast and profusion, they developed notions of themselves and of
their stars as heroes and servants of the people. They exalted the
people and were in turn exalted by them. Holland was 'the people's
caterer', another 'People's William' alongside the greatest of all
heroes of a virtuous people, William Gladstone.

What was at issue was the people's right to enter into the kingdom
of leisure in which everyone was equal, and distinctions of class did
not exist. That kingdom was predicated upon the idea of the good

time, upon new versions of bonhomie and liberality that purported to speak directly to the people in an era of nascent democracy. Bailey is quite right to draw a parallel between the development of notions of the fraternity of pleasure and the growth of democracy attendant upon the Second and Third Reform Acts. Just as the people were the rightful heirs of the democracy of pleasure, so too by their virtue had they earned the right of inclusion in the reformed political order. Their right to inclusion in the social order was thus argued by their tribunes, the two Williams. In other work I have shown how both party politics and employer paternalism in the manufacturing districts of the time depended heavily upon the exploitation of the virtues of bonhomie and liberality among those who purported to be the people's leaders and representatives.[17] Clearly, the classless, pseudo-egalitarianism evident in this cultivation of the people in the political and cultural spheres owed a great deal to the new sorts of social identity being pioneered and explored in music hall.

In turn such exploration was made possible because of the general intellectual climate of the times. The late nineteenth century and early twentieth century was a time when the vocabulary of 'mass' and 'masses' was at least as prominent as class in the language of social description.[18] The hero of 'mass culture' was the little man, the common man. The vocabularies of class and mass society overlapped here: the little man took on characteristics akin to those of the 'lower middle class', at a time when this stratum was increasingly given a class designation. But the 'little' or 'common' man, as we have seen in the ballads, was essentially socially indeterminate, indeed a marginal figure. The figure of the common man reaches one kind of apotheosis in the figure of Joyce's Leopold Bloom, the little man as hero, the mock-heroic at last ennobled.

Bloom finds an unlikely kinship in the world of popular art, in the 'liberal populism' of the music hall but also of the new, popular comic art of the 1880s. In the cartoon figure Ally Sloper it is apparent how in both forms there is the same reduction of social distance between 'high' and 'low'; the same guying of the high, but nonetheless the same inclusion of the mighty, for example the monarchy, as part of a common humanity. There are parallels here between the southern comic hero Sloper and the northern hero, 'Ab o' th' Yate': both were engaged in demystifying the social order, reducing it to the manageable proportions of the familiar, of 'folk' or 'ordinary people'. As Bailey indicates, Sloper is plebeian without being class bound, the first demotic hero of the period (along with Ab one should add) who was not a servant or a criminal.

Bailey has applied the term 'liberal populism' to the music hall, but it clearly extends to other forms of popular art, and to popular culture and popular politics more widely considered. It is apparent how the new, democratic and utopian vistas of leisure and consumption could serve the ends of a pseudo-egalitarian politics, manipulating these currents for its own purpose. Indeed, Gladstonian Liberalism can be seen partly in this light, and party politics more widely depended much on the exploitation of these rich veins of identity and aspiration. Outside the political sphere *per se*, 'liberal populism' needs to be traced in relation to the contextualised etymology of terms akin to 'the people', 'the masses' or 'the common man', namely 'the public', and those clustering around the idea of 'social citizenship', an idea of increasing significance in the early twentieth century.[19]

However, there is another side indicated by the figure of 'Ab': the sentiments focused in this figure were clearly capable of producing a politics that was not pseudo-egalitarian. One hesitates to emphasise a south-north distinction here, as the ethos of the music hall was national in scope. Nonetheless, the more radical potential of the associations clustering around the figure of Ab is apparent, just as the northern music hall itself injected very marked regional characteristics which distanced and to some extent undermined the consequences of the exaltation of consumption.

Music hall in both north and south also had characteristics that suggest a capacity to stamp 'liberal populism' with the character of people's own culture, and to some extent with a class impression. The link between individual halls and their local communities continued to be strong despite the growth of chain ownership by the entertainment entrepreneurs. The halls were expected to respond to local needs (mounting strike and accident benefits, for example), and audience groups exerted what Bailey calls a 'moral economy' of the halls, a set of expectations and sanctions expressing their own view of what the halls should be like.[20] Nonetheless, the example of the music hall suggests the development of new social identities which, however appropriated and developed, may be seen to occlude class understandings of society.

The same can generally be said of melodrama, a form which by 1900 had long been deeply entrenched in popular affections. Melodrama deserves much more attention than can be given it here, though some brief observations are in order. This form of theatre exemplified further the dominant 'populism' so far emerging in this examination of the different kinds of popular art. The idea of the virtues and value of labour is as marked as elsewhere, but so too is the human and moral explanation of oppression, injustice and social change. In one well-known example, *The Factory Lad*, economic change in the form of the introduction of steam power and the development of the factory system[21] is viewed as the product of moral failing. Instead of notions of social change the intensely polarised world of melodrama presented the battle of good and evil in its manifold forms as the cause of events: the ground of the 'social' is simply evacuated. Again, the religious sense is much in evidence.

Melodrama put a premium on presenting the world in a particular way that did not easily lend itself to understandings based on class. This may be briefly illustrated by *The Sign of the Cross*, the most popular play of the late nineteenth century, and arguably of the century as a whole.[22] This sort of historical romance was quite typical, much more typical than plays about strikes and factories (again one is aware how in the nineteenth century the historical sense was a privileged mode of interpretation). The opposition that is central in the play is that of Rome and the early Christians, the former symbolising the unholy alliance of the aristocracy, the Established Church, and the entrepreneur, the latter a people enslaved and excluded by this oppressive ruling class. Social discontent took religious form (the artisan, small tradesman and Nonconformist credentials of the Christians are apparent), but this discontent can hardly be given a class label, at least in the sense of class used here.

The same may be said on the basis of an examination of a fairly typical example of the proletarian vein of melodrama, namely the portable or 'fit-up' theatre of the Hodson family, just outside Sheffield.[23] In the early twentieth century the plays performed here, many written for local taste by J. C. Hodson, show just how late many of the elements previously discussed were to persist. The very popular historical romances played by the Hodsons frequently represent the struggle of 'the people of England' against oppressive rulers, as well as the virtue of English liberty against foreign tyranny.[24] As such, they represent a continuation of much older melodramatic accounts of the struggle of liberty against tyranny seen in plays like *Wat Tyler* and *William Tell*. Indeed, these plays themselves continued to be very popular throughout the century. Plays of unashamed patriotism were also put on, especially in the First World War,[25] reminding us of the politically conservative applications of ideas of English liberty and of the struggles of the English people.

It is Hodson's home-grown plays that are of particular interest: productions such as 'The Perils of A Miner's Life'.[26] These in fact bear a very strong resemblance to the romances printed in the textile operatives' union journals considered earlier.[27] The same emphasis on the dignity of labour is evident, but so too is the emphasis on fate and human morality as the moving principles of history. Above all, the melodrama of 'wish fulfilment' echoes the romance in its highly conventionalised but magical realisation of utopian justice and social reconciliation. The miner marries the mineowner's daughter and inherits the mine. The hero nonetheless retains the character and values of the workingman, yet the workingman is symbolically wedded with capital in a realisation of the human value that underlies social distinctions.

Having so far looked at a fairly representative range of examples of popular literature and entertainment, it is time to draw breath and consider how these help us understand popular conceptions of the social order in this period. The contrast between music hall and dialect literature highlights the place of the local and regional in the formation of popular culture and popular politics. Music hall seems to have been a response to pan-regional economic and cultural developments. There were clear tendencies towards centralisation in its direction and to a uniformity of response in its reception. Similarly, it is arguable that the ballads signified a broader popular culture than was later registered in dialect.[28] Contrary to teleological notions of the onward march of social and cultural centralisation and standardisation in the process of industrialisation, we may be seeing the development of a highly regionalised and heterogeneous 'working class'.

As witnessed by the example of dialect, this might be reflected in parochial and introspective attitudes. There is a degree of justice in these observations, but the qualifications one is forced to make suggest that something rather more complex and elusive was going on. It is indeed apparent that to a considerable extent regional diversity was more marked than is often thought, and that parochialism was one outcome. But at the same time it will be apparent how the socio-geographical 'stages' of collective identity were not mutually exclusive. Rather, they formed relationships. Consideration of these reveals that the provincial was not the same thing as the parochial. In what follows, therefore, the parochial and the catholic will be traced: it is apparent that this consideration of mental horizons is inseparable from the matter of class.

The picture of economic change so far presented here indicates how important were the staple industries in British industrialisation, and how intimately they were linked to particular regions. While recognising the significance of disruptive changes, the account of social and demographic change given in the previous chapter also emphasised the importance of continuity, in particular the prevailing patterns of migration to and settlement in industrial towns. A real degree of disruption was nonethless managed by material and cultural links to the past. These links constituted a very powerful recourse to local and regional cultural characteristics, evident above all in dialect. This was especially so in the northern industrial districts in, roughly, the second half of the century, the time when the pattern of what was later to be called 'traditional working-class culture' was formed. Aspects of development making for national and international integration should not be ignored (the railway system, world markets, and so on), but even so the enormously localised and concentrated nature of Victorian and Edwardian industry is apparent. This, and the concomitant endemic localism of popular culture, is sometimes lost to view in prevailing accounts.[29]

The parochialism and the conservatism of outlook consequent upon this localism is evident in a number of areas. The loyalties reflected in dialect literature were an important resource upon which contemporary employers drew: building upon real similarities of language use (however tactical),[30] employers in the manufacturing districts exploited regional and local patriotism in the creation of a populist style that was of the utmost use in the running of their own factory regimes and in their prosecution of party politics. The industrial deference I have considered in earlier work indicates, among other things, a positive response among workers to these overtures.[31] Though this response was probably less inward and more calculating, or at least conditional, than I earlier argued, it undoubtedly drew deeply on workers' cultural preoccupations. And these preoccupations were hardly fertile ground for a social and political mobilisation built upon class, which by definition depended upon the recognition of similarities obtaining across and between locales and regions. The uses of territorial chauvinism have been seen in other respects to be hardly radical, as, for instance, those of the British Army in peace and war. The dialect literature itself dwelt much upon the differences between workers, most of all in terms of the stigmatisation of the London labouring poor.

Just how socially conservative regional and local attachments could be is indicated by the case of cotton textiles considered above. As we have seen, there was a particularly close link between the development of the factory system and the rise of dialect, the literature always having a specially close relationship to its operative audience. In many respects, dialect mirrored the extraordinarily intense concentration, by unions and workers, upon the industry as a world unto itself. As has been seen, notions of the trade were developed in such a way as to emphasise the firm, the town trade, or the industry in general as communities of interest. Such communities of interest involved employers as well, non-conflictual notions of capital and labour – drawn from many sources – being uppermost. In turn the interests of the trade were heavily identified with both the interests and the identity of towns and regions, indeed with the interests and identity of the Empire and the nation as well. The extent to which the great battalions of nineteenth-century industry looked after their own first and foremost is well known. The extent to which this was underpinned by regional and local cultural allegiances is less familiar.

Certainly, the cultural and industrial chauvinism evident in cotton and other great staple industries and their unions was frequently a bar to the solidarities of class, and to a sense of what was common between industries being more important than what divided them. Nonetheless, chiefly after 1918 or so, it is arguable that a firmer sense of class did develop. As has been seen, the war and post-war conditions were important, as were the early century institutional arrangements of the unions and the Labour Party. But behind this conjuncture, it would seem that a heightened sense of class, if it was such, in fact eventuated precisely as a more marked sense of what was already present, namely the local and regional identity of popular values. The locale and the region and their accompanying sense of community were in fact the building blocks of 'class': this is more than a truism, in the sense that class in Britain was and still is indelibly marked by the ambiguities that attended its birth in the English industrial regions.

The example of textiles and of dialect is revealing: the sense of 'factory folk' emerging in the late nineteenth century was the product of changes beyond literature, but literature was capable of giving these changes a firmer grounding. This larger sense of the entire community of workers in a particular industry was a legacy drawn upon by the unions and the Labour Party. It could be a link to larger sympathies, an identification with labour in a more collective sense. This possibility was present in the dialect literature that accompanied this sense, as indeed it was in all the forms of popular art we have considered. These emphasised the dignity of labour and its value as the foundation of society. Socialism and the unions stood to inherit and use these large conceptions of labour. Perhaps we can call the enlarged, inter-regional awareness of the solidarity of labour a 'class' sense, though in fact – at the risk of compounding definitional confusion – perhaps the term 'labourist populism' is a better term. Whatever the description, what is evident still is how much this sense of labour was shaped by local industry and the local culture. As we have seen, there were bounds as well as possibilities inherent in notions such as 'factory folk': the parochial and the introspective could be very marked. This tension or ambiguity between local and larger sympathies may indeed be one of the chief distinguishing works of popular ideas of society in the twentieth as in the nineteenth century (the miners' strike of the early 1980s revealed something of this tension). The English, indeed the British, working class was, and is, the sum of its regional parts, and in some respects the parts have been greater than the whole.

Looked at another way, as forming a relationship with the 'national' stage, the local and regional were in many respects anything but parochial and introspective in their social effects. Cotton workers, for instance, might be taken up with their town and its trade, but they also had ideas of nation and Empire, ideas that both realised the trade for them and were realised by the trade. The wider world might serve as a convenient symbol of what was immediately pressing, but immediate circumstances could also articulate a larger vision. This is especially apparent in the case of dialect. The emphasis upon the integrity of the provincial might be the way in which a sense of Englishness or Britishness was achieved that united the country as a whole. But this emphasis could be a source of tension as well as agreement with the national centres of power and authority, the assertion of regional and local pride against the metropolis and the south. In turn, this implied the idea that the heart of the true nation beat in the north. This sense of the industrial north as the seat of productive activity and the obverse of southern privilege took many forms.

One form it took was a strong assertion of the independence and dignity of the labouring poor. Another was as an element in Liberalism. The two were closely related. As the gestation and reception of dialect in particular indicates, this emphasis upon the values and the identity of the labouring poor came out of the resources of the popular culture itself. Especially in its 'pre-factory', artisan-domestic industrial birthplaces, a sense of attachment to older values is apparent, particularly to traditions of dissent, both political and religious. One hesitates to describe this current as 'radical', for it took different forms, but what dialect clearly reveals is the sense of plebeian values and old plebeian identities being directly transposed upon a proletarian condition.

This combination of plebeian and proletarian characteristics in fact largely reflected the economic status of the workers to whom dialect appealed particularly strongly: textile workers in Lancashire and Yorkshire, and miners and to some degree shipyard and engineering workers on Tyneside. As has been seen, these workers were experiencing the uneven but sometimes powerful brunt of proletarianisation around the mid-nineteenth century, though the full social consequences of this were to be played out over a longer period. What is perhaps most striking about dialect is its distribution in districts undergoing rather similar economic change, and the broad similarity of theme and outlook evident in the literature across these different districts. In one sense, therefore, it is possible to see dialect as the expression of a class in the making.

In this regard, it is important to emphasise important contrasts with the ballads. There the sense of the value of work and of the pivotal role of labour in society were marked. In the dialect literature such values become fixed upon real and very distinctive industries and communities. The workers in these industries and communities become the explicit subject of the old emphases on work and labour, also in a sense the author of this new development. We can perhaps term this 'class'. The sense of labour identity is strong and now more firmly anchored in daily circumstances. As noted earlier, we can employ class here but recognise its non-conflictual character, the strength of identity but the weakness of the sense of opposition. But, as was argued previously, this weak sense of class may not ultimately be terribly helpful. It is arguably less a sense of class that is evident here than one of labour, a more emphatic 'labour consciousness' than hitherto. Perhaps for the latter part of the period of this book we do indeed need to speak less of class than of a new 'labourist' manifestation of populism. As has been seen in all the examples of popular art noted, music hall included, there were so many sources of social identity other than class, that perhaps we ought indeed to look beyond class.

Dialect shows clearly how a catholic outlook as well as a parochial one could be created out of the regional in its relation to the other 'stages' on which social identity was formed. In quite pragmatic ways, this has been seen in operation in the ways in which dialect actually increased the scope of communication beyond its previously localised, and often oral, forms. Dialect conventions worked in this way, providing, quite literally, a common language. This language involved more than the plebeian-cum-proletarian alone. As noted, dialect was popular with all sorts of workers. In many respects, therefore, rather than narrowing it broadened their perspective. This is also evident in the ways in which different dialect literatures enjoyed popularity beyond their immediate regions. Of course, they also enjoyed popularity among those outside the ranks of manual workers: the different characters of popular and 'high' dialect literature certainly measured a significant social difference in this respect, but there were many among the non-manual audience to whom the meanings and tastes apparent in higher class appro-priations of dialect would have been remote. What is evident, therefore, is a very diverse audience, with some groups in particular having a close affinity to the central concerns of the literature. Fixing a class label in these circumstances has its uses, though these uses are arguably rather limited. In the end, it is perhaps more important to argue for the historical specificity of both the social constituency of dialect, and the kind of outlook it expressed, to which the terms 'radical', 'democratic' and 'labourist' populism do some kind of justice in their different nuances of emphasis. The question of whether these terms or 'class' more properly apply is taken further in the conclusion.

The music hall may suggest the eclipse of this emphasis upon the values of local community in its different forms. The discussion so far has emphasised the significance of extra-local aspects, especially the emergence of what has been termed 'liberal populism'. However, while such aspects were very important, the development of the music hall from the late nineteenth century did not see the unfolding of 'mass culture' or 'mass society'. The local and regional roots of popular culture remained strong, and were reproduced in different ways in terms of the changing relationships of the various 'stages' upon which the social sense was played out. Dialect certainly did wane in popularity from the early twentieth century, but instead of old forms being superseded by new, what was evident in music hall – and beyond it in radio, films, and records – was the reconstitution of older patterns, adapted to serve new needs in new circumstances, but nonetheless enjoying real similarities with the past. Although dialect did not always directly influence what came after it, the kinds of sentiment, humour and characters it dealt in were part and parcel of what followed. In many respects the putatively new world of twentieth-century 'mass entertainment' developed directly out of dialect, if not in linear succession then certainly in terms of the significance of the regional and local archetypes it did so much to develop.

In this regard, for example, the idea of a Lancashire character and sense of humour was important. Lancashire attributes were delineated in the books of 'cracks' and 'buzzes' that circulated in the inter-war years, and which, though mostly written in standard English, served as a kind of bridge between dialect and what followed. (Allen Clarke, the dialect writer, was in fact an author of such books.)[32] These purveyed a specifically 'Lanky' sense of humour, and dealt in the homely or 'gradely' values of dialect. Frank Ormerod ('Owd Shunt') published his *Lancashire Cracks* in the 1920s, and this figured 'ordinary Lancashire working people' coping with the world through their knowing and understated humour[33] As the author maintained, inside all his readers, Lancashire factory lads and girls, was a budding George Formby trying to get out. The Formby Ormerod spoke of was George senior, renowned father of a son, George junior, who was soon to achieve national fame, and in so doing relate Lancashire and the nation in yet another permutation. The music hall of the Formbys was a decidedly different world from that of the dialect writers but nonetheless drew directly upon their creations, just at it played to audiences that were brought up in both worlds.

To varying degrees this is also apparent in the great line of northern comics, men such as Sandy Powell, Rob Wilton and Norman Evans, as well as Stanley Holloway. Above all, it is apparent in the figure of Gracie Fields, 'Our Gracie', 'Sally of our Alley', the Rochdale mill girl whose legendary fame between the wars reveals so much about contemporary attitudes. Fields' fame was national, but it is not far fetched to see in her a continuation of a Rochdale tradition begun by Tim Bobbin and continued through Waugh into the twentieth century. In turn, through Fields, it is also possible to see the perpetuation of a northern mythology into the present, particularly in that most popular of all celebrations of a mythologised proletariat, 'Coronation Street'.

To appreciate something of this it is necessary to turn to that most telling of accounts of twentieth-century popular values, Hoggart's *Uses of Literacy*.[34] Fields, and figures such as Wilfred Pickles, compere of the long-running and revealingly named radio programme, 'Have A Go', spoke to the sense of good neighbourly folk, a sense long since formed in dialect. According to Hoggart, what was present was the solidarity of 'ordinary folks', in some respects a conservative sense of identity based on limited scope for ambition. This was directed against 'stuck up' folk: Fields and Pickles were praised because they conquered the 'moneyed classes' with their 'working-class' manners and wit, and respected because their values earned appreciation 'down south'. Figures like these were of a piece with representations evident in the popular press examined by Hoggart, a periodical press surprisingly close to people's experience, and preceding the new popular (especially newspaper) press of the 1950s. These journals emphasised what were for Hoggart the defining marks of the northern, working-class culture he explored, namely the homely, the personal and the concrete. In turn, a host of radio programmes such as 'Mrs Dale's Diary', 'Family Favourites', and 'Down Your Way', were popular because they presented the people to the people as ordinary and heroic. Comedians such as Al Read and Norman Evans, popular in music hall and on radio, gave this demotic self-regard a comic twist.

These examples were of course creations of the era of the 'mass media'. No more than dialect before them were they simple expressions of the 'voice of the people'. But, just as dialect, they were decidedly more the creatures of popular invention than otherwise.

13 Self-image of an unregenerate working class: holiday portrait taken
in Blackpool, c. 1920.

One does not, therefore, need to labour the point that these
representations of sentiment in inter-war and mid-century Britain
were direct descendants of Victorian forbears. Making all allow-
ances, it is the substantial continuity of outlook between the 1880s
and the 1950s that is most striking. Likewise, the matter of the
content of these representations does not need elaboration. At times,
in the mid twentieth century, for example, when class enjoyed
perhaps a greater salience than ever before in the lexicon of social
description and social allegiance, the universalistic, demotic associations and values underlying class are amply evident in these notions
of 'folks', ordinary and otherwise.[35]

These indications of continuity in English popular culture are
illuminated by other aspects of Hoggart's work. In considering the
'discourse of modernity' evident in early twentieth-century Blackpool,[36] it was noted how older styles in fact encompassed and shaped
new ones rather than the reverse. Another example of this was inter-
war British cinema, the home-grown products of which for long held
out against Hollywood, not least in reproducing in celluloid the
older world of British music hall. Again, the cultural atavism of the
seemingly new is apparent. Popular conceptions of the 'good time'
overlaid newer variations, and in Hoggart's depiction of the working-
class 'baroque' one sees a popular appropriation of the cult of leisure

and consumption expressed in a rather different form in what was earlier termed 'liberal populism'. The ornate, sprawling, generous and indulgent were aspects of the music hall ethos of feast and profusion, yet the baroque continued to be inscribed in the routines of working-class life into the mid-twentieth century. Outside the home the ritualisation of leisure evident in the 'charabanc' trip saw this reproduction of the baroque. Inside the home the model for display was the sumptuous interior of the Victorian middle-class home.[37] What was evident in the baroque, indeed, as in the happy ending of popular fiction, was some vision of a better, fuller life than was evident in the common run of things. Utopian desires were only a little below the surface in all aspects of the culture considered here.

Perhaps the best way of approaching the relevance of twentieth-century forms of entertainment for an understanding of how the social order was perceived is through a closer consideration of the career of one of the most powerful of all contemporary icons of social identity, Gracie Fields. The symbolic power of Fields lay in her capacity to represent differently to different social groups the images of themselves and of others they most desired. It also lay in her capacity to represent the nation to itself, in ways which, if quite deliberately manufactured in many respects, nonetheless found an echo across different social elements, comprising a twentieth-century 'populism' very much akin to some of the earlier populisms that have so far been considered. What may be termed the socially specific meanings of Fields will be examined after the 'national' meanings, though both sets were related, just as re-combinations of the old relationship between the region and the nation were present in both sets. Looking at the 'classless' Fields, it is the cinema that provides the clearest evidence, film reproducing the music hall but developing it in new directions.[38]

These directions involved a 1930s film career which transformed her from mill girl to theatrical grande dame, infusing large doses of patriotism and self-help along the way. She became an embodiment of the myth of success. Something rather similar is also evident in the film career of George Formby junior: a progression which started with a music hall persona expressing sympathy and intimacy with a working-class Lancashire audience, developed in ways that were increasingly consensual in outlook.[39] At least in his film career, Formby gradually put the ironic saturnalia of 'Wigan Pier' behind him, though for his popular audience he never quite lost the capacity, inherited from his father who invented 'Wigan Pier', to represent both the spirit of the wakes, and the proletarian wise fool or little man. Fields became a figure of national fame: she was 'Our Gracie' to the monarchy, too, performing at royal command

14 Holiday portrait taken in Blackpool, c. 1920.

performances. Debates in the Commons reportedly finished early
because she was due to perform on the radio.[40] Her records and films
were popular throughout Britain. She in fact pioneered a 'showbiz'
path later to become very familiar. One landmark along this route
was recognition for her charity work in the CBE she received in
1939.

The source of this success lay in several areas. For those outside the
working classes she above all represented a desired image of the
worker. She was successful but retained her homely virtues; she was

15 Populism at play: the Kay family of Bolton portray authority in a
barrel, Blackpool, c. 1920.

vivacious but unthreatening. There was a clear sense, actively
engineered in her film career, in which she became the epitome of a
neutered working class: it is very striking how in the 1930s,
industrial Lancashire, not only in Fields and Formby, came to

symbolise for the English middle classes the acceptable face of the proletarian (and if not the acceptable face then still the essential working class, as is evident in Orwell's choice of Wigan as the destination of his journey into darkest England). But Fields functioned in other ways, too, which suggest that the unifying potential of her figure may have been more effective than her sectional role in the folk myths of the middle classes might indicate.

The historian of Fields' cinema work suggests that in the 1930s she figured as the symbol of a genuinely felt sense of patriotism and national unity evident at all levels of society.[41] In the conditions of that decade, it has been argued, she carried a message of hope, and hoped-for reconciliation (especially after the General Strike and the National Government of 1931). This message was amplified through the means of other embodiments of this 'national character': if Fields was the elder sister, Baldwin was the father, and King George V the grandfather of the nation. Consensus may have been evident but also needed promotion, yet there is little doubting how potent were the popular feelings underlying the consensual English populism given expression in the king, in Baldwin the re-assuring John Bull figure (combining country squire and paternalist employer), and in Fields the comforting emblem of the proletariat. It seems unlikely that the idea of a patriotic working class that was part of the national family was ever ineffective. However, a popular audience brought its own values to an understanding of Fields, and it is necessary to view 'Our Gracie' from another angle, that of the community from which she came, particularly the town of Rochdale. Socially specific or contextualised sets of meaning might differ from more generalised, 'national' ones.

Her Rochdale credentials were impeccable, above all in the form of town dialect. The souvenir booklet commemorating one of her periodic, triumphal returns to Rochdale in 1931 was entitled 'Gracie Comes Whoam'.[42] It opened with a quotation from that 'grand owd singer', 'Ned' Waugh (Edwin Waugh). Of her many stage personae the Lancashire mill girl was probably uppermost. On her departure for New York she carried a pair of clogs for luck, and descriptions of her in the American press invariably carried the Lancashire adjective. Her recorded output had real roots in Lancashire popular speech and popular life: characteristic titles were 'Nowt About Owt', 'Ee By Gum', 'Lancashire Blues', and 'Stop and Shop at the Co-op', as well as the current list of British and US 'hits'. Her appeal in fact combined old and new, and formed precisely that capacity of the old to colonise the new spoken of above. The *Manchester Guardian* of 1930 summed up much of this appeal, a combination of humour, mischief and sympathy, added to a powerful religious element evident in her singing of 'The Lord's Prayer'. It

commented that one would have to imagine Vesta Tilly in a
charwoman's garb, or Marie Lloyd in a dress of shimmering gold.[43]

This combination of the proletarian and the glamorous is of
interest. A long extract from her 1931 Rochdale souvenir described
her palatial south of England home. Here is an example of the poor
being permitted into the realm of the great, however vicariously.
Fields certainly offered to her northern audience this vicarious sense
of involvement in her southern success, but it is also apparent that
this is not the same as present-day venerations of the doings of the
great, royal or showbusiness. Fields was also the prisoner of her
audience – it was their version of glamour to which she had to
correspond. In the end, she offered her northern, popular audiences
real not spurious knowledge, knowledge which corroborated their
perception of their own value. Fields dealt in a proletarian glamour,
a northern, working-class royalty, which evinces the strengths of this
culture prior to its subsequent disintegration. Her southern home
has maids and butlers, but it is rumoured that these are northerners.
She likes to be surrounded by her own people.

Although the source of many conceptions of society, for her
working-class audiences she had a distinct set of meanings. If these
did not preclude others, it is clear that she was in many respects the
creation of her popular audience. There is every sign that she was
their willing prisoner, actively colluding with the image created by
them. These audiences were of course greater than the Lancashire
and the Rochdale working classes, for she was immensely popular
with the British working classes as a whole. It is indeed in her role
as the expression of the values of this larger group that she is most
interesting. But it was in her guise of the 'Lancashire lass' and
Rochdale mill girl that she most typically and effectively represented
this wider audience. In the inter-war years Lancashire was not only
a potent symbol for the middle classes.

She actively grounded her glamour and success in reminders of
her origins in the world of work and of Rochdale. The account of this
visit in 1933 given at the start of part IV will be recalled. She made
repeated returns to Rochdale for this purpose. In 1931 she
emphasised to her public how she always worked, never took a
holiday. The 'work' of performance counted, as well as that of
philanthropy. But she also represented the ambiguous feelings about
work which, as has been seen, very much characterised her audience.
She symbolised the aspiration to a world beyond work as well. She
started her stage career after being sacked for singing and dancing for
other mill girls during factory hours. She was the one who had
escaped, the spirit of song amid the toils of factory labour. She
represented the possibility of freedom beyond the mill, as well as the

humanity of the millworker. The possibility of escape did not signify a retreat from the life of the milltown. In 1931 she was met by a large crowd of mill girls, her greatest devotees, when visiting the Infirmary.[44] In 1933 she made a point of staying not at the best hotel but in the tiny bedroom above the beershop kept by her mother's dearest friend.[45] She was said to have talked to everyone in Rochdale's own dialect. In 1956 she visited to open a new Co-op shop and to play for charity at the Hippodrome, the performance being relayed to between 5,000 and 10,000 in the street. On her final visit in 1978, she was applauded by thousands in the streets.[46]

This was the end of a long chapter, a chapter that also concerns another geographical 'stage' of social identity which has so far not much concerned us in this account, namely that of the town. Fields' relationship with Rochdale stood in this respect for all the towns of industrial England. In 1954 she visited the carpet works of one of the latter-day Rochdale magnates, Cyril Lord. She supported industry, certainly, but also, earlier on, the Infirmary, which was run in the interest of, and supported by, the inhabitants of the town at large. Along with a capitalist town benefactor she was made an honorary freeman of the borough in 1937. Fields represented, therefore, not some undiluted sense of proletarian identity, but rather a sense of the town which included all in local society. In an era before the welfare state the pooling of the activities of all groups and classes in the interests of the town was a very important feature, being reflected not only in welfare activities but in the whole institutional life of the town.

The traditional institutions of working-class self-help; the Co-op, the burial society, the trade union and the friendly society, all asserted a distinct role for labour in furthering the interests of the town. Indeed, in the early twentieth century, with the proliferation of such institutions into the governance of the town, and the election into parliamentary and municipal office of the representatives of labour, there developed a sense in which working people came to see the town as *their* town. This was so in comparison with the nineteenth century, when the town was rather more the possession of the philanthropic magnates, at least in industrial Lancashire. But such magnates did not of course entirely disappear, and this sense of possession was always shared with all those who also lived in and contributed to the town. As in so many other respects, the sense of class was effected through the realisation of an entity, the town, that at once served to delineate the features of another set of social sympathies, capable of affirming but also qualifying class, and often broader and more potent than it in this very qualification.

These considerations of Fields and Rochdale are, of course, of very northern examples. In conclusion, therefore, it is desirable to widen the picture by turning from north to south, from industrial England to that other great source of images of the social order, London. The recent work of Stedman Jones on the history of representations of the Cockney enables this broader picture and suggests some comparisons.[47] The music hall in fact played a central part in the evolution of the Cockney, in the 1890s associating the figure with the coster and so fixing upon it an unreservedly lower-class origin. Like the northern, provincial myths and representations so far considered, the Cockney was taken up differently by different social elements, by the London poor on the one hand, and by higher social classes on the other.

In the latter aspect the Cockney was inserted into ideas of nation and empire, offering exemplary patterns of social relations in the particular conjuncture of the late nineteenth and early twentieth century. According to Stedman Jones the cockney offered to conservative feeling – of a party and a more general sort – a new language of 'class', not hierarchical in a traditional sense but domesticating and enshrining social differences in a greater unity. If a language of class in the simple sense of handling the social relations of contemporary society, the vocabulary and meaning of this language seems to have been populist in character. It was celebratory and conservative, rather than reformist, moralistic and elitist,[48] so representing a break with previous higher-class representations (a break, it should be added, not nearly so great in provincial England, where a moralistic, reforming strain long continued to be potent among the middle classes).

The populist label is also appropriate to the other aspect of appropriation and use, that of the lower classes, in this case the London poor, those in between the casual poor and the artisanate or craftsmen. Here generalisation is on limited ground (that of the so-called 'pearlies' among the poor), but the suggestion of a link between the peculiar socio-economic position of the poor – combining the element of dependence with a desire for independence – and their embrace of the Cockney figure is suggestive. The figure offered them a way of handling their ambiguous condition and of making their presence felt in the city at large. The associations and politics linked to this manifestation of the Cockney were monarchist and nationalist, yet not deferential, asserting in characteristically populist fashion the right of the poor as the people of London to a place in the national community.

In another, sense, too, one can trace populist motifs, but these are linked to a liberal rather than a conservative populism. The previous discussion of 'liberal populism' indicated how the music hall of the late nineteenth century developed in ways emphasising the exploration of new social styles, emanating from a variety of social locations, and intersecting one with another. Stedman Jones remarks of the 1890s music hall, of which the cockney was such a central part, that it represented the intersection of polite, bohemian and popular culture. One may see in this example, then, the same profferred equality and standing on the national stage evident in liberal populism's emphasis on the utopian egalitarianism found in the realms of leisure and consumption. Both manifestations had strong pseudo-democratic aspects. Both also involved the embrace or at least the exploration of new social styles and experiences: the old 'Cockney' Ally Sloper was in this respect father to the new Cockney of the 1890s.

So, the figure of the Cockney involves a continuing history, and one stretching far into the twentieth century. What had been used for Conservative purposes could take different forms, in which the class element was not at all excluded, even if it was always closely linked to populism. Conservatism spurned the Cockney in the inter-war years, identifying the nation not with the city and its people but with the shires. This is only partly so, however, for appropriations of northern industrial myths seem to have been very widespread in the inter-war years, Conservatives no doubt included. Nonetheless, the latent power of Cockney imagery was great, and was revived in the 1930s to be utilised by the state in the Second World War and by the Labour Party after the war. In the latter development ideas of 'the common people' linked class, democracy and nation, interweaving the language of the urban nation with the language of labour. This, however, is to trespass even further into the twentieth century than intended. Nonetheless, the example of the Cockney indicates differences as well as similarities between north and south.

A number of these will be already evident. The general importance and the operations of socially differentiated representations of social types and the social order is apparent, as are versions of populism linking north and south. As striking as these similarities, however, are the great differences obtaining between north and south (though of course in London there was a wider range of representations evident than the Cockney alone). The accent on work and productiveness suggests itself at once, as does the identification of the people with the nation through the medium of the town and industry. The idea of the true England, crusading against Privilege in its southern bastions was also strong, evident, for instance, in the northern-rootedness of the ILP, and in nineteenth-century Liberalism. The contrast in turn suggests many more aspects, each of which requires discussion. That discussion, albeit briefly, will follow in the final chapter, where the character of popular art and the northern, industrial examples are both set in their broader context. For the moment, it is worth recalling the figure of Ab o' th' Yate as one shorthand expression of these differences, just as the proletarian manifestations of Gracie Fields express other aspects of the contrast.[49] Ab was a true man of the industrial north in setting limits to the exaltation of consumption and to the acceptance of the status quo. If a product of one kind of populism, he and what he stood for were often far removed from the 'liberal' and 'conservative' populism considered here.

14

Summary and conclusion: the making of the English working class before 1914?

The icons of popular art suggest the force and longevity of populist notions over this period. They also indicate that rather than a single populism, it is a variety or 'family' of populisms that should be considered, a variety in which the capacity for change and adaptation was marked. In the northern, industrial districts there was, however, a decided continuity amidst this variety and change. This was evident in a radical populism conceiving of the true England as the industrial north in struggle with Privilege. The conception of a 'family' of populisms was invoked in the first part of this book, on politics. There the roots of social identity were in important measure seen to lie in ideas and associations taken from politics, in particular the populist traditions of popular radicalism and the many tranformations these went through up to 1914. The controlling narrative of popular politics appears to have concerned a righteous and dispossessed 'people' rather than a 'working class'. The political sphere paralleled the sphere of art here: the idea of the true, unadorned England of the north was a varient of the broader mythology of the true political nation of the excluded English.

The excluded English could be seen as the labouring English, and in this sense 'class' appropriations occurred, even though this was in practice rather limited. It was in the sphere of work and the operations of the trade union that class became more decidedly evident, particularly in the sense of class taken in this book to have most theoretical and empirical utility: conceptions of social relations as turning centrally upon the relationship of labour and capital, of this relationship as tending to conflict, and of society as more exclusive than inclusive in character; all these were evident increasingly from the 1860s and 70s, though they developed most markedly in the early twentieth century, especially post-1914. The late and gradual 'making' of the English working class in this sense should be noted. This sense of class in the English regions was highly particularistic, in respect both of its rootedness in particular locales, and its view of capitalism and the nature of industry, the 'trade' and employers. These aspects meant that the view of class that developed could be perfectly compatible with 'populist' appeals of a political and social sort. Class in England was largely built up out of the often ill-fitting bricks of these distinctive local and regional experiences, in which the parochial and the sectional were often finely balanced with the catholic and the solidaristic. It is amply evident from the consideration of politics and work that rather different conceptions of the social order were evident in different spheres of people's lives.

The section on culture enabled a closer consideration of these conceptions, and suggested that populist views were probably dominant. The importance of territorial aspects of 'community', such as nation, region, town and neighbourhood, was pursued more systematically here, and in chapter 6 it became evident how conceptions of the social order were related to attempts to bring order and decency to the experience of poverty, insecurity and labour. This attempt was a matter of investing the everyday *milieu* of people's lives with symbolic significance. This process produced a multiplicity of outcomes, class being only one of the ways in which people patterned and gave meaning to the social order. The major tension in the culture of the labouring poor between fatalism and utopia became evident in this study of the semiology of the social order, but it was indeed present in all areas of popular life. In the chapter on history a populist sense of the past was apparent, both in 'Protestant libertarianism' and in the expression of 'liberal culture' that succeeded this – the view of history as the unfolding of reason and progress. The close connection between political and historical views is also apparent here, politics being one expression of an historical sense widely disseminated in popular society. The populist dimensions of ideas about language and culture were also marked and these ideas were reproduced in popular life through the schoolroom and other agencies of cultural dissemination. Language use itself expressed something of the tensions evident in social conceptions, 'class' differences of a broad sort emerging (between educated and uneducated, or rich and poor), yet language was also the shared experience of different social levels in a broadly populist way, particularly in the industrial north.

The family of populisms makes itself known through the representations of popular art; the ballads showing a marked kinship with what was earlier termed a 'classical' populism, and the music hall evincing both a 'liberal' and a 'conservative' populism. Given this variety, the search for what was earlier called a dominant English popular tradition in these matters may be illusory.[1] Nonetheless, and assuming from the evidence so far presented that the possibilities here concern the range of populist outlooks more than they concern class, it seems to me that it is possible to identify what was earlier termed radical populism as the dominant strain. The evidence of dialect literature in particular points to this, and it does so in two senses of the word radical: the more clear-cut sense of provincial England, indeed, northern Britain as well as northern England as the seat of the crusade against privilege; and a more diffuse sense apparent in terms of the notions of popular justice, equality and fraternity tapped in the literature. This sense was exploited in other kinds of popular art, but in the development in dialect of a populist discourse about 'ordinary people', 'folk', (especially 'decent folk'), one sees it taking its most sustained and elaborate form. These senses of radical leave out of the account the assumed, but usually unstated, radical political sympathies of so many authors.

Dialect was obviously only one place where this radical populism was to be found. It was there in religious notions, especially in notions of both the past and the liberties of a Protestant people. Conceptions of religious identity were often fused with conceptions of the English national past. It was of course in politics itself that this sense was most developed, taking its most characteristic form in radical Liberalism. Looking again at politics in the light of the subsequent parts of this book, it is evident just how significant were notions of dispossession and exclusion in the broader popular culture beyond Liberalism, notions taking explicit political form in the idea of lost rights and liberties. The utopian impulse was also very widely evident, and with it the claim to the restitution both of rights and of a commonality of human feeling, a legacy lost with the waning of a golden age. In looking at politics one also becomes aware that what was earlier called its 'controlling narrative' applied far beyond politics alone. This narrative is one key to understanding what is here termed a dominant English tradition of radical populism. Another is the concrete experiences and feelings of those who embodied this tradition. The question of narrative can be addressed first.

Perhaps, in line with the emphasis on discourse evident in this book, it is better to talk of a 'master narrative' rather than of a 'master identity', though it does in fact seem the case that the labouring poor of the industrial England of the time interpreted this narrative in a remarkably uniform way, making out of it what is here called a dominant tradition. In respect of narrative, the work of American historians and scholars on the significance of such 'master plots' or narratives in American history is very revealing.[2] Perhaps in the English (and to some degree the British) case there was a single tale tying together a diversity of representations. In the American case there was, and is, the narrative of the Republic and its mission, a narrative closely tied to the religious sense through the identification with Providence.[3] But it is variation and conflict within bodies of national myth and narrative that also need emphasis. In nineteenth-century America there developed a particular craft or artisan appropriation of this central myth, the idea of the 'artisan Republic' as it were, seen in the fusion of the emblems and political language of the Republic with the social traditions and labour relations of the crafts.[4]

For the English case the notion of a master narrative is more difficult. So indeed is that of a dominant popular tradition, especially when one bears in mind the weight of fatalism and quiescence so often felt in the culture of the labouring poor. Nonetheless, a story emerges. The subject of this is the destiny of the nation, a destiny as in the American case often firmly tied to providential religion. The appropriation of this subject concerned the 'true people' of England, those who have been excluded from their birthright. England and Providence became identified with the history, character and fate of 'the people', and in many respects 'the people' itself becomes the subject of the narrative, its travail forming the stuff of legend. The principal player in the master plot became the subject of the drama, an excluded and virtuous people doing battle in its pilgrim's progress against the forces of privilege, faction, darkness and ignorance. 'The people' itself, as has been seen, could variously be seen as 'the poor', 'the labouring poor', even 'the working classes'. They might be the unenfranchised. But for the most part they were 'ordinary people' or 'decent folk', in short everyone who showed respect and was respected, but who were yet refused their proper place in the scheme of things.

This appropriation of a dominant myth, or myths, can be termed 'class'. This returns us to a sense of class noted in the introduction: in the words of Jameson, 'the dialogue of class struggle is (normally) one in which two opposed discourses fight it out within the general unity of a shared code'. In this sense of conflicting versions of the same body of narrative one can therefore see the 'making' of the English working class as this process of re-worked myth: utilisations of the myth of 'the English people' became the means by which a sense of common social identity developed. However, the same objections as were raised earlier still apply. The deployment of notions of 'the people' is indeed the means by which a common social identity was created, but when that identity seems, as in the English case, to have had more to do with broad terms of people at large than the narrow ones of class, then the value of applying the class label is open to doubt. The consciousness of *a class* need not, and has not, been the consciousness of *class*.

Of course, describing it as the consciousness of a class also has its own problems, not unlike those raised by the labelling of artisan traditions as class traditions in the American case. The marked heterogeneity of the social and economic condition of English workers in this period will be called to mind. And, even when looking at so decidedly a proletarian group as textile workers, and at the dialect literature that expressed so many of their concerns, we find that what seems at first glance to be the possession of a particular group could be pressed into service not only by many sorts of workers, but also by many who were not manual workers. Even more with other appropriations of 'the people'; the likes of shopkeepers, teachers, employers and so on would have defined themselves, and been accepted, as part of the people (not to mention people higher up the social scale who were often taken as part of the body of the people). Nor does it do to imagine that the terms in which groups are represented are ultimately redundant: the discourse of 'the people' did not express some higher 'class' identity or unity. It mattered in its own right. Language mattered in its own right. The notion of 'languages of class' carries great dangers.

Once these dangers are recognised, however, the idea that classes developed by inflecting shared discourses with their own meaning does have value. The problem is to decide on what their 'own meaning' amounts to: it still seems to me that for the term class to have much currency terms such as 'the people' must be understood in a way in which the attributes of manual labour have prominence. In short, there must be elements of my 'restricted' definition of class present. I shall return to this briefly later on. Readers will for the moment have had enough of the matter of definitions, and it is to one embodiment of 'radical populism' that I shall next turn, that of the journalist Ian Jack's Scots father, a steam mechanic by trade, born not in the Victorian but in the Edwardian years. The example is not typical, but no individual ever is typical: Jack was a skilled man, a self-educated and politically articulate Edwardian Scot. Ian Jack's account of his father tells us a great deal about values that I have attempted to explore in this book, values that clearly had a northern British as well as an English aspect, and an influence that extended far into the present century. Ian Jack talks first about his own childhood;[5]

> I suppose that what all this amounts to is a working-class childhood. I hesitate, not to fight shy of a cliché, but because I still can't be sure; whenever I read phrases such as a 'working class culture' or 'middle class values' I feel dizzy from sociological abstraction and the need to be steadied by a fact or two.

His father (a man who felt a kinship with Yorkshire's Wilfred Pickles!), he describes in the following terms:[6]

For all his socialist convictions, I don't think my father ever saw social division in purely political or economic terms. He would make ritual attacks on the big local landlords, the Earl of Elgin and the Marquis of Linlithgow, and on people who showed how they 'fancied themselves' by sending their children to piano and elocution lessons ('Aye, but do they have books in the house?'), but it was an older moral force which generated the most heat in him, and the class conflict as I most often heard it expressed was not so much between classes as internal to each of them: it was 'decent folk' versus the rest...A strict application of socialist theory would mean that our natural allies were the Davidsons (crash, thump; 'Where's ma fuckin' tea?') and that we would be bound to them for life. And bound not only to the Davidsons but also to another heart of darkness in our own family's past...the chaos and poverty which my father had caught the last whiff of as his family completed their trek through the volcanic industrialism of Victorian Scotland.

The embers of Calvinism, at heart a seemingly narrower philosophy, freed him from class-bound loyalty and gave him a much broader choice of the good and the bad. This is hindsight and may be no more than an over-elaboration of one of my father's favourite concluding statements, *There's good and bad every-where*...And so I never heard my father use 'working class' or 'middle class' as terms of approval or disapproval. The categories were far too broad and he liked clearer targets. Throughout the Fifties he took steady aim at the nearest approach to a class enemy: Edinburgh Scotsmen...[who] 'did not get their hands dirty' and 'lived off the back of other folk'...My father said: 'They've sold their birthright for a mess of porridge'. Behind the joke lay a genuine grievance. Edinburgh Scotsmen did not *make anything*, other than their wills.

The elder Jack was a man who manifestly did make things and get his hands dirty. There is therefore present in this case that pride in manual labour which was so evident throughout the period of this book. This can be seen as a 'class' pride, and the claim could be made with some justice that by dwelling on the various mani-festations of 'populism' I have in fact simply been describing the English (and British) case of class, in which class identity (but not class opposition) has been strong. This may be so, and ultimately it does not much matter what terms we use to define the creation and use of the popular identities we explore so long as their real character is revealed by this process of definition. However, when the actual ways in which a class vocabulary was used are considered, one is constantly aware how behind the explicit terms of class stood larger and more powerful social identities. The examination of the use of class revealed for instance the importance of moral and occupational distinctions *within* groups at the time.[7] Seemingly socio-economic descriptions of the social order turned out to have basically moral meanings, as well as political use and meanings. Behind class were more potent distinctions such as Gladstone's crusade of the 'masses' against the 'classes', or of 'the people' against the ruling class, or the rich and the poor. Class was most often subsumed in these broader categories, a process deliberately engineered in what was earlier called 'the management of class'.[8] In much the same way labour was seen as one 'interest' among many, an element in the larger entities of society and of the nation. What was there to be 'managed' was in fact often a 'class' vocabulary that really had very little to do with class as we would understand it, betokening instead dinstinctions of morality or social status, and not carrying all the distinctions of sub- and super-ordination, of solidarity and struggle, and of the exaltation of manual labour alone which were later to accrue around class. As has been seen, even in its most aggressive form in early Victorian popular radicalism,[9] it was the universalist, socially inclusive meanings of class that were uppermost. This went together with a stigmatisation of class as a reprehensible, selfish denial of the interest of all people. It was only later, and then less perhaps in Britain than in Europe, that class came to have these more restrictive meanings.[10]

It is necessary therefore to write the history of class in this historical way, exploring the roots of earlier usage in the legacy of Enlightenment notions of knowledge, reason and progress, say, or in the influence of notions of democracy and popular sovereignty issuing from the late eighteenth-century age of revolutions. Later developments, around 1900, would need to account for the permeation, among other things, of the language of Marxism. But this history of class language is another matter. Here the concern is with the roots of popular social identities. So, the argument here would be that far from describing what was really class in other clothes, even a cursory examination of class language reveals that behind it lay other and more deeply seated discourses and identities concerning the ordering of society. Nonetheless, when all reservations have been made, it is still of value to retain the concept of class. And this in the two senses used in this book; as the consciousness of a class if not of class, and of the consciousness of class itself, along the lines defined earlier. Just as the language of class could betoken other discourses, so too could other discourses betoken class.

Much has already been seen of this, the discourse of populism in the mid-century for instance taking on the values of working people, and 'people' often standing for 'working class'. The phenomenon of dialect literature and language indicates the emergence of class in both senses of the term. In the ballads the role of labour in society was much emphasised. In dialect literature, roughly in line with the expansion and consolidation of the factory system and the factory town, these values accruing around work became fixed upon real and distinctive communities. The workers in the industries of these communities became both the subject and the audience of this literature. Though not solely the literature of the factory operatives, it reflected their concerns and aspirations in a very direct way. Lancashire and Yorkshire were not alone in this, as the example of other industrial districts shows, especially the instance of the northeast. The literature can be seen therefore as the expression of a class, or, more properly, the expression of fragments of a class coming together slowly in the late nineteenth and early twentieth century. In this regard it was not yet an expression of a consciousness of class. Rather, along with populist interpretations more widely, it can be interpreted as a language of class, the consciousness of a class in the making. This making of class occurred under the impact of that large series of economic and other changes traced in the introduction, and taking marked form from the late century onwards. At a more fundamental level the real sequence of events was more protracted still, in the manufacturing districts occupying the epochal transition from domestic production to the rise and consolidation of factory industry. But class also occurred when the populist discourses interwoven in dialect took on a more decidedly labour identity: 'real' folk, the epitome of 'decent folk', became 'working folk' or 'factory foak'. It was those who had known poverty and labour who were the true people of England. The notion of 'the people' could therefore be a principle of social exclusion as well as of social inclusion, as the 'working class' increasingly stood proxy for the nation. These changes in the realm of the imagination mattered as much as the other, structural changes going on. All these changes were accompanied by the continuing emergence of the trade union as the foremost institutional expression of a more clearly distinct 'economic' sense of class.

This sense of class grew in importance, the process of regional fusion perhaps becoming more evident after 1914 than before this time. Class in Britain seems indeed to have grown in this cumulative, aggregate way; neighbourhood, town, region and nation being gradually pieced together in the outlook of working people. But the limits to this before (and after) 1914 are evident enough, the parochial and the universal existing cheek-by-jowl, and the sense of class itself being marked by the particularities of place and of the obtaining traditions of labour. However, it would be wrong to write the history of popular conceptions of the social order as simply the prelude to class. So much will by now be amply evident. And, should we desire to retain the terminology of class, in whatever sense we employ the term we come back again and again to the primacy of discourses concerning the people of England, and, to a lesser degree, the British people. If we wish to talk of the making of the English working class before 1914, or if, in the manner of the preceding chapter, the idea of a 'labourist' populism emerging out of earlier populisms suggests itself, then it is the identities culled from these discourses that we need to attend to. In attending to them this book makes plain that however broadly class is defined it is still only one among many understandings of the social order held by people at the time.

In being about such understandings this book has also been about the ways in which these understandings were created, about language, and the creation and reception of meaning. As such, it enters upon a number of areas until relatively recently new to historians. In seeking answers about class much else has been discussed, including the constitution of the historical sense, the workings of popular art, or the nature of 'religious' beliefs. However indirectly and inadequately this book attempts to contribute something to questions that exist independently of the question of class, and which are every bit as important as it. Bearing these observations in mind, the kind of answers provided here can only be provisional.

The dominating concern with meaning and its communication was taken up in the first two parts of this book, in terms of the discourses evident in the areas of politics and work. The senses in which the term 'political language' is used make plain that it is the form as well as the substance of political communication that needs consideration. The account of aspects of politics such as the appeal of party and of leaders points to the importance of the emotional and symbolic character of meaning as well as the discursive and literal. It suggests the need to explore the ritual and non-verbal nature of politics, a nature evident in the iconography of political movements for instance, or in the style and organisation of political gatherings. As the structure of political meetings makes plain, the verbal nature of political communication is every bit as important: the study of political oratory, just as oratory in general, is in its infancy. The chapters on politics are a small contribution to this much-needed account of these symbolic and discursive sides of popular politics, though to the latter somewhat more than the former.

What they do show, however, is that the distinction between form and content is in fact rather arbitrary; at best it helps bring out broad distinctions in the manner of these paragraphs. The chapters on work and on the role of the discourse and the organisation of the trade union also make this plain. Just as in politics, organisation served to symbolically enact the purposes and aspirations of movements, while discourse had quite pragmatic tasks in organising action and behaviour. So, the actual forms of political communication need systematic attention, for instance the meeting, or the press, a subject given some consideration in chapter 2. The discursive and the symbolic will need to be interpreted together when the objects of this attention are analysed: the foregoing account of the press made plain that it communicated particular views, but also dramatised in the symbolic nature of the composition of the newspaper and, in its rhetoric, what its purposes were felt to be.

The study of romanticism in political discourse suggests further the need to look at what might be termed the idioms of political language, the structures of thought and feeling, the sensibility, through which people made sense of their worlds. Precisely the same point could be made concerning the discussion of work above: between this and the discussion of politics something of the range and richness of these idioms is evident, extending from the romantic to religious feeling, melodrama, and much else. Both sections showed how such discourses actively structured perceptions, but did so only because they articulated the needs and desires of their audiences. The various models of economic and social purpose and identity the trade unions worked with, whether the trade, the industry or the factory community, worked (or failed to work) insofar as they related to conceptions of justice, of gender, or of community, for example, conceptions evident beyond work as well as within 'the interior life of the workshop'. This study only scratches the surface of an understanding of what such discursive idioms and rhetorical models were, and how they functioned. What it does show, however, is the elusiveness of the processes at work, and the great difficulty of tracking them down. In this respect one thinks for instance of how the quotidian life of the factory – 'factory culture' – could be the raw material for strikingly different rhetorical appeals, those of unions and employers. At the same time, superficially similar appeals or discourses – for instance those to do with respectability and rational conduct – could be interpreted or appropriated in very different ways.

As well as being about 'discourse', this book has been about the making of identity. Indeed, in its attention to a plebeian 'invention of tradition', this cultural making is in many respects the book's central subject. Whether this is described as the making of a class or of a people is of course of crucial importance. But however the question is decided, the processes and results of what went on are of profound significance. The making of identity was intimately tied up with the operations of memory and the construction of the historical sense. These combined concerns are evident early, and continue throughout the book. The chapters on politics deal with the appropriation of the radical tradition and its development into popular party politics, and thence into socialism. Those on work deal with customary notions of the trade and of working communities in a similar manner. The concern with custom as an ongoing cultural activity, seen in chapter 6, tackles these matters head on, as does the account of the historical sense itself. The account of populart art adopts another perspective, that of the vitally important creation of mythic identities through the operations of the imagination. The continuities and new departures, evident in the transition from the ballads to dialect and to the music hall and beyond, show the working people of England making their own identities.

More precisely, of course they show the creativity of the working people of the industrial north, particularly industrial Lancashire. This creativity was exercised within the constraints of a particular pattern of urban and industrial change (in chapter 12 the processes of dialect production were related to Lancashire's passage to a new industrial order). Yet this passage differed much in different parts of Britain. If the experience of change differed, so did the outcome, and there is nothing so striking as the regional diversity of the England of the time, the strong attachment to local traditions and experience. While I have strongly argued for the importance of broader processes at work of which these were different expressions, we should not lose sight of the very real differences between regions and localities. As knowledge of the culture of such places increases, particularly of the ways in which they made identity, attention will no doubt focus on these differences, the products of different contexts of time and place.

This is all to the good, and this applies equally to the resulting ways in which the social order was perceived. There is a strong need to look at what might be termed the short or the medium term, the particular instance created by a particular time and place. In chapter 4, the conception of the social order emerging in the throes of early industry, the product of an earlier 'moral economy' and of the customary ways of domestic-industrial communities as these confronted political change and the factory system, was referred to as a kind of 'corporate' outlook, not quite class and not quite populism. One could extend this attention to the disciplines of context to other periods, for instance the late nineteenth-century emergence of the notion of 'factory folk' among textile operatives, a consciousness of identity not at all easy to pin down – hence my deliberations as to whether 'class' or such terms as 'labourist populism' come nearer the mark. In fact, the worrying over definitions characteristic of this book comes precisely out of the recognition of the markedly individual nature of popular perceptions. However, it also comes out of the awareness that such differences often represented things held in common, as the comparison of Lancashire and the north-east shows. The underlying processes of cultural making were similar, as was the resonance of terms like 'class', 'people' and 'nation'. However inadequate are these more general terms in registering local peculiarities, they need to be used. We need to work on both fronts in fact, the individual and highly contextualised, and the more general.

An interest in the making of identity in this work extends further, into a concern with what the cultures were within which this making went on. This involves the social constituencies and the social relationships evident in culture. It also involves some account of what culture was, what it did. Trying to work on a broad canvas, I have no doubt handled these matters in a crude fashion. Nonetheless, however rough and ready, the distinctions and functions described here do seem to me to be important. These distinctions are apparent from the start, in the tension between the politics of reason, improvement and high-mindedness on the one hand, and of bonhomie, largesse and violence on the other. The politics of progress and of the good time do not readily translate themselves into party terms, though there are differences of note here between popular Liberalism and popular Toryism, as well as between Liberalism and certain strains of populist feeling. In different ways, this broad (very broad) distinction between the rough and the respectable is evident throughout the whole culture of the labouring populations.

It is present for instance in the distinction between the union activists and their emphasis on 'rational' conduct and organisation, and the more spontaneous, often customary, and sometimes violent activity of the rank and file. It is there in different guises in chapters 6 and 7 on the force of fatalism in popular beliefs, and the contending pull of reason and progress in the creation of the historical sense. It is as difficult to translate these distinctions into social as into political constituencies, though there is some merit in differentiating the 'high' from the poor, unskilled working classes. But not a great deal I think. Rather, the differences were ones of education and temperament (union activists were occupationally and socially very similar to their membership for instance). This book points up the very great importance of the self-taught workingman in popular culture. And if there were points of dissimilarity between the autodidact and his labouring fellows, then there was also much in common, particularly in the industrial north of the time.

So many of the appeals evident in the popular culture of the time – those of the dialect author, for example, or of the trade union – worked because their autodidact spokesmen knew how to talk the language of the majority. This language was made up of both tendencies in popular culture, the rough and the respectable, the hedonistic and the rational, the fatalistic and the progressive. It is in fact not as warring camps in the life of the poor, but as tendencies that we should conceive of these differences, tendencies sometimes working apart, more often in concert. This is especially plain when we come to consider the functions of culture, a subject broached in chapter 6. There the dialectic of fatalism and hope was seen as central to what culture was. Culture was a means of bringing meaning and dignity to a life of poverty and toil by emphasising order and control. This quest might as easily move inwards, as it were, to fatalism and a fixation with order, as outwards to hope. A rage for order might be self-consuming, but more often the quest for dignity present in the need for order seems to have brought with it the recognition that at bottom one person was as good as another. For respect to be freely given and received the fundamental sameness of people had to be recognised. The outcome was evident in the aspiration to equality and justice so evident in the culture of the time.

Equally evident was the aspiration to fraternity. The need for order brought with it the desire to transcend order. And it is here that one glimpses the utopian current so much emphasised in this work because so present in the culture of the labouring poor. This grew directly out of the exigencies of poverty, and seems to me a valuable means of understanding what this culture was about. So too are the tendencies and tensions evident within it. The ways in which these, like the dialectic of fatalism and hope, were played out within individuals and communities are usefully understood in terms of what is here called a 'culture of control'. Above all, the recognition that popular culture was as much shaped by the experience of poverty as by the experience of work needs to be emphasised. Poverty twisted aspiration into resignation, but also served as the spur to visions of a better life and a juster world. Existing accounts of popular culture have had too much to say about labour and ideology, too little to say about poverty, and hardly anything to say about utopia.

A concern with culture can be seen therefore to involve the relationships between the social constituencies involved in its production and reception. This is so in the sense of the relationships going on within popular life, such as those between the self-educated and the labouring majority, or between the 'rough' and the 'respectable' sections of the poor. But culture played out relationships between the labouring populations and those outside as well. All these serve as narratives of a sort. The narrative of culture that captures the relationship of 'high' and 'low' social levels best is that of custom and the rise of 'liberal culture', with the qualifications that custom and the ideas of reason and progress were by no means always antithetical, and that when they were opposed this opposition was as likely to take place within popular culture as between the vulgar and the polite. Nonetheless, as the third part of this book makes plain, there was a systematic attempt by the polite to reform the culture of the vulgar, these eighteenth-century terms being long retained, yet also in time translated into those of the 'educated' and the 'uneducated'. This assault of 'respectable' culture upon the culture of the multitude was seen in terms of attitudes to history and language, indeed in the emerging idea of 'culture' itself. The term 'custom' does not fully describe the culture of the many, but the capacity seen in the persistence and regeneration of custom to keep this assault at arms length suggests the at best pyrrhic victory of reform.

Much in 'liberal culture' fitted well with the values of the labouring poor, however. Indeed, in attitudes to reason, knowledge and political liberty, that culture emanated directly from the experience of labouring people. At root, of course, in the Englightenment origins of liberalism, the tenets of liberal culture were essentially classless. If this was not how it worked out in practice in the nineteenth century, then the emphasis on the classlessness of true knowledge and liberty was strong enough to ensure that 'liberal culture' was never the sole preserve of the higher classes, just as custom never gave a full account of the culture of the lower classes. However, the constituents of liberal culture – reason, progress, Improvement, Providence – took on the markedly prescriptive and aggressive tone noted. In the last section of this book, therefore, in the capacity of popular art to produce images of popular identity that resisted, or ignored, this cultural evangelism, one sees played out some of the results of conflicts about culture, conflicts that can only be touched upon here. There is therefore a story here, perhaps more than a pyrrhic victory this time, for the plebeian invention of tradition over the harsher, more 'class-ridden' aspects of liberal culture. If not the conflicts and inventions of class, these creations had their own integrity and autonomy. And they were durable, for when class came it was to be shaped by the rich legacy that preceded and accompanied its realisation. Class continued to be only one of the many ways in which the social order was envisaged, though in the integrity of the self-created traditions of the nineteenth-century labouring poor one can unmistakably detect more than the semblance of a class talking, if not of class talk.

Appendices

Appendix 1

J. R. Stephens, The Political Pulpit.
A Sermon, 1839, (Extract)

By the Rev. J. R. Stephens

Delivered at Staley-Bridge, on Sunday Evening, Feb. 10th, 1839

The Rev. Gentleman, in commencing his discourse, said, – I will take the word of God against the world. (Aye). The world at this hour is set against the word of God. The struggle must be a deadly one: there is now no helping it: Pray God to give us strength, for we shall need it according to our day. (Amen.) For many years England has been a mark at which the devil has shot his most insidious but most destructive bullets. Covert and unobserved for a while, but at length more openly, and now at last without any disguise, England is claimed by Satan as his lawful inheritance and prey. It rests with God, and he only knows, by and bye, whether (as I sometimes fear, and as almost all the tokens of the times declare) whether the sun of England's greatness will not have to set in black midnight, in the very midst of day … If as a land, we go down, – if, as a people, we be destroyed, we shall in all likelihood go down at once. – perish at a stroke, and be swept away from off the face of the earth, as chaff is driven before the wind. You can hardly point to one solitary redeeming feature in the present crisis of our national destiny. Where are you to look for any hope, or for any help? I have looked around and if those things have not come within my ken, it is not because I would not see them – it is because I have not been able to discover them. If I go to the court, what find I there? Do I find a scriptural queen, a queen who is a nursing mother to her people? (No, no.) I hesitate not to say, that the queen of these realms has it not in her power, if she have the will, to help, succour, and deliver her people. (Hear, hear.) … Then, God help you to fight for your wives, for your children, for your brethren, and for your homes! It has come to this now, that you have no right to your own children, and that your children have no right to life. Marcus says that a child was never asked whether it would be born or not, and that, never having been

345

asked whether it would be born or not, it could not give consent to
be born (great emotion), and, therefore, never having given any
sanction – any consent to be born, it has no right to life, no title to
existence, and consequently to take that existence away is not to rob
the child. The child suffers no injury because life does not belong to
it as a right; we take nothing from it but the chances of misery. That
is argument! that is logic! that is political economy! and philosophy
and political economy are to sit upon God's throne, and Jehovah is
to be chained to the wheels of the chariot of Abaddon, and to be the
servant of Beelzebub, of Mammon, and of Moloch! (Great emotion.)
They are to ride it over the earth. God is to be a liar, and Malthus
and Marcus are to be true. (Great emotion.) Does any man wonder
at these things? I do not. Nothing of this kind ever comes suddenly
upon the land. The book of Marcus is only one of the signs of the
times. I was not at all astonished when I saw it and read it. Long
before I had seen that book, I told you publicly that such like things
would follow. (You did.) They must follow. Have I not told you
again and again that I was not surprised at the passing of the new
poor law, and that I looked upon the passing of that law as the most
perfect index to the character of the British nation? (Aye.) The poor
law separates man and wife. But what, of that? The factory masters
have done it long since. And where is the odds between a man being
separated from his wife in a bastile called a union workhouse, or in
a bastile called a factory? The poor law separates parent and child;
it plucked your own children from your own breasts. The factory
system has taught mothers to look upon their children as a burden.
I know it for a fact, on the testimony of several medical men, of
irreproachable character and worthy of credit, that in scores and
scores of instances, when they have been called in to attend women
in childbed in these factory districts, the mother, herself, as soon as
she become aware that her child is loosened from her, has bid the
doctor – BEGGED, the doctor to take no pains to keep that child alive.
(Great emotion.) I have heard of such instances in Stalybridge and
many other parts of Lancashire; and I mention them to show you
that such things as the book of Marcus and the new poor law never
come suddenly upon a nation. They are always progressive. The
factory system has deprived you of almost all natural affection.
Children don't know their mothers. Those who are allowed to live;
those whom the doctors are too conscientious to destroy – and there
are some doctors that are ready to do your bidding – those that are
allowed to live, what becomes of them? They go to a nurse, a strange
woman; and if they are not fed upon Marcus's gas, they are fed by
the nurse upon treacle and water and laudanum, and that is almost
as destructive as certain death. We need not, then, be surprised. The

Government knows this: the Government knows how debased the people have become; and if there have been any opposition to this law (the poor law) in this district – I will tell the Government a secret – that opposition has been founded upon and has run parallel with the revival in your breasts of love for one another. Stephens has done his utmost to bring back that old feeling; and it is because the word of God upon Stephen's lips has not fallen like water split upon the ground that cannot be gathered up – It is because the word of God has restored those ancient and natural feelings, that the people in the Ashton district, and in South Lancashire generally, have risen up as one man, and have said –

> For child and for wife
> We will war to the knife.

"Down with the Bastiles;" "Our God and our rights." (hear, hear.)...

Appendix 2

From B. Grime, Memory Sketches (Oldham, 1887)

1

Fox is Sure To Go
(Tune: 'Henry Hunt'.)

With Fox, the champion of our rights,
    We'll fight with might and main;
In spite of Alick's humbug,
    We'll send him in again.
With Free Trade laws, that give cheap bread,
    And freedom of the mind,
The Fox shall proudly cock his tail,
    And leave the hounds behind.

Chorus—

Come, rally lads, both Whigs and Rads,
    The Fox is sure to go;
We'll wear the cap of liberty,
    And lay the factions low.

We guess you heard the song of late
    Named 'Fox, it is no go';
Then let us all, both great and small,
    A contradiction show.
For Fox, he is the poor man's friend;
    He keeps the taxes low,
He feeds the poor at every door—
    Then Fox is sure to go.

Chorus—

With William Fox we'll go, we'll go,
    With William Fox we'll go;
We'll show the blue-daub Tory crew
    That Fox is sure to go.

A red-haired fool, just come from school,
    Who dwells within this town,

He now declares, and often swears,
   He'll chase our good Fox down.
One British pound we'll lay the hound,
   If he will make a match;
A polling race shall be the chase
   To try our Fox to catch.

Chorus—

A bully great, who has of late
   Turned all his green to blue,
Now gives his vote, to those cut-throats
   Who were at Peterloo.   (p. 94)

2   *Oldham Election, or 'No Go, Fox'.*
   (A New Song to an Old Tune – 'With Wellington we'll go, we'll go.')

Electors all within this place,
   There soon will come a day
When you'll be called to join the chase
   To drive the Fox away.

Chorus—

   With Duncuft we will go, will go,
      With Cobbett we will go;
   We'll wear the cap of liberty,
      But Fox will be 'no go'.

From Chadderton will be a run,
   They'll come to poll in flocks;
Round Whitegate End, you may depend,
   They'll vote against a Fox.

      Chorus—With Duncuft, &c.

And Hollinwood is staunch and good,
   With reservoir and 'docks';
If he goes there, they loudly swear
   They'll surely drown a Fox.

      Chorus—With Cobbett, &c.

Now, many barbers in this town
   Would like to cut his locks;
They say his nob requires the job,
   And so they'll vote for Fox.

      Chorus—With Duncuft, &c.

Then Crompton folk, with hearts of oak,
   Will give him some hard knocks,
And men from Shaw and Crompton Ha'
   Will never vote for Fox.

      Chorus—With Cobbett, &c.

About Springhill some asses still
   Are stupid there as blocks,
Among the drones at Culver Stones,
   Are kennels for a Fox.

      Chorus—With Duncuft, &c.

But Fulwood men will muster then,
   And, firm as Greenfield rocks;
And Sholver poots are fast as roots,
   And will not vote for Fox.

      Chorus—With Cobbett, &c.

Some Tailor Pats and Grub-street flats
   Are stupid as an ox,
And one mad Jesse, if not two,
   Will surely vote for Fox.

      Chorus—With Duncuft, &c.   (p. 95)

3   *The Political Alphabet*

A stands for 'Alick', short o'weight badger,
B stands for 'Bendigo', place-hunting cadger.
C stands for 'Collinge', the self-taxing Mayor,
D stands for 'Dunce' and such they all are.
E stands for 'Earnshaw', the greatest of asses,
F stands for 'Fox', the friend of the masses.
G stands for 'Gammon', a thing we don't want,
H stands for 'Humbug', and such is their cant.
I stands for 'Ignorance', of which they may boast,
J stands for 'Just-assess', and Nat rules the roost.
K stands for 'Kindness' – I wish they would show it,
L stands for 'Lees', the crack brained poet.
M stands for 'Mumps Quack', with his hobbling gait,
N stands for 'Nat', with his sense-wanting pate.
O stands for 'Oldham', a queer-looking place,
P stands for 'Price', with his Ketch-looking face.
Q stands for 'Quack', a thing they delight in,

R stands for 'Roughheads', given to fighting.
S stands for 'Shout for the Tories' defeat',
T stands for 'Taylor', the political cheat.
U stands for 'Union for Fox', our true friend.
V stands for 'Vincent', whom next we will send.
W stands for 'War', a game the Tories delight in,
X is symbolic of a jerry Lord's writing.
Y stands for 'Youth', misled by Tory tools,
Z stands for 'Zanies', synonymous fools.   (p. 110)

4   *The Political Alphabet*

A stands for 'Amicus', who writes against the masses,
B stands for 'Blockheads', those Foxites, those asses.
C is our 'Country', which they don't respect,
D 'Declaration', which they must expect.
E's for old 'England', our glorious nation,
F stands for 'Fox', that imp of damnation.
G stands for 'God', whom no Foxites adore,
H stands for 'Honesty', oh! that they had more of it.
I's 'Infidelity', which all Foxites believe in,
J stands for 'Justice', which none of them deals in.
K stands for 'Kennel', to put in an old Fox,
L's 'Lancaster Castle', where they will all be boxed.
M stands for 'Money', which they much need,
N's 'No go, Fox', which is true indeed.
O stands for 'Oldham', that true honest town.
P stands for the 'Public', that won't gulph Fox down.
Q stands for 'Quarmby', that paid spouting fool,
R stands for 'Rough-heads', that want no such tool.
S is for 'Sure go' (not for Fox, bear in mind),
T is for 'Truth', which in them you can't find.
U stands for 'Ugly', which all of them are,
V's are good voters, whom threats cannot mar.
W for 'Wreck' of the ships on the stocks.
Y is for 'Yoicks' when chasing old Fox.   (*p.* 116)

5   *Alick i' th' Hop 'Ole*
           (O Gradely Original Song.) – Tune: 'Going to California'.

O, an yo' 'erd the latest news?
If not, ol tell yo' if yo' chuse,
Alick's beawnt to vote for t' Blues—
    Thoose chaps ut gun to th' Hop 'Ole.

Un if om tell my mind complete,
Aw dunno think ut felley's reet,
To go to th' Anker every neet—
The base, corroding counterfeit.
He reckons t' bi th' poor mon's friend,
But dunnot on his words depend,
He's sure to trick yo' in the end,
    Uz sure uz he guz to th' Hop 'Ole.
        Too-ral-oo.

In principuls political
He co's his sell o Radical
It's o mi i un fal-the-dal—
    He's one o thoose ut th' Hop 'Ole.
Uz lung uz foos un find him tin
He'll brawl, un sheawt, and mak' o din,
Un in his sleeve he'll laeeth un grin
To think eaw nicely thir ta'n in.
Oppun yor een, un look abeawt,
Such yuman varmin larn to sceawt,
For like Jim Crow, he'll wheel abeawt
    Un dance a jig at th' Hop 'Ole.

Like bullbaits o eawr meetin's are,
There two-legged asses do repair,
To bray alwead, un gape, un stare,
    Ut um ut guz to th' Hop 'Ole.
Un when o chap gets up to talk,
They hiss un whistle, hoot un bawk;
Like feighten' cocks they strut and stawk,
Us if the'd mak' o't town their wawk.
The seeds of mischief hav' bin sown—
See ho th' ranklin' weeds have grown,
Whet Reason's scythe un cut um deawn,
    Un send um off to th' Hop 'Ole.

Alick's becum a mity chief,
Un Oudum lads ud just as leef
Ate sawt and tatus witheawt beef
    Us question law o' th' Hop 'Ole.
O secret aw will tell to you—
Next week thu'll be o grand revu,
So every one prepare to goo,
Un see the rag o'muffin crew.
'Twill then be Alick's full intent
On roofyets' rights to mak' descent,
With his wur nor Falstaff's regiment—
    Slaverin lads fro' th' Hop 'Ole.

He met be useful iv he wud,
Un be o instrument o good,
But curse his Tory taynted blud,
    It's bin dy'd Blue it th' Hop 'Ole.
Win put a vessel out to sea,
It's name shall be 'Democracy';
Un Alick shall the pilot be,
Merely to test his honesty.
Witness the litenin's vivid flash,
The thunner's roar, the billus' dash,
The ship, in won tremendous crash,
    Sinks in the whirlpool Hop 'Ole.

Self-interest will his conscience sway,
Bribe him, un he'll turn ony way;
Like Judas with his frauds betray,
    To modern Jews o' th' Hop 'Ole.
Alick, the uther day, at Mumps,
In deep despair, un gloomy dumps,
Toud lads to fill their clugs with sumps,
Un feight like imps for Jack o' Trumps.
To Alick this ud bi rare fun;
But, ah! the race is welly run,
Cobbit's eawt o'wynt, un dun,
    So tak him off to th' Hop 'Ole.

So neaw aw will conclude mi song,
On Alick ov bin rather strung,
Aw think od better oud mi tung,
    An let him rest it th' Hop 'Ole.
But, ere aw close this bit o' chaff,
Ol rite yo Alick's epitaff;
So dunnot oathur smile or laff,
It's nobbut dun on his behaff.
'Beneath this stone lies Alick's *Dust*,
O man unworthy faith or trust;
The wastril, let him go to rust,
    His deeds are kept o'th Hop 'Ole.'

Appendix 3

Ernest Jones, Speech on Blackstone Edge, 1846 (Extract)

Speech at a demonstration of Yorkshire and Lancashire Chartists on Blackstone Edge (between Halifax and Rochdale) on Sunday, 2 August 1846. *Northern Star*, 8 August 1846. This was the first occasion Jones had spoken in the north. Ben Rushton, the veteran Halifax radical, was in the chair. Feargus O'Connor and Dr McDougall were the other main speakers.

...WHAT is it that we want? Is it something so unreasonable? It is mercy at the hands of monopoly – justice at the hands of power – and our own at the hands of luxurious rapacity. On what grounds, I say, do they oppose us? They say we are too ignorant to enjoy the franchise; we, ourselves, do not know what we want; we are no judges of what would be good for us. Does a man know what he wants when he is starving? and sees the rich rolling in riotous profusion? He'll tell you he wants food – but then, they say that's all his folly – it's the *workhouse* that he wants! Does a man know what he wants when he is sinking with over-work, that the wealthy may enjoy their sumptuous indolence? He'll tell you he wants some hours of rest; but then, they say that's idleness and crime! It's the *gaol* that he wants! Does a man know what he wants when he's ground to the dust by the accursed hand of monopoly? He'll shout, 'Death to monopoly that consigns me to the workhouse and to gaol!' but then they say, 'That's all his ignorance, poor man, he knows not his own interests!' – Oh! who so likely, as the sufferer, to know where the pain is seated and so likely, as the man conversant with the mechanism of labour and the burdens of poverty, to know what remedy should be applied? We are too ignorant? So ignorant, that with all their wisdom, they can deceive us no longer.

Appendix 4

John Bright, Speech at Manchester, September 1866 (Extract)

(Opening and closing words)

On the 24th of September, in the Free-trade Hall, Manchester, which was crowded almost to suffocation by upwards of 5,000 persons, Mr Bright was presented with an Address by the Reform League recently established in that city. In accepting it, Mr Bright spoke as follows:

I was not aware when I was invited to attend this meeting that anything different from the ordinary course of proceedings would take place. I was not informed that I should be honoured by the presentation of any address. I accept this address with many thanks for the kindness which you have shown me; at the same time I accept it with something like fear and trembling, because of the mighty responsibility which by this address you would throw upon me. I have never had any ambition for leadership; I do not feel myself to have fitness for such an office. I have worked hitherto wheresoever I chanced to be, whether in the ranks or in the front; and without pledging myself to undertake all that this address asks of me to undertake, and perform, I may, however, freely pledge myself to this, that wherever I find men willing to work for human freedom and human happiness, I trust I shall be ready to take my part with them. And now, as my eye has rested upon this wonderful assembly, I have thought it not wrong to ask myself whether there is any question that is great, that is sufficient, that is noble, that has called us together to-night, and I have come to the conclusion that great as this meeting, and transcendantly great the meeting which was held in the middle of the day, that the question which has brought us together is worthy of our assembly and worthy of every effort we can make. We are met for the purpose, so far as lies in our power, of widening the boundaries and making more stable the foundations of the freedom of the country in which we live. We are not as our fathers were 200 years ago, called upon to do battle with the Crown; we have no dynasty to complain of, no royal family to dispossess. In our day the wearer of the crown of England is in favour of freedom. For on many separate occasions, as you all know, the Queen has strongly, as strongly as became her station, urged upon Parliament the extension of the franchise of the people. Parliament has been less liberal than the Crown, and time after time these recommendations have been disregarded, and the offers of the monarch have been rejected and denied...I believe now that there is nothing which would tend so to sweeten the breath of British society as the admission of a large and generous number of the working classes to citizenship and the exercise of the franchise. Now, if my words should reach the ears and reach the heart of any man who is interested in the advancement of religion in this country, I ask him to consider whether there are not great political obstacles to the extension of civilisation and morality and religion within the bounds of the United Kingdom. We believe – these ministers, you, and I – we believe in a Supreme Ruler of the Universe. We believe in His omnipotence; we believe and we humbly trust in his mercy. We know that the strongest argument which is used against that belief, by those who reject it is an argument drawn from the misery, and the helplessness, and the darkness of so many of our race, even in countries which call themselves civilised and Christian. Is not that the fact? If I believed that that misery, and that helplessness, and that darkness could not be touched or transformed, I myself should be driven to admit the almost overwhelming force of that argument; but I am convinced that just laws, and enlightened administration of them, would change the face of the country. I believe that ignorance and suffering might be lessened to an incalculable extent, and that many an Eden, beauteous in flowers and rich in fruits, might be raised up in the waste wilderness which spreads before us. But no class can do that. The class which has hitherto ruled in this country has failed miserably. It revels in power and wealth, whilst at its feet, a terrible peril for its future lies – the multitude which it has neglected. If a class has failed, let us try the nation. That is our faith, that is our purpose, that is our cry – Let us try the nation. This it is which has called together these countless numbers of the people to demand a change; and, as I think of it, and of these gatherings, sublime in their vastness and in their resolution, I think I see, as it were, above the hilltops of time, the glimmerings of the dawn of a better and nobler day for the country and for the people that I love so well.

Appendix 5

W. E. Gladstone, Speech at the Public Hall, Warrington, October 1868 (Extract)

(Description of scene and close of speech)

Long before the hour fixed for the meeting the approaches to the hall and the neighbouring streets were thronged by large and excited crowds. It is many years since there has been a contested election for the borough of Warrington, and the combination of town and county contests has created an extraordinary degree of excitement. The hall is large, airy, and comfortable, but, 2500 tickets having been issued, the space was tested to the utmost. The gallery had been allotted to the county voters, of whom between 300 and 400 were present. In the body of the hall the audience, standing, were most densely packed. During the interval which elapsed between the opening of the doors and the commencement of the proceedings, the rather incommoded audience preserved excellent temper, which was certainly humoured by judicious selections played on the organ. When the organist ventured on 'Tramp, Tramp', the chorus was taken up with great vigour and effect. Across the ceiling in front of the platform was a large flag bearing the words 'Welcome to Gladstone and Grenfell' in red letters. A noticeable feature of the arrangements, and one deserving of imitation elsewhere, was the excellent accommodation provided for the press. Over fifty reporters were present and the table space was ample. Punctually to the minute the candidates appeared, and were received with long-continued and vehement applause, the organ playing 'See the conquering hero comes'.... The CHAIRMAN said he thought the sight of that meeting must be most gratifying to all who had the welfare of the nation at heart. He had no wish to occupy their time – they would all be anxious to hear Mr Gladstone and his friend; but he must remark that there was now a tide in their affairs when it became imperative for them to form opinions. They were about to hear one who from his past history they must be quite sure was quite competent to guide the counsels of the nation. Let them do their part to surround him with a phalanx of strong men with free opinions to enable him to pass those great measures which would conduce to the common welfare. (Cheers.) He would now call on the Right Hon. Mr Gladstone to address the meeting. (Great cheering.)

...Gentlemen, this is a great issue for you to consider and to decide. I think that we have done our duty in endeavouring to lay it before you. Its gravity is not to be disguised. It is said that we, forsooth, for mean motives, have made it a party question. Well, gentlemen, at all events you know this, that when we charged ourselves with the question of reform, and when we found that we must abandon either the question of reform or our offices, we determined to abandon our offices. (Loud applause.) After that we are not to be driven back by these idle imputations. We have made our appeal fairly, openly, in the face of day, to the people of England to abolish the church of Ireland as an establishment, with every consideration that equity can suggest in the arrangement of the measure necessary for the execution of our designs; to abolish along with it every other grant that involves the State in Ireland in the respectability of connection with any particular religion; and after we shall have done all that equity and indulgence can require in winding up this great scheme of policy, to establish no other church and no other form of religious teaching in its place. That, I say, is the design which we have laid before the country, and which the country can understand and does understand. There is no other scheme, gentlemen, before you. There is nothing but a crowd and a multitude of misty, vague, vaporous declarations. As far as they have meaning, they are in conflict with one another. One says he is for holding high the Protestant religion in Ireland; another says that undoubtedly the question of the Church of Ireland is difficult, and requires much consideration; another says that probably it will be necessary to give away some part of its property. I do not ask you to follow any one of these narrow, obscure, and devious paths, that will lead you into the desert, into the mist, and into the bog. Let us march steadily and straightforward along the road of civil justice and equal rights, giving unto others which we desire they should give to us, doing unto them as we in their place would be done by, confident that in serving the right we are serving the God of right and justice, and that wherever be our controversies of faith and religion, wherever be the superior claims of this or that ecclesiastical communion, the supreme interest of truth will and must be served by the adoption of such a policy.

The right honourable gentleman resumed his seat amidst vociferous cheering.

Appendix 6

McDouall's Chartist and Republican Journal, 3 April 1841 (Extract)

'The White Slaves of Great Britain: Lectures on the Factory System'

WHAT HAS THE FACTORY SYSTEM DESTROYED?

Regarding the condition of the country previous to the introduction of the Factory System, we have not to depend upon obscure records or questionable history. The experience of living men supplies us with all the requisite information.

We find the hand-loom weaver, scattered over a great extent of country, which is still marked by those old fashioned, but commodious houses of former times, with the broadseated hearthstones, and the ever opened porch for the passing traveller. To these ancient cottages of the hand-loom weaver, were attached a limited number of acres for grazing or tillage. You will still find in the upper stories of these ruins of the good old times, the mouldering loom of the industrious weaver, and honest farmer.

There he sat at his rattling loom, assisted by all of his family who could work; there the grown up child worked with the parent, and the mother left her other duties to taste recreation beside her husband. There you would find all the household manufacturers busily engaged together; there, too, the song and the laugh rose cheerily, and rung in chorus with the restless shuttle. Had you entered that dwelling you would have found the weaver at his light hearted easy task, the wife smiling amidst plenty. They were free, hospitable, and intelligent; no stranger was denied a meal in their home, no wandering beggar a welcome crust at their door. The children know no greater task than a schoolboy's lesson, and were acquainted with no more tiresome occupation than a schoolboy's game.

When the spring approached, and decked the fields with its splendid covering; when the summer ripened, and the autumn cast its blushing fruits in abundance at the feet of the farmer; then you heard the loom no more; the house was deserted, and the sickle and the scythe found a healthy employment for the weaver's family. They laughed amidst the joys of haymaking: they sang to the merry harvest home.

Young and old, husband and wife were rioting amidst the annual profusion of nature, and gathering health and riches from the acres of their forefathers. The children too were there, the little flock were there to roll amidst the scented hay, to pluck flowers from the waiving corn, or to paddle in the clear stream that rushed through the lovely valley.

There is no illusion of the fancy, this is no dream of the imagination; this is the truth, the whole truth, and nothing but the truth; this was the hand-loom weaver's condition in the olden times of our fathers.

Appendix 7

(a) Short Time Committee Placard, Cassidy MS

The Queen, her People, and the Ten Hours Bill

AGAINST THEIR OPPONENTS.

When the Monarch of these realms placed her signature to the Factory Act that limited the hours of labour, she said, " *No Bill of the Session had given her so much pleasure as that!* " and if it give pleasure to the best Sovereign that this country has ever known, the sensations of joy were no less great on the part of the Working Population and every lover of humanity and intellectual progress.

We conceive it to be a hardship of no ordinary kind that, after Queen, Lords, Commons, the light of science, and the voice of the people have so often proclaimed the truth, that from Six to Six, with proper time out for a little rest and to take necessary food, is long enough for human endurance, an insignificent fraction of the Manufacturers should bid defiance to all authority, and trample the constitutional usages of a great Country under their feet, and insultingly defy all law—human and divine. This has hitherto been triumphant in Glossop Dale and neighbourhood.

The eyes of Government and the whole of the United Kingdom have long been fixed on that valley, and all good men have asked themselves the question—How long wilt thou continue to insult us? The answer is,—Till an outraged people shall rise in their majesty, and, with the sense of right that dwells within them, swear upon the constitution and the altar of their country, that this hideous system of working frail woman and frailer children Twelve and Thirteen Hours per day, shall cease for ever. Let not the Manufacturers of Glossop deceive themselves, and lay the flattering unction to their souls that they can much longer set at defiance the humane principles of the age in which they live.

The Manufacturers of Glossop have large possessions. Let them set an example of obedience to the laws of their country, lest the thousands by whom they are surrounded, who have helped to raise those possessions, should learn a lesson from their book, and pay as little respect to law and order as they do. They are very great men, doubtless, and wise in their day and generation. So was Haman, the potent minister of the East ; but the unbending soul of the humble Mordecai, the Jew, brought his power to the dust, and him to the end he designed for others. The tax-gatherer, armed with the authority of Parliament to collect a poll-tax, was another hero, till his indecencies led him too far in the house of the brave English blacksmith—Wat Tyler, when the latter, by a father's love and a sense of outraged honour, dashed out the brains of the ruffian, and then headed an insurrection, which, if it did not overthrow the reigning dynasty, put an end to an abominable tax. The lessons of history are thrown away upon such men as the Glossop employers, and they will not believe a suffering people's wail, nor bend to a request, till they have broken the tie that binds society together, and driven their work-people into open rebellion.

We now implore the Masters of Glossop to follow the example of the whole Manufacturing Districts ; and, as they value their safety and property—as they reflect upon the influence their conduct must have on all around them, by violating the laws of their country—as they respect the peace of their valley, and the safety of society around—let them commence immediately to work from Six to Six, with one hour and a half out. And if this appeal to their better judgment has no effect, then we say to the Men, Woman, and Children of Glossop employed in the mills, take the power into your own hands, and nobly resolve to work no longer than your brethren and sisters elsewhere. You have too long been the serfs of mammon. You have nobler destinies to fill than to drag out a miserable existence in spinning 36's and weaving calico cuts ; whilst for all this toil, the majority of you are within a month's march of the Workhouse.

" The woes, the pains, the galling chains, that keep our spirits under ;
We'll break again, in proud disdain, and tear the yoke asunder."

If the people adopt the policy here recommended of ceasing labour at Six o'Clock in the Evening, and the spirit of persecution should drive any of them from their employment, we have funds to support them—the promise of thousands more—and the will and the power to appeal to the people of these islands to support an industrious people in a struggle, nobly resolving not to be worked to death for a bare existence. Then, Piecer Boys of Glossop, up with your souls and down with your jackets at Six o'Clock, and the will of a united people, taking that which Parliament has been unable to give, will settle the Ten Hours Question ; make factory life endurable, and place the Operatives on the same footing as their brethren of other trades throughout this empire.

MEN OF ASHTON AND NEIGHBOURHOOD,
WE HAVE MADE ARRANGEMENTS FOR A

CHEAP TRIP TO GLOSSOP!

On SATURDAY next the 4th day of JUNE, 1853,

To start from the Park Parade Station, Ashton, at half-past Three o'Clock in the Afternoon.
Tickets, There and Back, 9d. *each, may be had from the Committee, Brougham Inn.*

The Manchester men will meet us, per train, at Guide Bridge. **SIX BANDS** are already engaged; and if the Acts of the Imperial Parliament could never get through Mottram Toll Bar, the voice of a people struggling to be free shall echo over greenwood and vale, and hill and welkin shall ring with the shouts of the glorious children of toil, whose long loud cheer shall be the death-knell of the long-hour system.

(b) Short Time Committee Placard, Cassidy MS

To the Employers and Work-people of Mossley

The spirited movement that has been going on for the last three weeks in the towns adjacent to you, must have seized upon all your minds, and compelled the employers to admit the justice of the system of abbreviating the hours of labour, and impelled the workmen to see their long cherished object carried to a successful issue.

In our Addresses to our employers, we have argued the whole question of the effects the shortening of the hours of labour will have on their interests in competing with the other manufacturing states of the world; and we will simply say here, from years of observation of this industrial question, that what other masters are able to do in Manchester, Preston, Blackburn, Bolton, and other places, you in Mossley, are able to do the same.

We appeal to the good sense of the employers, and ask them this simple question – If, in the selling of their goods in Manchester, they ever find an American, French, German or Russian manufacturer, or their agents competing with them on 'Change? and the answer must be – NO! The fact is, the competition is amongst ourselves; and what we ask is simply this – that all men employed in the same trade, living in the same country, governed by the same laws, and surrounded by much the same circumstances, though living in different localities, should regulate their hours of labour by one uniform system of working from Six to Six, with one hour and a half out for relaxation and meals. And as this is done in a majority of places throughout Great Britain and Ireland, in the name of common sense, honour and humanity, is it unreasonable to demand that this established practise should extend to you? There is not an employer in Mossley, or any where else who would have the hardihood to get up in an intelligent assembly and assert the contrary, or publish a document with his name attached thereto endeavouring to overturn the chain of reasoning on which these truths are based. If we ask ourselves the question. Has the cotton trade been a remunerative one? we have nothing to do but look around us in Mossley, and the answer is found on your hill sides, and in the valleys, and the busy note of industry that resounds around the solemn old hills, and comes rushing through the mountain gorges, speaks of a persevering industry by both master and men. In the struggle for the accumulation of capital, has the thought ever struck you of the immense sacrifice required to build those colossal establishments that meet the eye?

Oh! gentlemen, many, very many, houses have been made desolate by the long-hour system. Many a fair and fragile form has sunk beneath the burthen. The angel of Death has too often swept his terrific and soul-subduing wing over the homes of your village; left many a house desolate; many a father and mother to weep for a loved one sent to an early grave, which under a wiser and more humane system, might have been spared them to assist their declining years, and cheer them up with the light of their countenances. If any of you have ever lost a dear relative think of the mental anguish it has cost you; what you would have given to restore animation or preserve life; and then think of the thousands of homes that have been desolated by the daily, hourly, and life exhausting system that has been carried on too – too long!

In the name of Christianity; in the name of humanity; by every tie, human and divine, by the light of science; by the ties of honour that ought to exist between man and man; by the wisdom of the most profound legislation; by the maxims of philanthropists and philosophical intelligence; by all that is great and noble in the character of human beings, we ask for the extinction of this life-destroying and mind-stunting system, and the uniform adoption of the same hours of labour as the Operatives enjoy throughout this United Kingdom.

A very short time will prove to all the wisdom of the policy we advise; it will again unite the silken cord of amity between employers and employed; the world we live in will appear more bright and beautiful; men will have time to learn, by geology, on your hills, the countless ages of this world's existence. The whole book of Nature may become unfolded to the Operative, if he seeks it; and the great philosophic axiom of the divine Shakespear, may be made apparent to all –

> "There are sermons in stones, tongues in the running brooks, and good in everything."

We have heard, with the deepest regret, that a dispute exists between a portion of the Spinners and Piecers of Mossley. We wish it to be distinctly understood that we, as a Committee, exist simply to shorten the hours of labour, and cannot, and will not, have anything to do with wages or any other question; but we can tender you our best advice, and for the sake of carrying our long-cherished object, we hope both Spinners and Piecers will take our advice.

Recollect this axion, that you can seldom accomplish a great good without a little evil somewhere. The Piecers of Ashton have acted in the most honourable manner, according at once to the Spinners' request. But if the Piecers demand the same Wages now for Ten Hours and a Half that they received for Thirteen Hours, it is evident that they are prepared to receive all the good with not a particle of the evil. Piecers and Spinners must both make concessions to each other; and we call upon you immediately to agree amongst yourselves, and return to your work. A shilling a week is not to be put in the scale against happiness; and it is our deliberate opinion, that if you do not resume labour, agree, and make mutual concessions to each other, you will do more harm than you can ever do good, however long you live.

Recollect, fellow workmen, that on this question you have the sympathies, as you will have the support, if needed, of the people of Great Britain and Ireland. Four fifths of the masters, and all the men are with you. Trade is good. Your demand is as just as ever emanated from the lips of human beings. With these things in your favour, you have only to be true to your-selves, and while Parliament and agitators are debating about details, you will accomplish that for yourselves that no power has hitherto done for you.

Be respectful to your employers. Serve them faithfully and diligently whilst you are in the mills; but let no blandishment, however soft; no threats, however hard; no promises, however insinuating and lofty, induce you to to work after or before the fingers of the clock are straight up. Up with your souls and down with your jackets, and let the words pass from mouth to mouth, and reverberate over hill and through valley – "SIX o'CLOCK, the Watchword and the Cry!" Then this great question of humanity will be settled for ever. The whole people will be more happy and contented than at any former period, and our own loved Island of the West shall continue to stand out proudly from the sea, the freest of the free and its merchants, manufacturers, and populations be models of all that makes a nation great, glorious, and irresistable in the eyes of an admiring world.

Appendix 8

'Our Merry Town', Pearson Collection (188), Manchester Central Library

(Tune – Kitty Jones)

_____

Gosh dang it lads, I've come again though many a mile I've been
    I'm —— lad bred and born and lots of sights have seen,
But when I came in town egad I nearly fell in fits
    Both times and folks so alter'd look'd I thought I'd lost my wits
I turned me north, I turn'd me south, I turn'd me east and west,
And everything look'd vastly changed and some were not the best
They even altered parish pump and turned it upside down
    And the wells are choked with paving stones since I left our
town.

When I left home some years ago old folks had lots of trade.
    Some right good jobs came tumbling in and every one were
paid.
We had good roast beef and pudding and of ale some decent swig
    In fact they lived like fighting cocks and got as fat as pigs.
But know egad ther's no such stuff poor folks have empty tripes
They've no roast beef to stuff their ribs but poor law soup and
swipes,
An honest working man's no chance grim death on him doth frown.
    I never thought things would come to this since I left our town.

In days gone by our fine young men ne'er told such dismal tales
    Not a man would not transport himself as far new south whales
We had honest men in parliament both tories, rads, & whigs
    They ne'er were known poor folks to rob, but now they turn
like prig
Our manufacturers wor'd full time the mills were seldom stop
    We had then no general turn outs cause folks wages was not
drot

366

The corn law chaps & chartist lads might talk till all was brown
  Without being sent to tread the mill when I left our town.

I never thought in days gone by such times would come as these
  When lads were all as gay as larks & wenches blythe as bees
Right merry they jog'd to the fair in clogs and light shaloon
  And every one could sport a face just like a harvest moon;
But now their clogs & light shaloons each one has flung aside
  The lasses moons are faded and they grown too proud to stride
The foolish frumps sport mutton pumps, & now their pride to
crown
  With bustle tied behind them half as large as our town.

But dang it lads I shall ne'er forget when first I came in town,
  A pretty wench came up to me & said where are you bound
Oh I said I'm not particular though my blood was in a stew,
  But hoo sed if I would go with her hoo'd show me something
new,
We got some drink and then I felt fuddled in my head
  We toddled to her lodgings where we'd supper & a bed,
Hoo stole my watch & all my brass nor left one single brown
  Thinks I thou's shown me something new in coming to our
town.

But wanton jokes let's put aside let's hope the times will mend
  There will a day come when the rich will prove a poor man's
friend
When work and honest poverty will meet with due regard,
  Then plotting knaves & fretting slaves will get their just reward
But soon or late as sure as fate such things will come to pass
  And when we all get lots of work we'll soon get lots of brass;
With right good trade & fairly paid I dare not bet a crown,
  There'll not be such a place ith world as our merry town.

Appendix 9

'Rich and Poor', Pearson Collection (99), Manchester Central Library

I pray give attention and listen to me,
I'll point out some facts with which you'll agree,
There's two classes of people the rich and the poor
Betwixt them there is a great difference I'm sure,
While they live in splendour you all are aware,
How the poor man is living they know not or care
But if you'll attend I've the object in view,
To show you the difference there is twixt the two.
    So don't be offended at what I shall say,
    For good and bad times I have seen in my day.

The rich live in castles with grandeur all round,
While the poor they are buried a mile under ground
The rich they have gold and it mouldering in bags
While the poor of old England are dressed up in rags
Their daughters can ride out with saddle and whip,
With a flounce down like the sail of a ship,
The rich they can go out a shooting at noon,
But the poor can shoot nothing except at the moon.

The rich they for pleasure to balls they do go,
Because they can't hear any thing that is low,
They dine on roast mutton roast turkey and duck,
While the poor they're glad of a sheep's head and pluck,
There are rich noble pensioners hatching gold eggs
And lots poor soldiers with old wooden legs,
If the rich they get drunk they can do as they chose
But poor often gets knocked about by the blues.

The rich often go to mess at the club,
Their guts they will stuff with the finest of grub,
Then cut away home at the first peep of day,
And off to the change where they prattle away,
They then speculate on the market and stock,

The hardworking men to the poor house must flock,
The rich they can live on the fat of the land,
But the poor they must work while they're able to stand.

There's Mrs Linney the publican's dame,
She can't take her tea without the best of good cream,
Her daughter Mary is going to get wed,
With a bustle as big as a jack-ass's head,
If you go in and call for a drop of good malt,
Her gown is the colour of pepper and salt,
If you kick up a row she will tell you at large,
She'll send for the Police and give you in charge.

The rich upon all kinds of dainties can dine,
On pies and plum puddings geese turkey and wine,
While the poor hungry people how sad for to tell,
For a day and a half often lives on the smell,
The rich care for nothing but eat right a head,
While the poor are as tight as three in a bed,
The rich of fine feathers can sleep at their ease,
While the poor are annoyed with the bugs and the flees.

The nobles can go it as daily does seem
To the d—l and back for a trifle by steam,
The rich like the Queen has a drawing room gay,
But where shall they be on the great judgement day?

Appendix 10

Extract from the preface of the Weyver's Awn Comic Olmenack, 1881, Leeds

T'PREFACE
Another year has passed away, —
Time swiftly glides along.

FELLA-CREATERS, – For t'seventh time I bring before ye, wi fear an tremlin, me little annewal. Nah when a weyver hez put six webs dahn t' slothoyl he sud hev getten to knaw summot abaht thrawin a gigbit an makkin a nice heeadin, an be able to put a piece together withaht makin reng picks or fleyks, or weyvin t' shuttle in. A! it's a job when ye catch t' shuttle e t' middle o' t' sheeard, izznt it! – So it may be supposed 'at nah 'at I've neearly sarved me 'prenticeship tut Olmenack bizness I sal be able ta du better for ye. Well I hope I sal.; I've heeard a story abaht a lad at wor prentice tuv an Olmenack-makker. Wun day his father ast him hah he wor gettin on like, an t' lad replied 'Haw, first-rate, father, – I've ommost getten up tut maister nah.' 'Hi!' sed t' owd chap, reight pleased, – 'ha's ta mak that aht, lad?' 'Well, he can tell at morn what sort o' wether there's bahn to be during t' day, an I can tell at neet.' I think t' lad must hev been Yorksher, – most on us can tell at neet what sort o' wether thare's been during t' day. It's bein able to tell aforehand at beats a deeal ov us. Bud thare's wun thing I can tell ye aforehand, an that is – I mean to coninny to du mi best to mak t' 'WEYVER'S AWN' as good as – well as misen – an if onny ov ye thinks it's worth thripence ye can pay that sum asteead o'tuppence, and I've no daht it'll be accepted. I don't think I can safely promise onny more ner this, – cos I harbour an owd-feshund opinyun at most men's wark is but a reflekshun ov thersens, – if thay've nowt in em, or are bad workmen, thay'll due poor wark; if thay're good an clever workmen there wark'll shew it. T' difficulty is ta get fowks alus to du ther best, for ov late yeears duin ther best hezznt supposed to 'pay.' Nah I've

370

anuther impression abaht this matter, an it's this – at gooid honest
wark on the pairt ov workmen, an honest deahn in an honest aikle
on the pairt of tradesmen, *will pay t' best e t' long run.* – if thay've
nobbud t' same chonce as tuther side. We've been tryin tuther side
for sumtime nah. We've belt hahses o' single bricks, endway up: we
watter t' milk, an put sand emeng wer sugar; we mak calico aht o'
China clay an cotton – mostly clay; an we mak cloath aht ov
shoddy, cotton, waiste, muck, – or aoany sort o' devilment, raither
ner wool; an we're sendin sitch stuff tut heathens abroad at'll mak
em wish thay'd nivver leearn'd to wear cloas. Nah hah the hengment
can sitch go ins-on as these stand t' peark? This is noan t' way at owd
England gat tut top o' tree wi her manifacters, an it's noan t' way
ta keep at top. I may be reng, bud I think I ammot; an if we wish
to keep at front ov all the world wi wer goods an workmanship I
beleeve at both men an maisters will hev to put more brains,
conscience an honesty into their bizness. As sooin as manifackturers
begin o' thinkin less abaht makking brass fast, ner makkin good,
honest, satisfactory artikles; an men think more abaht duin there
wark as well as it can be dun, rather ner getting t' most wage thay
possibly can for duin t' least an t' poorest possible kwantity o'wark,
– then I think we'se mend e all at's worth hevvin. At present I daht
were on t' reng track, as t' chap sed when he met a railway-engin on
t'line, an it put him o' wun side; an if we don't mind we'se be put
o' wun side an all. – Bud enif on that streyn for t' present...

Appendix 11

Extract from the 1885 Weyver's Awn almanac, entry for January and the facing page

Dear friends, I nah address you once again, an e'furst place let me thenk you for t'favours past, an also for't favours I trust ye're abaht to grant me ageean, e t' shape ov ivvery wun on ye buyin a coppy o' this almenack. A paper on health says at its wise to tak at least three quarters of an hahr for t'dinner, an anuther recommends at a bit ov meyt an porrates added to t'three quarters ov an hahr wondn't spoil it mitch. It certainly wod be a poorish job withat meyt an porrates, bud if ye knaw annyboddy at after heytin cannot manige to digest what they've hetten, tell em ta get a Weyver's Awn ta help dahn ther food. It'll dew more gooid ner awther pills or frewt salts, an it'll breeten em up all rahnd. Dewrin t' past year there's nut been soa mitch ta dew e t' country, different ta uther years, except this big franchise agitation which hez hahivver been a pretty busy time (especially for t'printers). I doan't pretend (like owed Moore) to be able ta say hah it'll end, bud this I dew say, at there's a deal o' ill-feeling created abaht it at's altogther uncalled for. Hesn't ivvery man at reight ta his awn opinion – an if he hes what duz he want to compel ivvery other man to fall to it, an thinks he's an idiot an a fooil if he doesn't. I dew believe at both parties mean weel – for thersen – bud who doesn't lewk aht for hissen? I believe at ivveryboddy owt to hev a vooat – wimmen an all, bless em – whether there fit to use it or noa. I shall next year happen be able to say hah things are then, bud I sooan't prophesy till O knaw it's reight.

Referring ta wimmen reminds me that the Farsla demonstration there wor a lot o'wimmen led t'Stannila lot e t'procession. Nah I wonder – if suppoasin there hed been a reyt bengin new feshon e wun o' t'shop windas – whether they woddn't hev forgotten abaht t' voat an' made for' t' shop winda? Takin abaht feshons I think they get moar brazzened ner ivver. Just fancy lasses puttin 'turkey peaks' at back on em, an callim em improvers; bud soa long as it's feshion it'll hev ta be kept up to. Bud is it trew at sin that bustle feshon com aht at t' regmen hev hed no employment? I think it's happen nobbut a tale, but if that lass at let t'bundil tumble aht ov her gearin up Lowtahn wun day be a sample, then there may be some truth in it.

An nah for t'futur. It is sed at society's composed ov two classes; them at's moar dinner ner appetite, an them at's moar appetite ner dinner. Well I trust at whatever occurs to ye, whether ye hev trubbles ov ivvery uther kind; whether its yer sad lot to get wed; or whether it's your sadder lot to hev barn's bi two, three, or fower at a time, at ye'll not belong ta them ats moar appetite ner dinner. I trust at all will at least hev sufficient for t'appetite dewrin t'year, an at you'll be able to trewly fill t' stayshun e life in which yer placed, an endeavour to feight shy o' that undesirable place – t' poleece stayshun. Speykin ov t' poleece stayshun reminds me at I owt to tell you ta determine ta mind yer duties better ner Mike Muffintin. He wor set on to be a poleeceman, an next day he wor 'seckt'. He sed wen ast why he'd neglected his duty, – 'I wor telled to watch, an I waited an watched an noaboddy com, soa I went hooam an went ta bed'. Do yer duty better ner than, an allah me to remain.
Yers trewly,
S.B.

FESTIVALS AN' HALLIDAYS.

Shrove Tuesday	Feb. 17	Easter Sunday...	Apr. 5
Palm Sunday	Mar. 29	Whit Sunday	May 24
Good Friday	Apr. 3	Michaelmas Day	Sep. 29
Lady Day	Mar. 25	Christmas Day	Dec. 25

BENK HALLIDAYS.

Good Friday, Easter Monday, Whit Monday, first Monday in August, Christmas Day and day following, every Sunday; an' all uther days when thay've nowt ta dew.

LOCAL FEEASTS AN' FAIRS.

("AN' THARE'LL BE BEEF AN' PLENTY.")

Bradford Pleasure Fair ...	Jan. 3	Kirkstall Feast	Aug. 16
Gomersal Feast	Mar. 23	Hunslet Feast	Aug. 16
Pudsey Fair	Mar. 30	Birstall Feast	Aug. 19
Otley Cattle Fair	Apr. 8	Horsforth, Rawdon, Yeadon,	
Adwalton Easter Fair ...	Apr. 9	and Guiseley Feasts ...	Aug. 23
Bramley Clash	May 4	Pudsey Feast	Aug. 23
Otley Cattle Fair	May 27	Cleckheaton Feast	Aug. 27
Adwalton Feast, and Horse		Halton Feast	Aug. 30
&c., Fair	May 28	Armley, Wortley, and Farn-	
Bradford Cattle Fair ...	June 17	ley (new) Feasts	Sep. 6
Halifax Fair	June 24	Holbeck Feast	Sep. 13
Bradford Pleasure Fair ...	July 6	Lee Fair	Sep. 17
Leeds Fair	July 10 and 11	Batley and Morley (old)	
Bramley Feast	July 19	Feasts	Sep. 18 & 19
Shipley and Saltaire Feasts	Aug. 2	Idle and Windhill Feasts ...	Sep. 27
Stanningley, Rodley and		Woodhouse Feast	Sep. 27
Calverley Feasts ...	Aug. 6 & 7	Pudsey Fair and Farnley	
Leeds 'Corporation' Holiday		Old Feast	Sep. 28
First Week in August	New Wortley Feast... ...	Oct. 4
Morley New Feast ...	Aug. 3 & 4	Barkerend Feast	Oct. 11
Tong Feast	Aug. 9	Halifax Fair...	Nov. 6
Apperley Bridge and Eccles-		Leeds Fair	Nov 8 & 9
hill Feasts...	Aug. 9	Bradford Cattle Fair ...	Dec. 9
Bowling & Tong Street Feasts	Aug. 9		
Gildersome Feast	Aug. 13		

1885. ## Jennewery. **31 Days.**

Changes ov t' Mooin.

Full Mooin	...	1st,	5 hr.	26 min. a.m.
Last Quarter	...	8th,	3 hr.	37 min a.m.
New Mooin	...	16th,	8 hr.	37 min. a.m.
First Quarter	...	24th,	1 hr.	26 min. a m.
Full Mooin	...	30th,	4 hr.	19 min. p m.

1 Th
2 F

I cud nobbut get this bit o' poetry for this year. I advertised for an acre, an ast for samples, an this wor wun,—

3 S
4 S

" I hooap dear frends at ye will lend,
Me yahr attenshun for a while,
An if ye will I'm sewer I'll try
To draw a tear or fetch a smile."

5 M
6 Tu
7 W

A lad at heard a man at wor at their hahse sayin t' well knawn line 'An honest man's the noblest work of God,' sez at it izzn't reit, for ' his muther wor better ner onny man at ivver wor made.'

8 Th
9 F
10 S
11 S
12 M
13 Tu
14 W
15 Th
16 F

He wor a 'masher' an noa mistak wor Billie Spruce—a dahn reight lady-killer in fact.—Bud he gat taen dahn a larp one day when he least expected it. He wor at Newla stayshun waitin for a train to tak him ta Apperla Brig, an on t' platform there wor a reight spenkin young lass bi hersen. Of course as sooin as Billie saw this he began plannin hah to hewk on. Enah he spies his opportunity an introduced hissen. Shoo seemed rayther capt wi his boldness, bud as he wor donned up to t' nines, an wor bi no means bad lewkin, shoo anserd him back. He thus encouraged grew bolder an wor sooin e his element He wor pilin on t' agony, an makin use of a lot o' long words he'd leearned aht o' t' dickshunary, when up cums a mate ov his, an witaht movin a single muscle or even smilin he sed ' Ah say lad hes ta taen that band-cart daahn ta Leeds ?' That floored him. T' lass just stopped a minnit, an then went off highly indignant. Billie of course hed nowt to dew wi noa hand carts, followin a mitch better occupayshun, an monny a laff he an his mates hev hed ower that little affair.

17 S
18 S

Mooinleet musing,—stoppin to ascertain what damage hes been dun to yer togs after yer eucaahnter wi t' dog e t' back yard.

19 M
20 Tu

He wor an owd sowlger an wor browt before t' magistrates for bein drunk. Ses t' great unpaid ' Have you ever been in a war ?' ' Yes,' replied t' sowlger, ' I sud think I hev, an hed it hoat tew ; *I've been wed fower times.*' They let him off.

21 W
22 Th

' You are goin to Hell my man,' sed a parson to a chap at Leeds station at wor drunk. ' Thart—a—a—a—liar,—ahm bahn to Armla.'

23 F
24 S

' Buy a bit o' fish ?' ast a fishmonger ov a woman wun Setterda neet e Pudsa market. ' Now,' shoo anserd ' nut to neet, beside it isn't fresh. ' Well,' replied t' fish chap, ' you sud a bowt it last Setterda neet wen I offered it to ye,—it's noan my fault.'

25 S
26 M
27 Tu

' Bi gow lad, bud that fish dus smell,' sed a fella tul a fish chap tuther day. ' Dus ta mean ta say at it smells bad ?' sharply ast t' fishmonger gettin his heckle up. ' Now, lad,' anserd t' chap, ' nut bad—fresh.'

28 W
29 Th
30 F
31 S

A chap wor up tuther day for steylin, an wen t' magistrate ast him if he wor guilty he thowt at if he appeared ta hev a ' slate off' at he'd get off raither easier, soa he anserd wi a grin, ' Tha knaws.' He wor then ast if he'd owt ta say ? ' Tha knaws,' he agean replied. An to ivvery question at was ast he allus gave t' same anser. At t' last judge gave him three months. ' What's that for ?' ast chap in astonishment ' Tha knaws,' quietly anserd t' judge wi a diabolical grin on his face, ' Tha knaws.'

Appendix 12

Extract from Bob Stubbs' Yorksher Awmynack, preface and entry for March 1910

Deead men's shoes dooant allus fit

T'PREFACE

Fower goin i'five! Anuther yeear's gooan by, an as ah sit mah darn to start anuther Awmynack, I feel inclined to lewk back o' t' past tooathery yeear, an see wot changes they've browt.

Five yeear seems a lot to lewk forrad tul, bud to lewk back on, wha! it dusn't seem as long as wun o'them dreeams when yo dreeam ye'r getting chased in aht ov a lot o'snickets bi a pig wi' three nooases an a horn a fut long grown up aht ov ivvery nooase, an ivvery time yo turn a corner the's anuther three nooas'd pig stood i' yer way! Them's t' sooart o' dreeams yo dreeam after a gurt fried fish an chip puttatey supper!

Still, the's been a lot o' changes this last five yeear for us all. Changes for better er for warr! For it's a world o'changes, an as long as we live we goa on changin, an wot happens after we're deead – well, th'es nivver nobody com'd back yet to tell us.

Five yeear owd! Little I thowt when I rate mi first AWMYNACK, wot a lot o' friends it 'd bring me. Bud it hez done, an ah'm bottom thenkful to feel wot thaasands upon thaasands o' Yorksher people taks a interest i' mi green-backed AWMYNACK, an hah kindley they lewk forrad to me plain hooamli tawks.

This yeear I hooap to give yo a better AWMYNACK ner ivver. I sallant awlus pander to frivolity, for all we'll hev wer share o' fun I'd rayther feel, when mi AWMYNACK gooas aht t' world, nut just 'at it's gooan aht to make fowk laff, bud also to mak fowk happier.

Ah'm darn abart happiness wi' long faces. If we're barn to hev wrinkles, let's hev 'em rahns wer maath corners wi' laffin, an nut rahns wer e'e corners, wi' rooarin. "God nivver intended us to rooar," wunce sed owd Jooany Beck, him 'at wor a local preysher at Queensbury an Clayton aboonn twenty yeear sin. "Wot's t' wotter i' wer e'es for, then? ax'd a poor owd woman at after t' sarmon, when t' pray'r meeting wor ower'd. "It's to wesh t' muck aht," sed Jooany, "the better to see God's goodness!" An, yo knaw, the wor a lot o' trewth i' wot Jooany sed, for we cause wersens a lot o' wer awn sorra. The's to be noa teears i' Heaven!

"Nothing suceeds like success!" It's trew. Bud if yo want to be successful, yo mooant goa abart wi' yer e'es shut, trustin to luck. "Put not thy thrust in princes," sed poor Archbishop Laud when they wor barn to shop his heead off; bud Bob Stubbs sez, "Put

376

not your trust in luck," If yo dew, dooan't be capt if yo loss yer heead, like poor Laud did!

T'YORKSHER AWMYNACK hesn't succeeded wi' trustin to luck. It's meant a lot o' hard graft for poor Bob Stubbs; monny a struggle; monny a restless neet. For the's a lot o' plannin an skeemin to make ends meet even i'bringin awmynacks aht.

T' main o' t' credit for wot it's already doe I give to mi reeaders. They've been lenient wi' mi faults an weeaknesses, an when ah've sed owt at didn't just pleease 'em, they've owerlewk'd it, an sed, "What! he's done his best, hez t' lad, an noa man can dew more!" Let's stick together, then friends. Lewk threw mi little AWMYNACK, not to criticise, bud to learn. It's reeal life, trew to Nature, and noa mak-up. Ther's men an wimmin in it I've met i' mi awn life. Happen ye'r in it yersen!

Let's hooap this year 'll be better ner t' last. We owt ta get happier as we get owder! We dooan't hev t' same pleasures when we get owd as we did when we wor young – an we dooan't want 'em. Owd age brings it awn pleasures. Nobbut t' sewerest way to be happy when we're awd is to be good when we're young.

Them at sets cabbages mooan't except to gether scarlet runners!

Here's mi, hand, friends. Tak hod, an give it a shak. Forget and forgive. Let bygones be bygones, an if yo've a enemy i' t' world clap t' AWMYNACK darn an goa an mak it up wi' him this minnit.

> "Life's too short to quarrel,
> Friends too precious to lose;
> Shake hands and let us be friends
> For old time's sake."

An nah, ah'll retire into t' backgrahn.

> I wish yo' health, I wish yo' wealth,
> May yo' nivver dew nowt bud injoy yerself,
> An live tuv a hundred an twenty,
> If yo're single I wish yo noa crosses, all crahns,
> If yo're wed, I wish yo plenty o' barns;
> As long as yo live may yo nivver want,
> May yer final hawp'ny nivver be spent;
> May yo live o' eggs, an milk, an beef,
> May yo nivver be short ov a set o'good teeth;
> May yer koilus be full, an yer kubberd be pack't,
> Hah to pay yer rent may yo nivver be rack't,
> May yo live till ye're stawl'd an then when yo dee,
> May yo fly up ta heaven, an keep a corner for me!

Ta-ta, an wishin yo wun an all a Merry Chris'mas an a Happy New Year.
Believe me,
Yer sincere fella Yorksherman and well-wisher,
BOB STUBBS

Its easy to be wise after t'event

A hungry hoss gallops to t'stable

NEW MOON 11th MARCH FULL MOON 25th

BOB STUBBS' WEATHER FOR THIS MONTH

March owta come in like a lion this yeear, bud unless I'm sadh mistaen it 'll be like a tame lion this time, bud when it gets to be abart t'third week then 'll be more umbrellas turn'd inside aht ner wot 'll be pleasant, an ah'm flay'd the'll be a cowd, wet Easter. Ah'm sorry, bud if the's a fine day at Gooad Frida, (that's t' last Frida i March) mak t' best o' t' day, for it's much if the's onny fine weather at after, unless it cleears up a bit at Easter Tuesda.

Yo'll heear mooar grummlin abar't weather this munth ner onny uther munth i' t' yeear. It's awther too wet, er too dry, er too warm, er too cowd, er too close, er too stuffy, er too winndy, er summat. It's gotten a bad name, hez this munth, an if a dog gets a bad name yo mud as weel heng it at wunce an it's same wi' a woman. Sally Nicholson wor as honest an deeasent a lass as ivver walk'd shoe leather between Horton Benk Top an Bradford tahn hall, but wun sorry day shoo went to Morecambe on a day trip wi' a lot o' singers i' t' singin seeat, an comin hooam throo Morecambe shoo gat sepperated throo all t' uther lasses an rade hooam in a carriage all bi hersen woll shoo gat ta Manningham, an at Manningham a man gat into t' carriage, an Sally wor seen getting aht o' t' carriage wi' t' man at Bradford station, an her mates set her darn to be wot shoo hedn't owta be, an for all Sally stopp'd i' t' same choir for yeears at after they nivver forgave her, an her name wor mix'd up wi ivvery scandal at Greeat Horton for ivver after. T' trewth o' t' matter wor, at t' man wor noa more reng between Sally an her uncle Jonathan ner ther ivver wor between Titus Salt monnyment i' Lister Park an Queen Victoria monnyment i' Morley Street, bud sum'dy saw 'em gettin aht o' t' train together, an started t' tale an it's stuck to poor Sally to this day. Bud when yo feel inclined to grummle yo can awlus grummle abart t' weather an call it all t' names yo can think on, withaht hurtin it, for

> Whether the weather be fine er wet,
> We s'll etta weather it, whether er net!

An if we nobbut gave it a thowt we can awlus finnd summat to be thenkful for, even at t' warrst o' times. If ye've a bad cough, er a pain i' yer back, an yo feel inclined to get dhan hearted and despondent, thinkin yer time's neearly up, an wunderin hah sooin yo'll be hevvin to livver yer checks in, tak a walk er a tram ride, as far as Undercliffe simmy-terry, an ask yersen. "Hah menny poor blokes is ther laid stiff an cow i' thid here miserable hoil 'ud be glad an fain to tak my cough an my granny back, an chonce anuther e'eful o' earthly woes an soora rayther ner be wheer they are?"

Hi! the's a lot to be thenkful for, even if we dooan't get ivverything just as we sud like it. It's summat to be alive, nivver heed owt else! As ahr Nanny sez, wiss'l be a long time deead!

Owd Martha Parkinson, shoo kept a mengle at a little cottage up a fold i' Bowlin Owl Loin at Bradford, an shoo'd nobbut a sorry puttin on. Me an ahr Nanny we wor wunce seekin a hahse i' Bowlin Back Loin to live in, an we call'd at Owd Martha's just bu luck, an t' owd lass wor just munjin away at a bit o' avverbreead an a morsel o' cheese. Her owd cheeks wor sunk in, an her chin an nooase neearli met as shoot chew'd away at

t'avverbreead, an ahr Nanny ass'd her if shoo'd lost all her teeth. "Nay," sed owd
Martha, her two little ferrity e'es sparkin like diamonds, "ah've two teeth left, nobbud
two, bud thenk God, they've booath opposite to wun another!"

Mucky windas an a cleean dooar-step doesn't match!

Keep yer pockets full o' brass, an yo'll nivver be short ov a "friend"!

A trew friend puts yo on yer guard when he sees yo runnin into danger. He dusn't
let yo goa blindly on, an wait till yo fall, an then jump on t' top on yo to hod yo darn!

When a workman feels 'a he dusn't get better thowt on for dewin his best, an doesn't
get paid accordin'ly, what wunder if he gets it intuv his heead at he might as weel laik
for nowt, as work for nowt!

A man 'at works hard at t' mill throo Munda morn to Setterda nooin, I dooan't fairly
knaw whether he's even justified i' shuttin hissen up in a chappil three hahrs ov a Sunda!
A ten mile walk across ov Ilkla moor it ud happen dew him mooar reeal gooid!

> "Who guides our footsteps while at play?
> Watches in sickness, day by day?
> Why, mother!
> Sometimes we may despise her,
> And say that she's to blame;
> No matter what her faults may be,
> She's mother – just the same!"

Note:
This is a simulation of the typeface of the original.

Appendix 13

Cover and extract from Tommy Toddles' Comic Almenac, 1875

—— falling in love with him begs him off.

But it was too bad to make him adopt the customs of the country, and not to let him see "the King's Umbrella" before he "swapped."

The Stones were bad enough,   But when he came to Snakes

He fled.

LIFE IN ASHANTEE.

"He blackened his face wi' chalk."—*Shakespeare.*

ASHANTEE—pronounced a-shanty—isant a shanty at all, bud a collection o' shanties. It is a country bounded on t'east bi t'rising sun, an' on t'west bi t'setting same, an' is a place whear warming pans ar unnawn, an' wear coils as bowt simply for ornaments. T'inhabitants ar a warlike race, an' feit wol ther black i't face, an' bankruptcy is a thing yet only dremt of, as they'd tak sa mich ta whitewesh 'em. Black, indeed, seems ta be t'prevailing colour, an' it's noa uncommon thing ta see a chap look black thear; he seldom looks owt else. Watter is never used bud as a drink; t'natives issant at all like ahr teetotalers; they doant abuse it be weshin' thersen in it. Thear a blackenin' hawker ad do weel, for every burthday they all blacken thersens up, an' a swell may generally be nawn bi t'shine ther is on him, just as they're nawn here. Spar-rib an' pig-fry is a great article o' food, and t'manufacture on it as a national affair. T'raw material consists o' human beings an' little dogs. It's varry comfortable tu a chap thear, when t'wet season starts, tu think 'at he's a dozen barns i't family; he feels a bit like a Yorkshireman wi' a pig hung up at t'bauk an' a pack o' flaar i't kist; he feels as if he woddant hev ta pine. It's varry nice is that, for suar. Thel noan hev t'care wi' barns thear 'at ah hev hear; thear ther's noa board skooils, an' if one o' t'barns taks t'mazzles, it's made inta sossige at once, afore t'infection spreids. As for clothing, two yards o' tuppenny-haupeny cotton al mak' suits for a family o' eighteen, an' t'fashions doant change aboon once in a lifetime. It's a cheap country for everything, an' noa bookkeeping's required, as a shopkeeper chalks his scores on his body wi' chalk. Thus we may see 'at a chap 'at's worth a deal al hev his body covered wi' white marks, an' all t'young women all be e love wi' him. It's a nice country is Ashantee for some fowk, bud t'fowk 'at it suits ar yet unborn. Na man's life is particularly safe thear; ther's nauther warkhahse nar prison tu tak care on 'em in. Things get streitened as they goa on, an' as sooin as a lodger hes gotten a fortnight's lodgings inta debt he's killed an' etten tu pay for it wi', an' things goas on as usual.—*Extracted from a work,* "*The late Ashantee War, an' Warser,*" *be T. Toddles, Esq.*

Appendix 14

An example of Sussex dialect literature

Tom Cladpole's jurney to Lunnun; Shewing the man Difficulties he met with, and how he got safe home at last (told by himself and written in pure Sussex doggerel, by his Uncle Tim)

PREFACE

Most people want to know when dey buy a book who is de author ov it. So one says to another, "An who is dis Tom Cladpole wot maaks sich a fuss about he's travels?" Why Tom ent ashamed ov he's clawney, so he wishes me to tell ye a liddle about un. Our family is an old feshioned one. *Ol' Cain* was de fust an um, an he jes wos a gurt Farmer: ye may be sure ov dat, fer he built a City; now uf any ov our Farmers build a Barn, a Stable, or even a Hog-poun, 'tis though much ov! Howsumever uf dis Cain wos a gurt man, he was loike a dunna-many other gurt men, *good for naun;* but good or bad, he wos de Father ov all de Cladpoles, an 'twood taak me up a wick to tell about um all.

So I shall onny goo back to Tom's Granfuther, dat is to say my Father, who about half a hundred years agoo or dereaway, used a Farm ov about twenty acres under one Sqyer Squeezer – about dat time de French kicked up a rout and cut der King's head off! Dat made our King so lamantable crass fer fear dey would cut he's head off too, dat he set to fighten de French at a robben ov a rate, an all dat was able was off a soageren: an ever since da time dere has been too families ov de Cladpoles – de gurt Cladpoles and de little Cladpoles. De Gurt uns wont own de Liddle uns fer ken now; howsumever dey *be* ken to us, and I can prove it, for Tom's granmother, whos name was *Sue Slapper*, was fust cousen to de present Squyer Slapper's Father, an he's own Mother wos a Cladpole, so ye see dat we be all ov a breed loike.

I think Tom is de fust dat ever told about he's travels, fer dis rasen, acus all de family be troubled wud sich bad eyes; fer as my ol' cousen, Sam Quizum, used to say, dere never wos a Cladpole dat ever could look higher dan de top ov de mow or deeper dan de plow went.

384

Now uf dere shud be ennybody wot don't loike to believe me about our Family, let um goo an ax de Parson, fer he's got all der names in he's gurt book; besides, ya know, wot de Parson says must be right, for he's paid fer tellen the truth.

Wel, dat is all we can say 'bout Tom at present: mayhap we may tell a liddle more about our family sum day – but now 'bout de book. Tom as sold another thousand ov um and lacks more now, so he's got sum more prented. It cums to a power of money for prenten, an wot it wus, Tom sent sum to a fellur at Lunnun, and never got the money for um, so Tom 'lows dat de Lunnuners be all a pack ov rubbage together, but dat dey sey is a trick ov trade, and so de trade beant a bit onester dan dey shud be – but 'tis no manner ov use grumblen, as I have sumwhere read, –

'Tho' fretting may make our calamities deeper,
It never can make bread and cheese to be cheaper.'

Tom has heerd say dat Lords, an Squyires, an Lawyers, an Doctors, an ev'n Parsons read he's book, an he thinks it's true, for he's sold a plague of a lot on um.

Sum folks say dat dis here book is all a pack ov nonsense, an very loily 'tis, but one ov my brother *poets* says that "nonsense has a charm," an uf my liddle book can charm its readers its wot a dunamany gurt books ten times as big as his'n never cud do. So all I can say 'bout it is, dat dey wot don't loike it may make it better.

Tom as no objection to reform, dat is to say, to mend our ways, but wants all his readers to know dat to make a good job ov dat dey must all begin at de right end, an dat end is at *number one!*

So no more at present, from Yer ol' Fren, TIM CLADPOLE.

(Printed and published by Farncombe and Co., *East Sussex News*, Lewes 1872)

Appendix 15

Samuel Laycock, Welcome, bonny brid

Tha'rt welcome, little bonny brid,
But shound't ha' come just when tha did;
    Toimes are bad.
We're short o' pobbies for eawr Joe,   *bread soaked in milk*
But that, of course, tha didn't know,
    Did ta, lad?

Aw've often yeard mi feyther tell,
'At when aw coom i' th' world misel'
    Trade wur slack;
And neaw it's hard wark pooin' throo—
But aw munno fear thee,—iv aw do   *mustn't frighten*
    Tha'll go back

Cheer up! these toimes 'ill awter soon;
Aw'm beawn to beigh another spoon—   *going to buy*
    One for thee;—
An', as tha's sich a pratty face
Aw'll let thi have eawr Charley's place
    On mi knee.

God bless thi, love! aw'm faint tha'rt come,
Just try and mak' thisel' awhoam:
    Here's thi nest;
Th'rt loike thi mother to a tee,
But tha's thi feyther's nose, aw see,
    Well, aw'm blest!

Come, come, tha needn't look so shy,
Aw am no' blamin' thee, not I;
    Settle deawn,
An' tak' this haupney for thisel',
The'r lots of sugar-sticks to sell
    Deawn i' th' teawn.

Aw know when first aw coom to th' leet,
Aw're fond o' owt 'at tasted sweet;
    Tha'll be th' same.

But come, tha's never towd thi dad
What he's to co' thi yet, mi lad,
   What's thi name?

Hush! hush! tha mustn't cry this way,
But get this sope o'cinder tay
   While it's warm;
My mother used to give it me,
When aw wur sich a lad as thee,
   In her arm.

Hush-a-babby, hush-a-bee,—
Oh, what a temper! dear-a-me
   Heaw tha strikes!
Here's a bit o' suger, sithee;
Howd thi noise, an' then aw'll gie thee
   Owt tha likes.

We've nobbut getten coarsish fare,
But, eawt o' this tha'll get thi' share,
   Never fear.
Aw hope tha'll never want a meal,
But allus fill thi bally weel
   While tha'rt here.

Thi feyther's noan been wed so lung,
An yet tha' sees he's middling' thrung   *rather crowded*
   Wi' yo' o.
Besides thi little brother Ted,
We've one upsteers, asleep i' bed
   Wi' eawr Joe.

But tho' we've childer two or three,
We'll mak' a bit o' reawm for thee,
   Bless thee, lad!
Tha'rt th' prattiest brid we have i' 'th' nest,
So hutch up closer to mi breast;
   Aw'm thi dad.

Appendix 16

B. Brierley, 'A Royal Visit'

from J. Dronsfield (ed.), *Ab' o' Th' Yate sketches*, vol. III, Oldham, 1896

Aw've had curious brastins-eaut i' my life. Sometimes aw've bin as loyal as an Orangeman; while, at another time aw'd rob th' Queen of her creawn, an'pone it for what aw could get on it. That's bin accordin' to th' ups an'd deawns aw've had. Ther's a good monny o' th' same soart, they're ruled by th' state o' th' buttery. Aw'm in a loyal fit neaw, becose loyalty's i' th' fashion,—an' beside that, th' pottito-pies we'n had lately han had moore stars on th' gravy. My owd ticket's i'th' same skoo'. Th' air has just bin stirred wi' puffs o' royal wynt, an' storms fro' loyal lungs; an' this has caused th' owd rib to hang eaut her flag—a check napkin pinned on a brush-stail, an' trim her bonnet wi' orange ribbin. An' ther' had bin some talk o' dooin' things even moore grand, but we geet th' wrung soart o' oil. It wouldno' brun. Eaur Sal said it wur Radical oil, an' that ackeaunted for it. Aw coome whoam t'other neet, an' sung her a new sung, o' mi own makkin, an' yo' shall have it, wi' an' apology to Ned Waugh.

Eaur prince's visit

Come, Sarah, get thi bonnet on,
  An' gang along wi' me,
An' we'n goo deawn to Manchester,
  This royal lad to see.
They say'n his face is like his mam's,
  His een are like his dad's;
But i' other things, if th' truth wur known,
  He's mich like other lads.

His pasture's bin too rich for him—
  He seldom porritch takes;
An' nob'dy'll e'er be plagued wi' fat
  Ut feeds on Eccles cakes.
If he'll coome deawn to Daisy Nook,

Wi' Charlie, Frank, an' me,
We'en show him heaw to ratch his rags
Wi' a cheese an' bacon spree.

We'n taich him heaw to swing his clogs,
An' heaw to use his spoon;
An' heaw to whet an' appetite
By peepin' into th' oon—
An' seein' there a bubblin' tin,
Just like a little sae;
An' aw'll be sworn when he goes whoam
He'll never ax for tay.

We'n pile some flesh on his bare bones,
Ut are showin' through his skin,
An' mak' him he'll no' know hissel'
Afore a week he's bin.
An' when wi' th' "Hencote's" fun an' sung
He's yerd th' owd rafters ring,
He'll say—"Sup up, lads! aw'll stond th' next—
Aw'm 'every inch a king!'"*

'Aw've towd thee!' th' owd rib said.

'Theau's towd me what?' aw axt her.

'Ut theau're oather drunken, or gooin' off thi year, or else theau'd
never write poetry. Theau'll be writin' volentines next, or a copy o'
verses on a hangin' do.'

'Well, doestno' co that sung a good un?'

'It's middlin' for thee. But what abeaut gooin' a-seein' this young
prince?'

'Aye, that's what aw're comin' to. Heaw dost think we con get to
see him?'

'Well, ther's Mary at mi Aint Ailse's lives i' Butler Street; hoo's two
or three windows up steears; we con surely stick eaur yeads through
one on 'em. It'll be as good seein' theere as onywhere aw know.'

'Reet, owd ticket' aw said. 'Aw've bin tryin' to plan some soart
of a watch teawer; but aw find a woman con plan things better nur
aw con. We'n goo theere.'

Th' mornin' after we set eaut to Manchester, an' it wur a grand
day. Th' bonnet blazed i' th' sun like a basketful o' oranges; an'
when we geet to Butler Street, wurno' ther' a sheaut? Folk thowt th'
prince wur comin'; an' th' band begun o' playin', an' th' so'diers
wur odered to do summat wi' the'r 'hums'. Ther' two or three on
hoss-back ut kept ridin' abeaut fort' let folk see heaw important they

* 'Aye, every inch a king.'—*King Lear*.

wur, an' heaw mich like th' Ash'n 'Blake Lad' they could rise; aw
reckon they'rn ossifers. If they'd bin privates they'd had to ha'
ridden like men ut knew th' difference between a hoss an' a feel-loss-
o'-speed. But they'rn happen dooin' the'r best.

We fund sich a creawd as aw never seed i' Owdham Road afore,
not even at a wakes; an' we could hardly see deawn Butler Street,
ther so mony clooas-lines stretched across, wi' o colours o' calico
flappin' an' flyin' fro' 'em as if it had bin a grand weshin' day. Every
window wur filled wi' yeads; some wi' nice faces, an' ut would ha'
bin nicer if the'r een hadno' bin hid i' yure. An' ther one face like a
harfest moon ut smiled a welcome to us ut seemed to flash across th'
street.

'Heaw arta, Sarah?'

'Heaw arta, Mary?'

'Didt' ever see sich a street?'

'Nawe, an' happen never shall agen.'

'Mind if th' Queen doesno' say summat abeaut it.'

'Aw shouldno' wonder. Aw'd have th' name changed to Victor
Street. But then, londlords ud raise th' rents, an' yo'd be bothered
wi' rich folk comin' to live i'th' street, so yo'n be betther as yo' are.'

'Aye, folk han to be used to Butler street afore they liken it. But
come upsteears, an' get fixed at th' window afore he comes.'

Well we went upsteers, an' geet mixed up wi' a lot o' yeads. But
Mary at Aint Ailse's preferred stondin' at th' dur; an' hoo filled it wi'
her own carcass. Ther mony a false alarm ut caused a bit ov a flutter
amung th' bunches o' yeads; an' ther lots o' fun an' meauntebankin'
gooin' on i'th' street ut geet time on, or else we should ha' bin weary
wi' waitin'.

But ther a sheaut set up at last ut couldno' be mistakken for a false
alarm as it rowled alung th' line till it wakkent th' so'diers ut stood
i' Owdham Road, an' they had to present 'hums'. Ther a cleaud an'
a glitter filled th' street as fur as we could see for th' clooas lines; an'
some bobbies on hoss-back broke eaut o'th cleaud, an' led up a lot
o' carriages wi' folk in 'em ut didno' seem to know heaw to sit for t'
look big enough. Then ther' coome a nice lot a chaps, led up wi' a
band ut didno' play. Aw reckon they didno' want to mak' tother
bands jealous. These wur th' Lancers an' they knew heaw to ride a
hoss an' look like a so'dier, too,—noane o' yo'r short pipe brigade.
Sandwiched between two squads o' these wur th' Prince, lookin' very
thin an' pale aside o'th' burly form o' Sir John, ut wur o there. An'
folk sheauted, an' waved o' soarts o' napkins, till th' royal lad looked
bewilder't. Aw dar'say he'd bin towd ut he're bein' driven through
th' lowest part o' Manchester, becose ther nowt but workin' folk
lived in it. Th' swells lived eautside. He favvort bein' surprised ut

ther no lads runnin' abeaut wi' calico tails, as they'rn used to do, an' wi' very hungry looks. He seed no toe-rags noather, an' nob'dy rowlin' i'th' gutter. He're surprised, too, ut seein' so mony healthy-lookin' faces, different to what he'd ever seen i' Whitechapel' an' for th' matter o' that, i' Mayfair. When he geet a-facin' wheere we wur, he stopt his carriage, took off his hat, an' bowed to th' pictur' ut wur framed by a certain dur-place. He seemed to be axin Sir John if that wur a gradely sample o' Lancashire women, an' Sir John seemed to be tellin' him hoo wur. They didno' live o' zeffers an' scent theere. They sowd moore tripe, an' trotters, an' keaw heels, an' fried feesh, an' beef, an' penky i' that street nur would be fund i' o Lunnon. Talk abeaut 'the food of the people', look at that show! Th' carriage drove on, an' th' Prince made a note, aw dar'say for t' show his mother an' grondmother when he geet whoam. A lung line o' what th' childer coed 'Coppers', browt up th' tail end o'th' procession, an' then coome th' scramble to get eaut o'th' street. We'd no change if we'd wanted, unless we'd gone eaut o'th' back dur an' deawn th' entry.

Mary at Aint Ailse's axt us to stop to eaur baggin; an' ther some fun, an' some good solid talk o'er it; but th' fun wurno' abeaut th' Prince. Everybody pitied him, an' said what a shawm it wur ut a poor delicate lad like him should be dragged abeaut th' country by a lot o' chaps ut thowt moore abeaut usin' a knife an' fork nur owt else, an' made a show on him, while they'rn showin' off the'rsels. Th' owd rib couldno' see ut they'rn dooin' ony good by it, nobbut gettin' folk ready for th' pone shop. Beside, what wur th' Prince to look at? If they'd stuck a wax candle i'th' corner o'th' carriage, an' put it a hat on, an' lapt plenty o' starched linen reaund it, it would ha' done as weel.

'He's a nice young chap, for o that,' Mary at Aint Alise's said, 'But he looks as if he're gettin' ready for a "job."'

'Well, he's young yet,' th' owd stockin-mender said. 'as he gets owder he may get fatter. Eaur Joe wur nobbut like a worm once, an' look at him neaw. He's so mich like a tub ut the'r Matty has to tee his soon, when he's ony to put on. His feyther, here, met ha' bin as big if he'd kept off his whisky an' stuck to ale.'

'Reet, owd ticket!' aw said; 'but ale tak's up to' mich reawm when they're like me, gan o'er grooin'. But yo'rn talkin' abeaut this Prince. Aw shall yer nowt ut's good if yo' talken abeaut me.'

'Aw'm fain theau knows it,' th'owd Mother Confessor said. 'But if th' Prince had bin browt up i' Walmsley Fowt, an' had to feight for his buttercakes, he'd ha' takken moore cloth for his clooas nur he does neaw. That's th' place for eddicatin 'em, booath i'thi yead an' th' body. This grey-toppined owd sinner would ha' bin as numb as onybody if he'd bin sent to a college. They makken 'em fit for nowt theere nobbu' partin' the'r yure i'th' middle an' saying' "haw!"'

'What abeaut these lad's clubs?' aw axt her.

'Well,' hoo said, 'aw dunno' think they're o' that importance ut royalty should be fotcht deawn fro' Lunnon for 't mak' 'em think they're little gods. Wheere ther's a lot o' lads t'gether ther's sure to be some mischief gooin' on, if not summat wurr. Aw know that by eaur board skoo. They're th' impidentist, mischievousist, swearinist little blackguards ut ever broke a window or yelled in a fowt.'

Aye, that's true,' aw said; 'an' if one spakes to 'em they gi'en three or four words for one, an' some on 'em arno' sich nice uns,—plenty o' slowter-heause abeaut 'em. An' they're aulus puncin' at summat, if they con find owt to punce at,—oather hauve a breek or a deead cat. It wur but t'other day ut an owd kettle coome crashin' through eaur window, but nob'dy had done it.'

'Theau forgets, Ab, ut theau's bin a lad thisel',' th' owd rib put in. 'Let's be fair to 'em'.

'Aye, aw know that, an' aw've bin made to know it mony a score o' times,' aw said. 'If a lad did owt wrung then he geet a warmin' for it, one ut he'd remember too. Neaw if they touchen a lad they're hauled afore th' magistrates, an' fine't. That's th' difference between bein' a lad then, an' bein' a lad neaw. What wouldt' think abeaut a wenches' club?'

'Eh,' th' owd crayther said, an' hoo threw up her honds, 'that 'ud be wurr nur a lads' club. They're wurr nur lads neaw, for if lads 'ud let 'em a-be, they winno' let lads a-be. Shawmful th' way they carryin' on, speshly ov a Sunday neet, when they should ha' bin towt betther. A wenches' club! They mit as weel start Knot Mill Fair agen, an' howd it every week.'

'Well, neaw, owd skoomissis,' aw said, 'if theau'd th' orderin' o' things what would theau do?'

'What would aw do wi' what?'

'Lads an' wenches.'

'Aw'd keep 'em separate till they'd sense enoogh to behave th'rsels'. I'stead o' havin' big skoos, an' clubs, aw'd have a lot o' little skoos, abeaut as big as this heause, it 'ud howd as mony as are fit to be t'gether; an' one body could taich 'em. Aw'd have 'em to loce at different times, so ut ther' wouldno' be sich a racket i' th' lone. Aw'd have 'em like little familiesk watched o'er by careful een, an' aw wouldno' stuff so mich into 'em. They arno' like turkeys ut fatten o' what they crom 'em wi'. It's moore like to turn 'em into loonies. Change these things, an' we shall see a diffeent race o' childer. Ther' wouldno' be so mony spectekles worn wi' young folk then.'

This browt th' lecture, an' th' 'jacky' to an end.

Appendix 17

Edwin Waugh, Eawr Folk

Er Johny gi's his mind to books;
Er Abram studies plants,—
He caps the dule for moss an' ferns
An' grooin' polyants;   *polyanthuses*
For aught abeawt mechanickin',
Er Ned's the very lad;
My uncle Jame roots i' th' stars,   *searches*
Enough to drive him mad.

Er Alick keeps a badger's shop,   *grocer's*
An' teyches Sunday schoo';
Er Joseph's welly blynt, poor lad;   *almost blind*
Er Timonthy's—a foo;—
He's tried three different maks o' trades,
An' olez miss'd his tip;   *throw*
But, then, he's th' prattiest whistler
That ever cock'd a lip!

Er Matty helps my mother, an'
Hoo seews, an' tents er Joe;   *looks after*
At doin' sums, an' sich as that,
Miy feyther licks them o;
Er Charley,—well,—there connot be
Another pate like his,—
It's o crom-full o' ancientry,
An' Roman haw-pennies!

Er Tummy's ta'en to preitchin'—
He's a topper at it, too;
But then,—what's th' use,—er Bill comes in,
An' swears it winnut do;
When t' ones bin strivin' o' he con
To awter wicked men,
Then t' other may's some marlocks, an'   *mischief*
Convarts 'em o'er again.

393

Er Abel's th' yung'st;—an'—next to Joe,—
My mother likes him t' best;
Hoo gi's him brass aboon his share,
To keep him nicely drest;—
He's gettin' in wi' th' quality,—
An' when his clarkin's done,
He's olez oather cricketin',
Or shootin' wi' a gun.

My uncle Sam's a fiddler; an'
Aw fain could yer him play
Fro' set o' sun till winter neet
Had melted into day;
For eh—sich glee—sich tenderness!
Through every changin' part,
It's th' heart that stirs his fiddle,—
An' his fiddle stirs his heart.

An when he touches th' tremblin' string,
It knows his thowt so weel,
It seawnds as if an angel tried
To tell what angels feel;
An', sometimes, th' wayter in his e'en,
'At fun has made to flow,
Can hardly roll away, afore
It's blent wi' drops o' woe.

Then, here's to Jone, an' Ab, an' Ned,
An' Matty, an' er Joe,—
My feyther, an' my mother; an'
Er t' other lads an' o;
An' thee, too, owd musicianer,
Aw wish lung life to thee,—
A man that plays the fiddle weel
Should never awse to dee!

Appendix 18

Samuel Laycock, Bowton's Yard

At number one, i' Bowton's Yard, mi gronny keeps a skoo,
Hoo hasna' mony scholars yet, hoo's nobbut one or two;   *she's only*
They sen th' owd woman's rayther cross, —well, well, it may be so;
Aw know hoo boxed me rarely once, an' poo'd mi ears an' o.

At number two lives Widow Burns, hoo weshes clooas for folk;
The'r Billy, that's her son, gets jobs at wheelin' coke;
They sen hoo cooarts wi' Sam-o'Neds's 'at lives at number three;
It may be so, aw conno tell, it matters nowt to me.

At number three, reet facin' th' pump, Ned Grimshaw keeps a shop;
He's Eccles-cakes, an' gingerbread, an' traycle beer an' pop;
He sells oat-cakes an' o' does Ned, he 'as boath soft an' hard,
An' everybody buys off him 'at lives i' Bowton's Yard.

At number four Jack Blunderick lives; he goes to th' mill an'
   wayves;
An' then, at th' weekend, when he's time, he pows a bit an' shaves;
                                                        cuts hair
He's badly off, is Jack, poor lad! he's rayther lawn, they sen,   *lame*
An' his childer keep him down a bit, aw think they'n nine or ten.

At number five aw live misel', wi' owd Susannah Grimes,
But dunno like so very weel, hoo turns me eawt sometimes;
An' when aw'm in ther's ne'er no leet, aw have to ceawer i' th'
   dark;
Aw conno pay mi lodgin' brass becose aw'm eawt o' wark.

At number six, next door to us, an' close to th' side o'th' speawt,
                                                      downspout
Owd Susie Collins sells smo' drink, but hoo's welly allus beawt;
                                                       without
An' heaw it is, ut that is so, aw'm sure aw conno' tell,
Hoo happen mak's it very sweet, an' sups it o hersel'.

At number seven ther's nob'dy lives, they laft it yesterday,
Th' bum-baylis coom an' marked the'r things, an' took 'em o away;
They took 'em in a donkey-cart—aw know nowt wheer they went—
Aw reckon they've bin ta'en an' sowd becose they owed some rent.

395

At number eight—they're Yawshur folk—ther's only th' mon an' th'
　　woife,　　　　　　　　　　　　　　　　　　　　　　　*Yorkshire*
Aw think aw ne'er seed nicer folk nor these i' o mi loife!
Yo'll neer see 'em foin' eawt, loike lots o' married folk,　　*quarrelling*
They allus seem good-temper't like, an' ready wi' a joke.

At number nine th' owd cobbler lives, th' owd chap ut mends mi
　　shoon,
He's gettin' very wake an' done, he'll ha' to leeov us soon;
He reads his Bible every day, an' sings just loike a lark,
He says he's pratisin' for heaven—he's welly done his wark.

At number ten James Bowton lives, he's th' noicest heawse i' th'
　　row;
He's allus plenty o' summat t' ate, an' lots o' brass an' o;
An' when he rides or walks abeawt he's dressed up very fine,
But he isn't hawve as near to heaven as him at number nine.

At number 'leven mi uncle lives, aw co him Uncle Tum,
He goes to concerts up an' deawn, an' plays a kettle-drum
I' bands o' music, an' sich things, he seems to tak' a pride,
An' allus makes as big a noise as o i' th' place beside.

At number twelve, an' th' eend o' th' row, Joe Stiggins deols i' ale;
He's sixpenny, an' fourpenny, dark-colour't, an' he's pale;
But aw ne'er touch it, for aw know it's ruin't mony a bard,
Aw'm th' only chap as doesn't drink 'at lives i' Bowton's Yard!

An neaw aw've done, aw'll say goodbye, an' lov yo' for a while;
Aw know aw haven't towd mi tale i' sich a fust-rate style;
But iv yo're pleas't aw'm satisfied, an' ax for no reward
For tellin' who mi neighbours are ut live i' Bowton's Yard.

Appendix 19

Sam Fitton, Cotton Fowd

We han some funny folk i' Cotton Fowd.
We'n big an' little folk, an' young an' owd;
We'n short an' tall uns too, an' fat an' smo;
So if yo' like I'll write abeawt 'em o.
Eawr Cotton Fowd ull bow the knee to noan,
It has a sort o' kingdom of its own;
We'n thick yeds, bawd yeds, bacon-yured an' curled.
It tak's o sorts o' folk to make a world.

Well, first of o, i' th' middle house,
Next dur to Rovin Joe,
There lives a chap wi' tons o' sense,
He thinks he has it o.
Yo'll never find him worchin' hard,
He's swanky, yo' con see.
He's what they coen—howd on a bit—   *call*
I think that beggar's me.

I' th' corner house there lives a chap
Who's never tasted boose.
For, when he isno' mindin' mules,   *i.e. spinning mules*
He minds his P's an' Q's.
He's getting rayther wake i' th' yed,
An' wackery at th' knees.
He's brass enough to live retire;
He will do when he dees.

Next dur to him lives Bob o' Sups,
He's allus seekin' trouble,
He conno' see mich good i' life,
Unless he's seein' double.
Last week he supped his Sunday shoon,
It's time he geet some new uns.
He conno' keep his spirits up:
And what he has are blue uns.

I' that big heawse at top o' th' hill,
There lives a millionaire.
He's o his loaves an' muffins baked,
His mind is free fro' care.
There's some think he's an angel, an'
He looks it, yo' con bet.
He happen wears a halo, but
I havno fun it yet.

He wears tay-party whiskers an'
They hang deawn on his chest.
They say he's quite a gentleman,
I reckon he knows best.
He never looks at sich as me,
He's one o' th' upper class.
I dunno like his whiskers, but
I weesh I had his brass.

A poor owd widow lives next door;   *almost*
Hoo's welly seventy-eight.
To keep hersel' alive at o,
Hoo fairly has to feight.
Hoo does a bit of charrin', then
Hoo goes round sellin' barm.   *yeast*
Of course hoo gets her pension, so
Hoo winno' tak' mich harm.

At number nine, next dur to t'church,
There lives a nice owd maid.
Hoo's very fond of gossipin',
Hoo mak's it in a trade.
Hoo's what they coen religious, an'
Hoo goes to t' Sunday schoo'.
If onybody plays her tricks,
Hoo'll curse 'em till they're blue.

Hoo's allus havin' bits o' fraps,   *arguments*
Wi' thoose at number seven.
By th' way hoo gets her dander up,
Hoo'll never get to Heaven.
Hoo towd a woman t' other day,
Hoo'd· knock her off her perch,
But this owd maid's a chapeller,
While t' woman goes to t' church.

We han a little shop an' o,
It's kept bi Mester Cant;
He'll sell yo' owt yo' may require,
And things yo'll never want.

O' th' folks i' th' Fowd look up to him,
They sen he's gettin' rich,
It's not becose he's clever, it's
Wi' chargin' folks too mich.

O' keeping friends wi' every one
He seems to have a knack.
When onybody goes i' th' shop
He smiles o down his back.
Yo' owt to yer him singin' hymns,
He gets 'em off his chest;
An' like a good church warden, he
Con sing "Amen" wi' th' best.

A widow woman lives next dur,
They coen her Mrs Green.
Hoo has a lot o' childer too,
I think hoo's seventeen.
If childer are a blessin', well,
Moor sweet 'ud be their cup,
If poor folks childer o were born
Wi' brass to bring 'em up.

We'n funny folks i' Cotton Fowd,
Some wrong, an' others reet,
They're nobbut humans after o,
There's noan of us so breet.
There's clever Dick an' crazy Joe,
An' others I could tell.
But what's the use o' sayin' moor,
Yo'n o met sich yo'rsel'!

All annotated Lancashire dialect verse in this appendix is taken from B. Hollingworth (ed.), *Songs of the People: Lancashire Dialect Poetry of the Industrial Revolution* (Manchester, 1977).

*Allen Clarke, Title page and opening
of a 'Tum Fowt' sketch*

(Second Edition, 6th to 10th Thousand.)

THE SPRIGGS SKETCHES.

PRICE ONE PENNY

BILL SPRIGGS

IN T' WEIVIN SHED
AS A TACKLER.

By TEDDY ASHTON

BOLTON:
PENDLEBURY & SONS, Printers, 54, Higher Bridge Street.

400

MANCHESTER:
J. HEYWOOD, Deansgate.
ALL RIGHTS RESERVED.

TUM FOWT SKETCHES — 1d.

MAY BE HAD FROM ANY NEWSAGENT

No. 1 – Heaw t Menociation were Formed. A Bit of a Feight o'er t Rules. Who's t' Gaffer?

No. 2 – Five Bob an' Costs. Sally Spriggs' Voluntine.

No. 3 – Smoking Concert at Tum Fowt. Sammy Snokes' Donkey an' th' Express Train.

No. 4 – Theau Greight April Foo. Bill Spriggs Sensus Papper.

No. 5 – Grand Futebaw Match. Heaw my Hat went Off—side.

No. 6 – Bradhsawgate Masher. Th' Return Match.

No. 7 – Th' Pickles of a Pic-nic. Heaw Bill Spriggs Leet New Year In.

No. 8 – Chep Trip to Blackpool.

No. 9 – Messmerisin' at Tum Fowt. Bet Spriggs Imitates Mrs. Jackson, an Bill gets Turn't Eaut.

No. 10 – Bill Spriggs puts a Bowd Front on an' Goes Whum. Cricket Match at Tum Fowt.

No. 11 – Bill Spriggs Goes to t' Field Day. Bill Spriggs an' t' Curate at th' Field Day.

No. 12 – Th' Curate Proposes at t' Field Day. Bill Spriggs an' t' Curate at Field Day.

No. 13 – Bill Spriggs on th' Ocean Wave. Threatening Letter from Bet Spriggs.

No. 14 – Bet Spriggs Besieges th' *Trotter* Office. Another Note from Betsy (*re* Fenton Cross). Bill Spriggs as a Newsagent.

No. 15 – Bill Sprigs at Turton Fair. Bet Kills th' Hoss.

No. 16 – Bill at Farnworth Wakes. Bet Finds Him.

No. 17 – Bill Spriggs i' t' Charge o' t' Leet Brigade. Bill Goes Canvassin – Election Sketch.

No. 18 – Bet Writes Abeaut Bill Votin. Bill tries t' Catch th' Speaker's Eye. Bill as a Vegetarian.

No. 19 – Th' Cuckoo Clock. Part I. and II.

No. 20 – Magic at Tum Fowt. Bill Spriggs Shoots a Goal.

No. 21 – Bill Moves a Vote o' Thanks. Bill an' Bet Get Snowbawned. Bill Decorates th' Heause for Xmas.

No. 22 – Th' Tum Fowt Menociation Roll Call. Th' Secretary's Report.

No. 23 – Not Love in a Tub, but Love in a Dolly Tub. Rhyme: –
The Feast and the Guests.

No. 24 – Th' Ghost that were fond o' Rockin. Rhyme: – Swoppin
Sam. The Baby that Never was Born.

No. 25 – Th' Carol Singers, – a recitation. Th' Disadvantages o'
Skennin. Cock-Eye's Tale. A Wooden Family. Joe Lung's
Story, an' "Auld Lang Syne."

Real Good Recitations.
– On Sheets, One Penny each.

Owd Bloouns an His Goose.   Public House Signs.
Good Bless aw these Wimmin wi Childer.   My Owd Bonnet.
Matty Hickleton's Dreeom: or the Dean Church Ghost.
A Brother's Wish. – Arranged also as a Friend or Parent's Wish
Suitable for Weddings
(*Read Teddy Ashton's Journal, halfpenny every Friday,
for Spriggs' Sketches.*)

Bill Spriggs in t' Weivin' Shed as a Tackler.

By TEDDY ASHTON

PART I

TH' Tum Fowt Debatin Menociation (it's cawd that because th'
members said they weren't donkeys an therefore wouldn't have it
christened Ass-ociation, but Men-ociation) met as usual on
Wednesday neet, Bill Spriggs, t' president bein in t' cheer, of course.

He towd t' members aw abeaut his experience as a minder, an said
as that chap what invented factories wanted chuckin nose-fust
deawn a factory chimbly, and then skewerin on t' wheel-yed.

He'd just finished his greit tale, and were tryin for t' persuade owd
Feighrface (t' landlord) for t' let him have another gill on tick when
in coom that manager again fro Black-lane.

'How do, Bill,' he says, 'heaw are ta gettin on?'

Bill looked at him reproachfully, 'Theau does weel to ax heaw I'm
gettin on,' he replied, 'after tryin for t' get me murdered same as
theau did t' other day.'

'Not I,' said t' manager, 'nowt o' t' sort.'

'That's aw gammon,' returned Bill. 'Look at my thumb, sithee.
It's black and sore yet, and t' nail's comin off.'

'Well theau shouldn't ha' put it under t' faller.'

'Why didn't ta tell me as there were such things as fallers, then? Theau never said nowt abeaut 'em.'

'There'll be no next time,' said Bill emphatically, 'no bloomin fear. T' next time as I goo a-mindin ull be when hosses is spinners an cats an dogs is little piecers, but not afore then.'

'Well,' said t' manager, 'I'm very sorry. It wer aw an accident. What are ta having to sup?'

'Neaw, theau't talkin summat sensible like,' cried Bill. 'I'll have a pint o' bitter. But theau mun trate my piecers too.'

'He mun that an aw,' exclaimed Joe Lung an Cock Eye, booath at once, 'for we're dreigh yet wi t' wark we did on that eautrageous mornin.'

'Oh, I'll trate yo aw,' said t' manager generously.

Th' ale soon put 'em aw on a good footin once mooar, an then t' manager said, 'Well, neaw, Bill, I've geet another job for thee.'

'Oh,' said Bill, lookin up suspiciously aw at once, 'if theau wants for t' keep on good drinking terms wi me, durn't thee be after findin me no mooar jobs. Th' next time I want a job I'll goo a-lookin for it mysel.'

'Oh, but it isn't mindin this time. Durn't think I'd willinly put thee into riskin thy life, Bill, for I wouldn't. This is a quiet, sober, respectable job, and would just suit thee.'

'What is it? One wi aw t' wark tan eaut on it?' inquired Bill.

'Ay, it's a proper gentleman's job, an I'm sure theau con manage it. I should be much obliged to thee if theau'd tak' it, for I'm in a big fix just neaw.'

'An what is t' job?' axed Bill. 'I durn't mind obligin thee if I con, for theaur't a dacent soart, but no mooar mindin, mind thee; I've had enoof o' that. I'm noan warking no mooar in no place wheer aw t' wa's an cilins an fences runs at thee for t'punch thee, an bites thy fingers like a mad dug if theau tries for t' stop 'em.'

'Rest yessy on that score, Bill,' said t' manager. 'It's noan a job o' that soart as I want thee for this time. There's one of eaur tacklers been suddenly tan ill wi t' liver complaint in his legs, and I want thee for t' tak his place for a day or two in t' weivin shed. A bit of a boss, theau knows.'

'An what shall I ha' for t' do?' axed Bill. 'Is there any machines abeaut it?'

Note:
This is a simulation of the typeface of the original.

Bibliographical note

Full guidance to the primary and secondary sources used in this book is given in the notes, and there seems little point in listing here all the many items drawn upon. However, further amplification concerning particular sources, and types of source, may be useful. The place of publication given in the notes is London unless otherwise stated.

The *Typographical Society's Monthly Circular* and the *Typographical Circular*, used in chapter 5, are held at the Modern Records Centre, University of Warwick. The *Cotton Factory Times* and the *Yorkshire Factory Times* are fairly widely available in northern reference libraries, also in the British Library. The journals used in chapter 7, *The British Working Man and Friend of the Sons of Toil* and *The Working Man* are available in Manchester Central Reference Library (MCR) and the British Library. Almost all the schoolbooks and works of self-education used in chapters 7 and 8 will be found in the Canon Marmion Collection, John Rylands University Library, University of Manchester. The journal of the Lancashire Authors' Association, *The Record*, used in chapter 8, is in MCR.

The Madden Collection of ballads in Cambridge University Library covers all the English counties. Despite its great size, it often does scant justice to the range of local ballad publishing. The importance of provincial publishing (and of the activity of provincial collectors) is indicated in the Manchester ballad sources cited in chapter 10. Similar collections will be found in other English cities, as well as in some towns, for instance the important Harkness collection at the Harris Library, Preston. For material similar to the ballads, though for a period earlier than the one considered in this book, see the Robert White Collection of chapbooks, the University Library, Newcastle-upon-Tyne (available in Harvester microfilm as *Popular Literature in Eighteenth- and Nineteenth-Century Britain*). Readers wishing to consult ballads in contemporary printed editions will find the following useful, though they are inevitably highly selective; Roy Palmer (ed.), *A Touch on the Times: Songs of Social Change 1770–1914* (1974). *Everyman's Book of British Ballads* (1980), *The Painful Plough* (Cambridge, 1982), and with J. Raven (eds.), *Rigs of the Fair* (Cambridge, 1976); M. Vicinus, *Broadside Ballads of the Industrial North* (Newcastle, 1975).

Unfortunately, dialect literature is far less easily accessible in recent editions. B. Hollingworth (ed.), *Songs of the People: Lancashire Dialect Poetry of the Industrial Revolution* (Manchester, 1977) remains the best collection of poetry, and B. Maidment (ed.), *The Poorhouse Fugitives: Self-Taught Poets and Poetry in Victorian Britain* (Manchester, 1987) has a useful selection. See also P. Salvesen (ed.), *Teddy Ashton's Lancashire Scrapbook. Selections from Allen Clarke* (Bolton, 1985); D. Harker (ed.), *Allan's Illustrated Edition of Tyneside Song* (Newcastle, 1972). Harker's edition of George Ridley, and Forbes' of Tommy Armstrong, both cited in the notes to chapter 11, may also be consulted. Dialect prose is not served at all in contemporary editions.

Almost every northern town, especially those with a dialect tradition, has a good run of dialect literature in its local library. However, the big regional libraries are best, particularly Newcastle, Leeds and Manchester. MCR has a very good collection covering the country as a whole. The British Library also has extensive

404

dialect holdings. Nonetheless, it is to the regional and local libraries that one must go, for dialect literature beyond as well as within the northern regions. Skeat and Bodal's bibliography of 1877 (cited in chapter 11) offers some guidance, as does, earlier on, J. Russell Smith, *A Bibliographical List of... the Provincial Dialects of England* (1839). However, the catalogues of county and city record offices and libraries yield a far larger harvest than is evident in these bibliographies. Even these catalogues do not always list ephemeral dialect publications held by these libraries. Some libraries have produced lists of their dialect holdings, among which the most useful is *Dialect Books in the West Country Studies Library*, Westcountry Studies Handlist, 6 (October 1985) (Castle Street, Exeter). See also *Norfolk and Region Dialect* (Coleman and Rye Library of Local History, Norfolk Country Library, Norwich) and on Cumberland and Westmorland the printed catalogue of the new Cumbria County Library, Carlisle, *Bibliotheca Jacksonia* (1913).

Among theatre collections consulted the most revealing was the Hodson Collection, covering the Hodson family's 'fit-up' melodrama theatre outside Sheffield. The Manchester University Drama Department also holds extensive material relating to George R. Sims, one of the major melodrama playwrights of the late nineteenth century.

Notes

1 Introduction

1. E. P. Thompson, *The Making of the English Working-Class* (1963).
2. E. J. Hobsbawm, 'The Formation of British Working-Class Culture' and 'The Making of the Working Class 1870–1914', in *Worlds of Labour: Further Studies in the History of Labour* (1984); see also 'Labour in the Great City', *New Left Review*, 166 (1987).
3. W. M. Reddy, *Money and Liberty in Modern Europe: A Critique of Historical Understanding* (Cambridge, 1987), for the most emphatic recent left-inclined attack. For some points of criticism see P. Joyce, 'In Pursuit of Class: Recent Studies in the History of Work and Class', *History Workshop Journal*, 25 (1988).
4. For a fuller account, upon which the present one rests, see P. Joyce, 'Work' in F. M. L. Thompson (ed.), *The Cambridge Social History of Great Britain 1750–1950*, 3 vols. (Cambridge, 1990), vol. II.
5. P. Joyce, 'Introduction' to Joyce (ed.), *The Historical Meanings of Work* (Cambridge, 1987), esp. pp. 6–8. The work of Burawoy has been important; esp. M. Burawoy, *The Politics of Production* (1985); *Manufacturing Consent* (Chicago, 1979).
6. P. Joyce, 'Work', pp. 139–48, 169–84.
7. P. Joyce, *Work, Society and Politics: The Culture of the Factory in Later Victorian England* (Brighton, 1980).
8. For further consideration of these aspects, see P. Joyce, 'Work', pp. 142–8.
9. *ibid.* pp. 181–9.
10. M. Mann, 'The Rise of the Working Class 1815–1914', chs. 14 and 15 of *The Sources of Social Power*, vol. 2, *A History of Power 1760–1914* (Cambridge, 1990).
11. Figures increased from 2·5 million in 1910 to almost 8·5 million in 1920, an increase in density from 14·62% to 45·2%. See J. E. Cronin, *Labour and Society in Britain 1918–1979* (1984), pp. 241–2.
12. E. J. Hobsbawm, 'Making', pp. 198–9. However, for the still powerful limits to these expanded horizons of labour see below, pp. 137–41.
13. *Ibid.*, and 'Formation'.
14. E. J. Hobsbawm, 'Making', p. 200.
15. B. Waites, *A Class Society at War: England 1914–18* (Leamington Spa, 1987); 'The Language and Imagery of "Class" in Early-Twentieth-Century England, c. 1900–1925' *Language and History*, (Autumn 1976).
16. The upshot of another fairly systematic account, that of Cronin, emphasises the long term but in fact suggests in its deployment of evidence how important the 1910–20 decade was; J. E. Cronin, *Labour and Society*, chs. 2, 3, 5.
17. B. Waites, *A Class Society*, pp. 55–71; 'Language and Imagery', pp. 43–4.
18. For the wider currency of this labelling see the student textbook by R. Morris, *Class and Class Consciousness in the Industrial Revolution 1780–1850* (1979). The most recent textbook, admirable in so many other respects, mostly ignores the problems of language and consciousness: D. G. Wright, *Popular Radicalism: The Working-Class Experience, 1780–1880* (1988).
19. See esp. G. Marshall, H. Newby, *et al.*, *Social Class in Modern Britain* (1988), esp. pp. 192–3, 202–6, 221; for a similar though more subtle approach M.

Savage, *The Dynamics of Working-Class Politics: The Labour Movement in Preston 1880–1940* (Cambridge, 1987).

20. W. H. Sewell Jr, *Work and Revolution in France: The Language of Labor from the Old Regime to 1848* (Cambridge, 1980); W. M. Reddy, *The Rise of Market Culture: The Textile Trade and French Society 1750–1900* (Cambridge, 1984).

21. As well as the citations there see also J. E. Cronin, 'Language, Politics and the Critique of Social History', *Journal of Social History*, 20 (1986–87); D. Thompson, 'The Language of Class', *Bulletin of the Society for the Study of Labour History*, 52 (1987); J. W. Scott, 'On Language, Gender and Working-Class History', *International Labour and Working-Class History*, 31 (1987); also 'Responses' by C. Stowell and A. Rabinbach; G. Claeys, 'Language, Class and Historical Consciousness in Nineteenth Century Britain', *Economy and Society*, 14:2 (1985); J. Epstein, 'Rethinking the Categories of Working-Class History', *Labour/Le Travail*, 18 (1986).

22. This despite its title, *Languages of Class* (Cambridge, 1983). The essay in question is 'Rethinking Chartism'.

23. C. Calhoun, *The Question of Class Struggle: Social Foundations of Popular Radicalism during the Industrial Revolution* (Oxford, 1982).

24. E. J. Hobsbawn, 'Formation', p. 191.

25. N. Abercrombie, S. Hill and B. S. Turner, *The Dominant Ideology Thesis* (1980), pp. 55–6.

26. W. H. Sewell Jr, *Work and Revolution*, pp. 282–3.

27. J. Epstein, 'Understanding the Cap of Liberty: Symbolic Practice and Social Conflict in Early Nineteenth-Century England', *Past and Present*, 122 (1989).

28. *ibid.*, p. 117.

29. D. Thompson, 'The Language of Class'.

30. E. P. Thompson, 'Eighteenth-Century English Society: Class Struggle without Class?' *Social History*, 3:2 (1978). For a useful rejoinder to this approach, see P. Anderson, *Arguments within English Marxism* (1980), ch. 2.

31. G. A. Cohen, *Karl Marx's Theory of History* (1984), pp. 73–7.

32. G. de Ste. Croix, 'Class in Marx's Conception of History, Ancient and Modern', *New Left Review*, 146 (1984).

33. As does E. Meiskins Wood, *The Retreat from Class: A New True Socialism* (1984), ch. 7.

34. See remarks in P. Joyce, 'Introduction', *Historical Meanings of Work*, pp. 8–9.

35. See the pioneering work of A. Briggs, 'The Language of "Class" in Early Nineteenth-century England' in A. Briggs and J. Saville (eds.), *Essays in Labour History* (1960) and 'The Language of "Mass" and "Masses" in Nineteenth-Century England' in D. E. Martin and D. Rubinstein (eds.), *Ideology and the Labour Movement, Essays Presented to John Saville* (1979). For a very different approach to class as a *solely* discursive, rhetorical formation see P. N. Furbank, *Unholy Pleasure: The Idea of Social Class* (Oxford, 1988). This is philistine about language and crude about class, seeing language as divorced from social and economic conditions and the idea of class as really rather a bad thing, a dangerous and irrelevant fixation of axe-grinding intellectuals and academics.

2 The languages of popular politics

1. G. Stedman Jones, 'Rethinking Chartism', in *Languages of Class: Studies in English Working Class History 1832–1982* (Cambridge, 1983).

2. See above, pp. 12–13.

3. See below, chs. 3 and 4.

4. W. H. Sewell, Jr, *Work and Revolution in France: The Language of Labor from the Old Regime to 1848* (Cambridge, 1980).

5. I am grateful to my research student, James Vernon, for this account of popular politics, part of his forthcoming thesis entitled 'Politics and the People: A Study of English Political Culture and Communication, 1808–1868', Manchester University.

6. For much elaboration see Vernon, 'Politics and the People'.

7. See below, pp. 97–102, 284–6.

8. See remarks of O'Connor, opening remarks of Richard Pilling and James Leach, also Leach (p. 253), *The Trial of Feargus O'Connor and Fifty Eight Others...1843* (Abel Heywood, Manchester, John Cleave, London, 1843: New York, 1970); *McDouall's Chartist and Republican Journal* (printed in Ashton, published in Manchester) 3 Apr., 10 Apr. 1841; J. Epstein, *The Lion of Freedom: Feargus O'Connor and the Chartist Movement 1832–42* (1982) ch. 6, 'The Promised Land'.

9. Rev J. R. Stephens, *Sermons and Trial, 'The Political Pulpit'* (1839).

10. *ibid.*, esp. sermons 1, 6, 7, 8, 9, and Afterword. For the significance of Stephens' religious message nationally, and for the importance of religion in Chartism, see J. Epstein, 'Some Organisational and Cultural Aspects of the Chartist Movement in Nottingham', in J. Epstein and D. Thompson (eds.), *The Chartist Experience: Studies in Working-Class Radicalism and Culture, 1830–1860* (1982); E. Yeo, 'Christianity in Chartist Struggle 1838–1842', *Past and Present*, 91 (1981).

11. R. Gray, 'Deconstructing the English Working Class', *Social History*, 11:3 (1986); J. Epstein, *The Lion of Freedom*, p. 10.

12. *ibid.*, p. 253.

13. On the recourse of radicals to the romantic imagery of the ballad, see below, p. 101, also A. Clark, 'The Politics of Seduction in English Popular Culture, 1748–1848', in J. Radford (ed.), *The Progress of Romance* (1986). See also L. James, *Fiction for the Working Man 1830–1850* (1973), chs. 2, 3, 5.

14. B. Grime, *Memory Sketches* (Oldham, 1887), *passim*. Grime, a Gladstonian Liberal in his later days, had lived through the period he describes, and he made this large collection of political ephemera at the time.

15. For these aspects in Oldham radicalism before 1850 see J. Vernon, 'Politics and the People'.

16. For different conclusions about class, made possible when attention is diverted from the literal to the spoken and symbolic, see P. A. Pickering, 'Class Without Words: Symbolic Communication in the Chartist Movement', *Past and Present*, 112 (1986). However, Pickering's claim that the symbolism of O'Connor's fustian and his invocation of 'blistered hands' and 'unshorn chins' represent a new class awareness in his audience seems to me entirely unproven. Invocation of the attributes of labour, an antique theme by then anyway, does not translate into working-class consciousness.

17. J. Foster, *Class Struggle and the Industrial Revolution* (1974), ch. 7, pp. 205–12, 238–50.

18. P. Joyce, *Work, Society and Politics: The Culture of the Factory in Later Victorian England* (Brighton, 1980), pp. 323–6.

19. *ibid.*, chs. 6–8.

20. B. Grime, *Memory Sketches*, account of 1847 and 1852 elections.

21. P. Joyce, *Work, Society and Politics*, pp. 187–91, 255–61.

22. *ibid.*, pp. 201–2, 272–82.

23. See his autobiography, *Ashton Reporter*, 18 Sept. – 23 Oct. 1869.

24. See his obituary, *Ashton Reporter*, 2 Oct. 1869.

25. S. Huxhorn, 'United We Stand, Divided we Fall: Chartist Celebrations in Ashton-under-Lyne in the 1840's', MS copy in Tameside Local Studies Library.
26. *ibid.*, section on 'Toasts'.
27. E. P. Thompson, *The Making of the English Working Class*, (1963), p. 809.
28. J. Garrard, *Leadership and Power in Victorian Industrial Towns 1830–1850* (Manchester, 1983), pp. 128–30.
29. *Ashton Reporter*, 2 Oct. 1869. See also obituary of Richard Pilling, like Aitken a leading workingman radical of the time. Despite being blacklisted in the town after his return in 1850, Pilling became an ardent Liberal, *Ashton Reporter*, 5 Dec. 1874.
30. E. P. Thompson, *Making*, p. 809.
31. On Reynolds, see *Dictionary of National Biography* (1896), vol. 48.
32. J. Saville, *Ernest Jones, Chartist* (1952), p. 230.
33. For the appeal of the land issue to Aitken for example, and to working men in the industrial Ashton of the 1860s, see Aitken's obituary.
34. See J. Saville, 'Introduction', *Ernest Jones*.
35. J. Epstein, *The Lion of Freedom*, pp. 10–11.
36. J. Mendilow, *The Romantic Tradition in British Political Thought*, (1986) ch. 6, pp. 10–11.
37. D. Vincent, *Bread, Knowledge and Freedom: A Study of Nineteenth-Century Working Class Autobiography* (1981), section 3, esp. ch. 7.
38. A. J. Lee, *The Origins of the Popular Press in England* (1976), chs. 2 and 3; R. D. Altick, *The English Common Reader* (1957), pp. 348–57.
39. J. Vincent, *The Formation of the Liberal Party 1857–1868* (1966) section 2, esp. pp. 58–65; A. J. Lee, *Origins of the Popular Press*; see also S. Maccoby, *English Radicalism 1832–1852* (1935), ch. XXV.
40. See below, pp. 273–4.
41. As well as Vincent, see also P. Joyce, *Work, Society and Politics*, pp. 316–18.
42. L. Brown, *Victorian News and Newspapers* (Oxford, 1985), chs. 4 and 11; and on the considerable popular taste for newspapers, especially of a local sort, see ch. 2 on distribution and circulation.
43. H. C. G. Matthew, 'Rhetoric and Politics in Great Britain 1860–1950', in P. J. Waller (ed.), *Politics and Social Change: Essays Presented to A. F. Thompson* (1987), pp. 51, 52–3.
44. For an interesting listing of town meetings see R. D. Mattley, *Annals of Rochdale* (Rochdale, 1899).
45. On Bright and the press, see J. Vincent, *Formation of the Liberal Party*, pp. 178–9, and for the national Liberal leaders and the press, see H. C. G. Matthew, 'Rhetoric and Politics', *passim*.
46. M. R. D. Foot, 'Introduction', W. E. Gladstone, *Midlothian Speeches*, 1879 (republished Leicester, 1971).
47. *ibid.*; see also ch. 10 below. The following paragraph is drawn from Foot's interesting observations on Gladstone's oratory.
48. See J. C. Belchem, '*Orator' Hunt: Henry Hunt and English Working-Class Radicalism* (Oxford, 1985).
49. For a valuable account of local leadership see R. Sykes, 'Popular Politics and Trade Unionism in South-east Lancashire 1829–1842', PhD dissertation, University of Manchester (1982), vol. 1, ch. 9.
50. See J. Epstein, *Lion of Freedom*, *passim*, and P. A. Pickering, 'Class Without Words'.
51. J. Epstein, *Lion of Freedom*, p. 92. This was often very marked later on, see below, pp. 126–7.

52. E. P. Thompson, *The Making of the English Working Class*, pp. 682–3, and ch. 5, 'Demagogues and Martyrs'.
53. See below, pp. 254–5.
54. P. Joyce, *Work, Society and Politics*, pp. 286–8.
55. *ibid.*, ch. 6, and pp. 274–7.
56. See the remarks of the artisan glass blower at the large meeting of the London trades, *Reynolds News*, 2 Dec. 1866.
57. At Grantham, *Reynolds News*, 2 Sept. 1866.
58. *Reynolds News*, 23 Sept. 1866.
59. J. Vincent, *Formation of the Liberal Party*, pp. 162–3.
60. J. Bright, *Mr. Bright's Speeches...Revised by Himself* (1859), 1859 Bradford meeting; hereafter Bright, *Speeches* (1859).
61. *ibid.*, beginning of Birmingham speech.
62. J. Bright, *Speeches on Parliamentary Reform by John Bright, revised by Himself...* (1866), beginning of Manchester Free Trade Hall speech, 24 Sept. 1866; hereafter Bright, *Speeches* (1866).
63. Public Breakfast at Cobden Hotel, Glasgow, 1866.
64. *Reynolds News*, 2 Sept. 1866.
65. Opening of Birmingham speech, and Mayor of Birmingham's address, Bright, *Speeches* (1859).
66. Bright, *Speeches* (1866), p. 20.
67. As does Reform League activity which represented one transposition of older forms to new purposes, in the form for instance of the town procession of the political hero (Beales). See the account of the junketing at the Norwich meeting, *Reynolds News*, 16 Sept. 1866. See the same issue for the old practice of effigy burning continuing in the Governor Eyre case. These practices marked party politics when it came.
68. See Joyce, *Work, Society and Politics*, pp. 279–82 for a brief account.
69. J. Vincent, *Formation of the Liberal Party*, pp. 230–1.
70. W. E. Gladstone, *Speeches of the Rt. Hon. W. E. Gladstone M.P. in South West Lancashire, October 1868* (1868).
71. F. B. Smith, *The Making of the Second Reform Bill* (Cambridge, 1966), pp. 30–1.
72. P. Smith, *Disraelian Conservatism and Social Reform* (1967).
73. See also J. Vincent, *Formation of the Liberal Party*, pp. 230–1ff. D. A. Hamer, 'Gladstone: The Making of a Political Myth', *Victorian Studies*, 22: 1 (1978).
74. *ibid.*; the distinction between the political party as a movement and as an organisation should perhaps be made here. Loyalty was to party in the former rather than the latter sense, where the charges of faction and self-interest long continued to stick. However, party organisation from the 1860s was always important in securing electoral success, particularly in industrial Lancashire. It should not be underestimated, though it was markedly less significant in London compared with the provinces, in the senses both of movement and institution.
75. See the comments of Samuel, 'Breaking Up is Hard to Do', *The Guardian*, 2 Dec. 1985.
76. *Reynolds News*, 2 Sept. 1866 (Birmingham speech).
77. Bright, *Speeches* (1866), Leeds.
78. Bright, *Speeches* (1859), Birmingham.
79. Bright, *Speeches* (1866), Glasgow speech.
80. J. Wilson, *Memoirs of a Labour Leader* (1910; 1980), pp. 218–19.
81. See below, pp. 129–30, 253–5.
82. See also J. Vincent, *Formation of the Liberal Party*, p. 233.
83. See chapter 1 of F. E. Gillespie, *Labor and Politics in England 1850–1867* (1927; New York, 1966).

84. See the address of the men of York cited in J. Vincent, *Formation of the Liberal Party*, p. 234.
85. *ibid.*, p. 230.
86. Leader, 2 Dec. 1866.
87. See below, pp. 110–12.
88. Leader, *Reynolds News*, 16 Sept. 1866.
89. Vincent, *Formation of the Liberal Party*, p. 216.
90. See below, pp. 246–53, 295–300.
91. *Reynolds News*, 2 Sept. 1866 (Birmingham meeting); *Speeches* (1866), Leeds Town Hall.
92. For the continuing importance of these issues see the meeting of the London trades, *Reynolds News*, 9 Dec. 1866, remarks of 'Northumbrian'.
93. *ibid.*, Beales at Birmingham Town Hall meeting.
94. J. Vincent, *Formation of the Liberal Party*, p. 217.
95. J. Bright, *Speeches* (1866), Free Trade Hall; *Reynolds News*, 30 Sept. 1866 for banners.
96. J. Vincent, *Formation of the Liberal Party*, p. 163.
97. *Reynolds News*, 30 Sept. 1866.
98. See the report of the stump speech of the Hollingworth working man outside the Free Trade Hall, *Reynolds News*, 14 Oct. 1866.
99. Bright, *Speeches* (1866), Glasgow City Hall; also Free Trade Hall.

3 Class, populism and socialism

1. J. Vincent, *The Formation of the Liberal Party 1857–1868* (1966), pp. 215–16, 217.
2. *The Times*, 24 July 1865.
3. *ibid.*, 13 Oct. 1864.
4. *ibid.*, 25 Sept. 1862 (Denbigh and Flint Agricultural Show).
5. *ibid.*, 11 Nov. 1864.
6. A. Briggs, 'The Language of "Class" in Early Nineteenth-century England', in A. Briggs and J. Saville (eds.), *Essays in Labour History* (1960); G. Crossick, 'Classes and the Masses in Victorian England', *History Today*, 37 (1987).
7. Thomas Wright, 'journeyman engineer' of the time, supplies one of the most telling accounts of the force and character of divisions internal to the labouring population of the day – divisions based on education, politics, employment, generation, behaviour, and much else. For an account of Wright, showing his awareness of the political uses of class language, see A. Reid, 'Hero of a Thousand Footnotes: Thomas Wright and the "Labour Aristocracy"', in J. Winter (ed.), *The Working Class in Modern British History* (Oxford, 1983).
8. *ibid.*
9. P. Bailey, '"Will the Real Bill Banks Please Stand Up?" A Role Analysis of Victorian Working-class Respectability', *Journal of Social History*, 12 (1979).
10. M. E. Rose, 'Rochdale Man and the Stalybridge Riot: Poor Relief during the Lancashire Cotton Famine 1861–5' in A. P. Donajgrodski (ed.), *Social Control in Nineteenth-Century Britain* (1977).
11. See F. B. Smith, *The Making of the Second Reform Bill* (Cambridge, 1966) p. 8. On 'Rochdale Man', R. Harrison, *Before the Socialists: Studies in Labour and Politics, 1861–1881* (1965), pp. 113–119.
12. See A. Reid, 'Hero of a Thousand Footnotes', and P. Bailey, 'Will the Real Bill Banks'; also below, pp. 151–7.
13. See esp. R. Gray, *The Labour Aristocracy in Victorian Edinburgh* (Oxford, 1976); *The Aristocracy of Labour in Nineteenth Century Britain c. 1850–1900* (1981); G. Crossick, *An Artisan Elite in Victorian Society* (1978).

14. On Earl Grey, Mill and Cobden see F. E. Gillespie, *Labor and Politics in England 1850–1867* (1927; New York, 1966), ch. 9.
15. R. Harrison, *Before the Socialists*, ch. 4, *passim*.
16. A. D. Taylor, 'Ernest Jones: His Later Career and the Structure of Manchester Politics 1861–69', MA dissertation, University of Birmingham, (1984), ch. 3.
17. R. Harrison, *Before the Socialists*, pp. 203–4.
18. A. D. Taylor, 'Ernest Jones', pp. 34–42.
19. P. Joyce, *Work, Society and Politics: The Culture of the Factory in Later Victorian England* (Brighton, 1980), pp. 187ff, 276ff.
20. For this concord on essentials, see *Ashton Reporter*, 20 Feb., 19 Jan., 14 Feb. 1856.
21. See 'A Plea for Poetry' by Elijah Moss, *Ashton Reporter*, 11 Aug. 1856.
22. For the significance of this common feeling even in the more troubled years of the early nineteenth century see D. Vincent, *Bread, Knowledge and Freedom: A Study of Nineteen-Century Working Class Autobiography* (1981), ch. 7.
23. *Ashton Reporter*, 14 Feb. 1857.
24. *ibid.*, 27 Sept. 1856.
25. *ibid.*, 7 March 1857, presentation to J. R. Stephens and meeting to organise a new workingman's college.
26. *ibid.*, 24 Jan. 1857.
27. See Hindley's comment, *ibid.*, 14 Feb. 1857.
28. *ibid.*, 14 March 1857.
29. See Bright's utilisation of Peterloo, Free Trade Hall Speech, Bright, *Speeches* (1866).
30. See below, pp. 99–100, 103–4.
31. See above, pp. 37–8.
32. W. Chadwick, *Pages From a Life of Strife* (1911). See also B. Grime, *Memory Sketches* (Oldham, 1887).
33. By the very important Manchester leader, the employer and MP, W. R. Callender, *Historic Conservatism* (Manchester, 1868); See also P. Joyce, *Work, Society and Politics*, pp. 296–8.
34. J. R. Stephens, *The Altar, The Throne and the Cottage* (Manchester, 1868).
35. See e.g. *Ashton Reporter*, 2, 7, 23 Feb. 1867.
36. *ibid.*, 26 Jan. 1867, Ashton Town Hall Meeting.
37. Account of Reform meeting in *ibid.*, 7 April 1860.
38. Mottram Reform meeting, *ibid.*, 26 Jan. 1867.
39. Stalybridge meeting, *ibid.*, 7 Feb. 1867.
40. *ibid.*, 27 July 1867.
41. See the 6,000-strong meeting of trades unionists to defend the legal rights of unions, *ibid.*
42. See below, pp. 65–9. Also see e.g. Leader, *Reynolds News*, 2 Sept. 1866.
43. *ibid.*, 16 Sept. 1866, 30 Sept. 1866. Beales, however, could at times give vent to the feeling that the League was a class movement in the sense that it belonged to the working man; cf. R. Harrison, *Before the Socialists*, p. 98.
44. *Ashton Reporter*, 16 Feb. 1856, also 27 Sept. 1856.
45. See above, note 7.
46. W. H. Sewell, Jr, *Work and Revolution in France: The Language of Labor from the Old Regime to 1848* (Cambridge, 1980).
47. See below, pp. 139–40.
48. For the best recent survey of the literature, D. G. Wright, *Popular Radicalism: The Working-Class Experience 1780–1880* (1988), esp. pp. 78–82; 98–9; 112–16.
49. W. H. Sewell, Jr, *Work and Revolution*, pp. 281–5.

50. V. Berridge, 'Popular Journalism and Working-Class Attitudes 1854–86: A Study of *Reynolds Newspaper, Lloyds Weekly Newspaper* and the *Weekly Times*', PhD dissertation, University of London (1976).

51. See above, p. 39.

52. V. Berridge, 'Popular Journalism', chs. 2, 3. For the sizeable Manchester readership in 1876, see J. H. Nodal, 'The Circulation of Newspapers and Periodicals in Manchester', *Papers of the Manchester Literary Club 1875–6*, vol. 2. (1876).

53. Particularly perhaps of older men. Thomas Wright (see note 7 above) gives this impression, conveying the idea that *Reynolds*' core-readership was men born before 1820, at once crudely chauvinist and full of 'class hatred'. However, I have found several instances of *Reynolds*' influence among younger, politically conscious, textile operatives.

54. V. Berridge, 'Popular Journalism', ch. 8.

55. *Reynolds News*, 5, 12, 19 July 1885.

56. *ibid.*, 23 April 1882, 'Words From the Workshop'.

57. *ibid.*, 16 April 1882, 'Gracchus'; 'Northumbrian', 19 July 1885.

58. *ibid.*, 2 July 1905, esp. pp. 1, 6.

59. *ibid.*, 23 April 1882 ('Northumbrian'). See also 18 June 1905, pp. 1, 2.

60. See reference to the 'Democratic Calendar', *ibid.*, 4 June 1905; also 2 July 1905.

61. *ibid.*, 12 July 1895; 24 Feb. 1895 ('Gracchus'), also 'Court and Aristocracy'; and 'Society's Pet Dogs', 11 June 1905.

62. See below, pp. 106–7.

63. P. Joyce, *Work, Society and Politics*, pp. 289–90, 296–7.

64. M. Roe, *Kenealy and the Tichborne Case: A Study in Mid-Victorian Populism* (Melbourne, 1974). The definitive account promises to be that of R. McWilliam, 'The Tichborne Claimant and the People: Investigations into Popular Culture, 1867–1886', PhD dissertation, University of Sussex (1990).

65. See below, pp. 252–5.

66. P. Joyce, *Work, Society and Politics*, ch. 7; and see pp. 173–9 below on the Protestant sense of the past characteristic of working men of various political persuasions.

67. See below, pp. 300–1.

68. These and all other aspects of the case are treated in the accounts of Roe and McWilliam, 'The Tichborne Claimant', upon which this account is based. See also R. McWilliam, 'The Tichborne Case and the Politics of "Fair Play"', in E. F. Biagini and A. J. Reid (eds.), *Currents of Radicalism: Popular Radicalism, Organised Labour and Party Politics in Britain 1850–1914* (Cambridge, 1991).

69. See below, pp. 295–300.

70. P. Joyce, *Work, Society and Politics*, pp. 15, 252, 275–81, 282.

71. C. Calhoun, *The Question of Class Struggle: Social Foundations of Popular Radicalism during the Industrial Revolution* (Oxford, 1982). A more rewarding account of early century populist radicalism can be found in T. W. Laquer, 'The Queen Caroline Affair: Politics as Art in the Reign of George V', *Journal of Modern History*, 54 (1982).

72. W. D. Rubinstein, 'British Radicalism and the "Dark Side" of Populism', in *Elites and the Wealthy in Modern British History* (Brighton, 1988).

73. G. Ionescu and E. Gellner (eds.), *Populism, its Meaning and Characteristics* (1969).

74. See end of D. MacRae's discussion, 'Populism As An Ideology', and P. Wiles, 'A Syndrome Not A Doctrine: Some Elementary Theses of Populism', which

also indicates the considerable degree of disagreement in the definition of populism; both in G. Ionescu and E. Gellner (eds.), *Populism*.

75. These examples and citations for them are discussed, briefly, in M. Roe, *Kenealy*, W. D. Rubinstein, 'British Radicalism', and P. Wiles 'Syndrome'.

76. M. Roe, *Kenealy*, ch. 8.

77. J. Harris, 'Did British Workers Want the Welfare State? G. D. H. Cole's Survey of 1942', in J. Winter (ed.), *The Working Class in Modern British History*; H. Pelling, 'The Working Class and the Origin of the Welfare State', in *Politics and Society in Late Victorian Britain* (1978).

78. R. Hoggart, *The Uses of Literacy* (1957), ch. 3, '"Them" and "Us"'.

79. *ibid.*, ch. 3, section C, 'Putting Up with Things', 'Living and Letting Live'.

80. G. Foote, *The Labour Party's Political Thought. A History* (1985), ch. 1.

81. See above, pp. 32–3, and below, pp. 93–102. Foote also dwells on these roots.

82. D. Howell, *British Workers and the I.L.P. 1888–1906* (Manchester, 1983).

83. *ibid.*, pp. 363ff.

84. *ibid.*, p. 352.

85. *ibid.*, p. 355. See also R. Mendilow, *The Romantic Tradition in British Political Thought* (1983), ch. 6.

86. See below, pp. 235–9, 284–5.

87. D. Howell, *British Workers*, p. 354.

88. *ibid.*, chs. 15, 16.

89. *ibid.*, pp. 352–62.

90. G. Foote, *The Labour Party's Political Thought*, pp. 43–5.

91. S. Yeo, 'The Religion of Socialism', *History Workshop Journal*, (1977).

92. D. Howell, *British Workers*, pp. 363–73.

93. *ibid.*, *passim*.

94. *ibid.*, p. 361.

95. G. Foote, *The Labour Party's Political Thought*, chs. 2, 6, 8.

96. Of course the class analysis of Fabianism took the eminently old-fashioned view of the struggle being not of capital and labour but of the idle versus the industrious classes.

97. J. Smith, 'Class, Skill and Sectarianism in Glasgow and Liverpool, 1880–1914' in R. J. Morris (ed.), *Class, Power and Social Structure in British Nineteenth-Century Towns* (Leicester, 1986).

98. J. Smith, 'Labour Tradition in Glasgow and Liverpool,' *History Workshop Journal*, 17 (1984).

99. S. Reynolds and B. and T. Woolley, *Seems So! A Working-Class View of Politics* (1911), ch. 15, p. 163.

100. P. Stead, 'The Language of Edwardian Politics' in D. Smith (ed.), *A People and A Proletariat: Essays in the History of Wales 1780–1980* (1980).

101. P. Joyce, *Work, Society and Politics*, pp. 164–5, 228–30, 335.

102. *ibid.*, pp. 164–5; also S. Yeo, 'The Religion of Socialism'.

103. P. Stead, 'Language of Edwardian Politics'.

104. C. Cross, *Philip Snowden* (1966), ch. 1, esp. pp. 2, 5.

105. On Snowden in the Blackburn election of 1906 see P. Clarke, *Lancashire and the New Liberalism* (Cambridge, 1971), pp. 312, 319, 332.

106. See below, pp. 126–8, 151–64.

107. Quoted in C. Cross, *Philip Snowden*, p. 27, also pp. 25–8 (Snowden's letter to the local press).

108. See R. Blatchford, *Britain For the British* (1902), and esp. *Merrie England* (1894).

109. For the tenacity of older party allegiances, before 1914, and for their capacity to re-assert themselves after 1918 as well, see the recent, detailed accounts of

popular politics in A. Reid, 'The Division of Labour in the British Shipbuilding Industry 1880–1920', PhD dissertation, Cambridge University (1980); Reid, 'The Division of Labour and Politics in Britain 1880–1920' in W. Mommsen, H-G. Husung (eds.), *The Development of Trade Unionism in Great Britain and Germany 1880–1914* (1985); J. Melling, 'Scottish Industrialists and the Changing Character of Class Relations on the Clyde, 1880–1918', in T. Dickson (ed.), *Capital and Class in Scotland* (Edinburgh, 1982).

Both writers show very clearly how it was chiefly the experience of the war itself that radicalised workers, albeit often temporarily. It changed their perception of what state power could achieve, linking a more positive view of the state with a new sense of class agency as expressed in independent labour politics.

For further corroboration of the view of politics presented in this and the preceding chapter, in particular the emphasis on continuity, and the debt of Liberalism and socialism to the radical tradition, see the papers presented to the conference at Churchill College, Cambridge, in April 1989, 'Popular Radicalism and Party Politics in Britain 1848–1914'. In particular, for the view of socialism as the recombination of earlier elements rather than a new departure see D. Tanner, 'Liberalism, Labourism and Socialism: The Ideological "Distinctiveness" of the Edwardian Labour Party' and P. Thane, 'Popular Radicalism and the Rise of the Labour Party, 1880s–1914'. The proceedings of this conference are published as E. F. Biagini and A. J. Reid (eds.), *Currents of Radicalism*.

4   Civilising capital

1. K. McClelland, 'Time to Work, Time to Live: Some Aspects of Work and the Re-formation of Class in Britain, 1850–1880', in P. Joyce (ed.), *The Historical Meanings of Work* (Cambridge, 1987); P. Joyce, *Work, Society and Politics: The Culture of the Factory in Later Victorian England* (Brighton, 1980).
2. For an extended examination of the implications for the idea of class of uneven industrial development see P. Joyce, 'Work', *The Cambridge Social History of Great Britain, 1750–1950*, vol. 2, ed. F. M. L. Thompson (Cambridge, 1990).
3. K. McClelland, 'Time to Work'.
4. *ibid.*, pp. 185–90.
5. Though Biagini's claim that the unions were and always had been 'economic' in aim betrays a narrow understanding of the contemporary union. E. F. Biagini, 'British Trade Unions and Popular Political Economy, 1860–1880', *The Historical Journal*, 30, 4 (1987), p. 814.
6. *ibid.*, esp. pp. 832–3, 837–40.
7. E. J. Hobsbawm, 'Custom, Wages and Work-load in Nineteenth-Century Industry', in *Labouring Men* (1964); C. Behagg, 'Secrecy, Ritual and Folk Violence: The Opacity of the Workplace in the First Half of the Nineteenth Century' in R. Storch (ed.), *Popular Culture and Custom in Nineteenth-Century England* (1982). See also the discussion in P. Joyce, 'Work', pp. 176–80. For the continuing importance of informal modes of labour regulation, and of custom, see R. Price, *Masters, Unions and Men* (Cambridge, 1980).
8. A. Reid, 'The Division of Labour in the British Shipbuilding Industry 1880–1920, With Special Reference to Clydeside' PhD dissertation, Cambridge University (1980), pp. 231–7; K. Burgess, *The Challenge of Labour: Shaping British Society 1850–1930* (1980), ch. 1. See also the exchange between myself and Richard Price in *Social History* 9:1 (1984), 9:2 (1984), esp. pp. 226–8 in the latter.

9. G. Stedman Jones, 'Rethinking Chartism', in *Languages of Class: Studies in English Working-Class History 1832–1982* (Cambridge, 1983), pp. 174–8.
10. J. Rule, 'The Property of Skill in the Period of Manufacture', in P. Joyce (ed.), *Meanings of Work*.
11. For an extended discussion see P. Joyce, 'Work', pp. 163–9.
12. K. McClelland, 'Time to Work', p. 196.
13. P. Joyce, 'Introduction', in Joyce (ed.), *Meanings of Work*.
14. See above, pp. 31–2.
15. K. McClelland, 'Time to Work', pp. 200–9.
16. W. M. Reddy, *The Rise of Market Culture: The Textile Trade and French Society 1750–1900* (Cambridge, 1984); *Money and Liberty in Modern Europe: A Critique of Historical Understanding* (Cambridge, 1987).
17. For a critique of the latter see P. Joyce, 'In Pursuit of Class: Recent Studies in the History of Work and Class', *History Workshop Journal*, 25 (1988).
18. G. Stedman Jones, 'Rethinking Chartism', 'Introduction', in *Languages of Class*.
19. See above, pp. 29–30.
20. G. Stedman Jones, 'Rethinking Chartism', pp. 137, 157.
21. P. Joyce, *Work, Society and Politics, passim*, also discussion in P. Joyce, 'Languages of Reciprocity and Conflict: A Further Response to Richard Price' *Social History*, 9:2 (1984), pp. 229–30.
22. The best critique is R. Gray, 'Deconstructing the English Working Class', *Social History*, 11:3 (1986).
23. *ibid.*, pp. 371–2.
24. D. Gadian, 'Class Formation and Class Action in North-West Industrial Towns, 1830–50', in R. Morris (ed.), *Class, Power and Social Structure in British Nineteenth-Century Towns* (Leicester, 1986), esp. pp. 34–5. R. Sykes, 'Popular Politics and Trade Unionism in South-East Lancashire, 1829–1842', PhD, University of Manchester (1982), 2 vols.; R. Sykes, 'Early Chartism and Trade Unionism in South-East Lancashire', in J. Epstein and D. Thompson (eds.), *The Chartist Experience: Studies in Working-Class Radicalism and Culture, 1830–60* (1982); J. Belchem, 'Radical Language and Ideology in Early Nineteenth-Century England: The Challenge of the Platform', *Albion*, 20:2 (1988). See also note 21, in chapter 1 above.
25. N. Kirk, 'In Defence of Class: A Critique of Recent Revisionist Writing upon the Nineteenth-Century English Working Class', *International Review of Social History*, 32 (1987).
26. *ibid.*, esp. pp. 16–32.
27. J. Epstein, 'Understanding the Cap of Liberty: Symbolic Practice and Social Conflict in Early Nineteenth-Century England', *Past and Present*, 122 (1989).
28. *ibid.*, p. 76.
29. *ibid.*, p. 117.
30. See above, ch. 2, n. 16.
31. See above, pp. 32–4.
32. *McDouall's Chartist and Republican Journal*, 3 April, 10 April, 1841, and following numbers for 'The White Slaves of Great Britain: Lectures on the Factory System'. The journal was printed in Ashton. See also N. Kirk, 'In Defence of Class', pp. 20–5.
33. D. Thompson, *The Chartists* (1984), *passim*; but see especially J. Epstein, 'Some Organisational and Cultural Aspects of the Chartist Movement in Nottingham', in J. Epstein and D. Thompson (eds.), *The Chartist Experience*.
34. E. P. Thompson, *The Making of the English Working Class* (1963), ch. 9.
35. In particular see D. Thompson, *The Chartists*.

36. C. Calhoun, *The Question of Class Struggle: Social Foundations of Popular Radicalism during the Industrial Revolution* (Oxford, 1982).

37. S. Alexander, 'Women, Class and Sexual Differences in the 1830s and 1860s: Some Reflections on the Writing of Feminist History', *History Workshop Journal*, 17 (1984).

38. *ibid.*, pp. 136–40.

39. G. Stedman Jones, 'Rethinking Chartism', pp. 168–70.

40. J. Smail, 'New Languages for Labour and Capital: The Transformation of Discourse in the Early Years of the Industrial Revolution', *Social History*, 12:1 (1987).

41. *ibid.*, p. 54.

42. R. Gray, 'The Languages of Factory Reform in Britain, c. 1830–1860', in P. Joyce (ed.), *The Historical Meanings of Work*, esp. pp. 146–56.

43. P. Joyce, *Work, Society and Politics, passim.*

44. R. Gray, 'Languages of Factory Reform', pp. 146–7.

45. J. Epstein, *The Lion of Freedom: Feargus O'Connor and the Chartist Movement 1832–42* (1982), ch. 6.

46. See the evidence of James Leach and Richard Pilling, as well as O'Connor in the introduction to *The Trial of Feargus O'Connor and Fifty Eight Others...1843* (Manchester and London, 1843; New York, 1970).

47. *ibid.*, 'Address of the South Lancashire Delegates'.

48. A. Clark, 'The Politics of Seduction in English Popular Culture, 1748–1848' in J. Radford (ed.), *The Progress of Romance: The Politics of Popular Fiction* (1986).

49. R. Colls, *The Colliers Rant*, p. 127.

50. E. P. Thompson, 'The Moral Economy of the English Crowd in the Eighteenth Century', *Past and Present*, 50 (1971).

51. Cassidy MSS, DD 13/24/11. Tameside Public Library, Stalybridge.

52. See above, pp. 36–8.

53. Obituary, *Ashton Reporter*, 20 Oct. 1869.

54. Dated 1 June 1853.

55. 'To the Inhabitants of Millbrook, nr. Stalybridge' (all references are to the Cassidy MSS).

56. 'To the Employers and Work People of Mossley'.

57. 'To the Factory Operatives of Ashton, Mossley'.

58. 'To the Operatives of Stalybridge'.

59. Address dated April 19 1853.

60. See placard dated 16 June 1853 (also *Manchester Guardian* for factory operatives' demonstration at Glossop, 8 June 1853).

61. 'To the Inhabitants of Millbrook'.

62. R. Gray, 'The languages of factory reform', pp. 154–6.

63. 'Six o'clock'.

64. 'To the Factory Operatives of Oldham', 4 March 1853.

65. See above, pp. 235–9, 284–5.

66. S. A. Weaver, *John Fielden and the Politics of Popular Radicalism in 1832–1847* (Oxford, 1987), esp. pp. 29–30, 97–8, 109–10.

67. 'To the Hand-Mule Spinners of Ashton and Neighbourhood'; 'To the Master Cotton Spinners of Preston'; 'The Late John Fielden of Todmorden'.

68. 'To the Manufacturers...Spinners in Your Employ' (title obscure, 1857? 1858?).

69. 'To the Manufacturers of Glossop – To the Weavers in your Employ'.

70. 'On the Need for Discipline in the Mills', Short Time Committee material, 'To the Self-Acting Minders of the Hurst District' (near Ashton).

71. *Ashton Reporter*, 2 Oct. 1869 (Autobiography).
72. 'To the Self-Acting Minders of the Hurst District'.
73. 'Memorial to be Adopted, Rejected, etc.' (1857/8?)
74. W. Reddy, *Money and Liberty in Modern Europe*, ch. 5.
75. See n. 69 above.
76. See the spinners' address on the occasion of John Fielden's death, cited above note 67; also 'Elegy to Joseph Brotherton M.P.' (1857), 'The Man of the People and their Greatest Sire'.
77. P. Joyce, *Work, Society and Politics*, esp. ch. 4.
78. H. I. Dutton and J. E. King, *'Ten Per Cent and No Surrender' The Preston Strike, 1853–4* (Cambridge, 1981).
79. H. I. Dutton and J. E. King, 'The Limits of Paternalism: The Cotton Tyrants of North Lancashire, 1836–54', *Social History*, 7:1 (1982).
80. N. Kirk, *The Growth of Working-Class Reformism in Mid-Victorian England* (1985), pp. 258–65.
81. *ibid.*, pp. 251–7.
82. J. E. King, '"We Could Eat the Police!": Popular Violence in the North Lancashire Cotton Strike of 1878', *Victorian Studies*, 28:3 (1985).
83. *ibid.*, pp. 466–70.
84. Cassidy MSS, 'To the Factory Operatives of Oldham' (Ashton Short Time Committee).
85. 'To the Manufacturers of…[?] The Spinners and Minders in Your Employ'.
86. 'The Queen, Her People and the Ten Hours Bill'.
87. For a welcome defence of the radical credentials of the so-called 'old unionism' see A. Reid, 'Old Unionism Reconsidered: The Radicalism of Robert Knight 1870–1900', in E. F. Biagini and A. J. Reid (eds.), *Currents of Radicalism: Popular Radicalism, Organized Labour and Party Politics in Britain, 1850–1914* (Cambridge, 1991).

5   Building the union

1. R. McKibbin, 'Why Was There No Marxism in Great Britain?', *English Historical Review*, 99:391 (1984).
2. K. McClelland, 'Time to Work, Time to Live: Some Aspects of Work and the Re-formation of Class in Britain, 1850–1880' in P. Joyce (ed.), *The Historical Meanings of Work* (Cambridge, 1987), pp. 204–9.
3. Oldham Public Library, Oldham Cotton Spinners' Trade Union, TU/1/2/94, Misc. Reports, for the many placards and addresses on the issue, esp. 'Hurrah, Hurrah, Hurrah: For the Demonstration…' (1871); 'Address to the Factory Operatives by the Fifty Four Hours Movement'; 'To the Rt. Hon. the Commons of Great Britain and Ireland' (1872?).
4. See the conduct of the Oldham spinners' strike of 1895, *Cotton Factory Times*, 24 July – 23 Oct. 1895, also of Stalybridge Lock Out in *ibid*, Nov. 1892 – March 1893.
5. E. Thorpe, 'Industrial Relations and the Social Structure: A Case Study of the Bolton Cotton Mule Spinners, 1884–1960', MSc dissertation, University of Salford (1969), ch. 2, section II; J. T. Fielding, *Speech on Foreign Competition in the Cotton Trade* (Bolton, 1879).
6. *Ashton Reporter*, 4 March 1893.
7. P. Harris, 'Class Conflict, the Trade Unions, and Working-Class Politics in Bolton, 1875–1896', MA dissertation, Lancaster University (1971).
8. *Cotton Factory Times*, 7 April 1893 ('The Late Lock Out').

9. Printed and published by Wood in Salford, copy at Oldham Public Library, TU/1/2/130.

10. Which is perhaps the tendency in Kirk's otherwise useful discrimination between the statements and bargaining positions of the weavers and spinners, N. Kirk, *The Growth of Working-Class Reformism in Mid-Victorian England* (1985), pp. 276–92.

11. This can be followed in W. H. Wood, 'Reasons', 11, 2, 3, 9, 12, 10, 18, 5.

12. *The Typographical Society's Monthly Circular*, Jan. 1853.

13. *ibid.*, June 1853. See also February report on Newport.

14. *ibid.*, Feb., March 1853. Also May for the example of the discharged scab worker loitering around the town in his torn coat.

15. J. Burrell, 'Trade Economies', *The Typographical Circular*, Sept. 1901.

16. *ibid.*, Jan. 1901, Newton-le-Willows branch.

17. *ibid.*, Liverpool branch.

18. *ibid.*, Nov. 1900, St Albans branch.

19. *ibid.*, Leader, 'Capital and Labour'.

20. G. H. Roberts, 'Some Economic Reflections' *ibid.*, Nov. 1901; and 'Capital and Labour'.

21. As evidenced for instance by the attendance of some employers at union meetings, or the very frequently reported workers' outings in which employers often took a central part, to the apparent satisfaction of all concerned.

22. *Cotton Factory Times*, 18, 25 Nov. 1892 (editorials), also 10 Jan. 1893. For corroboration of the strength of the unions' ideology of the trade see the discussion of similar themes in relation to the example of the cotton spinners, A. Bullen, 'A Modern Spinners Union', in A. Fowler and T. Wyke, *The Barefoot Aristocrats, A History of the Amalgamated Association of Operative Cotton Spinners* (Littleborough, 1987).

23. *Cotton Factory Times*, 16 Jan. 1885, and see comments of Ben Brierley at the inaugural meeting, cited by P. Joyce, *Work, Society and Politics: The Culture of the Factory in Later Victorian England*, (Brighton, 1980), p. 50.

24. *Cotton Factory Times*, 10 May 1887, cardroom officials at Mossley meeting.

25. *ibid.*, 11 Feb. 1887 (editorial).

26. *ibid.*, 3 June 1887, 'Notes on Passing Events'.

27. P. Joyce, 'Work', *Cambridge Social History of Great Britain 1750–1950*, ed. F. M. L. Thompson (Cambridge, 1990), vol. II.

28. D. Farnie, *The English Cotton Industry and the World Market 1815–1896* (Oxford, 1979), chs. 2, 8.

29. *Cotton Factory Times*, 7 April 1893.

30. *ibid.*, 27 May; 3, 10 June 1887.

31. *ibid.*, 23 Dec. 1885.

32. Joint activity was seen in the development of the Indian market, and support for factory legislation and limited liability. See H. A. Turner, *Trade Union Growth, Structure and Policy: A Comparative Study of the Cotton Unions* (1962), esp. pp. 356–61.

33. See comments of the union leaders J. Andrew, James Mawdsley and Wright Wood at the *Times* dinner, *Cotton Factory Times*, 1 July 1887.

34. H. A. Turner, *Trade Union Growth*, pp. 358–9.

35. On the need for capital and labour to pull together expressed as a 'duty', see *Cotton Factory Times*, 9 Dec. 1887.

36. Account of Co-op Congress in Carlisle, *ibid.*, 3 June 1887.

37. *Barnsla Foaks Annual or Pogmoor Olmenack* (1873), copy in Manchester Central Reference Library.

38. See for example, *The Weyver's Awn Comic Olmenack* (1881), Preface; also the

adages in these almanacs, e.g. 'If theers nowt in thee thou'll do bad work', or 'A Good Master Makes Good Workmen' in *Bob Stubbs' Yorksher Awymynack* (1910).

39. B. Brierley, 'A Christmas Dinner' in *A Bundle o' Fents, From a Lancashire Loom* (Manchester, 1883).
40. 'Club Train Yarns' and 'Chaps On Change' in *Teddy Ashton's Lancashire Annual* (1925, 1926); see also 'Lancashire Lads and Lasses' in *Teddy Ashton's Journal* (1896); 'Tamsie...' *Teddy Ashton's Northern Weekly*, 20 May 1899, for very favourable treatments of employers.
41. See the account of 'Billy Bobbin', the gullible Lancashire cotton operative, in his *Journal* (1896), and in the *Northern Weekly*, 16 Sept. 1899.
42. See below, pp. 226–7.
43. *Cotton Factory Times*, Nov. 1905 – March 1906; See also, from March, 'Maggie Ray: The Story of a Lancashire Factory Lass'. 'The Old Factory' appeared in Dec. 1885, and is an instance of the longevity and continuity of this literature.
44. On its organisation and unions see H. A. Turner, *Trade Union Growth*; P. Joyce, *Work, Society and Politics*, chs. 2 and 3; K. Burgess, *The Origins of Modern British Industrial Relations* (1975), ch. 4.
45. See Alan Gee on the difficulties of organising women, *Cotton Factory Times*, 5 Jan. 1900.
46. See 'Do Women Keep Men From Success?', a question answered in the affirmative, *ibid.*, 23 Feb. 1906.
47. For the attempts to organise the chiefly female weavers of Ashton see *ibid.*, 4 Feb. 1887. For exceptions to the general rule of women's quiescence, especially among younger women, see J. Liddington and J. Norris, *One Hand Tied Behind Us. The Rise of the Women's Suffrage Movement* (1978), ch. 5, also chs. 2, 7, 9.
48. P. Joyce, *Work, Society and Politics*, pp. 311–12.
49. *Blackburn Times*, 3 April 1869.
50. E.g., *Cotton Factory Times*, 2 Feb. 1906.
51. P. Joyce, *Work, Society and Politics*, pp. 96–103.
52. Quoted in *ibid.*, p. 90.
53. J. R. Clynes, *The Right Honourable J. R. Clynes, P.C., M.P., Memoirs 1869–1924* (1924), p. 33.
54. R. Blatchford, *Economic Ballads, The Clarion Ballads, Clarion Pamphlet No. 14*, (1896); *Merrie England* (1894), chs. 7, 3, 4; also *Britain For the British* (1902).
55. *Ashton Reporter*, 17 Nov. 1887; see also *Cotton Factory Times*, 7 Jan., 1 April 1887.
56. *ibid.*, 19 Jan. 1906.
57. Nathan Ratcliffe, Robinson Bradley Dodgson, H. Heap, Joshua Barrows, Thomas Birtwistle, all in 'Our Portrait Gallery', *Blackburn Times*, undated (1888/9?); George Barker, John Whalley, undated press cuttings, Blackburn Public Library. See also the obituaries of the Blackburn and area union activists, which substantiate the points made here: William Crossley (*Blackburn Times*, 13, 20 Feb. 1875), Thomas Fenton, spinners' leader (*ibid.*, 7 Nov. 1891), David Holmes of Burnley, (*Cotton Factory Times*, 19 Jan. 1906); also the obituaries of textile union leaders of a somewhat later date, Joseph Cross (*Blackburn Times*, 17 Jan. 1925), Luke Bates (*ibid.*, 28 March, 18 Sept. 1936).
58. See below, pp. 175, 210–11.
59. On past and present see *Cotton Factory Times*, 16 Jan. 1885; and comments of Thomas Birtwistle, *ibid.*, 10 July 1885.
60. *ibid.*, report on Mossley cardroom hands, 6 May 1887; see also editorial 11 Feb. 1887, and 14 Jan. 1887.
61. Blackburn report, *ibid.*, 7 Jan. 1887.

62. *ibid.*, Leader, 21 Jan. 1887.
63. For complaints about overlookers, *ibid.*, 11 Feb. 1887.
64. J. Lambert, 'Sexual Harassment in the Nineteenth Century English Cotton Industry', *History Workshop Journal*, 19 (1985).
65. *Cotton Factory Times*, 1 April 1887.
66. *ibid.*, editorial, 8 July 1887.
67. *ibid.*, 14 Jan. 1887 (Clitheroe report), 4 March 1887. For an example of the weavers' unions being brought in to adjudicate on the quality of yarn and finding in favour of the employer, *ibid.*, 7 Jan. 1887 (Colne report).
68. See below, ch. 12.
69. This was also reflected in the glowing portraits the *Cotton Factory Times* presented of the perseverance, invention and usefulness of the great entrepreneurs. See the account of the Bradford silkmaster S. C. Lister, *ibid.*, 9 Feb. 1906.
70. See e.g. *ibid.*, 23 Feb., 9 March, 23 Nov. 1906.
71. See account of Mutual Cotton Classes, *ibid.*, Jan. 1906, but see also 'Bruce' in Nov. 1914.
72. P. Joyce, *Work, Society and Politics*, esp. ch. 5.
73. J. Burnley, *Phases of Bradford Life* (Bradford, 1875), 'A Day in the Mill'.
74. J. Barlow Brooks, *Lancashire Bred*, 2 vols. (privately printed, Stalybridge, 1926), vol. 1, pp. 121–31.
75. B. Messenger, *Picking Up the Linen Threads*, (Austin, Texas 1975), esp. chs. 6, 7.
76. P. Joyce, 'Introduction' in P. Joyce (ed.), *The Historial Meanings of Work*, pp. 20–1.
77. P. Joyce, *Work, Society and Politics*, pp. 113–15.
78. *Cotton Factory Times*, Jan., Feb. 1893.
79. See below, ch. 11.
80. E.g., *Cotton Factory Times*, Jan., Feb., Oct., Sept. 1900; *Yorkshire Factory Times*, Jan. 1906, Oct. 1909; also *CFT*, July 1928.
81. See esp. *ibid.*, 13 Jan. 1911, also Jan., Feb. 1911, and 16 Jan. 1914.
82. See e.g. 'Children's Corner' in *ibid.*, 6 Jan. 1911.
83. *Ashton Reporter*, 2 Nov. 1872, 9 Nov. 1870 (miners' tea party); 18 Jan. 1871 (spinners and grinders).
84. For interesting examples of a spinners' social gathering, *Blackburn Times*, 24 May 1871, and *Ashton Reporter*, 12 March 1870 (Mossley spinners).
85. H. Benyon, *Masters and Servants: Class and Paternalism in the Making of a Labour Organisation* (1990).
86. See above, pp. 92–3.
87. E. J. Hobsbawm, *Worlds of Labour* (1984), pp. 198–9. See 'Introduction' above. For *Cotton Factory Times* columnists actively developing this broader feeling, see 'Bruce', Jan. 1914.
88. For corroboration of the intensely sectionalist character of the spinners' support for labour representation see J. McHugh and B. Ripley, 'The Spinners and the Rise of Labour', in A. Fowler and T. Wyke (eds.), *The Barefoot Aristocrats*.
89. M. Perrot, 'On the Formation of the French Working Class', in I. Katznelson and A. Zolberg (eds.), *Working Class Formation: Nineteenth Century Patterns in Western Europe and the United States* (1986), esp. pp. 96–101.
90. See leaders, *Cotton Factory Times*, 12 Jan., 2 Feb. 1906.

6 *Custom and the symbolic structure of the social order*

1. For an informative account see P. Schöttler, 'Historians and Discourse Analysis', *History Workshop*, 27 (1989).
2. The main exception is P. Burke and R. Porter (eds.), *The Social History of Language* (Cambridge, 1988). See also the comments of P. Joyce, 'The People's English: Language and Class in Nineteenth-Century England' in P. Burke and R. Porter (eds.), *The Social History of Language* (Cambridge, 1990), vol. II.
3. For custom in a chiefly rural setting, see B. Bushaway, *By Rite: Custom, Ceremony and Community in England 1700–1850* (1982).
4. See for example, R. Storch, 'Introduction', in R. Storch (ed.), *Popular Culture and Custom in Nineteenth Century England* (1982); D. Vincent, *Bread, Knowledge and Freedom: A Study of Nineteenth-Century Working-Class Autobiography* (1981), esp. parts 1 and 3. See also the very interesting remarks of D. Thompson, 'Conclusion', in *The Chartists* (1984).
5. J. Langton, 'The Industrial Revolution and the Regional Geography of England', *Transactions of the Institute of British Geographers*, 9: 145–67 (1984).
6. B. Bushaway, *By Rite*, ch. 7. See also J. Obelkevich, *Religion and Rural Society in South Lindsey, 1825–1875* (1976).
7. H. Cunningham, *Leisure in the Industrial Revolution c. 1780–1880* (1980), ch. 2.
8. Persistence is the keynote, often too insistently, in J. M. Golby and A. W. Purdue, *The Civilization of the Crowd: Popular Culture in England 1750–1900* (1984), an account itself marred at times by its authors' decided populism.
9. E. J. Hobsbawm, 'Introduction', in E. J. Hobsbawm and T. O. Ranger (eds.), *The Invention of Tradition* (Cambridge, 1983).
10. For an illuminating discussion see G. M. Sider, 'Fun in Starve Harbour: Custom, History, and Confrontation in Village Newfoundland', in H. Medick and D. W. Sabean (eds.), *Interests and Emotion: Essays on the Study of Family and Kinship* (Cambridge, 1984), esp. p. 363.
11. See above, pp. 97–102.
12. See H. Medick and D. W. Sabean, 'Introduction' and 'Interest and Emotion in Family and Kinship Studies: A Critique of Social History and Anthropology', in *Interests and Emotion*.
13. B. Martin, *A Sociology of Contemporary Cultural Change* (Oxford, 1981), esp. chs. 3 and 4.
14. S. Hall, 'On Deconstructing the Popular', in R. Samuel (ed.), *People's History and Socialist Theory* (1981); T. Bennett, 'Introduction: Popular Culture and "The Turn to Gramsci"' and S. Hall, 'Popular Culture and the State' in T. Bennett *et al.* (eds.), *Popular Culture and Social Relations* (Milton Keynes, 1986); D. Hall 'Introduction', in S. L. Kaplan (ed.), *Understanding Popular Culture: Europe from the Middle Ages to the Nineteenth Century* (Berlin and New York, 1984); S. Clark, 'French Historians and Early Modern Popular Culture', *Past and Present*, 100 (1983).
15. B. Martin, *Sociology of Contemporary Cultural Change*, pp. 62, 68.
16. R. Roberts, *The Classic Slum. Salford Life in the First Quarter of the Century* (Manchester, 1971), esp. ch. 1.
17. *ibid.*, ch. 9, 'The Great Release'.
18. *ibid.*, pp. 15–16.
19. R. Hoggart, *The Uses of Literacy* (1957), esp. ch. 3.
20. See below, pp. 318–20.
21. A. Clarke, *The Effects of the Factory System* (1889), pp. 44–52. For the earlier citation of Clarke and Snowden see above, pp. 83–4, 126–7.
22. *ibid.*, pp. 26–34.

23. See e.g. *Kipps, The Story of A Simple Soul* (1905; 1966), pp. 30–1, 98–9, 186–7, 286–7.

24. S. Reynolds, *Seems So! A Working-Class View of Politics* (1911), ch. 13, esp. pp. 116, 118.

25. The work of Seed and Gunn is extremely suggestive here; J. Seed, 'Unitarianism, Political Economy and the Antinomies of Liberal Culture in Manchester 1830–1850', *Social History*, 7:1 (1982); 'Theologies of Power: Unitarianism and the Social Relations of Religious Discourse, 1800–1850', in R. Morris (ed.), *Class, Power and Social Structure in British Nineteenth-Century Towns* (Leicester, 1986), esp. pp. 129–46; S. Gunn, 'The Manchester Middle Class 1850–1880', PhD dissertation, University of Manchester, (1990). See also P. Bourdieu, *Distinction. A Social Critique of the Judgement of Taste* (1984).

26. R. Hoggart, *The Uses of Literacy*, ch. 4.

27. G. Stedman Jones, 'Working-Class Culture and Working-Class Politics in London, 1870–1900: Notes on the Remaking of a Working Class', in *Languages of Class* (Cambridge, 1983).

28. R. Hoggart, *The Uses of Literacy*, p. 92, also pp. 91–101, 149–166, esp. p. 164.

29. *ibid.*, pp. 24–5.

30. J. Seabrook, *The Unprivileged* (1967), pp. 40–1.

31. J. Wilson, *Memoirs of a Labour Leader* (1910; 1980), p. 95, also pp. 76–7.

32. J. Rule, 'Methodism, Popular Beliefs and Village Culture in Cornwall, 1800–1850', in R. Storch (ed.), *Popular Culture and Custom*.

33. J. Obelkevich, *Religion and Rural Society*, esp. chs. 6, 7.

34. R. Hoggart, *The Uses of Literacy*, ch 5, A.

35. W. E. A. Axon, *The Black Knight of Ashton* (Manchester, 188?), p. 5.

36. C. Hardwick, *Traditions, Superstitions and Folk Lore...Chiefly of Lancashire and the North of England* (Manchester and London, 1872), discussion of fortune telling.

37. J. Harland and T. T. Wilkinson, *Lancashire Folk Lore* (Manchester and London, 1882; Wakefield, 1973), p. 121.

38. W. E. A. Axon, *Folk Song and Folk Speech of Lancashire* (Manchester and London, 187?), pp. 93ff., also pp. 90–2.

39. J. Harland and T. T. Wilkinson, *Lancashire Folk Lore*, p. 164, see also pp. 41, 121–2, 145–9, 164, 229–31, 233, 262–3. See also J. Harland and T. Wilkinson, *Lancashire Legends, Traditions, Pageant...* (Manchester and London, 1882), pp. 143, 145, 159, and section on popular rhymes and proverbs.

40. M. Penn, *Manchester Fourteen Miles* (1947; 1979), ch. 5.

41. W. Lovett, *The Life and Struggles of William Lovett...* (1876; 1967), pp. 9–11.

42. T. Burt, *An Autobiography* (1924; 1984), p. 125.

43. J. Barlow Brooks, *Lancashire Bred* (privately printed, Stalybridge, 1929), vol. 1, pp. 47, 48.

44. B. Capp, *Astrology and the Popular Press. English Almanacs 1500–1800* (1979), chs. 8, 9.

45. W. Hone, *Hone's Poor Humphrey...* (1829).

46. J. Obelkevich, *Religion and Rural Society*, pp. 301–13.

47. S. Clarke, *Clitheroe in Its Railway Days* (Clitheroe, 1900); J. Sugden, *Slaithwaite Notes of the Past and Present* (Manchester, 1905); J. Sykes, *Slawit' in the Sixties* (Huddersfield, 1926), also the voluminous works of Ammon Wrigley, for example *Rakings up* (Rochdale, 1949), pp. 19–22, 23, 44–5, 50–1, 84.

48. J. Barlow Brooks, *Lancashire Bred*, vol. 1, pp. 30–1. Brooks was born in 1874 and recalled the 1880s.

49. P. Bailey, *Leisure and Class in Victorian England* (1978); P. Cunningham, *Leisure in the Industrial Revolution* (1980).

50. Though new sports and gambling were in fact often intimately related to older

pastimes; see P. Joyce, *Work, Society and Politics: The Culture of the Factory in Later Victorian England* (Brighton 1980), pp. 286–8.

51. E. P. Thompson, 'Folklore, Anthropology and Social History', *Indian Historical Review*, 3:2 (1978), (*Studies in Labour History Pamphlet*, 1979).

52. See the comments and citations in P. Joyce, 'Introduction', in P. Joyce (ed.), *The Historical Meanings of Work* (Cambridge, 1987), pp. 16, 27–8.

53. J. Barlow Brooks, *Lancashire Bred*, vol. 1.

54. See M. Anderson, *Family Structure in Nineteenth Century Lancashire* (Cambridge, 1971). For a critique of this emphasis on the short-run 'instrumental' nature of family and kin ties see H. Medick and D. W. Sabean, 'Interest and emotion in family and kinship studies', pp. 21–3.

55. J. Benson, *The Penny Capitalists. A Study of Nineteenth-Century Working-Class Entrepreneurs* (Dublin, 1983). Credit is also another area of interest, see M. Tebbutt, *Making Ends Meet. Pawnbroking and Working-Class Credit* (1983).

56. R. Poole, 'Oldham Wakes', in J. K. Walton and J. Walvin (eds.), *Leisure in Britain 1780–1939* (Manchester, 1983); also J. K. Walton and R. Poole, 'The Lancashire Wakes in the Nineteenth Century', in R. Storch (ed.), *Popular Culture and Custom*.

57. R. Poole, 'Oldham Wakes', p. 87.

58. See below, ch. 12.

59. R. Poole, 'Oldham Wakes', pp. 90–3.

60. T. Bennett, 'Hegemony, Ideology and Pleasure: Blackpool', in T. Bennett, *et al.* (eds.), *Popular Culture and Social Relations*.

61. P. Joyce, *Work, Society and Politics, passim*.

62. See above, ch. 5.

63. Bennett also underestimates the subversive, critical edge to this populism, writing it off as incapable of 'rupturing' dominant discourses.

64. T. Bennett, 'Hegemony', p. 145.

65. *ibid.*, pp. 141–2ff.

66. For the limits to carnivalesque inversion see R. Poole, 'Oldham Wakes', p. 92.

67. J. K. Walton, *The Blackpool Landlady: A Social History* (Manchester, 1978), pp. 35–40.

68. *ibid.*, p. 139.

69. Postcard Collection of Mrs Olive Halliwell, near Bolton, kindly loaned to me by the owner. There is also a collection in the Documentary Photography Archive, Manchester Polytechnic.

70. J. K. Walton, *The Blackpool Landlady*, pp. 52–7, also ch. 7.

71. A. Clarke, *Teddy Ashton's Gradely Guide to Blackpool* (Bolton, 1908).

72. Clarke is discussed below, pp. 301–2.

73. *ibid.*, 'The Trippers' Choice'.

74. B. Martin, *Sociology of Contemporary Cultural Change*, p. 65.

75. R. Hoggart, *The Uses of Literacy*, p. 29.

76. W. J. Ong, *Orality and Literacy. The Technologizing of the Word* (1982).

7   *The sense of the past*

1. D. Vincent, *Bread, Knowledge and Freedom* (1981), ch. 2, esp. pp. 19–29, also ch. 9, *Literary and Popular Culture in England 1750–1914* (Cambridge, 1989).

2. *ibid.*, chs. 5, 6.

3. Popular Memory Group, 'Popular Memory: Theory, Politics, Method', in R. Johnson (ed.), *Making Histories: Studies in History Writing and Politics* (1982).

4. R. Samuel, *Theatres of Memory* (1990).

5. 'Popular Memory', pp. 244–9.

6. See above, ch. 2.

7. P. Hollis, *The Pauper Press* (Oxford, 1970).

8. O. Smith, *The Politics of Language 1791–1819* (Oxford, 1984).

9. *ibid.*, pp. 105–6.

10. *ibid.*, p. 192.

11. K. Snell, *Annals of the Labouring Poor* (Cambridge, 1985), pp. 336–43.

12. See below, pp. 210–11, 274–6.

13. This synthesis seems to have been most marked in the kinds of community where pre-factory forms of production continued longest, also where the symbiosis of the rural and the urban was longest retained. In these situations custom and local traditions lived longest. See below, pp. 280–2.

14. D. Vincent, *Bread, Knowledge and Freedom*, ch 6, also pp. 189–90; *Literacy and Popular Culture*, ch. 2.

15. A. Everitt, *The Pattern of Rural Discontent: The Nineteenth Century*, Department of English Local History, Occasional Papers, 2nd series, 4 (1972). See also C. B. Turner, 'Revivalism and Welsh Society in the 19th Century', in J. Obelkevich *et al.* (eds.), *Disciplines of Faith: Studies in Religion, Politics and Patriarchy* (1987).

16. B. Capp, *Astrology and the Popular Press: English Almanacs 1550–1800* (1979).

17. *ibid.*, chs. 8, 9.

18. W. Hone, *Hone's Poor Humphrey* ... (1829).

19. W. Hone, *The Year Book of Daily Recreations and Information* ... (1832); later, 1833–7, *The Everyday Book and Table Book* ....

20. Copy in Manchester Central Reference Library (MCR).

21. *The Christian Almanac for 1833* (MCR). There were also family, parochial, commercial and institutional almanacs as well as those considered here.

22. For example, *Preston Guardian Almanac for 1854; Bolton Almanac and Advertiser* (1853).

23. See above, ch. 2.

24. For discussion of these aspects of the dialect almanacs, see below, pp. 287–8.

25. F. Furet and B. Ozouf, *Reading and Writing: Literacy in France from Calvin to Jules Ferry* (Cambridge, 1982), ch. 3.

26. T. Cooper, *The Life of Thomas Cooper by Himself* (1872), chs. 1–4; T. Burt, *An Autobiography* (1924; 1984), chs. 1–3, 9; J. Wilson, *Memoirs of a Labour Leader* (1910; 1980), pp. 38–9, 42–3, 48–9, 208; F. M. Leventhal, *Respectable Radical: George Howell and Victorian Working-Class Politics* (1977), ch. 1.

27. T. Cooper, *Life*, chs. 8, 9, 24; T. Burt, *Autobiography*, chs. 9, 11, 6.

28. M. Rutherford, *The Revolution in Tanners Lane* (1887; 1984), p. 132, see also pp. 268–9.

29. See Vincent's discussion of Burns' 'The Cotter's Saturday Night', in 'The Decline of Oral Tradition in Popular Culture' in R. Storch (ed.), *Popular Culture and Custom in Nineteenth-Century England* (1982).

30. See above, pp. 57–8.

31. T. Cooper, *Life*, chs. 30, 31.

32. W. Robertson, *Rochdale and the Vale of Whitworth* (Rochdale, 1897); *Old and New Rochdale* (Rochdale, n.d.); *Rochdale Past and Present* (Rochdale, 1875); *Rochdale Social and Political* (Rochdale, n.d.).

33. W. E. A. Axon, *Folk Song and Folk Speech of Lancashire* (Manchester, 187?) pp. 93ff.

34. S. Clarke, *Clitheroe In Its Railway Days* (Clitheroe, 1900); *Clitheroe in the Old Coaching Days* (Clitheroe, 1929). The best available account of the new provincial interest in history and antiquities, extending across the whole country, is C. Dellheim, *The Face of the Past: The Preservation of the Medieval*

Inheritance in Victorian England (Cambridge, 1982). The radical, progressive nature of this interest is rightly emphasised (ch. 1). Particularly in industrial Lancashire, but more widely too, interest developed earlier and was more broadly based socially than Dellheim's account (of antiquarianism and archaeology rather more than of history) indicates (ch. 2).

35. W. Robertson, *Rochdale and the Vale of Whitworth, passim.*
36. See for instance W. A. Abram, *Blackburn Characters of a Past Generation* (Blackburn, 1894), *History of Blackburn* (Blackburn, 1877), also J. G. Shaw, *History and Traditions of Darwen and its People* (Darwen, 1889). For an earlier example see P. A. Whittle, *Blackburn As It Is* (Preston, 1852).
37. Examples are R. D. Mattley, *Annals of Rochdale* (Rochdale, 1899); W. A. Abram, *Chronological Notes on the History of the Town and Parish of Blackburn* (3rd ed., Blackburn, 1884). Mattley was a solicitor, Abram a local newspaper editor. The Blackburn notes first appeared briefly in the *Preston Guardian*. See also *Blackburn Weekly Telegraph Year Book* (Blackburn, 1904). Town Councils also sometimes issued year books and town directories often contained historical material. The craze for chronicling came early, and chroniclers needed little encouragement to chronicle. See *The Chronicles of Blackburn during the Mayoralty of Robert Hopwood Hutchinson esq.* (Blackburn, 1863).
38. See below.
39. *Historic Society of Lancashire and Cheshire, Proceedings, Papers, session 1, 1848–9* (Liverpool, 1849), inaugural address of Rev. A. Hulme.
40. A. Darbyshire and G. Milner, *A. Booke of Olde Manchester and Salford* (Manchester, 1887).
41. On the building and iconography of the town hall see C. Dellheim, *The Face of the Past,* ch. 4.
42. *Mural Painting in the Large Hall, Town Hall, Manchester* (Manchester, n.d.). On the mural, see also C. Dellheim, *Face of the Past,* ch. 4; J. Treuherz, 'Ford Madox Brown and the Manchester murals', in J. H. G. Archer, *Art and Architecture in Victorian Manchester,* (Manchester, 1985).
43. M. Wiener, *English Culture and the Decline of the Industrial Spirit 1850–1980* (Cambridge, 1981), esp. ch. 4.
44. E.g. H. Fishwick, *A History of Lancashire* (1894).
45. C. Cunningham, *Victorian and Edwardian Town Halls* (1981); J. H. G. Archer, *Art and Architecture.*
46. D. Cannadine, 'The Transformation of Civic Ritual in Modern Britain: The Colchester Oyster Feast', *Past and Present,* 94 (1982).
47. D. Cannadine, 'Conflict and Consensus on a Ceremonial Occasion: The Diamond Jubilee in Cambridge in 1897', *Historical Journal,* 24 (1981).
48. E. J. Hobsbawm, 'Introduction' and 'Mass-Producing Traditions: Europe 1870–1914', in E. J. Hobsbawm and T. O. Ranger (eds.), *The Invention of Tradition* (Cambridge, 1983).
49. This was in part the Cambridge case in 1887, Cannadine, 'Conflict and Consensus'.
50. As well as the southern emphasis in Colchester and Cambridge see R. D. Storch, 'Please to Remember the Fifth of November: Conflict, Solidarity and Public Order in England 1815–1900', in Storch (ed.), *Popular Culture.*
51. This account is based mostly on the BA thesis of A. Walker, 'A Study of the Celebration of the Preston Guilds Merchant 1842–1922' (BA thesis, Manchester University, 1987), also on W. Dobson and J. Harland, *A History of the Preston Guilds* (Preston, 1862) and W. Dobson, *An Account of the Celebration of the Preston Guilds in 1862* (Preston, 1862).
52. See n. 41 above, also P. Joyce, *Work, Society and Politics* (1980), pp. 276–9.

53. For full details see Walker's account, n. 51.

54. See above, ch. 3.

55. D. Vincent, *Bread, Knowledge and Freedom*, p. 165, also ch. 7.

56. T. Tholfsen, *Working-Class Radicalism in Mid-Victorian England* (1978).

57. *The British Working Man and Friend of the Sons of Toil* (1859–60) was one instance of the perpetuation of the older condescending, didactic tone. See e.g., no. 51, Jan. 1860.

58. Especially as after the 1840s it was much more frankly commercial in character and had to respond to its readers rather than lecture them. See *The Workingman: A Weekly Record of Social and Political Progress*, published 1860s. The historical perspective in this was akin to *Cassell's Historical Educator*, the source of much of Thomas Burt's history.

59. A. Ellis, *Educating Our Masters: Influences on the Growth of Literacy in Victorian Working Class Children* (Aldershot, 1985), *passim* but esp. ch. 6.

60. A. Ellis, *Books in Victorian Elementary Schools*, Library Association Pamphlet no. 34, (1971).

61. *ibid.*, pp. 21, 35, 37–8.

62. See the essays of T. Bateson and E. A. Haworth in T. F. Tout and J. Tait (eds.), *Historical Essays By Members of Owens College Manchester* (1902).

63. J. M. Golstrom, *The Social Content of Education 1808–1870* (Dublin, 1972).

64. A. Ellis, *Books*, pp. 32–3.

65. V. E. Chancellor, *History for their Masters: Opinion in the English History Textbook 1808–1914* (Bath, 1970).

66. *ibid.*, ch. 2.

67. R. Gray, 'The Languages of Factory Reform in Britain c. 1830–1860', in P. Joyce (ed.), *The Historical Meanings of Work* (Cambridge, 1987).

68. V. E. Chancellor, *History*, ch. 4.

69. D. Vincent, *Bread, Knowledge and Freedom* pp. 27–9.

70. A. Clarke, *The Effects of the Factory System* (1889), pp. 145–7, 149.

71. The weight of neglect Chartism suffered is evident in accounts that were of a more radical inclination, for example George Saintsbury's heterodox history of Manchester, which while unforgiving about *Manchestertum* has comparatively little to say about Chartism; G. Saintsbury, *Manchester* (1887).

72. This account is based on the Marmion Collection of these books in Manchester University Library. The collection comprises several hundred books, most of which have been examined. It also covers manuals for teachers, and books of self-education. These have also been consulted.

73. A typical example is *Pinnock's Catechism of the History of England...* (1822).

74. Mrs Markham, *A History of England...for Young Persons* (1866); O. Browning, *Modern English History 1815–1885* (1891). In the older vein, though much re-issued, see Lady Calcott, *Little Arthur's History of England* (1834).

75. S.P.C.K., *English History*, New Reading Series (1860?); see also *An Outline of English History for Junior Classes. A First Book* (1860).

76. See also *Arnold's Historical Reader* (Editions of 1880s and 1890s); also 80s and 90s editions of Mrs Creighton's *The Rise of the People and the Growth of Parliament* and her *Shilling History of England*.

77. See esp. chs 1. and 2., also pp. 198ff; also in the same 'English Citizen' series see H. D. Traill on central government and T. W. Fowler on the poor law.

78. For this and other veins of Wyatt repeated, E. L. Elias, *This England of Ours* (1914) and *Modern Times Since 1760* (n.d., post-1918).

79. The most radical examples are the works of J. R. R. Green; see also the work of the Oxford don, F. York Powell, *Old Stories From British History* (1895).

80. W. S. Thomson, *English Composition* (1894).

81. On 'national manners' see H. Price, *Outline of English History...* (1884), reputedly with sales of 595,000; see also the earlier *Royal Readers, Stories From English History Simply Told* (1882), and *Blackies Composition, School Series, Sixth Reader* (1871).
82. R. Colls and P. Dodd, *Englishness: Essays in Politics and Culture 1880–1920* (Manchester, 1986).
83. See below, ch. 13.
84. *John Heywood's Manchester Readers: A New Series for Elementary Schools of All Grades – The Third Book* (London and Manchester, n.d. [1880s]). See also W. S. Thomson, *English Composition*, 'National Songs'. On the racial characteristics of the Anglo-Saxon see V. E. Chancellor, *History For Their Masters*, pp. 118–20, where the message of racial character could be a moderate one. However, Britain's mission in the world was not in doubt.
85. R. Roberts, *The Classic Slum* (Manchester, 1971), pp. 110–14.
86. As in the case of Birmingham and Manchester, M. Blanch, 'Imperialism, Nationalism and Organised Youth', in J. Clarke, C. Critcher, R. Johnson (eds.), *Working Class Culture: Studies in History and Theory* (1979).

8 The people's English

1. Cited, from *Pygmalion* (1912), by P. J. Waller, 'Democracy and Dialect, Speech and Class', in P. J. Waller (ed.), *Politics and Social Change in Modern Britain: Essays Presented to A. F. Thompson* (Brighton, 1987), p. 1.
2. See above, pp. 157–8.
3. The exception is P. Burke, 'Introduction', in P. Burke and R. Porter (eds.), *The Social History of Language* (Cambridge, 1987), which offers the most succinct guide.
4. B. Bernstein, *Class, Codes and Culture*, (1971–75) vols. 1–3; see the criticisms in the following, especially of Bernstein's simplistic model of class and his underestimation of the creativeness of popular speech; H. Rosen, *Language and Class: A Critical Look at the Theories of Basil Bernstein* (Falling Wall Press pamphlet, Bristol, 1972); W. P. Robinson, *Language and Social Behaviour* (1972), ch. 9; D. Leith, *A Social History of English* (1983), ch. 4, also the works of Labov cited below, note 8.
5. On the study of language as interactional discourse, showing how gender, class and other social distinctions are not given as constants but are communicatively produced, see ch. 1 of J. J. Gumperz (ed.), *Language and Social Identity* (Cambridge, 1982). See also G. Steiner, *After Babel: Aspects of Language and Translation* (Oxford, 1975), ch. 1.
6. Cited in J. Steinberg, 'The Historian and the *Questione della Lingua*', in P. Burke and R. Porter (eds.), *Social History of Language*, p. 199.
7. M. A. K. Halliday, *Language as Social Semiotic* (1978).
8. W. Labov, *The Social Stratification of English in New York City* (Washington, 1966); see also *Language in the Inner City* (Oxford, 1977).
9. See the discussion of Labov in W. Downes, *Language and Society* (1984), ch. 7. In the Europe of the present, dialect use appears to be increasing rather than decreasing in several countries; see J. Steinberg, 'The historian', p. 204.
10. L. Milroy, *Language and Social Networks* (Oxford, 1980), ch. 1.
11. As in the case of Martha's Vineyard discussed by Labov, see W. Downes, *Language*, ch. 7.
12. L. Milroy, *Language*, pp. 27–8.
13. See *ibid.*, p. 18 as well as the work of Labov.
14. An analogous, slightly different example would be that of students who

believed they always retained dialect, but, when talking about extra-local experience, took up the standard form picked up at university. For this see *ibid.*, pp. 31–2.

15. For nineteenth-century examples see R. Waller, 'Democracy and Dialect', pp. 15–16.
16. L. Milroy, *Language*. Milroy's argument is that the denser, the more complex, and the more territorial the social networks of the people involved, the greater is their retention of dialect. Though contentious, the argument points to the great importance of language in communal identity.
17. P. J. Waller, 'Democracy and Dialect'.
18. It should be noted that Waller recognises the danger of imagining a 'pure' dialect prior to industrialisation. He also notes how urban growth in fact multiplied dialects by generating new combinations. Further limits to change before 1914 are evident in an educational system that was still highly localised in character. New forms of communication, e.g. print, also increased opportunities for oral, indeed dialect, forms of expression. Nonetheless, the whiggish, teleological account of dialect is still uppermost, as it is more generally as part of the commonsense of the historical profession in England. For another whig see L. Colley on dialect in 'Whose Nation? Class and National Consciousness in Britain, 1750–1830', *Past and Present*, 113 (1986), p. 102.
19. See below, ch. 13.
20. S. Bamford, *The Dialect of South Lancashire or Tim Bobbin's " Tummus und Meary" Revised and Corrected...* (Manchester, 1850).
21. *The Record*, 2:25, (1917), p. 9 (this was the journal of the Lancashire Authors' Association).
22. There are revealing resemblances between the perceived decline of dialect and the shifting historical threshold held to mark the demise of the English countryside. Both involved myths akin to the idea of a vanished golden age. See R. Williams, *The Country and the City* (1973).
23. T. H. Gough, *Black Country Stories*, 5 vols. (reprinted from *Dudley Herald*, 1935–37), vol. 5, pp. 30–2, 71–2. For very clear signs as to the strength of dialect speaking in, respectively, 1890s rural east Yorkshire, and the industrial district of the Potteries in the 1930s and 1960s; M. C. F. Morris, *Yorkshire Folk-Talk...* (London and York, 1892); R. Nicholls, *Dialect Words and Phrases Used in the Staffordshire Potteries* (1934); J. Levitt, *North Staffordshire Speech* (Stoke-on-Trent, n.d. [1968?]).
24. *The Record*, 2:25 (1917); 21:100 (1936), 'Lancashire Life'. For the frequently expressed association of the decline of dialect with new-fangled ways, in this case the fall from fashion of the shawl and the wearing of shoes instead of clogs (also the heinous modern crazes for music halls and billiard rooms), see J. Baron's introduction to his *A Lancashire Dictionary* (Blackburn, 1907).
25. L. Milroy, 'Urban Dialects in the British Isles', in P. Trudgill (ed.), *Language in the British Isles* (Cambridge, 1984), p. 214.
26. See below, ch. 12.
27. 'Report on the State of Popular Education in England', *Parliamentary Papers* (1861), **XXI**; part II (reports on Rochdale and Bradford, and on Durham and Cumberland).
28. *ibid*, part II (J. S. Winder on Rochdale and Bradford), p. 175.
29. See the introduction to J. Trafford Clegg, *The Works of J. Trafford Clegg (Th' owd Weighver)* (Rochdale, 1898).
30. J. Barlow Brooks, *Lancashire Bred*, 2 vols. (privately printed, Stalybridge, 1926), vol. 1, pp. 137–8.

31. *Parliamentary Papers* (1861), XXI, part II, p. 339.
32. The compiler of the great *English Dialect Dictionary*, Joseph Wright, knew nothing of standard English, little indeed of reading and writing, on leaving school around 1870; E. M. Wright, *The Life of Joseph Wright*, 2 vols. (1932), vol. 1, ch. 1.
33. *Parliamentary Papers* (1861), XXI, part II, p. 340.
34. *ibid.*
35. D. Leith, *Social History of English, passim.*; B. M. H. Strang, *A History of English* (1970).
36. O. Smith, *The Politics of Language, 1791–1819* (Oxford, 1984), ch. 1.
37. Cited by P. J. Waller, 'Democracy and Dialect', p. 18, see also pp. 16–17.
38. *ibid.*, p. 23.
39. P. Joyce, *Work, Society and Politics: The Culture of the Factory in Later Victorian England* (Brighton 1980), pp. 188–91, 285–8.
40. For a useful but wholly unsystematic study of higher-class usage see K. C. Philips, *Language and Class in Victorian England* (Oxford, 1984).
41. A. Bennett, *Tales of the Five Towns* (1905; 1964).
42. Advertisements for 'universal' pronouncing dictionaries and for books claiming to teach the reader how to write letters in the correct standard form regularly appeared in the big-selling West Riding dialect almanacs, for example, *The Halifax Illuminated Clock Almanac*. See below, pp. 277–8.
43. Mrs Loane is an interesting but rather patronising and not altogether reliable guide, 'The Art of Polite Conversation As Practiced Among the Poor', ch. 4 of *The Queen's Poor* (1905). A revealing instance of code-switching, standard to dialect, in order to guy the 'lady' and 'gentleman' and exalt ordinary folk is evident in Vicinus' discussion of the 'Geordie' music hall entertainer Billy Purvis. M. Vicinus, *The Industrial Muse* (1974), p. 242.
44. See above, ch. 6.
45. Eric Partridge is not only a great glossarist of slang but a very suggestive interpreter of its social meanings. See, respectively, his *Historical Dictionary of Slang* and *Slang Today and Yesterday* (1954).
46. A. Bennett, *Tales*, pp. 19, 25, 37.
47. J. Barlow Brooks, *Lancashire Bred*, vol. 1, pp. 72–8.
48. W. A. Abram, *Blackburn Characters of a Past Generation* (Blackburn, 1894), p. 3.
49. P. Joyce, *Work, Society and Politics*, ch. 1.
50. P. J. Waller, 'Democracy and Dialect', p. 16.
51. D. Vincent, *Literacy and Popular Culture in England, 1750–1914* (Cambridge, 1989), ch. 3.
52. *ibid.*; on the limitations of the use of writing in popular culture see also D. Vincent on the penny post, 'Communication, Community and the State', in C. Emsley and J. Walvin (eds.), *Artisans, Peasants and Proletarians* (1985).
53. This account is based on the Marmion Collection, Manchester University Library, discussed above pp. 189–90. For a general account of language prescriptiveness see J. and L. Milroy, *Authority in Language: Investigating Language Prescription and Standardisation* (1985).
54. L. Murray, *English Adapted to the Different Classes of Learners* (1842); also *English Exercises... Adapted to Murray's English Grammar* (n.d., 1840s edition seen).
55. H. Butter, *The Etymological Spelling Book and Expositor* (1846).
56. *Chambers Elocution*, introduction (revised ed. seen, London n.d. [1890s?]).
57. See especially the extraordinary *Enquire Within Upon Everything*, selling about 600,000 copies by 1877. This compendium of advice on all matters of social skill is a classic in the voluminous literature of Victorian self-improvement. It contains a large section with hundreds of rules and hints about 'correct'

speaking and writing. It is at once absurdly prim, hyper-correct and extremely supercilious about popular usage. Imitation of the 'educated' is the key to success. The most reprehensible errors reside in dialect, especially cockney. The tone is taken from *Punch* and its guying of popular speech. Nine versions of cockney are identified and denounced, including 'Low', 'Genteel', Cockney Flunkey', 'Feminine', and 'Domestic'. Similar treatment is meted out to the Irish and Scots, and to provincial 'brogues', 'provincialism' being the chief term of abuse. The reader is assured that though he may not be educated he may yet become 'cultivated' through the proper exercise of language.

58. Published 1906.
59. Published in Oxford, and duly spelling out the linguistic failures of 'the lower orders'.
60. O. Smith, *The Politics of Language*, ch. 1.
61. *ibid*, ch. 6.
62. See H. Aarslef, *The Study of Language in England* (Princeton, 1967), chs. 1–4 for an excellent account. See also G. Steiner, 'To Civilize Our Gentlemen', in *Language and Silence: Essays 1958–1966* (1967).
63. Also of Hone's *Year Book*; see above. Particularly important was J. Brand's *Observations on Popular Antiquities* (1777). On the 'discovery of the people' from this time see part 1:1 of P. Burke, *Popular Culture in Early Modern Europe* (1977).
64. See above, pp. 189–92.
65. For a full account see H. Aarslef, *Study of Language*, chs. 5, 6.
66. R. Williams, *Culture and Society, 1780–1950* (1963).
67. On this see J. Milroy, *The Language of Gerard Manley Hopkins* (1977), chs. 2, 3. For the quite crucial role of language and language study in European nineteenth-century nationalism, itself often liberal or radical, see B. Anderson, *Imagined Communities* (1983).
68. For an account of Trench see H. Aarslef, *Study of Language*, ch. 6.
69. R. C. Trench, *English Past and Present*, pp. 8–9.
70. D. J. Palmer, *The Rise of English Studies* (1965), chs. 1–4, also the later chapters on the creation of the Oxford English School.
71. For example, C. D. Yonge, *A Short English Grammar...For the Use of Schools* (1879), chs. 1 and 2.
72. R. Morris (president of the Philological Society), *Elementary Lessons in Historical English Grammar* (1874).
73. Rev. Canon Daniel, *Grammar, History and Derivation of the English Language* (1896).
74. Nelson's *Senior Reader* of 1864.
75. On the development of the idea of literary history at this time see T. Davies, 'Education, Ideology and Literature' in T. Bennett and S. Martin (eds.), *Culture, Ideology and Social Process* (1981).
76. 1855, 9th thousand.
77. See Reed, *Introduction*, pp. 6–19. The debt of Reed, an American, to Thomas Arnold seems to have been considerable. Arnold's own *Manual of English Literary History* was in its fourth edition by 1874.
78. See pp. 3ff., where great literature is seen as coming about by great historical changes which stir up the people.
79. R. Samuel, 'British Marxist Historians 1880–1920', *New Left Review*, 120 (1980).
80. H. Alford, *The Queen's English*, p. 4.
81. Cited in T. Paulin, *A New Look at the Language Question* (Field Day Theatre pamphlet, Derry, 1983), p. 8. For the late nineteenth-century development of

English studies as part of a new, often socially and politically conservative, definition of Englishness see B. Doyle, 'The Invention of English' in R. Colls and P. Dodd, *Englishness: Essays in Politics and Culture* (1986).

82. Including a very early crop of books of the prescriptive kind, see e.g. D. Baxter, *The Queen's English* (Liverpool, 1888); Eis Electikwan, *Language in Relation to Commerce, Missions, and Government. England's Ascendancy and the World's Destiny* (Manchester, 1846).

83. K. M. E. Murray, *Caught in the Web of Words: James A. H. Murray and the Oxford English Dictionary* (1977), esp. chs. 1, 3, 10.

84. E. M. Wright, *The Life of Joseph Wright*, vol. 1, ch. 1.

85. See above, chs. 6, 7.

86. D. Vincent, *Bread, Knowledge and Freedom* (1982), pp. 192–3.

9 Investigating popular art

1. *Sunday Chronicle*, 5 March 1933.

2. W. H. Reddy, *The Rise of Market Culture: The Textile Trade and French Society 1750–1900* (Cambridge, 1984), p. 239.

3. On the public persona of the dialect writer as performer see M. Vicinus, *The Industrial Muse* (1974), p. 194. See also S. Fitton, *Gradely Lancashire* (Stalybridge, 1929), 'Introduction'.

4. J. Bratton, *The Victorian Popular Ballad* (1975).

5. Cited in M. Booth, *English Melodrama* (1965), p. 62.

6. P. Burke, *Popular Culture in Early Modern Europe* (1978), chs. 3, 4.

7. R. Finnegan, *Oral Poetry. Its Nature, Significance and Social Context* (Cambridge, 1977), esp. pp. 28–30, 88–90, 267–72.

8. P. Burke, *Popular Culture*, p. 115.

9. M. Denning, *Mechanic Accents: Dime Novels and Working-class Culture in America* (1987), ch. 5.

10. R. de V. Renwick, citing Flora Thompson on ballad performance among the nineteenth-century rural poor, *English Folk Poetry: Structure and Meaning* (1980), ch. 3, pp. 114–16.

11. J. Bratton, *The Victorian Popular Ballad*, chs. 1–3. This communality of setting was in turn reflected in the form of the nineteenth-century ballad, both 'drawing room' and 'popular'. If not anonymous, the ballad was impersonal, public persona and not individual experience being presented.

12. See below, p. 283.

13. P. Bailey, 'Introduction: Making Sense of Music Hall', in P. Bailey (ed.), *The Victorian Music Hall. The Business of Pleasure* (Milton Keynes, 1987).

14. C. E. B. Russel, 'Poor People's Music Hall in Lancashire', *The Economic Review*, April 1900. See also D. Höher, 'The Composition of Music Hall Audiences 1850–1900', in P. Bailey (ed.), *The Victorian Music Hall*.

15. See for example S. Powell, '*Can You Hear Me, Mother?*': *Sandy Powell's Lifetime of Music Hall* (1975), p. 16.

16. D. C. Calthorp, 'The Patter Comedians', *Music Hall Nights* (1925). On the high degree of interplay between performers and audiences in the Ashton-under-Lyne music hall of the 1920s and 30s see B. Dickinson, 'In the Audience', *Oral History*, 1983.

17. J. Burnley, 'Music Hall Life', *Phases of Bradford Life* (Bradford, 1875).

18. P. Bailey, 'The Swell Song', in J. Bratton (ed.), *The Victorian Music Hall. Performance and Style* (Milton Keynes, 1987).

19. P. Bailey, 'Custom, Capital and Culture in the Victorian Music Hall', in R. D. Storch (ed.), *Popular Culture and Custom in Nineteenth Century England* (1982).

20. M. Denning, *Mechanic Accents*, 146–7, and 'Cheap Stories: Notes on Popular Fiction and Working-Class Culture in Nineteenth-Century America', *History Workshop Journal*, 22 (1986).

21. R. Darnton, 'Peasants Tell Tales: The Meaning of Mother Goose', in *The Great Cat Massacre and Other Episodes in French Cultural History* (1985), p. 70.

22. M. Segalen, *Love and Power in the Peasant Family* (Oxford, 1983).

23. M. Vicinus, *The Industrial Muse*, pp. 26–38.

24. R. Darnton, 'Peasants Tell Tales', pp. 60–8.

25. G. Stedman Jones, 'Working Class Culture and Working Class Politics in London, 1870–1900', *Journal of Social History*, 7:4 (1974).

26. B. Sharrat, 'The Politics of the Popular? – From Melodrama to Television' in D. Bradbury, L. Jones, B. Sharrat (eds.), *Performance and Politics in Popular Drama* (Cambridge, 1980).

27. J. Radford, 'Introduction', in J. Radford (ed.), *The Progress of Romance: The Politics of Popular Fiction* (1986).

28. See above, p. 10.

29. On the radical potential of the myths and motifs of inversion see V. Turner 'Comments and Conclusions', in B. A. Babcock (ed.), *The Reversible World: Symbolic Inversion in Art and Society* (1978).

30. See above, ch. 6.

31. See above, pp. 82–4, 126–8, 151–63.

10 *The broadside ballad*

1. B. Hollingworth, *Songs of the People: Lancashire Dialect Poetry of the Industrial Revolution* (Manchester, 1977), pp. 4–5; J. Barlow Brooks *Lancashire Bred*, 2 vols. (privately printed, Stalybridge 1926), vol. 1, 'Mendicants and Street Singers'.

2. R. de V. Renwick, *English Folk Poetry: Structure and Meaning* (1980), ch. 3.

3. J. Bratton, *The Victorian Popular Ballad* (1975), pp. 3–11, 23–4.

4. See the Library guide to the 30,000-strong collection; also a thesis which makes much use of the collection, R. S. Thomson, 'The Development of the Broadside Ballad Tradition and Its Influence upon the Transmission of Folk Songs', PhD dissertation, Cambridge University (1974).

5. Pearson collection, 4 vols., BRQ 398.8S9, Manchester Central Reference Library. The following have been consulted in the same library:- J. F. Moseley Ballad Songbook, 821.04.B3; Harland's Ballad Collections, MS f821.04 B25; 'Manchester Ballads, collected by Fred Leary', MS 821.04 M51. As well as these there are also other collections of early nineteenth- and eighteenth-century ballads at BR F821.04 Ba.1., B2, B3, BR f398.8 B1 (Ba.1, vols. 3 and 5 has material, *c.* 1840s–60s).

6. On ballads see M. Vicinus, *The Industrial Muse* (1974), ch. 1, esp. pp. 13–26 on printers, sellers and the organisation of the trade; A. L. Lloyd, *Folk Song in England* (1967); L. Shepherd, *The History of Street Literature* (1962).

7. R. S. Thomson, 'Development of the Broadside Ballad', part II, ch. 1, for a discussion of the middle-class commentators on the ballads. It is to Mayhew of course that we owe much of our knowledge of the London ballad trade, H. Mayhew, *London Labour and the London Poor*, 4 vols. (1861–62; New York, 1968) vol. 1, pp. 213–51, 272–85; vol. 3, pp. 151–5, 195–7.

8. Manchester Central Reference Library, MS 821.04 M51.

9. R. McWilliam, 'The Tichborne Case and the Broadside Tradition', draft chapter of his thesis, 'The Tichborne Claimant and the People: Investigations into Popular Culture 1867–1886', PhD, University of Sussex (1990). This

assembles a good deal of material showing the decidedly plebeian character of the trade. Printers, writers and singers were out to make money, not to influence or preach. They gave people what they wanted.

10. 'Felix Folio' (J. Page), *The Hawkers and Street Dealers of the North of England Manufacturing Districts*, 2nd edn. (Manchester, 1858). See also article on the ballad trade, *Manchester Quarterly*, 1913.

11. R. S. Thomson, 'Development of the Broadside Ballad', part II, chs. 1, 3. See also M. Vicinus, 'Introduction', *Broadside Ballads of the Industrial North* (Newcastle, 1975).

12. R. Elbourne, *Music and Tradition in Early Industrial Lancashire 1780–1840* (1980) pp. 29–32. See also R. Colls, *The Colliers' Rant: Song and Culture in the Industrial Village* (1977).

13. 'Ballads, Broadsides, Songs', collected by the former overseer of Oldham workhouse, donated 1902, Oldham Public Library.

14. The Oldham collection has songs from Rawtenstall and Middleton reproducing on a smaller stage this local intimacy of reference.

15. Oldham Collection. Jone drew on the early 'Jone O'Grinfilt' ballads (see subsequent discussion), and took form in songs such as 'Ma, Aunt, Child and the Professional Robert by Gentle Jone' (on the police).

16. This is amply evident in the Madden collection and in the many printed selections of ballads, e.g. L. Jewitt, *Ballads and Songs of Derbyshire* (1867), C. F. Forshaw, *Holroyd's Collection of Yorkshire Ballads* (1892).

17. H. I. Dutton and J. E. King, '*Ten Per Cent and No Surrender*' (Cambridge, 1981), pp. 43, 100, 125.

18. R. de V. Renwick, *English Folk Poetry*, pp. 134–5.

19. Cited in *ibid.*, ch. 3, pp. 114–16.

20. B. Grime, *Memory Sketches* (Oldham, 1887), pp. 168–9.

21. J. Harland, *Ballads and Songs of Lancashire Ancient and Modern*, 3rd edn. (1882), pp. 162–75.

22. Sub-titled: 'Or the Burning of Both Houses of Parliament', Harland Collection, Manchester Central Reference Library (MCR).

23. J. Harland, *Ballads and Songs of Lancashire, Chiefly Older than the Nineteenth Century* (1865), pp. 212–16.

24. See below, ch. 13.

25. See M. Vicinus, *The Industrial Muse*, pp. 45, 287–8 (for 'Lament'). 'Hand Loom etc.' in Harland, *Ballads and Songs*, p. 188.

26. *ibid.*, pp. 190–3, 202–4.

27. J. Stafford, *Songs Commercial and Sentimental* (Ashton, 1840).

28. Harland Collection (MCR).

29. *ibid.*; 'Girls of Lancashire' in Moseley Collection.

30. Named ballads in the text are given the sheet numbers they bear in the Pearson collection, hence 17, 170, 268, 277. On the Free Born Englishman theme see also 'William Tell', 'Liberty's Island', 'Britons Never Shall Be Slaves' (273).

31. Yorkshire ballads, Madden Collection; also 'Things I Should Like to See' (235), 'What Will Old England Come To' (282), 'The Days When We Were Boys' (170), 'An Interesting Dialogue Between the Poor Law Commissioners and People That Apply for Relief' (237) and on 'poor law soup', 'Our Merry Town' (188).

32. See above, chs. 2, 4.

33. 'Claughton Wood' at Pearson (180); other examples are in the Harland collection of ballads circulating around mid-century. On the longevity and urban popularity of poaching songs see A. C. Lloyd, *Folk Song*, pp. 243–7.

34. See above, pp. 38–9.
35. V. Neuberg, *Popular Literature*, pp. 123–43; L. James, *Fiction for the Working Man, 1830–1850* (1974), ch. 6.
36. R. Colls, *The Colliers Rant*, pp. 117, 118–31.
37. Pearson, 16, 183.
38. Pearson, 215, 11, 99.
39. J. Stafford, *Songs Commercial*.
40. Pearson, 238.
41. *ibid.*, 60. See also Madden Yorkshire collection, 'The Ragged Coat', 'Plato's Advice', 'The Honest Workingman'; Moseley Collection, 'If I Had £1000 A Year'.
42. Pearson, 95.
43. R. McWilliam, 'The Tichborne Claimant and the People'.
44. See above, ch. 3.
45. V. Turner, *The Ritual Process: Structure and Anti-Structure* (1967); B. A. Babcock (ed.), *The Reversible World: Symbolic Inversion in Art and Society* (1978).
46. P. Bailey, 'Ally Sloper's Half-Holiday: Comic Art in the 1880s', *History Workshop Journal*, 16 (1983).

11   *The voice of the people?*

1. B. Hollingworth (ed.), 'Introduction', *Songs of the People. Lancashire Dialect Literature of the Industrial Revolution* (Manchester, 1977). This is the best published selection of the Lancashire literature.
2. E. Waugh, *Poems and Songs*, ed. G. Milner (Manchester, 1895?). On Waugh see G. Milner, 'E. Waugh, An Estimate and a Biographical Sketch', *Manchester Quarterly*, 12 (1893).
3. On higher class influences on Lancashire ballads see J. Harland, *Ballads and Songs of Lancashire Ancient and Modern* (1882), *passim*; on the north-east, see the citations of D. Harker, below, notes 7 and 27, and 'John Bell, the Great Collector' in Bell, *Rhymes of Northern Bards* (1812; Newcastle, 1971).
4. Also on the north-east, R. Colls, *The Collier's Rant: Song and Culture in the Industrial Village* (1977), ch. 2. See also M. Vicinus, *The Industrial Muse* (1974), p. 33.
5. *ibid.*, ch. 5 is the best account of dialect (though one much disagreed with here).
6. For some valuable remarks on the diverse social and cultural inheritance of dialect see B. Maidment (ed.), *The Poorhouse Fugitives: Self-Taught Poets and Poetry in Victorian Britain* (Manchester, 1987), pp. 355–9, also pp. 359–69 (for contemporary 'defences' of the dialect), and pp. 231–66 (for a selection of Lancashire dialect poetry).
7. D. Harker, 'Introduction', *Allan's Illustrated Edition of Tyneside Songs* (Newcastle, 1972), pp. xi–xii.
8. See n. 19 below.
9. Almost all these can be consulted in the large collection in Leeds Central Reference Library.
10. Copies in Blackburn Central Library; Tameside Local Studies Library, Stalybridge.
11. Staton was an operative printer, an advanced radical, and eventually the editor of one of the Liberal Bolton weekly newspapers. Copies of the *Loominary* and Clarke's journals are in both Manchester and Bolton Central Reference Libraries.
12. However, the number of very local, very ephemeral journals is unknown, and

may be considerable. An example in the author's possession is *Dick Snowdrop's Comic Journal*, May, June 1878, (Tockholes, near Darwen). This mixed comedy, burlesque and the righting of local wrongs.

13. B. Hollingworth, *Songs of the People*, p. 5.
14. M. Vicinus, *The Industrial Muse*, ch. 5, section II.
15. B. Turner, *About Myself 1863–1930* (1930), pp. 19, 24, ch. 2, pp. 32–3, 48.
16. Thomas Wright, *Some Habits and Customs of the Working Classes* (1867), part II, pp. 174–5. Dialect theatre was another venue for the orality of the literature.
17. *Teddy Ashton's Lancashire Annual*, Dec. 1924.
18. For information on sales, M. Vicinus, *The Industrial Muse*, ch. 5, *passim*.
19. W. W. Skeat and J. H. Nodal, *English Dialect Society. A Bibliographical List* (1877).
20. See the praise of urban growth and of trade in *Seets i Yorkshire and Lancashire: Grimes' Comical Trip from Leeds to Liverpool by Canal* (Wakefield, n.d.).
21. *Bill o' Jack's Monthly*, May 1909.
22. R. Forbes (ed.), *Pollises and Candymen: The Complete Works of Tommy Armstrong* (Consett, 1987). See also J. Burgess, *A Potential Poet? His Autobiography and Verse* (Ilford, privately printed, n.d.); S. Fitton, *Gradely Lancashire* (Stalybridge, 1929), esp. 'Introduction'; H. Mitchell, *The Hard Way Up* (1968), p. 116.
23. On Turner see K. E. Smith, *West Yorkshire Dialect Poets* (Ruined Cottage Publications, Wetherby, 1982).
24. See above, ch. 4.
25. The *Yorkshire Factory Times* ran a similar column. See for example, the *CFT*, Jan., Feb. 1911. 'Mirth In The Mill' ran for decades.
26. Postcards in the collection of Mrs Olive, Halliwell, near Bolton.
27. Along with Vicinus, Maidment and Harker cited above; see also M. Beetham, 'Healthy Reading: The Periodical Press in Late Victorian Manchester', and B. Maidment, 'Class and Cultural Production in the Industrial City,' in A. J. Kidd and K. W. Roberts (eds.), *City, Class and Culture: Studies of Social Policy and Cultural Production in Victorian Manchester* (Manchester, 1985). See also D. Harker, 'Joe Wilson', in P. Bailey and J. Bratton (eds.), *The Victorian Music Hall*, vol. 2 (Milton Keynes, 1986), and Harker, cited below and above, also 'The Making of the Tyneside Concert Hall', *Popular Music*, vol. 1 (1981).
28. That of Maidment, 'Class and Cultural Production', pp. 149, 151, 161, in which class is 'not far enough developed at the time', or else is 'confused'.
29. That of Harker in all the works cited. Beetham's account, while subtler, tends to stereotype the literature as sexually chauvinist.
30. J. Gladstone, draft chapters of forthcoming thesis, '"A Way of Happening, a Mouth": Health-Image and Self-Image During the Dialect Enlightenment... 1674–1824...', PhD dissertation, Harvard University.
31. See above, pp. 210–11.
32. Robert Anderson, *Cumberland Ballads*, ed. Sidney Gilpin, (Carlisle, 1866), and subsequent editions.
33. See above, ch. 8.
34. For further consideration see my projected study of dialect language and literature, provisionally entitled *The People's English*.
35. I have examined the dialect holdings of most of the major county libraries of England. Almost every county has examples, the ones cited being especially important. Dialect was a national as well as a regional phenomenon, as the coincidence of the rise and decline of dialect in the north and beyond makes plain. For Sussex and Wiltshire see *Tom Cladpole's Jurney to Lunnun, Jan Cladpole's Trip to Merricur*, (both Lewes, 1872); E. Slow, *The Adventures of Farmer John Bray at the Wilton Festivities, In Honour of the Coming of Age of the Earl*

of Pembroke (n.d., 1871/2?), *Rhymes of the Wiltshire Peasantry* (n.d., 1870s), *Wiltshire Tales*, esp. 'Dick Dafter'.

36. W. Gregory Harris, *West-Country Volk* (1923).
37. Anon, *Jack Jawkin's First Vote, and How He Won Polly Pawkins* (Norwich, 1880); E. Slow, *Rhymes of the Wiltshire Peasantry*; I. T. Tregallas, *Cornish Tales in Prose and Verse* (Truro, 1868); T. H. Higham, *Four Tales in Verse and Prose in the Cornish Dialect* (Truro, n.d.); Nathan Hogg, *Nathan Hogg's Letters* (Exeter, 1846, 1847).
38. See for example the Harland Collection, Manchester, Central Reference Library; 'Wednesbury Cocking', 'Dashing Steam Loom Weaver', 'Black Your Eye', for the very explicit violence. The sexual is less explicit but amply evident, especially in comparison with the later dialect literature.
39. Edward Corven (*sic*), *Random Rhymes, Being a Collection of Local Songs and Ballads Illustrative of the Habits and Character of the Sons of the Coaly Tyne* (Newcastle-upon-Tyne, 1850). Keelmen transported coal by barge along the Tyne. Their trade was in decline from the 1820s.
40. Robert ('Bobby') Nunn, 'The Keelman's Reason for Attending Church', in *Allan's Illustrated Edition of Tyneside Songs* (Newcastle-upon-Tyne, 1891); George Ridley, 'The Blaydon Keelman', 'Cushy Butterfield' in D. Harker (ed.), *George,Ridley Gateshead Poet and Vocalist* (Newcastle, 1973). The 'domestic' Wilson was perfectly capable of work in this vein.
41. R. Forbes (ed.), *Pollises and Candymen*; T. Gilfellon (ed.), *Tommy Armstrong Sings* (Newcastle, 1971), see Introduction; A. Barrass, *The Pitman's Social Neet* (Consett, 1897). The briefest examination of Tyneside popular culture indicates how Colls' picture of popular traditions subordinated to union and Methodist needs is greatly exaggerated (as indeed is the wider influence of Methodism in the north-east). See also the work of Marshall Creswell in *Allan's Illustrated Edition* (1891).
42. See D. Harker, Introduction to *Allan's* (1972), p.xiv, and notes on songs, poets, vocalists and patrons of dialect (e.g. Joseph Cowen the Liberal magnate and newspaper owner, also J. P. Robson) in *Allan's* (1891).
43. See accounts of Rowland Harrison, John Taylor, George Baron, Ralph Blackett, John Craggs in *Allan's* (1891).
44. See above, pp. 179–83.
45. Address by Rev. A. Hume, *Historic Society of Lancashire and Cheshire, Proceedings and Papers, Session 1, 1848–9* (Liverpool, 1849).
46. R. Samuel, 'The Tory Interpretation of History', presented for a conference entitled 'Patriotism: The Making and Unmaking of British National Identity', Oxford, 1986; the proceedings of which were published as three volumes under this title (1989).
47. M. Beetham, 'Healthy Reading', p. 174.
48. M. Vicinus, *The Industrial Muse*, p. 190.
49. T. Thomas, 'Representation of the Manchester Working Class in Fiction, 1850–1900', in A. J. Kidd and K. W. Roberts, *City, Class and Culture*.
50. P. Joyce, *Work, Society and Politics* (Brighton, 1980), chs 1, 5.
51. See above, ch. 8.
52. For defences of the dialect rejecting privileged, metropolitan values and culture, see B. Maidment, *The Poorhouse Fugitives*, pp. 354–71 (esp. Ben Brierley and Elizabeth Gaskell, for the common feeling of those of vastly different backgrounds).
53. M. Vicinus, *The Industrial Muse*, pp. 203–4.
54. C. F. Forshaw, *John Hartley, Poet and Author. An Appreciation* (Bradford, 1909).
55. Vicinus, *The Industrial Muse*, pp. 194, 210–12.

56. M. Beetham, 'Healthy Reading', pp. 168–174, 190–1.
57. For example, *Country Words* (1866–7); or *Bradshaws Journal*, (1841–3).
58. J. Harland, Preface to J. Harland (ed.), *Ballads and Songs of Lancashire Ancient and Modern* (1882).
59. G. Milner, Introduction to G. Milner (ed.), *Poems and Songs of Waugh*.
60. See *Ben Brierley's Journal*, Dec. 1871; *The Record* (journal of the Lancashire Authors' Association) Aug. 1917; J. T. Clegg, Introduction to *The Works of J. Trafford Clegg* (*Th' Owd Weyver*) (Rochdale, 1898).
61. See 'Jonathan Oldbuck' (John Harland) in *Country Words*, 5 Jan. 1867, 26 Jan. 1867; G. Milner, Introduction to *Waugh*.
62. D. Vincent, *Bread, Knowledge and Freedom: A Study of Nineteenth-Century Working Class Autobiography* (1981), pp. 192–3.
63. B. Maidment, 'Class and Cultural Production'.
64. S. Laycock, *Warblins Fro' An Owd Songster* (Oldham, 1893), for instance 'Only A Poet', 'Lancashire Lyrics Written During The Cotton Famine'.
65. Sim Schofield, *Short Stories About Failsworth Folk* (Blackpool, 1905), pp. 43–6.
66. Joseph Ramsbottom, 'Writing in Dialect', *Country Words*, 15 Dec. 1866.
67. K. E. Smith, *The Dialect Muse* (Ruined Cottage Publications, Wetherby, 1979).
68. See above, p. 202.
69. T. Paulin, *A New Look at the Language Question* (Field Day Theatre Pamphlets, Derry, 1983).
70. K. E. Smith, *The Dialect Muse*.

12   *Dialect and the making of social identity*

1. W. Reddy, *The Rise of Market Culture: The Textile Trade and French Society 1750–1900* (Cambridge, 1984), p. 259. Cited further above, p. 216.
2. See above, pp. 170–1.
3. P. Joyce, 'Work' in *Cambridge Social History of Great Britain 1750–1950*, ed. F. M. L. Thompson (Cambridge 1990), vol. II.
4. A. E. Smailes, *North England* (1960), ch. 9.
5. M. Anderson, *Family Structure in Nineteenth-Century Lancashire* (Cambridge, 1971); R. Dennis, *English Industrial Cities in the Nineteenth Century. A Social Geography* (Cambridge, 1984); P. Joyce, *Work, Society and Politics: The Culture of the Factory in Later Victorian England* (Brighton, 1980), chs. 3, 5.
6. J. T. Danson and T: A. Welton, 'On the Population of Lancashire and Cheshire 1801–1852', *Transactions of Historic Society of Lancashire and Cheshire*, II, (1858–59).
7. D. J. Rowe, 'The Population of Nineteenth-Century Tyneside', in N. McCord (ed.), *Essays in Tyneside Labour History* (Newcastle, 1977).
8. See above, pp. 210–11.
9. A. D. Gilbert, *Religion and Society in Industrial England* (1976), pp. 110–15.
10. H. Pelling, *Social Geography of British Elections 1885–1910* (1967), pp. 316–23.
11. E. P. Thompson, *The Making of the English Working Class* (1963), chs. 8–10, 12; See also R. Elbourne, *Music and Tradition in Early Industrial Lancashire, 1780–1840* (1980).
12. J. Sykes, *Slawit in the 'Sixties* (Huddersfield, 1926); J. Sugden, *Slaithwaite Notes of the Past and Present* (Manchester, 1905); D. F. E. Sykes, *History of the Colne Valley and its Vicinity* (Huddersfield, 1897). See also the work of Ammon Wrigley.
13. See above, pp. 111–12.
14. See above, pp. 267–9. Examples of dialect literature in these non-northern

industrial districts are W. Morgan, *Our Anuk and Other Black Country Stories* (Oldbury, 1909); 'A Darbyshire Mon' (J. P. Robinson), *Owd Sammy Twitcher's Crismas Bowk for the Year 1870* (Derby, 1870); F. W. Grove, *Advenchurs of Tew Pottery Chaps at the Paris Eggsibishun* (Longton, 1867), G. Squiers, *Aerbut Paerks of Baernegum* (Birmingham, 1917).

15. Mimicry and recitation were a vital part of Victorian culture. In the second half of the century the publishing house of Abel Heywood in Manchester turned out large numbers of reciters featuring the linguistic traits of the Scots, Dutch, American negroes ('niggerosities'), Germans, and many more, including the Irish.

16. Oliver Ormerod, *O Ful, Tru, Un Pertikler Okeawnt, O Bwoth Wat Aw Seed Un Wat Aw Yerd We Gooin To Th' Greight Eggsibishun E Lundun...* (Rochdale, 1856). Sales of 12,000 were claimed since the first edition of 1851.

17. See above, pp. 122–4, 268.

18. See above, pp. 257–9, 265–6.

19. See above, ch. 10.

20. See above, ch. 11.

21. G. Ridley, 'Bob Chambers', 'The Bobby Cure' in *Allans Illustrated Edition of Tyneside Song* (Newcastle, 1891).

22. B. Brierley, 'Bein Gradely', 'Walmsley Fowt Goose Club' in vols. II, III, J. Dronsfield (ed.) *Ab o' th' Yate Sketches*, 3 vols. (Oldham, 1896), or see *Daisy Nook Sketches* (Manchester and London, 1881); 'Treadlepin Fold', in *Tales and Sketches of Lancashire Life* (Manchester, 1884).

23. G. Milner (ed.), *Besom Ben Stories* (Manchester, n.d., 1880s).

24. John Hartley's famous Yorkshire character 'Sammywell Grimes' was a chip off the block of Ab and Ben.

25. K. E. Smith, *The Dialect Muse* (Wetherby, 1979).

26. S. Schofield, *Short Stories About Failsworth Folk* (Blackpool, 1905).

27. See above, chs. 6, 7.

28. E. P. Thompson, *Making of the English Working Class*, pp. 321–6.

29. Particularly in his autobiographical works, *Home Memories and Recollections of a Life* (Manchester, 1886); 'Failsworth My Native Village', in J. Dronfield (ed.), *Ab o' th' Yate Sketches*, vol. 3 (hereafter *Sketches*).

30. *Sketches*, vol. 2.

31. *ibid*, vol. 1.

32. 'Ab...An' Chep Beef', 'Shoiny Jim's Kesmas Dinner', in *ibid*, vol. 3.

33. P. Joyce, *Work, Society and Politics*.

34. See above, p. 114.

35. S. Laycock, 'Mashers', *Warblins Fro' An' Owd Songster* (Oldham, 1893), p. 183.

36. See for example the lesser-known J. Barnes, 'We Couldno' Stand It Neaw', in *Heywood's Samples of Lancashire Verse and Prose* (Manchester, n.d., 1880s?)

37. See above, pp. 177–9.

38. B. Brierley, 'A Day At Bolton Abbey', in *Sketches*, vol. 3; J. Hartley, 'My Gronfayther's Days', 'What Aw Want', also prose pieces on 'Progress' and 'Machinery', in *Yorkshire Ditties* (2nd series, Wakefield, n.d.).

39. The sense and uses of the past are explored above, ch. 7. Dialect representations of the past are more complex and many sided than can be registered here. In particular there were non-radical representations, and the dominant radical version had a profound effect on later socialist authors.

40. See above, pp. 259–62.

41. *Weyver's Awn Olmenack*, 1881. See appendix.

42. *Weyver's Awn* (1873); *Bishop Blaize Olmenac* (Bradford, 1857).

43. *Chimney Nook* (1908), stories and sayings.

44. J. Baron (Tom o' Dick's o Bobs), 'Naybers', in *Short Studies on Important Subjects* (Manchester, 1892); B. Brierley, 'Dooin One's Own', in J. Dronsfield (ed.), *Sketches*, vol. II; B. Wood, *Sparks From the Smithy: Lancashire Rhymes and Recitations*, (Bury, 1879).

45. In B. Hollingworth (ed.), *Songs of the People: Lancashire Dialect Poetry of the Industrial Revolution* (Manchester, 1977) p. 139.

46. Text from *Teddy Ashton's Lancashire Annual* (1923).

47. See above, ch. 8.

48. They were also fostered by the local press, and higher-class friends of the dialect. Bobby Nunn was the laureate of what was reported to be the first of the great employer-sponsored outings on Tyneside; see Nunn in *Allan's Illustrated Edition* (1891).

49. See above, ch. 5.

50. Corvan could be a keen critic of Progress (e.g. 'The Toon Improvement Bill, or Ne Pleyce Noo Te Play') but also praise the new industry and prosperity (e.g., 'The Comet: Or, the Skipper's Fright'). Ridley used sport and invention as symbols of the great strides taken on industrial Tyneside; see 'The Stephenson Monument', a tribute to the invention of the railway nearby. See also John Peacock, J. P. Robson ('The High Level Bridge'), all in *Allans* (1891). Also, Joe Wilson, 'Tyneside Lads for Me', from *Tyneside Songs and Drolleries* (Newcastle, 1890).

51. Copies in Manchester Central Reference Library, vol. 1 (1886), vol. 2 (1887).

52. See above, pp. 202–3.

53. B. Brierley, *Ab o' th' Yate's Dictionary; or the Walmsley Fowt Skoomaster* (Manchester, 1881). See also the illuminating definitions of 'clown', what condescending 'furriners' call Lancastrians.

54. 'Ab...in London', *Sketches*, vol. 1.

55. See above, ch. 5.

56. See the citations to the discussion above, pp. 130–1.

57. W. H. Hampson, *Yorkshire Tykes Abroad* (Wakefield, 1911).

58. 'E Defence On Az Awn Taane Like'; see also *BFA*, 1852. *Tykes Own Almanac* (1924); *Yorkshireman's Almanac* (Otley, 1904).

59. E. M. Wright, *Life of Joseph Wright* (1932), pp. 438, 442.

60. *Yorkshireman's Almanac* (1904).

61. See also January, in *Bob Stubbs* (1911). See appendix.

62. *Chimney Nook* (1908).

63. J. Hartley, *Yorkshire Ditties*, see also 'Heart Broken'.

64. 'A Fearful Mistak', and mottoes. See appendix.

65. February section. See appendix.

66. Hartley, 'The Honest Hard Worker', *Yorkshire Ditties*; E. Waugh, 'Among The Preston Operatives', in G. Milner (ed.), Edwin Waugh, *Lancashire Sketches* (n.d.).

67. See above, chs. 2, 10.

68. 'A Bad Sooart', *Yorkshire Ditties*, also 'The Honest Hard Worker'.

69. In *ibid.*

70. *ibid.*

71. See the religious poems in *Bob Stubbs* (1911).

72. *Chimney Nook* (1908); 'A Happy New Year', *Weyver's Awn* (1881).

73. E. Waugh, 'God Bless These Poor Folks', also 'Hard Weather' and 'Tickle Times' in G. Milner (ed.), *Poems and Songs*, (Manchester, n.d., 1895?).

74. 'To Poverty', 'Starved to Death', in *Warblins Fro an Owd Songster*.

75. J. Baron, *Short Studies...* See also *Some Lankisher Sayings* (1891) and *A Lankisher Dickshonary* (4th ed., Blackburn, 1907).

76. 'Th' Ship Cannell', 'Doin One's Own', 'A Day at Llandudno', in *Sketches*, vols. 2, 3.
77. *Sketches*, vol. 2.
78. *Sketches*, vol. 3.
79. M. Vicinus, *The Industrial Muse*, pp. 225–31.
80. See above, ch. 6.
81. *Sketches*, vol. 2.
82. See above, pp. 121–4.
83. 'Goosegrove Penny Readings', *Sketches*, vol. 3.
84. *ibid.*
85. See note 31 above.
86. *Sketches*, vol. 3.
87. *Barnsla Foaks Annual* (1840, 1852, 1873).
88. *Sketches*, vol. 3. See also stories on Prince of Wales in vol. 1.
89. S. Laycock, *Warblins Fro' An Owd Songster*.
90. See Hartley's 'Give It Em Hot', cited above, note 68, (*Yorkshire Ditties*).
91. B. Wood, *Sparks from the Smithy: Lancashire Rhymes and Recitations* (Bury, 1879).
92. See Brierley's 'Failsworth' for a strong sense of how potent political loyalties were, also P. Joyce, *Work, Society and Politics*, chs. 5–8.
93. See 'Th' Ship Cannell' story, cited above, note 76.
94. See B. Brierley, *Old Radicals and Young Reformers* (Manchester, 1860).
95. See above, ch. 3.
96. J. Baron, 'Pollaticks', in *Short Studies*.
97. *Barnsla Foaks Annual* (1892), 'Hah T' Soashalists Laid Sheffield E Ruins'.
98. B. Wood, 'Different Opinions', *Sparks*; *Leeds Loiner* (1879); *Tommy Toddles* (1875); *Weyver's Awn* (1885, 1881); *Chimney Nook* (1912). These ideas were also reflected in the growing *Cotton Factory Times* disillusion with party politics, e.g. Oct. Sept. 1900.
99. There was also a flourishing Lancashire school of workingman novelists, men with close links to socialism and dialect; see P. Salvesen, 'Allen Clarke and the Lancashire School of Working Class Novelists', typescript kindly provided by Mr Salvesen.
100. P. Salvesen, 'Introduction', *Teddy Ashton's Lancashire Scrapbook. Selections from Allen Clarke* (Bolton, 1985).
101. See above, ch. 5.
102. These aspects are very well revealed in 'The Bully of Barlow's Shed', in P. Salvesen (ed.), *Teddy Ashton's Scrapbook*.
103. A. Clarke, *Tim Bobbin Resurrected* (Blackpool, 1911).
104. For fiction put to political uses which reflected these beliefs see his dialect addresses to the people and electors of Rochdale, for which he stood in the 1900 parliamentary election. He was defeated, polling 901 votes. 'My Say To The People of Rochdale' and 'An Election Address To Th' Rochda Folk', in P. Salvesen (ed.), *Teddy Ashton's Scrapbook*. 1900 was still early days for labour independence.
105. *Bill a' Bet Spriggs Visit to Princess May... An' Her Majesty T'Queen* (Manchester, n.d., 1900s?).
106. See above, p. 123.
107. *Teddy Ashton's Northern Weekly*, 26 June 1900.
108. *Teddy Ashton's Lancashire Annual* (1892). Bolton Central Reference Library has the best collection of Clarke's work, especially the hugely popular 'Tum Fowt' sketches.

13   *Stages of class*

  1. D. Höher 'The Composition of Music Hall Audiences 1850–1900', in P. Bailey (ed.), *The Victorian Music Hall. The Business of Pleasure* (Milton Keynes, 1987). On the character of the audience for melodrama, see M. Booth, *English Melodrama* (1965), chs. 2, 7.
  2. See above, pp. 224–5.
  3. P. Bailey, 'The Swell Song', in J. Bratton (ed.), *The Victorian Music Hall. Performance and Style* (Milton Keynes, 1987).
  4. J. Travis, 'Jones and the Working Girl: Class Marginality in Music Hall Song 1860–1900', in *ibid.*
  5. M. Vicinus, *The Industrial Muse*, pp. 263–6, 276.
  6. P. Bailey, 'Introduction. Making Sense of Music Hall', in P. Bailey (ed.), *The Victorian Music Hall*, pp. xiv, xviii.
  7. J. Bratton, *The Victorian Popular Ballad* (1975), ch. 7.
  8. *ibid.*
  9. M. Booth, *English Melodrama*, ch. 2.
 10. R. Darnton, *The Great Cat Massacre And Other Episodes in French Cultural History* (1985), p. 71.
 11. J. Bratton, *The Victorian Popular Ballad*, chs. 3, 4. T. S. Eliot's essay on Marie Lloyd is a revealing attempt to relate music hall to national character, very much in the vein of conservative populism; T. S. Eliot, 'Marie Lloyd', *Selected Essays* (1951).
 12. See above, ch. 10.
 13. P. Bailey, 'Making Sense of Music Hall'.
 14. P. Johnson, *Saving and Spending: The Working Class Economy in Britain 1870–1939* (Oxford 1985). See also H. Cunningham, 'Leisure', in J. Benson (ed.), *The Working Class in England 1875–1914* (1985).
 15. See above, pp. 88–9, 114–15.
 16. P. Bailey, 'Ally Sloper's Half-Holiday: Comic Art in the 1880s', *History Workshop Journal*, 16 (1983).
 17. P. Joyce, *Work, Society and Politics: The Culture of the Factory in Later Victorian England* (Brighton, 1980), ch. 5.
 18. A. Briggs, 'The Language of "Mass" and "Masses" in Nineteenth-Century England', in D. E. Martin and D. Rubinstein (eds.), *Ideology and the Labour Movement. Essays presented to John Saville* (1979).
 19. See above, pp. 190–1.
 20. P. Bailey, 'Custom, Capital and Culture in the Victorian Music Hall', in R. Storch (ed.), *Popular Culture and Custom in Nineteenth Century England* (1982).
 21. John Walker, *The Factory Lad* (n.d., 1830s) is the best known example of the industrial melodrama, though the genre was not large. The play was performed in the 1830s in that mecca of factory lads, Oldham.
 22. D. Mayer, 'The Romans in Britain 1886–1910: Pain's "The Last Days of Pompeii"', *Theatrephile*, 2: 5 (1984–85).
 23. The Hodson Collection, Drama Department, University of Manchester. My thanks are due to Dr David Mayer for allowing me access to the collection, and for giving me the benefit of his expert knowledge of the popular stage.
 24. See e.g. 'Jane Shore', 'Napoleon King of Spain'.
 25. For *Wat Tyler* playing to packed houses in London see *Penny Illustrated Paper*, 1 Jan. 1870. See 'Nurse Cavell, The Angel of War', 'British Born, An Englishman's Pluck', Hodson Collection.
 26. See also 'The Mystery of the Hansom Cab' on the wool trade, for another play in the same vein.

27. See above, ch. 5.
28. See above, ch. 10.
29. For a useful corrective see J. Langton, 'The Industrial Revolution and the Regional Geography of England', *Transactions of the Institute of British Geographers*, n.s. 9 (1984), pp. 145–67.
30. See above, pp. 201–3.
31. P. Joyce, *Work, Society and Politics*, ch. 6.
32. A. Clarke, *Lancashire Buzzes. A Collection of Gradely Lancashire Jokes* (Bolton, 1932).
33. F. Ormerod, *Lancashire Cracks* (Manchester, n.d. *c.* 1920?).
34. R. Hoggart, *The Uses of Literacy* (1957; 1965), ch. 3.
35. See above, pp. 156ff.
36. See above, ch. 6.
37. R. Hoggart, *The Uses of Literacy*, pp. 140–9. For an especially revealing examination of the extraordinary degree of continuity evident in twentieth-century popular culture, particularly its rootedness in the Victorian era, see *ibid.*, pp. 121–31, 146–66.
38. See J. Richards, *The Age of the Dream Palace: Cinema and Society in Britain 1930–1939* (1984), ch. 10, upon which the following account of cinema draws heavily.
39. *ibid.*, ch. 11, also ch. 17.
40. M. Burgess and T. Keen, *Gracie Fields*, p. 86.
41. J. Richards, *Age of the Dream Palace*, esp. pp. 173–7.
42. 'Gracie Comes Whoam, Souvenir of the Visit of Miss Gracie Fields to her Native Town…Her Efforts in Aid of Local Charities' (Rochdale, 1931). There is much information on Fields in this booklet, and in the cuttings file on Fields in Rochdale Public Library. I have drawn on these sources for the following account. I acknowledge with gratitude the help of the Rochdale Local History Librarian, Mr John Cole.
43. Cited in 'Gracie Comes Whoam'.
44. *Rochdale Observer*, 19 Jan. 1931. See also programme for 'Admission of Miss Gracie Fields…to be Honorary Freeman of the Borough, 19 May 1937', (Rochdale Public Library).
45. *Sunday Chronicle*, 5 March 1933.
46. On the Lancashire reputation of Fields and Formby see W. R. Mitchell, *Lancashire Mill Town Traditions* (Clapham, via Lancaster, 1977), pp. 8–10.
47. G. Stedman Jones, 'The "Cockney" and the Nation: 1780–1988', in D. Feldman and G. Stedman Jones (eds.), *Between Nationhood and Nation* (1989).
48. *ibid.*
49. See above, pp. 284–7.

14   *Conclusion*

1. See above, p. 220.
2. See the interesting discussion in M. Denning, *Mechanic Accents: Dime Novels and Working-Class Culture in America* (1987), ch. 5, esp. pp. 72–4.
3. S. Bercovitch, *The American Jeremiad* (Madison, 1978).
4. S. Wilentz, *Charts Democratic: New York City and the Rise of the American Working Class* (1984).
5. I. Jack, 'Finished with Engines', in *Before The Oil Ran Out: Britain 1977–86* (1988), p. 32.

6. *ibid.*, pp. 33–4.
7. See above, p. 57.
8. See above, ch. 3.
9. See above, ch. 2.
10. See above, pp. 139–40.

Index